ECOLINGUISTICS

Open Linguistics Series

The *Open Linguistics Series*, to which this book makes a significant contribution, is 'open' in two senses. First, it provides an open forum for works associated with any school of linguistics or with none. Linguistics has now emerged from a period in which many (but never all) of the most lively minds in the subject seemed to assume that transformational-generative grammar — or at least something fairly closely derived from it — would provide the main theoretical framework for linguistics for the foreseeable future. In Kuhn's terms, linguistics had appeared to some to have reached the 'paradigm' stage. Reality today is very different. More and more scholars are working to improve and expand theories that were formerly scorned for not accepting as central the particular set of concerns highlighted in the Chomskyan approach — such as Halliday's systemic theory (as exemplified in this book), Lamb's stratificational model and Pike's tagmemics — while others are developing new theories. The series is open to all approaches, then — including work in the generativist-formalist tradition.

The second sense in which the series is 'open' is that it encourages works that open out 'core' linguistics in various ways: to encompass discourse and the description of natural texts; to explore the relationship between linguistics and its neighbouring disciplines such as psychology, sociology, philosophy, artificial intelligence, and cultural and literary studies; and to apply it in fields such as education and language pathology.

Open Linguistics Series Editor
Robin F. Fawcett, University of Wales College of Cardiff

Modal Expressions in English, Michael R. Perkins
Text and Tagmeme, Kenneth L. Pike and Evelyn G. Pike
The Semiotics of Culture and Language, eds: Robin P. Fawcett, M.A.K. Halliday, Sydney M. Lamb and Adam Makkai
Into the Mother Tongue: A Case Study in Early Language Development, Clare Painter
Language and the Nuclear Arms Debate: Nukespeak Today, ed: Paul Chilton
The Structure of Social Interaction: A Systemic Approach to the Semiotics of Service Encounters, Eija Ventola
Grammar in the Construction of Texts, ed.: James Monaghan
On Meaning, A.J. Griemas, trans. by Paul Perron and Frank Collins
Biological Metaphor and Cladistic Classification: An Interdisciplinary Approach, eds: Henry M. Hoenigswald and Linda F. Wiener
New Developments in Systemic Linguistics, Volume 1: Theory and Description, eds: M.A.K. Halliday and Robin P. Fawcett
Volume 2: Theory and Application, eds: Robin P. Fawcett and David Young
Eloquence and Power: The Rise of Language Standards and Standard Language, John Earl Joseph
Functions of Style, eds: David Birch and Michael O'Toole
Registers of Written English: Situational Factors and Linguistic Features, ed.: Mohsen Ghadessy
Pragmatics, Discourse and Text, ed.: Erich H. Steiner and Robert Veltman
The Communicative Syallabus, Robin Melrose
Advances in Systemic Linguistics: Recent Theory and Practice, eds.: Martin Davies and Louise Ravelli
Studies in Systemic Phonology, ed: Paul Tench
*Ecolinguistics: ¿Toward a New **Paradigm** for the Science of Language?*, Adam Makkai

ECOLINGUISTICS

¿Toward a New **Paradigm** for the Science of Language?

ADAM MAKKAI

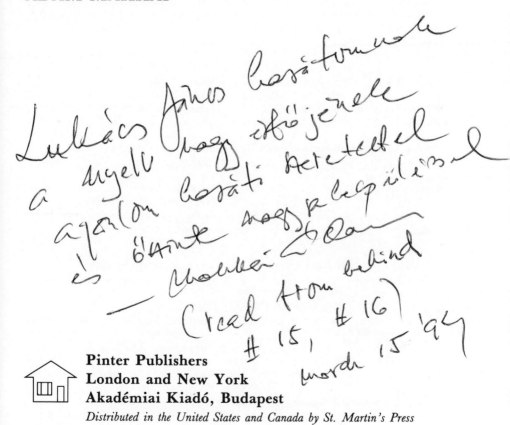

Pinter Publishers
London and New York
Akadémiai Kiadó, Budapest
Distributed in the United States and Canada by St. Martin's Press

Pinter Publishers Ltd.
25 Floral Street, Covent Garden, London WC2E 9DS, United Kingdom
and
Akadémiai Kiadó
Budapest

First published in 1993

Distributed exclusively in the USA and Canada by St. Martin's Press, Inc., Room 400, 175 Fifth Avenue, New York, NY10010, USA

Adam Makkai is hereby identified as the author of this work as provided under Section 77 of the Copyright, Designs and Patents Act, 1988.

British Library Cataloguing in Publication Data
A CIP catalogue record for this book is available from the British Library

ISBN 1 85567 018 6

Library of Congress Cataloging-in-Publication Data
Makkai, Adam.
    Ecolinguistics: toward a new paradigm for the science of language/
Adam Makkai.
        p. cm. – (Open linguistics series)
    Includes bibliographical references and index.
    ISBN 1-85567-018-6
    1. Linguistics – Methodology. I. Title. II. Series.
P126.M35 1993
410'.1–dc20   92–44119
                                                                                  CIP

Typeset by Mayhew Typesetting, Rhayader, Powys
Printed and bound in Great Britain by Biddles Ltd., Guildford and King's Lynn

Contents

This book is dedicated to the past, present and future members of LACUS, the Linguistic Association of Canada and the United States, our 'university without walls' which has taught us the 'LACUS spirit' of friendly co-operation, courteous debate and creative tolerance of one another's quite often very different views.

LACUS was inaugurated on 20 August 1974 at Lake Forest College in Lake Forest, Illinois, U.S.A.

Why **ECOLINGUISTICS**:
in lieu of introduction

The second half of the 20th century has seen a number of 'breakthroughs' and 'counter-breakthroughs' in linguistics; so much, in fact, that the diversity of this once modest field of study invites comparison with medicine with its diverse range from podiatry to psychiatry. Linguistics, too, it would seem, has its 'podiatrists' and its 'psychiatrists'; a wide variety of 'gynecolinguists' and 'paedolinguists' have also come into existence during the discipline's recent past.

It cannot be the task of this brief characterization of my present contribution to the field to place actual nominations on the floor either by name or by 'school of thought' as to who and whose groups are the foot-doctors and who enjoy the loftier quarters of the psychiatrists' suite on the penthouse floor of the linguimedical complex: readers are invited to draw their own conclusions and make their own comparisons. I do very much want to make ONE SINGLE POINT, however, and it is this: I vigorously object to the characterization of some linguists as 'noble unicorns' (the theoreticians [of the Transformational-Generative persuasion]), and the 'coyotes tugging at the carnage' (the field workers), an unnecessarily provocative and unbecoming division of linguistics perpetrated by Langacker (quoted in Abercrombie 1980).

Perhaps a word or two might be in order here to explain the title of this book and the inverted Spanish question mark in front of the subtitle with two asterisks surrounding one word in the middle ¿Towards a new **paradigm** for the science of language?, for such punctuation is not in the English tradition, which I respect and do not wish to violate. My purpose is to call attention to the abused and misunderstood word paradigm and what it can reasonably be expected to stand for in the present ecological context.

Ever since the appearance of Thomas Kuhn's famous book The Structure of Scientific Revolutions (Kuhn 1962), a number of linguists have been busy comparing the Chomskian revolution of 1957–65 to a major 'paradigm shift' in linguistics – a paradigm shift comparable to the Copernican-Newtonian-Einsteinian revolutions in physics and to Siegmund Freud's appearance on the scene of psychiatry. Whereas it is undoubtedly true that interesting questions have arisen in the wake of 1957–65 and since, it is not too difficult to demonstrate (although it may be an unpopular stance to take in some circles of established power) that the changes that have ruled linguistics are NOT REALLY IN THE NATURE OF A TRUE SCIENTIFIC REVOLUTION, BUT RATHER IN THE NATURE OF A SOCIAL COUP D'ÉTAT. I am not the first writer to say so in print: Raimo Anttila was (Anttila 1974). I have subsequently come to understand how much social coups d'état work and how their propagators manage to make them seem as true scientific revolutions: the answers are given in Berger and Luckmann's revealing book *The Social Construction of Reality* (Berger and Luckmann 1967).

A researcher who shows that a so-called 'scientific revolution' was, in fact, merely a social coup d'état, can be characterized as a PARADIGM DEBUNKER. A writer on the other hand, who is anxiously declaring the scientific paradigm-shift status of any minor footnote issuing from the pen of a practitioner in power, can be called a PARADIGM MONGERER. The problem, of course, is that the very word *paradigm* has picked up the connotations of prestige, acceptance, regularity, normalcy, funding – in short, the overtones of desirability, success and social acceptance. Practitioners outside a given 'paradigm' are viewed with suspicion; they meet up with scorn, ridicule and rejection – sometimes also a certain amount of envy and admiration.

This book is, in its first part, an iconoclastic indictment of the Transformational-Generative 'paradigm' in many of its aspects. The papers from which 1, 2 and 3 were later constructed were written in the early and middle 1970s, shortly before I was promoted from Associate to full Professor at the University of Illinois at Chicago, whose linguists were obviously laboring somewhat in vain in the shadow of the University of Chicago's 'Generative Semantics' movement that entirely dominated the annual gatherings of the *Chicago Linguistic Society* (CLS) and its program committees consisting largely of graduate students anxious to ride the latest fad. It was obvious that there had been a rift between orthodox TGG *à la* MIT and the University of Chicago's 'Generative Semantics' movement with James D. McCawley as one of its main exponents, and my sympathies lay with the CLS. I, and many others with me, have felt that the CLS did not go far enough in questioning what was wrong with orthodox TGG, and so it came to pass that in August of 1974 we decided to found an independent binational linguistics society with the Great Lakes as its center. The name LACUS (for *Linguistic Association of Canada and the United States*) was actually invented by my colleague J. Peter Maher of Northeastern Illinois University; this most fitting acronym occurred to him while I was pacing the floor and talking about the Great Lakes, Canada, and the USA. Since the appearance of this book will coincide with the 20th anniversary of this Association, it seems only fitting that I explain 'ecology' and 'paradigms' in the spirit of LACUS and its growing, enthusiastic membership, to whom collectively this book is dedicated.

We have felt from the very start that if there ever was a field in the so-called humanities that depended for verification and relevance on mass data, it was linguistics. Yet the handling of large amounts of data on a mass basis has remained an overwhelmingly difficult task – until recently.

The relatively easy and nearly universal availability of the personal computer is bound gradually to remove the curse of unwieldy taxonomies from linguistics, essentially a behavioral and social science.

We in LACUS have always felt that perhaps no other field should deliberately avoid compartmentalization into 'theory' versus 'practice' than linguistics, since human language is a democratic commodity of all humankind, given naturally – if not in equal measure of quality – to the educated and the uneducated. The proof of the proverbial pudding, therefore, ought to be in the eating, and irrelevant theories should be discarded and only studied as historical aberrations or curiosities.

Consider the case of Professor Marr in the former USSR. He maintained that language belonged to the 'superstructure', which, in a certain interpretation of Marx, ought to be influenced by the 'base structure', that is the tools of production and their ownership and political administration. It soon became obvious, however, that the Russian language had not really changed appreciably because of the country's change from the Czar's rule to Lenin's (some of the orthography was actually simplified and some new phraseology had sprung up), so that eventually Stalin himself had to intervene and declare Marr's teachings as erroneous. Since before Stalin's denunciation of Marr the politically advantageous thing to do was to practice Marrism, a number of Soviet linguists, who dedicated their careers to Marr, lost their jobs or were otherwise disgraced and humiliated.

What manners of 'eating' the contemporary North American linguistic 'pudding' are there that have been under-explored by all of the great linguistic cook-books to date? Language learning is one; Language acquisition is the other, beyond serious doubt. Consider the following, however: suppose there were a tried and tested way of teaching Spanish, French, Latin, German and Russian in American high schools and colleges that would somehow be based on Chomsky's insights emanating from MIT and that it could be statistically proven that pupils so taught have achieved accentless and fully grammatical, indeed near-native fluency in these languages, whereas those unfortunate ones who were taught the traditional way stayed at their customary low level. Also consider the following possibility: if in the teaching of English as a second language (ESL/TESL) statistically tested masses of live populations could exhibit the innate superiority of consciously choosing or not choosing the 'passive transformation' via consciously applied ordered rules by writing in a lively and superior style cleverly alternating these two voices, having resulted in numerous Pulitzer Prizes for fiction and poetry written by non-native speakers, such that all of these great successes could objectively and unanimously be traced back to the advantages of transformational-generative language learning, there would be socially verifiable proof that grammars in the TGG mode are better for human beings than non-TGG-based ones.

But is that the case?

That Chomsky and Transformational-Generative Grammar (TGG) have no use for language pedagogy is one of the major calamities of modern linguistics. As a reaction to the anti-practical stance of TGG (in all its extant versions), numerous former TGG practitioners declared that ALL of theoretical linguistics is dead and withdrew into language typology, pragmatics, or into ESL/TEFL, which is still rather amorphous and struggling to shape its own identity.

It would almost seem as if there COULD BE no theoretical approach to second language pedagogy – at least from the point of view of TGG, since all such matters have been relegated to 'performance', with 'competence' being the only true goal of actual linguistics. (See the first chapter in this book about this issue.) Other theories, alas, have not done too much better, especially the more formal theories.

S.K. Shaumyan's Applicative Generative Grammar (AGG), developed during Shaumyan's Soviet years, is also heavily formal and based on symbolic logic. Unlike TGG, however, it is soundly based on semiotics and for that reason it offers a much more realistic set of analogies for human natural language use. AGG still owes us answers on two major issues: the role of the lexicon in 'phenotype' (i.e., actual spoken) grammars, and how human beings acquire their language. AGG may yet surprise us in this regard as Shaumyan, transplanted to Yale and subsequently to private consultancies in America from the former USSR, continues to develop and modify his views.

Lamb and Cognitive Stratificational Grammar (CSG) have been somewhat remiss in not addressing the problem of pedagogy in a sufficient number of publications, although several practitioners have indicated that both sociolinguistic issues and matters of language acquisition can be elegantly handled in CSG (Herrick 1984; also cf. the *LACUS Forum Series* in the bibliography).

This leaves two major contemporary theoretical approaches to language, both of which have distinguished themselves by addressing concrete needs of concrete people in various parts of the world. The older of the two – internationally – is the British Firthian tradition, known today primarily through the works of Michael A.K. Halliday and his Systemic-Functional Grammar (SFG).

Originally invented in the USA, but now globally practiced through the work of the Summer Institute of Linguistics (SIL), there is the Tagmemics of Kenneth L. Pike, Robert E. Longacre and others. Pike and his more than five thousand collaborators in the SIL have been particularly successful with the phonemics-based devising of alphabets for preliterate language groups and the writing of grammars for the same. They have achieved lasting and impressive results in the area of translation theory and practice (Nida 1974, Beekman and Callow 1974).

Halliday and the Systemic Functionalists have achieved the equally lasting results of producing grammars (mostly of English) which can deal with what people actually say and write; furthermore, Halliday's model is the first major modern theoretical model that successfully treats language not only as a social semiotic (Halliday 1978), but in such a way that our literary colleagues can make better use of it through the systematic inclusion of register or personal tenor, functional tenor, written or spoken mode, and lexis as a linguistic level.

What we still lack on a global basis are some of the following accounts:

1. How does a writer of good literary prose marshall his or her thoughts in the developing of literary plots? How do the various plot structures interdepend with the level of diction (vocabulary) and the syntax of a given writer?

2. How do poets and translators of good poetry produce their texts?

3. What is the relationship between the 'social status' and the 'ego state' of a speaker-writer as reflected by that person's diction, the meaning potential and the syntax of the text under investigation? In other words, can there be such a thing as a 'psychiatric psycholinguistics' which would, then, be meaningfully linked to the more traditional sociolinguistic approach?

4. Why is not anyone seriously working on Social Interaction Psychology (SIP) in the West? (Karácsony 1938).

5. Why is no one trying to produce a model in which the features of the aforementioned models could come to a new synthesis? Is this impossible? Would it be offensive to anyone? If so, why?

6. In this day and age of general computational expertise in so many other fields, why are logicians too shy or reluctant to express the assumptions and premises of Theory A in terms of Theories B, C, and D? Would this not show us something useful about the human mind, everyone's ultimate goal of study?

7. Why are not more linguists looking into literature and why are not more writers taking a serious look at what modern linguistics has to offer?

We are living in an age when humanity has, at long last, become aware of the importance of both the macro-environment and the micro-environment we live in. The general cover term for this New Age awareness, ECOLOGISM, has made its influence felt on conservation both on sea and land; in both urban and rural sociology and economics; in agriculture and in space exploration. We all tend to be aware nowadays that in addition to the ECOLOGY OF PHYSICAL SPACE there is also an ECOLOGY OF MIND. We live in 'mind sets', in more or less socio-psychologically premanufactured MODES OF THINKING, such as the 'pre-scientific', the 'scientific' and the 'post-scientific' mode. A pre-scientific thinker is one who puts his hands on two objects and declares 'this is cold' about the one and 'this is hot' about the other. A scientific thinker is one who invents the thermometer – whether in Fahrenheit, the Réaumur, or the Celsius – and starts to measure the relative temperatures of things. A post-scientific thinker, in contrast, is one who has dozens of various thermometers and uses them profusely, but at the same time questions the source of 'heat' in the Universe and links this intergalactic query to well-grounded doubt about the ability of human consciousness in general to be objective at all, due to the Heisenbergian recognition that observations interfere with the nature of most observed phenomena (Lukacs 1968; see Chapter 2 in Part I of this book). *Mutatis mutandis*, 19th century philology may have been pre-scientific; Bloomfield, Hockett, Chomsky, Pike and Shaumyan are scientific – each one uses a different thermometer – Lamb, Halliday and to a certain extent Roy Harris can be credited with being post-scientific as they all three, each in a different way, are questioning or rather re-questioning basics.

ECOLINGUISTICS, as its name implies, is trying to ask those questions which will, hopefully, usher the new generation of linguists toward a philosophically more tolerant and generally INCLUSIVE, not an EXCLUSIVE, view of human language.

Maybe this will explain the title and its unusual Spanish question mark and the two asterisks.

I have no intention of claiming the start of any new paradigm. *The Structure of Scientific Revolutions* is simply NOT APPLICABLE TO LINGUISTICS. Our field has had but one 'paradigm' ever since the learned debates of the ancient Greeks regarding whether language was subject to rules (the 'analogies' of the Alexandrians) or a matter of random lists (the School of Pergamon) (Dinneen 1967: 94–5). The argument is even older and can be traced back to the debate between the Heraclitean and the Parmenidian view (Heraclitus said 'everything flows' or 'becomes'; Parmenides said 'everything IS' (cf. Algeo 1972). It does not take too great an effort to see the 'reincarnation' of the ancient Greek regularists and the Heracliteans in the Junggrammatiker movement of the 19th century in Germany whose indirect but obvious intellectual continuation is Transformational-Generative Grammar with its mutation rules; by the same token it would be quite logical to see Hugo Schuhardt (1889) and the seekers of exceptions to the Junggrammatikers' 'Ausnahmslosigkeit der Lautwandel' (= 'the exceptionlessness of sound changes') continuing in urban sociolinguistics and latter-day variationism. Lamb's stratificational Grammar, as was convincingly shown by Algeo in his classical comparison (1972) would be the 'reincarnation' of Parmenidean philosophy which, in dialectical opposition to Heraclitus, seeks 'being' and 'realization' over 'motion' and 'becoming'.

How big and how old does a 'paradigm' have to be to count for a genuine 'Paradigm' with a capital P? How many 'sub-paradigms' are we ready, willing and able to recognize inside the truly major ones, such as the two thousand five hundred-year old macro-Aristotelian paradigm, which can encompass Copernicus, Kepler, Newton, Einstein and Heisenberg?

Physicists may disagree. Yet the fact remains that the INTERNATIONAL NOMENCLATURE OF LOGIC was worked out in Aristotle's works and relying on those insights the subsequent changes in world-views as indicated by the major inventors above, ALL MAKE CUMULATIVE, HISTORICAL SENSE WHETHER SEVERALLY OR JOINTLY. The same is not true of Thales, Anaximandros, Pythagoras, or Plato for that matter, as these pre-

Aristotelian giants of Greek thought still lived in the world of mysticism to a large extent.

Fritjof Capra, the author of *The Tao of Physics* (1980), while still belonging to the macro-Aristotelian paradigm of 20th-century science, already points beyond it, and this 'beyond', curiously, points back to the ancients and to the mystical Far East. I thus see a major 'paradigm of consciousness shift' along the following lines:

(a) The world before Aristotle
(b) The Aristotelian-Judaeo-Christian-materialistic world view
(c) The post-Hiroshima and the post-lunar landing world view gradually changing into 'New Age Thinking'.

All of linguistics as we know it belongs in the Aristotelian-Judaeo-Christian-materialistic world view and offers nothing but sometimes major and sometimes minor variations on the theme announced by the Greeks around 400 B.C.: we are either rule-builders (or 'tough-minded' to borrow a phrase from Halliday's Inaugural Lecture at the University of Sydney) as the TGG and the Chomskians, or we follow 'softer lines' along the lines of the ethnography of speech (to quote a phrase and title by Dell Hymes).

SO LET US FIRST MANUMIT, THEN EXPROPRIATE, AND ULTIMATELY MONGER OFF AT WHOLE-SALE PRICES
NO NEW **PARADIGMS**, PLEASE!

Let us live out and complete as best we can the one in whose midst we all are with some measure of human dignity and scholarly decorum! I would like to suggest that the word *claim* be officially struck from the vocabulary of all practising linguists and replaced by *suggest, hypothesize, surmize* and *intend to show* followed by data and objective proof.

My characterization above of the 'post-scientific' mode of thought as perhaps more advanced than the previous 'scientific' mode is not intended to suggest that all 'scientific issues' in linguistics have been cleared up – far from it. The three modes 'pre-scientific', 'scientific' and 'post-scientific' are still inextricably intermixed in the work of most practising linguists and many leading figures have distributed themselves quite unevenly along the scale of all three. Chomsky, for example, who has been aiming at being the critic of everything that was ever written about linguistics, and who introduced the notions of 'observational adequacy', 'descriptive adequacy' and 'explanatory adequacy', is often inaccurate about actual, simple observables of human speech – e.g. the interdependence of meaning and stress. If being 'scientific' means going by overt data, he fails to qualify, as Yngve (1986) so convincingly implies. Yet, in so far as he, too, is concerned with the process of explanation itself, Chomsky, too, is, up to a point, functioning in the post-scientific mode. These categories, therefore, are not clear-cut and we should be beware of attaching value-labels to them. A superficial reading of Yngve's epistemological statement could easily lead someone to think that a good linguist must perforce be a philosophical materialist who views language as videotapable and audiotapable electric impulses. This is, of course, part and parcel of the objectively observable behavior of Yngve's 'communicating individual'. From a higher platform we are also able to see that the 'communicating individual' who makes those tapable and electronically codable impulses is also a member of a social class, a family, a nation, a dialect area or two (or three or seventeen, as the case may be), holder or non-holder of educational degrees, holder of philosophical, political, and religious views, broadcasting at a given time in an 'adult ego state', a 'parental ego state' or in a 'child ego state'. None of these categories are *ipso facto* unscientific; they only become so if people are forced into them subjectively and without democratic consent or public verifiability. Undoubtedly, it is easier to videotape a bargaining session in an open-air market than to 'prove scientifically' that speaker 'A' is merely teasing speaker 'B' and is merely mock-bargaining for something he does not intend to buy at all. But it can be done. The questions asked must be carefully constructed and submitted to scrutiny; the subjects must be interviewed and their responses recorded and analyzed according to new methods of data management that will make the responses accessible to objective panels of observer-judges and descriptivists.

ECOLINGUISTICS is merely *in statu nascendi* and has a long way to go before it can fulfil any of its own goals and aspirations. The career of a single linguist will, in all likelihood, go through its own 'pre-scientific', 'scientific' and 'post-scientific' phases, all well within what a trained Ph.D. does in a way which is understood to be plainly 'scientific linguistics' by members of other professions.

But let me word the matter differently: 'pre-scientific' really means non-analytical, or naively catalytical. In the history of philosophy the great sage Plato can be seen as a major pre-scientific figure in this sense. 'Scientific' is a mode of thought which is primarily analytical; that which takes observables in chunks or holons and then reduces these chunks to their smallest atomic constituents – whether to leave it at that or to pretend that from these small elementary particles one can actually re-assemble the original holons, somewhat as the generativists do, frequently without giving much thought to the matter. 'Post-scientific' is a mode of thought which has been through the analytical stage and can count on its technics in analyzing observables, but which aims at providing 'outlook' to 'insight'; to describe the uses of linguistic structures, for example, in larger contexts. The development of sociolinguistics and text-linguistics in the wake of the TGG 'breakthrough' can be seen as a neo-catalytical phase following upon a highly analytical phase in the history of linguistics.

Earlier in this introduction I have singled out Pike's tagmemics and Halliday's systemic-functional grammar, with which I wish to ally ecolinguistics, and here is why: these are the two modern movements in the field which show relatively equal amounts of analyticity and catalyticity, both in their aims and in their methodology. TGG, in contrast, is primarily an analytical undertaking, even if the 'semantic features' and the 'phonetic features' are sometimes seen by some as the starting point of human language rather than the cemetery of its *disiecta membra*. Lamb and SCG were also primarily analytical, but in Lamb's later thinking EPISTEMOLOGY began to play an increasingly important part and this, in turn, has led to a recognition of both the difference between and the interdependence of analyticity and catalyticity in linguistic theorizing. The least practical of the compatible theoreticians, Shaumyan (1983) clearly recognizes the two-sided nature of linguistics when he speaks of 'centaur-concepts'. Analysis and catalysis are clearly implied in Shaumyan's dividing language into GENOTYPE and PHENOTYPE: any description of a real, spoken human phenotype language must start by analytical methods with the results of such analysis being deposited in an inter-lingual theoretical construct, the universal algebra of the GENOTYPE language, as a catalytical activity. *Mutatis mutandis*, Shaumyan, then, is acting 'scientifically' as analyst of real (phenotype) languages, and 'post-scientifically' when he writes (i.e. creates) genotype algebraic sentences in symbolic logic.

None of this makes the task of the ECOLINGUIST any easier. In fact, it pits him against the best minds in the field; scholars who are his teachers and his seniors; people whom he admires and respects. The dictates of the writing process and the translation process as well as the daily realities of an active multilingual existence are such, however, that the questions outlined above (1–7) must be asked; furthermore, they must be asked in a way that allows the ecolinguist to proceed undaunted, even if the answers reaching him from the generation of his teachers should be negatively critical.

I hope not to offend anyone with my attempted suggestions of 'theory mapping' as in the chapters 'The lexocentric approach to descriptive linguistics' or 'A pragmo-ecological view of linguistic structure and language universals: towards a new synthesis of linguistics and anthropology'. That more than just 'linguistic' scholarship is needed in explicating a text has been known for a very long time. The paper 'The "Illumination" of Giuseppe Ungaretti' is a case in point. After showing what the grammar of the text does from several theoretical points of view, the task yet remains to delve into the historical and philosophical background of both the author and the genre the author was working in.

All of this would probably have been termed just common sense in the 19th-century philological tradition. The pragmo-ecological linguist has no difficulty in being identified with 'philology' as long as it is understood that 19th-century and early 20th-century philology are perceived today as belonging to the 'pre-scientific' *modus operandi*. Philology has never really been superseded by structural linguistics; these two fields of inquiry can only benefit from each other's experience. Facing the end of this century it is perhaps not premature to say that ECOLINGUISTICS may be seen as 'post-scientific philology', or catalytic neo-philology. The composition process of a given sonnet (as in the chapters 'How to put the pieces of a poem together and ' "Lexical insertion" as sociolinguistic activity: evidence from poetic behavior' or the analysis of a poem written by someone else

as in the chapter 'The meaning of Noel Coward's "Venice"') can both be
seen as instances of ecolinguistic neo-philology.

ECOLINGUISTICS, as a term, was suggested to me by Professor Einar
Haugen in Chicago at the occasion of the Ninth International Congress of
the Anthropological and Ethnographic Sciences, where an early version of
Chapter 2 was presented. Professor Haugen is in no way responsible for
my particular use of the term as I use it throughout this collection of
essays.

My indebtedness to cognitive stratificational linguistics (CSL) and
Professor Sydney M. Lamb throughout will be obvious to anyone. Despite
this indebtedness, the views expressed here are my own and no one
associated with stratificational linguistics should be held responsible for
them.

Most of the chapters have appeared elsewhere in earlier forms between
the years 1968 and 1991. The volume thus contains the work of twenty-
three years, during which time my thinking has not remained the same on
any topic. Earlier attempts at dividing the material into sections on
'Phonology', 'Morphology', 'Syntax', 'Semantics', 'Lexicography',
'Idiomaticity', 'Literary Aspects' and 'Diachronic and Sociolinguistic
Aspects' seemed forced and essentially unnecessary after further soul-
searching. The paper 'The "Illumination" of Giuseppe Ungaretti' is in the
literary, idiomatic and translation section, but in a real sense it belongs in
a section on phonology and perhaps semantics. One of the results of
writing this book over the years has been that I can no longer see any clear
borderline between these traditional disciplines. The case of a poem, short
or long, must certainly amalgamate and accommodate all aspects of
language from the phonological and the graphic 'upward' to word formation, sentence formation, stanza formation, syntax, semantics, literary
intention, the historic setting, etc.

I was originally educated in the European tradition as a student of
Sándor Eckhardt, Albert Gyergyai, János Győri and Jolán Kelemen at the
University of Budapest; prior to my two years in the French Department
there, the greatest influence on my thinking came from our Hungarian and
Latin teacher at the Academy of the Hungarian Reformed Church, Dr
Lajos Lengyel, whom we called 'Zeus'. It was with this Central European
background, rooted in Hungarian, French, German, Latin, and Russian,
that I arrived in the United States as a 21-year-old on January 1, 1957.
At Harvard University, where I became the first refugee student of my
generation, I took French courses from René Jasinski and Old French and
Provençal courses from Professor F. Solano; in the Slavic Department I
took courses from Professor Sechkareff, Hugh McLean, H.G. Lunt and
Roman Jakobson. Although strikingly different in detail, Budapest and
Harvard had one underlying theme in common: they taught me a healthy
respect for the text.

From 1958 to 1960 I taught French, German, Latin and Russian at
Iolani College Preparatory Academy in Honolulu, Hawaii. Here the local
boys of Japanese, Chinese, Hawaiian, Philipino and Portuguese, besides

Mainland American ancestries, became as much my teachers as they were my students. I spoke Hungarian at home with my wife and father, English at work, and listened to all the national languages of the various ethnicities mentioned as well as to a good deal of 'Hawaiian Pidgin' characteristic of the late 1950s and early 1960s. By the time the Ford Foundation sent me to Yale in the Fall of 1960, my mind was no '*tabula rasa*' as far as language and its various uses were concerned. My first poems were published back in Hungary in 1954 and 1955; several translations from French, Old French and Provençal appeared in print or were read over Radio Budapest in a variety of literary programs. I must also mention my work as literary secretary to my mother, Rózsa Ignácz (1909–1979), author of some forty novels and numerous translations, mostly from Rumanian and French. From the ages of 14 to 21, when I left Hungary in the wake of the Soviet military intervention after the 1956 National Uprising, I lived in an intense literary atmosphere with regular visits by novelists, editors, stage directors, composers, painters, sculptors, poets and translators – all friends of my mother and the larger extended family. Language was perceived by these people as a medium, as a means to an end, that of self-expression in a social setting designed to communicate with others. I do not think I would ever have become a linguist if I had stayed in my native country.

The structuralist doctrines of 'once a phoneme always a phoneme', 'complementary distribution', 'do not be teleological', 'meaning is unimportant', etc., that floated around in the air at Yale, were as much something tolerantly to learn in order to see where they might lead, as a big insider's joke. 'Do you think Bernard Bloch means all of this?', we used to ask one another, somewhat frightened and bemused at the same time. It soon became apparent that one had to 'act as if' these tenets were true, because to say otherwise would have meant losing a grip on objectivity, which was the hard-earned foreign currency of the trade, accumulated since the 1880s, when William Dwight Whitney had taught at Yale. The heavy emphasis on Indo-European, two years of Sanskrit, classical and Vedic, as well as Gothic, Old Church Slavic, and the Comparative Grammar of Greek and Latin under teachers such as Paul Tedesco, Konstantin Reichardt, Ralph Ward, and Warren Cowgill had one common denominator which, again, seemed to go hand in hand with the Budapest–Harvard experience: the importance of the ancient (written) text. Whereas we all made up sentences in Greek, Latin, and Sanskrit, it was yet overwhelmingly obvious that we could never become speakers of these languages and so Albrecht Goetze's half-joking, half-serious remark, according to which 'in the beginning there was the text', seemed to be reliable wisdom to build upon for later years as well.

The militant claims of the early TGG converts seemed both interesting and frightening: interesting, because they were going to make up their own texts, and frightening, because once the linguist became his/her own informant, the control of objectivity over what was being looked at seemed to go by the wayside. I was still only a first-year graduate student when I concluded that the dialect issue and the relativity of 'what is grammatical for what speaker' would lead to many a crack and many a tumbling fortification along the occupied territories of TGG.

Sydney M. Lamb's arrival on the scene in the Fall of 1964 was like a breath of fresh air inside a mausoleum. All of a sudden one could talk about 'meaning': it was removed from the blacklist of no-nos; the possibility of discussing computers became a reality; idioms, allusions, puns, quotations and literary texts all became possible areas of research as did linguistic decipherment and serious discussion about the pros and cons of TGG and the stratificational alternative. With structural semantics strongly established at Yale thanks to Rulon S. Wells and Floyd G. Lounsbury, both of whom were sympathetic to the new trend in theoretical linguistics, my choice for a doctoral dissertation became English idioms. My advisors were Professor Wells, Lamb, Lounsbury, Cowgill and Stimson. When it became ready, *Idiom Structure in English* (Makkai 1965) was the first Ph.D. written at Yale on modern American English from a stratificational point of view by a non-native speaker. These were three 'firsts' in one bag, and not everyone was equally glad in seeing me pull it off. In 1972 the work was published in book form, enlarged to three times its original size (Makkai 1972a).

By that time I had been working at the University of Illinois at Chicago where I started in the Fall of 1967. Chicago turned out a stimulating place to be: the vicinity of the University of Chicago, James D. McCawley and the generative semanticists and their yearly gatherings which resulted in the CLS series, made for interesting discussion. But the TGG establishment was still oppressive, even in its 2nd- and 3rd-generation forms, and so it came to pass that in August of 1974, with the help of M.A.K. Halliday, J. Peter Maher, Valerie Becker Makkai, Jean-Luc Garneau, Peter A. Reich, Robert J. Di Pietro and Fred C.C. Peng, LACUS, Inc., The Linguistic Association of Canada and the United States, was born. It has been my privilege to serve as its Foundation Executive Director and Director of Publications from the start, which is a commitment lasting even as I write these words. The lively and stimulating membership of LACUS has provided me with endless input in the writing of these essays. We have all learned a very great deal from our Past Presidents, Dwight L. Bolinger (1975–1976), Roger W. Wescott (1976–1977), Kenneth L. Pike (1977–1978), Ernst Pulgram (1978–1979), H.A. Gleason, Jr (1979–1980), Saul Levin (1980–1981), Charles F. Hockett (1981–1982), M.A.K. Halliday (1982–1983), Sydney M. Lamb (1983–1984), Robert A. Hall, Jr (1984–1985), Victor H. Yngve (1985–1986), Allen Walker Read (1986–1987), Carleton T. Hodge (1987–1988), Walter Hirtle (1988–1989), Robert J. Di Pietro (1989–1990), Velma B. Pickett (1990–1991) and Sebastian K. Shaumyan (1991–1992). Our featured speakers have included Paul L. Garvin, Yakov Malkiel, Rulon S. Wells, Isidore Dyen, Fred W. Householder and Roy Harris, to mention just a few. The extant volumes of LACUS take up a whole shelf. This organization draws its membership from twenty-seven countries on five continents and is a 'university without walls'. It has been my singular fortune and privilege to have been permitted to conceive of, start and run LACUS – perhaps the most significant educational experience I have ever had. LACUS is no one theory's club-house: among other things, it is a school of tolerance and goodwill in an intolerant, pugnacious and often quite unnecessarily nasty field full of oversized egos and their outlandish 'claims'. ECOLINGUISTICS is, to a very significant extent, a child of LACUS, to whose collective membership, past, present and future, this collection of essays is dedicated.

ADAM MAKKAI
July 4, Hong Kong –
October 23, Chicago, 1992

Part I. Theoretical considerations

1 Pragmo-ecological answers to unbridgeable gaps in the TGG paradigm: translation, idiomaticity and multiple coding

0.0. This chapter surveys some areas of recent linguistic theory that have proven the Chomskyan paradigm (and its various notational variants) to be unworkable, if by a 'working grammatical theory' we mean a theory that squarely faces the task of informing us of what people actually do. Hence the main argument of this chapter will be that the Chomskyan distinction between 'competence' and 'performance' must be understood in the light of the pragmatics and the ecology of human interaction in a non-imaginary society. My solutions are suggested within the framework of Stratificational-Cognitive Grammar (henceforth SG) and Pragmo-Ecological Grammar (PEG), my own approach within the family of stratificational grammars. The areas covered here will be (1) translation, (2) deep structure, (3) idioms and, finally, (4) multiple coding in speech.

1.0. It is by now more than intuition that tells us that TG cannot handle translation in any systematic, non-*ad hoc* manner. It is a moot point whether transformationalists have dealt with the problem, for the reply could always be made that the problem simply did not occupy their attention. My point here is that it is a LOGICAL IMPOSSIBILITY to achieve any sort of adequate translation from L_1 to L_2 under TG assumption, whether one espouses the Chomsky–Katz–Jackendoff 'lexicalist-interpretivist' position, or the McCawley–Lakoff–Ross 'generative semantics' position. It will be shown that, if TG is to work at all, one would have to practice both the semantics-centered versions of TG and the syntax-centered ones which, according to Emmon Bach (1971), has been proven to be impossible. Essentially Bach says that according to advanced mathematical testing by Stanley Peters and R.W. Ritchie the lexicalist-interpretivist and the generative semantics positions are logically incompatible. The question arises whether or not 'mathematical testing' is relevant for evaluating human grammars, and whether competence and performance are indeed two truly separate sides of the coin of human speech. For linguists in the TG and PEG traditions, competence and performance coincide in many areas. The stratificationalist David G. Lockwood, for instance, speaks about 'ideal performance' in his *Introduction to Stratificational Linguistics* (1972).

1.1. In what follows, I will describe the various TG positions AS IF THEY ATTEMPTED TO DESCRIBE WHAT HUMAN BEINGS REALLY DO. That the TG-oriented reader will cry 'this is not cricket' is to be expected. My reply to such a defense is: A LINGUISTIC THEORY OUGHT TO BE ABOUT WHAT HUMAN BEINGS DO, AND IF IT IS NOT, IT IS NOT A VIABLE, SERIOUS LINGUISTICS THEORY, BUT MERELY AN INTELLECTUAL GAME. Intellectual games, as all games, subdivide into (a) harmless, entertaining games, (b) challenging, sporting games, designed to strengthen the mind and the body, and (c) crooked games, designed to get the better of a socially or emotionally inferior victim by an aggressor. (For a theory of games from the emotional point of view, see Eric Berne's popular psychological study of 1966, *Games People Play*.) It is my contention that viewed as a game, TG exhibits all three of these characteristics. In so far as it is harmlessly entertaining and challenging, there is nothing one could object to. Alas, it also exhibits the characteristics of crooked games and as such has caused the profession of linguistics as well as individuals actual harm. Aspects of this will be documented and discussed below.

1.2. In his forthcoming book, *Introduction to Human Linguistics*, Victor H. Yngve of the University of Chicago, recalling his conversations with Chomsky at MIT writes:

> The freeing of linguistic data from personal bias is far from a trivial point, for it is all too easy to be led astray. One of the most serious problems with Chomsky's early (1957) monograph was an inadequate treatment of the relation between theory and observation in science. In that study we find recurrent discussions of this issue, for example: 'One function of this theory is to provide a general method for selecting a grammar for each language, given a corpus of sentences in that language' (p. 11). 'Clearly, every grammar will have to meet certain *external conditions of adequacy*; e.g., the sentences generated will have to be acceptable to the native speaker' (pp. 49–50).
> Yet these were not the strictures actually employed in that monograph: 'One way to test the adequacy of a grammar proposed for L is to determine whether or not the sentences that it generates are actually grammatical, i.e., acceptable to a native speaker, etc. We can take certain steps toward providing a behavioral criterion for grammaticalness so that this test of adequacy can be carried out. For the purposes of this discussion, however, suppose that we assume intuitive knowledge of the grammatical sentences of English and ask what sort of grammar will be able to do the job of producing these in some effective and illuminating way. We thus face a familiar task of explication of some intuitive concept, in this case the concept of "grammatical in English", and more generally, the concept of "grammatical"' (p. 13).
> Now the task of explication has its place, but it brings the danger of mistaking the intuitive concept either for solid data or for some self-evident theory that somehow *need not be tested against data* (emphasis added, A.M.). There is the

further danger that the author's 'intuitive knowledge of the grammatical sentences of English' may be biased by his theoretical preconceptions in such a way as to bolster his arguments *at the expense of scientific truth* (emphasis added, A.M.). Let's see what Chomsky is led to do when what his intuition would include as 'grammatical in English' differs from what is acceptable to a native speaker.

The whole point of that monograph was to argue the merits of the author's transformational approach to grammar, with the author taking a strong point of advocacy. In the course of the arguments, certain simple processes of sentence formation are postulated and accepted intuitively as characteristics of English (p. 21). These processes involve the embedding of sentences in other sentences, and would generate such strings as '*If either the man who said that if either the woman who reported that it is raining, is wrong, or the boy rode his bicycle, then I will be happy, is arriving today, or you are sad, then Bill was right.*' The further course of the argument hinges on whether strings such as these are grammatical English sentences or not. Now it would seem that any realistic criterion of 'external adequacy' would reject such strings as not being acceptable to the native speaker. This is particularly true in light of the fact that Chomsky intends no limit to the recursive processes used, so that much more complex examples would also be produced. BUT THEN HE COULD NOT GO ON TO 'PROVE' THAT 'ENGLISH IS NOT A FINITE STATE LANGUAGE' AND HIS ARGUMENT IN FAVOR OF TRANSFORMATIONS WOULD CRUMBLE (special emphasis added, A.M.).

Faced with a discrepancy between observed facts and the predictions of theory, one would expect a revision of theory: 'We shall continue to revise our notions of simplicity and characterization of the form of grammars until the grammars selected by the theory do meet the external conditions' (p. 54).

But we find instead an argument for keeping the theory and removing the discrepancy by actually accepting such sentences as grammatical: 'Note that many of the sentences of the form (. . . of the one cited above) will be quite strange and unusual' (they can be made less strange by replacing 'if' by 'whenever', 'on the assumption that', 'if it is the case that', etc., without changing the substance of our remarks). BUT THEY ARE ALL GRAMMATICAL SENTENCES, formed by processes of sentence construction so simple and elementary that even the most rudimentary English grammar would contain them. They can be understood, and we can even state quite simply the conditions under which they can be true. (Yngve, *Introduction to Human Linguistics*, pp. 16–18, quoted from a privately-circulated manuscript, by permission of the author.)

In the rest of the chapter Yngve recalls how Chomsky was immediately and widely criticized for this contradiction. Having been at MIT at the time, and having engaged Chomsky personally in the conversation about these matters, Yngve recalls the birth of the forced distinction between 'competence' and 'performance'. Chomsky's answer was that for a sentence to be grammatical in English, it can meet adequacy conditions in the competence which it does not necessarily meet in performance. Between competence and performance, competence is the more important one; it is, in fact, the basis of the description of the language.

In this manner, then, Chomsky may have patched up the most glaring contradiction of his theory by creating (for his purposes) an unbridgeable gap between competence and performance. So far it would have been merely an entertaining or a challenging game, but alas, in its later stages the game also became a crooked one. Whenever a critic of the 'Chomskyan paradigm' pointed out an irreconcilable contradiction between fact and theory, Chomsky and his disciples intoned: 'You are not interested in real linguistics . . . You are talking about matters of performance. Real linguistics is the description of competence in terms of transformations and symbolic logic'. By using this form of rhetoric, the MIT-establishment accomplished several things at once:

(a) They explained away the contradictions found by the critics;
(b) they projected an image of progress, mentalism, sophistication, and revolution in science;
(c) they succeeded in intimidating everybody who dared disagree with them. Since 'performance' always carries the attribute 'mere' whereas 'competence' was equated with true linguistics, interest in data and facts became peripheral; honest, data-oriented linguists became 'lowly taxonomical data gatherers' perhaps not worthy of promotion and salary. Incredible and unprecedented inequality in hiring and publishing (at least in the United States) was the result. The MIT-establishment became rigid and impenetrable; in short, a closed system alien in spirit to democracy and academic freedom.

1.3. I will now raise the question of what is better to do: Play a crooked game while staying honest (as if playing poker with a group that cheats thereby losing one's shirt); get out of the game and change professions; or, devise a counter-game, whose apparent crookedness is but a means to show to the onlookers that the opponent is the one, whose game is really crooked. Since I have tried the first solution and found it not to work, and since I will not change professions, I beg the reader's indulgence in allowing me to devise a counter-game of my own. It is very simply this: I will interpret Chomsky's position at face value, AS IF HE DID NOT HAVE THE CONVENIENT EXCUSE OF RELEGATING MY OBSERVATIONS TO 'PERFORMANCE'; IN SHORT, AS IF THE COMPETENCE–PERFORMANCE DICHOTOMY DID NOT EXIST. I trust that this is not a 'crooked game', but merely a challenging or an entertaining one. I predict that it will help understand what makes me object to the Chomskyan paradigm thereby enabling those who believe in it to remove some of its useless ballast and retain only that which is actually useful in it: The study of surface syntax and its sadly neglected pedagogical applicability in teaching English to foreigners or the teaching of composition to children.

1.4. According to my face-value reading of Chomsky's *Aspects of the Theory of Syntax* (1965) the meaning of a sentence (or a set of sentences) is understood by the ideal speaker-hearer only after semantic projection has taken place, where the semantic component is supposed to interpret the syntactically 'creative' component, the deep structure of what has been said or found in writing. It can be argued, of course, that Chomsky did not mean to say that this is what people do. My answer, as before, is that

(a) he either ought to have meant it (in which case he would have been plainly wrong), or (b) he ought not to have said it (in which case there would have been no linguistic revolution). Since my declared purpose is to engage the reader in the logic of a counter-game whose purpose is to show the motivation of the opposition, I will turn tables on Chomsky and pretend that he does not have the convenient excuse of invoking the 'but I am not talking performance' injunction. I do not recognize the relevance and the intellectual legitimacy of using the performance–competence distinction in order not to have to make a theory account for what people do while at the same time promoting an irrelevant and secretly computer-oriented linguistic theory alien to life, people's needs, encoding and decoding, the translation process, poetry, psychology, puns, and double coding. Hence I will deliberately pretend that semantic projection is something that happens in the human brain, right after reading or hearing something, as if happening a few split seconds after the received sentence was processed by human perception. Let us imagine that we are confronted with the following stanza by Horace:

(1)   *Integer vitae, scelerisque purus,*
          Non eget mauris iaculis neque arcu,
          Nec Venenatis gravida sagittis
          Phusce, Pharetra.

If I were a native Roman living in Horace's days, I would, no doubt, have an easier time of 'interpreting' the meandering syntax of this sentence, forced, as it happens to be, by the metrical constraints of the Alcaeic meter. The non-native student of Latin, of course, cannot really grasp this sentence until and unless they had rearranged it in prose form, somewhat as follows: *(Homo) purus sceleris (et) integer vitae, non eget iaculis mauris (obligatory ablative where the logical case is accusative) neque arcu, nec pharetra gravida venenatis sagittis, (O) Phusce!* After the syntactic relationships of modifier and modified, the use of the ablative after *egeo, -ere* 'need' have been 'projected', i.e., looked up in the internalized grammar with the lexemes found ('looked up') in the internalized lexicon, the translator 'reads' the sentence as: 'Phuscus, (I am telling you that) (one, a man) with a life of integrity and pure from sins, needs no Moorish javelins nor a quiver heavy with poisoned arrows!' The sentence simply remains unintelligible as long as the agreements and governments demanded by Latin syntax are not worked out. A native speaker of Latin probably did it in much shorter time by using intuitive jumps, the contemporary foreign student of Classical literature labors at the sentence with dictionary in hand at a relatively slow pace. This, of course, has been known from antiquity to the present. It is a basic move in my deliberately devised counter-game to state that if 'semantic projection rules' in the sense of Katz and Fodor (1963) and Katz and Postal (1964) were to be relevant to human behavior, that is the linguistics of what people do, they would have to be understood and reinterpreted as DECODING PROCEDURES PERFORMED BY THE HUMAN

HEARER-TRANSLATOR'S BRAIN. But human speakers, unlike computers, have no decoding algorithms built into their brains, that is algorithms which function in ordered fashion taking one step at a time. The human brain, being infinitely more subtle and complex than any computer, is of course capable of pretending that it is taking one linear step at a time, and struggling students of Latin who look up each word in a dictionary before understanding Horace's stanza quoted above, may approximate the computer in slowness and inefficiency. But even these slow students, by virtue of being human, will eventually discover that the sentence is in the Alcaeic meter and that it, therefore, exhibits aesthetic beauty. The point I am making here is simply that by asserting that the meaning of sentences is intimately tied to their structure, Chomsky has not said anything new.

1.5. We may enquire what happens when a person has to translate the sentence:

   (2)   visiting relatives can be a nuisance.

If Chomsky's 'semantic projection rules' had any relevance for human linguistics (to borrow Yngve's term), one would expect that these semantic projection rules would tell us whether the gerundival or the participial meaning of the form *-ing* was intended depending on what the deep structure of the sentence was. Thus DS_1 would read something like (somebody visits relatives (((it)) is capable of being a nuisance); with DS_2 being approximately (relatives visit) (((they)) are capable of being a nuisance). Thus, assuming again that performance and competence have been hammered apart artificially in order to save the theory, the real human hearer-reader would perform projection$_1$ (the gerundival interpretation), and match it against the immediately preceding linguistic and extra-linguistic context; if it does not fit, he would perform projection$_2$ (the participial interpretation) and accept it if it fits. The question I am asking is this: Is this, in fact, what people do? Do not be hasty and prejudge your answer. I am not necessarily saying that people never do this at all, under any circumstances. As a matter of fact – as we saw above in the case of the student struggling with Horace's verse – under certain pedagogically relevant circumstances, such a composition, laborious, slow translation, etc., the person engaged in his work might quite possibly try to literally 'interpret' a given sentence once this way, then the other. This old and experimentally proven fact of language pedagogy is, however, not the reason why this analysis has become so popular. Rather it is said that it can claim theoretical advantages of 'descriptive adequacy' over Neo-Bloomfieldian Immediate Constituent analysis; that the IC analysis cannot account for the two different meanings and that, therefore, IC analysis is mechanistic, taxonomical and inferior, with TG being mentalistic, able to approximate 'explanatory adequacy' in addition to 'descriptive adequacy' and that it has these prestigious advantages because of positing a level of linguistic competence underneath the surface structure, known as deep structure. It is an ironic fact that Latinate traditional grammar can deal with the situation perfectly well by using the concepts of 'gerund', 'present active participle', 'singular', and 'plural'.

It is becoming increasingly clear that Chomsky was following a definite sales strategy resembling Madison Avenue advertising replete with both seduction and intimidation when he invented the notion of deep structure. The ingredients were as follows:

(1)   Sentence syntax is the central axis of language.
(2)   If ambiguity is seen in the meaning of a sentence, there must be two nonambiguous sentences (emphasis on SENTENCES) that are the two respective meanings of the observable ambiguous sentence.
(3)   The surface sentence relates to 'performance' as the underlying sentence-like proposition (i.e., the 'deep structure') relates to 'competence'.
(4)   Surface structure is to mechanism and taxonomical data gathering, as deep structure is to mentalist theory-orientedness.
(5)   Surface structure might exhibit observational adequacy, but only deep structure can exhibit descriptive or explanatory adequacy.
(6)   If a sentence is judged unacceptable by native speakers while nevertheless being a logically constructed, hence laboriously retrievable, sentence the unacceptability of the sentence is merely a matter of limitations on performance which does not interfere with the grammaticality of the sentence in competence.
(7)   Surface structure oriented linguists are reactionaries and lack insight; deep structure oriented transformationalists, on the other hand, are revolutionary, daring, and are blessed by the gift of insight.

This is the simple script of seven steps that has conquered the world of linguistic scholarship during the past thirty-five years. It is as simple-minded and as effective as a television advertisement promoting a new kind of mouthwash which posits that clear breath means social success and bad breath means social failure; that smart people who want not to offend their lovers, bosses, fellow-travellers in a crowded Volkswagen, will use the mouthwash, while those who are slow, stupid, and sluggish will go on offending.

We must now take a look at how SG could deal with the ambiguous sentence (2). Stratificational linguistics recognizes that neutralization is a multi-stratum phenomenon, not limited to phonology alone, as was practiced – by and large – in Praguean linguistics.

The 'surface structure' of the sentence, of course, remains ambiguous in isolation, when we do not know who uttered it to whom, under what circumstances, and for what purpose. In stratificational thought we recognize that the sentence is either the realization of sememic trace $(ST)_1$ or of $(ST)_2$.

Figures 2, 3 and 4 show the 'participial', the 'gerundival', and the joint either participial or gerundival interpretation or the sentence in a

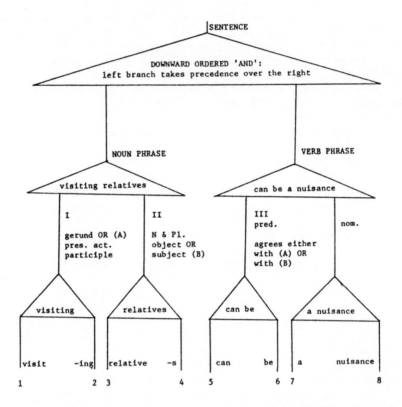

Figure 1 A simplified relational network analysis of the 'surface structure' of *visiting relatives can be a nuisance*. The Lexo-Morphemic constituents 1–8 are ORDERED, that is, we read them off from left to right. The status of the higher constituents I, II, and III, which depends on the SEMEMIC TRACES here realized in NEUTRALIZATION, is the source of the ambiguity, if the sentence is encountered out of context.

stratificational relational network description. Figure 4, in other words, builds together ST_1 and ST_2 without repeating, however, what is common in the two, that is, the predication that is made of the *visiting relatives₁* and the *visiting relatives₂*, namely, *can be dangerous*.

How does this influence our picture of the nature of the translation process and of the concept of 'Deep Structure'?

If the semantic component of a TG grammar 'interprets' the 'Deep Structure', the most we can hope to achieve is to decode the sentence as it was given in the source language. The problem now arises as to how we shall express the sentence in the target language. Let us look at *visiting relatives can be a nuisance* in French. A convenient translation of the sentence would be:

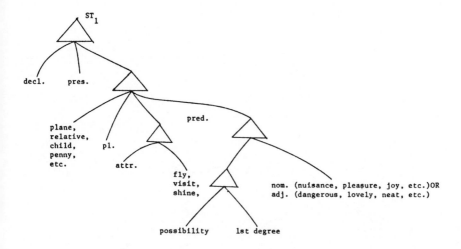

Figure 2   A simplified relational network description of the sememic trace giving rise to the 'present active participle' interpretation with *can* realizing the ˢ/Plural/. Depending what content sememes are used, the network will account for *visiting relatives can be a nuisance, shining pennies can be a joy, visiting children can be neat, flying planes can be dangerous, etc.* Some outcomes will be nonsensical, e.g., *visiting pennies can be neat, shining relatives can be a nuisance, flying relatives can be a joy, etc.* None of these are, of course, 'ungrammatical'; their ill-formedness rests elsewhere. See below. The ˢ/possibility/ in conjunction with the ˢ/first degree/ gives rise to *can*, in conjunction with ˢ/second degree/ to *may*, with ˢ/third degree/ to *might*, etc. Thus a morpheme in 'Deep Structure' such as Auxiliary will not do in a sememic trace. *Will have been, would have been, should have been*, etc., are all different sememic propositions accidentally realized by a set of verbs known as Auxiliaries, but their auxiliary nature is not a sememic, but a lexotactic fact of the English language.

3.   *Les parents qui visitent peuvent être ennuyeux, or*
4.   *Visiter les parents peut être ennuyeux.*

I take it for granted that the following facts are obvious:

(1)   We have not mapped the phonology of the English sentence onto two different French sentences in an algorithmic way without regard for meaning. (By 'meaning' I mean here morphology, lexology, and semology lumped together.)
(2)   Neither have we mapped the morphology of the English onto the morphology of the French. That, incidentally, may be a possibility. Let us see what it would yield:

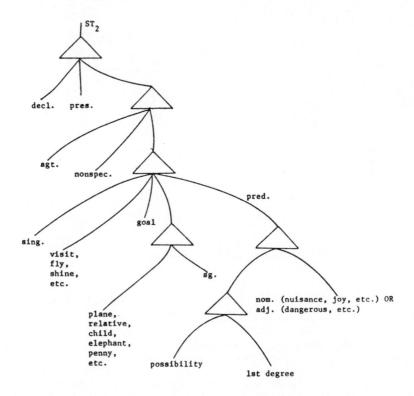

Figure 3   A simplified relational network description of the sememic trace giving rise to the 'gerundival interpretation' with *can* realizing the ^{S}/Sing./. Whereas ST_1 had 5 unordered AND nodes, ST_2 has 6; whereas ST_1 had the Plural sememe in it, ST_2 has the Singular sememe; whereas ST_1 indicates that a predication is made of something we attribute to relatives (i.e., a fact that they visit), ST_2 shows that a predication is made of a non-specific agent's doing something to some goal (i.e., some one flies planes, or some one visits relatives). This non-specific agent is not the Deep Structure Dummy SOME ONE later to be deleted, it is simply realized as 0 on the lexemic stratum with the action sememe realized as the gerund that can carry an object.

English:	*French:*
visit	visit-
-ing	-er
relatives	parents
can	peut, peuvent
be	être
a	un, une
nuisance	ennui, incommodité

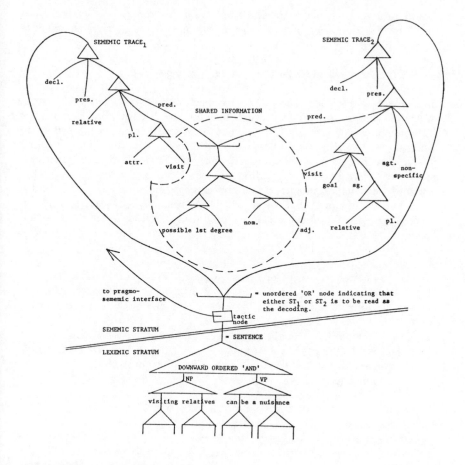

Figure 4

Lining the French up we get:

5.   *visiter parents peut être un ennui, or
6.   *visiter parents peuvent être une incommodité

or any conceivable combination of morphological quasi-equivalences. It is obvious that a syntactically undoctored morpheme look-up, no matter how detailed, cannot render justice to translating the sentence even in one sense (say, the 'gerundival') let alone in both. If we transfer the lexotactics ('surface structure') of the English into the French, accommodating the French habit of using *les* or *des* before *parents* and substituting the adjective *ennuyeux* (both sing. and pl. here) for the nouns *ennui*, *incommodité*, etc., we would probably get sentence 4, that is *visiter les parents peut être ennuyeux*, aided by the similarity of word order, but not 3, which retranslated into English gives:

> 7.   ** The relatives who visit can be bothersome.*

The only possibility left would be to attempt mapping the 'Deep Structure' of the English onto the 'Deep Structure' of the French. But that cannot be done either. First of all, it cannot be done, because – according to Chomsky – the English sentence has two deep structures. The dilemma arises: Which one is to be mapped onto the French structure? Furthermore: Are there two corresponding French 'Deep Structures'? If so, what are they? But let us imagine, that the English sentence has a DS_1 and a DS_2. Let us imagine that these are straightforwardly available and, in accordance with Chomsky's claims, practically identical. Then we would have:

	English:		*French:*
DS_1	(SOMEONE visits relatives ((this act)) is capable of being a nuisance)	:	(QUELQU'UN visite les parents ((cette activité)) est capable d'être ennuyeuse)
DS_2	(relatives are visiting SOMEONE, ((they)) are capable of being a nuisance)	:	(les parents visitent QUELQU'UN ((ils)) peuvent être ennuyeux)

Translation, however, STILL CANNOT BE ACHIEVED. After all, the 'Deep Structures' exist in order to be interpreted semantically, and not to be transformed from one language to the next without semantic interpretation! But this is the lesser objection. The main objection is that the translator simply does not know whether to transfer DS_1 or DS_2 unless and until he interpreted them semantically. Thus he could transfer English DS_1 as French DS_1, but he could just as well transfer it as French DS_2, and that would be an error. Thus the separate availability (and partial similarity) of DS_1 and DS_2 both in English and in French is by no means sufficient in order to translate from English to French, and vice versa.

There may be one way out of this dilemma, and it is the following: If the person engaged in translation INTERPRETS the meaning of the sentence of the source language, he has managed to get hold of its MEANING. He could, then, for the purposes of expressing the same MEANING in the target language, GENERATE THAT SAME SEMANTIC REPRESENTATION based on the knowledge of what the meaning of the original sentence was. But this amounts to having to be BOTH AN INTERPRETIVIST AND A GENERATIVIST AT THE SAME TIME!

If TG – Bach's statement notwithstanding – can indeed tolerate such duplicity, it will have remedied the greatest malady that plagues it at the present time. But the price for such a double-standard will be the admission THAT LANGUAGE IS STRATIFIED. The interpretivist is, of course, the DECODER, and the generativist the ENCODER.

Now, whether one is in the process of ENCODING or in the process of DECODING depends on the pragmo-ecological fact that human speech occurs not in a vacuum, but in definable and describable circumstances understandable as SWITCHABLE ROLES. Both the speaker and the hearer are role players; the roles they play are regulated by SOCIAL INTER-ACTION PSYCHOLOGY (SIP). A person speaking (or singing) out loud without anybody to hear him is either mad, trying to make the time pass quicker in solitary confinement, or walking through a dark forest after midnight; additionally he may be practicing for a recital, dictating to himself as he types, practicing reading in a foreign language, etc. But TG has not even reached the insight that a person either encodes or decodes, let alone the even more basic fact, that a human being is a role player under SIP.

1.6. The translation process works essentially as it has been presented in my article 'The Transformation of the Turkish Pasha into a Big Fat Dummy' (Makkai (1971a), Makkai and Lockwood (1972)), and can be schematically represented as shown in Figure 5.

The translator receives through the transmitting channel (air, marks on paper, etc.) minimal morpheme building signals, PHONEMES, or MORPHONS; in writing GRAPHEMES or GRAPHOMORPHONS. (The morphons are comparable to the 'morphophoneme' and the graphomorphon to the written version of the 'morphophoneme'.) These morpheme-building, or rather, morpheme-realizing elements are decoded into morphemes, and words. The morpheme and word sequences are further decoded into clauses and sentences, and the clauses and sentences are decoded as one, in some instances as two, or more sememic traces, of which these clauses and sentences are the realizations. Having reached the sememic stratum, the decoder-translator switches roles, and becomes the encoder-translator. Due to his cognitive apparatus he will be able to tell WHICH LANGUAGE TO CHOOSE in a given situation, hence the box on the figure called the 'language switch'. In the re-encoding process he now chooses the appropriate sememic trace for the target language. The sememic trace of the source language and that of the target language may frequently be similar, even identical, if the clauses involved are of an ordinary science article type, or of a political-international newspaper article style and, especially, if the languages involved are TYPOLOGICALLY SIMILAR. Thus between German, English, and French there will be many more similar, even structurally identical sememic traces than between English and Hungarian, English and Eskimo, English and Hopi. Whereas this is not the place for me to enter into a detailed criticism of the TG 'universalist' hypothesis, I would like to suggest that it, too, can be met head-on (cf. Birnbaum 1977, Makkai 1973 and 1974a,b). Having chosen the appropriate sememic trace, the translator-re-encoder proceeds to realize

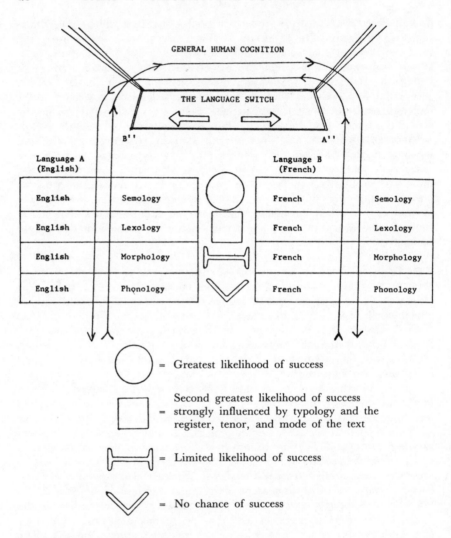

Figure 5 The translation process
A = Translation from French to English, where A′ is the French input and A the English result.
B = Translation from English to French, where B′ is the English input, and B the French result.
B″ is the point in the translation of English into French at which the translator, having properly decoded (i.e., understood) the English text, appropriately chooses the French medium (and not, say, Spanish) for the rendition, and at which general human knowledge must aid the translation process in conjunction with what is available in French.
A″ serves the same purpose when we proceed the other way round, from French to English, without accidentally winding up speaking German, for instance.

that trace according to the lexotactic patterns of the target language. These, too, may bear greater or lesser similarity with the sentence structures of the source language, but any resemblance is strictly accidental and is NOT the result of an underlying identical 'Deep Structure'. Again, typological similarity will have a large part in any similarities. The same holds for the morphological stratum. It has been noticed throughout the past 150 years of linguistic scholarship, that languages differ the most in the arrangement of morphemes, that is, in their morphosyntax. This is why traditional typology has been concentrating on the morphologies of the languages compared. (See Chapter 3, Makkai 1973, in which this fact is discussed in detail and is graphically illustrated in terms of a 4,500-sided diamond in space.) After the appropriate morphotactic arrangements have been made, the re-encoder realizes the morphological material in terms of morphons and phonemes, or grapho-morphons and graphemes. Additionally, he may realize them as motions of the hand (as in the American Sign Language for the deaf) or as distinctive configurations of bumps on paper (as in Braille).

2.0. What is 'Deep Structure', really? An imperfect approximation of the sememic traces of stratificational grammar, additionally hampered by the inept admixture of surface elements and assertion that 'Deep Structure' is synonymous with Language Universals. (See Lamb's review of Chomsky's *Aspects*, Lamb 1967). For a detailed treatment of sememic traces and their interrelationships with sentences see D.G. Lockwood's *Introduction to Stratificational Linguistics* (1972).

To illustrate the untenability of the 'Deep Structure' hypothesis, I will list below a number of sentences all of which, according to the 'Standard Extended Theory' of 1965, would have identical 'Deep Structure' slightly altered by a number of surface transformations:

8. *Jim and George hope to save Noam's paradigm by throwing pornography at the public.*

9. *It is hoped by Jim and George that Noam's paradigm would be saved by throwing pornography at the public.*

10. *By throwing pornography at the public, Jim and George hope to save Noam's paradigm.*

11. *Noam's paradigm will be saved, Jim and George hope, by their throwing pornography at the public.*

12. *It is by throwing pornography at the public that Jim and George hope to save Noam's paradigm.*

13. *It is Noam's paradigm that Jim and George hope to save by throwing pornography at the public.*

14. *It is by throwing PORNOGRAPHY at the public, that Jim and George hope to save Noam's paradigm.*

15. *It is by throwing pornography AT THE PUBLIC that Jim and George hope to save Noam's paradigm.*

16. *It is NOAM's paradigm that is hoped to be saved by Jim and George by throwing pornography at the public.*

17. *It is Noam's PARADIGM Jim and George hope to save by throwing pornography at the public.*
18. *It is Jim and George who hope to save Noam's paradigm by throwing pornography at the public.*
19. *It is AT THE PUBLIC that Jim and George are throwing pornography whereby they hope to save Noam's paradigm.*

Figure 6 is in no way meant as the only possible TG analysis of sentence 8; it will, however, serve our purposes here since it represents (with simplifications and omissions) that version of 'Deep Structure' which is commonly taught in linguistics courses in the USA these days. It can be represented also as:

(20) # ((((Jim and George)) hope to save paradigm ((Noam has paradigm)) ((Jim and George)) throw pornography at the public) #

TG has claimed ever since its early inception, THAT TRANSFORMATIONS ARE MEANING-PRESERVING. TG has also claimed that transformations apply in terms of ORDERED RULES. But the arrangement of 8–19 has nothing about it that forces say, 14 to follow 13, and not the other way round. The order of these sentences makes no difference at all; we might as well start with 19 and work our way back to 8. This is the first observation that needs to be made. Second, and more important, is the fact that native speakers of English DO NOT MEAN THE SAME when saying 8 through 19. The truth is that EACH OF THESE SENTENCES MEANS SOMETHING ELSE. Let us take a brief look at the main differences in meaning:

8. This is the 'neutral' or unmarked version of the sentence. *Jim and George* are thematic, *paradigm* and *public* carry the predictable 'new information stress' in accordance with their clause and sentence final positions, respectively.
9. *Hope* is thematic, *Jim and George* are shifted down to agents, *saved* has clause final stress, the rest is as in 8.
10. *Throwing pornography* is thematic, *public* has clause final stress, *Jim and George* are downshifted to agents in the adjoined clause, *public* carries the sentence final stress signalling new information.
11. *Noam's paradigm* carries the theme, *Jim and George* are downshifted as agents in a secondary clause, and *public* carries the sentence final stress of 'new information'.
12. This sentence implies that it is precisely *by throwing pornography at the public* (and not by some other means) that Jim and George hope to save Noam's paradigm. That is, *throwing pornography* is topicalized sememically; the result is the cleft sentence construction on the lexotactic level.
13. Here it is *Noam's paradigm* that is topicalized; the implication is that it is not anything else they hope to save with their verbal habits, but precisely Noam's paradigm.

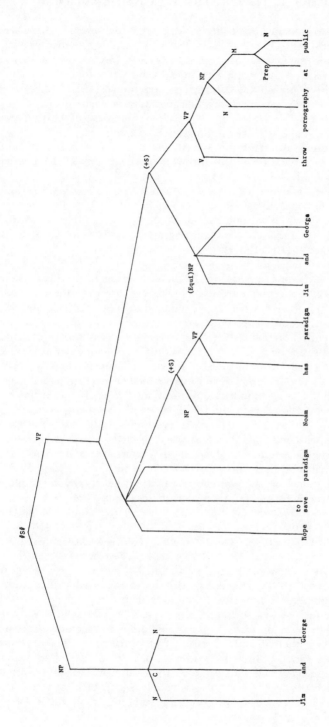

Figure 6 'Deep Structure' of *Jim and George hope to save Noam's paradigm by throwing pornography at the public*

14. This sentence has contrastive stress, which implies a difference in meaning. Otherwise identical with 12, this sentence implies that precisely by throwing PORNOGRAPHY (and not kindness) at the public, do they hope to save Noam's paradigm.
15. This sentence has contrastive stress on AT THE PUBLIC implying that they do not throw pornography at each other.
16. Contrastive stress on NOAM. It is not BLOOMFIELD's paradigm they hope to save, but precisely Noam's.
17. Contrastive stress on PARADIGM. It is not Noam's income tax they hope to save by throwing pornography at the public, but precisely his PARADIGM.
18. Cleft sentence construction topicalizing *Jim and George* and not Edith and Elizabeth.
19. Cleft sentence topicalizing AT THE PUBLIC. The implication is that they do not throw pornography at a few isolated individuals, but AT THE PUBLIC.

Needless to say, these explications of the differences in meaning holding in sentences 8–19 are greatly oversimplified; nor are they the only possible explications possible. Further implications arise if we realize that each cleft sentence construction creates a different thematic structure and that within each differently thematicized cleft structure a number of different contrastive stresses are possible. Hence the number of permutations and variations on each basic, neutral ('unmarked') construction is very high indeed. The number of possible varieties (each grammatical) accommodating all tenses and modes, topicalization/clefting, focus shifting via the passible construction, re-thematicization, and contrastive stress is most probably up in the millions. It thus makes obviously no sense to order these events with relation to one another. Neither do speakers ever think of an underlying sentence first which they then proceed to 'transform' in order to carry just the right desired shade of meaning. How could they? After all, the meaning of a sentence cannot be clear to anybody unless and until the structure of it is there for them to interpret it semantically. Ludicrous as it sounds, it is true: IF THE TRANSFORMATIONAL-GENERATIVE ASSUMPTION OF CHOMSKY THAT THE MEANING OF A SENTENCE IS DERIVED BY SEMANTIC PROJECTION RULES FROM ITS DEEP STRUCTURE WERE TRUE, PEOPLE WOULD BE UNABLE TO TALK. The only way they could talk would be if they said first what they were going to say, and then listened to themselves in order to determine what they said. This is a sad comment on the great 'mentalist revolution' indeed!

The basic task of this section of the present chapter is to point out that since sentences 8–19 do have demonstrably different meanings, it makes no sense to derive them from the same 'Deep Structure'. The truth of the matter is that each of the above sentences has its own sememic trace, each differing from every other in some real and appreciable way. This is not to deny, of course, that they also resemble each other to a considerable extent. But just because two brothers resemble each other (to quote

Lamb's striking analogy offered during his talk at the University of Washington in Seattle in August 1973) it does not follow that they can be explained as deriving from one another. In fact, just as even two closely resembling brothers are the descendants of their parents (and their parents at DIFFERENT STATES OF THEIR LIVES, even if the brothers are twins!), two AGNATE sentences (the term is Gleason's) (or, for that matter ANY NUMBER of agnate sentences) are related to one another as daughter languages are related to one another via the proto-language and never as thought of by beginning undergraduates taking a course in linguistics who think that English has descended from Sanskrit.

TG supporters might object at this point insisting that for sentences 8–19 to come out as they are, a separate sememic trace had to be formed for each, which is repetitious. It would be simpler, one could suggest, to PERFORM MINOR OPERATIONS ON THE SAME TRACE. (The reader is referred here to Lockwood's *Introduction*, 1972, and especially Chapter 5 'Sememic Phenomena'.) The problem with this suggestion is that it presupposes that the speaker had an earlier (say, the 'unmarked') version on his mind before he came out, say, with 18 *It is Jim and George who* . . . etc. This is definitely not the case in ordinary speech. The speaker forms THE RIGHT TRACE IMMEDIATELY based on the contextual evidence available to him – as far as possible. Admittedly, there are exceptions. The most significant exception is when a person 'has something on his mind' but 'doesn't quite know how to say it', and tries a number of different ways. This sort of behavior is most evident during composition; the writer will scratch out several sentences, sometimes even whole paragraphs and pages and start all over again. Our intention is to tell THE STORY in the most effective way; we are searching for alternative realizations of the same set of contextually interlinked sememic traces. We must, therefore, not dismiss entirely the possibility of performing minor surgery on the same trace for better stylistic effect during composition. But such trace-surgery is not TRANSFORMATION in any conceivable sense of the term. For one thing the meaning is thereby appreciably altered; second, the basic proposition has not been altered totally, but only partially. The term ANASEMIOSIS seems appropriate to use for trace-surgery. We must remember that anasemiosis only applies when there has in fact been a previous attempt at forming the right trace, but for some reason or other the speaker (and most often the writer) chooses to edit it.

Every once in a while we encounter different wordings which do NOT carry any appreciable difference in meaning. Consider:

20.   It bothers me that she snores.
21.   Her snoring bothers me.

If these two mean different things to my readers, they are entitled to regard them as results of different traces. It is arguable that *bothers* is thematic in 20, whereas *snoring* is thematic in 21. (I do not mean for 21 to read *her SNORING bothers me* which implies contrastive stress.) I would like to suggest the term ANALOGOSIS for varieties of this sort. Clearly, 1–19 are all instances of analogosis, but they are instances of SEMEMICALLY CONSEQUENTIAL ANALOGOSIS, where 20 and 21 (for those speakers at least to whom theme does not matter much) may be viewed as SEMEMICALLY NONCONSEQUENTIAL ANALOGOSIS. Analogosis, then, is also not a case of 'transformation' but is motivated by (a) thematic choices, (b) cognate vocabulary structure, or (c) frequency of patterns. Thus if I say:

    22.   It irritates me that she breathes so loud.

I have uttered a sentence that is closely related to 20 (the syntactic structures are ENATE), but also one which differs from 20 in VOCABULARY. Is saying the same sentence in different words a matter of transformation. Hardly. Consider:

    23.   He had to go to the foot-doctor.
    24.   He had to go to the podiatrist.

Several questions arise, none of which has been faced by TGG grammarians. Is *podiatrist* a transformation of *foot-doctor*, or the other way round?

    TG has consistently failed to face up to this problem. I would suggest that these are instances of ANALEXIS. The existence of analexis proves that the vocabulary of the English language, for one, is diachronically and dialectally stratified, and that this diachronic and dialectal stratification can reveal itself in the speech of the same person at a given time as synchronic stratification. If I say

    25.   *The teacher walked around the building*, versus
    26.   *The educator circumambulated the edifice*,

I talked plain English in 25 and stilted Latinate English in 26. This choice may mark me socially as normal and young, or weird, old, and pedantic; it may show the informal nature of the situation in which 25 was uttered, and the utmost rigidity of the situation in which 26 developed. ANALEXIS and ANALOGOSIS may co-operate in the production of different sentences whose traces may differ markedly, or only minimally:

    27.   *Around the building walked the teacher*, versus
    28.   *The edifice was circumambulated by the educator*.

I hasten to add here that *foot-doctor* COULD, in fact, be derived from *podiatrist*, especially the *foot* from the **pod-(os)*. So could, additionally, *niece* and *nephew* from **nepot(ism)*, *governor* and *gubernational* from **kybern(es, -etics*, cf. *cybernetics*) along with *father, mother* and *brother* from **patri(cide)*, **matri(cide)* and **fratri(cide)*. What would need to be done would be to reinvent Grimm's Law, Verner's Law, and most of the work carried out on

Indo-European in the 19th century. There would still, I think, remain insurmountable problems, as it would be almost impossible to derive *dog* from *can(ine patrol)*, *bird* from *aviary*, *moon* from *selen(ology)* or *lun(ar)*, or *grass* from *herb(arium)* along with *water* from *aqua(rium)*. The reason why I mention these semantically linked pairs in modern English is that ETYMOLOGICAL PHONOLOGY, a contemporary of TG-style NATURAL PHONOLOGY, has attempted similar derivations. (See Lockwood 1975, Lightner 1975.) The way things are, here and now, modern English is a complex ecological system in which POLYCHRONOLOGICAL SYMBIOSIS is overtly manifest. I can walk into a camera shop and ask for a *three-foot tripod* without contradicting myself, although I have repeated the same *IE words for '3' and 'foot', respectively; once as processed by Grimm's Law for the Germanic languages, and once as borrowed into modern English from Greek, where Grimm's Law has not been operative. Thus, from the point of view of modern English *three-foot* is 'older', if we evaluate age from the point of view of English by itself (this would be the ENDO-ECOLOGICAL VIEW), but, of course, *tripod* is the older form, if we look at the question from the EXO-ECOLOGICAL point of view. Here and now, endo-ecologically speaking, *tripod* is by far the 'younger' form, recorded in the OED as occurring first in 1611 in the sense of 'three-legged vessel', and in the photographic sense first in 1825.

Analexis, in point of fact, is ecologically analogous to the various ways in which the sentence *Jim and George hope to save Noam's paradigm by throwing pornography at the public* can be re-encoded in a number of agnate structures. Just as the various realizations of the sentence do not derive from one another but from the sememic network, analectical lexemes, as the ones cited above, do not derive from one another synchronically. Diachronic derivations are sometimes valid, and sometimes not; the language must tolerate symbiosis. The implications of 27 and 28 are obvious to native speakers of English.

To illustrate how meaning (semology) can be related to sentences (syntax, lexotactics) without transformations yet in such a way that AGNATE and ENATE structures are accounted for (indeed 'generativity' is nothing else but a confusion regarding enate and agnate structures), I will present here one possible stratificational analysis of a set of related German sentences.

Figure 7 describes the German sentences:

29. Die Kinder schlafen
30. Das Kind schläft
31. Schläft das Kind?
32. Schlafen die Kinder?

Under *nouns* (also eligible in the sememic trace) we have *Katze, Pferd, Kuh, Ochs, Hund, Mann, Frau*, etc., under *verbs* (also eligible in the trace) we have *weinen, lachen, spazieren, gehen, sitzen, rennen, atmen*, etc. The unordered 'AND' node on top indicates that the speakers, before committing themselves to one

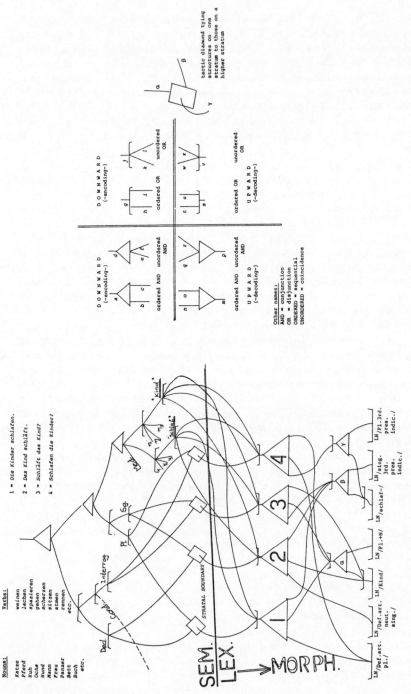

Figure 7 A key to stratificational diagramming

Other names: AND = conjunction ORDERED = sequential
OR = disjunction UNORDERED = coincidental

structure or the other, have the freedom to form ANY on the appropriate traces as the pragmatics of the situation demand it, without having to resort to any given sentence structure (real or abstract) from which to 'derive' any one alternative. The first choice (unordered 'OR') allows the speaker to choose between declarative, interrogative and conditional; as it happens the German conditional (or at least one variety of it) has the same word order as the interrogative, e.g.,

33.   Schläft das Kind? (interrogative, 'does the child sleep'?)
34.   Schläft das Kind, so können wir ins Kino (conditional, 'if the child sleeps, we can go to the movies')

On the right hand side of the trace the speaker can choose between plural or singular, hence the trace will 'generate' either

35.   Die Kinder schlafen ('the children are asleep') or
36.   Das Kind schläft ('the child is asleep')

Since sleeping is not any sort of agency, the sememe ^{S}/Medium/ is next conjoined with the various verbs and nouns that are pragmatically eligible for this family of traces.

The actual sentences are ordered downward 'AND' nodes 1, 2, 3, and 4, on the lexemic stratum. These sentences, in turn, are realized by the lexons *definite article plural, definite article sg. neut., Kind, plural verb ending-n-en, the verbal stem schlaf- the present singular indicative, and the plural third indicative.* Depending on which one is needed, *schlaf* will be *schlaf + en*, or *schläf- + t*, which is a morphemic-morphophonemic matter, no longer under the jurisdiction of the lexotactics, hence omitted on this diagram. Notice, incidentally, that the 'generativity' of such a TRACE FAMILY is very powerful indeed.

37.   Atmen die Männer? ('are the men breathing'?)
38.   Die Frau sitzt. ('the woman is sitting'.)
39.   Die Frauen sitzen. ('the women are sitting'.)

are merely some of the possibilities accounted for (or 'generated') by this particular trace family. Given the very large number of nouns and verbs that can be predicated to each other in German in some real or imaginary sense, this trace family generates millions of sentences without a single grammatical transformation or any ordered rules. It simply shows what is stored in the human brain and what paths the speaker selects when he encodes his experience.

I will rest the case of sememic traces versus 'Deep Structure' here by saying that 'Deep Structure' was an aborted attempt on the part of Chomsky and followers to explain the meaning in syntax, by using the artificial examples of 'ambiguous sentences' out of context. The attempt failed, however, because transformationalists were unable to give up the idea that sentences can only derive from other sentences (or sentence-like abstract pre-sentences) and because of the computer-inspired fixation of rule ordering. Since a digital computer can only allow or disallow electricity to cross a set of wires, its choices are always binary and must be ordered. Even though Chomsky and his followers are no longer actively involved in computer work, without the mechanical translation fad of the late 1950s and 1960s financed by the Army, Navy, and other branches of the US government, TG would not have developed into the binary-logic bound mechanical artifact that it is today in all of its forms.

3.0. In this section I will focus my attention on idioms (cf. Makkai 1972). That TG has had nothing of value to say on the matter has been admitted in print by transformationalists (Binnick 1974).

3.1. LEXICAL IDIOMS are multi-morpheme or multi-word sequences which correlate with a definite syntactic function (verb, noun, etc.) and whose meaning does not follow from the standard lexical meaning of the parts when occurring in other environments. Thus *hót dòg* is not a *dog* that is *hot*, but a 'Frankfurter in a bun'. This simple observation in itself completely defeats TG in one simple shot, since this fact cannot be accounted for by any derivation, transformation, or any other artifact of the system. If you start with a DS derivation predicating of a certain N to BE ADJ., you will wind up with a surface construction *hôt dóg*, which, however, will be stressed the wrong way. The same goes for *rédcàp*, which is not a *rêd cáp*. The *Whíte Hòuse*, which is not *whíte hóuse*, and *bláckbìrd*, which is not *blâck bírd*. Lees in his *Grammar of English Nominalizations* (Lees 1960) openly admitted that the generative method has no way of accounting for such semantically aberrant and irregularly stressed forms. The point I must reiterate here is that these idioms do not DERIVE from any underlying and syntactically mechanically produceable form. (That these forms, too, have syntax, is commonplace knowledge; but the internal syntax of idioms and their behavior in sentences are two independent matters.) In SG the lexical idiom is a complex 'AND' node that leads 'downward' to its constituent lexons and morphemes which, in other environments, are the realizates of other lexemes and sememes with the idiomatic lexeme having its own separate sememe. SG does not commit the error, in other words, of trying to derive *hót dòg* from some fictitious (the dog (WH dog BE hot))) while due to the sensitivity and flexibility of the relational network system it can accurately show what an idiom means, how it is realized, and what it does in the sentence.

3.2. SEMEMIC IDIOMS are sentence or clause-length, institutionalized utterances which are the realizations of more than one sememic trace. In this regard, then, sememic idioms resemble 'ambiguous sentences'. Figure 8 shows the sememic idiom *don't count your chickens before they're hatched*. The CONTEXTUAL ADJUSTABILITY PRINCIPLE (CAP) as a function of cognition signals to the individual whether to encode the sentence in the sense 'do

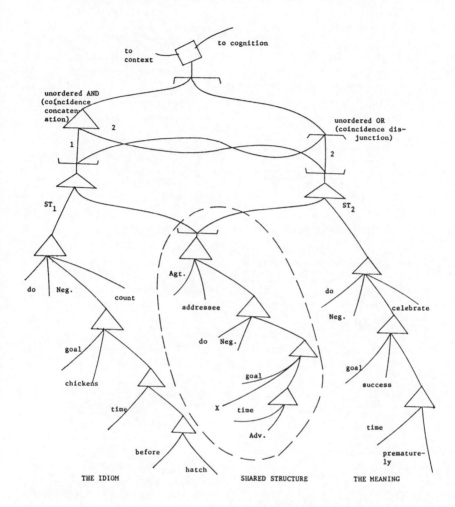

Figure 8 A relational network description of *Don't count your chickens before they're hatched*

not enumerate your fledgling chicks before they are out of their shells'
(ST₁) or in the idiomatic sense 'refrain from celebrating prematurely'
(ST₂). The black unordered 'AND' on the left may or may not be called
into play regulated by the unordered 'OR' above it; if it is, the decoder
decodes IN BOTH SENSES which amounts to PUNNING ON THE IDIOM. Such
a situation can arise if a farmer actually counts yet unhatched chicks and
someone warns him by saying the proverb; it would be signaled that he
is foolish for celebrating prematurely and that he is enumerating unhatched
chicks. Failing the activation of this unordered 'AND' node, the decoder

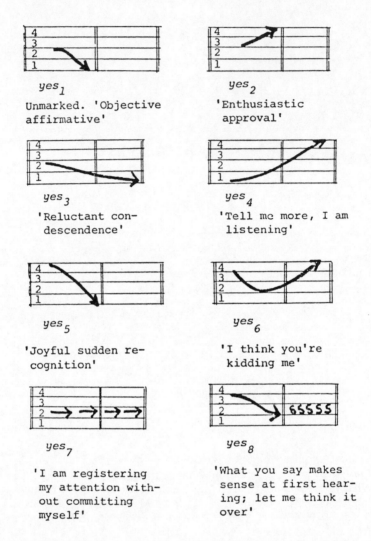

yes_1
Unmarked. 'Objective
affirmative'

yes_2
'Enthusiastic
approval'

yes_3
'Reluctant con-
descendence'

yes_4
'Tell me more, I am
listening'

yes_5
'Joyful sudden re-
cognition'

yes_6
'I think you're
kidding me'

yes_7
'I am registering
my attention with-
out committing
myself'

yes_8
'What you say makes
sense at first hear-
ing; let me think it
over'

Figure 9 Eight commonly recognized meanings of *yes* in American English. (See opposite page for detailed analysis.)

Eight commonly recognized meanings of *yes* in American English

---

(1) Is by far the commonest; hence we regard it the 'unmarked' form. The intonation falls from 2.8 or 2.9 to 1 and signals objective consent. It is typically heard in exchanges such as *Q: Do you have change for a dollar? A: Yes₁.*

(2) Means something like 'great' or 'wow!' The pitch rises sharply and briefly from 3 to 4. *Q: Would you like me to take you to Hawaii for Christmas? A: Yes₂.*

(3) Takes up twice as much time as (1) or (2). The pitch drops from 2.3 or 2.5 to a low, drawn-out 1. *Q: Are you going to do the dishes? A: Yes₃.*

(4) Has the voice rising in pitch from a low 1 to the top of the scale; the rise is drawn out over two measures. It sounds almost like a question. Typically heard when an unknown salesman approaches a customer over the telephone and starts making an appealing proposal. *Q: Sir, I am telling you about our new investment possibilities on Grand Bahama Island where we take our customers by jet economy all paid by us – do you have a minute to talk? A: Yes₄.*

(5) The pitch drops suddenly and sharply from 4 to 1 in one measure. An old, almost forgotten friend announces himself over the telephone: *Q: This is Jack Mulligan calling, your old room mate from college? A: Yes₅.*

(6) The voice starts at 4, dips down to 2 in a drawn out manner, and goes back up again to 4 filling up two measures. *Q: There is this strange costume party at the Taylors tomorrow and I was asked if you'd care to come alone – you see, it is supposed to be surprise for Joanna. A: Yes₅.*

(7) The word *yes* is repeated three or four times in the time of two measures in a colorless, even-keyed fashion held at level 2, as if the speaker is just making noise to keep his interlocutor talking but is not really paying serious attention.

(8) Indicates that the person saying *yes* has heard this kind of question or argument before; is not totally surprised by it; that he is considering it; that he thinks the interlocutor has a point but not one that could not be better stated or improved. Typically heard from university lecturers who are interrupted by a student.

---

reads the sentence either in the sense of ST_1 or in the sense of ST_2, as the pragmatics of the situation demands it.

What matters is that there is no legitimate sense in which the one sense can be 'derived' from the other, except historically. TRANSDERIVATION, as used by Newmeyer (1972), is [+ tricky – honest]. Historically, of course, the proverbial idiom 'derives' from one of Aesop's Fables in which a foolish person did count chickens before they hatched, just as *The White House* is a *house* that is, incidentally, *white*, and as a *blackbird* is also a *bird* that is, incidentally, *black*. (But notice: *The Texas White House is a yellow barn, the flying White House is Air Force No. 1, this baby blackbird is white, it must be an albino*.)

SG, as can be readily seen, handles idioms in a much more elegant and efficient way than other theories. It accounts for their literal versus their idiomatic sense, indicates what sememic traces they are realizations of, and does NOT, unwarrantedly, mix diachronic with synchronic considerations.

4.0. What, we may ask, is the COMMON DENOMINATOR of the various failings of TG. The basic inadequacy of TG is that it regards human language through MUTATION RULES, instead of looking at it as a SYSTEM OF RELATIONSHIPS. (See Lamb (1975a).)

4.1. As a closing argument, I will address myself to the common human experience of DOUBLE CODING. Double coding occurs when a lexeme, a phrase, or a whole paragraph in spoken discourse has a discernible second (or even a third and fourth) meaning beyond the institutionalized, lexico-grammatically retrievable meaning.

4.1.1. The simple lexeme *yes* has – at least – eight commonly recognizable meanings, depending on the intonation and the length.

4.1.2. If we were to take transformationalism seriously, we ought to posit a 'Deep Structure' for 'yes' of which these (as well as many other possibilities) would be 'transformations'. They could be called the 'Enthusiasm Transformation', the 'Reluctance Transformation', the Tell Me More Transformation', the 'I am So Glad Transformation', the 'Kidding Transformation', the 'Noncommittal Transformation', and the 'I heard that Before Transformation', respectively. The first one may be regarded as the 'Deep Structure of yes'. I have no idea how these transformations would be ordered, or what would trigger them. Depending on where the grammarian stood with regard to phonological theory, he might attempt to generate these intonations as phonetic representations of the 'surface structure' of *yes*. But I do not think that would really work. For it seems to me that it is in the very nature of these intonations that the MEANING of the given *yes* rests; as if phonetics were NOT the end result of a transformational cycle that maps surface structures into systematic phonetics, but – in cases such as these – an integral part of the SEMANTICS of the speech act.

Stratificational grammar can easily handle situations like this by virtue of the UNORDERED AND (the coincidence concatenation) concept in COGNITION. The one line of the node goes directly to the sememe, the lexeme, and the morpheme, realized by the phonemes /y/, /e/, /s/, with the socially institutionalized major meaning 'affirmative' activated. At the same time – and without any order – another line from the same unordered AND node in cognition can go to the sememes ^{s}/yes$_1$/, ^{s}/yes$_2$/, ^{s}/yes$_3$/, ^{s}/yes$_4$/, ^{s}/yes$_5$/, ^{s}/yes$_6$/, ^{s}/yes$_7$/, and ^{s}/yes$_8$/ IN ANY ORDER, and at ANY TIME during the same conversation, several times.

Playwrights, actors, and stage directors know this rather well. Additionally, there will be stage instructions as to what kind of facial expression to put on while pronouncing one of the appropriate 'yes'-affirmatives.

4.2. The phenomenon of poetry is, as I see it, not explainable without double (or multiple) coding. The simple fact that two words rhyme in a certain environment changes their relative meanings *vis-à-vis* one another. If a child says

The *cat*
In the *hat*
That chased the *rat*
Sat on a *mat*
And did this
And did *that*
But he looked very *sad*

one of the meanings of each marked item – in addition to what it means institutionally – is that it RHYMES with each other marked item. In the common tongue-twister

Peter *P*iper *p*icked a *p*eck of *p*ickled *p*eppers;
't is a *p*eck of *p*ickled *p*eppers Peter *P*iper *p*icked

perhaps the MAJOR MEANING of the entire tongue-twister is the difficulty of pronouncing a series of aspirated initial /p/-s; a fact very much on the speaker's mind when performing the familiar tongue-twister. (For a more detailed treatment of tongue-twisters, see the next chapter.)

4.2.1. Pursuing my previous line of attack, that is, pretending that TG can be taken at face value, let us imagine what kind of transformational rules we would need to make a statement in 'Deep Structure' BECOME a tongue-twister, difficult to pronounce.

We would probably start out with a logical proposition stating that SOMEBODY with a GIVEN NAME and a SURNAME performed in the PAST an ACTION, the action was CHOOSING and the ITEM chosen was CUCUMBERS that were made SOUR.

Our problem now is this: how does this BECOME a tongue-twister? X. Y. must first of all, undergo the PERSONALIZATION TRANSFORMATION, so we can call him John Smith. But this is not enough; John Smith does not 'pop' with heavily aspirated initial /p/-s; so we have to submit John Smith to the POPPING TRANSFORMATION. How does this work? The ideal speaker-hearer searches his memory until he finds sounds that 'pop'. /t/ and /k/ are also eligible, in a sense, since initially, they, too, are heavily aspirated. Thus, strictly speaking, there is no reason why the deep structure cannot become something like *Tommy Tinker took a tank of tangy tomatoes*, where the POPPING TRANSFORMATION (= initially aspirated stop) would be present. So we have to specify that /t/ and /k/ must be out; by having a P-POPPING TRANSFORMATION, a T-POPPING TRANSFORMATION, and finally, a K-POPPING TRANSFORMATION, unless we want to run the risk of winding up with the wrong tongue-twister, such as *Tommy Tinker*, or, with the /k/-popping, *Kelly Calley collected a kilo of chlorinated cucumbers*.

Each specific tongue-twister would have to go its own specific POPPING TRANSFORMATION, and even then we are still not in the clear. For *Tommy Tinker took a tank* and *Kelly Calley collected a kilo* would result in AD HOC TONGUE-TWISTERS, whereas *Peter Piper* would result in a widely recognized, INSTITUTIONALIZED TONGUE-TWISTER. Thus the transformational rules would have to be rendered context sensitive with regard to INSTITUTIONALIZED OUTCOME versus RANDOM OUTCOME.

The import of this observation cannot be overemphasized. It simply means that GENERATING SOMETHING IS NOT THE SAME AS CREATING IT. Generating an utterance logically implies that we knew IN ADVANCE what the utterance was going to be, and then laboriously accounted for it by re-assembling it. Functionalists and structuralists were, then, more honest because they never claimed to have done anything else BUT decompose utterances that were ready-made; the TG grammarian, on the other hand, prides himself on 'generating' new sentences when what he, in fact, DOES do is merely re-assemble new sentences from the parts of previously observed and analyzed ones. Being a speedier way of operating, this creates the mirage of progress and 'mentalism': people themselves are in control behind the gears. But are they?

5.0. In this chapter I have deliberately chosen those areas of our linguistic behavior which, if TG were to be understood as a theory describing WHAT PEOPLE DO, would show beyond a reasonable doubt THAT THIS IS NOT HOW WE BEHAVE. In so doing I may have been prejudiced and unfair to transformational-generative grammar. It could be argued that there is no justification for doing this. But there is. TG, and especially its earlier militant phase, has accused the 'Neo-Bloomfieldians' of all sorts of omissions and intellectual neglect of which they were not really guilty. Yet, in doing so, TG achieved its greatest positive contribution to modern linguistics: It has managed to ask a set of questions that was previously asked only very timidly and occasionally, or not at all. TG, in its systematic war against behaviorism accomplished a clear understanding of what is REAL about human language behavior, and what is IMAGINARY. As it often happens in the history of science, TG became the victim of its own method. It is only fitting and just, therefore, that we linguists, in the name of progress and fair play, do the same to TG as TG did to structuralism: even at the cost of drawing deliberate caricatures of the system. For in such caricatures the objective researcher will see the vestiges of positive accomplishment as well as the swamps and the quicksands whence there is no return.

If by drawing such a caricature of TG I arouse the reader's interest in stratificational linguistics, I have achieved my goal.

Postword

The stratificational analysis of *visiting relations can be a nuisance* presented in this chapter is not the only possible one. In fact, it is possible to show that already on the lexemic level two tactic analyses can be carried out. It was my intention throughout this chapter to keep the stratificational diagramming – a taxing technicality – to a bare minimum and present the 'philosophy' of the matter at hand.

2 A pragmo-ecological view of linguistic structure and language universals: toward a new synthesis of linguistics and anthropology

The thesis of this chapter is that grammar is to language as autopsy is to general human medicine. This is not to downgrade grammar. Just as you cannot graduate from medical school without knowing your anatomy, a real understanding of language can only be accomplished by a person who masters the grammar of that language both analytically and synthetically.

But as the ability to carve up cadavers scientifically does not make a Whole Physician – and certainly not one who has also insight into the patient's emotional problems – grammatical expertise, indeed theoretician-ship, does not make a Whole Linguist. In order to become a Whole Linguist the student of language must look beyond the grammar and understand the society and culture that uses the grammar under investigation. That this is the case has always been known by anthropologists, but modern linguistic theoreticians have been guilty of neglect in the important area of cultural anthropology. This is an odd fact of life indeed, since anthropology has every right to claim the parenthood of modern linguistics.

It is even more curious that the inadequacy of grammar to account for language should have become increasingly evident at just the time when grammar, after half a century's worth of subservience to phonology, is beginning to emerge as a meaningful subdiscipline in its own right. But the essential emptiness of previous achievements usually reveals itself to the objective observer at the peak of the cognitive cycle in question.

The years 1933 and 1951, the respective publication dates of Bloom-field's *Language* and Harris's *Methods in Structural Linguistics* mark the HIGH PLATEAU and the APOGEE of the essentially surface-oriented Bloomfieldian paradigm. It took less than seven years to 1957, the publication of Chom-sky's *Syntactic Structures*, for linguists to begin asking an altogether different set of questions in view of which the previous high plateau and apogee suddenly seemed shallow and desolate places. Previously static structural relationships could be seen in the light of the new questions as having a potentiality for changing into one another, as if a structural relationship

were a PROCESS. The chief term of the new movement, TRANSFORMA-
TION, TRANSFORMATIONAL GRAMMAR, was borrowed from mathematics,
and the resultant sensation, make-believe though it was, had the power of
entertaining the imagination with an impression of dynamic motion, a
treat enjoyed previously only in the course of arduous historic studies of
languages. The transformer thus luckily escaped the diligence required by
an Edgerton, a Thieme, a Sturtevant, a Tedesco, or a Cowgill, and also
got rid of the taxing field work of a Boas, a Sapir, or their modern
followers Pike, Lounsbury, Longacre, and the five thousand-or-so workers
of the Summer Institute of Linguistics deployed around the globe.

The Chomskyan paradigm, which started out by being avowedly
asemantical (Chomsky 1957), compared to the earlier autopsy-by-candle-
light-and-scalpel style of linguistic analysis as a high capacity computer
compares to a hand-cranked desk calculator, or to computer-aided
postmortems in well-equipped modern hospitals. Excuses for the expiration
of certain sentences were now seen from a different vantage point, at a
greater power of magnification, as it were.

But autopsy is autopsy, no matter how sophisticated or dynamic the
methodology. You can dissect the heart of a dead body, but you cannot
take the person's pulse; and not being able to take the person's pulse
certainly precludes any further guesses as to whether the live patient was
easy-going or irritable in the face of challenges. The practitioners of the
new paradigm opted for discussing what an abstract body CAN do, and
not what a real body DOES. The former was called, with indirect borrowing from Saussure's *langue-parole* distinction, COMPETENCE, and the latter,
PERFORMANCE. A generative description of the body's working was based
on extrapolation from the cadaver's structure, but a direct observation and
recording of the live person's movements and reactions were derided as
merely 'taxonomical', hence uninteresting.

At this stage in linguistics (Lamb 1964a, 1965a, 1966a), a counter-
movement was born which has accurately recognized that autopsy is but
the first step in the process of becoming a Whole Physician. It was known
as STRATIFICATIONAL GRAMMAR, and I have devoted numerous publications to explaining and furthering it (Makkai 1965, 1968, 1969a, 1969b,
1970, 1971a, 1971b, 1972a, 1972b, 1973, 1974a, 1974b, 1974c, 1974d,
1975a, 1975b, 1975c, and Makkai and Lockwood 1973). With stratificational theory we have managed to build a humanoid robot that can almost
stand up on its feet and exhibit bodily motion, like a marionette pulled by
the puppeteer's strings. We have done away with the artificial competence–performance distinction, and speak of IDEAL PERFORMANCE
instead (Lockwood 1972); we have avoided the pitfall of transformationalism by speaking of higher-level realizates and their lower-level
realizations, but a direct observation and recording of the live person's
movements was still not achieved in this theory either, at least not by the
time of the publication of *Reading in Stratificational Linguistics* (Makkai and
Lockwood 1973).

1. Pragmo-ecological grammar (PEG) is an attempt to outline the structure of a theory of language, which, in accordance with Hjelmslev's desideratum (Hjelmslev 1943), does not study the *dislecta membra* of language, but LANGUAGE itself as it functions. Hence the double name, pragmo-ecological: the theory must be practical, or more precisely pragmatic (in the sense of William James (1907–1965)) and must recognize the ecology of language (in the sense of Haugen (1972) and beyond).

1.1. The philosophy of pragmatism can be best illustrated with a quote from William James' lecture, 'What pragmatism means'.

Some years ago, being with a camping party in the mountains, I returned from a solitary ramble to find every one engaged in a ferocious metaphysical dispute. The *corpus* of the dispute was a squirrel – a live squirrel supposed to be clinging to one side of a tree-trunk; while over against the tree's opposite side a human being was imagined to stand. The human witness tried to get sight of the squirrel by moving rapidly around the tree, but no matter how fast he goes, the squirrel moves as fast in the opposite direction, and always keeps the tree between himself and the man, so that never a glimpse of him is caught. The resultant metaphysical problem now is this: *Does the man go round the squirrel or not?* He goes round the tree, sure enough, and the squirrel is on the tree; but does he go round the squirrel? In the unlimited leisure of the wilderness, discussion had been worn threadbare. Everyone had taken sides, and was obstinate; and the numbers on both sides were even. Each side, when I appeared therefore appealed to me to make it a majority. Mindful of the scholastic adage that whenever you meet a contradiction you must make a distinction, I immediately sought and found one as follows: 'Which party is right', I said, 'depends on what you *practically mean* by "going round" the squirrel. If you mean passing from the north of him to the east, then to the south, then to the west, and then to the north of him again, obviously the man does go round him, for he occupies these successive positions. But if on the contrary you mean being first in front of him, then on the right of him, then behind him, then on his left, and finally in front again, it is quite as obvious that the man fails to go round him, for by the compensating movements the squirrel makes, he keeps his belly turned towards the man all the time, and his back turned away. Make this distinction, and there is no occasion for further dispute. You are both right and both wrong according as you conceive the verb "to go round" in one practical fashion or the other' (1965, pp. 41–2).

It has been pointed out (Lamb, personal communication) that pragmatism in this particular instance could be understood as sensible linguistics: William James seeks and finds the two conflicting semological realizates of the lexemic expression 'to go round'. In so far as stratificational linguistics already has made such disambiguations (see Bennet 1968, 1973), it is true that 'pragmatism' means sensible linguistics. As will be seen below, PEG belongs in the family of stratificational grammars for this reason. The pragmatic component of PEG is this: the theory seeks to dissolve interminable metaphysical debates about the nature of language. Some such seemingly unanswerable questions raised during the past thirty-five years are:

A. Is linguistic theory to be mechanistic on mentalistic?

B. Is a language to be described from the point of view of competence or performance?

C. Is sentence syntax in natural languages finite or infinite?

D. Is language acquisition rule-governed, or based on analogy, imitations, i.e. mimicry of the early environment?

E. Does a child acquire his mother tongue because of innate ability or because of exposure and overuse of certain basic patterns?

F. Are natural languages stratified, or are they sets of quasi-algebraic rules which will generate well-formed sentences and reject ill-formed ones?

G. Is a taxonomy of 'rules' inherently superior to a taxonomy of facts?

And so on. Most researchers and students in the field are quite familiar with these questions. The list above is by no means meant to be complete or to be the exact wording of how any linguist would express some of the major issues we are concerned with. It is hoped, nevertheless, that for purposes of illustrating the pragmatic method in theoretical linguistics these seven points will suffice. In what follows I shall attempt to give in a nutshell the appropriate pragmatic answer to each of these apparently irresolvable debates.

A. The metaphysical debate between 'mentalism' and 'mechanism' is a misunderstanding. If 'mechanism' is limited to dealing with facts and data that can be observed with the naked eye (perhaps aided with the microscope or the telescope), scientists should never have discovered, strictly speaking, that the Earth revolves around the Sun, and not the other way around. The heliocentric view of the universe does not follow from direct observation, if follows from speculations based on secondary experiments. Speculations, in turn, are mental activities, hence the mechanically simpler account of the rotation of celestial bodies in this solar system was achieved by mental activity. This well-known explanation is aimed to illustrate that mentalism and mechanism need not be mutually exclusive notions, and that the two approaches can, in fact, be used to shed light on the same phenomenon. From the nonirresolvable pseudo-conflict of 'mentalism' and 'mechanism', it follows that the problem of behaviorism can be similarly dealt with. What is and what is not properly describable under behaviorist assumptions depends on whether we 'spell' behavior with a lower-case b or with an upper-case B, impressionistically speaking. If we espouse the lower-case, narrow approach, only those facts of languages should be worthy of scholarly discussion which have been elicited from a naive informant, transcribed phonetically, then phonemicized, and further analyzed into morpheme sequences without attributing mental rules of how the sentence works. Grammatical is what occurs, and ungrammatical what does not occur. On the other hand, if we spell Behavior with an upper-case B and include the analysis of literary passages, jokes, songs, rituals, and so on, we will have enlarged the scope of our investigation in a way that will include cultural concepts. There are few real linguists who doubt that certain sentences are grammatical only under certain social conditions. This recognition is known as the CONTEXTUAL ADJUSTABILITY PRINCIPLE (see Chapter 3) and without it linguistics is doomed to remain a dull and narrow exercise in artificial sentence patterns and features below the sentence. We can understand, then, that the pragmatic re-evaluation of the concepts of mentalism, mechanism, and behaviorism can help us in elevating linguistics into areas of more rewarding research while maintaining the precision and the scientific rigor that has been achieved during the earlier mechanistic period.

B. The pragmatist approach to the competence–performance controversy would thus be stated: IT IS ILLOGICAL TO SUPPOSE THAT A HUMAN BEING SHOULD BE CAPABLE OF OUTPERFORMING HIS OWN COMPETENCE. The importance of this insight cannot be overemphasized. It happens with great regularity and frequency that people, on the spur of the moment, say things that their grammar, properly spoken, should not allow. Puns, neologisms, jokes, double entendres, allusions are all integral parts of the total use of language. Competence-based rule-oriented grammars are inherently unable to account for matters of this sort. Typically, when generative transformationalists are confronted with the question of artistic use of language, art translation of verse, etc., they will shrug their shoulders and declare that 'that's a matter of special performance'. What is happening is that the TG theoretician sweeps unpleasant problems under the rug by pleading irrelevance.

Let us turn to another example concerning the competence–performance distinction and look at how a pianist functions. Here we see an art whose success or failure depends almost exclusively on practice. But practice is tentative performance intended to build up the performer's competence. What is the competence of a Horowitz or a Rubinstein? Their potential performance. But how did they come by his competence? By practice, which is a kind of low-level performance. Thus in the performing arts, such as music, we see that performance actually antedates competence; it is the very foundation on which competence is built. Now there is reason to believe that human speech is a highly complex musical act, at least in part. Without the constant trial-and-error of early low-level practice, no human being would have any competence on which the rules of his performance could be based for synchronic description. Yet, on the other hand, it is clear that two native speakers of the same dialect can understand each other even if they never met before and even if they discuss matters new to both of them. It follows from these two observations that competence and performance cannot really be separated one from another, except artificially. They are really two sides of the same coin, functioning as a dialectical entity.

C. The pragmatist's answer to the question of whether natural languages are finite or infinite is relatively easy to answer. The question is merely this: What is the game you are playing? If you start on an 'infinite' sentence consisting of an enumeration of the integers of the decimal system: the first number of the decimal system is one, the second is two, the third is three, the fourth is four, the fifth is five . . ., you have committed yourself to an unimaginative pattern which is truly infinite, in the mathematical sense of the term. But there are other arguments for the 'infinity' of syntax. It is possible to enlarge sentences artificially by adding an arbitrarily large number of embedded clauses by using *which* or *that*. The point is that these are abstract, theoretical possibilities that real users of the language only indulge in for the sake of playing memory games, similar to their interest in tongue-twisters. It is also true that tomorrow's novels, newspaper articles and poems have not been written yet; hence, the argument goes, syntax is infinite. Here again is a trivial half-truth, magnified out of proportion. That tomorrow's prose, verse, etc., has not yet been written does not mean that the basic sentence patterns of a language are infinite within a given time period. Needless to say, problems abound in designating relevant time periods, styles, and dialect, but, nevertheless, it is possible to summarize and say that 20th-century American prose has the syntactic patterns a, b, c, d, . . . and q, which is true for 79 per cent of the adult population between 1950 and 2000 with syntactic patterns w, x, y, and z heavily restricted to educated districts of London, England, during the same period of time. If approached from this angle, the finiteness–infinity controversy becomes a Jamesian squirrel chase: obviously everybody is right, hence the argument is a nonargument, and the discussants must specify their vantage points, i.e. their specific interests in the game. The mathematically trained linguist is interested in abstract (read: 'empty', *menschenfremd*) theory, hence he ignores differences in society, social class, dialect, the distinction between prose, verse, and journalism; he shuns statistics and strives for elegant formulae destined to have eternal truth. The anthropologically trained linguist is much more modest, hence also much more realistic: he will strive to give a credible account of how people talked during his lifetime, and also what the main topics of their discourse were. The pragmatist judge in these debates would add that in order to understand such debates it is necessary to know who is the sponsor. The TG-mathematician linguist, typically, has been sponsored by the Army and Navy Signalling Corps, and only more recently by the more civilian agencies of the government which are concerned with mental health and the humanities. Hence computerization and machine translation loomed large as desiderata, and real people were largely left out of the account. The anthropological linguist is apt to be sponsored by modestly financed Protestant churches doing field work in the jungle. As the Romans said: *sapienti sat*. Everybody deserves his sponsor, and the sponsor's prejudices.

D. The language-acquisition debate is similarly resolvable by pragmaticist disambiguation of the issues. Experience has shown that an infant of any race, if brought up by people who speak a language different from that of the natural parents of the infant, will acquire the language of their environment as native speakers. Millions of immigrants to the United States alone testify to this basic proposition. Immigration from Western countries to places where 'exotic' tongues are spoken are, of course, much rarer, but instances of the latter also occur. I believe it can be stated once and for all that (i) the choice of the mother tongue is determined by the grown-ups who take care of the infant irrespective of race, and that (ii) whether a language is 'exotic' or well known makes no difference in this instance.

What is remarkable about the human beings is that they will learn ANY language. Now the TG-Universalist argument usually states that the deep structures of languages are much more similar to one another than the surface structures and that it is the logic of the deep structure relations which is an unconsciously (i.e. genetically) inherited common characteristic of all human babies. There the TG-Universalists have a significant piece of half-truth which then got magnified out of proportion and, consequently, misunderstood by their own students as well as their opponents. What is common between even two typologically most different languages (say, Eskimo and English) is that being natural human languages of the planet they (i) offer a system of systems between general human cognition and a phonological code, (ii) tend to encapsulate the most common human experiences at the cognitive end of the system (birth-pains, hunger, thirst, self-identity, possession, instrumentality, agency, joy, fear, etc.) expressed by (iii) the common human articulatory organs, and perceived by (iv) the common human auditory organs. That is to say, every human language (v) encodes and (vi) decodes culturally absorbed information; furthermore, there is evidence that a large amount of cognitive development takes place in the infant (recognition of mother, fear of strangers, etc.) before it begins to symbolize these recognitions in terms of the social code that it is about to inherit. This may be summarized as the principle (vii) of the supremacy of cognition over the code. These observations (i–vii) may be regarded as unquestionable universals. How the various grammars of the various languages encountered deal with the general human condition and the infant's future culture may be reflected on various levels of the grammar of the language; furthermore, a large number of languages may share specific similarities due to common historical provenience or typological similarity.

It seems idle metaphysics, in view of the above, to distinguish squarely between 'rule-governed behavior' and 'analogical learning', since on a higher level of sophistication analogies are restatable as rules, and rules may be viewed as the results of analogy. The inheritance issue is, of course, another red herring, and must be properly understood. The human being has a brain which is far more complex than that of even the highest mammals. (See Koestler (1967).) It makes little sense, therefore, to argue that we inherit the structure of our languages because we are more sophisticated than the rat or the ape. What we inherit as humans from our parents is our typically human neocortex and its incredible adaptability. Nobody inherits genetically the phrase structure universal whereby

S ⇒ NP + VP; what we DO inherit is our ability to conform to this heavily prevailing pattern in a large number of human languages. (A consequence of the above finding is that, if sentences were not so widely spread all over the world or if their basic structure were somehow different, the human being would use that different structure instead of the familiar pattern above.) The language-acquisition debate's pragmatic bipolarization and resultant disambiguation, then, hinge on the logical INTERCONVERTIBILITY OF RULES AND ANALOGY, in the first instance, and, secondly, on the proper understanding of the RELATIONSHIP OF THE HUMAN NEOCORTEX, ITS FLEXIBILITY, AND THE STATISTICS OF HOW COMMON HUMAN EXPERIENCE HAPPENS TO BE ENCODED IN VARIOUS HUMAN CULTURES. (The answer to question 'E' is contained in this section, so we can skip to the last two questions.)

F-G. As these two popular pseudo-questions are also interdependent, they will be analyzed as one problem rather than two. They are easy to dispose of. A heap of stuff is a heap of stuff, whether it is facts, words, morphemes, features, or what have you. The most tragicomical aspect of recent TG theory is that, in its attempt to dispose of 'taxonomies', it created the most vast and complex taxonomy ever encountered in the humanities. Chomsky and Halle's *The Sound Pattern of English* (1968) is the prime example of one kind of taxonomy replacing an earlier kind with pretentions to innate superiority. At this point, the pragmatist's position can only be Carroll's classical point, when Humpty Dumpty speaks to Alice and explains that the real point is 'who is to be master'. (Read: my taxonomy is not a taxonomy because it is the result of a fashionable theory, hence I am nice and modern; your taxonomy is a dirty and lowly taxonomy because your theory is no theory at all.)

Of more interest is the question whether natural languages are stratified or not, whether they are sets of algebraic rules that will generate only correct sentences. The pragmatist's answer here is: look at the data, and then decide what game you want to play, and how far you want to go. If you are not too data-oriented and like to work on just your mother tongue, and if you are not too interested in what real people do in real life situations, it is indeed possible to argue that language is describable by pseudo-algebraic progressions, equations, and rules. The trouble with TG is not that it does not work, but that it works too expensively, noisily, tyrannically, and arbitrarily, to the exclusion of encoding and decoding, psychology, literature, singing, etc., to mention just a few of its deficiencies.

Whether any given language has strata or not is again an empirical question. Three seem to be the absolute minimum for human languages (ranging from Chinese to Sanskrit), in this order: 1. Semology–Cognition; 2. Lexology–Morphology; 3. Upper and Lower Phonology.

1.2. I will now turn to the ecological component of PEG. I view natural language as a quadripartite system of systems (representable as a funnel-

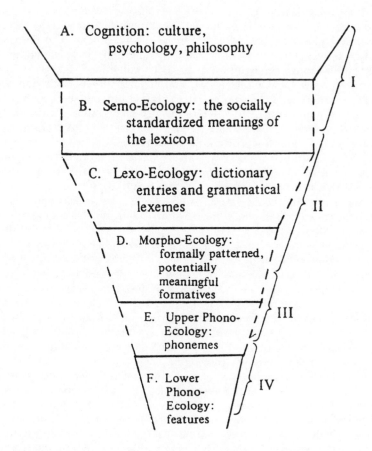

A. Cognition: culture,
   psychology, philosophy

B. Semo-Ecology: the socially
   standardized meanings of
   the lexicon

I

C. Lexo-Ecology: dictionary
   entries and grammatical
   lexemes

II

D. Morpho-Ecology:
   formally patterned,
   potentially
   meaningful
   formatives

E. Upper Phono-
   Ecology:
   phonemes

III

F. Lower
   Phono-
   Ecology:
   features

IV

I   = Semology
II = Lexology
III = Morphology
IV = Phonology

Figure 1

shaped building with four stories in it) whose role is to offer a bridge mediating between the conceptual world and the phonological (or some other phonology-based) code used by the speech community under investigation.[1] (See Figure 1.) The phonological code is, of course, for members of a given speech community culturally inherited, whereas for the foreign observer-investigator it seems entirely arbitrary. The concepts that such a code expresses are much less arbitrary even for the foreign descriptivist; if a missionary becomes thirsty in the Malaysian jungle the new noises he must learn to convey the meaning of 'water' may be totally surprising, but the common human sensation of thirst is a cognitive-biological 'universal'. We can refer to the substance known to the chemist as H_2O in roughly 4,000 or 4,500 different languages, in addition to being able to make differentiations as to its condition; e.g., we may find expressions referring to salt water, fresh water, rivers, drinking water, puddles, various types of frozen water, and so on; but we may also refer to it in the commonly used international chemical abbreviation as H_2O. Such an awareness of water would be DENOTATIVE rather than CONNOTATIVE, but this is the kind of awareness of 'water' that enables any person to translate the English lexeme *water* into the corresponding German *Wasser*, French *eau*, Indonesian *ajer*, Hungarian *víz*, etc. When I refer to the denotation of the LEXEME *water* I am dealing with the SEMEME *water*; this is the normal unit of meaning which allows translation. The connotations of the term would belong in the cognitive system of each speaker.

It appears that the funnel-shaped structure of Figure 1 can be drawn from the point of view of an individual speaker as well as from the point of view of the ecology of our planet's 4,000 ($\pm$500) languages. An individual speaker (as well as an individual language) has disproportionately more material stored in his cognition than he has articulatory-acoustic distinctive features in his phonological system. Hence the staggered funnel of Figure 1 becomes narrow near the bottom, indicating a lesser domain, whereas the top part flares outward, indicating expansion. Phonological analyses of English vary widely as to school of thought, sophistication, and vintage, but almost all linguists, when it comes to written representations of the phonological material, use maybe forty or forty-two symbols, regarded in some traditions as PHONEMES. Now forty-two is certainly a much smaller number than 15,000 or 20,000 – a conservative estimate of the number of vocabulary items used by an average native speaker of American English. Note also that vocabulary items can be highly complex and be merely the surface realizations of a great many more semantic elements, of which the speaker is aware consciously or unconsciously. As a typical example we say rather easily *UNESCO* or *LM*. As phonological units they are /yunéskow/ and /lém/, respectively. Most people using the word *UNESCO* would probably realize after some prodding that it stands for 'United Nations Educational, Scientific, and Cultural Organization' and that *LM* stands for 'Lunar Module', but if they try to relate the concepts to their cognitive counterparts we find much diversification. Just to explain satisfactorily what *nation* means, then what *United Nations* means, is very complex and the number of defining concepts brought into play is very large.

Nor do words need to be abbreviations of sophisticated instruments or social institutions in order to be semantically and cognitively complex. This becomes immediately apparent when one tries *really* to explain the concepts *Sun*, *Moon* or *Earth*. It is obvious, then, that our phonological apparatus is a great deal simpler and a great deal more repetitious than our conceptual universe. The top portion of the funnel, then, is wider in relation to the middle and the lower portions, as it houses the concepts (and their components) we humans carry around in our heads. It is an expandable bag, a flexible component, capable of growth (learning) and of forgetting (this would amount to shrinkage)[2] and is populated by a number of universal human concepts[3] (*hot, cold, night, day, Sun, Moon, male, female, adult, child, yes, no,* etc.) along with the more technical subcomponents of such concepts, and some culture-specific ones (e.g. *hominy grits, bubble and squeak, sauerkraut, beef goulash, stars and stripes, hammer and sickle, social security, de-Stalinization, laua pig, wildcat strike, dark horse candidate, lame duck president, to gerrymander*).

The fact that we use WORDS to express CONCEPTS is indicative of the general human condition: we are all language-captives. The natural sciences of physics, chemistry, botany, etc., have managed to make use of mathematics as a metalanguage in expressing their meaningful relationships, and the transformational-generative grammarians have also been hopeful that mathematics and symbolic logic would turn out to be adequate metalanguages of human language. As Hockett (1968) has convincingly pointed out, however, mathematics is more appropriately viewed as a *result* of human language rather than its principal cause or justification. The most vulnerable of all sciences in this regard is linguistics. While it is clearly in need of a metalanguage, it is, by necessity, the most prone to use the object of its study, natural language, as its own scientific metalanguage. Few linguists have faced this dire fact, but the psychologists Oller, Sales and Harrington came to grips with the dilemma in their 1969 paper. The point is reiterated in Oller (1971). A pragmo-ecological theory of language seeks to relate linguistic elements (words, monomorphemic or polymorphemic lexemes, idioms of various size-levels) to units in the physical and social culture and is, thus, closely related to Pike's (1967) general theory of human behavior, with language as part of that behavior as well.

Just as it is true that tomorrow's poetry has not yet been written, it is also true that I can inform any intelligent English speaking person of some unfamiliar fact or an institution existing in some other country, as long as I embed the new information in a matrix that is basically familiar to him, the listener. Thus I can describe *chicken paprika* or *beef goulash* to any American who has never had it by likening it (and simultaneously contrasting it) with the various types of stew and stroganoff-like dishes he might be familiar with, then going into the details of how it is made, what the role of onions and red paprika is during the preparation, whether to add sour cream or not, etc. This is essentially why cookbooks may work, if they work at all; in fact, why any instruction booklet works. The instructions invariably describe some familiar set of actions in a new ecological setting and thus engender a new act, by re-employing certain already familiar habits or motions. The acquisition of any such new information (on whatever subject) if done systematically over the course of four years in a structured environment, is known as a university education. The student acquires, no doubt, some new vocabulary as he goes along, e.g. new lexemes such as *de-Stalinization, gerrymandering, Demilitarized Zone,* and *Civil Disobedience* in social sciences, *Van Allen radiation belt* in astrophysics, *cardiovascular insufficiency* in medicine, *iambic tetrameter* in poetics, *morphophoneme* in linguistics, but in many cases, especially if the person comes from an exceptionally good high school, the number of new vocabulary items *per se* might turn out to be negligible in comparison with the total amount of new information acquired through the remobilization of his old vocabulary during his stay in college. Clearly, then, the new information (such as ability to recount the history of the United States with major dates and corresponding events) is a matter of the person's having acquired new interconnections (perhaps in bundles or in elaborate networks) of cognitive-semological material, all of which may express itself in the vocabulary he brought with him from his high school days.

By analogy, consider a person's task in learning new morphemes in order to acquire a new vocabulary. In the examples cited above few of the morphemes will be unfamiliar to the uninitiated; maybe *vascul-* in *vascular, iamb* in *iambic,* and *tetra* in *tetrameter*; *Stalin* and *Van Allen* are names and one always learns new morphological material when encountering an unfamiliar type of name; *-mander* of *gerrymander* may also be thought of as new; but *de-X-ization, de-X-ized Y,* etc., may all be familiar material.

Also consider the number of irregular words in English, which is finite, and does not seem to grow. Whereas we do not innovate freely by creating verbs on the *sink–sank–sunk* or the *hit–hit–hit* pattern, we do often create new verbs whose past tense and past participle end in *-ed.* Rhyme and analogy are the principal ecological factors that make this uniformly predictable. Thus new vocabulary is most often created through recombinations of already known morphemes. It follows that a natural language such as English has far fewer morphemes than lexemes, just as it has fewer lexemes than sememes, and fewer stock sememes than cognitive units whose 'free and flexible' recombinations amount to the constant flux of thought passing through a person's mind.

Thus we witness the unfolding of a most efficient ECOLOGICAL STRUC-TURE, whose basic architecture shows the wisdom of PRESERVATION BY RECYCLING (see Figure 2).

The nature of every ecological system is that every member in it functions in relation to the other members, somewhat as a violinist or an oboist does during the performance of Beethoven's Ninth Symphony. In a symphony, every orchestra member plays his part in order to contribute to the composer's concept of the whole: he is subservient to the unity's function-ing. Notice, however, that each instrument can, nevertheless, at the composer's will, become a solo instrument temporarily, or the instrument which carries the main theme. The analogy with language (and its ecological subsystems) bears some examination. When a violin or a flute plays the theme in a certain section of the symphony, it is an ELEVATED INSTRU-MENT which does not merely ACCOMPANY, but CARRIES the main theme. Yet two moments later it can fade again into the general accompaniment.

	ESTIMATED POPULATION:
Conceptual world	
Semo-Ecology	millions
Lexo-Ecology	tens of thousands
Morpho-Ecology	thousands
Phono-Ecology	dozens

The relevant 'tactics'

A = if the units in this section are organized into chains branching out to the right, we approximate a 'tactics' of the semantics, which could be called 'thought'.

B = If we concatenate the SEMEMES of a language before committing ourselves to any particular wording, we are in the midst of producing abstract 'pre-sentence sentence structures', that is, we create traces that are the possibility of many sentences. This is called SEMOTACTICS. This is what 'Deep Structure' ought to be.

C = If the LEXEMES of a language are concatenated, one is producing CLAUSES and SENTENCES without yet having taken care of the finer morphological and morphophonemic adjustments that still need to be made. (This is the LEXOTACTICS.)

D = Morphophonemically ready-to-adjust clauses and morphological words are the results of the horizontal combinations of the MORPHOTACTICS.

E = Syllables and nonsense words result from the horizontal combinations on this level, known as the PHONOTACTICS.

F = This is the PHONETIC STRATUM below the PHONOLOGY. It, too, has a 'tactics' whose output is bundles of features; segments and clusters.

Important note: Far from shying away from syntax, a Pragmo-Ecological Grammar actually recognizes 6 different levels of operation for syntax from 'thought' to 'noise' with TRACES, CLAUSES, SENTENCES, WORDS, and SYLLABLES are the mediating output of each tactic level.

Figure 2

Similarly, cognition can light up sharply, or only dimly, certain linguistic elements in the given ecological setting.

Take the expressions *old wife* and *Emperor of Japan*. If I embed these in a sentence such as *The Emperor of Japan has an old wife*, every element in the sentence receives sharp cognitive illumination. The ecological setting of the sentence is such that all of the morphemes (*emperor*, *of*, *Japan*, etc.) receive the degree of cognitive luminosity we associate with them as lexemes when they refer to 'a kind of potentate', 'provenience', 'certain

Asian country', etc. However, I can also say *My cat devoured my old wife and my Emperor of Japan*, and persons not familiar with the terms *old wife* and *Emperor of Japan* in the ichthyological sense may wonder what was said. It so happens that for complicated lexo-ecological reasons, the English language has reserved the morpheme combination *old wife* and *Emperor of Japan* for certain kinds of fish. In a way this is a saving, since the namer of these fishes did not have to think up a new pronounceable phoneme string to create a new morpheme for each of these creatures – but it could have happened the other way, too. The *old wife* could conceivably be called a *nootch, and the *Emperor of Japan* fish could, in fact, be called a *bootch. If we had the morphemes *nootch and *bootch in English referring to these two fishes, we would have two morphemes which we presently lack; this, in turn, would lessen the potential misunderstandability of the expressions *old wife* and *Emperor of Japan*. Thus to say that *old wife* and *Emperor of Japan* are somehow a 'saving' is only partially true, for there is a reverse consideration. It could, in fact, be true that all such lexical idioms are a matter of SENSE POLLUTION, the inevitable result of the increase in functional load of reinvested morphemes.[4]

It appears that what one saves by inventing a new morpheme, one must pay for in the multiple reinvestment of phonemes, and so on, upward, in the entire quadripartite ecological system of language. (Cf. Lamb (1964), reprinted in Makkai and Lockwood (1973), and Chafe (1967, 1970).) Yet one would have a hard time redesigning natural languages to make them 'more economical' or 'more efficient' than they already are. Planned interference may turn out to be a pollutant. Ecological systems have a remarkable way of working out entirely on their own and without human meddling, their ratio of growth and waste, and that is exactly what languages have done (English in particular), centuries before any speaker thought of linguistics, structural, tagmemic, transformational, or stratificational grammar. If the estimated population numbers of Figure 2 are approximately correct (and there is reason to believe that they are, at least on the order of magnitude), it seems reasonable to suspect that the lower the population number within a given ecological system, the greater the chances of the members of that subpopulation to be multiply reinvested in order to realize units of the neighboring higher ecological subsystem. If we compare the 'phonemes' of English to the keys on a typewriter, we can immediately see what is involved: entirely contradictory philosophical volumes may be typed on the identical typewriter by two diametrically opposite personalities. The syllable-ecology may be viewed as a much larger (in fact, enormous) typewriter which, instead of typing letters, types syllables. It is theoretically possible to construct such a syllable typewriter for English, but the waste would be fantastic. Imagine that every possible syllable in English, whether in real, or made-up words, beginning with the consonant cluster /fl/, as in *flank, flute, float, flue, fluid, flicker, flame, flag*, etc., could be typed only by striking a separate key for each! There would also have to be a key for *fle*, one for *flo*, and one for *fla*, and so on. Even such a device would not be a morpheme typewriter but merely a syllable typewriter, yet even so the number of keys needed to type ordinary English would have to be in the thousands; the size of such a machine would be prohibitive. The next step would be to have a morpheme or a lexeme typewriter. Imagine, for the sake of argument, that the only way to type English would be to have a separate key (or symbol) for every entry in the unabridged *Oxford English Dictionary*. The proposition is far from being as absurd as it sounds: certain old-fashioned Japanese and Chinese type-writers which use characters rather than Romanized spelling come close to the syllabary (Japanese) and the to morpheme typewriter (Chinese). Yet an average size phonetic typewriter with a few dozen extra symbols stored where we ordinarily have upper case, can do justice even to the phono-logically most demanding languages. Thus, there is something in the very nature of human languages that makes their phonologies the most multiply reinvestable of their stock, the morphologies their next highest multiply reemployable reservoir and, finally, their lexeme stocks, which are more often in a one-to-one relationship with the concepts expressed by these individual lexemes. But here, too, as we saw from the examples of *old wife* and *Emperor of Japan*, human nature has brought it about that, instead of using phonological ingenuity in creating some new morpheme, conceptual and imagistic ingenuity is used at the cost of displaying poverty on the level of morpho-ecological creativity. The fish known as *old wife* has a rotund shape and a fairly large mouth, hence the person(s) responsible for naming the fish *old wife* may have thought of some real person(s) who distantly resembled the fish so described; likewise, the *Emperor of Japan* fish may have traceable logical connections with the name it echoes either by origin, resemblance, original provenience and ownership, or any logical connection that seems to make sense.

2. On the diversity of human languages vis-à-vis the common human condition: a reverse view of language ecology As the foregoing discus-sion and Figures 1 and 2 suggest, it is the cognitive portion of man's language that is the vastest and the richest, and his phonology that is, relatively, the narrowest. This is indeed the picture that emerges if we view the organization of language as the language of one speaker.

In contrast to this view of language, we must entertain the picture that emerges if we realize that there are, roughly, 4,000 languages in the world *vis-à-vis* one general, human condition on this planet. It is true of every human being that we come into the world by being born of a woman; we all have a male and a female parent (artificial insemination notwithstand-ing);[5] we live, on average, under 100 terrestrial years, and then die. Virtually all members of the species *Homo sapiens* have a spinal cord, a pair of kidneys, a heart, a lung, two eyes, two ears, two legs, two arms, and so on. We differ as to the color of our skins, the sizes of our lips: the commonly known characteristics studied in physical anthropology. These, however, seem not to warrant the separate existence of 4,000–5,000 separate languages, since whatever our separate appraisals of the world we live in, whatever our particular cultures and their particular orientations,

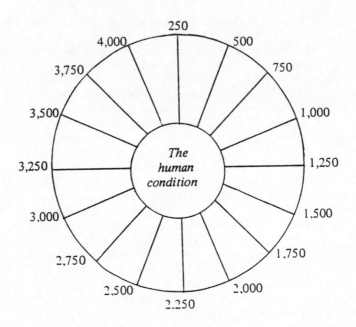

Figure 3   Each spoke of the wheel represents 250 natural languages of the planet

we do all share the BASIC HUMAN CONDITION of pleasure, pain, joy, sadness, hunger, secretion, reproduction, etc. Our interpretations of these experiences are, no doubt, as many as there are human beings on the planet, and so the oral and written expressions about these experiences will differ as well. As the French say, *le style c'est l'homme*, and that is, I fear, our only real chance for any originality on this planet. It is not so much *what* we see, but *how* we see it; not so much *what* we express in statues and music, but *how* we express it, that marks us as separate individuals with separate biographies, separate destinies.

If we take the pragmo-ecological view of language, according to which human languages are the natural precipitations of the collective awareness of discrete groups of humanity on the planet, we must conclude that we live in a natural state of primordial sound-pollution (see Figure 3). The important thing to realize is that both the state of affairs depicted in Figures 1 and 2, and that described in Figure 3 are not all contradictory, but co-exist simultaneously. In other words, for an individual speaker of English, it is true that the concepts he stores in his brain are up in the millions with only forty or so phonemes to express them; yet it is also true that English is only one of the natural languages of the planet, many of whose concepts (and sounds, for that matter) are also found in other languages.

To take an example of two unrelated languages, a speaker of English and a speaker of Hungarian have their own linguistic structures which are, abstractly speaking, similar. Both the Hungarian and the English speaker have a phonology, a morphology, a lexology, a semology, and a cognition. These two cognitive systems, however, are special. Separate though they may be in relation to the two discrete languages which they feed from 'above', only they, and certain portions of the phonologies, can be mixed with one another, while a great deal less is available for common use in the areas of the morpho-ecology and the lexo-ecology. The reason for the 'mixability' of the cognitive component is that cognition, by its very nature, is tangential simultaneously to the particular linguistic system it feeds and to the general human condition; the 'mixability' of the phono-ecological subsystem is due to the fact that the biological characteristics of human mouths and ears on the planet, though slightly different, are reducible to a limited set of universal features. An average Hungarian immigrant in the United States is able to communicate entirely with his native Hungarian phonemes which he substitutes for the corresponding native American English ones. He is, of course, marked sociologically as a foreigner; depending on the situation, this may be a disadvantage or an advantage. If his grammar and vocabulary are in order and he manages to communicate with the native speakers by successfully conveying his cognitive message, the fact that he has no American English phonemes at all may frequently be overlooked.

Figure 4 should be visualized as a 4,000-sided diamond in space. The greatest degrees of universality are found at the 'North Pole' and at the 'South Pole' tips of the diamond; these are the places where, due to features of the universal human condition, the things people talk about and the bodily organs with which they talk and hear make the features of various languages converge. On the North Pole (cognition) these are the basic experiences of birth and death – this being the exceptionless base-axiom of the human condition.[6] Below this point matters move farther apart, but they are still very close; pain, hunger, pleasure, eating, and love-making, for example, are all common human experiences. Matters of family and what we think about them are more specific. These, then, would belong at the lower portions of the cognitive level (A) giving room for particular cultures and the way they analyze the world for themselves. The pragmo-ecological approach to the Humboldtian–Whorfian hypothesis in this connection would be the following: the linguist can make only two mistakes, namely (1) if he takes the suggestion that language structure determines one's cognitive outlook seriously, and (2) if he ignores it. A pragmatic course must be steered between Scylla and Charybdis, and the way to do it is to take along the diamond of Figure 4 as the ecological compass. The detailed and extremely valuable work carried out by anthropologists such as Floyd Lounsbury with regard to kinship terminology (cf. Lamb (1965)) is based essentially on the use of such a compass in unknown waters: the universal concepts of ego, male, female, male parent, female parent, patrilateral, matrilateral, etc., are matched against the individual lexicons of the languages under investigation. Each

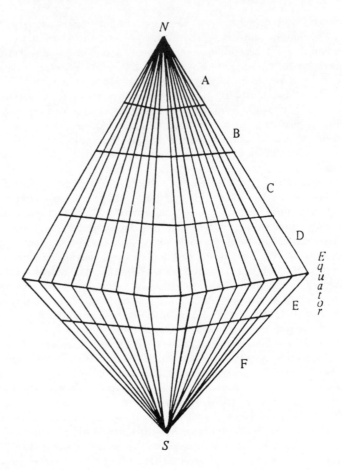

Figure 4   The diamond of language universals

A = Cognition
B = Semo-Ecology
C = Lexo-Ecology
D = Morpho-Ecology
E = Upper Phono-Ecology
F = Lower Phono-Ecology
N = 'North Pole' (the human condition)
S = 'South Pole' (human articulatory and auditive organs and linguistic
        features)
'*Equator*' (widest band of linguistic diversity).

term found in the culture is then describable by an appropriate quasi-algebraic line-up of the universal concepts whose network functions as the eliciting matrix during field work. The types of structures that emerge can then be compared for typological purposes showing both diversification and congruence.

Levels B, C, and D (semo-ecologies, lexo-ecologies, and the morpho-ecologies) widen out gradually on the diamond, as languages become more and more dissimilar in their surface grammars. Depending on the genetic and typological classification of the languages concerned, certain North-to-South bands of the diamond will be wider or narrowing down to thin meridians, depending on how many languages share certain features in common. The drawing is thus deceptive, since it suggests that the diamond is completely symmetrical and well formed, which certainly cannot be the case. It is also apparent that the 'Northern Hemisphere' of the diamond (housing cognition, meaning, lexicons, and morphologies) is a much busier hemisphere than the southern one which, to bring the diamond to its 'South Pole', has but the upper phono-ecology (phonemics) and the lower phono-ecology (phonetics). It appears to be a pragmo-ecological fact that symmetry and realism do not always go hand in hand.

As the angular Equator of the diamond suggests, there is, no doubt, A THEORETICALLY CALCULABLE WIDEST BAND OF LINGUISTIC DIVERSITY ON EARTH. It is no accident that if we continue marking off the boundaries of the sub-ecologies on the diamond, this theoretical widest band of diversity will fall roughly in the area of morphosyntax, the area referred to by many recent linguists as 'surface structure'. Traditional typology will bear out this observation: the more conceptual we make the grammars of any two languages, the more we will find that by some device or another, the same basic denotative content can, in fact, be expressed in the other language. Traditional language typology (Sapir (1921)) and its more recent, but still pre-transformationalist-universalist applications (Greenberg (1957), etc.), were instinctively correct in seeking the most suitable theater of their operations in the border area between morphology and syntax. This fact cannot be overemphasized. The insight that languages differ most in the way they realize inner relationships (innere Sprachformen) in their outer manifestations (Ausdruck) goes back to Wilhelm von Humboldt's 1836 *Über die Verschiedenheit des menschlichen Sprachbaues und ihren Einfluss auf die geistige Entwicklung des Menschengeschlechts* (see the 1960 facsimile edition, Ferd. Dümmlers Verlag, Bonn). This great milestone of linguistic history and human intelligence in general is an enigmatic masterpiece which was misunderstood and belittled by the Neo-Bloomfieldians and callously misexpropriated by some MIT-universalists. The morpho-ecologies of the planet's natural languages may be viewed as petrified fragments of conceptual material precipitated in various forms of phonic substance. On p. 94 (Chapter 5) of his *Language*, Edward Sapir wrote concerning the structure of the sentence *The farmer killed the duckling*: 'The sentence is the outgrowth of historical and of unreasoning psychological forces rather than of a logical synthesis of elements that have been clearly grasped in their individuality.' On p. 105 we read:

It is almost as though at some period in the past the unconscious mind of the race had made a hasty inventory of experience, committed itself to a premature classification that allowed of no revision, and saddled the inheritors of its language with a science that they no longer quite believed in nor had the strength to overthrow. Dogma, rigidly prescribed by tradition, stiffens into formalism. Linguistic categories make up a system of surviving dogma – dogma of the unconscious. They are often but half as real as concepts; their left tends ever to languish away into form for form's sake.

No better wording of morpho-ecology is available to date. I can only add: this dogmatic and unconscious inventory taking became deposited along the Equator of the diamond of language universals, as if the centrifugal force of a spinning top had helped to hurl it there. Thus when we translate from one language into the other, we must climb the unreasoning Rocky Mountains of morphosyntax to find the hidden passages that lead from meaning lurking in the valleys on the content sides of the participating languages involved. But the contents, at least denotatively, are there. This is the reason why the Communist Manifesto, the Bible, Chairman Mao's collected works, and the American Declaration of Independence can be and are being translated into practically all known languages in the world.

Notice that the diamond cannot depict numerical relations. The fact that an individual speaker carries perhaps millions of concepts in his head but only uses a few dozen articulatory-acoustic distinctive features (see Figure 2) must be visualized simultaneously with the insight offered by the diamond of linguistic diversity. It is as if the specific gravity of the Northern Hemisphere allowed much denser molecular packing than the Southern Hemisphere. Our species appears to be much more universally human in its relative poverty of archaic resources (features of the upper and lower phono-ecologies) than in its proliferation of conceptual material. This, too, however, may be perfectly natural. Biologists have known for some time that the human cortex is disproportionately large if compared to other portions of the brain (cf. Koestler (1967), particularly Chapter 16, 'The Three Brains'), characterizable as a tumorous overgrowth. To put it briefly: *Homo sapiens* is concept-rich and sound-poor. It may be worthwhile to quote Koestler's summary of Chapter 16:

> The evolution of arthropods and marsupials shows that mistakes in brain building do occur. The strategy of evolution is subject to trial and error, and there is nothing particularly improbable in the assumption that in the course of explosive growth of the human neocortex evolution has erred once more. The Papez-MacLean theory offers strong evidence for the dissonant functioning of the phylogenetically old and new cortex, and the resulting 'schizophysiology' built into our species. This would provide a physiological basis for the paranoid streak running through human history, and point the direction of the search for a cure (pp. 295–6).

It would also explain what I have been referring to as the multiple reinvestability principle of the sub-ecologies of language from sound through form, up to sense. A proliferation of senses sponsored by the neocortex lives in symbiosis with an essentially static inventory of sounds (i.e. the conceptually inarticulate archi-language of screams, laughter, plaintive or threatening intonations, etc., which are present in the language behavior of children and provide the basis of the kind of double coding in speech which has occupied analysts of poetic language; cf. Fónagy (1971, 1976b, 1983), which may change historically, but do not proliferate at the same rate as does the inventory of human concepts.

3. On the inverse proportion between universality and the descriptive value of discovered linguistic features Despite the vast amount of literature on linguistic universals produced during the present and the recent past in linguistics (cf. Greenberg (1963, 1966); Howard (1971); see also the *Working Papers* of the Linguistic Universals Project of Stanford University), we have no commonly agreed upon, rigorous definition of what universality really means, how it is established, and whether it can come in degrees. The subject remains highly controversial, as shown by Howard (1971).

In English we have some gradable and some ungradable adjectives and I think most of us would agree that the adjective *universal* is not commonly gradable. Yet perhaps by semantic doctoring we might be able to call some linguistic features *universal*, some **more universal* and other **most universal*, where the degrees of universality refer to countable features and express their statistical spread over a given population of tested languages.

But universality might be graded qualitatively as well. Do we, for example, find more or fewer similarities between languages nearer their phono-ecologies or nearer their lexo- and semo-ecologies? What is the precise role of language relationship in positing universals and how does typology affect our understanding of universals?

As mentioned in the preceding section, the pragmo-ecological view holds that the theoretical linguist can make only two mistakes concerning universals: first, he is in error if he ignores them, but second, he errs even worse if he advocates the study of universals without the proper statistical constraints. I further wish to suggest that the value of a discovered linguistic universal for descriptive purposes is in inverse proportion to its statistical spread. The wider the statistical spread, the more predictable the feature, hence also the more descriptively trivial. Conversely, if a feature ranks low on the curve of statistical spread, and seems quite clearly to be restricted to two languages which are not related genetically, the descriptive value of those features will be high because of their power to set off the two unrelated languages in which they occurred from all others in the test group.

This point needs further elaboration. In order to clarify our notions, let us separate at the outset DISCOVERED UNIVERSALS (DUs) from POSITED AND LATER VERIFIED UNIVERSALS (PUs). DUs are the result of careful and slow field work on numerous, dissimilar languages, using essentially the same discovery procedure. Less fashionable nowadays, but once the only respectable *modus operandi* in linguistics, discovery, whether of particulars or of universals, still seems more reliable than merely positing them philosophically, because with DUs one proceeds from the data to some generalization about the data, whereas with PUs one assumes certain metaphysical characteristics of unknown languages basing one's guesses (whether consciously or unconsciously) on the structure of the language or languages one *does* know.[7] Hence PUs are much riskier to operate with. But let us now look at a few hypothetical examples of how one might evaluate DUs and PUs, respectively.

Basing one's expectations on familiarity with English, one posits that the feature ZX will be found in Hungarian and in Hawaiian only to discover that whereas Hungarian has it, Hawaiian does not. What statistical inferences could one possibly draw from such a discovery? Obviously none. This is due to the fact that the test language population has only two members. Clearly it is idle to talk about universals of any sort if only two languages are considered. So let us take the case of 100 languages being investigated simultaneously. Let us imagine that the PU Q is found to exist in 75 of them, but not to exist in the other 25. Could we then say that the feature Q has a 75 per cent universality index? One hundred languages are certainly only a fraction more than 2 per cent of the 4,000 (± 500) natural languages of this planet, so we must submit our 75 per cent finding to X^2 or other appropriate tests of significance based on the size of the test population and random sampling. Such X^2 tests could reveal, for instance, that the feature Q scoring 75 per cent among 100 languages is indeed a genuine universal and would be found in additional languages as well, so that the fact that it scored relatively high can be due to chance in, say, only a 1:100 proportion. A negative test result would reveal the opposite, namely that the high score of feature Q was accidental and that the 100 languages which contained it were somehow stacked and others are not likely to contain it. (In statistical terminology such a stacking of data is known as *prejudiced sample*.) Let us suppose, however, that the hypothetical feature Q and an X^2 test proven, *bona fide* universality, tested in 100 randomly selected test languages where its 75 per cent status can be due to chance only once in a hundred. We may then safely label the feature Q a 75 per cent universal feature. The question arises: What is the use of such a finding and how do we proceed from here? NOTE THAT WE ARE DEALING WITH A PU WHICH HAS BEEN MATERIALLY VERIFIED. This statistical verification turns the posited universal into a STATISTICALLY PRIVILEGED POTENTIAL ELICITABLE, whose chances of occurrence in other languages would be 75 per cent. The meaning of such a finding is that we can now enter the feature Q into our universal metagrammar. Such a universal metagrammar is not to be confused with the Chomskyan mirage of a Cartesian *grammaire raisonnée* (it has been satisfactorily proven that 'Cartesian' linguistics as advocated in Chomsky (1966) and (1968) is a misnomer; cf. Aarsleff (1970), Verhaar (1971), Aarsleff (1971)), but should rather be viewed as a post-theoretical and neo-pragmatic discovery procedure.[8]

Given a verified 75 per cent universality index of the feature Q over 100 random test languages, in field work, one may proceed rapidly to establish whether the feature in fact exists for Language no. 119 as well, or not; indeed one may try to elicit it sooner than another hypothetical feature W, whose statistically validated occurrence ratio is only around 60 per cent.

Let us imagine that a PU actually has 100 per cent confirmation over 100 languages. What kind of implications might we draw from so high a number? On the positive side, we would note that the feature (given further X^2 test confirmation) is truly universal and must be entered in the universal metagrammar among the UNCONDITIONAL ELICITABLES (i.e. elicitables of highest privilege). Such would be, for example, the existence of at least some modest set of numerals, some basic personal pronouns and body terms, as well as some of the other entries found on Morris Swadesh's 100- and 200-word lexicostatistical list.

If the descriptive linguist's task is to uncover strange, new facts about unknown languages, A 100 PER CENT UNIVERSAL WOULD, IN FACT, HAVE TO BE A DESCRIPTIVELY TRIVIAL ONE. Note that such a descriptively uninformative universal is, paradoxically, highly valuable from an epistemological-semantic point of view, as it tells us certain basic facts about human languages in general. This cannot be overemphasized. We are, after all, talking about the value of discovered universals, and the only sensible, pragmatic way to establish value is to specify one's point of view.

3.1 More on pragmatism William James has thus properly reminded us of the virtue of specifying our RELATIVE VANTAGE POINTS, in addition to suggesting that we in linguistics take a hard look at the literature of natural science.

One such recent account of modern physics accessible to the non-technical readership is found, curiously, in a book on the philosophy of history, written by John Lukacs (1968, pp. 273–315); on p. 276 we read:

Since physics deals with all matter, sooner or later its systematic investigations will bounce against the most difficult and elusive of physical questions: what are the properties of light? Pythagoras solved this simply. He did not bother to define whether light consisted of waves or particles. He stated that light flows from luminous bodies in every possible direction (a statement which, incidentally, corresponds to some of the present rediscoveries of modern physics). Two thousand years later Newton defined light as formed by luminous particles. This theory began to be questioned during the nineteenth century until Maxwell's theories in the 1870s 'established' that light consisted not of particles but of waves. In 1887 the experiments of Hertz found that Maxwell's electromagnetic waves had the same properties as waves of light.

But then, in 1900, Planck found that the pulsations of these waves did not flow regularly. They came in irregular jerks, representing bundles of energy. These he named *quanta*.

In 1905 Einstein found that, instead of being a wave, a quantum of energy was a particle – but that such a quantum of energy changes in time, and that thus matter and energy in certain circumstances, are dependent on the dimension of time. This is the basis of the relativity theory (one of the implications of which, stated *vulgo*, is that two by two does not *always* make four).

But about 1920 confusion set in among physicists. Light was at once a wave and a particle: but if so, how could one possibly imagine its size and shape? This was the central question. By 1923 de Broglie found that particles turn into waves as they move; he said that light was *both* particle and wave.

Between 1925 and 1927 Heisenberg confirmed that, indeed, *both* statements were true. The result was his principle of uncertainty or indeterminacy (amounting to the recognition, among other things, that we may never be able to see the atomic particle 'as it is', since we cannot determine precisely either its position or its speed).

Lukacs then goes on and summarizes (pp. 278–86) in ten points Heisenberg's 'recognitions'. Of particular importance for the pragmoecological view of language in the spirit of William James are these:

Heisenberg's third recognition (p. 280): Definitions are illusory; scientists are, in general, in the habit of giving newly discovered things names that ought to 'fit'. The postulate-corollary and definition method of Neo-Bloomfieldian structuralism lingered on for a long time; even in earlier stages of stratificational linguistics itself there was no dearth of new terms for new linguistic units. Yet at later stages of the theory it became clearly recognized that terms such as morpheme, phoneme, morphophoneme, to mention but the three most commonly recognized ones among linguists, are really superfluous since really all they are are certain nodes, that is, points of connection or disjunction in a network leading from content (meaning) to expression (phonology) and vice versa (cf. Lamb 1969).

Heisenberg's fourth recognition ('The illusory nature of the absolute truthfulness of mathematics') is also highly relevant here. Especially so, since the transformational-generative grammarians of Chomsky's persuasion seem to feel that borrowing mathematical symbolism (equation-type sentences replete with Greek letters and special symbols; indeed the very term TRANSFORMATION is borrowed from mathematics) enhances the scientific reliability of a linguistic description. The notion that mathematics is the only truth available to man is by no means new. But it could very well be false. Lukacs writes on p. 288 (fn. 15):

> Galileo (like Descartes) said: 'The book of nature is written in the language of mathematics.' This statement would have seemed revolutionary (and perhaps even nonsensical) to, say, Machiavelli, a century before Galileo: and now, three centuries later, it is becoming nonsense again. The absolutist Hobbes wrote on mathematical geometry: 'The only science that it hath pleased God hitherto to bestow upon mankind.' Spinoza: 'If mathematics did not exist, man would not know what truth is.'

Here the humanist-historian Lukacs interjects his own opinion: 'No: if man did not exist, there would be no mathematics, and if truth did not exist, there would be no man.' Lukacs quotes Goethe (p. 81, fn. 7), who in his *Theory of Colors* wrote: 'What is there exact in mathematics except its own exactitude?'

Heisenberg's fifth and sixth recognitions ('The illusory nature of "factual truth"' and the breakdown of the mechanical concepts of causality', pp. 282–3), though interesting for a general philosophy including the philosophy of language, are less significant for our purposes here than his seventh and eighth recognitions (pp. 282–4). According to the seventh recognition, 'quantum physics brought the concept of potentiality back into physical science'. Tendencies and potentialities are of principal importance since they can be described (at least statistically, hence the pragmo-ecological grammarian's relative confidence in statistical measurements), whereas abstract 'objects' and 'rules' actually do not exist. Lukacs quotes Heisenberg on p. 284:

> Probability in mathematics or in statistical mechanics means a statement about our degree of knowledge of the actual situation. In throwing dice we do not know the fine details of the motion of our hands which determine the fall of the dice and therefore we say the probability for throwing a special number is just one in six. The probability wave of Bohr, Kramers, Slater, however, meant more than that; it meant a tendency for something. It was a quantitative version of the old concept of *potentia* in Aristotelian philosophy.

Why is this important for linguistics? Vast numbers of examples of 'grammatical', 'semi-grammatical' and 'ungrammatical' sentences (marked by asterisks) have been introduced in recent theoretical discussion (cf. J.R. Ross' *Constraints on Variables in Syntax*, and G. Lakoff's *On The Nature of Syntactic Irregularity* (1965)) in order to prove that natural languages have certain underlying principles not overtly manifest in the data, and that the observable data are somehow regulated by the rules of the invisible systems that language harbors on its inside. These are valid observations and few linguists object to the exploration of such tendencies and potentialities which were ignored or rendered taboo during the Stalinist period of the post-Bloomfieldian era. The debate, rather, is this: do the nature of syntactic irregularity and that of constraints on variables belong to the level of sentence syntax (in other words: does syntax regulate itself), or are there principles and tendencies on a higher ecological subsystem (such as the semo-ecology) whose systematic exploration can give a simpler account of these phenomena? As William James would point out, obviously our vantage points differ.

For some in the transformationalist camp, there is a deep-structure/surface-structure dichotomy with semantics and phonology being interpretive; in this 'standard theory' held by Chomsky and Katz, the creative-generative portion of one's linguistic competence would be in the deep-structure syntax. The Rebellious Disciples Movement (headed by McCawley and Lakoff) would eliminate deep structure and lift the generative-creative process up into semantics. Here we have two different vantage points within TG itself. An entirely new unidirectional (encoding) approach with semantics as the chief component is advocated, independently from anyone else, by Chafe ((1970), reviewed in Makkai (1972b)). In stratificational linguistics 'thinking' or 'conceptual decision making' belongs in one's cognitive system, which has been called by Lamb gnostemic, or hypersememic, formalized in the sememic system. (Cf. Lamb's 'The Crooked Path of Cognitive Linguistics', reprinted in Makkai and Lockwood (1973).)

The unique nature of linguistics among the other sciences is that, given sufficient ingenuity and sophistication, both the two-fold transformational-generative, and the two-fold stratificational view can be upheld and elaborated upon without material repercussions or bodily harm to the practitioners. This is because linguistics is a 'soft science'. If it were like the space industry, the smallest error in calculation could lead to death and destruction (as, for example, when space-suit pressure or oxygen level in a LM is in error). The evaluation process of competing grammars and beyond that, of competing linguistic theories, is one of the hardest problems facing us today. We must remember that such an evaluation procedure was one of Chomsky's earliest (1957) and most ambitious promises, unfulfilled to date. The stratificationalist Lockwood in his '"Replacives" Without Process' (Makkai and Lockwood (1973), ch. 8), by using the relational network model of language, did succeed in offering an evaluation procedure via a 'simplicity count' involving the number of nodes in a diagram. A solution is said to be better (read 'simpler') if a smallest number of lines can adequately describe the data. But sometimes the data to be explicated are not overt but covert, such as the past tense in *hit*, *spit*, the plural in *deer*, *sheep*, etc. Thus the evaluation of a given description as good, better, or best, or conversely, as *bad*, *worse*, or *worst*, does not necessarily always rest with overt and tangible data, but rather with the analyst's ability to grasp the meaning of a system. But this ability (or the lack thereof) may depend on the scientific vantage point of the investigator, and here is where, for the time being, linguistics is a 'softer' science than physics, though modern quantum physics has its own philosophical mysteries.

Just as potentialities and tendencies are being rehabilitated in natural science, we must recognize that scientific vantage points themselves are subject to potentialities and tendencies – but of an entirely different nature. This is not the place to elaborate on what these tendencies and potentialities are, but it is safe to imagine that they have to do with the linguist's life philosophy, his psychological make-up, and last but not least, what his undergraduate major was in college. Chomsky started out as a mathematician working on symbolic logic. Roman Jakobson was a poet and a phonologist, also a literary historian and critic. Sydney Lamb majored in economics. It is no coincidence that their linguistic theories reflect this fact.

According to Heisenberg's eighth recognition (Lukacs (1968), p. 284) 'not the "essence" of factors but their relationship counts'. (Cf. Hjelmslev (1961).) Lukacs writes:

Modern physics now admits, as we have seen, that important factors may not have clear definitions: but, on the other hand, these factors *may* be clearly defined, as Heisenberg puts it, 'with regard to their connections'. These relationships are of primary importance: just as no 'fact' can stand alone apart from its associations with other 'facts' and other matters, modern physics now tends to divide its world not into 'different groups of objects' but into 'different groups of connections'.

4. A brief but necessary digression on real and phony ancestors In this section I shall devote a few remarks to the question of who is whose real and fake ancestor in the history of thought. The foregoing passages reflecting the thinking of one of the modern world's greatest natural scientists, Werner Heisenberg, offer clear evidence regarding the provenience of pragmo-ecological grammar. PEG is a further development of stratificational grammar. My indebtedness to Lamb is so obvious that it hardly needs step-by-step documentation. Where PEG, once it is fully worked out, will further SG will be in the hitherto neglected areas of context, literary texts, poetic language, and linguistic creativity; also in the organic reintegration of statistics into the philosophy of language. The basic insight that a language is not a set of 'objects' but a network of relationships, is essential for PEG as well. PEG, then, does not depart from SG in ideology, but extends it into areas which already exist in its potential.

This, however, in the last analysis, is a Hjelmslevian idea (Hjelmslev (1943–1961)). It is important to remember here that Hjelmslev's father was a professor of mathematics – in Copenhagen, the very city where in 1927 the World Congress of Modern Physics was held. Heisenberg, then a young man, attended that conference, as did Hjelmslev's father. The insight that light consists of BOTH waves AND particles stands out as one of the twin intellectual ancestors of the Hjelmslevian notion of 'either-or' and 'both-and', clearly recognized and put to modern use by the Lambian stratificational conjunction (AND) and disjunction (OR) nodes (cf. Lamb (1966a,b)). The better known one is, of course, Saussure's distinction between syntagmatic relations and associative relations. Thus we have, in addition to the recognized Saussure–Hjelmslev–Lamb line, a clearly traceable Saussure–Planck–Heisenberg–Hjelmslev–Lamb line as well. The significance of this *bona fida* ancestry cannot be overemphasized. In it we witness the paradox that genuine natural science may be less materialistic and mechanical than the self-styled 'mentalists' *à la* Chomsky who, in order to justify and exonerate their own unrealistic views of human languages, had to resort to (an essentially misunderstood) Cartesian dualism, not to mention their reliance on substance (e.g. phonetic features in the grammar).

The pragmo-ecological observation about the Chomsky–Aarsleff–Verhaar debate is that an extremely important point has been missed by all sides, namely the question of MOTIVE on Chomsky's part. This may be summarized as follows: having a system in which syntax is the central axis of language, which is creative, with phonology and semantics being interpretive, Chomsky needed a SECOND SYNTAX (this is what became deep structure) to account for generalities as opposed to the particulars on the surface. In other words, he needed two sets of values for the explication of the same phenomenon, especially if he was going to save the increasingly unlikely view according to which syntax was the axis of natural language. Then came the performance–competence dichotomy which was modelled to suit the already existing deep-structure–surface-structure dualism. They make a neat quasi-logical pair: DEEP STRUCTURE IS TO COMPETENCE AS SURFACE STRUCTURE IS TO PERFORMANCE.

But then this needed to be justified historically. Here Chomsky's vague familiarity with French literature and philosophy offered an easy way out. If he were able to show that Descartes' rationalism (which happily rhymed with 'mentalism', the new -ism designed to destroy the 'mechanists') was adequate to explain both man's place in the world and how the Port Royal grammarians wrote 'universal reasoned grammars', he would have justified his own desperate need for a dualistic *Weltanschauung*, without which the epistemological basis of transformational-generative grammar, questioned by many, would collapse. The rest is recorded history. Aarsleff has convincingly demonstrated that Chomsky misread his sources and, to summarize, that the rationalism–empiricism issue is a phony dichotomy. To put it in Heisenbergian terms: Chomsky resembles the kind of pre-1927 physicist who is unable to comprehend that light can be BOTH wave AND particle at once, depending on the investigator's vantage point.[9]

The natural opposite of a dualistic philosophy is a post-dualistic neo-monism, or as the modern Hindu philosophers call it, ādvaithā, 'non-twoness'. Pragmo-ecological grammar espouses ādvaithā: competence and performance are a dialectically evolving, nonseparable unity; diachrony and synchrony may be reflected together, but on separate strata and without ordered, artificial mutation rules (cf. V.B. Makkai 1969, 1972); natural languages are the depositories of BOTH ordered AND unordered phenomena, and so on.

5. A pragmo-ecological reappraisal of language universals How do the foregoing observations relate to the question of language universals? I think the connection is obvious and immediate: it must be made clear what our vantage point is. Are we talking about the DESCRIPTIVE VALUE, or about the EPISTEMOLOGICAL VALUE of a given universal?

In order to illustrate the notion of epistemological value, let us consider the following PUs, all of which would, it seems, have a statistical value of 100 per cent:

(1) Natural languages are systems of systems, relating codes to cognition, and cognition to codes.
(2) Natural languages utilize phonologies as their primary code.
(3) Natural language phonologies can be analyzed either in articulatory or in acoustic terms into a basic dichotomy, traditionally known as the vowel–consonant dichotomy.
(4) Natural languages have morphological combinations of size-levels determined by the tactics of the given morphologies which have systematic positions in the sentence syntax and certain semantic roles.
(5) Natural languages have a sentence syntax.

(6) Natural languages have vocabularies, some of whose corresponding cognitive realizates, stemming from the universality of the human condition, are denotatively, if not connotatively, intraconvertible for purposes of translation.

(7) A natural language is an integral part of the culture of the speech community using that language for purposes of human communications.

Such properties of languages are truly universal; disqualifying these as universals could only be achieved at the cost of sophistry. These seven universals are philosophical-epistemological assumptions about human speech in general, but they tell us nothing about what there might be in common, if anything at all, between, say, English, Hawaiian, and Hungarian grammar.

Let us now imagine that we are interested in the descriptive value of universals rather than in their epistemological value. THE POLAR OPPOSITE OF A LINGUISTIC UNIVERSAL IS A LINGUISTIC IDIOSYNCRASY. A linguistic idiosyncrasy can be formulaically expressed as the imaginary fact that among 100 languages only Language no. 77 exhibits the feature Z while the other 99 do not. Now the statistical verification must move in the opposite direction. Whereas previously our task was to calculate the chances of the supposed universal Q turning up in more than 100 languages, we must now ascertain whether Z is truly restricted to no. 77, making it its exclusive idiosyncrasy, or whether the chances are that it would recur in a yet untested language. Statistical chances for verifying true randomness also exist, but are too complicated to go into here. The descriptive value of such a discovered idiosyncrasy would be rather obvious because of its power of distinguishing Language no. 77 as opposed to all the other languages participating in the test. Yet no. 77 may share a large set of (statistically verified) universals with the other test languages, with the idiosyncrasy Z being, say, its erratic morphological encoding of an otherwise quite common semantic relationship. In terms of universals, then, Language no. 77 would have to be characterized as an intersection between the statistically verified universal features Q, W, Y, and R, and the idiosyncrasy Z.

Let me illustrate such an idiosyncrasy from Hungarian. Verbs in Hungarian morphology can be inflected transitively or intransitively, with a handful of verbs being restricted to transitive or intransitive alone, on semantic grounds. All the transitive verbs, in addition to having the usual personal endings, may add a different suffix whose meaning is 'I do it to thee'. Thus *szeretlek* 'I love thee', *látlak* 'I see thee', *nézlek* 'I behold thee', and so on. (The forms -*lak* and -*lek* are vowel-harmonically conditioned allomorphs and present no special problem.) In this case the agent's relationship to the patient, in terms of what is being signalled by the semo-ecology, is a high-ranking universal, as one can express such a content in all known languages, whether the language has a transitive–intransitive distinction, a you–thou distinction, and a marked object case or not. Yet the fact that Hungarian has this vowel-harmonically conditioned special morpheme in its transitive verbal paradigm to express that semantic relationship is an idiosyncrasy. Now, if it were true of ALL known Finno-Ugric languages that they express the 'I V_t thee' relation by a single unsegmentable portmanteau morpheme, the existence of such a morpheme would become a feature genetically characteristic of the F-U family of languages. But that happens not to be the case. Neither is it the case that a number of unrelated languages, each on its own, shares this particular morphemic encoding of the mentioned semantic relationship. If it were, we could talk about the typological fact that languages 23, 25, 33, 34, 35, 38, 89, and 92, though unrelated, share the feature of having a portmanteau morpheme whose meaning is 'I V_t thee', as we can talk about unrelated languages sharing the so-called classical vowel triangle, or the /p, t, k, b, d, g/ stop series.

So far we have been concerned with discovered linguistic features as they relate to posited universals, and have suggested that if we work from a set of fixed universals toward actual description, the description becomes in fact more rewarding to the linguist if he does NOT find what he set out to discover. The logical opposite of this operation is to assume that the method of description is standardized according to a universal meta-grammar, in the sense discussed above, and that the universals are not presupposed, but discovered. At this point the question arises: How does a linguist actually discover universal features without presuming their existence in the first place? What universals can a monolingual English grammarian DISCOVER? Obviously none. A trustworthy record of statistically significant findings can only come from the skilled, preferably multilingual descriptive artist. Such people are not likely to be vociferous advocates of universals à la MIT, but are probably tagmemicists, struc-turalists, or stratificationalists in the field.

Let us take another hypothetical case. Let us imagine that a descriptivist in the field has analyzed and described 100 languages, all of which had definite and indefinite articles. In all of the languages but one, the definite and indefinite articles always precede the noun, and never follow it, with the exception of Language no. 20, which, under certain conditions, has the articles either before or after the noun, and under different conditions only after the noun. Would the fact that in 99 cases the articles, definite and indefinite, preceded the nouns amount to a discovered syntactic universal on the constituent structure level? One would probably argue that it did. Yet Language no. 20 showed an exception. (Note that this hypothetical case has not dealt with Russian and Latin type languages that have no articles at all.) This trivially easy problem has been chosen to make the main point here: IN ORDER TO ATTAIN PRAGMO-ECOLOGICAL HUMAN RELEVANCE, YOU CANNOT GET AWAY FROM STATISTICS.

Ninety-nine out of 100 is a very high percentage, but just as before, one must bear in mind that 100 is barely more than 2 per cent of the world's spoken natural languages, added to which must be the cautionary note that some languages do not have articles at all. Our discovered phrase-structure syntactic universal of the shape:

Art/def-indef + N; * N + Art/def-indef

is not really universal at all in the epistemological sense of the word, but merely a statistically high-ranking factual observation, having the index 99 over the range of tested languages 1 through 100, and not including articleless languages.

What then is the true value, not of a posited and later verified universal, but of a genuinely discovered linguistic universal? Pragmo-ecologically speaking, the value of a discovered universal is in direct proportion to its statistical significance for a given population of test languages, whereby the analyst can turn the discovered universal into a posited one, to be later verified, or disproved for other languages that are not members of the original test group.

Notice that the relationship between posited universals and discovered universals must, by necessity, be a dialectically tenuous one. Even the monolingual, mathematically and dualistically inclined MIT theoretician working on English syntax has, by virtue of being a native speaker, unconsciously discovered, or as we euphemistically say, 'acquired' his mother tongue. Since discovery has been rendered a stigmatized expression, a 'dirty word' by the pressure-group tactics of the dominant, but now gradually ebbing MIT trend, we prefer to concentrate on children and talk about 'language acquisition'. Chomsky claims that the native speaker has acquired his grammar because he has certain inherent genetic linguistic faculties. But just as you cannot discover a mountain or a river that was not there in nature to discover, neither can you acquire something that has no objective reality outside of yourself.[10] The point is that, in order to dispel some of the fog around the subject, we must recognize that language acquisition and linguistic discovery are really the same undertaking, except that language acquisition is done unconsciously by children, and language discovery is done by methodologically trained individuals. Or to put it pragmo-ecologically: the tasks are identical, but the settings and the participating sieves differ.

6. Einar Haugen in his *The Ecology of Language* (1972) gives the relevant bibliographies of work carried out by researchers in this evolving new field. The names range from Uriel Weinreich to Joan Rubin. As a general characterization of the work of language ecologists to date, we can state that the main thrust of the work has been the examination of what happens to different LANGUAGES IN CONTACT, DIALECTS IN CONTACT, and SOCIAL STRATIFICATION. This type of work is then best characterized as the EXO-ECOLOGY OF LANGUAGE. By exo-ecology we mean development, distribution, social characteristics, population statistics, status within national states as minority or majority languages, legal situation, chances of survival, educational facilities, and so forth, of individual languages and dialects looked at as entities or cultural bodies.

The logical counterpart of the exo-ecology of language is what I propose to call its ENDO-ECOLOGY. Endo-ecology studies and describes the inner relationships of the lower to the upper phono-ecological subsystem; the inner relationship of the phono-ecological subsystem to the morpho-ecology, and that of the morpho-ecology to the lexo- and semo-ecologies. (These subecologies will be defined and illustrated below.)

The synthesis of the exo-ecology and the endo-ecology may be defined as jointly amounting to the PAN-ECOLOGY of the language. The notion of pan-ecology becomes indispensable because of the numerous interactions that exist between a language's exo-ecology and its endo-ecology. Certain lexemes may change because of exo-ecological contacts and this may cause changes in the endo-ecology of the morpheme to lexeme ratio. Pronunciations may also change because of contact with another language, thus leading to recalculations of the relations of the phoneme stock to the available morpheme combinations, and so forth.

6.1. The status of diachronic or synchronic account becomes involved in the question of endo- versus exo-ecology as well. The internal evolution of a language examined on its own terms may be called DIACHRONIC ENDO-ECOLOGY, but as students of language are well aware, it happens rather rarely that a language should not, during the course of its evolution, come into contact with other languages which, then, have a modifying influence on its structure. Consider in this regard the fate of English before and after 1066, when the influx of Old French via Normandy altered its vocabulary, its syllabification, phonology, morphology, and semology. The events of 1066 and their results, then, are not a matter of diachronic endo-ecology, but a matter of DIACHRONIC EXO-ECOLOGY. Once suffused with the morphemes, lexemes, and new phonological elements of medieval French, the English language followed its own course of development nevertheless, and thus the events of the Great Vowel Shift (1400–1500), though indirectly connected to the fact that Romance words now heavily populated the language, must be viewed as a matter of diachronic endo-ecology. A proper recognition of the fact that diachronic events come both exo-ecologically and endo-ecologically forces one to recognize that, just as synchronic exo- and endo-ecology reach their synthesis in synchronic pan-ecology, diachronic exo- and endo-ecology reach theirs in DIACHRONIC PAN-ECOLOGY.

6.2. The endo-ecology of language (i.e. its internal subecologies) has been well understood for some time in stratificational linguistics, even though the ecological considerations were not made explicit in theory. Lamb (1964a,b, 1965a,b, 1966a,b and 1969) recognized the stratification of language and proved that this recognition was in fact a continuation of the early insights of Noreen, and the more explicit work of de Saussure, Troubetzkoy, and, most significantly, Hjelmslev. That a language should have not just a lexicon but a MORPHICON and a SEMICON was suggested in Lamb's *Outline of Stratificational Grammar* (1966a). In my usage the *i* in these terms has been replaced by an *e*, hence instead of *-icons* I have *-econs* in keeping with the contention that these are *eco*-logies.

Speakers of Standard American English use forty-six phonemes (according to the Trager and Smith system), which can be reduced to a few dozen or so articulatory features. The number of morphemes that can be built from these few phonemes, however, is up in the thousands, but still significantly below the number of longer, complex lexemes that can be built by multiply reinvesting the morphemes. For example, the prefix *trans-* is built of the phonemes /t/, /r/, /æ/, /n/, /z/ (five segmental phonemes), but the single morpheme *trans-* recurs in a large number of lexemes (cf. *trans*late, *trans*fer, *trans*pire, *trans*migrate, *trans*duce, *trans*ducer, *trans*pose, *trans*position, etc.). On a lower level we witness the same phonemes that built the morpheme *trans-* functioning as building blocks for such morphemes as *rat*, *ran*, *Nat*, *-traz* (as in Alcatraz), *at*, and so forth. Lexemes such as *transposition* and *transducer* necessitate many words to define them, i.e. the sememes they tie in with for definition in the speaker's cognitive system are very many. Thus we witness the unfolding of a most efficient ecological structure whose basic architecture shows the wisdom of preservation by multiple reinvestment, as shown in Figure 1.

6.3. The inventory of the endo-ecology of a language is its ECOLOGICAL DICTIONARY, with the tactics of each subecology (i.e. the 'grammar' of the given subecology) being the ECOTAXIS of that level. First we shall examine the Ecological Dictionary of English (EDE), and afterwards a brief sketch of the ecotaxis of English will be attempted.

6.4. Nothing significantly new has happened in lexicography since Gutenberg invented the printing of books. This is not to deny the steady stream of small, step-by-step technical improvements in the field of dictionary making as new and more insights were gained into the nature of the word stock, but all currently available dictionaries (note the single exception below) have this in common: they start with the letter A and end with the letter Z. These dictionaries are characterizable with the invented acronym HABIT for 'Heterogenous Alphabetical Inventory'. HABIT is ruled by the tyranny of the alphabet. Some HABIT dictionaries offer phonological transcriptions, some do not; some offer etymologies, some do not; some include the biographies of famous people, some do not; again, some include illustrations of objects, others do not. Better HABIT dictionaries indicate if a term is an 'Americanism', as is done in the *Oxford English Dictionary*, but one never finds a marker indicating where else that 'Americanism' may be found and understood, or where it is definitely NOT understood, or, to what part of the USA it is restricted, if any. Thus entries like *hominy grits*, *dark horse candidate*, *wild-cat strike*, *lame duck president*, *maverick*, and *gerrymander*, to name just a few, are found marked (US), but the user never finds out that whereas *maverick* 'loner, outsider' (after a real person named Maverick) is frequent, *hominy grits* is practically unknown outside certain southern states.

Pronunciations are usually given for one dialect only. There is usually no indication in HABIT dictionaries of how the words *no, dog, money, matter, ladder, after, London* are pronounced in New York City, Boston, Chicago, Tennessee, London, Sydney, or Auckland.

HABIT dictionaries list everything according to the establish habit, that is, alphabetically. The harder the editors try to be complete, the more dead ballast they have to carry in their dictionaries for the benefit of that nondescript entity known as the 'general educated public'. Hence constant problems arise: just how much chemical information should a good dictionary carry? How many new space terms? Medical terms? Real estate and legal terms? How much of modern slang? And so on.

Let us now take a look at how the dictionary could be reorganized to accommodate everything where it is needed and truly useful for the 'general educated public' as well as the not-so-well-educated-public; after all, the purpose of a dictionary should be, among other things, to offer a way to foreigners and people with incipient literacy towards a better use and understanding of the language. There is nothing wrong with a dictionary serving pedagogical purposes as well, if that can be simultaneously integrated into its other functions.

7. What would a TRUE dictionary be like? The proposed Ecological Dictionary of English (EDE) would be a TRUE dictionary, as opposed to HABIT dictionaries. The letters of this acronym stand for 'Thesaurus Rendered Updated Ecologically'. It is our contention that the only really significant change in dictionary making occurred when Roget published his first *Thesaurus* in the latter decades of the 19th century in England.

In Roget's *Thesaurus* and subsequent editions thereof, the user finds a handy nest of synonyms worked out carefully for each entry. These SEMANTIC NESTS, as I propose to call them, do fairly good justice to the entries covered, as far as the knowledge and patience of the original compilers permitted. But the markings in Roget, again, are inconsistent. The many attempts at modernization of the dictionary have disturbed Roget's original mode of organization and the additions suffer from not being truly systematic in our sense. And again, everything is arranged according to the tyranny of the alphabet as before.

The question arises: why do we find alphabetization a negative rather than a positive feature, and what do we have to offer instead of it? Alphabetization in itself is not all bad, unmotivated though it may seem, since we are used to it, and usually know what letter the entry we are looking for starts with. But have we not all noticed how certain sections of HABIT dictionaries get dirty and worn, with others barely touched? The reason is that entries used by the 'general public' tend to be clustered in certain portions of the dictionary and this clustering sometimes agrees with the essentially arbitrary order of the alphabet, and sometimes it does not. (Also note that a student, or a foreigner, or a foreign student will look up different entries in a dictionary than a native speaker specialist in a certain technical field.)

What we, therefore, need is a primarily unalphabetized dictionary in which the entries – resembling Roget's synonym groups, but improved – would occur not in the alphabetical order but in their order of frequency in the spoken and written language. Such word frequency lists are badly needed and not too easily available: the ones that do exist are mostly old-fashioned and unreliable. One of the best known such word frequency lists is E.L. Thorndike's *The Teacher's Manual of the 20,000 Most Frequent Words in English* (1920), republished in an enlarged and improved version in 1952 with the coauthorship of Lorge. The main problem with the Thorndike–Lorge word list is that no indication is given as to a certain word's frequency as it relates to its position in the sentence. For example, is the entry *man* marked 1a (i.e. belonging to the 500 most frequent words in English) qua noun, as in *John is a nice man*, or qua verb, as in *John will man the post*? One suspects, of course, the noun to be far more frequent than the verb, but the compilers ignore even the traditional school syntax of the Latinate 'parts of speech'. On the other hand, the RAND Corporation in Santa Monica, California, has forty years' worth of *Time Magazine* on computerized tape, and search programs for frequencies with syntactic functions indicated could easily be written and made available for the purposes of the EDE.

A TRUE dictionary would start say, with a set of words such as *yes, no, I, you, man, go, get, put, take, run, make, water, eat, food, buy, where, who, today, tomorrow*, etc. But how, then, would the user find the entry he is looking for? Let us imagine that the entire corpus consists of these nineteen words only. Also imagine that they occur in the order of frequency listed above (*yes* the first entry, *tomorrow* the last). At the end of the dictionary there would be an alphabetical indicator, merely for the sake of convenience, without any definitions. In the present hypothetical case this would look as follows:

buy	15
eat	13
food	14
get	7
go	6
I	3
make	11
man	5
no	2
put	8
run	10
take	9
today	18
tomorrow	19
water	12
where	16
who	17

yes	1
you	4

Next to the serial number of frequency there would be a page number indicator as well.

7.1. The two faces of HABIT are the ecology of expression versus the ecology of content. Let us take as an arbitrary example some of the meanings that the verb *take* can enter into expressing in Standard American English:

be taken aback	'be startled'
take after somebody	'resemble'
take back	'renege on promise'
take down	'write upon diction'
take sy. for sg.	'consider to be'
take in (1)	'be able to hold physically'
take in (2)	'absorb mentally'
take off (1)	'start to go at high speed'
take off (2)	'become airborne'
take on (1)	'engage in combat'
take on (2)	'employ new workers'
take on (3)	'assume (new) responsibilities'
take over	'assume control'
take up	'begin to study'
take sy. up on sg.	'make sy. keep his promise'
take sg. up with sy.	'discuss, start discussing'
take to sy.	'have an instinctive liking for'

These seventeen examples are all verbal in nature. On the nominal side we have the following:

intake	'capacity'
take-off (1)	'parody'
take-off (2)	'period during which plane becomes airborne'
take-over	'coup d'état'
uptake	'mental ability, capacity'

There are far more members of the *take* family, to be sure. The point to be made here is that, as we can see, the examples listed here deal with the verb as expression. In other words, here we have listed some of the occurrences of *take*, whatever they happen to mean. (Similarly, by the way, in a TRUE dictionary, one would indicate that the prepositional-adverbial particles *back, down, in, off, on, over, up*, etc., co-occur with these expressions headed by *take*.)

How would the content side be organized, by contrast? Let us take the meaning (not the expression) 'happen' as an example. We would list, thesaurus-like, the following expressions all of which share denotatively, if not connotatively, the meaning of 'happen': *come about, come out, be up, fall out, work out, turn out*, etc. Test sentences (examples) would be provided to show the validity of the choices. The matrix sentence in this case would be *this is the way it X-ed*. We have thus: *this is the way it happened, this is the way it came about, this is the way it came out, this is the way it fell out, this is the way it turned out, this is the way it worked out*, but **this is the way it was up*, because *be up* as in *what's up?* 'what's happening?' is restricted to the present tense. Additional expressions for the meaning 'happen' would be *transpire (what has transpired, how did it transpire?), come to pass (in the year 1914 it came to pass that . . .)* etc.

One of the shortcomings of the traditional thesaurus is that it fails to give sufficient specification as to when two words can be used as synonyms and when not. The expression *this is how it fell out*, while certainly carrying the denotatum 'happen', also carries the connotatum 'by chance, accidentally', whereas the expression *this is the way it worked out* carries the implication that the problem evolved in its own manner and resolved itself without outside interference.

In TRUE, then, we would endeavor to imitate what the human brain does when a native speaker of English stores this kind of information unconsciously. TRUE would cross-refer the user from any occurrence of the expression *take* to all or any one of the possible meanings that have to do with 'get hold of', 'grab', 'acquire', etc., but TRUE, by being genuinely ecological in its orientation, would also show just where the limits of such correspondences are.

7.2. The morpheme–lexeme ratio deserves special discussion. English has a much smaller number of morphemes than it has lexemes. No currently available dictionary makes that distinction explicitly and no reliable statistics of the morpheme–lexeme reinvestment ratio are available to date. There is only one *trans-, re-, de-, in-, con-, per-, pro-*, etc. in English, but because of the unpredictability of some of the resultant meanings in combination with the verbal stems *-late, -fer, -duce, -ceive, -ject, -primand, -mand*, (cf. *translate, transfer, transduce, transceive, *transject, *transprimand, *perdemand, *prodemand, reduce, deduce, induce, *conduce, conducive, conductor, *preduct, product, production, produce*, etc., to mention just a few. Observe the asterisked non-occurrences for each of which a 'logical' sense could be invented based on the Latin etymologies and current English analogies involved). TRUE would establish, for the first time, a reliable morpheme reinvestment count. Questions raised and answered would include: (1) what is the lexeme-building load of a prefix such as *trans-*? what are its statistically most likely meanings (e.g. 'across' from Latin)? (2) what is the lexeme-building load of a verbal stem such as *-late, -ceive, -duct, -fer*? What are the statistically prevalent meanings of these stems based on the Latin etymologies and the contemporary English analogies? Any truly unpredictable anomalies? These morpheme reinvestment counts could show what morphemes are alive and productive in the language, hence available for building names for new technical inventions, and which ones are frozen and unproductive, such as the stem -*trol*, of the lexeme *control*.

7.3. The next portion of a TRUE dictionary to consider would be the retro-depository, acronymizable as HARD for 'Heterogeneous Alphabetical Retro-Depository'. HARD within TRUE serves a function which is actually hard to see at first glance, hence its name. It spells the whole dictionary backwards. The words themselves are not spelled backwards, i.e. *window* is never presented as *wodniw; the principle rather is that the compiling program looks at the last letter of the word first. I will reproduce here a brief sample from Papp (1969):

```
          A   B   C   D   E   F   G
     BABA
PRÓBABABA
   FABABA
 FÖLDBABA
KUGLIBABA
JÁTÉKBABA
 ALVÓBABA
  KISBABA
```

The meanings in this instance, are 'doll', 'mannequin', 'wooden doll', 'earthen doll', 'bowling pin' 'toy doll', 'closing-eyes play doll', 'baby'. The categories A–G allow the compiler of HARD to indicate the number of syllables, the number of morphemes, the frequency of usage, the page in the TRUE section where the definition is found, etc. This principle of retro-alphabetization also yields in one cluster all the words of the language that end in the same suffix, say, all the English nouns that end in the suffix, -*ness*, -*dom*, -*ship*, or -*hood*. Interesting and revealing statistical calculations can be made of bi-letter, tri-letter, and quadri-letter word-ends, their rhyming potentials, and so forth.

Both the retro-depository and the straightforward alphabetical look-up would be made into appendices to the main body of TRUE itself. The overall organization of an Ecological Dictionary, then, would look as follows:

A. The expression forms in frequency order with interspersed definitions, cross-reference given to the appropriate semantic nest.
B. The contents (meanings) in frequency order; cross-references given to the relevant expression forms.
C. The alphabetical look-up with page indicators and section indicators.
D. The Retro-Depository.

8. The grammar of a language in PEG may be defined as the simultaneous functions of the tactics of each of its subecologies (lower and upper phonology, morphology and lexology, semology and cognition) amounting to the language's ECOTAXIS.

8.1. The features/elements of the lower phono-ecology are the articulatory/acoustic concepts of voiced, voiceless, labial, nasal, alveolar, palatal, dorsal, retroflex, etc., high, mid, low, front, back, etc. PEG seeks to unite the most important articulatory features with the most important acoustic ones into one single lower phono-ecology. The reason for this synthetization is that PEG recognizes that human beings speak with their mouths and hear with their ears; besides that, people, for psychological reasons, tend to hear what they think they hear, and what they think they hear is heavily influenced by their articulatory habits. Strange as it may sound, it is nevertheless true that people hear not so much what they actually should be hearing (based on sound spectrography printouts) but what they expect they might hear. This is one of the reasons, incidentally, why, above a certain age, foreigners with perfect hearing, when learning a foreign language, never lose their 'foreign accent': they hear in terms of their native patterns of overlearned and overpracticed articulatory habits.

The articulatory-acoustic features/elements according to what tactic combinations are allowed in the language, will yield the phonemes of the language.

Phonemes /n/ and /m/, have in common the fact that they are nasal; /m/, /b/, and /p/ have in common that they are labial; /n/, /m/, and /b/ are all voiced, with /p/ alone being voiceless. Thus the tactics of the lower phono-ecology describes, yields, reassembles, or if you insist 'generates' the phonemes, the linguistic phenomena of the higher phono-ecology. There are far fewer features and segments in any natural language than there are phonemes, and the reinvestment ratio of the stock of the lower phono-ecology *vis-à-vis* the higher is a matter that deserves careful study and tabulation for both individual languages and typological studies.

8.2. The morpho-ecology of a language studies, describes, and explains the behavior of the morphemes in the language as they relate to (i) content, i.e. what lexemic elements they happen to realize and in what alternations, and to (ii) expression.

8.3. The fact that Indo-European languages have irregular adjective gradation of the type *bonus, melior, optimus*; *malus, peior, pessimus*; *gut, besser, best*; *good, better, best*; *bad, worse, worst* is a clear and convincing example of the behavior of the morpho-ecology *vis-à-vis* the lexemic subecology. Characteristically, stratificational linguistics (cf. Lamb 1966a) has made a great deal of such alternations, describing them in terms of lexo-morphemic alternations. The pragmo-ecological point to be made here is that languages in the course of their evolution act erratically and prodigally, quite similar to nature itself, which has no logical plans as to how many species of cactus will develop during a few million years or as to whether or not a new species of clam will be allowed to develop in certain tropical waters. The point is that phenomena that seem wasteful do happen, and the linguist-anthropologist does best if he accounts for these prodigal facts as reasonably and economically as he can. English (as well as the other IE languages) could be regularized by fiat. Then there would be only one kind of adjective gradation, namely *good, more good,* and *most good,* to go along with *extravagant, more extravagant,* and *most extravagant;* or *good, gooder,* and *goodest,* together with *bad, bader,* and *badest.* At present we view these as monstrosities, but they are by no means illogical.

The fact that the lexeme *good* is expressed morphologically by the morpheme *bet-(t)* in front of -*er* and by *be-* in front of -*st* is a phenomenon of lexo-morphemic ecology; quite literally, this phenomenon (or 'rule', if you insist) reveals something of the life and habitat of the entity stored in our brains as the adjective *good.* The lexo-ecology and the morpho-ecology are inextricably intermingled, as if in real biological symbiosis, with certain areas of clear separation and certain areas where the separation is actually impossible. The example of *good, better, best* constitutes an instance of lexomorphemic symbiosis, where the separation of morphemes and lexemes can only ·be achieved artificially. Yet morphemes and lexemes have separate existences in the following instances:

go is to *went* as *undergo* is to *underwent;*
stand is to *stood* as *understand* is to *understood;*
stand is to *stood* as *withstand* is to *withstood;*
man is to *men* as *man-o'-war* is to *men-o'-war;*
venir is to *que je vienne* as *prévenir* is to *que je prévienne,* etc.

What these examples show is that the multiple reinvestment of morphemes during the course of the natural history of English resulted in morpheme combinations whose meaning is not predictable from the meanings of individual morphemes, looked at as lexemes in their own right. These larger, multi-morpheme lexemes with an unpredictable meaning are known as LEXEMIC IDIOMS (see Makkai 1972c).

The separation of the lexo-ecology from the morpho-ecology would seem an unwarranted luxury if the language under examination had only monomorphemic lexemes and no semantically endocentric (unpredictable) combinations of morphemes. But this is unlikely to happen. Just as morphemes are the result of the multiple reinvestment of the phoneme stock, lexemes, in most natural languages, are the result of the multiple reinvestment of morphemes. In the English lexemic idioms *Emperor of Japan, old wife, hot potato,* and *red herring* (the first two are fish names, the last two mean 'embarrassing' and 'phony' respectively), the participant morphemes once had (and in other environments still have) separate lexemic status with separate sememic realizates, and these past (or elsewhere still active) meanings have a definite shining-through effect, suffusing the meaning of these lexemic idioms with the old, suppressed, literal meanings. The denotatum in each case is the primary or lexical meaning, and the TRANSLUCENT CONNOTATUM is the original literal meaning of the form. What makes lexical idioms unusual is that they, therefore, have two meanings simultaneously, i.e. the REFLECTING DENOTATUM together with the TRANSLUCENT CONNOTATUM. Whether a language has a heavy morpheme reinvestment ratio or not in its lexeme inventory becomes an interesting typological question, but there is little doubt that there are any real languages that do not somehow utilize morpheme reinvestment in the building of new lexemes.

The foregoing was a brief account of the upper boundary between morphemes and lexemes in the morpho-ecology. The morpho-ecology, however, has a lower boundary with the phono-ecology as well.

8.3.1. This area of language is what has been known in structuralist terms as morphophonemics. It is a well-observed phenomenon of a vast number of natural languages that the phonemes as realizors of certain morphemes change under the impact of the vicinity of other morphemes. Hence in English we have *wife-wives, wolf-wolves, booth-booths* (in the latter with alternation between /θ/ and / ✗ /). Whereas the paradigm alternants expressing the same idea 'good' in various forms were a matter of the lexemic subecology preying on the morpho-ecology, morphophonemic alternations are a matter of the morpho-ecology preying on the phono-ecology. This hierarchy of exploitation clearly resembles the pecking order of biological species in symbiosis elsewhere in nature. The arbitrariness of this downward exploitation can be seen by the fact that the /f/-/v/ alternation seen in *wife-wives, wolf-wolves, knife-knives*, does not carry through logically to such pairs as *dwarf-*dwarves*, the correct plural being *dwarfs*, with a good deal of variation left over to behold: *hoof-hooves* and *roof-rooves* co-exist with *hoof-hoofs* and *roof-roofs* in certain areas.

8.3.2. Just as in the case of the above-mentioned lexical idioms, morphophonemic alternation, too, displays antiquity by translucence. Troubetzkoy called the ancestor of the /f/-/v/-alternation an archiphoneme, symbolizable as //VF//. /v/ and /f/ share the features labial, dental, and fricative; what distinguishes them is the presence or absence of voice. (The same presence or absence of voice differentiations /θ/ from / ✗ /, /s/ from /z/, which are some of the most widespread consonantal morphophonemic alternants in English.)

In the *sane-sanity, vain-vanity, Spain-Spanish, nation-national* type, as well as in the *invite-invitation, ignite-ignition, deride-derision* type of vowel morphophonemic alternation the regulating feature has been convincingly shown to be a matter of length which, during the century 1400–1500 (the Great Vowel Shift), developed further until it reached the current phonemic realization. All these are well-known facts about English and so the point here is not to repeat but rather to show how they can be interpreted from the basic point of view that a language is an evolving ecology. That morphophonemics and internal reconstruction are complementary disciplines is well known in linguistic scholarship. What concerns us here, from the point of view of the diachronic endo-ecology of language (for a definition of this concept, see above), is that the historically reconstructed protophoneme in most cases coincide with the synchronically most logical 'archiphoneme' (or 'morphon', as it has been called in stratificational terms). The construct //V̶//, then, reveals itself both as a historical and as a synchronic entity, and constitutes an example of the panchronic endo-ecology of language. In the realm of vocalic morphophonemic alternants the 'archiphonemes' (i.e. 'morphons') //ằ// and //ĭ//, depending on whether the length or the shortness prevailed (notice that both a macron and a micron appears on both vowels), evolved into the surface phonemes /ey/, /æ/, /ay/, and /i/, respectively.

8.3.3. The question arises whether *wife-wives* and *invite-invitation* can be handled together from the ecological point of view. The reason is that *wife* is an old Anglo-Saxon word and *invite-invitation* was adopted after the Norman-French invasion. The pragmo-ecological answer here is that at the time when *invite-invitation* was acquired, it (along with thousands of other borrowed elements) altered the English language exo-ecologically. In the 300 years that followed, these Norman-French elements were naturalized to the extent that the phenomenon appears to us in 1973 as an endo-ecological matter. The exo-ecological effect on endo-ecological matters is most crucial, therefore, in the case of developing languages, especially where language planning is involved, as in the case of Bahasa Indonesia, Malay, etc.

8.4. The lexo-ecology of a natural language studies and describes the lexicon of a language. Having discussed this in greater detail under the Ecological Dictionary of English (EDE), we shall now pass to an examination of the tactics of the subecologies so far discussed. The ecotaxis of the semology-cognition will be discussed later.

8.4.1. The EDE marks for each lexemic entry its function in the ecotaxis. *Man* is a noun in *John is a good man*, but a verb in *John cannot man the post*; they are also separate morphemes, because *man* pluralizes as *men* and the verb inflects as *man, mans, manned, manning*.

The ecotaxis of the lexemic subecology distinguishes between SKELETON SENTENCES and COMMUNICATIVE SENTENCES. A skeleton sentence is one which does not display the actual lexeme, but only its ecotactical ('grammatical') function. Chomskyan phrase-structure rules before lexical insertion are all instances of skeleton sentences. A 'string' such as

S ⇒ (Skeleton 1)
DET + (def. art.) + N + (sing.) + MODEL + (time ±) + HAVE +
EN + V (trans) + DET + (def. art.) + (S) + DET + (def. art.) +
N + (sing.) + V (intrans) + ADV

is viewed pragmo-ecologically as a skeleton of a sentence, or as an abstract paradigm for a very large number of enate sentences. (This string above does not purport to represent any transformationalist's current or past views; it is simply an abbreviated formula which is easy to read and add real lexemes to.)

The string can be clad with real lexemes in two ways:

(i) the resultant 'real sentence' makes pragmo-ecological sense in a human-to-human communication situation, or
(ii) it is an INCURRENCE (that is, an occurring non-occurrence) perpetrated by an idiot, a fumbling foreigner, a person under the influence of alcohol or drugs, or a playful poet, or a desperate linguist trying to make a point.

The Skeleton 1 will admit a tremendous variety of lexical clothing:

(a) *the man may have seen the boy who ran away*
(b) *the boy should have heard the man who ambled off*
(c) *the dog may have smelled the rabbit that jumped away*
(d) *the elephant could have trampled the mouse that squeaked,* etc.

These sentences might be regarded as 'meaningful', i.e. as communicating a socially recognizable sense. (We are not concerned here with the equally important question whether the sentence is *à propos* of anything or not, that is, whether it is something said *ex abrupto* and without motivation, or whether it fits a certain definite sociosemantic context. PEG is judging the adequacy of sentences on all of those criteria simultaneously.)

The equally 'grammatical' sentences

(e) *the chair may have seen the trumpet that ran away*
(f) *the trumpet should have heard the fiddle which ambled off*
(g) *the dog may have swallowed the elephant that chanted loudly,* etc.

are the nonsensical sentences which can be built (if you insist, 'generated') on Skeleton 1.

8.4.2. The skeleton-building ability of the ecotaxis of the lexemic subecology has been erroneously called 'deep structure' in the past. The very concepts 'deep' and 'surface' are misleading and ill-chosen. The real question is whether the sentence communicates, or whether it merely shows how the sentence might be constructed if it were to communicate. Now PEG does not deny the value of pointing out potential constructions versus actual constructions, but it insists that the distinction be made from the point of view of human communication.

8.4.3. At this point the question might be raised how PEG envisages the celebrated question of 'transformations' and transformational-generative linguistics in general.

Let us take the basic proposition *Brutus killed Caesar* and examine the various possibilities that present themselves. In standard TG theory the corresponding passive, *Caesar was killed by Brutus* is said to be the 'passive transformation'. In 1957 when TG was still an asemantic theory, this passive transformation was said to be derived by optional transformation rules from the active sentence; later it was proposed that the passive is in fact a modality: and more recently it has been suggested that a quasi-active 'deep structure' gives rise to both the active and the passive sentence as surface transformations. (Of course, this is a simplified condensation of the various TG proposals.) In contrast, stratificational theory points out (Lockwood 1972) that a sememic trace, having unordered *and* (coincidence concatenation) nodes, is realized either as passive or as active, depending on whether the agent (Brutus) or the goal (Caesar) is in focus. PEG recognizes the stratification of language and is a member of the stratificational family of grammars, but with an important distinction: PEG realizes that the proto-proposition is activoid in nature and therefore closer to the actual active than to the passive sentence. To use an analogy introduced by Lamb (1966a): if both man and the ape are descendants of a now extinct ancestor, it remains true that the ape, in his *cul de sac*, is much closer to this extinct ancestor than is man. Therefore there is room to argue that the passive sentence is, in a real sense, not a 'transformation', but a variation on the basic theme of the underlying activoid proto-sentence. But how are we to reconcile this conflict?

PEG, on the one hand, does not believe in 'transformations', because they are psychologically counterintuitive and do not properly describe what humans engaged in conversation really do. It does agree with stratificational grammar that the same trace (with minor emphases moved around appropriately) can function as the parent of a large number of agnate sentences. The question is this: just what do we humans do when we move the focus marker from the agent to the goal? I suggest that we do something similar to the composer when he takes off on a theme in a sonata and starts to write variations on that theme. *It was Caesar Brutus killed, it was Brutus who killed Caesar, it* WAS *Brutus who killed Caesar, it* WAS *Caesar Brutus killed, Caesar* WAS *killed by Brutus, it was killing Brutus did to Caesar*, etc., are all such variations on the basic theme *Brutus killed Caesar.*

Here PEG may have one of its best chances to disambiguate a metaphysical debate, namely the disagreement between TG and SG. TG claims that the derivation of one sentence from its prototype is a process; SG claims that it is a matter of simultaneous options. PEG would attempt to point out that we are confronted here with a classical instance of the Jamesian squirrel chase. Both TG and SG are right, hence, neither is right; both possess partial glimpses of the pragmo-ecological truth. PEG, like SG, would posit a semo-ecological reticulum (roughly equivalent to the SG sememic trace, on the one hand, and to the activoid 'deep structure', on the other) recognizing that the choices between active and passive are simultaneous, and, if conditioned at all, are probably conditioned by stylistic or additional semantic criteria. Yet the fact that the semo-ecological reticulum must undergo minor operations (such as the moving of the focus from agent to goal) is a kind of activity which the speaker performs at will. The passive sentence does not derive from the active via any process, but the semo-ecological operation which takes place in the semo-ecological reticulum does amount to a minor process, where process is understood more in the sense of 'activity' than in the sense of 'linear progression'.

In most instances where two related meanings are expressed by two structurally different sentences, two ecologies are involved: the semo-ecological-cognitive, and the lexemic subecology. The moving of the focus sememe from agent to goal, then, results both in difference in meaning and a different string of lexemes. The resultant change in meaning can be assigned the label ANASEMIOSIS, and the resultant difference in lexotactic arrangement may appropriately be called ANALOGOSIS. Now metasemiosis and metalogosis are most frequently interdependent. As we saw above, *Brutus killed Caesar, Caesar was killed by Brutus* 'tells the same story from a legal eye-witness point of view', and therefore appear to 'mean the same'. Linguists have become aware, however, that only this gross 'legal mean-ing' is identical and that the active–passive distinction carries real differences in meaning (see Bolinger 1975). If we accept the fact that the active and the passive have a difference in meaning, we can say that the two sentences above show anasemiosis and analogosis together.

8.5. Each level of a Pragmo-Ecological Grammar sponsors a number of possible horizontal tactics. These are the SYNTAX of each given level. The basic assumption throughout this study has, of course, been that ANY CHANGE in the deployment of ANY ELEMENT on ANY LEVEL involves a change in meaning, no matter how minute or difficult to paraphrase.

> *He came slowly   vs.*
> *slowly he came*

imply different emphases in the interpretation of the report of someone's arrival, with *he slowly came, *came slowly he being rejected by the ECOTAC-TICS which is, basically, a computationally assembled and managed statistical report of native speaker responses to alternate suggestions proposed by the investigators. ?Came he slowly and ?he slowly came are of the conditionally acceptable variety, the condition being the right intonational contours and pausing between the words. Thus in an actor-performed narrative a sequence such as *and then came he, slowly but with determination* and another such as *and finally he – slowly – came and announced* would become plausible. My reason for assuming that minimal differences in expression always and invariably carry minimal differences in meaning rests on systematic observations of such syntactic minimal pairs. If a huge billboard along a major highway says *build we must* instead of *we must build*, I assume that the people who put that billboard up had a reason for inver-ting the word order. The 'thought' behind each version is 'basically' the same: there is a necessity to build on the part of the bringers of this message. But if the message should read in the ordinary word order *we must build*, the effect created by the message could be a lesser one. The first word *we* allows the reader/hearer of this sentence to insert a mental pause and to say an inter-sentence pause filler such as *we* (*as far as we are concerned/on our part/the inhabitants of this county/city/village* etc.) *must build.* Thus the necessity to build becomes somehow less prominent, less urgent as it is being shielded by the doers, the word *we.* Taken the other way round, *build we must,* this mental pause with the insertable silent comment, is forced to occur after the word *build.* Thus we have *build* (*if anything at all/if it is the last thing we do/no matter what/under any circumstances* etc.) *we must.* Now this, to me, is a very different statement from the neutral *we must build.* I find that most grammars, TGG or otherwise, with the possible exception of Halliday's systemic-functional grammar which deals with such differences in word order as THEME, have precious little to say about just what the difference between a given version *a* and another version *b* is. Grammarians, by and large, have not yet learned from their colleagues in literature the art of 'reading between the lines', sometimes actually between the words. The reason for this reluctance, in turn, is most likely due to the lack of preparation of grammarians to see sentences as parts of dialogs within scenarios. The objection could be raised that the billboard along the highway is not a partner in real dialog – but that is only seemingly so. The billboard with its emphatic word order is an official mouthpiece of a state or a municipal government and the intention is to convince you, the traveller, that this place you are traversing is seriously intent on building as a high priority item. This message is, of course, ignorable if you so choose; generally not too many linguists have bothered analyzing it.

In my graduate student days at Yale (1960–1965) there was a minimal pair that was often quoted as practically impossible to differentiate in meaning. It was asserted that *once I had lunch there* and *once I had a lunch there* are extremely difficult to analyze as to their intended meaning. The discussion revolved around whether the indefinite article *a* made having lunch somewhere less of an almost institutionalized 'routine' than saying *to have lunch.* In retrospect it seems fairly obvious that the expression *to have lunch* would be unnaturally tampered with through the insertion of the indefinite article in expressions such as *it's good to have lunch on time,* vs. *it's good to have* *a lunch on time; *people on a hunger strike just don't have lunch,* vs. *people on a hunger strike just don't have* **a lunch.* Examples of this sort seem to reveal that the expression *to have lunch* without the indefinite article is approaching the status of a single closed lexeme whose meaning is ever so slightly more than the sum of its parts, i.e., it is approaching idiomatic status. *To have lunch* means, besides the expected 'to partake of the noon-time meal' also means 'to be in the habit of partaking of the noon-time meal as socialized communal activity'. The other meals one can have during the course of the day display similar ambivalence, once in the 'institutional-cultural' sense, once in the sense of an individual occurrence:

once I had a dinner served to me in an ice bucket vs.
once I had dinner in a catamaran in the Caribbean, and
once I had a breakfast while standing in the shower, and

once I had breakfast at midnight in Alaska

show a systematic alternation between an articleless, more socially institutionalized way of thinking of the meal in question versus a more haphazard, or anecdotal one signalled by the presence of the article.

Any change in the word order in PEG is a case of ANALOGOSIS. As the obvious etymology of this term implies, the idea is expressed in OTHER WORDS and those different words carry perhaps the same basic idea but with slightly – or significantly – different implications.

The pre-lexical counterpart of ANALOGOSIS is ANASEMIOSIS. Here the words or lexemes remain the same, but you start 'inflecting' the entire sentence. The sentence *the boy chewed the apple* vs. its negation, rendition in the various tenses with interrogation and negation added as in *the boy did not chew the apple, hasn't the boy chewed the apple?, the boy must have been chewing the apple* etc., all mean different things. What has remained the same is the topic of the discussion: whether you are asking a question about it or making a guess as to what probably happened, you are not suddenly talking about the waxing or the waning of the Moon, but about a boy chewing an apple. By the time we reach the present perfect continuous passive negative interrogative as in *hasn't the apple been being chewed by the boy?* we are probably invoking indirect evidence observable through the boy's strange behavior of chewing the apple for such a long time, probably to create a diversion while his fellows were holding up a liquor store. Whatever the appropriate interpretation as justified by the given context, it is an unwanted inheritance from the meaning-shy days of Harrisian distributionalism (Harris 1951) to see the resultant possibilities as 'meaning preserving transformations' of an underlying simple active sentence that says *the boy chewed the apple*. There is NO SUCH THING AS A MEANING-PRESERVING TRANSFORMATION in a natural language. Perhaps in mathematics one sees no essential difference between expressing the half of a sum as ½ or as 0.5, in real life a 'half watermelon' can be crushed on a dirt road and heated by the Sun, or pleasingly displayed in the cooler of a neat supermarket and chilled ready to eat. (Compare Gleason's treatment of AGNATE vs. ENATE structures as they relate to what I propose to call ANALOGOSIS vs. ANASEMIOSIS, Gleason 1966.)

There is no hierarchy to be observed in the edifice of these relationships prefixable with *ana-*.

ANASEMIOSIS – a change of meaning – must by necessity always be accompanied by SOME change in expression, whether this is a matter of syntax, the choice of word, a morphological feature, or a change in pronunciation as from loud to soft, threatening or pleading, slow or fast, etc.

ANALOGOSIS – a change in word order without added morphological material – while seemingly carrying no extra meaning at cursory examination, always reveals a hidden agenda.

ANAMORPHOSIS is at hand when the lexically unaltered topical proposition is altered as to its meaning through the use of additional morphological building blocks, such as *chewed* being recast as *will be chewing, could have been chewing, must chew*, etc. In inflectional and agglutinating languages these different meanings are often expressed in the same word, as in Latin and Hungarian.

ANAPHONOSIS is the means whereby we alter a meaning through the primary use of our voice. Observe the following basic facts of spoken English generally missing from ALL grammars:

Whereas yes-or-no questions generally have a rising intonation contour in North America and a rise-dip-rise intonation in British English, questions introduced by *wh-* (hence commonly referred to as *wh-* questions) have a falling terminal contour. Thus we say *has the mailman come yet?* and bring the voice straight up in the US, performing the familiar rise-dip-rise contour of some major British dialects, but in the sentences *what's for dinner? Who's coming? Where's my key?* etc., the voice goes uniformly down. Now, if one wants to produce a CHALLENGE QUESTION, all one has to do is to pronounce the interrogative *wh-* question on a rising (US) or rise-dip-rise (British) contour to indicate surprise, dissatisfaction and disdain of one's interlocutor.

A: *What's for dinner?* (objectively, falling intonation)
B: ¿*What's for dinner???* (rising intonation, showing great indignation). *I tell you what's for dinner, nothing! You left me no money to go shopping!*
A: *Who's coming to dinner?* (Objective question, falling intonation)
B: ¿*Who's coming to dinner???* – *What's the matter with you? How could you forget? It's my mother, of course . . .*

The interrogative word order is not alone in being contradictable by a challenge intonation. The ordinary declarative sentence has a falling terminal contour as in *Max is smart*. A speaker who objectively tries to find out if Max is smart or not would normally ask *is Max smart?* and expect a yes–no answer. But a person wanting to challenge the assertion *Max is smart* has the option of saying ¿*Max is smart????* meaning 'you must be kidding me'. Also consider: *This is inexpensive . . .* vs. ¿*This is inexpensive???* (implication: you must be very wealthy to think so.) Or: *It's warm in here* vs. ¿*It's warm in here???* (implication: I am actually cold, I disagree with you.)

The non-*wh-* yes/no question intonation (rising in US speech) as in *has the mailman come yet?* if repeated by one's interlocutor on a falling intonation contour while leaving the interrogative word order unchanged ¡*has the mailman come yet!!!* indicates the respondent's disgust felt at the obviousness of the question in view of some visual evidence such as letters carelessly scattered on the floor. *Have the boys come in yet?* replied to as ¡*have the boys come in yet!!!* implies disapproval of the way they came in; perhaps they were trekking in snow or mud on their shoes which is ample and negative evidence of the fact that they did come in which makes the original question unnecessary.

Imagine for a moment what the speaker would have to do if the device of METAPHONOSIS were not there to issue a challenge question. A said *have the boys come in yet?* and B wishes to indicate indignation at the way they in fact came in while simultaneously indicating to A that the evidence of the boys' inappropriate entry is in plain sight rendering A's question unnecessary. Lacking the device of ANAPHONOSIS B would have to reply 'yes they did and look at the mess they made of it' or 'can't you see that they did? Who else could have trekked all that muddy snow in?' Replies of this sort do, of course, occur and may be regarded as more explicit or more polite than the literal repetition of A's question riding the intonational curve of a challenge question.

The 'challenge' need not always be a negative one. Suppose someone asked *Is Max smart?* A strongly affirmative answer can take the form ¡Is Max smart!!! and be taken as a friendly admonition saying 'yes he is smart, and far more so than you think'. B is, in fact, saying that A has understated the case.

The reply ¡is it ever!!! (on a falling, declarative intonation curve) reiterates and underlines the truth value of the first speaker's statement: A: *This ring is too expensive.* B: ¡Is it ever!!! The words *is it ever/are they ever?*, if spoken on the interrogative upward curve, become an objective yes/no question and not an emphatic agreement with an admixture of minor admonition. A: *These employees just aren't satisfied with their wages.* B: *Are they ever?*

As we can see from these and other examples, the HUMAN VOICE ALONE, without any alteration in syntax (word order, etc.) can alter the meaning of a sentence entirely. ANASEMIOSIS, therefore, can be realized in English by ANAPHONOSIS.

9. It is now time to devote our attention to the ecotaxis of the sememic-cognitive subecology. In PEG this is the most important part of the description of how real people actually use a language. Instead of going into great detail here, I would simply like to enumerate a few points of principle.

A. Sentences do not occur in isolation, except in grammar books. Thus a sentence such as *dogs bark* is preeminently ill chosen for purposes of illustrating the 'declarative sentence'. *Dogs bark* only makes sense in the ecological setting (henceforth abbreviated ECOSET) of enumerating the kinds of noises animals make, e.g. in explaining to a young child: *Cats meow, donkeys he-haw, birds whistle, roosters crow, dogs bark. Now can you repeat this, Johnny?* – or some similar situation.

B. The supposed grammaticality or ungrammaticality of individual sentences is correlative with the ecoset in which they were observed. If a foreigner manages to make himself understood even though he piles error upon error, his sentences are correlatively grammatical to the intended speech act he is engaged in. If this were not so, immigrants to the USA with very bad English-speaking habits could not make a living. The fact that they do, proves that grammaticality is ecoset-relative.

C. People seldom soliloquize; people normally talk to each other. The language that gets exchanged between speaker 1 and speaker 2 is correlative with their mutual regard for one another, their respective ages and sexes, their respective superior or inferior social status. We might call this the sociological dimension of the ecoset of normal human dialog.

D. The human responsibility is not monolithic but structured within the conscious and the unconscious. PEG finds it most convenient to adopt the scheme developed by Dr Eric Berne, the founder of transactional psychoanalysis in this regard. According to Berne (1969), the human personality has a threefold stratification: parental ego state (roughly the same as Freud's 'super-ego'), or the neo-psychic ego state; the adult ego state (roughly analogous to Freud's 'ego') or the meso-psychic ego state; and finally, the child ego state (roughly the same as Freud's 'id') or the archepsychic ego state. An adult-to adult conversation would typically be a university lecture, reading certain usage labels, man's ability to process cerebral information without subterfuges, or any ulterior motives.

A parent-to-child exchange is typically what passes between a mother and her four-year-old or, later in life, when we 'talk down' to somebody who either solicits this, or actually resents it. A child-to-parent exchange is when a psychologically dependent person whines or complains to his fellow-adult subconsciously treated as a parent figure; in its natural elementary state this is the four-year-old addressing its mother or father about a bodily or emotional need. Parent-to-parent exchanges occur in committee meetings, conferences, or when teachers and parents get together at school. Child-to-child exchanges are the creative, free talk that little children engage in when not suspicious of being overheard by their elders; later in life when liberated adults engage in playful activity, the adults' sex-play, if uninhibited and normal, is a child-to-child type exchange.

Berne classifies these types of exchanges as TRANSACTIONS, and PEG, in its attempt at bringing the true anthropological relevance back into a non-reactionary, progressive linguistics, finds the notion of transactions particularly appealing.

Berne gives the following example of a 'crooked transaction': An impressionable lady buyer enters a store and tries to choose between two pairs of shoes. The salesman, eager to make a sale, engages her in conversation:

Salesman: 'That's the better pair, but you can't afford it.'
Lady: 'That's the pair I'll take' (pointing at the more expensive pair).

SPEAKER I   SPEAKER II

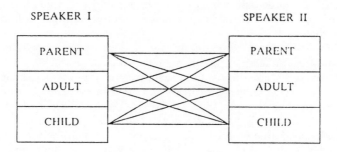

Figure 5

What has happened here?

No currently available grammatical theory could describe what passes between the salesman and the lady. It could be argued that the sentences are not even logically related, for the lady ought to answer: 'Oh, in that case, I'll come back some other time' or: 'You are correct on both accounts' and simply leave. But she accepts the salesman's challenge and buys the more expensive pair of shoes she probably cannot afford. According to Berne, what happens in a situation like this is that the adult-to-adult 'straight transaction' occurs only on the surface underneath which there is another 'crossed' or 'crooked' one. The overt 'straight' and the covert 'crooked' transactions are, of course, simultaneous, and one of the parties is usually unaware of the 'crooked transaction'. What happens in this exchange is that the salesman's adult cleverly attacks the lady's child, challenging her, as it were, to show that she is no cheapskate. The fact that she accepts the challenge and falls for the salesman's dishonest sales pitch indicates that she has a vulnerable 'child' in her unconscious make-up, and that when she says 'that's the pair I'll take', she is talking as an adult only on the surface; subconsciously, in fact, she is talking as a child, really saying: 'I'll show you that I am no low-class customer who is willing to settle for the cheaper pair of shoes', or something similar. (We reiterate that her child's reply is essentially unconscious.) The sale, i.e. the exchange of shoes and money occurs overtly on the adult level, that is, the sale is concluded, and the transaction ends with the salesman's victory and the lady's defeat. In Berne's terminology both get their 'payoffs': the salesman, who is a winner, wins; the lady, who is a loser, loses; hence each gets his/her unconscious psychological satisfaction of the 'game' they played.

I would not have entered on an explanation of transactional psycho-analysis were it not so sorely needed for a better understanding of how our modern society operates. In an ecology-minded late 20th-century America when the fates of millions are influenced by mass media persuasion techniques (such as Madison Avenue sales techniques based on motivational research), anthropological linguistics can ill afford to remain unaware of some of the major types of psychiatric motivation that influences the human dialog.

In summary, we may say that the ecotaxis of the cognitive-semantic subecology is, in fact, the main area to which anthropological linguistics should devote its attention. (The exchange between the salesman and the lady above may be unheard of in certain African countries or in Southeast Asia; it may be symptomatic of Anglo-Saxon North America, hence heavily culture-specific.) It is also evident that this is the least explored and least understood area of our human behavior, and that the work of scholars such as Halliday (see especially Halliday (1973)) is an important addition to traditional linguistics.

The ecotaxis of the sememic-cognitive subecology could be called THOUGHT, thought in the sense that we can talk about 19th-century Russian thought, or 18th-century French thought. What we mean by 'thought' in these instances is, of course, the most important cultural products of that age, and the cultural trends shown in them. The salesman–lady exchange is a kind of 'thought' as well, not very elevating, not very artistic, and with little entertainment value, if any; but is a characteristic thought-pattern of a certain culture in a certain age. 'Thought', then, is not meant here in the cerebro-neurological sense.

10. Linguistics, at least in North America, began as a subdiscipline of anthropology. This was to a large extent a reaction to the philosophy and practices of the German *Junggrammatiker* of the 19th century, but also due to the fact that there was a real need on this continent to describe Indian languages of which little or nothing was known. It was obvious to Franz Boas that the traditional categories of IE grammars did not apply to the Uto-Aztecan, or the Algonquian languages. 'Behaviorism' and 'mechanism', for Boas, would simply have meant that he was not going to prejudice the chances of successfully describing Menomini or Ojibwa, if he wanted the data to yield the terminology needed and not to have the old, inherited terminology mold the data into a Procrustean bed.

10.1. Bloomfield's insistence on 'mechanism' was a reaction to all things German. During and after World War II, for a scholar of German-Jewish descent it was more than natural to be fearful and suspicious of *Sprachgeist*, *Volkgeist*, *Zeitgeist*, or anything that ended in *-geist*. Bloomfield, however, went too far when, in *Language* (1933), he declared that he was not interested (as a linguist) in why a person would say the utterance *I am hungry*. He insisted that it was irrelevant whether the sentence was produced by a hungry beggar or by a naughty child not wanting to go to bed. The lesson to be learned was that *I am hungry*, as a sentence, is built on the sentence skeleton Pers. Pron. 1st pers. (sing.) + BE + (pres. 1st pers. sing.) + ADJ. and that this kind of X-ray insight into the sentence structure of any language can only help the linguist in his work. Again, it is like anatomy for the student physician. Would you go to a physician who had not been through regular anatomy? I would not. But if you had an infected middle-ear and the doctor gave you some diagrams and a lecture on how the ear is built instead of prescribing the appropriate antibiotic, you would be cheated. The adequate physician is not only one who knows all about the anatomy and physiology of the ear, but is also one who can diagnose the probable reasons for an infection, and suggest the right medicine; furthermore, he is even better if he can make an educated guess that the infection took hold in the first place because you were so exhausted. Thus in linguistics today we have reached the age when the skeletal structure of sentences are rather well understood. A synthesis of structuralism, tagmemics, and TG can certainly add up to a lot of information; if on top of it the anthropologist acquires a sound knowledge of stratificational theory, he will be rather well equipped in dealing with 'grammar'.

10.2. But we are now past the stage when scientific detachment is enough. Leading American philosophers of history (Lukacs 1968, 1972) have recognized that we live in the post-scientific age. The moral postulates of the post-scientific age include that, among other things, we have to step beyond science WITH the aid of our acquired scientific skills, NOT despite or without them. Stepping beyond 'science' simply means that we now have to enlarge the scope of our investigations or that we now have to start applying scientific integrity to areas of culture that were hitherto only discussible in terms of vague generalities.

Leading intellectuals in North America have called attention to the fact that our planet is an ecology living rather alone in space. (Alone in the sense that no life form similar to ours exists in this solar system and in the sense that we are unlikely, within this century, to get to other solar systems.) This recognition has led to the environmentalist movement concerned with the preservation of energy, the cleaning up of rivers and lakes, the water we drink, and the air we breathe. Few people have remarked, however, that there is also an intellectual pollution in our society. Egos and charisma dominate; fears and insecurity cower, or vociferously jump on bandwagons. Much work needs to be done to clear up our intellectual pollution as well.

Significant work has begun on the area of language as an ecological entity. At the beginning of this chapter I referred to that work (by Haugen and others) as the exo-ecology of language, because these scholars have been concerned primarily with how various languages (and dialects) co-exist. Due to the insights gained by stratificational theory, however, it can now be said without danger of fadism or exaggeration that the internal organization of languages also shows close kinship to ecological systems. I have opted for the term endo-ecology to express that thought.

It is now time for anthropology to reclaim scientific linguistics, to which it gave birth. By understanding that language has both an endo- and an exo-ecology (i.e. its organic inventory, its properly stratified 'grammar', and certain territorial and sociological relationships both in the present and in the past), anthropology may be able to rise to the task and become once again synonymous with her most prestigious daughter discipline.

11. Concluding Remarks In the wake of the industrial revolution came behaviorism; in the wake of the nuclear bomb came structuralism; in the wake of the digital computer came generative grammar; and in the wake of space travel came stratificational-cognitive linguists. Mankind has entered the self-destructive age of PROGRESS-POLLUTION and must read-dress itself to the questions of humanism and social relevance. The questions of social usefulness, public verifiability, and statistical accountability mark the present passing of the syntactic age and the unfolding of the new age of resource-minded responsibility.

Objective and numerically verifiable investigations of natural languages show that human language is an ecology consisting of ecological subsystems, yielding the ENDO-ECOLOGY of human language. Languages in contact (cf. Haugen (1972)) with the exterior environment yield the EXO-ECOLOGY of human language.

Pragmatism is the method of inquiry that dispels the fog of metaphysics by stating the vantage point of the inquirer. Pragmo-ecological solutions to questions raised by current linguistic speculation show that modern physics (à la Heisenberg) has a better chance of accounting for the most typically human manifestation, language, than artificially resurrected ancient 'rationalists'. The Heisenbergian indeterminacy principle compels anyone aspiring to the rank of scientist to include statistical tests and measurements in any and all of the social sciences while realizing that what he measures is not a chunk of matter but a node in a network of relationships.

Notes

1. For more formalized accounts of what has come to be known as the 'stratificational' model of language see Lamb (1966a), Lockwood (1972), A. Makkai (1972a) and A. Makkai and Lockwood (1973).
2. 'Shrinkage' is not meant literally here. Recent neurophysiological evidence indicates that there is in fact no material loss of neuremic networks. This information is, in other words, not 'lost', it just becomes inaccessible to normal consciousness, while it may still be available to expanded consciousness, e.g. when under hypnosis, in medically controlled experiments with LSD, or in certain types of mediation.
3. The question arises when to consider two concepts identical in two unrelated languages. According to S.M. Lamb (personal communication), 'two concepts would be the same if the BOUNDARIES OF SCOPE are the same'. This, however, would decrease the number of truly universal concepts to a relatively small number. If we accept the boundary of scope restriction, *water* for a native speaker of Navajo and a Chicago high-rise dweller, speaking only English, will greatly differ in scope; 'stream' will be more likely the Navajo's association and 'faucet' that of the city dweller. A higher number of universal concepts can be

identified if instead of allowing only concepts whose boundary of scope is the same we admit concepts whose SEMANTIC CENTER OF GRAVITY is the same. The semantic center of gravity for *water* would be the subelements *liquid*, (normally) *drinkable*, (normally) *cold*, *boilable*, *for ingestion*, *for bodily immersion*, *swimming*, etc. If such a semantic center of gravity can be established, we can, for the time being, ignore the questions of deities that dwell in streams and lakes, and the state of water pollution in the big cities.

4. The study of idiomaticity has been traditionally weak and unconvincing in linguistics. Yet it appears that in languages such as English idioms are of such importance that a mastery of them can make or break the user of the language, especially if he is a foreigner. For linguistic studies of idiomaticity see the bibliography in Makkai (1972b).

5. I ignore here the possibility of parthenogenesis. Christians believe that Jesus had no father, and the same claim has been made by the mother of Alexander the Great. Medicine may yet have a few surprises in store for us.

6. It could be argued here that the 'basic human condition' which is shared by all terrestrial physical humans is only a small part of the total conceptual system; it is the small common core. As B.L. Whorf has shown, for the most part, conceptual systems differ. Hence the differences could become great, since conceptual systems are so large. This point has, in fact, been raised by Lamb, upon reading an earlier draft of this chapter. I have two explanations to offer: (1) If we accept the semantic center of gravity criterion for universal concepts as opposed to the boundaries of scope restriction, as explained in note 3, we gain a solid percentage of thoroughly all-human universal concepts; (2) even the cognition and the semology widen out with relation to the North Pole as we come down towards the 'Equator'. This allows us to accommodate different conceptual systems with different boundaries of scope, which I expect to be reflected in the grammatical structures of the individual languages at least partially, if not completely. Whorf, too, approached the differences in conceptual systems through overt differences in grammar. The more 'southern' portions of the cognition and the semology are beginning to widen, hence differ, significantly, thus showing that differences in cognitive systems due to nonmatching boundaries of scope may be correlated in contrastive typology with lexical and grammatical matters. I am further indebted to Lamb for pointing out that 'it is at the top and bottom that diachronic change (hence dialect variation) is most frequently observed. The middle is the most stable part, hence the best for determining distant genetic relationships; cf. Edward Sapir.'

7. On this point see Noss (1972, p. 12), who gives some highly convincing bogus rules a transformationalist trained in Thai would have to posit in order to account for such sequences in English as *one stick of dynamite* (OK), *two bottles of wine* (OK), *three head of cattle* (OK, *s* deleted), but *four chairs*, which must be merely the surface form of an underlying **four bodies of chair* with an obligatory deletion of *bodies*.

8. Such a universal metagrammar would be constructed of questions in terms of open-ended network connections which would seal up and solidify as soon as the data come into contact with the master network itself. The following analogy will clarify what I mean. The universal metagrammar I am suggesting would be comparable to a sonar guided sieve whose holes would expand and contract according to a program allowing the sieve to deposit the common sand in one box and transport the rarer gold nuggets into another. That experienced field workers carry such 'sonar sieves' in their heads designed to catch linguistic gold is common knowledge, yet the statistical probability calculations

with which they operate have never been worked out and have, in fact, been artificially suppressed by static visions of a universal grammar based, of course, on English, French, and Russian, i.e., the better-known European languages.

9. Sometimes one cannot, in fact, afford to have inflexible vantage points. The age we live in demands that we be realistically mobile. We must build factories in rural areas and we must build parks in industrial-urban centers. Pushing urbanization or neglecting it pollutes, and pollution can kill mankind. Linguistics has not yet become lethal to the same extent as industrial civilization has, but it has run into a severe problem of relevance and a massive credibility gap. TG grammarians gave longer and worse-looking taxonomies than their Bloomfieldian predecessors, and the language teaching profession is totally lost with regard to the practical applicability of TG. I do not exaggerate if I say that TG has become entirely *menschenfremd*; it is deeply afraid of psychology, ignores literary and creative uses of language, and turns a deaf ear to social dialects, encoding and decoding, jokes, allusion, double entendres, to mention just some of its defects.

10. Notice that 'inherent human linguistic ability' is not questioned here but is merely being assigned a more plausible pragmo-ecological role; this is that the bio-psychological nucleus in the human brain will, through childhood, adolescence, and adulthood, grow into the person's cognitive sieve. For elderly monolinguals the cognitive sieve ossifies according to the language he speaks; bi- and trilinguals have a much more flexible one, and the linguistic descriptive artist, at least, ideally, could have the ability of constantly loosening his cognitive sieve and zeroing it in on any new object that he approaches.

3 Degrees of nonsense, or transformation, stratification, and the contextual adjustability principle

This title is no pun. Yet I must warn the reader that this chapter is the spoof, the whole spoof, and nothing but the spoof. May I be denied a place in Noam's Ark when the flood comes if I lie to you about this. What happened was that I was so busy generating all the sentences that I had no time to interpret what they meant; so I cannot be held responsible for what I am saying. As beauty is always in the eye of the beholder, perhaps it is true that the meaning of a set of sentences belongs properly in the head of the listener. Or does it? I shall leave this delicate question up to you, and get on with my subversive remarks.

As you know, we live in an age of general pollution. Next to atmosphere-, soil-, and water-pollution, we are currently sustaining a pollution of ideas, in both the socio-economical and the humanistic fields. This universal condition of PROGRESS POLLUTION henceforth abbreviated PP) has affected our discipline in several ways. The first great pseudo-liberation occurred in 1957 when Chomsky so gallantly set grammar free from its semantic bondage with *Syntactic Structures*. But as the Good Book says, alas, 'as ye sow, so shall ye reap'. Thus it came to pass that ever since 1957 those colorless green ideas have been dormitating rather furiously in every linguist's mind. They keep periodically erupting into the foreground of linguistic research from their irate slumber in the untapped recesses of the unconscious, demanding their rightful place under the sun as asterisked sentences, and they have now become the prime target of PP, bringing about a singularly unruly set of transformations of asterisked sentences, which are steadily becoming more and more *asterisquée*.

As it has always been one of my genetically inherited universal assumptions about context-sensitive natural languages (which no conditioning of academic survival reflexes could curb or restrain) that too much INSIGHT inevitably results in a pitiful loss of OUTLOOK, I decided to take it upon myself to lay aside temporarily the virtue of being insightful, and practice instead the neglected virtue of being *outlook-some.

Perhaps a word or two might be in order here to elucidate the concept of *outlooksomeness* as a tentative first step in clearing up some of our current ASTERISK POLLUTION in linguistics. According to current establishment mythology, the insightful linguist is a person who, in contrast to the lowly taxonomical data-gatherer, seeks a coherent system underneath the gamut of facts encountered and classified, whereupon he can say that his insightfully drawn map of the inner mechanism explicates the exterior structure. This is indeed a great boon to mankind. However, knotty problems arise. First and foremost the question must be answered: if collected and classified structural facts can actually be better explicated by sighting this inner system, maybe the inner system *itself* can be viewed as another set of facts which have further systems underlying *them*, capable of explicating *their* nature and organization. Thus insight led us from phrase structure grammars to deep structure in 1965, and the earlier independence of grammar from semantics was seen a new light. It was nevertheless maintained that the syntactic component of a grammar generated creatively and the semantic component interpreted restrictively. Then, from a number of independent sources it began to be questioned whether deep structure was in reality deep enough at its 1965 depth, and various scholars, each for his own reasons and each in his own way, pushed the underlying system a few steps further.

Thus it is easy to see how *insight*, if carefully practiced, inevitably must lead to *outlook*. But outlook, as its name properly implies, leads us to previously unsuspected New Frontiers of the Great Society of Common Sense where, the square footage of Noam's Ark permitting, we may eventually find an entire Generation of Peace among linguists after the flood of asterisk pollution has properly subsided.

Chomsky's position on the '"Cognitive U" of Linguistic Philosophy' is, therefore, a uniquely complex and, in point of fact, a very lonely one. Belonging by intellectual lineage to the Neo-Bloomfieldians, he yet became their severest critic. Denouncing their mechanistic behaviorism, he proposed that linguistic competence was a mental quality, inherent in human beings, only to come up with a huge taxonomy of rules which turned out to be only a few degrees more abstract than a straight Bloomfieldian inventory of forms presented in item-and-arrangement fashion. Answering the call of the cognitive impulse, Chomsky, after inadvertently separating and liberating grammar from semantics, and semantics from grammar, now moved toward a systematic incorporation of semantics into transformational grammar, but under the domination of the syntactic component. Thus we note that the cognitive impulse is clearly understood and recognized but is answered – and most paradoxically in the name of mentalism – along essentially mechanistic lines. I am tempted to characterize his role in the cognitive development of the discipline as that

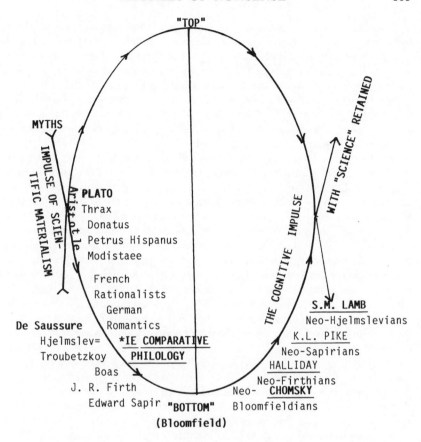

FIGURE 1

LEGEND: Left upper branch starts with 'myths' & continues with Plato, Aristotle,
Thrax, etc., culminating in INDO-EUROPEAN PHILOLOGY. To the left of IE we see
Saussure, Hjelmslev, Troubetzkoy, Boas, Firth and Sapir; the line ends at the 'bottom'
where we see Bloomfield. The left descending branch of the 'Cognitive "U" ' represents the 'Impulse of Materialism in Science', whereas the right ascending branch
represents 'The "Cognitive Impulse" with Science Retained'. Bloomfield is in the 'pit'
or — in a mirror image — on the 'top', depending on one's philosophical inclinations,
as 1933 was the height of mechanism-behaviorism [overt data ruling the field]. For
advocates of 'materialistic science' 1933 was the 'peak' and Bloomfield is on the 'top'
of an inverse parabola. On Bloomfield's right on the ascending branch we find the
Neo-Bloomfieldians, the Neo-Firthians, the Neo-Sapirians and the Neo-Hjelmslevians
with the names of CHOMSKY, HALLIDAY, PIKE and LAMB. Whereas Bloch, Z. Harris,
Hockett, R.A. Hall Jr., etc. were more 'Neo-Bloomfieldian', Chomsky is placed here
because of his inability to see Human Language as a meaning-driven social semiotic
that serves the purposes of human communication. He is a 'half-mentalist' at best, who
remained under the influence of his teacher, Z. Harris, the a-semantic distributionalist.

of Copernicus or the Sorcerer's apprentice. Chomsky had asked all the right questions and come up with all the wrong answers; or to express myself more metaphorically, he opened up Pandora's box, and to everybody's utter amazement out leapt our most respected colleague, Professor Quang Phuc Dong from the South Hanoi Institute of Technology.

Neo-Sapirians and Neo-Hjelmslevians, on the other hand, have always had a different approach to meaning, and cognition in general. Whereas in 1965-depth transformational grammar (and recent metamorphoses thereof) an aberrant sentence must be explained by SYNTACTIC CONSTRAINTS (Ross (1967), Lakoff (1965), etc.), tagmemicists and stratificationalists, jointly and severally, and each for their own reasons, were regarding non-occurrences as utterances wrought against the grain of familiar patterns, such that each of them was motivated by a different set of circumstances. In the terminology of Pike's tagmemics (Pike 1967) - emes of each and every level, from phoneme through morpheme and tagmeme, all the way to the behavioreme, had to be analyzed in terms of their feature modes (i.e. meanings) and their manifestation modes (i.e. distribution over a given field). In Lamb's stratificational model errors or violations occur on the same respective levels as do well-formed utterances. This is due to the fact that instead of transformational grammar's one central generative mechanism with two interpretive components mediated by transformations, in stratificational grammar there are minimally four interrelated tactic mechanisms, namely a phonotactics, a morphotactics, a lexotactics, and a semotactics. Optimally, there may be, pending further research, a fifth tactic system on the 'top' known as hypersemotactics or the tactics of the cognitive system, with a sixth one at the bottom, known as hypophonotactics. For an excellent comparison of the transformational grammar model and the stratificational grammar model in this regard the reader is referred to 'On Defining a Stratum' by John Algeo (1970).

My purpose here is not to rehash an old argument and to say to followers of one brand of grammar or another that 'your grammar can't do what my grammar can', because there is essentially no grammar in use today that will not work. The challenged party can always withdraw to his study, and, at the cost of a sleepless night and a small increase in his coffee consumption, indeed handle what he has neglected to handle previously. The problem with most grammars is precisely that they WORK, that is, they quite literally creak, shift gears, take matter in and put matter out, become heated to the bursting point, and pollute the intellectual atmosphere with their refuse. Some grammars use the 'direct shot approach' similar to abortive Soviet attempts to land on the Moon, while others use a 'graduated descent approach' – more stratified, if you will – similar to Apollos 11, 12, and 14. Errors and aborted missions abound in both camps.

I propose that the thirteen sentences enumerated below are all erratic and wrong, each for a different reason, and that no theory has so far been able to propose a sensible method of dealing with them. It is not enough for a theory to say simply that the sentences are wrong and to throw them out. This is just what previous theories have done, and this is the main source of the continual arguments among linguists over what is, or is not, ungrammatical. No theory has yet systematically incorporated the fact that grammaticality is a RELATIVE matter. Not only is it relative in the sense that some things can be considered more ungrammatical than others; but, more importantly, it is relative in the sense that a sentence which appears blatantly ungrammatical, given the right context, may be shown to be in fact quite grammatical. This is most obviously true on the semantic level. Each of the sentences below appears to be ungrammatical or nonsensical in one way or another; and yet I can suggest for each one a perfectly plausible explanation for its occurrence, such that it would make perfect sense in the context in which it was used.

(1) The little boy married his grandmother despite his parents' violent disapproval.
(2) The little boy married his grandfather despite his parents' violent approval.
(3) It was five years before he was born and seven years after she died that the baby divorced his grandmother.
(4) Chicago is two pounds and three ounces away from New York.
(5) MIT is in Cambridge, England.
(6) The milkshakes devoured Johnny.
(7) The square root of the nuclear thrust of a man-paddled canoe equals the sum of an albino polar bear's tail feathers if and only if said albino polar bear is simultaneously the first cousin twice removed of that alcoholic duck-billed platypus whom – my eyes almost bursting with joyous tears of amazement – I saw yesterday on television presiding over the 299th session of the United States Senate wearing an astonishingly exact replica of Liberace's second most expensive golden tuxedo.
(8) If the length of a nuclear submarine is 4,000 feet, its width 236 feet, its height 124 feet, and its gross weight 98,000 tons – how old is the Captain?
(9) I have three things to announce: first, I am being subversive, and second, that you will benefit from it.
(10) I have two things to announce: first, that every grammar works; second, that that is exactly what is wrong with linguistics; and third, that I am adding a third point to this announcement to illustrate how I can step on my own throat in public.
(11) Baron Münchhausen grabbed his own hair and pulled himself out of the quicksand.
(12) one two three testing one two three testing one two three testing one two three testing one two three testing roger and out
(13) thrushes// are/ silent/ now// in silvery// notqu/-it-/ eness// dre(is)ams// a/the/o// f moon
     Or in its original form:

t,h;r:u;s,h;e:s
are
silent
now
.in silvery
notqu
-it-
eness
dre(is)ams
a
the
o
f moon

– e.e. cummings, 'Poem 48'
(*73 poems*, 1962.)

Before getting down to the sentences themselves, I wish to indulge myself in a brief diversion to enhance further my subversiveness. Notice that I am particularly concerned here with the salvaging of semantically aberrant sentences and not so much with the adjusting of syntactically ill-formed ones. There are many reasons for this. We have, at this point, been so heavily overtaxed for the sins of the Neo-Bloomfieldians that our discipline grew into an imbalanced monster of National Debt of sin-tax. This National Debt, to be sure, we really do owe to ourselves. The remedy is to view syntactically ill-formed sentences as sentences which are actually well-formed, but dance to a different tune. They are uttered by foreigners, children, speakers of non-standard dialects, and the occasional otherwise fluent native speaker who gets tangled up in his lexotactics due to a discoordination of thought and verbiage. It is my considered opinion that all the other syntactically ill-formed sentences of recent linguistics are deliberate contrivances made up by the linguist. I view sentences such as *Max did away with someone but I don't know who with* (incurred by Ross) as the heap of shavings that lie around an emerging wood carving. You could reconstruct the statue NEGATIVELY by building a hollow cavity from the disjointed shavings – unless you lost or misplaced a fragment here or there. If you lose or misplace such a fragment and thus your hollow cast does not match the statue, you exclaim and say: 'Aha! I have discovered a syntactic constraint'. But this is, of course, pure fantasy and fiction enthroned by the fad of lending respectability and credence ONLY to statements that manage to state a taxonomical fact (Sentence A occurs but B does not) as if such a fact were the consequence of a quasi-mathematical equation. The development of the '"Cognitive U" of Linguistic Philosophy' has brought us to this peculiar and unnatural situation in the post-Neo-Bloomfieldian era under the still misunderstood initial inklings of the now rapidly growing Cognitive Impulse. Many have felt that direct, positive statements are naive, while indirect, rule-type results ground out by a central machine are intriguing, relevant, and beautiful.

I am confident that our sin-tax has been fully paid. The syntactic religion has run its course but has left behind a powerful antitoxin. This antitoxin, of course, is semantics, and the discovery of the fact that if anything in man's linguistic behavior is supremely creative it is our ability to recombine and actually create conceptual networks, whereas if there is something essentially finite, narrow, and restrictive about human languages, it is their sentence-syntax. Thus the sentences discussed here illustrate the almost infinite semantic creativity which is inherent in language.

Sentences (1) and (2) seem nonsensical by surface-semantical standards, with (2) more so than (1) because little children do not marry their grandparents whether their parents approve or not; and if need be, a little boy would sooner marry a grandparent of the opposite sex, and certainly not 'despite the parents' approval'. Thus in sentence (2) the felonies of (1) are compounded by a more transparent error, the *despite their approval* construction. Yet each sentence is perfectly sensical provided it has been contextually adjusted.

In the family about which we are talking, the child likes to act out a wedding ceremony wearing colorful odds and ends grabbed for the occasion. The grandmother is frail of health and must not be jostled around. The grandfather, on the other hand, is agile and eager to play, but the little boy thinks his grandmother is more fun. This little boy has an additional habit, namely, that he will gladly do everything his parents discourage, and eagerly avoid doing all the things his is permitted to do. In short, he is a spoiled brat. Sentences (1) and (2) are now completely sensical and might occur in an account given to a visiting social worker who looks in on the family for counselling.

Sentence (3) presents somewhat deeper problems. We are bothered by a strange shift in gender in the middle; either the *he* refers to the baby and the *she* to the grandmother, or else the baby must have changed sexes between the two successive incarnations. As it happens the sentence is completely salvageable on both accounts and all we need is some decision whether we can entertain reincarnation as a possibility and what the precise shade of meaning of *divorced* is in the given context. Let us assume that in this sentence we are talking about a family who practices a certain brand of occultism. They assume that people are in a state of limbo for twelve earth years between successive incarnations, and he who departed as male shall return as female, and vice versa. They further assume that one's spiritual guardian is the grandparent of the opposite sex at the moment of death, which guardianship constitutes a karmic link between the two individuals. The verb *divorce*, then, has a logical subsense here meaning 'freed itself from the guardianship of' or 'became karmically independent'. Since the family believes in reincarnation, the order of events is perfectly logical, the baby is born twelve years after its death; at the moment of death it is female, then seven years into her death she becomes male and freed from the karmic link to grandma.

Sentence (4) is relatively simple. What happens is that a man wants to fly from Chicago to New York and is found two pounds and three ounces too heavy to be allowed on a certain airliner where, according to a new ruling, they weigh passengers. Hence his overweight becomes the expression of the distance between the two cities.

Sentence (5) seems blatantly false, but if Professors Katz, Chomsky, Ross, and Jackendoff should all, some year, take a joint sabbatical in Cambridge, England, the sentence would become quite logical.

Sentence (6) is a little more complicated, but no problem either. What we have here is an obsessive eater of sweets who has grown unnaturally obese and is unattentive in school because of his preoccupation with milkshakes. Johnny is psychologically possessed by the milkshakes he devours, so that it is appropriate to view HIM as being devoured by the milkshakes. The sentence might easily occur at a meeting between anguished mother and mildly surprised teacher.

Sentence (7) offers a different set of problems because of the non-sequitur of the original proposition, the non-commensurable entities that go into that first proposition, then the non-commensurability of the *if and only* clause, compounded by the rest. This sentence is easiest to salvage contextually if it is taken in its totality as a coded message. This, however, would depend on where and when it occurred. If it should be an intercepted message going by wireless from enemy headquarters to outposts during war, it might very well mean 'commence attack only under certain conditions'. As it happens it is probably too long for such a purpose. On the other hand, when the Allies invaded Europe during World War II they actually informed the French resistance of the fact by broadcasting the famous line from Verlaine, *les sanglots longs des violons de l'automne blessent mon coeur d'une longeur monotone* (for further discussion of this see Makkai (1969)).

As it happens, I wrote sentence (7) so one could argue that it has no meaning at all. Yet if nothing else it could be regarded as a feeble attempt at humor, similar to the well known 'speech' which begins, 'Ladies and Gentlemen, I stand before you to sit behind you to tell you something I know nothing about'.

Sentence (8) is an example of the infinite variety of riddles all based on the principle that the information given in the first part has nothing to do with the question asked at the end. It is to be interpreted as a red herring dragged across the trail with the deliberate purpose of misleading the listener.

Sentences (9) and (10) carry a kind of semantic deviation which could be characterized as forgetfulness for (9) and as smart aleckiness for (10).

Sentence (11) may seem difficult to perform under ordinary terrestrial gravity conditions, but in Central Europe where tales of Münchhausen are as common a staple food for juvenile minds as Jack and the Beanstalk or Superman in the USA, this passes as no marvel at all. It appears that in a grammar using semantic features, a feature such as [plus Münchhausen–Superman] ordinarily would have to be entered for relevant items in the lexicon. The trouble with this solution is, of course, that it may be criticized for being plus tricky, minus honest.

Sentence (12) is a bit unusual, both as spoken in soliloquy by one person, or if the *one two three* part is said by one ham radio operator to an unknown party, from whom he receives the message *Roger and out*. Formally speaking there is nothing wrong with the utterance, except that it is a classic case of UNDERCOMMUNICATION, where this term indicates that the number of words in the string is disproportionately too many for the semantic ground covered. The meaning of (12), at best, may be something like 'lo and behold, we established voice contact'.

Sentence (13) is a linear arrangement of a poem by e.e. cummings, with its actual printed format reproduced below. Everything is all right here until we reach the word *notqu-it-eness* which is, as cummings deliberately intended, multiply decodable. We can read it as a nominalization of *not quite* yielding *notquiteness*, i.e. the condition of being *not quite*. He must have intended to communicate here that all analogies are inherently weak and if you have not shared the experience of seeing the silent thrushes, words will not do the trick. But he spells the letters *i* and *t* on a separate line, so the sequence could additionally mean that even if it is *not quite*, it is nevertheless an *it*, a *Ding an sich*. The following lines show another masterly touch at letter symbolism. Cummings opens up the word *dream* into *dre* and *am*, associates *am* with the verb *be*, and inserts its third person singular present form in parentheses; thus we obtain *dre(is)ams*. (How this is to be pronounced is another matter; but, then, these poems were written for visual consumption.) *Of a moon*, or *of the moon* is easily derived by reading the last elements in a leapfrogging manner. The point with all of this is that good nonsense is hard to come by and seems to be the prerogative of poets such as e.e. cummings. Nevertheless even a poem can, and in fact should, be decipherable in some meaningful way.

I leave it up to the reader's imagination to figure out further appropriate contexts in which these sentences make sense. The main point here is that by adjusting the context, many things which at first glance would be labelled ungrammatical turn out not to be ungrammatical at all. (Maybe the word *ungrammatical* should be spelled with an * in all future linguistic work.) Any grammar which purports to handle any and all sentences of a language must make provision for this fact.

A complete grammar of a language must incorporate what I propose to call the CONTEXTUAL ADJUSTABILITY PRINCIPLE; a grammar which is able to do so systematically, I will call a pragmatic-ecological, or a PRAGMO-ECOLOGICAL GRAMMAR.

In summary, I would like to present a set of seven definitions for the future:

(1) Words, phrases, sentences, entire paragraphs and texts or various mockeries thereof, under linguistic analysis, which were not found in a natural context (spoken or written) are *OCCURRING NONOCCURENCES, or briefly, INCURRENCES. An incurrence, as the term suggests, is a public debt to the society of listeners; the perpetrator must pay for it by explaining himself.

(2) The explanation of an incurrence is an act of SENTENCE CAPPING,

where the letters CAP stand for CONTEXTUAL ADJUSTABILITY PRINCIPLE. It is a universal property of all natural languages that not all utterances that need CAPping are incurrences.

(3) It is a universal property of native speakers of natural languages that even deliberately constructed incurrences can be CAPped by resorting to pattern formations within the THEORY OF THE UNCONSCIOUS.

(4) It is a universal property of incurrences that they come in a hierarchically organized pyramid thus:

← thoughts
incurred texts
incurred sememic sentences
incurred lexotactic sentences
incurred morphotactic arrangements
incurred phonotactic arrangements, glossolalia

(5) It is a universal and axiomatic truth that native speakers of natural languages cannot OUTPERFORM THEIR OWN COMPETENCE.

(6) Since sentence CAPping is well within the competence of every native speaker of a natural language, a complete linguistic theory has to account for the CONTEXTUAL ADJUSTABILITY PRINCIPLE. As soon as such an account will be reached, the competence–performance dichotomy must, by logical necessity, fade away and yield to being *PEGged* (where the letters PEG stand for Pragmatic and Ecological Grammar, or Pragmo-Ecological Grammar).

(7) Grammars of the Pragmo-Ecological persuasion will be de-mathematicized, de-computerized, de-context-insensitivized, fully re-CAPped, and rehumanized.

There can be no more appropriate way to close this chapter than by paraphrasing the late Right Reverend Karl Marx, patron saint of modern intellectuals:

GRAMMARIANS OF THE WORLD UNITE! YOU HAVE NOTHING BUT YOUR *

Notes

1. This chapter was originally written in Hungarian for delivery at the Maastricht Conference on Context in Linguistics and Literature. In the meantime I have also given a paper, originally written in English, at the VIIth Regional Meeting of the Chicago Linguistic Society. It so happened that the Chicago Regional Meeting took place first, and the Maastricht Conference afterwards. What was said in Maastricht was nevertheless, no exact repetition of the paper given in Chicago, since it was a free-flowing Hungarian lecture aided by only one printed handout page, the figure of the 'Cognitive U'. That lecture relied heavily on Hungarian examples not worth translating into English. The two papers, then, were very different, yet they treated the same subject. I have decided, therefore, to reprint here that version which was given at the VIIth Regional Meeting of the Chicago Linguistic Society. There are several reasons

for this decision. The Chicago version has become widely discussed. The comment that was made after it by John A. Rea of the University of Kentucky received such an ovation that the editors of that conference decided to make it the motto of the *Papers from the VIIth Regional Meeting*. James D. McCawley at the University of Wisconsin Conference on 'Limiting the Field of Linguistics' gave a paper called 'Interpreting the Theme of this Conference' in which he dealt with my paper in detail, making interesting suggestions about inappropriate contexts. What I say in 'Degrees of Nonsense' is as well said as I know how; there seems to be little justification in rewording my argument.

2. The decoding of this all-powerful symbol must fall well within the competence of any reader of this chapter and, hence, need not be performed. I am gratefully indebted to Jack Rea of the University of Kentucky for bringing its profound appropriateness to our minds by orally performing * in a CAPped occurrence, thereby ensuring the immortality of this chapter.

4 On 'positive' and 'negative' kinds of logic in modern linguistics: a Vichian perspective on the evolution of the science of language

1. Introduction

Our uniquely human ability to use logic in mathematics, physics, chemistry – all of the sciences that can use mathematics as their 'metalanguage' – has emboldened us towards the end of the 19th century and throughout the 20th, soon drawing to a close, to seek opportunities creating systems based on logic that can also serve as metalanguages for natural human languages themselves.

Although the term NATURAL LANGUAGE is common enough and seldom causes misunderstanding, it would still be worth, I think, briefly to define natural languages (NL, NLs) in contrast to ARTIFICIAL or REGULAR LANGUAGES (RL, RLs).

An NL is one that is spoken by indigenous populations on our planet, whether educated and literate or not; whether the speakers can or cannot give reasoned explanations of how the grammar of their language works. NLs serve as primary media of communication in NATURAL SOCIETIES (NS, NSs) as contrastable with ARBITRARY SOCIETIES (AS, ASs). A natural society, by way of exemplification, is that of France, England, Hungary, Indonesia, etc., to which correspond the NLs French, English, Hungarian, Indonesian, etc. (The matter of subsections of these societies with their corresponding language varieties, or dialects belongs in a separate discussion in fine detail; it must, however, briefly be mentioned here in order to indicate that modern linguistics is aware of the non-homogeneity ('variationism') of all NLs and their corresponding NSs.)

An arbitrary society, in contrast, can be seen in the Singapore Royal Jockey Club, the Linguistics Society of America, the International Society of Applied Linguistics, the American Anthropological Association, the American Medical Association, and so on – all of which have developed sub-languages of their own. Philosophy and religion, our two oldest ways of pursuing knowledge and once, especially in Ancient Greece, free-flowing and 'natural', have also developed in the direction of artificiality. ASs of applied and research mathematics abound world-wide; various associations promoting the study of computers and artificial intelligence are perhaps the most obvious cases. Consider the payroll of a major university or a big hospital. In the old days employees worked for weeks to issue the paychecks of everyone concerned; calculations were made by hand. This kind of manual accounting was replaced by the hand-cranked desk-top calculator; towards the end of World War II these had been replaced by electric counting machines that could carry out complex arithmetic calculations. The computer revolution of the 1950s and 1960s saw the arrival of punched-card IBM machines that worked faster and more accurately than even the best electric desk-top calculators, but they were still relatively slow and cumbersome. A program would easily consist of 2–3 kgs of punched cards which had to be carried in boxes; mechanical obstacles, 'bugs' in the programs frequently resulted not just because of inaccuracies in the programming language used, but the cards themselves could jam. Yet, by the time the Microchip Revolution ushered in the mini-computers and their personalized varieties, the industry had already developed and had been using a sub-language of English well marked by its characteristic vocabulary and syntax.

From the common phrasal verb *to put in* we inherited the computer-language expression *to input*; this inflects not like the ordinary verb *put* but like a 'weak verb': *they inputted the data*, not *they *input the data*. The term *output*, once designating the end-result of one's labor, as in *Michener's literary output is amazing*, became more or less the property of the computer industry, it now means the printed or otherwise stored information that a computer produces as a result of the information inserted into its 'memory' and the instructions regarding what to do with that information.

With *input, inputted, inputting* and *output, outputted, outputting* having thus entered the mainstream vocabulary, the sub-language of a sub-society of international English users has spread from the AS and AL of the computer specialists and became the common property of NL English users in NSs all over the English-speaking world. In other words there is no North American monopoly on *input, inputted, output, outputted*; these 'monstrosities' enjoy a pan-global territoriality and are just as easily used in the USA as in the UK, Canada, New Zealand, Australia, or India, Singapore and Hong Kong, where other types of English are used less frequently and with lesser regularity. To put it another way: the once almost private professional slang of the computer specialist spread out into natural human societies at large; frequently, however, WITHOUT THE PRECISE IMPLICATIONS OF FORMAL AND SYMBOLIC LOGIC THE TERMS ORIGINALLY ENTAILED AND STILL ENTAIL IN NARROWLY DEFINED TECHNICAL USAGE.

This phenomenon of the loosening of originally technical meaning by being 'watered down' in popular usage, can be illustrated from another highly technical field as well, astronautics. The word *go*, with its well-known past and past-participles being *went* and *gone*, respectively, is still regarded as a verb. Yet in Space English (Makkai 1972), it has become a predicate adjective. When a rocket, such as the Saturn IV that took the American Astronauts to the Moon in June of 1969, is ready for firing, the command center issued the brief statement *All systems are GO*. Obviously, *go* here is functioning not as a verb but as a predicate adjective; the replacements *all systems are good, all systems are bad; functioning; faulty, excellent, in order,* etc. prove the point. The public has started to imitate this space usage of *go*, and so today one frequently hears sentences such as *their marriage is a go, their marriage is a no-go; the dean gave the go-no-go decision; we must wait for Daddy to give the go-no-go decision on our trip.*

It seems as if English, one of the world's most dynamic and still developing NLs, has avenged itself on the particularizers and the special meaning developers gathered in special societies and taken back what might be considered as having been its genuine property at the beginning.

2. Where does the language of logic come from?

But where does the tradition of using special logic-based languages originate and what enables us to develop the ability to do logical reasoning in the first place? There are various views on this subject one of which, briefly characterizable as 'Innatism in Logic', is a mixed bag of half-truths and, as such, pregnant with the danger of easy generalization and, hence, various kinds of misunderstanding.

One of the most trouble-ridden areas of modern linguistic theorizing, which originates in the various metamorphoses of Chomsky's Transformational-Generative Grammar (TGG), as manifest in Chomsky (1957) and (1965), is the question of how a child learns to distinguish what is 'logical' from what is 'illogical'. Behavioristic argumentation, characteristic of the first half of the 20th century and ultimately traceable back to Ivan Pavlov and the theory of 'Conditioned Reflexes', would have us believe that logic is learned by humans, just as experimental rats in mazes learn and remember that turning in the wrong direction results in punishment (an electric shock), whereas turning in the right direction results in a small reward (the dropping of a sugar pellet from a dispenser). Academia has been far too tolerant for much too long with the vulgar-Pavlovian view of human behavior. After all, human beings can select various behavior modes that are not dependent on immediate reward or punishment and such human behavior can go as far as encompassing charity on the one hand, and voluntary martyrdom on the other, none of which is 'logical', if by 'logical' we mean that which narrowly and immediately benefits us in the material sense. Chomsky's well-publicized rebellion against narrow behaviorism associated with the name of Professor Skinner at Harvard was, therefore, a much overdue and most timely reminder that there is a great deal more to human behavior, and especially to human language use, than one might extrapolate from rat-experiments. But just as narrow Skinnerian behaviorism was founded on exaggeration, so was the Chomskian reaction, and perhaps predictably so. In rejecting

Skinner and his rat experiments as irrelevant to human beings Chomsky had to supply an alternative explanation for our ability to learn grammars and thereby understand and create actual utterances that we ourselves have never heard or produced before. For if 'logic' is not learned by children as the rat learns the equation that says: 'Right turn = pain; left turn = sugar'; there must be something INHERENT IN HUMAN BEINGS THAT DOES NOT IMPART 'LOGIC' EXPERIENTIALLY BUT THAT ALLOWS 'LOGIC' TO EMERGE FROM A PRE-EXISTENT, MOST PROBABLY UNCONSCIOUS STATE. If this is the case, however, 'logic' must be genetically inherited, probably by DNA. By implying this, TGG advocates begged a still unanswered question which is: does mankind's inherent logical ability develop on account of language acquisition or is it independent of languages? Can non-lingual logic of some sort also be detected in the work of composers, painters and sculptors, or is artistic ability some kind of 'special performance' which Linguistics as a science is not accountable for?

Careful observation indicates that children, as they learn human languages (Halliday 1974) do not only acquire 'grammar' and 'logic', but a general ability to obtain 'goods and services' from the attendant adults; the ability to build inventories (the 'mathetic' function), and last but not least, to play and experiment with language. It is especially important to point out that neither poetry nor prose-literature are materially necessary for immediate survival as are oxygen, food and shelter. Yet human existence without the 'superfluous arts' would be a dreary existence hardly worth living. Sincere and unbiased introspection into our own past development and present value-systems tends to reveal that no matter how important logic is in our daily lives, it is, at best, an equal partner with metaphors, understatements, hyperbole, humor, teasing, allusions, subterfuges, indirect persuasion, emotional language use, and so forth. Obviously, a professional mathematician or professor of symbolic logic 'loves' logic more than a poet or a painter, after all, the family paycheck is derived from the practitioner's daily involvement with logic as a subject matter of research and instruction. The same is true about colors and sounds. A painter, who makes his living by teaching art in a college, is more concerned with the spectrum of the rainbow and what he can bring out on his palette by mixing basic colors than the brick-layer, the computer operator or the music teacher in the same school; the musician, in turn, will have a tendency to think about the world as a gigantic composite of sounds. If such a musician is also interested in mathematics, (s)he may have heard of the Italian mathematician Fibonacci, who calculated the 'harmonics' of the distances between the various planets in our Solar System, thereby coming to the conclusion that mathematics, logic, music and ancient mysticism stem from a common, now largely forgotten source.

Trial attorneys must also rely on specialized kinds of logic, mostly verbal inferences. If an accused person offers an alibi during a murder trial that does not hold up under cross-examination, it is most likely that there was a 'logical flaw' in the argumentation. It is incumbent on the presiding judge and jury to pay detailed attention to the 'logic' presented by both the prosecution and the defense.

The point to be made here is that once 'Logic' or some logically-based profession becomes someone's livelihood, the importance of logic increases immensely in that person's conscious appreciation of what logic has to offer. A prima ballerina in the Bolshoi Ballet, by contrast, may live a glamorous and successful life without being aware of logic at all, no matter how 'logical' a particular piece of choreography may or not be. If 'sadness' or 'mourning' in ballet are symbolized by a downward, collapsing gesture, and joy and victory with upward leaps and rapid turns, is there 'logic' at work, or something else? In the following sections I shall try to formulate some kind of acceptable answer to this and related questions.

Before attempting a quasi-formal answer, however, I wish to enter a motion for general consideration regarding the relationship between 'Logic' and its various relatives such as 'Analogy', 'Metaphor', 'Anaphora', 'Cataphora', 'Puns', 'Jokes', 'Understatements', 'Hyperbole', and the rest of humanity's rhetorical rèpertoire.

If we assume that all of humanity is engaged in the manipulation of SIGNS OF VARIOUS KINDS AND AT VARIOUS DEGREES OF CONSCIOUS INTENSITY, we can come to a view of human nature that makes the apparent contradiction between 'Logic' and 'Non-logic' dissolve in a dynamic synthesis.

This view of humankind as various social conglomerates of signal-producing and signal-receiving conscious entities is the SEMIOTIC VIEW OF THE HUMAN CONDITION. It is my firm belief that we are all members of the species *homo signans*, and that nature-provided membership in this anthropological category brings with it the common human ability of using various kinds of logic at various levels of consciousness to varying degrees of social significance both for ourselves and for our fellow human beings.

3. *'Homo signans'*, language, logic, and the principle of 'semiotic relevance' in linguistics and all other logic-based disciplines

It is at this point that the philosophy of Giambattista Vico becomes enlightening and relevant in thinking about logic and linguistics.

Let us try to restate briefly in essential outline Vico's GREAT CYCLES as presented in his *Szienza nuova*, and see if, without forcing the issue, some similarities can be detected as regards the evolution of linguistic theorizing.

In Vico's scheme mankind's first stage of development is the DIVINE STAGE. This, he explains, came expressed not in modern language, but in GESTURAL LANGUAGE, an archaic way of communication. The Divine State was followed in Vico's scheme by the HEROIC STAGE. For this Vico uses the examples of Homeric Greek, a language characterized by METRIC MEMORY, specifically the GREEK HEXAMETER. (It is well known that both the *Iliad* and the *Odyssey* were orally recited for centuries before they were ever written down.) The Heroic Age produced HEROIC LANGUAGE, a language replete with the standing epithet ('hypotheton ornans'), the set phrase and the set comparison embedded in memory-enhancing rhythmical speech.

The Heroic Age is followed by the HUMAN AGE, whose language is the language of common day-time consciousness and rational discourse depending on lexico-grammar and the semantics of the lexicon. It is interesting to note that the invention of the CLASSICAL SYLLOGISM ('All men are mortal: Socrates is a man: Socrates is mortal') can be timed to be co-aeval with the appearance of Aristotle, whose work signals the beginning of human logic, as we know it today.

The Human Age gives way, in Vico's philosophy, to the AGE OF CHAOS, from which, after much pain and parturition, there will emerge a new cycle, having its own Divine, Heroic and Human stages.

That this is but a gross over-simplification goes without saying. It is, nevertheless, desirable for us to see if both recent events in human history and the development of the individual can suggest possible parallels. Scientific proof, in the sense of modern physics or chemistry, would be a misplaced desideratum here, as the very essence of Vichian thinking is more in keeping with ANALOGICAL LOGIC than with the modern linguist's set-theoretical logic, borrowed from a sub-discipline of mathematics.

Let us look at the individual human being first:

Children, as was shown by Halliday (1974), create their own ARCHE-LANGUAGE between the age of two and ten months. It is naive to suppose that they have no language at all; the evidence of the now famous *Nigel Corpus* directly indicates that meaning-manipulation, interaction with others and the obtaining of 'goods and services' is well on its way before the young child 'breaks into the adult language'. Halliday makes no mention of Vico in any of his writings, but this does not obligate us to ignore the obvious connection between Halliday's modern observations and Vico's 18th-century philosophy: Halliday, in fact, can be credited with having unwittingly provided REAL PROOF of Vico's contention whereby a pre-adult language user, by re-discovering the magic of the universe, lives in a mini-scale Divine World of his own. And how could it be otherwise? A sound is emitted, and lo and behold an adult appears and makes one's hunger, cold, itch, pain go away. This is instant magic! All one has to do is open and close one's lips while letting the vocal chords vibrate, and out comes the sound /mama-mama/! with a variety of emotive intonations, and the most significant human being of all, one's mother, takes that to be her name and furnishes constant proof of the fact by her spontaneously volunteered full-time availability.

Between ages one and seven, a youngster is a 'hero' in a very real sense. One fights dragons and dwarfs; one may have a leaping-gown in the fashion of Superman and one gets into one's first fights with other children. The time-slots may, of course, be cut up differently as well. It can be also analogized with some justification that ages one to seven constitute the Divine Age in miniature replica, for this is the age of primary socialization during which the acquisition of word-meanings as well as syntax is entirely unconscious. Words such as *milk, bread, Mom, Dad, sun, yes, no, me, he, she, go, sit, doggy,* along with countless others, do not necessitate conscious definitions of the kind becoming commonplace in the next stage of development. It is between ages seven and fourteen, during secondary socialization, that one learns 'meanings' for words such as *anticipate* and *procrastinate* paraphrased in plainer language as 'can hardly wait for something to happen' and 'put off til tomorrow'.

The school-age, therefore, is 'heroic' as we must fight the dragons of COGNOSEMEMES, the 'vocabulary words' we take home from school. Language acquisition during primary socialization was PSYCHOSEMEMIC in comparison: the 'meanings' of *sun* and *moon* were a 'gesture' such as 'up there' and not the high school science book's elaborate wordings: *sun*: 'medium-sized yellow star in the Milky Way Galaxy emitting heat and light through thermo-nuclear fission around which orbit Mercury, Venus, Earth . . .', etc.

With the third metabolic cycle of seven years, at age twenty-one one reaches 'adulthood', i.e. the beginning of the 'human phase'. Conscious decisions are taken, a profession or field of work is chosen with a view to finances and one is more likely to leave the security of the family nest.

Age twenty-eight, the fourth metabolic cycle of seven, is likely to see one as a young parent – the obvious beginning of a new cycle of life. What was once, in early childhood, a discovery of the universe, replete with the naming of things, becomes parental care, explaining, rearing, in short – being the educator instead of the educated.

How, then, should we see LOGIC in terms of a Vichian development in the individual?

What is most probably INNATE in human beings is not ADULT LOGIC *per se*, but an INNATE CAPACITY OF A DEVELOPING CONSCIOUSNESS, which is best expressed by the Greek term, LOGOS.

By 'adult logic' I mean the knowledge that the Pythagorean theorem is always considered to be correct in terrestrial, Euclidian geometry, regardless of the size of the triangle concerned, as long as it has a 90-degree angle. Chomsky, in his eagerness to liberate linguistics from behaviorism, was initially responding correctly to the call of the times, but he missed and is continuing to miss the real insight which is this: whereas the human being is certainly not 'Pavlov's dog' responding to conditioned reflexes, nor a hungry rat in a Skinnerean maze pushing certain levers expecting the reward of a lump of sugar, NEITHER ARE WE ADULTS LOGIC-DRIVEN AUTOMATA whose main concern is whether a string of morphemes is 'syntactically grammatical' or not.

The human being's main purpose in using language is to COMMUNICATE VIA SIGNS with fellow members of human societies. If this is a 'teleological' statement: I am guilty of seeing a 'purpose' in human language, where PURPOSE must be defined loosely enough to accommodate PLAYFULNESS. One of the most wonderful purposes of human language is language play: from the nursery rhyme and the tongue-twister through the limerick to the Petrarcan and the Shakespearian sonnet. Poetry is essential to life, and anybody blind to this is condemning us to live life as if we were hapless interns in a concentration camp where there is only duty and work without the bio-psychologically necessary intervals of rest and recuperation. To understand poetry, however, one must understand the ever-present CHILD in human psycho-cognitive organization, and Chomsky and his adult logic have no tolerance for the 'child', not even in his transformed adult forms when the underlying child is realized as e.e. cummings, T.S. Eliot, or Ezra Pound.

Due to the basic synchronic nature of the present study, my goal is not so much to characterize the last decade of the 20th century in Vichian terms as 'chaotic' in essence but with certain latent tendencies at recapitulation of 'divine', 'heroic' and 'human elements' – that will have to wait for another occasion. My primary goal is to examine how we use logic, and in coming to grips with that problem, the Vichian view of human pre-history TELESCOPED INTO INDIVIDUAL PERSONALITY STRUC-TURES cries out for identification. I am referring to Eric Berne's and Dr Harris's theory of the THREE-FOLD ORGANIZATION OF HUMAN PERSONALITY. According to this theory, every human being carries inside a PARENT, an ADULT and a CHILD. *Mutatis mutandis*, these stages corres-pond to Siegmund Freud's SUPER-EGO, the EGO, and the ID.

How does this three-folding of our personalities compare to the Vichian phases of human history? The CHILD (Freud's ID) is the archaic stage of our personality structure. As such, it corresponds to the DIVINE PHASE of human pre-history. The ADULT (Freud's EGO) should really correspond to Vico's HUMAN AGE, but we must realize that we must tolerate an asym-metrical overlap in comparing Vico's FOUR PHASES to Berne–Harris's THREE STRUCTURES. The ADULT is, accordingly, a mixture of the HEROIC and of the HUMAN. The PARENT (Freud's SUPER-EGO) is the 'judgmental component' of modern human personality, and as such it corresponds to Vico's *ricorso*, the 'trial', while also containing many of the features of the 'human stage'. The Bernian-Harrisian-Freudian PARENT also waxes 'divine' in its New Testamental, law-giving phases, thereby indicating that Divine–Heroic–Human–Chaotic are SIMULTANEOUSLY PRESENT in the modern human being; furthermore that these four basic elements of human personality structure can surface at rapid intervals several times within the same one-hour conversation with another human being. The three-fold Ego-structure with 'chaos' as its fourth solvent makes perfect ONTOGENETIC SENSE, exactly the same way as does Ernst Haeckel's theory (which states that ontogenesis recapitulates philogenesis). In fact we can look at Vico's phases in the reverse and say: since the human being can act like a Divine Child, like a Conquering Hero, like a Reasoning Adult, like a Judgmental Parent and like a quasi-Divine Law-Giving Parent, it would be in keeping with our knowledge of ontogenesis and philogenesis to suppose that such phases might have pre-existed in human history, whereby the Haeckelian theory of recapitulation is once again seen to work – this time not in our biological evolution from embryo to infant, but as functional, INTERACTING SOCIAL BEINGS.

We can produce logic 'logically' (adult mode, the work of a mathematician). We can produce logic 'playfully': the work of a Child or a prankster. We can produce 'logic' in a painting or in the composition of a symphonic poem praeter-logically, but with professional training and expertise: this is a combination of the Divine Child held over into adulthood and bolstered by Parental-Divine guidance.

Logic can also be used negatively, as by Inquisitors and mind-benders who try to influence our consciousness without our consent. This happens when the 'Parent' waxes imperious and decrees that it has all the answers; nobody else does. It is also known in world literature as the 'Raskolnikov Complex' and in Transactional Analysis as the 'Criminal Attitude', 'I'm OK – You're *not* OK'. More of this below.

I do not intend to imply what is sometimes said against logic by the general public at large: that there is something more inherently 'noble', more 'elegant' or more 'chivalrous' about trusting one's 'raw instinct' and let insurance policies – which are comparable to certain programs – reassure the cowardly. What I am trying to say is that there must be a HIGHER TRIBUNAL that adjudicates and evaluates just what 'logic' really is and what it does in a given human situation.

I believe, and am ready to defend by rational argumentation, that the common source of LOGIC, MEMORY, LANGUAGE, MUSIC, SPORTS and THE ARTS is one and the same, and that it can be identified as that life-force which is simultaneously responsible for 'reason' in crystalline rock-formations; 'reason' in the symmetry of plants and plant propagation; in the rapid, though unconscious calculations a tiger or a leopard makes when deciding how fast and how high to jump to catch its prey; 'reason' in the human skeletal structure (*sic!* Try- to calculate the most advantageous geometrical proportions of the head of the thigh-bone and place in the pelvis where it fits to ensure bipedal locomotion in humans!); reason in the human eye's iris and retina; reason in the human brain's hemispheric lateralization; reason in elementary trigonometry in the grade schools and reason in J.S. Bach's historic act of tempering the scales so that a piece written in C-major can be transposed and played in D sharp major instead. For all of this is 'reason', although sometimes it is UNCONSCIOUS REASON.

At this point I must beg the reader's kind indulgence. 'Reason', we commonly think, is synonymous with 'consciousness', that is, awareness and deliberate intention. But this is a common fallacy. Rock formations, replete with the intricate logic of crystallization processes, are entirely unconscious, as far as we can tell. The amazing beauty seen in the symmetry of plant leaves and flower petals is also unconscious since neither rocks nor plants have a nervous system which alone, as far as we are concerned, can lead to consciousness and, therefore, to logic. But is this really so? Vegetarians, who refuse to eat meat because they believe that animals suffer when slaughtered, hesitate when asked whether scallops and oysters feel pain when eaten (raw or cooked). Some will eat them perfectly cheerfully and maintain that oysters and scallops do not suffer; others count scallops and oysters along with various kinds of fish which, as is obvious when they are seen fleeing, must feel fright and must, therefore, suffer when caught, cooked and eaten. Not even the most sensitive vegetarians, however, hesitate in eating an apple. Who is to say that apples do not suffer when plucked from their tree? I heard a Hindu sage in Singapore in 1986 explain that vegetables feel pleasure when you eat them . . . they live in a self-sacrificial state and feel bad when they cannot participate in the metabolism of higher beings. This 'reverence for life'-syndrome can go as far as Don Juan Matus' exhortations to Carlos Castaneda (Castaneda 1975) that 'one must apologize to a vegetable before picking it for consumption'. A Western-trained mathematician or symbolic logician may very well dismiss any such speculation as fancifully irrelevant, or (s)he may admit to read Castaneda and authors similar to him for 'mere relaxation and entertainment' without paying 'any serious attention to his thought'. Others will waiver between the two extremes and say something such as 'Institution, games, religion, even magic are OK on week-ends, but not when I do my serious work in the laboratory or in my study'. To say that we human beings live a somewhat schizoid existence is no exaggeration.

One additional observation seems necessary before we attempt naming the common lowest (or highest?) denominator of all the things we know. Consider a native of Papua New Guinea who, for all practical purposes, lives a stone-age existence. He hops from rock to rock in the nude and uses a boomerang to hit birds with; the bird is a couple of dozen yards BEHIND HIM, yet the boomerang hits it right on the head when the native throws it FORWARDS, WITHOUT SEEING HIS INTENDED TARGET. Is the boomerang, as a projectile, thrown along the curve of a consciously calculated trajectory or is it moved accidentally? Considering the amazing success-rate of Papuan boomerang throwers, whose average score is a tantalizing 98 hits out of 100 attempts, one is truly amazed at the phenomenon. Numerous Europeans and other 'civilizados' have tried to acquire the skill, but only a very few have succeeded to any degree at all. Papuans, on the other hand, can be drafted into the Western mind-set via literacy, urbanization, clothing, and being given a name, an identity card and a motor vehicle operator's licence. What is it that passes between the civilized television watchers applauding Armstrong and Aldrin on the Moon, and staring, amazed, at the unfathomable skill of the Papua New Guinea native, who hits a bird, intended for supper, with a backward-flying-but-forward-hurled boomerang? One tentative answer might go somewhat as follows: The westernized television watcher and the Papua New Guinea native live in different mind-sets; i.e. they possess DIFFERENT MODES OF CONSCIOUSNESS. The civilized Westerner grasps only what he can see with his physical eyes. Thus the utterly phantastic unreality of 'men on the Moon' of one hundred years ago is 'reality'; but what the Papua New Guinea native does is 'weird', 'incomprehensible', 'magical', 'tricky', something that is quite out of the ordinary.

But what about the perspective of the Papua New Guinea native? Would he not have the right to insist that 'only spirits can walk on the Moon but any boy can be taught how to hit a bird behind his back with a boomerang being thrown forwards'? And then consider the phenomenon of inter-cultural transplants: the son of a Papua New Guinea hunter may go the University of Port Moresby and become a mathematician, while the son of the Australian or American mathematics professor at the same univer-sity may decide to become a cultural anthropologist who, during the course of his studies, spends a number of years with the tribe his counterpart comes from, and learns the 'magic skill' of boomerang hunting. Far-fetched? Not really. Maybe rare or off the beaten track, but such exchanges and mutual interpenetrations do occur, indeed they seem to do so with increasing frequency. The North American Indian Movement ('AIM'), the numerous anthropological treatises and studies written and published in the wake of Europeans becoming Witch Doctors in South Africa (personal communication from Mrs Joan Van Gogh Boshier, whose late husband did become a South African Witch Doctor), the works of Castaneda (1975) indicate that mankind still lives in largely separate mind-sets (or cultural compartments) and that these, no matter how far apart, can on occasion, be bridged by a dedicated minority.

I have started this section with the LOGOS; then mentioned rock and crystal formations, vegetables, animals, and finally human beings in strik-ingly different civilizations and modes of thinking. At present all of this co-exists on Earth and no matter what our particular prejudice, we must admit that, whether we like it or not, the mathematician's son can enter the consciousness of a pre-literate tribe, and a member of a pre-literate tribe can become a Medical Doctor. (This latter event happened when Ms Yahuaraqui Canayo, a native Piro Indian from Peruvian Amazonia, became the first Indian M.D. to have graduated from San Marcos Univer-sity, the oldest Medical School in the Western Hemisphere (Makkai 1983).) I must now try to show that none of this is accidental or random and that the principle that regulates our enormous diversity is as old as physical existence itself and that it was known to the Ancients but largely forgotten; furthermore that this forgotten knowledge did survive in hidden pockets of European thought, in Germany in Goethe's world view, and in 18th-century Italy in Giambattista Vico's profound thought of the Great Cycles of pre-history.

The common life-force, imaginable as a 'principle' though not at all as abstract and imaginary, that allows rocks to crystallize according to 'quasi-logical programs', that causes plants to have geometrical proportions whose drawing would necessitate the comprehension of 'π' well beyond 3.1452 – perhaps even up to several hundred or several thousand decimals –; that enables/causes/allows/encourages/determines/orchestrates/plans/draws   the Chambered Nautilus, this rarest of sea-shells, to exact mathematical proportions identical to the spiral-formation of a Galaxy; this Thought-Form, this Super-Program that brings about the music of Bach, Mozart and Beethoven as well as allowing Pythagoras to have discovered and taught that '$A^2 + B^2 = C^2$' in triangles that have a 90-degree angle; this

Force which, *inter alia*, can also cause us to draw a difference between 'moral' and 'immoral' behavior, can only be one which is intimately connected with the very *raison d'être* of our planet, our solar system, our galaxy, the Milky Way, and ultimately, the universe itself. Whether such a 'Force' or 'Principle' or 'Being' is 'rational-logical' or a matter of 'religious faith' hardly matters: the arguments one has heard and participated in and the ones that still lie ahead as 'progress' (however we interpret the term) are as numerous and multifarious as are the human personalities and their long range and *ad hoc* interests in entering such debates. This chapter is not about theology and I do not wish to promote any organized religion. This chapter is the attempt of a cognitive linguist to examine LOGIC in Vichian-semiotic terms. Arithmetico-mathematical common sense of the most compelling nature forces me to conclude that human cognition (or 'intelligence'), diversified though it may be, must have a common source.

In the mind-set of the ancient 'initiates' the 'logical' and the 'mystical' may very well have coincided without leading to nervous breakdowns or paranoia. That this was the case in all probability can be seen in the work of scholars such as the renowned former Soviet, now American scholar S.K. Shaumyan (1980) who, in agreement with Fritjof Capra, the author of *The Tao of Physics*, believes that it is precisely modern science – above all mathematically-based theoretical physics – that will ultimately tear down the remaining barriers between science and religion. The Capra–Shaumyan line of thinking calls attention to the fact that Pythagoras was a mystic who ran an initiation school in Ancient Greece and that Albert Einstein, the inventor of the theory of relativity, attributed nature's properties to a cosmic wisdom which he identified with God. Why indeed, do certain minerals crystallize octogonally while others do so hexagonally? Have these 'unconscious' materials a secret will or some secret self-programming ability that allows them to choose between becoming octogonal versus hexagonal? The answer must be that although rocks, plants, invertebrate animals and the intricately architectured junction between pelvis and upper thigh-bone have no 'consciousness' of their own, there must exist, somewhere and somehow, within our universe, a force, a power, a set of potentialities that has the unique function, duty, charge and force to dispense VARIOUS LEVELS AND KINDS OF LOGIC TO THE KINGDOMS OF NATURE IN A STRICTLY HIERARCHICAL ORDER.

Accordingly:

a)   Crystals and minerals are endowed with 'crystalline logic' which, due to the inorganic nature of the mineral kingdom, must be several degrees removed from the very crystals and minerals in whose nature this logic and consciousness is manifest.

b)   Vegetables, flowers, sea-shells, etc. are endowed with 'vegetable-lower-animal-logic' which, in accordance with the biological reality of non-vertebrate life-organisms must be only partly present in the creatures of this category, and largely outside of them. In contrast with minerals, 'logic/consciousness' is more 'in the flesh', i.e., 'incarnated' in the leaves, petals, mussels and sea-urchins than in the quartz and salt crystal formations.

c) Higher animals (from the vertebrates up to the primates) are endowed with manifestly larger and qualitatively superior kinds of 'logic-consciousness' which is, due to the central nervous system and the brain, far more 'in the flesh' (i.e. 'incarnated') in these creatures than in the mineral and the vegetable kingdoms. Think of the well-trained sheep-dog in this respect: the Hungarian *puli* can recognize over 200 commands performed by hand-signal and can control a flock of over 300 sheep. The circus performances of man-trained animals are another good example to show how close these creatures are to us humans: chimpanzees can 'ape' human behavior closely enough to cause uproarious laughter in the attendant human audiences.

d) 'Logic' and 'consciousness' have penetrated most deeply into human beings, as it is our species and our species alone that is capable of performing integral and differential calculus, comprehend and teach to the young the Pythagorean theorem; find Euclidian geometry insufficient and declare with Gauss and Bolyai that 'parallels will meet in infinity'; we alone can compose two- and three-part inventions and symphonies for ninety instruments and 250 voices; we alone can send a fellow of our species to the moon; we alone can build thermo-nuclear warheads powerful enough to destroy all 'bios' on the planet; we alone can martyrize ourselves for a 'religion'; we alone can die on the barricades for a set of ideas such as LIBERTY, EQUALITY and FRATERNITY, as the 200th anniversary of the French Revolution and the European democratic revolutions of the Fall of 1989 reminded us.

Since we seem to be able to bring 'logical behavior' to the surface of social behavior from our own consciousness, it must be the case that this 'Logic-Consciousness' is most deeply 'seated in the flesh' ('incarnated') in us, human beings.

The Vichian view of the universe allows logic to be seen in the mineral kingdom, the vegetable kingdom and in the animal kingdom as well, but it shows in its pre-eminately essential and human-Aristotelian form in the functioning adult human being. The other kingdoms of nature must, in Vichian terms, have been pre-programmed by the cosmic divine intelligence in such a way that the consciousness of logical behavior is not manifest in the beings that carry it. Crystalline consciousness exists but outside of actual crystals; vegetable consciousness, similarly, can only exist outside of actual vegetables, with animal consciousness being an interesting borderline case: the animal's consciousness is, in all likelihood, comparable to the dreaming-state consciousness of human beings. This is not spelled out in any of Vico's writings, but it follows from them. The great German poet, scientist and statesman, Johann Wolfgang van Goethe, clearly implies it in his scientific writings which were edited by Dr Rudolf Steiner in Weimar in the early part of the 20th century (see the References under Steiner).

4. Our moral duties as possessors of 'logic' and 'consciousness'

Whether 'logic' and 'consciousness' are divine and transcendental or caused by biological evolution, and therefore human and immanent, IS NOT THE ESSENTIAL QUESTION. The essential question is: WHAT ARE WE GOING TO DO WITH OUR LOGICAL CONSCIOUSNESS? ARE WE GOING TO USE IT TO DOMINATE AND EXPLOIT OTHER HUMAN BEINGS, OR ARE WE GOING TO USE IT TO BUILD BETTER SOCIETIES FOR THE BENEFIT OF ALL? Voltaire said: 'If God didn't exist, it would be necessary to invent him'. Confucius said: 'Treat the mundane as sacred and Earth will become Heaven'.

In what follows I will try to give some personally experienced illustrations of 'morally indefensible logic' versus 'morally compelling logic'.

4.1. Morally indefensible logic – from the ridiculous to the diabolical

Youngsters often indulge in verbal games of the following sort: 'If the length of a boat is 120 feet and the width 22 feet, how old was the owner when he first got married?' The question is supposed to be answered with an appropriate snarl, a wave of the fist, or be countered by an even more unlikely repartee of a pseudo-question garbed in the verbiage of quasi-logic. The game was invented by the Ancient Greeks and is perhaps best illustrated by what is known as Zeno's Paradox. The thesis is that 'you cannot go to the wall'. How is this proven? It is proven by stating that in order to go to the wall, one must, obviously, first cross the half of the distance that separates one from one's target. Having done that, there still remains half of the half-distance. When you have crossed that, there remains 25 per cent of the original distance, which, too, cannot be crossed in one step, but has to be halved first. Continuing this line of 'reasoning' one reaches the 'conclusion' that it is truly impossible to reach the wall, because no matter how small the distance remaining, its half must still be crossed which has a half, which has a half and which has a half . . . *ad infinitum*. Ergo, one never reaches the wall. This game, much enjoyed by Zeno and the original sophists, is rather easily foiled by pointing out that it is a self-imposed and unnecessary condition to state that 'only 50 per cent of any given distance may be crossed at a given time'. Why the half? Why not 75 per cent, after which one leaps there instantaneously covering the remaining 25 per cent. Why not make a 100 per cent jump at the very start, and have it done with? Is not that how we move, intentionally and, in most instances, successfully? The pitfall here is that there is a certain partial truth in the proposition that 'you cannot get there at once'. Reaching a goal in physical distance IS a process, and since it is a process, it is easy enough to claim that only a certain proportion of a process can be finished in a finite amount of time. The 'cheating' in Zeno's paradox occurs when the 'joker' (the 'logician') tells the straight-man (the 'pupil') that it is precisely half, i.e. 50 per cent of the distance that one manages to cover. This artificial imposition brings in the necessity of creating further subdivisions of the remaining distances – always at the preset 50 per cent mark – so that the 'pupil' is driven to the conclusion that, since the half of the half of the half, etc., is finite, reaching the wall is actually impossible. That this, *in natura et in realitate*, is not so, it is not an argument *ex principio* but rather one *ex perceptione*.

What is, in most probability, 'innate' in human beings is not 'logic' *per se* – that is, some kind of pre-programmed knowledge that the Pythagorean theorem is always necessarily correct in a Euclidian geometry regardless of the size of the triangle concerned as long as it has a 90-degree angle – but an innate capacity of consciousness which is best expressed by the Greek term LOGOS. I am all too aware of the dangers of equating 'logic' as well as 'intuition' and 'art' with the LOGOS as that term has been vastly misunderstood by the theologians who have used it for their own selfish purposes. The non-theological use of the word, especially in modern academic writing, is far from being well established. Most readers will probably identify the term LOGOS with the 'WORD' as it is given in the first sentence of the Gospel according to St. John, which says 'In the beginning was the Word, and the Word was with God, and the Word was God . . . And the Word was made flesh and dwelt among us . . .'. It cannot be the purpose of the present essay on the proper and improper uses of 'logic' to offer a detailed, non-sectarian exegesis of the opening lines of the Gospel according to St. John.

We must observe, however, that despite the innumerable good and bad translations of the Scriptures into hundreds of languages, we ourselves have not yet necessarily understood what John was trying to tell us. Precisely in order to be 'scientific', that is, unbiased about it, we must give the evangelist the 'benefit of doubt', this most precious legal privilege that characterizes Anglo-Saxon case law in contradistinction to the European *Code Napoléon*, and the various abuses of the legal process seen under Nazi and Communist tyranny in this century. In Anglo-Saxon jurisprudence the 'accused is assumed innocent until found guilty', whereas in Continental practice, going back to the age of the Inquisition and the infamous witch-hunts, the accused was *eo ipso* considered guilty and only rarely acquitted. 'When did you stop sleeping with the Devil?' is such a typical witch-hunter's question, also exhibiting one of the foremost and most widely spread abuses of logic. If the accused answered 'last year', she was guilty of having slept with the Devil until said time; if she said 'never', meaning 'never slept with him', the inquisitor could interpret it as 'never stopped sleeping with the Devil, ergo still sleeps with him'; if the accused said 'I have never done so and will never do so' the inquisitor could say 'The Devil alone can give you the strength to deny your guilt' and the verdict was the predictable 'guilty as accused'. Although we think that the age of the witch-hunts is over, it remains sadly true that we still very often employ similar 'logic' as did the notorious inquisitors. We tend to trust only the five physical senses and little else; 'logic', as we understand it, is an electrical function of the brain which consists of billions of neurons.

Why we have such complex brains, and what makes them function electrically, are questions one does not usually ask; they tend to be dismissed as 'uninformed questions'. The truth is more likely that they are questions extremely difficult to answer based on today's general materialist world view and since all of respectable science must be explainable in terms of materialism, everything that smacks of 'Creation', 'God', 'the Spirit', etc. is automatically unscientific and inadmissible as evidence. Yet the very nature of our universe is not quite 'logical'. How can we reconcile the Einsteinian position of a perpetually expanding universe with the equally likely, if unproven, hypothesis of the 'oscillating universe', which states that the universe has 'expanding phases' (the present one) and 'collapsing phases'? How many 'big bangs' were there? Just one? Why did it start? Where did primordial matter come from, endowed with forces of magnetism and gravity, such that globules of gas could condense into incandescent stars, solar systems, and entire galaxies? Where did primordial matter obtain the 'programming intelligence' that permitted it to evolve into a) the mineral kingdom, b) the vegetable kingdom, c) the animal kingdom, and d) into *homo faber/sapiens/signans*? Material science has no answer for these questions. 'That is just how it is', we are told, and it is regarded as 'bad form', 'naïveté', and 'immaturity' to inquire into primal causes and origins. Yet the structures of the simplest living organisms, the algae and other primitive sea-creatures, show complex 'programming' in their DNA structures, just as if some sophisticated computer programmer had been at work in designing their structures and their abilities to remember their structures in order to transmit them to their offspring. That we are genetically programmed, both philogenetically and ontogenetically, was discovered by Haeckel in the 19th century and today every fourteen-year old who took a class in biology knows that the human embryo repeats in the womb mankind's philogenetic evolution: we grow from amoeba-like cell to fish-like aquatic creature, then into a mammalian state, finally into a primate state, until at nine months, full-term babies with full human abilities, including the capacity to learn languages and engage in 'logic' both professionally and in a variety of applied modes. Where does this 'logical programming' start? In the father's sperm? In the mother's egg? In a random combination of both? How can the child of a chamber-maid and a truck driver become a brilliant poet, trial attorney, or mathematician? Is this predictable? Certainly not. Yet it happens. If heredity were strictly 'logical', should not all of Johann Sebastian Bach's sons have become equally famous and productive as JSB himself? Why was it frail Wolfgang Amadeus, of all the Mozarts, who composed *Don Giovanni*, *The Requiem Mass*, *The Symphony in G-minor*, and not his father, Leopold, who 'knew more about music' than Wolfgang, the four-year old prodigy? Why did Beethoven, whose family was saddled with tuberculosis and syphilis, succeed, even after going deaf, in composing some of mankind's greatest music? Is this 'logical' in any sense of the word?

What can be more 'logical' than a modern, high-capacity computer?

Hardly anything. Why is it then that the average fourteen-year old high school chess player of advanced standing can invariably beat the best computers programmed to play chess?

The answer I got to this last question came from actual computer specialists at the RAND Corporation in Santa Monica, California, where I spent a year studying computers, on a post-doctoral grant from the National Science Foundation in 1965–66. The answer was that the computer invariably gets beaten because it is too 'logical'. When I wondered what that meant, it was explained that the human mind, in contrast to the computer, 'goes to sleep every thirty seconds' and 'works by intuitive leaps and bounds'; furthermore, the human chess player is 'driven by the desire to win' whereas 'the computer has no emotions'. It has become clear that logic and nothing but logic is a DISTINCT DISADVANTAGE IN MANY HUMAN SITUATIONS.

Anyone who has ever watched the popular science fiction series *Star Trek*, or seen any of the motion pictures based on it, will remember that the 'Vulcan', Mr Spock, always goes 'by logic alone' as he has no human emotions. Yet, whenever the *Starship Enterprise* gets into serious trouble, Captain Kirk (who is merely human) saves the ship and the crew by using 'human intuition' and 'raw courage' which is, according to Spock 'strangely illogical'. But let us look at the real event. When Armstrong and Aldrin landed on the moon in June, 1966, during the last phases of the descent, Armstrong took the manual controls and sidestepped the computerized landing program. He discerned that the computerized program would have dropped the *Eagle* too fast and too soon so that it might have crash-landed. A 'parental-adult' program was thus overridden by a heroic half-Child half-Adult; survival won out over routine logical behavior.

None of this is meant to say that 'logic' is somehow not at work in the thinking of the fourteen-year old chess player who defeats the computer program, or in Mr Armstrong's last-minute decision to abandon the automatic landing program and to take Aldrin's and his own life into his own hands. The distinctly human-Adult ability to act logically is there 'all the time' in trained individuals, but the tri-partite organization of human personality structure often suppresses the logical component, driven, according to medical science, by the dominant left hemisphere of the human brain (cf. Jaynes 1976).

In what follows we ought to look at praeter-logical self-defense in legal cases where the prosecutors use a warped, evil kind of logic. I take my examples from the Chinese *Cultural Revolution, Marxist-dominated Hungary*, an *American shoe-store* and finally a fable by Aesop.

4.1.1. Some actual case histories of the abuse of logic in the legal sphere: China, Hungary and the United States

In the tormented and crazy world we live in, an actual defendant in a trial may be found 'guilty' or 'innocent', depending NOT ON THE INTRINSIC MERIT OF THE ARGUMENT PER SE, BUT ACCORDING TO THE MORAL INCLINATIONS OF THE 'TUTOR/JOKER'. AND THIS IS THE IMMENSE TRAGEDY OF 'FALSE LOGIC'; THE FACT THAT IT CANNOT BE COUNTERED BY LOGIC ALONE, BUT ONLY BY A COGNITIVE PARADIGM-SHIFT TO THE 'MORAL SPHERE'.

Let us make a jump in time to the decade between 1968 and 1978, the decade of the 'Cultural Revolution' in China under Mao Zedong. A member of the Party who believes in a modicum of free enterprise is accused by the Red Guard that he is fostering capitalism and is a hireling of the Kuomintang from Taiwan. The captors ask: 'Are you or are you not saying that agricultural productivity increases if the peasant owns his own land?' The prisoner answers: 'No, I am not saying that.' The captors: 'Aha, you support the Kuomintang because you have the audacity to deny that you advocate private ownership; only well-fed people have the energy to make such a denial and only people who own their own land are well-fed. Therefore, you are guilty.' Suppose that the prisoner says: 'Yes, I admit that I believe that private ownership increases productivity.' The captors can actually have him shot as having made an outright confession. Suppose, however, that the prisoner is exceptionally smart and says the following: 'Although you Comrades want me to say that I believe in private ownership so that you can have me shot, and although you Comrades want me to deny my belief in private ownership so that you can have me shot for THAT reason, I hereby declare my eternal love and loyalty to the Party and Comrade Mao Zedong and simply insist that it was the Great Chairman Mao himself who said that we should "let a hundred flowers bloom and a thousand ideas contend" . . . I meant no harm to Mao Zedong's Thought and I have not advocated private ownership; I merely dedicated twenty square yards around my living quarters to one of Chairman Mao's own Thoughts and this has resulted in more potatoes and onions. The honored Comrades can plainly see that I have acted with Red Guard Revolutionary Fervor in the best interests of the Party.' (This incident was related to me in Changchun, Jilin Province, July of 1986 by a former Professor of English who was in deportation during the Cultural Revolution and who grew vegetables around his hut. He saved his and his family's life by outsmarting the captors and by sounding more Maoist than Mao himself while obviously being 'guilty' of successful vegetable gardening.)

The success of the defense here is brought about by the prisoner cleverly rejecting the 'logical premiss' (i.e. the trap) set by the captors which is so organized that he turns out to be 'guilty' whether he confesses or not. The prisoner has turned tables on the captors and intimidates them by his 'superior knowledge of Maoism'. It is entirely irrelevant whether the argument used is true Maoism or not; it works not because of 'logic' or the lack of it; rather it wins because the prisoner has succeeded in foiling the power-plot of the captors. His strategy is one of side-stepping the question of entrapment set by the captors and appealing to the higher tribunal of

Chairman Mao's Thought, his prestige, before which the captors, who are not prepared to deal with the prisoner's sophistication, are powerless.

A similar incident was reported to me from 1944, towards the end of World War II, in Budapest, Hungary. Two members of the Arrow Cross Party (Hungary's Nazi Party) were trying to get a young man to confess to being Jewish. (The young man was Jewish and he was hiding with false documents in the basement of a friend.) Captors: 'You look Jewish, so you must be Jewish.' Accused: 'But I am not!' Captors: 'Take off your pants!' Accused: 'Why on Earth?' Captors: 'We need to inspect your penis.' Accused (pretending astonishment): 'What on Earth for?' (Pretending embarrassment and modesty mixed with submission to authority): 'I don't get it, but if you want to see my penis, I'll take off my pants.' (He knows that they want to see whether he is circumcised or not, and knowing that he is NOT, although being Jewish, he can play his hand): 'Here, I dropped my pants . . . Now what?' Captor 1 to Captor 2: 'Eh what, this kid is no Jew, why he doesn't even know what it is we're looking for . . . He did take off his pants.' (They leave, the young man is saved.) Here the 'logic' of survival works as follows: the young man knows that visual verification of circumcision is a verdict of death; he must therefore, not refuse undressing. If he were circumcised, undressing would be his death. He knows that the Arrow Cross gangsters assume that all Jews are circumcised, no matter what; he knows that they fail to realize that ethnic Jews, so classified by Hitler's laws, who were born Christian, did not get circumcised. He, therefore knows, that despite his Jewish looks, the lack of circumcision will prove his 'innocence', i.e., that he is a non-Jewish Gentile (not matter what religion). He therefore pretends ignorance of the Nazis' assumption about circumcision equalling Judaism (by ethnicity or faith) and drops his pants counting on the right outcome. His insurance is his knowledge that he is NOT circumcised and his guess that the Nazis will (erroneously) interpret this with his being a Gentile. His guess works out and he saves himself.

Here is a third example from Soviet-Marxist dominated Eastern Europe, Hungary of shortly before the Uprising of 1956. This is a personal experience. I was taking an obligatory seminar in Marxism–Leninism at the Law School of Budapest. The question of 'private ownership of tools of production' was being discussed. We had concluded earlier that 'existence determines consciousness' and not the other way around and that 'existence' was to be equated with 'the tools of production'. Therefore, we were taught, in feudalism, when the land was cultivated by oxen pulling wooden ploughs, the consciousness of the given society was 'determined' by wooden ploughs. Once the urban proletariat got to work with steam engines and electric dynamos, their consciousness was determined by these products of industrial revolution and this gave them their strength and stamina to fight the exploiting bourgeoisie. Writers of Communist persuasion [among them State Idol Attila József, in actuality a gentle schizophrenic who believed in Jesus, Freud, and committed suicide by jumping in front of a train], usually owned their own typewriters. Attila József's personal property was legendary; we were taught how his Jewish brother-in-law gave him jackets, shirts, an overcoat, and a used manual typewriter. Thus no matter how poor Attila József was, he did own a personal typewriter – in his case, clearly a 'tool of production'. I said to the instructor, an angry and repulsive female in her fifties: 'Comrade Instructress, if the poet Attila József owned his personal typewriter, was it not the case that he must have been dominated by his own "tool of production", that is, his typewriter? He owned a tool of production like a capitalist and yet he wrote Communist/Socialist poetry. Is this not a contradiction?' I was obviously the 'aggressor', but it was 'aggressiveness directed at the political oppressor' and as such it was, seen from within, as an act of intellectual self-defense. The twenty-three other members of the seminar cried out loud 'Yes! Yes! Makkai's question is most relevant.' The instructress was caught between a rock and a hard place. If she admits that the poet owned his own tool of production, it becomes illogical that he was a Communist poet; if she admits that the poet could write Communist verse on a capitalist typewriter, she drives herself into contradiction, hence ridicule in front of the class. She did manage to save her face at the cost of a *tour de force*: 'Comrades, I agree that Comrade Makkai's question is relevant. I puzzled over such questions myself in my younger days. The beauty of Marxism–Leninism lies precisely in the dialectical flexibility of Marxist thought as modified by the Great Comrade Lenin to suit individual circumstances . . . In the case of a Great Socialist Poet, such as A.J., we must distinguish between PRIVATE PROPERTY and PERSONAL PROPERTY. A.J.'s typewriter, you see, is a classical case of "individual" or "personal property" as opposed to "private property". Private property can be owned by a group or a consortium as opposed to an individual, with which one produces something in such a way that others do the work, you just reap the profit, whereas in the case of personal property you do the work yourself. Consequently there is no contradiction.'

She had just won her case when I thought of the following: 'What if a small clothing manufacturer, say a single woman, owns nothing but a sewing machine and a pair of knitting needles and makes sweaters and skirts? She has no employees; rents no room; her factory is on the top of her bed in a one-room apartment. She makes more money than the Secretary of the Party, because her skirts and sweaters are extremely popular; they sell at competitive prices and are far better made than the stuff you buy at the state-owned supermarket. Is she or is she not a capitalist? She exploits but one person: herself. Comrade Instructress, I know such a woman. She was arrested as a counter-revolutionary. Can you tell us why?' There was deadly silence in the room. The woman was turning green in the face. She appeared to be trembling. 'Well now' she said, 'Comrade Makkai has come up once again with a very challenging question . . .' Loud ring. The electric buzzer went off; the class was over. She sighed a sigh of relief and cried as we rushed out of the room: 'To be continued day after tomorrow! There IS an answer, you know . . .' It was

October 21, 1956. Two days later, on the 23rd, the Hungarian Uprising started. I left the country on November the 29th after the second Soviet armed intervention with a World War II-sized Army. We never got our answer. Or did we? Hungary had just legalized the multi-party system and free elections, like Poland. It has taken merely thirty-three years. I think it was worth waiting for the answer.

The reader will surely realize that customs vary from country to country and from continent to continent. Indonesia and most of South-East Asia are bargaining societies; a North-American supermarket or a department store has 'fixed prices'. In what follows, then, the sociological-anthropological dimension must be taken into consideration. Having lived both in the East and in the West, I think I can compare them with a fair amount of objectivity. It is not my intention to defend capitalism and extol the virtues of free enterprise; faults and criminal misuses of logic abound in the capitalist West as well. The following example is taken from Eric Berne's *What Do You Say After You Say 'Hello'?* (1978). An elderly lady enters a store that deals in leather goods and is beginning to look at ladies' purses. She picks up one and walks with it towards the counter. The salesman takes at look at what she is holding in her hand and points at another purse. He says: 'That's the better one, but you can't afford it'. The lady drops the purse she chose, takes hold of the one the salesman pointed out to her as one 'she cannot afford' and says: 'That's the one I'll take!'. Now who has acted 'logically' here? The salesman certainly did not, as he could not have predicted the lady's answer. She could have said: 'You're right on both accounts, young man' and walked out the door. That would have been a 'logical reply'. Or would it have been? The riddle is unsolvable unless we resort to the three-fold nature of human personality as proposed in TA ('Transactional (Psycho)Analysis'). Normal commercial interaction between speaker 1 and speaker 2 is on the Adult-to-Adult level, for instance when we tender exact change fare on a bus. Paying one's rent, telephone, gas and electricity bill is also a matter-of-fact 'adult' affair; little if any discussion takes place. If I ask for instructions in a strange city for the nearest hospital, chances are that I will get an Adult-to-Adult, serious, non-joking answer, unless I have picked a drunk who wants to give me a 'bum-steer'. Parent-to-Parent discussions are witnessed between actual Parents and the teachers of their children at teacher-sessions in a school; among irate tax-payers displaying dissatisfaction with their system of taxation, etc. Child-to-Child interaction is seen among actual children in a sand-box, or adults taking a 'roll in the hay'. Berne calls these 'straight transactions'. They are 'straight' because Speakers 1 and 2 do not maliciously attack one another at a level inappropriate for the occasion and so no 'illogical' exploitation of any interactant against any other is present during the transaction. When Speaker 1 uses his 'Adult' to attack Speaker 2's 'Child', we are witnessing a 'Crooked Transaction', one which results in exploitation. Berne uses the example of the salesman's 'Adult' attacking the old lady's 'Child'. The salesman's ploy is to make the lady spend more and thereby make the salesman get a larger commission. Since he hits her

'Child' (luckily for him) she responds as a 'Child' and is, in fact, trying to show him that she is no cheapskate. Her satisfaction comes from showing how well off she is when, in fact, she may indeed be unable to afford the more expensive purse. The 'logical answer' 'You are right, young man, on both accounts', however, would shame her as it would seem as an admission of her poverty. Berne's solution to the scenario is truly ingenious: he manages to show how the 'logical answer' is a confession of economic inferiority and as such a 'loss of face'; he also shows that the salesman's strategy is one of 'I'm OK, you're not OK' which describes an attitude of superiority, or the well-known 'Raskolinikov Complex' from Dostoevsky's *Crime and Punishment*. If two people talk to one another on a mutually appropriate level, they are in the 'I'm OK – You're OK' mode, which is most often the Adult-to-Adult. When someone whimpers at another always admiringly while complaining about oneself, that is the 'You're OK, I'm not OK' mode which is Child-to-Adult. In the little scene above the salesman's Adult attacks the lady's Child (criminal attitude) and the lady's Child falls for the ploy of the salesman's Adult (victim's attitude, Child to Adult). Since a great many conversations in our daily lives run along lines resembling this script, the question arises how linguistics can deal with the 'logic' of such texts? I believe that 'logic' is indeed a major part of the Lady-vs-Salesman scenario, but that this 'logic' is psychiatrically and cognitively stratified into a) the Adult's straight logic, b) the Adult's crooked logic, c) the Child's straight logic, d) the Child's crooked logic, e) the Parent's straight logic and f) the Parent's crooked logic. The term 'crooked' must, in each instance, be multiplied by 2 for 'inferior' and 'superior'.

In contemporary linguistics there has been a great deal of false advertising, not dissimilar to the salesman's attack on the lady's 'Child'. The implications were that unless one acted in accordance with the beliefs and tenets of Professor so-and-so, one was not deserving of one's rank and salary. I have written this up elsewhere (Makkai 1974/1975) under the title 'Madison Avenue Advertising: a Scenario'. I will merely repeat the most essential points made in that paper that helped inaugurate the Linguistic Association of Canada and the United States (LACUS, Inc.). I pointed out that Professor Noam Chomsky of MIT has succeeded in setting himself up as Mr Linguistics and that people who did not follow him have become outcasts in the profession. The TGG movement has, in many areas, come full circle in 25–30 years and so it seems superfluous at this point in time to repeat those arguments. It is still not all right for non-MIT graduates to say that transformations are unmotivated, that sentences in isolation are artificial contrivances and that the phonology of any sentence is in a direct relationship to its meaning. TGG linguists only brag (James Thorne, personal communication) 'that there is only one rule left: "move ALPHA anywhere"'; when one says 'I thought so twenty years ago', one gets the answer 'yes, but we came to this insight by reasoning!' What is reminiscent of the scenario in such an attitude is the assumption on the part of TGG that they alone used 'reason'; never mind that others knew twenty years ago what they know today; such knowledge is invalid because it was not achieved by reason! After all, to admit that others, too, have reason, would make it unbearably uncomfortable to be reminded that twenty-five years have been spent on re-inventing the wheel, for instance, that intonation carries meaning.

In sum, I have argued in the past and must, with regret, still maintain that a great deal of pressure-argumentation has been used in recent linguistic theorizing and that the simple integrity and elementary courage of speaking up in the defense of old ideas was shouted down with remarks that one was 'aggressive'.

Aesop summed it all up two and a half millennia ago. I present it in Latin on the left with the English translation on the right, and there will be a brief conclusion at the end:

Lupus et agnus ad rivum eundem	The wolf and the lamb [had gone] to
venerant, siti compulsi. Superior stabat	the same river, driven by thirst. Further up stood the wolf,
lupus, longeque inferior, agnus.	and farther downstream, the lamb.
Tunc fauce improba latro incitatus	Then, urged by a voracious throat, the scoundrel brought in
iurgii causam intulit: 'Cur', inquit	the cause of a quarrel. 'Why', he asked, 'did you make the water
'turulentam fecisti mihi aquam bibenti?'	turbulent for me as I drank?'
'Qui possum quaeso facere quod quereris	'How could I do what you ask, O Wolf, the drinking water
Lupe? Ab te decurrit ad meum haustus liquor.	flows from your direction down towards me'.
Repulsus ille veritatis viribus: 'Ante hoc	Thus repulsed by the strength of the truth [the wolf said]:
sex menses male' – ait – 'dixisti mihi.'	'Six months ago you cursed me!'
'Equidem natus non eram', respondit agnus.	'I wasn't even born yet', replied the lamb.
'Pater, Hercle, tuus' – ille inquit –	'By Jove then' the wolf said, 'it must have been your father
'maledixit mihi'	who cursed me' and he ferociously
agnumgue innocentem ferociter devoravit.	devoured the innocent lamb.
Haec propter illos homines scripta est fabula.	This story was written on account of those
qui fictis causis innocentes opprimunt.	who with fictitious causes oppress the innocent.

The 'wolf logic' is the aggressor's criminal logic; the lamb's logic is that of the oppressed; in this case the oppressed victim happens to be the actual truth as we might have observed the events.

4.2. The structure of a mathematical joke

On a bulletin board at the State University of New York at Buffalo the following 'equation' was posted by an anonymous author:

ENGINEERING PROCEDURE
FROM AN UNKNOWN BUT ASTUTE SOURCE

Every new engineer must learn early that it is never good taste to designate the sum of two quantities in the form:

(1) $$1 + 1 = 2$$

Anyone who has made a study of advanced mathematics is aware that

$$1 = \ln e$$

and that

$$1 = \sin^2 x + \cos^2 x$$

Additionally,

$$2 = \sum_{n=0}^{\infty} \frac{1}{2^n}$$

Therefore, Equation (1) may be expressed more scientifically as

(2) $$\ln e + (\sin^2 x + \cos^2 x) = \sum_{n=0}^{\infty} \frac{1}{2^n}$$

This may be further simplified by use of the relations

$$1 = \cosh y \sqrt{1 - \tanh^2 y}$$

and

$$e = \lim_{z \to \infty} \left(1 + \frac{1}{z}\right)^z$$

Equation (2) may therefore be rewritten

(3) $$\ln \left\{ \lim_{z \to \infty} \left(1 + \frac{1}{z}\right)^z \right\} + (\sin^2 x + \cos^2 x) = \sum_{n=0}^{\infty} \frac{\cosh y \sqrt{1 - \tanh^2 y}}{2^n}$$

At this point, it should be obvious that Equation (3) is much clearer and more easily understood than Equation (1). Other methods of a similar nature could be used to clarify Equation (1), but these are easily discovered once the reader grasps the underlying principles.

It cannot be argued that this fanciful, though mathematically entirely correct reformulation of $1 + 1 = 2$ is 'harmful deception' that causes harm to any one. In fact, it may be argued that seeing through the logic of this equation sharpens the mind and increases one's awareness regarding the usefulness of abstractions in contrast with simplifications.

How does this mathematical joke resemble linguistics? I would like to offer a couple of simple examples below:

4.2.1. The 'passive transformation' in classical TGG

The sentence *Brutus killed Caesar* can be said to be 'transformable' into the corresponding passive *Caesar was killed by Brutus*. In the TGG practice of the 'extended standard theory' which became school doctrine in the wake of Chomsky's *Aspects of the Theory of Syntax* (1965), the 'passive transformation' of the active sentence was 'derived' in a number of steps. The active sentence could be seen as having a tree-like structure as in Figure 1.

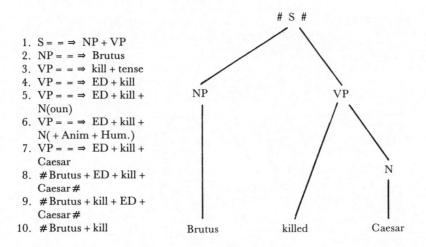

1. S = = ⇒ NP + VP
2. NP = = ⇒ Brutus
3. VP = = ⇒ kill + tense
4. VP = = ⇒ ED + kill
5. VP = = ⇒ ED + kill + N(oun)
6. VP = = ⇒ ED + kill + N(+ Anim + Hum.)
7. VP = = ⇒ ED + kill + Caesar
8. # Brutus + ED + kill + Caesar #
9. # Brutus + kill + ED + Caesar #
10. # Brutus + kill

Figure 1

These ten steps of generating the active declarative sentence must now be submitted to various transformational manipulations in order to derive not only the declarative passive *Caesar was killed by Brutus*, but any other 'semantic inflection' of the sentence, such as *It wasn't Caesar [that/whom] Brutus killed; Caesar was not killed by Brutus; Was Caesar killed by Brutus? Was it Caesar [that/who] was killed by Brutus?* and so forth, until one runs out of possibilities that 'make sense'. Herein, of course, lies one of the greatest weaknesses of TGG: who is to say what ultimate 'transformation' makes sense and what does not? Is it acceptable, for instance, to come out with the 'transformation' *it was KILLING ALL RIGHT (extra heavy stress) that was done unto Caesar by Brutus*! Many grammarians, when asked, blush and hesitate. 'In another dialect, perhaps' some say; others claim that no 20th-century speaker could say this but Nathaniel Hawthorne could have. Be this as it may, one is still expected in most institutions to 'explain' the passive version as the result of a number of transformational steps. They might go somewhat as follows:

1. $S = = \Rightarrow NP + VP$
2. $NP = = \Rightarrow n(7)$ of active derivation (= Caesar)
3. $VP = = \Rightarrow Aux + Tns + Vtr$
4. $VP = = \Rightarrow BE + Past + ED + kill$
5. $VP = = \Rightarrow BE + Past + ED + kill + Agent$
6. $VP = = \Rightarrow BE + Past + ED + kill + by + N$
7. $VP = = \Rightarrow E + Past + ED + kill + by + Brutus$
8. $VP = = \Rightarrow was + kill + ED + by + Brutus$
9. $VP = = \Rightarrow \# was + kill + ed + by + Brutus \#$
10. $S \# Caesar + was + kill + ed + by + Brutus \#$
11. $S = $ *Caesar was killed by Brutus*

This is presented in tree format in Figure 2.

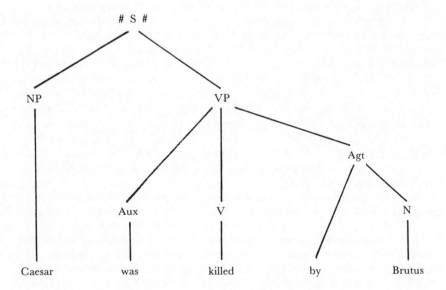

Figure 2

TGG has never quite satisfactorily resolved the question of just what *was V-ed by Agt. (N)* really means; some have placed it under a node called

M(anner) in deep structure so that it could be read somewhat as follows:
,$S = = \Rightarrow$ //([$NP = Brutus$]) + ([$Past + kill$] + [$NP = Caesar$] + [$Mnr.PASSIVE$])//.

Just as in the case of the mathematical joke, one can say with a relatively clear conscience that this is a harmless exercise in applied logic; that it causes no cardiac arrest or brain hemorrhage whether in high school, college or graduate school. I do, nevertheless, consider it 'harmful' in a higher sense. Although TGG advocates have insisted in paper upon paper that this is not what a native speaker does deliberately and consciously which, they add, would be a matter of performance-awareness, they are, nevertheless, 'competent' in doing this, albeit unconsciously. The TGG manner of indoctrination has the harmful effect that students begin to believe that sentence production is a process that follows ordered rewrite rules. Just about when this piece of ideology sinks in, MIT changes its mind; textbooks such as Owen Thomas's *Transformational Grammar and the Teacher of English* (1966) on which the foregoing example was largely based, must be thrown out and the teachers can attend summer school in order to retool and relearn Chomsky's latest version of the creed.

In cognitive-stratificational grammar (CSG), by contrast, there is a much simpler and intuitively much more satisfactory way of handling both 'deep structures' and 'transformations'. We start with a SEMEMIC TRACE or SEMEMIC RETICULUM, which is not responsible for the particular way in which the speaker/writer will REALIZE the reticulum *qua* SENTENCE.

Sentence-realization of essentially neutral reticula proceeds according to CONVENTIONS OF TEXTUAL AND CONTEXTUAL SEMANTICS. One major consideration, for instance, is this: Is *Brutus*'s identity essential for the message at hand, or is it somehow of secondary importance, well stored in and recallable from memory? Is *Caesar*'s identity of particular importance, or is it secondary in a similar sense? In terms of Halliday's Systemic-Functional Grammar one can ask the question: is *Caesar* THEMATIC in the sentence, or is that *Brutus*'s role? T(hematicity) in a sememic reticulum can be indicated by the Sememe /T/ for 'theme' and this sememe is NATURALLY MOBILE IN ANY GIVEN SEMEMIC TRACE, JUST AS IS THE SPEAKER'S TOTAL FREEDOM TO REALIZE THE TRACE AS SILENCE, A LIE, and EXAGGERATION, etc.

A typical and somewhat simplified sememic trace/reticulum of the same sentence *Brutus killed Caesar* might look something like that shown in Figure 3.

The sememes *male, ancient, Roman* and *177* or *001* will identify *Brutus* and *Caesar*, respectively; if one wishes to use shorthand notation, one can simply spell out their names. The action of *occidere/'render lifeless'* can be expressed as *kill* in the unmarked way; *assassinate*, if one wants to mark it for [+ political dignitary], in the customary manner. If the sememe /T/ for 'Theme' is under the 'Agent', the transduction protocol (= 'grammatical "rule"') will indicate that in the sentence grammar (the 'syntax') or LEXO-TACTICS, the Agent will be S(ubject) and will occupy the front position in the sentence. A second transduction protocol specifies that if the Agent is Subject the Goal/Target will be Direct Object in an active voice

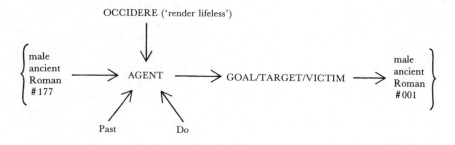

OCCIDERE ('render lifeless')

AGENT ——→ GOAL/TARGET/VICTIM ——→

male ancient Roman #177

male ancient Roman #001

Past   Do

Figure 3

sentence which will NOT employ the Agent Construction (reversed word order, past participle of the transitive verb and by + Noun). If, on the other hand, /T/ stands under the N or NP marked as GOAL/TARGET/ VICTIM, the transduction protocol will thematicize the DO noun, in our case *Caesar*, and the rest of the lexo-tactics, independently learned and remembered by the speakers, will adjust the verb as *Aux + Tense + V + Past Participle* and the original Agent/Subject of the trace will show up as *by + N* in sentence final position.

I have been told by some colleagues that this is far more complicated than the TGG 'rules' presented above. There is no denying that individual taste may play a certain role here, yet the majority of my respondents have indicated over the years that the CSG reticulum notation is intuitively far more satisfactory than the TGG 'rules' and resultant 'trees', because they do not unnecessarily presume the PRIMACY OF THE ACTIVE VOICE WHICH IS A DANGEROUS AND UNWARRANTED SUPPOSITION IN THE TGG VERSION.

If the 'active voice' IS somehow 'primary', we have no credible explanation for sentences such as *I was born in Kalamazoo* and *that isn't done in polite company*. Under classical TGG assumptions these two quasi-passive sentences must somehow be derived from 'underlying actives' that would have to be expressed as //([*my mother*]) + ([*bore me*] [*in K.*])//, and //([*A GOOD CHILD*]) + ([*doesn't do that*] + [*in polite company*])//, respectively. The former must undergo some mysterious and unmotivated MOTHER-DELETION TRANSFORMATION and the latter some kind of GOOD CHILD DELETION TRANSFORMATION. But this is surely absurd. No native speaker I have spoken to in the past thirty-five years spent in the English-speaking world has the faintest awareness of 'mother' or 'good child' in connections with these two sentences. Talmy Givón suggested to me (personal communication) in 1978 in Buffalo, N.Y. that *born* in *I was born in X* could be treated as some kind of a 'special adjective'. Indeed, *green, smart, little, big*, etc. all seem to fit in the frame *I was green/smart/little in X*, but does not such quasi-slot-and-filter substitution smack of the very a-semantical structuralism associated with the names of C.C. Fries, Zellig Harris and Leonard Bloomfield that Chomsky called his faithful followers into Holy Linguistics War to defeat? Givón, in order to sidestep the need to debate the issue just what the 'deep structure' ought to contain here, resolved the issue with a structuralist argument in spirit of the 1940s and the pre-Chomskian 1950s. I still disagree: *born* is no adjective in my book; it is the familiar, classical, if old-fashioned, past participle of the verb *bear*, *bore*, *born*, except that the past participial form *born* need not be occasioned by the notoriously pseudo-logical 'passive transformation' but one must recognize the possibility of PRIMARY PASSIVES IN ENGLISH in the sense of Winter (1965).

4.3. The structure of a linguistic joke and its literary result: the Classical example of stylistic constipation and suffocation

One of Chomsky's favorite arguments in the early days between 1957 and 1965 used to be that central embedding is E-grammatical *ad infinitum*, that is, grammatical in English whether a normal native speaker can recall what NP goes with what VP. To illustrate the absurdity of Chomsky's claim, Peter A. Reich (1978) wrote the following version of *This is the house that Jack built*:

THE HOUSE THAT NOAM BUILT
Peter A. Reich
University of Toronto

Once upon a time there was a famous linguist who had a little daughter. 'Daddy', she said, 'would you please tell me a story?' And so the famous linguist told his daughter the following tale.

This is the house that Jack built.
This is the malt that the house that Jack built contained.
This is the rat that the malt that the house that Jack built contained was eaten by.
This is the cat that the rat that the malt that the house that Jack built contained was eaten by was killed by.
This is the dog that the cat that the rat that the malt that the house that Jack built contained was eaten by was killed by was worried by.
This is the cow with the crumpled horn that the dog that the cat that the rat that the malt that the house that Jack built contained was eaten by was killed by was worried by was tossed by.
This is the maiden all forlorn that the cow with the crumpled horn that the dog that the cat that the rat that the malt that the house that Jack built contained was eaten by was killed by was worried by was tossed by was milked by.
This is the man all tattered and torn that the maiden all forlorn that the cow with the crumpled horn that the dog that the cat that the rat that the malt that the house that Jack built contained was eaten by was killed by was worried by was tossed by was milked by was kissed by.

This is the priest all shaven and shorn that the man all tattered and torn that the maiden all forlorn that the cow with the crumpled horn that the dog that the cat that the rat that the malt that the house that Jack built contained was eaten by was killed by was worried by was tossed by was milked by was kissed by was married by.

This is the cock that crowed in the morn that the priest all shaven and shorn that the man all tattered and torn that the maiden all forlorn that the cow with the crumpled horn that the dog that the cat that the rat that the malt that the house that Jack built contained was eaten by was killed by was worried by was tossed by was milked by was kissed by was married by was awakened by.

This the farmer sowing the corn that the cock that crowed in the morn that the priest all shaven and shorn that the man all tattered and torn that the maiden all forlorn that the cow with the crumpled horn that the dog that the cat that the rat that the malt that the house that Jack built contained was eaten by was killed by was worried by was tossed by was milked by was kissed by was married by was awakened by was kept by.

As the linguist finished telling his tale, his daughter looked up at him and said, 'Nobody can tell a story like you can, daddy.'

It is reasonably clear that it is indeed possible to factor out all the NPs on the left and all the corresponding VPs on the right; you need a large board to do so or a large sheet of paper; optimally a word processor. The 'logic' is flawless, but the product is not fit for human consumption. But what does this tell us about 'logic'? Is not the centrally multi-embedded version of *This is the house that Jack built* somewhat like the mathematical joke that gives us a 'simplification' of $1 + 1 = 2$? I am convinced that the same fallacy is at work in both cases: quasi-mathematical logic is infelicitously injected into the structure of an NL (English), which, by virtue of being the social product of an NS, has extreme difficulty assimilating the special technical dialect of symbolic logicians.

We are now ready to present (in abbreviated and simplified format) the ecological definition of language:

A LANGUAGE is a system of partly dependent and partly interdependent subsystems that form a two-way bridge between HUMAN COGNITION and a variety of CODES and such CODES to HUMAN COGNITION by means of which real human beings in real terrestrial societies communicate with one another in DIALOG, or with themselves in MONOLOG (as in mediation, prayer, writing, etc.). The primary CODE on TERRA is PHONOLOGY and the primary CHANNEL is the ATMOSPHERE. A speaker 'sends' and a hearer 'receives'; both the hearer and the sender change roles in mid-conversation, i.e., that 'take turns' and 'interrupt' one another.

LANGUAGE can serve as METALANGUAGE for sciences such as physics, chemistry, mathematics, biology, etc., but the elevation of a language-derived metalanguage (such as mathematics or set theory) to act as an adequate metalanguage for language, results in distortions. Language is a 'very large system' and as such, it must remain ill-defined and amenable to formal manipulations only by decontextualization and removal from the

SPOKEN MEDIUM in which INTONATION and other phonological properties of real tellurian speech are constantly interlaced with SEMANTICS.

This definition can, of course, be challenged. I respectfully invite professional logicians and logic-oriented linguists alike to do so. I do believe, however, that whereas this definition of language does no violence to the science of mathematics and logic, any definition of NLs that ignores the ontogenetic and philogenetic primacy of speech does, on the other hand, distort reality and thereby cause 'indirect cognitive harm' by a) promising undeliverable goods, b) fostering a false image of human cognition and communication and last, but not least, by creating human pressure-groups (ASs) which, for purposes of selfish interest with the deliberate exclusion of others, will propagate unrealistic tenets about human language whose surface-plausibility is derived from an immoral application of 'logic'.

5. Kinds of 'logic' and kinds of computerization

In this section I should like to list the various kinds of logic that I am aware of at the time of writing, with a few comments on the less familiar varieties of 'logic'.

5.1. Mathematical logic

This kind of logic is the best known. It originated in Ancient Greece and can be easily illustrated with the Pythagorean theorem, a simple exercise in logic everyone knows. Advanced mathematical logic can be encountered in every college course dealing with the subject in a wide variety of textbooks. Mathematical logic has an old history: It is an evolving science. 'Euclidean geometry' does not recognize, for instance, the insights of Bolyai and Gauss whereby 'parallels meet in infinity'. This is commonly taught today.

5.2. Set-theoretical logic

Set theory is a relative of mathematics, although a step closer to 'linguistics', if by linguistics we mean the human ability to perform logic-oriented or set-theoretical operations on an NL. Set theory uses very few numbers if any and can designate any conglomerate of objects with any number of Greek letters and symbols; thus one can describe ten eggs as the union of two sets of five eggs; 'intersections' and 'disjunctions'; 'X implies Z'; 'Q is true if and only if X, Y and Z are true', etc.

5.3. Inductive and deductive logic

Familiar from classical logic since Aristotle, inference and deduction are the two commonest kinds of everyday logic humans perform even if not engaged in philosophy or linguistics at all. The elementary syllogism is built on the ability of the human mind to deduce and to infer; thus we can say *All men are mortal; Socrates is a man; therefore, Socrates is a mortal.* Legal argumentation could not exist without INFERENCE, DEDUCTION and INDUCTION; elementary scientific hypotheses are also dependent on our ability to draw conclusions from premises and to judge whether a 'conclusion' is based on correct or false premises. Induction, deduction, entailment, inference, etc., are all possible informalized versions BECAUSE THEY ARE NL PROPERTIES AND NOT VICE VERSA. Principles such as RECIPROCITY can be abstracted out of NL relations such as *buy:sell, offer:demand, seek:find, reward:punish*, etc. (See my review of Geoffrey Leech's *Towards a Semantic Description of English* (Makkai 1972c).)

5.5. Symbolic logic

Thought to be the intellectual property of Chomsky, who made the most 'newsworthy' use of it in linguistics, symbolic logic was actually invented by the philosophers of the Vienna Circle, Ernst Cassirer, Rudolph Carnap and Ludwig Wittgenstein, who jointly influenced Yehoshuah Bar Hillel and those followers of Chomsky who were willing to read beyond the MIT literature in logic. The work of James D. McCawley, Barbara Hall Partee, etc., is heavily based on symbolic logic. Richard Montagu of UCLA, who was killed in Los Angeles in his creative prime, had created a special use of symbolic logic applied to English; this has become known as 'Montagu Grammar'.

5.6. Ana-logic from 'analogy' and 'analogical'

The terms *analogy, analogic/al/ly* are familiar and well established in general academic use. The form *ANA-LOGIC is, therefore, 'logically' derivable from the Greek *ana-* plus *-logic* by backformation. If *analogy* means 'paradigmatically compelling similarity', ANA-LOGIC would be the kind of logic that works more by 'rhyme' than by 'reason', although the TWO MUST WORK IN TANDEM FOR ANALOGY TO BE AT ISSUE. Paradigmatic association which is singularly important for retaining the lexis of a language in human memory, would not be possible without *ANA-LOGIC. Foreign language learners who make a 'good mistake' by over-generalizing a pattern are using *ana-logic, as in he **singed** a song; native-speaker children, similarly use *analogic when they over-generalize a pattern such as *look what I've **brung** ya!* The fact that syndicated columnist Art Buchwald was able to characterize the firing of Secretary of State

MacNamara by President L.B. Johnson by making him President of the World Bank as neither 'promotion' nor 'demotion' but a case of **transmotion** meaning 'lateral removal of a dignitary allowing him to save face' clearly indicates that *analogic is at work when we innovate, neologize, or pun. *Analogic is unreservedly underestimated as a major force in the shaping of NLs on the planet as well as other human affairs.

5.7. KATA-LOGIC from 'catalog(ue)', *CATALOGY, *CATALOGOUS

Just as *analog* ('*analog computers*') can be formed from 'analogy', *analogous*, etc., we can (and ought to!) form the word **catalogic**, **catalogical**, **catalogically**, etc. from the familiar form *catalog(ue)*. Human beings possess **catalogic**, i.e. the ability to build inventories and name the objects therein. Halliday in his classic *Learning How to Mean* (1974) calls this the 'mathetic function' harking back to the word *mathematics* which, perhaps surprisingly to some, reveals its primitive, language-like origins through the etymology of its very name. The word *mathematics* derives from Greek *mathēma*, 'science' or 'knowledge'. Whether 'science' and 'knowledge' depend more on facts, taxa, taxonomies and lists of objects or on our ability to combine one thing with another tactically, is a meaningless question since neither 'lists' alone, nor 'tactical rules' alone can deliver meaning in social action. Chomsky's greatest mistake in this regard has been his constant belittling of 'taxonomical linguistics'; he acted both in speeches and in writings as if 'taxonomy' were a dirty word that a true scientist must not utter. Yet the discovery of the planet Pluto in 1934 was simultaneously a victory of mathematical logic and mankind's taxonomy building activity in astronomy. Entomologists, ichthyologists, and botanists keep finding new specimens of flora and fauna whose description and classification can be a paleontological or a contemporary classification problem; certainly no one would deny the Nobel Prize to the biochemist who could build the ultimate taxonomy of viruses and bacteria threatening human health. *Catalogical thinking, therefore, is imperative: we all indulge in it when we learn our first hesitant words in the mother-tongue as children and in a foreign language as adolescents or adults. The DICTIONARY OF LANGUAGE, such as the *Oxford English Dictionary* (OED) is a gigantic catalog; yet, in spite of its very large size it is certainly not infinite; the number of items contained in its most recently computerized version available on one compact disk is on the order of magnitude of half a million; the number of words used to define this half million is approximately 22 000 000. This CATALOG of the English language also contains 'operators', of course, which we are generally accustomed to think of as the 'grammar' of a given language.

5.8. APOLOGIC, APOLOGICAL from APOLOGY, APOLOGIZE; **APOLOGOUS**

Apology/apologize is commonly associated with 'seeking forgiveness', 'pardon', etc. An *apology* is a speech act intended to elicit forgiveness or pardon; a person's speech is deemed to be *apologetic* if the person seeks to justify his/her own previous behaviour or is making a similar speech on someone else's behalf. What, then could **Apo-logic** mean? I think it would be possible to approach the sphere of meaning suggested by **apo-logic** (due to **ana-logic**, to be sure!) as 'sub(servient) speech' or 'speech designed to support or expiate a person, an action or some circumstance'. This kind of supplying reason to something can serve the function of explanation; hence **apologous** can mean 'explanatory' as well as 'expiatory'; a sentence such as *Max is **apologous** to Herman* could, then, be interpreted as 'Max is on the defensive *vis-à-vis* Herman'.

5.9. HYPOLOGIC, HYPOLOGUE, HYPOLOGOUS; HYPERLOGIC, HYPERLOG(UE), HYPERLOGOUS; PARALOGIC(-AL), PARALOG(UE), PARALOGOUS; METALOGIC(-AL), METALOG(UE), METALOGOUS

The Greek prefixes *hypo-, hyper-, para-, meta-*, etc. all suggest **analogical** possibilities for kinds of 'logic'. The problem is that *-logic* has been used as a suffix by other disciplines, hence we have *zooLOGICal, anthropoLOGICal, geoLOGICal*, with traditional 'logic' itself already in Greek developed *-logía* in the sense 'the study of'. But why should the study of something be DISSOCIATED from logic? Because study requires diligence and diligence, in turn, sounds too much like a 'taxonomy' which is more sweat than smarts. The suffix *-logy*, 'the study of', in contrast to the suffix *-nomy* 'the laws of, or the rigorous, mathematical study of' has developed with the familiar arbitrariness exhibited by most of NL development throughout history. If *geology* is a respectable science why is *astrology* a mere superstition? We do have *astronomy* to designate the mathematical, materially objective study of the stars, planets and galaxies, but why do we lack *astrography*? After, all, the surface description of the Earth is *geography*, not *geonomy*, which it certainly could have become, but did not. We need to become more actively aware of the possibilities present in this Greek morphological heritage we own, as science progresses and widens. Is the description of the moon's morphology properly called *lunar geography* or should it be *selenology*? Should the study of the inner structure of the moon be called *lunar geology, lunar *geonomy*, or *selenology*? There are numerous choices and linguistics ought to be able to advise agencies such as NASA when they need a new term.

The tactics of word-coining have eluded modern linguistics. This is understandable if we take into consideration that the linguist's primary preoccupation was sentence-syntax followed by semantics that still looked very much like sentence-syntax. Some people coined funny terms such as *SemanTAX* in order to blend the two; I doubt that *semanTAX* will survive the 20th century.

Chomskian linguistics in general looks very much like the output of the IBM computers of the late 1950s and early 1960s. Early computers used relatively small databases; to get the maximum results therefore necessitated complex syntaxes. This situation has changed drastically in the 1970s and the 1980s. I will finish this section with some remarks on the role of the new generation of computers in linguistics.

5.10. Does grammar belong to lexis or lexis to grammar? The computer-logical synthesis and solution of a seemingly unmanageable problem

In M.A.K. Halliday's Systemic-Functional Grammar (Halliday 1973, 1974, 1976, 1984) the ultimate step in 'delicacy' is the resolution of grammar into lexis. Readers not familiar with Halliday's thought should imagine that there exists a potential description of English grammar so detailed and so finely drawn that by the time the rules and exemplifications have come to an end, all 500,000 entries of the OED have been used up. That there is nothing wrong with the logic of Halliday's view can be seen from the fact that systemic-functional descriptions of English have yielded more insight into more phenomena than have other systems to date.

In Sydney M. Lamb's Cognitive-Stratificational Grammar the lexis if properly computerized, absorbs the grammar. Stated *vulgo et breviter*, this is what I see as the greatest attraction of Lamb's model. Furthermore, I see no logical contradiction between Lamb's and Halliday's respective views; both propositions are valid AND feasible with today's computational technology. A lexis that contains the grammar and a grammar that contains the lexis are not a contradiction, but a PARADOX, where PARADOX means 'an apparent contradiction that reveals a deeper truth'. How can this truth emerge? By observing children acquiring their mother-tongues. Children do not learn vocabulary in the abstract and they do not learn grammatical rules without words to operate upon. Children, luckily, do not go to linguists to learn how to mean and speak, but to their mothers, siblings and fathers. Since most honest people, unlike we linguists, do not speculate much about what makes them able to talk, they talk normally, and normal speech is an unconscious display of larger or smaller internalized lexicons, as the socio-psychological and educational situation of speakers warrants. Lexis and grammar co-select one another automatically and largely unconsciously, as native speakers go about their daily business of exacting 'goods and services' from people (to quote Halliday), and to 'gain friends and influence people' (to quote Dale Carnegie).

This section cannot end without mentioning the great significance of the work of the most significant Soviet linguist in this century S.K. Shaumyan, who has taught the last ten active years of his career at Yale University and lives in New Haven, CT as an American citizen. In Shaumyan's applicative-generative grammar (AGG) the central component is the GENOTYPE LANGUAGE which is an international algebra. This genotype international algebra can be mapped onto real languages (such as English, Russian, Chinese, etc.) which Shaumyan calls PHENOTYPE languages. Each act of mapping is a 'transformation', but the term 'transformation' is not to be understood in the TGG sense; no transformation can be 'meaning-preserving' by definition; in fact, transformations are 'semantic acts' of 'semiotic significance' in Shaumyan's work. Translation is, therefore, the greatest logical paradox of all in linguistics for NOTHING is translatable if we want TRUE EQUIVALENCE; yet everything is RE-ENCODABLE in another phenotype language (e.g. Shakespeare's *Hamlet* from English into Welsh, Hungarian, or Mandarin). The central and international GENOTYPE GRAMMAR consists of OPERATORS and OPERANDS; the former loosely compare to 'grammatical rules' and the latter to 'lexical entries' or 'lexemes'. The problem with Shaumyan's grammar is that the place and role of the lexicon is not specified, but is somehow taken for granted and subsumed under the other operations. I understand from Professor Shaumyan (personal communication) that he is currently working on a newer model of AGG in which the place and role of the LEXICON will be much more specific.

The computerization of large lexical databases (e.g. the OED) can only benefit the entire profession, since beside grammatical valences additional features relating to usage, style, educational level, sex, occupation, diploma or degree, regional accent, frequency, synonyms, antonyms, etc., can all be added to individual entries (*lemmas* or *lemmeta* technically). Even diachronic information can be handled economically and efficiently in a large, computerized lexical database.

5.11. Some closing remarks: the LOGOS?

We live in an age when terrorism, kidnapping, drug abuse, etc. are common fare on television, radio and in the newspapers. We have seen that 'logic' can be used in a large number of forms and for quite a variety of purposes. If there were no LOGIC, one could not tell a lie or spot a liar as (s)he lies. If there were no LOGIC, one could not tell a joke, make or appreciate a pun, make an allusion or an indirect request. Primarily, of course, one could not perform any sort of calculation whether with natural numbers or symbols; lastly, one could not program a computer, old-fashioned or modern.

In conversation-management one would be at a loss when dealing with IMPLICATURE and PRESUPPOSITION as those terms have become known in the discipline of PRAGMATICS (see Levinson 1983).

The LOGOS is the possibility of doing any and/or all of the above named. The LOGOS enables us to make moral as well as logical choices. When logic and morality coincide, we can speak of 'straight talk', or 'the truth', or 'generally successful and straightforward human communication'. Humans, however, also lie, prevaricate and obfuscate; we engage in double-talk and double-think with all of the Orwellian trimmings these terms remind us of. Apparently the LOGOS has enemies, such as terror, falsehood, sophistry, ill-chosen premises for a pre-figured, loaded 'conclusion'; mind-benders; in short those forces of thinking that serve the interests of anti-social groups and individuals.

Vico's theory of the GREAT CYCLES OF HUMAN PRE-HISTORY and the more-than-likely recapitulation of the same as seen in the interactional theory of pschyo-analysis and human personality structure as advocated by Eric Berne and Dr Harris jointly suggest that *prima facie* LOGIC, as we commonly understand it, is a left-hemisphere driven, conscious, day-time mode of thinking characteristic of ADULT BEHAVIOR. Since linguistics is supposedly the 'scientific study of language', it would make sense to suppose that a more or less exclusively logical approach to linguistics should be desirable, necessary and sufficient to do an adequate job in describing the NLs of planet Earth. It so happens, however, that we do not always and consistently speak with the adult portion of our personality. The behavior of poets is not explainable with nothing but logic. In poetic language the archetypal divine child, who rediscovers the universe and gives a name to everything encountered, like Adam in the Garden of Eden, claims his birth-right and goes against accepted conventions. Grammar is violated and nonsense words suddenly appear and claim their right to existence with a meaning all of their own, derivable mostly through the context. An unsocialized 'child' in an adult person shows arrested development, and the result can be insanity or crime. If the 'child' is successfully socialized, it can become the most powerful blessing that a person can have: it can be his or her GENIUS. In the successful social behavior of a successful artist, the mundane Adult ego (human stage) co-exists with the divine child and the conquering hero, and it is by no means certain how and when they alternate. Most likely the alternation is unconscious. (For a more formal elaboration of poetic language and musical elements in speech see Chapter 11.)

I believe with Dwight Bolinger that 'Truth is a Linguistic Question' (1976b). Truth, in turn, is super-ecclesiastically and inter-theologico-scientifically superior to all of our miserable contrivances, almost as if it were DIVINE. And what if it is? It is far better to live with the LOGOS than to die on account of some ideology, especially an alien one, imposed by an evil ruling class or a foreign occupying army. Certainly the Americans thought so on 4 July 1776; the French on 14 July 1789, the Hungarians on 15 March 1848 and on 23 October 1956; so did the students on Tiananmen Square in Beijing, China, on 4 June 1989; so thought six European nations: Poland, Czechoslovakia, East Germany, Hungary, Bulgaria and Romania in the three short months of the Fall of 1989 that culminated on 25 December in the execution of the Ceaşescus in Bucharest. Living by the LOGOS seems indeed so important to some human beings that they are willing to lay down their physical bodies for it as if biological survival for an ideology's sake under the Big Lie were worse than physical death. The convinced revolutionary does not fear death, *necros*, what he fears is moral death, *thanatos*. Thus, for some martyrdom or exile can be the only 'logical' way out. *Nomos*, the unbending Law, must give way to *dikē*, 'justice', for in justice and truth resides that higher tribunal to whose judgement mundane logic, even if provable correct by a computer, must yield to the hyperlogical trinity of *liberty*, *equality* and *fraternity*.

Part II. Syntax and semantics

5 What does a native speaker know about the verb *kill*?

The author searches in vain for a reliable Native Speaker to discuss the intricacies of the verb *kill* but is unable to find one single eligible soul – Winnebagos, truck drivers – every one is out to lunch. In desperation he latches on to Jerome Q. Nemportky, the resident poet and polymath on campus, professor of comparative literature. JQN, in turn, instead of instructing the author about *kill*, performs an act of intellectual sadism on his would-be-interviewer by outperforming both his own, and the interviewer's competence. The result is truly amazing and, to everyone's genuine surprise, replete with various and sundry arboreal excretions with roots and crowns and foliage dashing away in a variety of unexpected directions this abstract cannot even possibly hint at. Warning: *Curiosity killed the cat.* Fasten your seat belt and start reading.

My problem was a genuinely acute one. For as my colleagues and friends know, I am no native speaker of ANY language. I have now lived the longer half of my life in the English-speaking world (twenty-three years), but I was already 21 when I arrived here from Hungary. Optimistically, one could call me a 'bilingual', but I am not so sure about that. Thus I really had no choice: introspection was out of the question. I just had to find an ideal Native Speaker and fast. I tried all the tricks in the book and called, first of all, the local chapter of the Teamsters' Union. Truck drivers, you see, make excellent native speaker informants, as I have found out when adding the C(itizens) B(and) jargon to our *Dictionary of American Idioms* (Boatner, Gates, and Makkai 1975). However, there was a strike, and no one would inform me about anything, let alone the verb *kill*. In desperation I tried the Bureau of American Indian Affairs, remembering that top notch native informants used to be available among the Winnebagos of Wisconsin. Not one soul volunteered. 'We're civilized, you know' Chief Whirling Thunder, also knows as Mr Johnson, indignantly declared. 'You wouldn't be working for the CIA or something? . . . I used to do this for a fellow from up Canada way . . . way back in the thirties . . . Ed . . . Ed . . . S . . . something.' 'Do you mean Edward Sapir?', I asked with my mouth wide open. 'That's the one' the Chief assured me, 'he was nice though . . . He never asked me about *killing* people.' Utterly defeated, I tried stopping women in the street and I even called up the local television station and several radio stations that host talk shows in the larger Chicago Metropolitan Area. No luck at all. I got extremely depressed.

As I was walking the UICC campus to lunch, exuding sadness, gloom, and diffidence, a familiar voice addressed me from behind: 'Hello there, Makkai my man, me thinks you are suffering from the linguistics blues . . . Have I not warned you before that a man of your caliber belongs with us in comparative literature . . .?'

It was Professor Jean Nemportky, himself a former refugee immigrant in the United States. The Nemportkys were half French and half Polish and as commonly known in Chicago, this particular ethnic combination produces extraordinarily high IQs in that subset of the population who are fortunate enough to have descended from such lineage. Jean barely misses being the Mezzofanti of the last quarter of the 20th century. Why, the man is simply PANGLOTTIC and OMNISCIENT. Hurriedly and as best as I could, I told him about my pressing problems to which he replied in more than paternal tones:

'It is not true that Native Speakers abound in every bush, highrise, suburban house, or urban tenement, my friend . . . Native Speakers are extremely rare specimens these days . . . And it is even less true that they know anything about their language at all . . . You have to spend a lot of time and exert a great effort in order to find any Native Speaker at all, and once you found one, you have to be ever so careful in determining whether his Language Acquisition Device was operating normally before puberty.' I groaned: 'But what am I going to do? My paper is due in Düsseldorf honoring the Native Speaker, and all you can tell me is that I won't even find one?' Lunch was nearly over, and Prof. Nemportky generously insisted that we continue the conversation in his apartment, only a short ten minute walk from campus. I was now admiringly sitting at his feet, full of newly rekindled confidence. Jean was comfortably reclining in his hand-carved African arm chair, lined with a most unusual looking black-and-white skin. 'Is that an oversized skunk?', I asked naively. 'Your ignorance kills me', Dr Nemportky said. 'This is a *Colubus* monkey. No, no, not *Columbus*, kill the *m* in the middle . . .' 'Got you', I said, and added half-apologetically: 'nice way to kill time, these etymologies, don't you agree?' 'That depends on who it is you're talking to', he replied. 'Take Dr Quasimodo, my neighbor, for instance. He is the biggest bore in the world. He thinks of himself as an etymologist and keeps bursting in on me with his ideas. He's in the real estate game, you know, big guns, one huge, fat kill after another, but he is unsatisfied with his life. All he wants is more and more etymologies. I start by asking him about safe investments, and the kill-joy turns right around and hits me with yet another hare-brained etymological derivation. Worse yet, sometimes he borrows money from me, a poor comparative literature man at an upstart third-rate state university, where rampant inflation kills the value of every raise we get . . . This guy is absolutely killing me with his nervy demands on my time and on my purse.' 'Surely he pays you back, perhaps even with a meaningful interest, doesn't he?' – I timidly tried to mollify Nemportky's wrath. 'I wouldn't accept a penny of interest from a neighbor, not even that creep' – Nemportky thundered, 'the embarrassment would just about kill me.'

'Not to change the subject' – I said, 'but is it true that your family name derives from the French *n'importe qui?*'

Nemportky's glassy stare practically rendered me lifeless. 'We have an old mansion in the Kills, you know, between Staten Island and Bergen Neck. I am sure some of the old family records are still there in the attic . . . My aunt Mathilda, whom you met last year, may have taken lots of them to the hunting lodge in the Catskill Mountains where she lives these days, so if you're that keen on the subject you could go there and burn up some of your excess energy by digging into the records.'

'I'm not sure I could manage that right now' – I said, 'I have a terrible tooth ache that's been killing me for well over a week, and I have an unalterable dentist's appointment for later this afternoon and also one tomorrow morning.'

'How about some 96 proof Jack Daniels Sippin' Whiskey', Jean asked benevolently, 'it will kill the pain instantly'. 'Gee – how nice of you', I murmured. 'Many thanks . . . But I really came up here to ask you about the verb *kill* which is of great linguistic . . . uh . . . pardon me, I mean LITERARY interest to me. I was just on the verge of giving up on the entire project in lack of a Native Speaker when you suddenly materialized on campus . . . You have been perceptive enough to identify my problem immediately and you were kind enough to invite me here to talk about *kill*. This is a free gift from Heaven: you are a scholar, a poet, a general polymath. Could we please get on with it?'

'Yes, yes, I remember now, you poor linguistician', Nemportky continued to patronize me, 'that's why you looked so gloomy before lunch. The trouble is, you see, that I am fresh out of ideas on that one . . . Actually, Makkai, I am under considerable pressure myself. You see, that State legislature in Lincolnville killed Congressman Zolotorechny's proposed tax bill regarding the faculty merit raises, and I was caught right in the middle of the verbal slaughter . . . The legislature, as you may know, is heavily populated by spokesmen of the farm interest, and as you may also have heard, the farmers just won't kill more beef unless and until they're subsidized . . . So the subsidy has to be their first priority. Here is what happened: I got a phone call urgently requesting that I drive 300 miles from Great Lakes City to Lincolnville – by the way, the driving conditions were killingly hazardous; freezing rain, snow, mud, bottle-necks, you name it – so that I, as president of the Academic Senate, could bolster Zolotorechny's position. So my car stalls on me right in the middle of all this mud and slosh. I almost managed to restart it once, but as it turns out I kept killing the engine by flooding it . . . Finally the AAA came after 3 hours of waiting and got me out of the mess . . . I finally got there. I just caught the last critical half-hour session. But just when I was ready to move in for the kill . . .'

'Don't tell me', I exclaimed excitedly, 'let me guess what happened . . . They had to shut the power off in the Capitol . . . I heard there was some major electric disturbance there that day . . .' 'Yeah, you've got it', Nemportky groaned, 'the sergeant at arms rushed into the Assembly Hall and shouted: *"Kill the current!!! Kill the current!!!"* and then suddenly all the lights went dead.'

'So what did you do then?', I asked. 'Well', Nemportky mused, 'we went down into the basement, lit some candles, and tried to play some ping-pong in the semi-darkness not to kill but just to mark time, you know'. 'How did it go?', I asked, always the table tennis fan. 'Were you guys able to see at all?' 'Well, I hate mediocre players, you know', Nemportky continued somewhat self-praisingly, 'I kind'o feel sorry for guys who always lose . . . There was this middle-aged spinster who was absolutely mortified whenever she lost a point . . .' 'Oh yeah?', I egged him on admiringly. 'Well, first I deliberately killed every ball she served with my legendary back-hand twist – you just can't return those, remember?' – the bastard was grinning, 'but soon enough I discovered that I had to be extragenerous to this lady. I find women's tears mortiferous . . . So I changed tactics and deliberately started killing a few balls not by smashing them, but by hitting them into the net, which enabled her to score a few points and save face.' 'That was very nice of you', I said. In fact I was ready to kill the loquacious bastard, to strangle him to death with my bare hands, or hit him on the head with the poker near the fire place, a hammer, a string – give me anything! My eyes were avidly searching the room.

'By the way and not to change the subject', Nemportky said, 'this old Colubus monkey here I am sitting on must have killed well over one hundred pounds, guessing from the uncommon size of the skin, don't you think?'

By this time I was good and determined to get even with him and asked in an urgent voice: 'Did you hear that plaintive and penetrating cry just now . . . ? What could it have been?', and I rushed to the half-open window. After a minute's watchful gaze I said: 'I didn't know you had kill-deer in this part of the country, enough of them to have a couple of *habitués* representing the whole breed right here in your own backyard.' Nemportky's voice stabbed back in quick repartée, 'you will see a bird feeder slightly to the right of it. Can you see that bucket next to it?' 'Yeah, I can see it all right. How about the bucket?', I asked. 'That's where I keep the killfish for bait,' Nemportky said all too knowingly, as he squinted with his left eye, adding: 'Killfish or killdeer . . . I bet most of your silly linguist colleagues wouldn't even know whether they're talking about fish or fowl.' 'Well now, Jean', I protested mildly, 'that was literary overkill . . . My colleagues, you see, may indeed not be the brightest people in the world, but after all . . .'

'Come off it, Makkai', Nemportky sneered, 'your crazy colleagues are so firmly entrenched in killing the goose that lays the golden egg that they don't even notice how they unwittingly wind up cutting the very branches of the trees they sit on! Is this some kind of collective death-wish? More and more pseudo-arboreal irrelevance about less and less? It kills the point of your whole silly profession man, I tell you, if you guys don't watch out, they'll keep torturing the speakers, the informants, the data – the language, in short – until some day they succeed in killing it good and dead.'

'Well now', I interjected in great agitation, 'you sounded now almost like a native born Appalachian . . . But seriously, Jean, whereas no one denies that there has been a gradual killing back, an atrophying, if you will, of actual field work in recent linguistics, you still cannot say that . . .'

'Don't kill the punch line, Makkai', Nemportky intoned thunderously, 'and try to remember your historical linguistics!'

'My WHAT?', I asked with genuine horror in my voice and no little indignation. 'What has historical linguistics got to do with the description of the verb *kill* about which, by the way, you still haven't said a word to me?'

'Makkai, du quälst mich, lieber Mensch . . . Du langweilst und quälst mich immer . . . Don't you remember?' Nemportky was a notorious user of foreign words and phrases in the midst of English conversations, especially when he got emotionally involved. 'OK – I have to jog your memory . . . Come on, let's kill this bottle here, you have barely touched your glass!'

'Wait . . . Wait', I said in great excitement. 'Are you by any chance referring to stuff like the Old English "þa het se cwellere þæs caseres cempan" from *cweljan* "torture, torment" and later also "kill"'?'

'No, no, no! A thousand times no!', Nemportky cried angrily. 'You are the naivest creature in the world! Are you some kind of REACTIONARY or something? I say "history" and right away, like a good little robot that has been pre-programmed, you turn to the sermon of Ælfric as if "history" could only be interpreted historically!!!

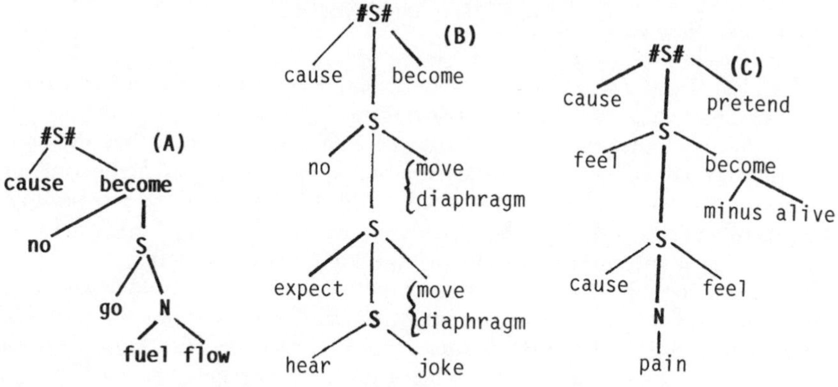

FIGURE 1

Nemportky's drawings of the 'derivational histories' of (A) *to kill the engine*, (B) *to kill a joke*, and (C) *my toothache's been killing me*.

Where on earth have you been these past few decades? Don't you know anything about the DERIVATIONAL HISTORIES of surface verbs? We do this sort of thing in mathematical botany, musicology, creative writing, comparative plot analysis and new criticism all the time!' He furiously grabbed a wrinkled napkin and scribbled with fiendish speed: 'This is what you do Makkai, pay attention!' (See Figure 1 on p. 154.)

I was flabbergasted. 'But where do you get all this amazing intuitive information?', I asked, hemming and hawing. 'Jean, you are absolutely brilliant . . . I feel I can't hold a candle to you! You . . . you, a literary scholar, a poet, a multiple native speaker! Why, man you do this almost better than . . .'

'Nomina sunt odiosa, mein lieber Freund!', Nemportky pulled one of his superior Europeanisms on me. 'By the way – and I do not mean to kill the subject by innuendo – ', he grinned maliciously, 'but as a poet I ought to tell you that your precious kill is far more than just a verb, whether transitive or intransitive, or some sort of nominalization of one of those underlying nouns!'

'How do you mean?', I asked, always the straight man, mesmerized by this sadistic joker.

'Well, Adam my boy, it's like this: part of the meaning of your precious verb kill derives from the fact that it associates with bill, Bill, chill, dill, fill, Phil, gill, Gil, Jill, hill, mill, nil, sill, quill, and will . . . are you following me?'

'Ah the rhymes', I muttered, 'the associative counterpart to morphological paradigms, as already de Saussure, and later qua "Gesamt-bedeutungen" Jakobson . . .'

My eyes were about to jump out of my skull. But there was no stopping him now. 'And certainly don't overlook this one!' he cried, as if in a trance: '. . . since this is one of my favorites. This one really cuts the tree . . . I mean it really goes to town.'

Nemportky rudely interrupted: 'Rhymes, rhymes, what's a rhyme? Go home, Makkai, don't be a pill'.

I was livid with anger.

Standing by the door, my fists clenched, I was talking more to myself than to him: 'Associations . . . associations . . . and what if I choose not to rhyme but instead invoke a fixed piece of text in some other manner? Wouldn't I be killing two birds with one stone if, instead of beating up Professor Nemportky, I forgave him? After all, he is only a comparative literature man. I, on the other hand, am a real linguist. To lift a finger against this gentle savant would be like killing a mockingbird.'

He must have heard me, or must have read my mind (maybe my lips, come to think of it) because I could hear him say as I was shutting the door behind me: 'By the way, Adam my boy, just because I do playfully enjoy word games I am no mockingbird . . . I am the real McCoy . . . sort of like a false killer whale . . . Cross my heart and hope to cause me to be minus alive!'

6 A lexocentric approach to descriptive linguistics

0. We live in an age when one of our most precious tools for increasing human consciousness, linguistics, has become compartmentalized to an unprecedented degree. Chomsky, and theoreticians of his persuasion, all seem to agree that theory and language teaching have nothing in common and, further, that 'the' theory of linguistics is not to be confused with 'discovery procedure' which has been belittled as 'mechanistical data-gathering'. Yet most of the jobs in 'linguistics' are in the applied or 'hyphenated' areas: neuro-linguistics, psycho-linguistics, socio-linguistics which are, by necessity, performance-oriented. So what does the 'pure theoretician' do under the circumstances? We see a general withdrawal from reality into more abstraction and even more philosophizing with fewer and fewer Ph.Ds in theory being employable, while the 'hyphenated areas' in the field are teaming with young talent as well as seasoned professionals who, on the other hand, have become almost anti-theory oriented.

The trouble, obviously, lies in the fact that 'theory' has been narrowly misunderstood to mean 'Transformational-Generative Grammar', and that alone. For there are other theories in the field which are all capable of dealing with data from the field. If united into a super-theory of typologically compatible views of human language, a particular union of three highly innovative and stimulating theories (to be outlined below) could deliver everything we expect from a linguistic theory: observational as well as descriptive adequacy, capped, as a bonus, by explanatory adequacy. The three theories are the following:

1. Pike's and Longacre's tagmemics.
2. Halliday's Systemic-Functional Grammar (known earlier as 'Scale-and-Category Grammar'), and
3. Lamb's Cognitive-Stratificational Grammar.

The reason why these three categories are compatible is that they can be mapped onto one another without loss of information or making logical errors, and they all three have a sound and central locus for the most important concept in descriptive linguistics, and that is the lexeme.

1. In what follows, I will try to discuss why and how one theory can be mapped onto another without loss of information or incurring logical distortion and I will show, specifically, how Tagmemics, SFG and STRAT have a logical, if sometimes inexplicit, place for the notion of lexeme.

1.1. Theory mapping. The best way to show what I mean by theory mapping would be to take a simple example, such as the sentence (1) below, and show by what methods of parsing it can be shown to be equivalent from a variety of points of view (see Figure 1). I have borrowed the sentence *the three old ladies upstairs own a boxer with a mean temper* from Gleason (1965) in order to show that given enough patience, anyone can easily accomplish the following:

(a)   Draw a 'Chinese Box' (cf. Bolinger 1975, 1980) Immediate Constituent analysis of the sentence, following the procedure originally outlined in Wells (1947);
(b)   Draw a 'Downward ICs' model as done in Gleason (1965);
(c)   Project a mirror-image of the 'downward ICs' upward and thereby derive a TGG-style surface structure labelled node tree of the identical sentence.

1.1.1. Possible objections. It is easy to imagine what objections might be raised against points (a), (b) and (c) as outlined in 1.1. 'A theory is not a drawing' would be the mildest form of such an objection. Whereas that may be true on a certain very abstract level, it is also true that the visual-aid media of various competing theories have, in recent years, become almost synonymous with the theories themselves. I have, therefore, deliberately executed this exercise in drawing-projections (downwards from the Chinese Boxes into ICs and upward into the labelled node S tree) so that a theoretically obvious, yet all too often unillustrated point can be rendered visible for all who care to see it. One immediate upshot of the combined three-fold drawing is that ICs, whether Chinese Box-style, downward tree style, or otherwise, have, traditionally, not been able to inform the user as to possible alternatives including omissions, replacements, substitutions, lexical replacements, entire grammatical re-encodings (= 'transformations'), which I say between unquotes because they are not ' "transformations" ' in the proper mathematical or musical sense. (More about this below.)

Drawings and theories reveal meaning in a SEMIOTIC SYMBIOSIS with one another. Hence the objection to the three-fold projection must disappear. Indeed a way of drawing can, by itself, become a PRESTIGE SYMBOL. It is our duty as scientists of language to remove any and all special status symbols as well as taboos from the object of our investigation, if we are to succeed with the description of natural languages.

Another possible objection might be that it is illegitimate to add 'tactic circles' to an IC structure.

I would have to regard that objection invalid for the simple reason that it would be a voice from the past. There is no intrinsic reason why a static IC analysis could not indicate OPTIONS FOR OMISSION AND REPLACEMENT in any given analysis, just as traditional language pedagogy books have always tried to show beginners what words in a given sentence were 'essential parts of the sentence', what was an 'additional element', etc.

The most crucial objection, of course, would come from practitioners of Generative Semantics and the Extended Standard Theory (GS and EST), whereby the projectability of the IC tree into a labelled node # S # tree would be trivialized as a 'notational variant' that left it unsaid whether the sentence was found in print as it is or whether is was 'generated as new' by a speaker who has never heard it before. My answer to such an objection would be that neither has any GS or EST model ever EXPLICITLY STATED whether the sentence(s) under investigation were found in the field as said (then tape-recorded and transcribed), or 'created anew *ex nihilo*' by an 'ideal speaker-hearer in a homogeneous speech community', Chomsky's convenient fiction of 1965. The crux of the entire matter, now shrouded in the obfuscations of a quarter of a century, lies in just what we mean by the term GENERATE and GENERATIVE GRAMMAR. The TGG debating stance has traditionally been this: whenever a linguist of a non-TGG persuasion took exception to something any generativist said, the generativist would invariably change the meaning of the term GENERATE, GENERATIVE so as to drive the interlocutor into real or apparent self-contradiction. Thus, if I say that 'you cannot generate anything that is not already given by nature', my opponent can answer, 'but of course. Nor did we ever say that we meant anything else. We are merely showing the logically precise, quasi-mathematical way, explicitly, of how we can enumerate grammatical utterances . . .' Should I choose to say, however, that 'all you do is render mathematically explicit what everybody knows anyhow', the objection is made, 'on the contrary, we in TGG try to show how a native speaker makes up entirely new utterances on an infinite basis from a finite set of materials and rules'. The arguments have somewhat subsided by the time of this writing (Fall 1984), but the lack of common understanding is still as glaring as ever.

For whatever its worth, I will proceed on the assumptions that THEORY MAPPING is not only permissible, but actually desirable. I believe that the minutest difference in graphic representation will entail, however subtly, some set of minimal assumptions about how language works. This is entirely analogous to the Bolingerian view (1977) that a minimal difference in expression entails a minimal difference in meaning. If a minimal difference in graphic representation also entails a minimal difference in theoretical approach as it very well might, it is all the more necessary to try to project equivalent drawings onto a plain where their lowest common denominator can be made more tangible.

1.2. Accidental theory mapping. Deliberate theory mapping occurs when a descriptivist tries to compare theories that are well known to be compatible with each other, e.g. IC analysis of one type with IC analysis of two other types (Wells 1947, Gleason 1965, and Bolinger 1975). Accidental theory mapping occurs when, to one's surprise, one comes to the realization that a set of drawings hitherto shrouded with the mystery of the in-jargon of a prestige group, suddenly resemble older, well understood methods. This is what happens when anyone tries to project downward IC trees into upward labelled-node S trees. (The downward trees are squared off at the intersections, the downward trees starting with the #S# node that dominates the NP and VP nodes are usually gathered into triangular shapes and are given a label before the appropriate lexeme is attached to them.)

We thus have several matters to consider at once. The #S# node on top is, in a sense, equivalent to the downward tree, but there are some essential differences which become clear only if one adds to this rather mechanical mapping the lexico-sememic sets given at the top of Figure 1 (this would roughly correspond to the area of GENERATIVE SEMANTICS) and the 'directed graph-sememic reticulum' (lower half, top section) which would roughly correspond to earlier versions of cognitive stratificational grammar.

The version with the #S# node on top assumes that LEXICAL INSERTION has not yet taken place but that somehow, in a way that nobody ever explained with any degree of realism, the labelled nodes, by virtue of their grammatical magnetism, will/can/might/appear etc. to DRAW TO THEMSELVES lexemes of an appropriate nature. This may be, because the lexemes themselves have certain 'semantic valences' that regulate their attaching behavior (+ mass, + count, + animate, + human, + animal, etc.), or it may be because the grammatically labelled nodes themselves have quasi-lexical valences attached to them. At the risk of exaggerating, I would like to characterize the first approach as the 'lexicalism approach' to TGG, and the latter as the 'Generative-Semantics approach' to TGG. As is well known from the literature, both camps have agreed (Newmayer 1980) that either the debate is logically irresolvable, or that it is not worth resolving, because they collapse into 'notational variants' of one another. Whatever the case may be, it is clear that theory mapping has allowed this two-way view to emerge. It is not expected, then, that theory mapping will always reveal identical views of a given problem: rather it will reveal, more precisely than before, what the actual differences between two competing views are.

1.3. The benefits of theory mapping. Theory mapping, then, whether purposeful or accidental, has the virtue of showing in a more explicit, visual-graphic form both different views that are truly only 'notational variants' (the various modes of IC mapping), as well as different views that entail an ENTIRE PHILOSOPHICAL ATTITUDE. The real difference is truly between the structural, static views that take the lexemes and their deployment as 'given' (all of the IC methods) and the TGG view, according to which neither the sentence, as a structure, nor the lexis, as building-blocks of that structure, are 'ready' at the moment of the generation of a given sentence. The EST view and the GS view, then, are as close to one another as the various IC models; the difference between the EST and GS is that the one pulls the white rabbit out of the helper's left ear, and the other one from the right. In truth there was no rabbit in anybody's left or right ear to begin with; the analyst had, in both cases (whether the EST or the GS view), created a structure that inexplicitly remembered the very words that would later populate the sentence-skeleton after the miracle of 'lexical insertion' was performed in due course.

2. What theories map out in Figure 1? Inasmuch as Tagmemics is a refined form of structuralism that recognizes a triplicity of linguistic organization in particle, wave and field, Figure 1 is, *mutatis mutandis*, a reasonable approximation of tagmemic assumptions about language, even if not in the actual slot-and-filler sorting modules of tagmemics. As an outgrowth of Fries' structural analysis of American English, Pikean tagmemics is a data-oriented theory or discovery procedure that accounts for entire texts via paragraphs, sentences, clauses, words, morphemes, allomorphs, phonemes and allophones. Inasmuch as the drawings in Figure 1 give an acceptable IC analysis of the sentence *the three old ladies upstairs own a boxer with a mean temper*, the assumptions of tagmemics are not contradicted by the mapping. The question of LEXIS versus GRAMMAR, however, is about as unresolved in tagmemics as in any other theory I know of with the exception of one, to be outlined at the end of this chapter.

Versions:

(1)   Three elderly spinsters above me possess a canine beast that is hostile.

(2)   A threesome of superannuated females are endowed with an unfriendly hound.

(3)   A triad of antiquated humans of the feminine gender co-habit with a domesticated canine of the boxer family.

(4)   A triplicity of withering women one flight up the stairs from me have a dangerous canine that is a boxer . . . etc. [Instances of ANASEMIOTIC ANALEXIS, i.e. near-synonyms with discernible differences in meaning assume the same syntactic position as the original sentence.]

(5)   A boxer with a mean temper is owned by the three ladies upstairs.

(6)   It is a BOXER with a mean temper that the three ladies upstairs own.

(7)   It is a boxer WITH A MEAN TEMPER that the three ladies upstairs own.

(8)   It is UPSTAIRS that the three old ladies own a boxer with a mean temper.

(9)   It is the boxer that has the mean temper that the three ladies upstairs own.

(10)   It is the three ladies upstairs that have a mean temper that own a boxer.

(11)   The three ladies upstairs with a mean temper, own a boxer.

(12)   The three old ladies upstairs OWN a boxer with a mean temper. Etc. [Instances of ANASEMIOTIC AND ANALEXICAL ANAMORPHOSIS, i.e., the same lexemes in different lexotactic deployment with extra construction-marking morphemes, e.g. -ed, by, it is . . . that . . . etc.]

(13)   X(T) is movable to the sememic Agent (= unmarked or normal transduction,

active voice); to the sememic object (= marked, or passive transduction); to any of the sememic adjuncts with the result that the corresponding lexemic material will show up in a cleft or pseudo-cleft 'pedestal construction'. This can be done with simply moving the contractive accent (= 'sememic stress') around as in the sentences I am walking home NOW, I am walking HOME now, I am WALKING home now, I AM walking home now, *I* am walking home now. *No. #2 is the unmarked case here, that is* I am walking *home* now.

Semo-lexemic relationships

Adult (1)	Possess, (2)	dog (3)	having (4)	mood (5)	bad, (6)
Human	own,	bulldog –	endowed	atmosphere,	unfriendly,
Female =	have, be in	poodle –	with,	disposition,	hostile,
woman	possession of	boxer +	encumbered	manners,	irritable,
+ HON. =	. . . (be)		with,	temper,	dangerous,
lady	owner of . . .		accompanied	etc. . . .	mean . . .
	(be) in		by,		etc.
	charge of		exhibiting		
	. . . (have)		. . . etc.		
	in one's				
	control				

A. Semo-lexemic relationship search precedes trace or reticulum-formation and is dictated by the ECO-SET (= 'pragmatics') of the utterance to be made.

B. Sememic 'trace' or reticulum-formation procedes AFTER the semo-lexemic relationship search. The non-sentence or 'pre-sentence' trace is formed with tense, mode, etc., in mind for the appropriate lexo-tactic encoding. See "transduction procedures"

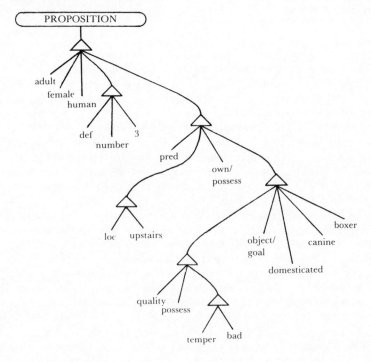

CONSTITUENT STRUCTURE IN
TGG – 'Surface Structure Style'

C. During lexo-tactic encoding the speaker-writer enters the 'editing phase'. It is here that new or additional semo-lexemic relationship searches may be undertaken to 'put it in other words'. Each 'different way of putting it' results, of course, in a slightly different set of meanings both *via* the lexis and the lexotactics (= grammar).

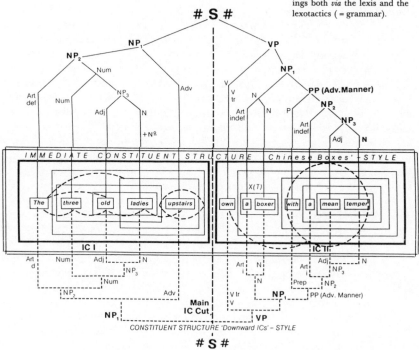

E. PROCEDURE FOR TRANSDUCTION OF A MARKED RETICULUM:

a) If the Sememe X(T) [(X) = 'marked'; (T) = 'as theme'], shows up on the Goal or OBJ of the reticulum, it will be realized in the lexemic structure as Subject N. of the **Passive lexotactic encoding protocol**.

b) If X(T) marks the sememic OBJ., the Agt/predicandum is realized as agentive marked by **by** in the lexotactics.

The sentence, as it is, is a TRANSDUCTION of the **unmarked version** of the sememic reticulum.

D. PROCEDURE FOR TRANSDUCTION OF AN UNMARKED RETICULUM:

a) If **Predicandum** or **Agens** is not marked for relocation due to THEMATIZATION or FOCUS, it will be the Subject NP of the lexemic structure.

b) The PRED of the Agt is realized as a V or as a VP in the Tense and Mode indicated by the Sememe attached to Pred or Agt.

c) the OBJ or GOAL Sememe is realized as the Object NP if the V is transitive.

d) QUAL(ity) sememes are realized as adjectives or as WH-clauses, optionally. Etc.

Figure 1

Legend of constituent structure analysis: Traditional constituent structure analysis has been criticised on the grounds that it does not reveal alternate options and gives a given sentence simply the way it is found. The staggered circles in the 'Chinese Box' and 'IC' structure lay-out indicate that not all of the elements given are necessary to have a grammatical sentence. *The ladies upstairs own a boxer* is just as possible an English sentence as is the fuller original version specifying their age, their location, and the boxer's disposition. Also possible are the following: *The three old ladies upstairs . . . The old ladies upstairs . . .* The headline-style sentence *LADIES OWN BOXER WITH MEAN TEMPER* is semantically weird because ownership as such is not newsworthy; if the boxer was killed, and was a boxer that had some sought-after military secret sewed in its ear, *LADIES KILL BOXER WITH MEAN TEMPER* would make sense in a local newspaper. *The ladies upstairs own a boxer, the ladies own a boxer with a mean temper, three ladies* (with or without *upstairs*) *own a boxer* (with our without) *with a mean temper,* all add up to grammatical English sentences. IC grammars were an easy target for advocates of the TGG movement both in 1957, 1965 and since, because it was seldom, if ever, specified that the descriptive analysis of a given sentence *hic et nunc* could, in fact, admit of alternative versions at the cost of certain modifications in meaning. The Lexo-Centric approach of Descriptive Linguistics wishes to emphasize that THE SLIGHTEST DIFFERENCE IN EXPRESSION ALWAYS RESULTS IN SOME SUBTLE CHANGE IN MEANING. In other words, THERE IS NO SUCH THING AS A 'MEANING-PRESERVING TRANSFORMATION'. It is possible, at the same time, to show alternate possibilities for lexotactic re-encoding without 'process'. *LDCL* views the linguistics structure as a large highway map which offers the user more than one possible way to make a certain trip; not to make a trip at all; change one's mind in mid-trip, turn around and go another way etc. Furthermore, it gives the CHOICE OF VEHICLE DESIRED. (The 'tactics' is like the turns to the North, South, East and West, and the 'words', semo-lexemic choices are the 'vehicles' and, due to the nature of language, the 'origins' and 'destinations' as well.)

The presence of standard structuralism is subsumed under tagmemics, since tagmemics is a text-oriented and context-sensitized enlargement of structuralism, as if *behavior* were spelled with a lower case '*b*' in structuralism and with an upper case '*B*' in tagmemics, so as to include culture, meditation and the myriad of invisible motivations that make speakers choose certain alternatives over others.

Early, 1957-style TGG is implicity present in the drawings, since as discussed above, the #S# node on top does in a way logically mirror the downward-drawn IC structures (in all three versions, Chinese Boxes, downward square trees, and Wellsian IC cuts). All sorts of issues remain, of course, unclear from the TGG point of view. Is the construction of *old ladies* to be regarded as the transformational result of a deep structure sentence that says *The ladies BE old?* Is *The three old ladies upstairs* to be regarded as a double-transform of the underlying sentences that say *the ladies BE old* and *the ladies ((WH-ladies) BE old) BE upstairs?* How about *a boxer with a mean temper?* Does this 'derive from' some underlying sentence that says *there EXISTS an animal* STOP *The (there EXISTS an animal) BE a boxer, The (there EXISTS an animal) Be a Boxer HAVE a temper* STOP *The (there EXISTS an animal) BE a boxer HAVE a temper (WH temper Be mean)* yielding, after appropriate deletion transformations, *a boxer with a mean temper?* And what about the fact that *a boxer with a mean temper* could also be, say, *a bulldog with a menacing disposition, a great dane with a hostile look on his face,* or any substitute with the ECO–EST range of canines and their unfriendly countenance? By the same token, *the three old ladies upstairs* could have shown up as *the threesome of elderly spinsters living one floor above us* or *the triad of superannuated female human beings which reside on the next higher elevation from my apartment.* But it did not. The sentence was, and remains, *the three old ladies upstairs own a boxer with a mean temper* and not any of the following amalgamated NP + VP versions: *The trio of antiquated female fellow-humans on the floor above me possess a domesticated canine of the boxer family that has a threatening disposition,* or *the triad of superannuated spinsters one flight up are the owners of a bulldog that has a nasty temperament.*

3. The problem of sentences that structurally resemble each other while displaying widely different, even clashing lexemes, versus the set of sentences whose grammar keeps changing while the words remain constant has been dealt with effectively by Gleason (1965) who calls structurally identical and lexically different sentences AGNATE, with grammatically changing sentences using the same words being termed ENATE. Thus, for example, the 'skeleton' Art (Def) Sing + Adj + N + Aux (Have) + en + ed Art (Def) Sing + Adj + N, whatever the lexis it carries, will always be the source of a set of ENATE SENTENCES whether one of them says *The naughty boy has stolen the delicious candy,* a sensible, if stale sentence, or if one of them should yield the 'grammatical but nonsensical' sequence *the gigantic colibri has eaten the tiny elephant.* (It is a difficult matter why the second sentence may make sense, as in an animated television commercial (cf. Makkai 1971)). AGNATION is said to occur when *the naughty boy has stolen the delicious candy* is said to undergo the 'negative', the 'interrogative', the 'passive' etc. ' "transformations" ' yielding sentences such as *the naughty boy didn't steal the delicious candy,* or *the candy the naughty boy stole wasn't delicious,* or *the delicious candy has been stolen by the naughty boy,* or *has the delicious candy been stolen by the naughty boy?* etc. Enation, in the Gleasonian sense, is some kind of TOPICAL COHESION. We are assured that the subject of discussion has not been shifted to colibries and elephants, but we have faithfully remained in the realm of naughty boys stealing allegedly delicious candy. Somehow the terms AGNATE and ENATE have not caught on as widely as they deserve. Perhaps the Latin etymologies involved are to blame. I would like to propose that we call enate, i.e. structurally identical and lexically different sentences IDENTI-SKELETAL SENTENCES and that we call lexically identical and structurally different ones IDENTILEXICAL SENTENCES. My analogy is no better than

Gleason's; it is perhaps more easily identifiable visually. The grammatical structure is like the skeleton of a human body; the lexis is like the flesh, muscles and nerves that ride on the skeleton. The importance of both the skeleton and the lexical flesh is equal. It is, perhaps, no idle coincidence that archeologists and police artists are trained in drawing full-fledged, i.e. fully-fleshed human faces on the basis of a skull. This skull-to-full-face vision of the matter would seem to advocate for the primacy of grammar over lexis. On the other hand, we know that all skeletal structures develop genetically from the human endodermic structures and that such endodermic structures are anything but hard bone, at the time of conception. Hard substances (bones, skulls, delexicalized grammar-skeletons) may allow the investigator to arrive at the softer outer layering more easily in biology; the converse would entail a full (as yet unavailable) understanding of the genetic code programmed in the human cells that interpenetrate during the conception of an embryo. Forcing the analogy a step further in linguistics, this would mean that the SEMANTICS OF WHAT ONE HAS TO SAY (the least tangible part of any utterance) SOMEHOW SECRETES ITS LEXICAL SHELL WHICH, in turn, CONTINUES TO SECRETE ITS GRAMMATICAL SCAFFOLDING ON WHICH TO DEPOSIT ITSELF, once the carrier has been built.

The choice seems undesirable both ways and awkwardly unwieldy in either event. The skeleton-to-flesh theory somehow requires that grammar be able to attract pragmatically and situationally appropriate lexis in all the right places for humans to make meaningful sentences, and that is extremely unlikely. The opposite, that pragmatically-semantically appropriate lexis generates its own grammar is, to my view, equally unwieldy, though intrinsically more credible than the opposite. To quote Angus McIntosh of the University of Edinburgh (personal communication):

If you were shipwrecked on an island inhabited by natives whose language you do not understand and whose willingness not to harm you depends on your ability to communicate with them, and your fairy god-mother gave you two wishes to choose from: (a) all the lexemes of the language and none of the grammar, or (b) all of the grammar of the language, but none of the lexis, which would you choose?

I, for one, would unhesitatingly choose the 'all of the lexis and none of the grammar', because, as I will try to demonstrate below, the TRANSMISSION OF MEANINGFUL MESSAGES, i.e. the act of SOCIO-PSYCHOLOGICAL TRANSEMIOSIS AMONG HUMANS is indeed possible with ZERO GRAMMAR, provided that the lexis, by nature of its ICONICITY IN DEPLOYMENT, is capable of yielding a PARAGRAMMATICAL HYPERSEMEMIC TRACE.

3.1. Possible objections. I can imagine that some might object: 'The reason why you can make sense and be understood in Broken English or Broken Anything is because all languages, basically, have similar deep structures and the hearer, who is, after all, smart, makes the necessary adjustments and interprets your intentions correctly the way(s) he would have put it in words.' Undoubtedly there is a communality to the kinds of things we humans can say, or try to say, to each other under dire circumstances, e.g. *me, now, want, eat*, or *me, afraid, now, die*, or *me, now, want, drink*, or even *drink, me, now, want*. Let us also not forget that a good actor can perform, as if on stage, any single word. With the word *afraid* can come a scared facial expression and with *die* the act of lying down on the floor and playing dead. With the word *me*, or *I* can come the obvious hand-gesture of pointing to oneself (*you, we, they, us, all*, etc. can all be performed by hand motions), and *eat* and *drink* being universal human favorites for mime performance through hand motions. Notice that all of this can, in extreme need, be done without any words at all. A person whose voice is temporarily lost by desiccation in the desert, can still make drinking motions with his hands and open his mouth as if drinking. Would such an unrehearsed sequence of nonconventional signs (we are not dealing with American Sign Language here!) have a 'deep structure' worth the name, as used by the linguist? It is hard to imagine Noam Chomsky agreeing that *I, want, eat, I want, drink* performed by hands, face and mouth WORDLESSLY have a 'GRAMMATICAL DEEP STRUCTURE', but I am willing to bet that, if forced by the appropriate circumstances, Chomsky, the HUMAN BEING, WOULD USE A SIMILAR OR IDENTICAL SURVIVAL STRATEGY in trying to obtain food and drink from the islanders.

4. The nature of field work in a monolingual setting. Those fortunate enough to own or have seen Kenneth L. Pike's monolingual elicitation lecture as filmed by the Television Studio of the University of Michigan (1979) entitled 'Pike on Language' (in four parts), or who have, by training or by necessity, ever invented or followed a real discovery procedure in the field, will probably agree with me when I opt for 'all the lexis and zero grammar' from the imaginary fairy god-mother, as offered by Prof. McIntosh.

Why and how does monolingual elicitation work? What theoretical assumptions must we share before we enter into such a situation?

For those who have not yet seen Professor Pike's 30-minute program, or observed him in real life, let me briefly summarize what goes on in the studio room:

Pike enters a well-lit room with a large table in the middle on which there lies a rich assortment of objects, e.g. stones of various sizes, leaves of varying magnitude; twigs, small and large, as many as there is room for. There will be flowers and small animals on the table, e.g. a tiny stuffed alligator and orchids. (SIL does a lot of its work in tropical rain forests.) There are no tiny motorcycles or imitation Hondas or imitation Volkswagens; these are irrelevant. The native may very well have seen such objects, but again, he may not have. Rags and cloths of various colors we call white, black, red, yellow, brown or green are also on the table. Beside the table stands a language helper (earlier known as an 'informant'), a woman or a man, wearing some local shirt, e.g. made from Batik or similar material. Pike will say 'hello' in Mixtec, an Oto-Manguean language of Central America which he speaks fluently and into which, with several native speakers and SIL colleagues, he translated the New Testament in just over a decade. The native speaker of the language Pike is investigating responds in the appropriate manner. Pike immediately goes to the blackboard and writes down what he heard, or what he thinks he heard. We cannot assume at the outset that the writing he uses is phonemic or phonetic; that sort of analysis will come later. Pike, with a questioning look, lifts one of the rocks and asks (either in Mixtec, which his language helper has certainly never heard) or by gesticulation something like 'what's this?' or 'what do you call this?' The helper responds by saying something that Pike perceives as [kø]. He then points at two stones and repeats the same questioning gesture or noise. The helper responds with [*ke:t kø*]. (Pike does not know the orthography of the language nor what language it is.) He will probably write the first utterance as [kø] and the second one as [ke:t kø]. He will reach for three stones and make the same interrogative facial expression. The speaker says [ha:rom kø] which Pike tentatively notes as [ha:rom kø]. He has realized by this time that the form [kø] for 'stone' does not seem to change with the 'numeral' before it, or what goes as a numeral in this strange tongue. He holds up five fingers and asks, facially, 'how many?' to which the helper answers [öt], then he holds up ten fingers, to which the answer is [ti:z]. Pike has barely been in the room for 3 minutes, when he is enabled by this information to make a bold generalization: NOUNS DO NOT 'PLURALIZE' IN THIS LANGUAGE, BUT ARE UNCHANGED AFTER THE NUMERAL. He is now ready to test this hypothesis and risks his own first construction: [ti:z kø]. He looks at his helper expectantly. The native speaker smiles and nods, and repeats the utterance [ti:z kø] holding up both of his hands. This confirms Pike's hypothesis that whether you say 'one stone,' 'two stones', 'three stones', or 'ten stones', the form for 'stone' will not change in this language. He now holds up one finger and says questioningly: [kø], uh, uh, uh, [kø]? His helper gets his meaning (Pike wants him to say 'one stone') and says [ɛd'kø]. Pike now has the numerals 1, 2, 3, and 10, and testing his hypothesis starts to count out loud: [ɛd'], [ke:t], [ha:rom] . . . [ti:z]? Amused, the helper smiles and shakes his head. He says, helpfully: [ɛd'], [ket:ø], [ha:rom], [ne:d'], [öt], [hɔt], [he:t], [ñolts], [kilents], and [ti:z]. Pike now tries all forms for 'one' through 'ten' with the word for 'stone' only to realize that the word for '2' [ke:t – ket:ø] is the only one to have a double form, one for counting, one for use before a noun. He is now ready to test whether this language has no plural form at all, and points at one stone first, then at a larger heap of uncounted stones. The speaker replies with a smile: [kø – kövɛk]. This gives Pike the idea of making collections of uncounted objects and, he then holds up one of the objects and points at the whole heap. He starts with 'leaf' and gets the following result: [lɛve:l – lɛvɛlɛk]. He points at a 'chair' then at many chairs and gets [se:k – se:kɛk]. For the pair 'tree' vs. 'trees' (these may be out of a color picture book) he gets [fɔ – fa:k]. He now retests the nonpluralization hypothesis by saying the numerals before the singular form of each noun with the exception that he uses the form [ke:t] as a numeral modifier before a noun. His hypothesis is confirmed; all nouns (so far) seem to behave identically. He reaches for a green rag and for a green leaf and holds the two objects beside each other. He then takes a white rag and holds that before the green leaf. The helper understands his intention and pointing to the green objects says [zöld]. When Pike says the word for green and holds up the object he wishes so characterized, the speaker responds: [zöld lɛve:l] for 'green leaf', and [zöld roñd'] for the green rag. Pike now gets more objects of the same color and gestures as before. The native answers, surprisingly: [zöld lɛvɛlɛk] and [zöld roñd'ok] for 'green leaves' and 'green rags', respectively. Pike tentatively concludes that this language has no adjective-noun agreement as the adjective (if that's what it turns out to be) stays in the 'singular' form; even though the noun was pluralized. He suspects some kind of V[k] structure is at work in the pluralization in this language and tries the form [zöldɛk lɛvɛlɛk] on the helper. The helper laughs and corrects him by saying: [zöldɛk ɔ lɛvɛlɛk] and by also volunteering [ɔ lɛvɛlɛk zöldɛk] with a rising intonation and an interrogative look *his* face. Then he answers his own question: [igɛn. ɔ lɛvɛlɛk zöldɛk]. From this Pike hypothesizes that adjectives will co-pluralize with the noun they refer to not as Head-Noun modifiers with the noun phrase, but as predicating adjectives. He correctly guesses that the helper said 'the leaves are green' and that he also asked 'are the leaves green?' The helper's intonation had a lot to do with guessing that the one was a question and the other was an assertion or a statement.

Pike now moves in for the first verb. (He has realized that in order to say 'the leaves are green' or 'are the leaves green?' this language uses no verbs.) He sits down in a chair, gets up, and motions to the man to sit down. The helper says: [ülök, üls, ül, ülünk, ültök, ülnɛk] and gestures first at himself, then at Pike, with the third utterance he obviously pretends that a third person is present; with the fourth he makes Pike sit down while he, too, sits down, etc. This makes him realize that the language has morpheme endings on the end of which seem to be 'verbs' and that these 'verbs' seem somehow to be 'inflected' in the six persons corresponding to 'I', 'thou', 'she/he/it', 'we', 'you', 'they'. There are some toy dogs on the table. This enables Pike to create a situation in which some dogs sit (these are the ones nearer him), and the other ones (farther from him) stand. He gets [ɛzɛk ɔ kut'a:k ülnɛk, ɔ zok ɔ kutya:k a:l:n ɔ k.]. He correctly concludes that this means 'these dogs are sitting, those dogs are standing'.

Barely fifteen minutes into the elicitation, he has the rudimentary alphabet, presumably a phonemic script of some sort, figured out; he has vowels, consonants, word initial stress; and due to the strange behavior of the plural suffix *k*, he begins to guess that this is a vowel-harmony language. Moreover, he has taken steps to discover and to describe the morphology of the language, which – lacking gender and number agreement – seems to be an agglutinating Asian tongue. The absence of the copula in stative sentences of the sort 'these leaves (are) green' reminds him of Russian, but he rules out Slavic, because of the lack of gender and the probable presence of vowel-harmony. He has begun to build a theory of Noun Phrase and Verb Phrase in the sentence and at the end of the 20th minute can ask questions of the type 'what is this?', 'what are these?', 'what are those?', since his helper has inadvertently slipped him the right lexis to do so.

I can attest to the exactitude of this procedure, since I WAS THE INFORMANT. Pike, I have found out, had never done Hungarian and I thought it would be fun to surprise him. I dressed up as an old Hungarian peasant, replete with moustache, beard and white wig; torn, old clothes, and a shepherd's drinking flask on my shoulders and a walking cane. My make-up helpers assured me that I was unrecognizable and that I looked 98 years old. Pike knew I was in Dallas that week, but he just saw me a few minutes before wearing a business suit with a white shirt and tie, and was assured that an illiterate old peasant from Asia was to be interviewed that evening. In thirty-eight minutes (I looked at my watch stealthily when he turned to the board) he had the main sketch of Hungarian morphosyntax worked out. When he got to the point he could ask questions, he knew it was a Finno-Ugric language, and laughter from the audience tipped him off. I lifted my garb and the show, for that night, was over. But on the University of Michigan tape he interviews a man who speaks the rural Javanese dialect, similar to Bahasa Indonesia, but sufficiently different, and he does this year in and year out in Africa, Papua New Guinea, and other distant points on the planet somewhat like a tournament chess-master who plays forty games simultaneously. These 'games' are, of course, the workshops Ken and Evelyn Pike hold both in the States and abroad, when they go on one of their numerous around-the-world trips and teach beginners in language description.

5. Field work with an interpreter. Needless to say, field work with an interpreter goes much faster and requires less theatrical back-up material. The essential point is always the same: never assume that the native speaker knows any 'grammar': what the native speaker provides is utterances of varying lengths. The numerous pitfalls one can fall into due to the helper's eagerness to help are well documented in the literature.

6. Underlying assumptions. Why and how does elicitation work at all? This is the real question we must ask ourselves. 'Why walk into a one-in-a-thousand-chance of ignorance?' asks Pike in the narrative portion of the Michigan tape with the Javanese informant. 'Because of just one assumption: That all mankind is one.' Obviously what he means is that we are all members of the species *homo signans*. I am not sure that we are all *sapient* at all times or that we are, at least morally speaking, always 'erectus'; nor do we always make things deserving the name of *homo faber*. We are just as destructive as we are constructive. We play, however (the very reason why Huizinga called us *homo ludens*) and whatever else we may do: we emit signals. All human language is, therefore, a matter of applied semiotics.

6.1. Consequences of language as applied semiotics. If language is indeed applied semiotics, and I am convinced that it is, it stands to reason to believe that concrete objects that are shared in human experience between the elicitor and the informant, will somehow be DESIGNATED BY A SIGN. Just as the object is discrete (e.g. a twig is a twig and a rock is a rock, although all twigs differ from all other twigs and all rocks from all other rocks), one can reasonably expect that the sign referring to it will be discrete, even if under certain circumstances one confuses one sign with another. Certainly the display of discrete, if regionally and climatically non-clashing, 'tropical', objects are discrete enough: why should evolution have played an irrational trick on the users of the language and given them one sign for 500 dissimilar objects? Since this does not happen typically, some instances of NEUTRALIZATION in the expression system notwithstanding, one can trust that a discrete object, or a number, or a personal pronoun, will correspond to a discrete sign.

6.2. At what level do the signs come in? At the outset the investigator has no idea whether he is dealing with an inflecting language, an agglutinating language, or a polysynthetic (incorporating) one; he can, therefore, have no idea if the utterances he receives as answers to the objects pointed at will be monomorphemic, or polymorphemic. He can rest assured, however, that the sign given for an object, if otherwise a linguistic event (i.e. a sequence of sounds that were heard elsewhere in another combination or in the neigborhood of other sounds) will be a LEXEME, i.e. AN UTTERANCE OF BONA FIDA SOCIAL STATUS IN THE COMMUNITY SUCH THAT DIFFERENT INDIVIDUALS WITHOUT PREVIOUSLY HAVING SEEN IT AS AN OBJECT OF ELICITATION WILL, DISCOUNTING INDIVIDUAL IDIOSYNCRASIES, PRODUCE THE SAME VERBAL SIGN FOR THE SAME OBJECT. 'Same' and 'different' need no particular epistemological defense in 1993. Nevertheless, I must reiterate that the Pikean distinction between etic and emic in the sense of Pike (1967) and (1982) is of lasting descriptive value. Discarding it is tantamount to putting on blindfolders in the dark instead of accepting a flashlight from someone who offers one to you.

To say, then, that ELICITED UTTERANCES come in at the lexemic level means several things at once. First, it means that regardless of the monomorphemic or polymorphemic status of the utterance (which will be determined later), the item solicited has been given a sign by a society of conscious interactants who, unless they engage in playful behavior, will try to preserve the INTEGRITY OF THE SIGN, certainly within the conscious memory of at least one generation. This needs stating, since linguistic change is a common event and it results in temporal as well as regional dialects. We are assuming throughout that the investigation is taking place in one dialect area at a time, such as one village in Central America, Papua New Guinea, or Africa.

7. Some tentative theoretical conclusions and work for the future. Whatever else a field linguist may do in the field, the result of serious work will invariably involve a LEXICAL STATEMENT of the language. This may take the form of an exhaustive lexicon featuring 35,000 to 50,000 entries, or it may be a thin glossary. As the grammar emerges during the work of description, lexemes will be used to illustrate grammatical points made. Words ending in *-o*, *-or*, *-os*, and *-er* in Latin belong to the 'masculine gender', I was taught in the 8th grade; one of my rules said *idus, tribus, porticus, acus manus* and *domus*, all ending in *-us*, were 'feminine' 4th declension nouns. To this day I remember the prepositions of Latin that take the 'accusative'; I recite the list even if roused from deep sleep: *ante, apud, ad, adversus, circum, circa, citra, cis; contra, extra, infra, inter, intra, iuxta, ob, supra, versus, ultra,* and *trans.* The Russian verbs *rukovod'it'* 'to lead' and *pravit'* 'to drive' are said to take (or govern) the instrumental case, when one would expect the accusative, the normal vehicle carrying the direct object function in most Indo-European languages. 'Be glad', 'Rejoice' is a semi-deponent verb in Latin with the principal parts *gaudeo, gaudere, gavisus sum*; the Hungarian vowel-harmonically conditions suffix pairs [lɔk ~ lɛk] meaning 'I do it to you, unto thee', and from which no subject 'I' and no object 'you-thee' can be subtracted, is an idiosyncratic feature of Hungarian grammar – as logically unwarranted as the existence of the English *serendipity*, coined by Horace Walpole in 1780. To know a language really well means far more than mastering its grammar; it means the ability to NEGOTIATE THE VAST MAJORITY OF THE LEXEMES of that language. By its very nature, THE LEXEME IS A STRATIFIED ENTITY. It has meaning; thus it is semantically sponsored. It has tactic properties in clause and sentence formation; the old-fashioned term would be that it correlates with a 'part of speech'. The lexeme, then, is best seen as that set of junctions in a language where socially coded and recognized meanings (with referents in the culture) intersect with tactic patterns in clause and sentence formation while one level lower they can be segmented morphemically, or turn out to be monomorphemic in size. Whichever side (the semantic or the grammatical) of the lexeme a speaker chooses to ignore or to handle aberrantly (i.e. in ways that markedly differ from socially accepted usage) is going to cost specific penalties; manipulating the semantics results in misunderstanding, intentional or deliberate; can lead to the reputation of being a clever or trite punster; an inventor of new terms; a namer of new inventions; a poet; a liar, or a schizophrenic: all of these are possibilities. Mismanaging the grammar (and the pronunciation that carries it) costs being labelled as a 'foreigner'; being a 'foreigner' can be a 'plus' if you are Maurice Chevalier in Hollywood where you are asked 'to keep your charming accent' or it can cost being asked to leave a certain position or not being offered it in the first place.

To paraphrase a talk by S.K. Shaumyan (Fall 1983, Chicago), manipulation by linguists of the meaning-portion of the lexeme has led to generative semantics, and manipulation of the phonology/morphophonemics of lexemes has led to generative phonology. Shaumyan's argument was that in either case the natural ecology of the lexeme is disturbed. A 'causative' structure is only truly causative for instance, if there is a real paradigm to bear out causativity, as in

> *sit* is to *set*
> *fall* is to *fell* and as
> *drink* is to *drench* ['cause to absorb water']

To treat *kill* as 'cause to become minus alive' is meaningless. Shaumyan argues because 'kill' has no counterpair such as *kell or *kall that would mean 'pass away on one's own'. Actually *kill* (cf. Chapter 5) also has the sense 'torture, torment' as in *my toothache has been killing me* and it is impossible to claim that the meaning here is 'my toothache renders me lifeless'.

In Shaumyan's most appropriate wording, the cohesion between a lexeme's semantic field and its morphosyntactic, grammatical behavior is a matter of what he calls the PRINCIPLE OF SEMIOTIC RELEVANCE.

As mentioned before, human language, in toto, can be justifiably seen as applied semiotics. As the sign is the crux of any semiotic system, so the lexeme is to any natural language on the planet. It is high time to recognize this central fact about human language and to put our theoretical and methodological debates into the proper pragmatic perspective offered by the insight available through observing the Principle of Semiotic Relevance.

The 50-year old Summer Institute of Linguistics is unique among international bodies of linguistics in the sense that it has consistently aimed for practical and verifiable results. In so doing, the SIL has been successful primarily because its practitioners, whether they consciously knew it or not, were in fact observing the Principle of Semiotic Relevance which, in the area of human language, hinges on the concept of the semantically sponsored, tactically deployable, morphologically combinable, and morphophonemically/phonemically spellable and pronounceable lexeme.

7 Periods of mystery, or syntax and the semantic pause

1. The known facts

Imagine that you have observed the following event: a little white dog, a poodle, known as Fifi, who belongs to my neighbor, the orthodontist, snatches a piece of soup bone from my dog, a black puli, called Pogi, and runs across the street. Just at that time a drunken driver, pursued by the local police, comes tearing down the street and hits the little white dog before it reaches safety; it dies on the spot. The neighbor was not there to see this happen and you are now trying to relate to him what happened.

1.1. Suppose I do not know my neighbor too well

If I do not really know my neighbor and also happen to be a somewhat cautious person, I might say (and expect to receive replies to as I go along) the following:

I: Do you own a dog, Sir?
N: Yes.
I: Is it a white poodle?
N: Yes, his name is Fifi.
I: I see . . . Well . . .
N: Anything wrong?
I: Well, your little white poodle, Fifi stole a bone.
N: Really . . .? Who from?
I: Well, it was my dog's chewing bone.
N: When did this happen?
I: Just a few minutes ago . . .
N: What happened?
I: Fifi snatched the bone, and started out across the street . . .
N: And?

I: There was a drunken driver tearing down the street being chased by
    the police . . .
N: Oh no . . . Did anything happen?
I: I am afraid so . . . Your dog was killed. I am awfully sorry.

In this possible exchange it actually matters more that the speaker 'I' is
cautious and breaks the news gradually to the neighbor after establishing
the dog's identity, than the fact that 'I' might also be genuinely sorry for
Fifi. Let us imagine, by contrast, that I am quite familiar with both my
neighbor and his dog. What might I say under those circumstances?

1.2. I know both my neighbor and his dog

I: Hey, Jack, come on over here! Quick! Look what happened . . .
N: What's wrong?
I: Fifi was running across the street with a bone in his mouth he
    snatched from our Pogi, and just that moment this car comes tearing
    along at a million miles an hour with the police after them . . .
N: Oh no . . .
I: I am afraid he's had it Jack . . . Look . . . This is really awful.

There are, of course, other ways in which my neighbor and I, if we are
really close friends, can talk about such an event. But suppose now that
I am the social columnist in this suburb and am writing a short piece in
the weekly newspaper to fill a page:

1.3. I am the social columnist for the local newspaper

'Dr John R. Quasimodo's valuable champion poodle, the snow-white
Fifi, winner of many a trophy, met a tragic death yesterday, when a hit-
and-run driver hit him on the corner of Westminster and Tara in
Whispering Oaks at 3:30 P.M. Fifi was last seen when he, having
snatched a bone from the front porch of Mr and Mrs Murgatroyd, ran
across Westminster. To the great sadness of both the owner and the
onlookers, he died on the spot. There having been a spate of careless
driving in the area, residents are requested to keep the local police
notified of any suspicious vehicles in the area.'

The columnist has, of course, other concerns than the death of a dog,
and so we should forgive him for making a plea to local residents about
careless drivers. This is an unimportant item anyway designed mostly to
fill the page, and talking just about a dog's death would seem meaningless,
hence the added phrase.

1.4. I am telling my wife about what happened to Fifi

I: Oh, hi, I'm so glad you're home . . . Guess what happened just a
    few minutes ago?

W: Bad news?

I: It's kind o' gory . . . Poor thing . . . Fifi got hit by a car . . .

W: You mean the Quasimodos' dog?

I: Yeah, yeah – our little daily visitor . . . He snatched Pogi's chewing
    bone and as he darted across the street . . .

W: Oh no, I bet it was one of those drunken drivers! When will our
    police department do anything about *them*??!!

I: I know . . . It's awful . . . Poor Jack . . .

W: He just loved that animal so . . . Does he know already?

I: That's just it . . . They're gone . . . I sure hate to have to break the
    news to him . . . Do *you* want to tell Carmelita?

W: She'd be too upset . . . You call Jack first thing when his car pulls in.

I think it is obvious from this particular exchange that both 'I' and 'W'
know all of the participants involved.

1.5. The unlikely sentence

Imagine that someone endeavors to write one elegant and exhaustive
sentence mentioning all of the relevant facts (such as who was the victim,
who was the aggressor, what attributes did the participants have, etc.),
while taking nothing for granted. Here are some of the ways it might be
put:

(a) At 3:30 P.M., yesterday, while my neighbor, Dr John R.
    Quasimodo, an orthodontist, was gone, his little white male poodle,
    called Fifi, ran over to our porch and snatched my black Puli's
    (Pogi's) bone, after which it started out across the street for safety
    when, suddenly, a drunken driver, pursued by the local police, hit
    and killed him.

(b) Fifi, who belongs to Dr John R. Quasimodo, my neighbor, who is
    an orthodontist, was hit by a drunken driver who was being chased
    by the police yesterday afternoon at 3:30 as he was trying to run
    across the street with a chewing bone in his mouth that he'd just
    snatched away from my black puli, Pogi, on our front porch.

(c) Just after he had snatched a chewing bone from my black puli, Pogi,
    my orthodontist neighbor's white poodle, Fifi, Dr John R.
    Quasimodo's dog, tried to run across the street for safety when a
    drunken driver, chased by the police, hit and killed him, just across
    from our porch where it had all started.

I call these sentences 'unlikely' because in contrast to the other situations they try to pack too much information into one sentence – as if the desired goal of making the information come out in one sentence were more important than the naturalness of the message. So let us again adjust our focus. There will be no live participants in conversation involved; this is to be just a written message, as if in one's diary, but now our goal is to make the message sound more natural, closer to real speech. We are less concerned with the one-sentence status of the message. What are some of the possibilities?

1.6. Some more likely sentences

(a) (Letter to mother living overseas; she vaguely remembers my neighbor but needs reminding.)
There isn't too much else in the way of interesting news. Oh yes, I almost forgot the mini-tragedy that we were unwilling witnesses to the other day. Remember Carmelita and Jack, next door? He's the orthodontist who's been straightening Sylvia's teeth, and the wife made that delicious dessert while you were here last July. Anyway, they're the ones with that cute little white dog, Fifi. You even remarked that it is unusual for a male dog to have a female name. Well, Fifi came over the other day and stole one of Pogi's chewing bones. So far so good, this has happened before, and he always brought them back. This time, unfortunately, he got wild and started running across the street, when suddenly a drunken driver came out of nowhere at great speed, and hit the poor little poodle. There was a cop chasing the drunken driver, that's why he must not have noticed what was in front of him. Well, poor Fifi died on the spot, and I had the sad duty of breaking the news to the Quasimodos. Carmelita sends her regards. They were wondering when you're coming again.

(b) (Letter to the owner who is at a doctors' convention in Florida. The wife can't make herself tell him what happened and asked me to do so.)
Dear Jack,
    I'm afraid I've got a piece of dreary news for you. (You may, in fact, be surprised to hear from me, but Carmelita asked that I write to you.) I hasten to add that she is fine and so are Timmy and Dawn – everyone's fine – they just miss you and wish you were here. It's about Fifi. Remember how I've been suggesting that you keep him on a leash? It wasn't that I was trying to bug you about the leash law here in Whispering Oaks, I was just worried that something might happen to him. He's – hang in there Jack, *was* – such a cute little sonovabitch. Jack, I am really terribly sad about this as I know how much Fifi meant to you! OK, here is what happened: You know Fifi; he ran over once again and snatched one of Pogi's chewing bones right on our front porch. Pogi was inside, so there was no nasty fight or anything. Then he headed across the street with the booty, when suddenly this drunken driver comes tearing down the road a million miles an hour trying to escape a cop who's behind him in hot pursuit. Well, Fifi got hit, and died on the spot. Jack, I am really awfully sorry about it! Your children were very brave and gave him a decent Christian funeral. Hope to see you soon, Sincerely, etc.

(c) (Lake County Animal Coroner's log entry)
Male, white, toy poodle 'Fifi', age 3 years; completely smashed, drunken driver, on corner of Tara and Westminster, Whispering Oaks; 3:30 Wednesday May 10, 1979. Owners: Dr and Mrs John R. Quasimodo, 510 N. Tara Lane, Whispering Oaks, Lake County, Wisconsin. Witness: Mr Alphonse Q. Murgatroyd (next-door neighbor), attorney-at-law. Was registered with the American Kennel Club, valued at $1,600.

2. The basic proposition

All of the sentences in section 1 tell 'the same story' with a different slant. A great deal of the given slant has to do with the familiarity of the interactants; with the formality or the informality of the situation, or what in British linguistics is known as the PERSONAL TENOR, the FUNCTIONAL TENOR, the MODE OF DISCOURSE, the FIELD OF DISCOURSE, and the CONTEXT OF SITUATION (see Benson and Greaves 1973; Halliday 1973). Part of the functional and the personal tenor, however, is formally interwoven with the fact that the same basic proposition can be realized as one long, labored sentence (1.5a, b, c) or as a number of smaller sentences in sequences. One of the functional tenors (1.6c) is extreme; even though the mode is 'written', the text is not intended to be read either silently or aloud, nor to be spoken, but for the sole purpose of being filed away like the record of a sale or an otherwise closed transaction. Thanks to stratificational diagramming (see Lockwood 1972) as well as to earlier versions of sememic networks, known as 'directed graphs' (Makkai 1972a:130–3), it is now possible to represent all of this information in a psychologically believable model of cognitive 'deep structure'. Deep structure is not, however, meant here in the sense of Chomsky (1965) or, for instance, Owen Thomas (1966), or any other transformationalist work that sees deep structure as abstract 'sentenceoids' whether before or after 'lexical insertion'. I assume that lexical insertion is SIMULTANEOUS WITH SEMEMIC TRACE FORMATION simply because lexemes (whose meanings, i.e., whose 'sememes', are known) are more likely to suggest appropriate sentences in which they can participate than the other way round: sentence structures, close to the surface, and ready to be pronounced, but free of actual lexemes, can elicit a large number of both sensible and nonsensical sentences from a respondent. Sentence structures and appropriate lexemes co-select each other, as it were. The words in capital letters in the sememic trace (Figure 1) are simply sememes in short-hand notation.

A Sememic Trace in Directed Graph format (henceforth STDG) is like a syntactic Dependency Tree, except that its primes are not sentence-formatives (lexemes) but pre-sentence network formatives, i.e., sememes. A sememe in this sense, is the POSSIBILITY OF THE OCCURRENCE OF A CERTAIN LEXEME or a set of related lexemes, and a SEMEMIC TRACE is the POSSIBILITY OF A SENTENCE, or A RELATED SET OF SENTENCES. Whenever more than one arrowhead points at the sememe, that sememe is ELEVATED and hence there is the possibility of

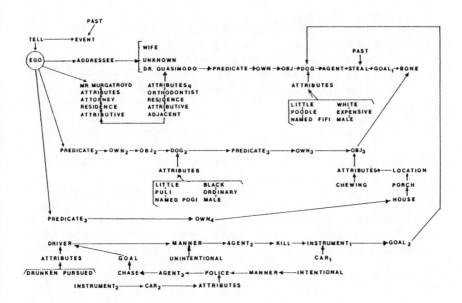

Figure 1

THEMATIZATION in a resultant clause. A sememe with one arrow leading away from it in one direction, and another pointing elsewhere, belongs to both immediately connecting sememes simultaneously. Thus the sememe ^{S}/adjacent/, located between the Attributes ^{S}/residence/ leading to the orthodontist Dr Quasimodo on the one hand, and to the narrator, Mr Murgatroyd, on the other, indicates that these residences are mutually adjacent to one another, i.e., that they are neighbors, which is an inherently reciprocal relationship. Converging arrows occur at the sememes ^{S}/Driver/, ^{S}/Obj.$_3$-bone/, ^{S}/Dog$_1$/, i.e., Fifi, the victim in our story; ^{S}/Dog$_2$/, the owner of the bone of contention that leads to Fifi's demise; the ^{S}/Attr./ for the location of the bone and the kind of bone that it is, etc.

When an arrow hits a vertical bracket (as in Addressee to Wife, Unknown, and Dr Quasimodo), the STDG indicates that either one in the set in any order is eligible, or all of them at once, or all in any order. Since the consequence in each case is a different text, the STDG, like a road map, is not responsible for which exit the driver takes, although the exit taken will have further consequences with regard to the journey as a whole. When more than one line leads away from a given sememe (as in the case of Ego to Mr Murgatroyd, Predicate$_2$ and Predicate$_3$ and, of course, to the Addressee), we are faced with a ZERO THEME or a NATURAL THEME. Zero or natural themes occur, in fact, in every simple one-word exclamation such as *Ouch! Gosh! Wow!* and even *No!* etc. (where the theme is the unannounced fact that the speaker is obviously announcing something). This common, everyday occurrence has caused transformationalists some degree of difficulty since they, in accordance with the neat symmetry of the Np-Vp structuring of all sentences, were looking for subjects and predicates for every sentence, even if there were none to see with the naked eye. Thus *Ouch!* can be MADE to conform to the Np-Vp pattern if one imagines that it is the dependent direct object morpheme hung on a tree which begins, as all normal sentences do, with a subject noun phrase *I* with the verb phrase continuing *say to you* and ending in the dependent object, the utterance *Ouch!* itself. The trouble with this 'performative' deep structure analysis is, of course, that both the *I* and the *say to you* must be deleted before we arrive at *ouch!*, the form we want. If, on the other hand, we recognize zero or natural themes, we do not have to go through the unnecessary process of generating a fully formed sentence only to have to destroy it later in order to describe what we had in the first place, i.e., the exclamation itself. A zero or natural theme, however, CAN be realized optionally; in the case of the present STDG we would have to look for the closest sememe that has two arrows pointing to it, and this is the ^{S}/Event/. Since it is the Ego who relates the event to the addressee (as normally in every human society), the narrator now has a choice of (a) either going into his story directly, or (b) first announcing that he is about to do so.

The available NARRATION OPENERS differ from genre to genre, from tenor to tenor, and depend largely on the situation of context of the interlocutors. Thus, if this is in the genre of a fairy tale, Murgatroyd can start the story of Fifi by saying *Once upon at time there was a little white poodle by the name of Fifi* . . ., or he can use the reminding device of the letter (as in 1.6a), or the 'breaking of the bad news via cushioning the blow' as in 1.6b. If he were testifying under oath, Murgatroyd could, of course, also say, 'I, Alphonse Q. Murgatroyd, attorney-at-law, residing at such-and-such-an-address, having personally witnessed the accident on the corner of Tara and Westminster Lanes . . . do solemnly testify that Fifi, a 3-year old white poodle, belonging to . . . was killed . . . by a drunken driver.' But then, being an attorney, Murgatroyd knows when he is testifying in court, when he is talking to his wife, when he is writing to his elderly mother who lives overseas, or when he is notifying his friend or neighbor of the death of his pet dog at the request of the saddened and timid wife, etc. At the risk of belaboring the obvious, grammarians should take note that people usually know who they are and who their interlocutor is (even if they do not know him, since then THAT is what they know); they know what is more important about a given message than something else also marginally contained in that message; they know whether what they say is true or false (save the occasional case of 'moral insanity' when the speaker actually does not know truth from falsehood); and they also know if the mode is spoken or written language that has a definite purpose. The degree of consciousness with which people are aware of these factors will vary with health, age, education, occupation, etc. but a normal, sane, legally responsible adult (and I do NOT mean Chomsky's 'Ideal Speaker-Hearer in the Ideal Speech Community') who is communicatively competent (to use Dell Hymes's term) in the national language spoken around him, whether as native or as immigrant, will be able to comment on an actual event as he or she perceived it. This is why legally sane, normal adults can, after all, be drafted to serve on juries. Their ability to analyze events and the roles of the participants in them does not automatically enable them also to make valid observations about the CODE they have been using i.e. the language and its mechanisms. People are people, not linguists, BUT linguists are also people. Many a modern grammarian, especially of the mathematically oriented mutationist varieties, likes to pretend to be in the possession of a certain computationally oriented omniscience and specificity, even if the knowledge represented in a given derivation turns out to be irrelevant (e.g. the fact that *Ouch!* is an exclamation issued by me, the sufferer, to you, the hearer, or to myself when there is no hearer around to commiserate) and even if some of the information given is totally alien to our average, adult, legally sane human psychology.

3. The semantic pause

What, then, is the mechanism most likely to be responsible for making us realize a certain amount of information as one sentence or as several shorter sentences? I believe that such a mechanism can be found in the notion of the SEMANTIC PAUSE. The remainder of this chapter accordingly will be devoted to explaining the notion of the semantic pause, how it operates, and what causes semantic pauses to occur in certain places.

3.1. Use of semantic pause

A semantic pause (henceforth SP) is a CHANCE TO CHANGE YOUR MIND IN MID-UTTERANCE. Written texts, especially of the academic variety, are rather poor examples of SPs, since academic writing, by its very nature, is consciously controlled and edited. What we need are copious transcripts of spontaneous oral conversations. In creating the examples above of how one might tell the story of Fifi, I was trying to give several appropriate genres, including a letter sent overseas, a coroner's report, and several oral versions.

The start of every communication is, by definition, the breaking of a semantic pause; let us call it 0 SP. 0 SP→U (utterance) symbolizes the fact that the addressor is engaging the addressee (who can be the addressor himself, as in soliloquy) in a speech act. Every subsequent period (full stop) is a SUBSEQUENT SEMANTIC PAUSE (SSP). SSPs are optional, as the U may continue in one sentence. SSPs are favored in normal speech, however, since not availing oneself of the possible pauses leads to the considerable strain of COMPOSED SPEECH (CS). CS can be observed under natural conditions also, but the places and occasions where it arises are marked by social formality, e.g. the university classroom, the court of law, the office where one speaks into a dictaphone for eventual transcription and written editing. The opposite of CS is SPONTANEOUS SPEECH (SS). One of the most striking characteristics of SS is that the semantic pauses observable in it do not necessarily get realized as periods ('full stops') replete with the customary falling intonation; rather, the person engaged in SS realizes his SPs as run-on clauses with suspended comma intonation between the various parts.

In what follows I will try to show how various realizations of Figure 1 can be accomplished using the SP and SSP method; // symbolizes SSPs.

    1. 0 SP → U

(a)   I // I saw // I saw your dog // I saw your dog Fifi // I saw your dog Fifi snatch the bone //

(b)   I saw // I saw Fifi // I saw Fifi running across the street //

(c)   Fifi // Fifi came and snatched Pogi's bone //

(d)   A drunken driver // A drunken driver chased by the police //

(e)   The police // were chasing a drunken driver //

(f)   The police were chasing // a drunken driver down the street //

(g)   My dog's chewing bone // my dog's chewing bone was snatched by your dog Fifi //

(h)   Say, Jack // Say, Jack, I've got some bad news I'm afraid //

(i)   Jack, say I've got //

(j)   Jack I'm afraid I've got some //

(k)   Bad news, Jack, I'm afraid //

(l)   On the porch of our house // there lay Pogi's chewing bone //

(m)   Pogi's chewing bone // lay on our front porch when Fifi //

(n)   Pogi's chewing bone lay on our porch when a drunken driver chased by the police //

Sentences (a) through (n) are all possible 0 SP→U events, but intermixing them is also a possibility, indeed a rather frequent one. The person who so intermixes his starts 'hems and haws': he cannot seem to get the message out correctly. Consider the following:

(1)   I saw // hey Jack // I'm afraid // the police were chasing a drunken driver // my dog's chewing bone // Fifi came and snatched Pogi's bone // Pogi's chewing bone lay on our front porch when Fifi //

(2)   My dog's chewing bone // hey Jack I'm afraid I've got some bad news // the police were chasing a drunken driver down the street //

(3)   Fifi came and snatched Pogi's chewing bone // bad news, Jack, I'm afraid // the police were chasing a drunken driver down the street

It seems that (3) is the most 'logical' of the possible sentences presented here, but this does not mean that other less fortunate sequencings do not occur with rather high frequency. The person so speaking is not really being illogical; he speaks in the mode of spontaneous speech, which is not composed, hence he can take the various chunks of information between semantic pauses and string them together with a variety of phonologically appropriate intonation patterns. The stress of having to relate the bad news of Fifi's accident to the owner will certainly favor SS rather than CS, hence the greater likelihood of loosely ordered sentence chunks being shifted around.

3.2. The correlation of semantic pauses and structural pauses

Let us take one of the 'unlikely' sentences and see if the structural breaks in its surface structure also happen to coincide with places where the narrator could actually change his mind. Let us take the sentence

Jack, your little white dog Fifi came and snatched away one of Pogi's chewing bones from our porch and then headed across the street with it just at the very moment when a drunken driver, chased by the police, came tearing down the street and hit poor Fifi.

The structural break after the vocative *Jack* is also a SP; the narrator could bargain for more time here and say *I'm afraid I've got some bad news*, or come right to the theme of the message, Fifi. *Your little white dog, Fifi*, as Subject NP in the clause, also serves as the theme of the entire sentence; after *Fifi* (followed here by *came*) the narrator could 'change his mind' and say *whom all love so dearly*, or *whom we know you love so much*, or skip any of these and move right to the predicate. *Your little white dog Fifi came* (period) would be a possibility; the speaker could then pick up the theme by saying *Well, he snatched* . . . etc., giving himself time to catch his breath and/or to prepare Quasimodo for the bad news. Continuing in this manner one could show that the traditional structural analyses associated with 'post-Bloomfieldianism' and the Wellesian IC analysis method tend to yield SSPs as well where the speaker could, to varying degrees of freedom, change his mind in the course of a given narrative realized as a sequence of sentences. One implication of this is that everything in a natural language is inextricably a part of meaning and of signification, i.e., that there is no such thing as a separate semantic component or a separate semological stratum. Human languages are PANSEMANTIC; pansemanticity is more obviously present on some structural levels than on others. The model I would like to propose here ultimately derives from standard stratificationalism (Lamb 1966; Lockwood 1972) but is one that, generally, de-emphasizes the importance of grammar over the lexicon.

4. Outline of the pansemantic model of the stratification of language

4.1. Verbal description of the model shown in Figure 2

The four central 'strata' of natural languages (I. Semology, II. Lexology, III. Morphology, and IV. Phonology) are surrounded by the SEMANTIC STRATUM. The major portion of this (left side of diagram) is called INPUT SEMANTICS; the 'top' of the system is called COGNITIVE SEMANTICS (Storage), and SOCIALIZATION OF STANDARD MEANINGS; the right side is called OUTPUT SEMANTICS, hearer's and reader's meaning, etc.

The structure inside this cortex-like hull is a funnel, wider at the top than on the bottom, because of the statistics of concepts (millions) versus sememes (hundreds of thousands), as against words and morphemes (thousands) and phonemes and syllables (dozens, or hundreds). The pansemantic nature of linguistic structure suggests that the first level (top) should be called SEMO-SEMANTICS. I believe that this is THE level of linguistic creativity. The SITUATION OF CONTEXT is taken into account at this level; also at this level the speaker decides his or her role as Ego in any statement, question, command, or narrative that will follow. The various outcomes of the network in Figure 1, depending on who the speaker is and whom he is talking to, depend on the cumulative INPUT SEMANTICS reaching level I from the left. The four levels in unison, acting as a huge filter, decide on the actualization of the output (our various texts dealing with Fifi's demise in various styles and ways). Semo-semantics is THE creative component, because major novelists, who use standard grammar and standard vocabulary, are nevertheless capable of creating new plots, new characters, and new situations all the time. (If they also create new vocabulary as they go along, all is fine, but the new vocabulary created will be explicable only in the context of the situation they have created as writers. This also goes for new sentence patterns.)

The horizonal left-to-right corridors called First Order of Restrictions, Second Order of Restrictions, and Third Order of Restrictions are the three major tactics that every natural language must have; i.e., the Semo-Lexotactics (between I and II), the Lexo-Morphotactics (between II and III) and the Morpho-Phonotactics (between III and IV). The double-shafted arrows leading 'up' and 'down' from each of these corridors show some of the internal mechanics of the system. The fact that Fifi is a white poodle and a male enters the hearer's consciousness at level I, but levels II, III and IV also fire simultaneously, though at a lesser power. Fifi walks into the reader's life as a concept realizable as a fairly tightly definable sememe that, further down, is realized as the lexeme ^{L}/Fifi/, a noun. This noun has a foreign 'French' ring to it, as the vowels involved resemble English /iy/, but without the glide. The morphology 'lets the item Fifi through', as it were – it does not stop to segment into *Fi* plus *fi*.

Fifi could also walk into your consciousness as a contextually disembodied lexeme. Suppose I write you a memo that says *please get me half a*

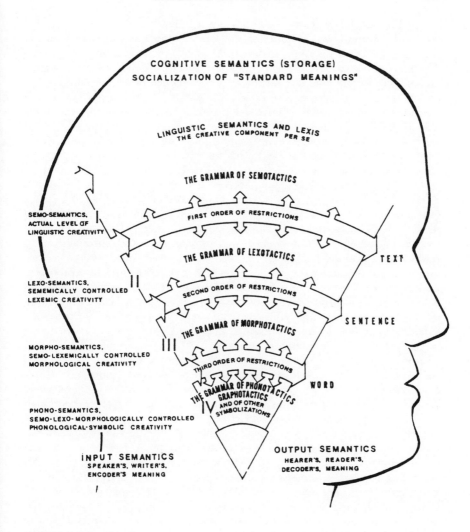

Figure 2

dozen fifis at K-Mart. You would have the right to turn to me and ask *What's a 'fifi'?* The explanation I might give would be the building of some sort of sememe via CIRCUMLEXICALIZATION so that you might understand what it is I want. Suppose I define ^L/fifi/ as 'that kind of newly imported French flea collar that poodles love to wear on hot, sticky summer days, selling for $1.20 each' – you would have a reasonably clear idea of what I am asking you to buy; certainly, at least, you would not go to the frozen food section or to the automotive department, but much more likely towards the pet shop.

The First Order of Restrictions is the most liberal; yet it, too, constrains the world around us. It functions differently during sleep from during conscious alertness. My knowledge of the world constrains my behavior so that I do not step out of the window on the 20th floor; yet I can safely dream that I step out and just float away. Types of fiction, fairy tales, poetry, ancient sagas, etc., function somewhat as 'dreams'; they create universes in which certain things are possible that we accept for the duration of the movie watched or the novel read and do not worry whether it is possible to have a space colony near Alpha Centauri in 2002 (see Jaynes 1976). Transformationalists have insisted in book upon book that the syntactic component is the creative one, with the semantics being interpretive and the phonology being interpretive as well.

The argument, repeated *ad nauseam* by all of its practitioners, is that we can produce sentences we have never heard before and can interpret sentences we have never heard before. Consequently, syntax must be creative. It never ceases to amaze me how such a valid observation can lead learned scholars to such an erroneous conclusion! The reason that we can indeed utter sentences we have never heard before and interpret ones we have never experienced is precisely that syntax, both in production and in reception, is a fairly narrow and restrictive domain, which, by repeating its standard patterns time after time, allows us to assimilate the speaker's meaning in terms of our own 'hearer's meaning', the two being mediated by the socialization of 'standard meanings'. The sentence *Fifi, my neighbor's white male poodle, was killed in the street by a drunken driver after he snatched away my dog's, Pogi's, bone from our porch* was never uttered before and never heard before by anyone, yet the various ways of telling the story unfolded themselves rather naturally in the earlier part of this chapter. The reason is that the experience of dogs snatching bones and running hither and thither is not uncommon; dogs getting killed by hit-and-run drivers is also fairly common. The lexical items *Fifi* and *Pogi* are certainly new to the reader, but they come tagged as 'dogs' names', hence they make sense. No other lexeme (hence sememe) in the sentence is new and neither is the sentence pattern. The sentence skeleton is *My N's Adj Adjs N was V-ed LOC by Adj N after Pron. V-ed adv. Poss, Pers N. 's N Prep. Poss, N* and it could be 'filled' by a variety of both sensible and nonsensical lexis, both as sentence-building practice in a class for foreigners, or for domestic amusement. The end-product of the channel called 'First Order of Restrictions' is a text or several texts, possibly one single text which is produced from time to time during the individual's lifetime. Most people create texts that are not too memorable; most of them never even write them down. Conversely, the simple fact that someone decides to write his texts down does not make him a good novelist, let alone one who leaves a mark on his generation or changes the awareness of life of his contemporaries. Yet if 'creativity' means anything at all, it should be used in this pristine, philosophical-artistic sense, the sense in which Shakespeare and Goethe are qualitatively different individuals from the rest of mankind.

Lexo-semantic creativity is describable by giving some real examples.

French has an expression *petit bourgeois endimanché*, which means something like 'a lower middle-class person having a Sunday picnic', or 'all Sundayed up'. (The image suggested is that he is lying under a tree, had too much to eat and drink, is huffing and puffing and can barely get up.) On one occasion at an open air picnic in Ravinia during a Mozart marathon, I dropped some food on my shirt. I was in French company, and thinking of 'making a pig of oneself' in English and not quite knowing how this is said in French, I suggested *je ne peux pas manger plus, je me suis complètement encochonné*, 'I can't eat any more, I am all *pigged up'. The response was copious laughter and the suspicion that I heard this from French people. All of those present, including the director of the Maison Française de Chicago, were commenting on how completely well-formed French this word *encochonné* 'all pigged up' (from *cochon* 'pig') was and that they never heard it before. (Even though this word does not legally exist in French, we all agreed that a female speaker would have to spell it as *encochonnée*.) Numerous examples could be given from English, but I believe this example will suffice.

As we reach level III, it becomes harder and harder to be 'creative' and make something new really stick in the language. The noun formative suffix *-th* of the forms *warmth, length, breadth, width*, etc., may give rise to an occasional analogy giving *slowth* for *slowness*, and the like, but these have very little chance of surviving the moment they are created. Note that this suffix is of early Anglo-Saxon origin in English. Speakers of English enjoy much greater creative freedom on the morphological level when they are dealing with Latinate prefixes and suffixes, or elements of Greek origin. One look at the *Dictionary of Space English* (Makkai 1973) will convince the reader that neologisms are most frequently coined out of Graeco-Latin morphological material such as *transduce, transducer, ablative cone*, etc.

The creative manipulation of level IV is the prerogative of talented poets writing in their native medium. Other than that, phonology IS and CAN BE interfered with by (a) immigrants, (b) children, (c) speakers of different dialects; this may lead to morphological changes in the language, which, ultimately, may also affect the syntax and the semantics. The history of English as traced in many standard textbooks (e.g. Pyles 1971) shows that this is exactly what happened between Old English and Middle English, and between Middle English and Modern English.

5. Why do we make periods (full stops)?

A sentence – like any object – is more than the sum of its parts. This is particularly true in live speech, since the intonation, the speed, and the rhythm are all intrinsic parts of the message. This period (full stop), which I have tried to characterize as a Semantic Pause, is also a signal that the speaker's mind is not so firmly made up as to be intolerant of someone else entering the conversation and registering doubt or disagreement. In order to test this hypothesis, try to SPEAK IN A COMPOSED MANNER in a situation and about a topic that by its nature does not call for such composed speech. Suppose you have guests in your house and are offering them the choice between tea and coffee; tea with lemon or cream, and coffee with cream and sugar or without. Since the normal ways of making such gestures are all too well known, I will not reproduce them here in any length (*Coffee any one? Tea? Lemon, cream and sugar?*) but I will report an instance told by an embarrassed participant in someone's house who offered coffee and tea as follows:

> Well, now then, if we are all agreed, I would like to propose that we leave the dinner table at this point in order to feel a little more comfortable and, while we do so, permit me to ask you if you would like to have some coffee or tea at this time also asking you, by the way, if, in case you would like to have coffee, you would also like to have cream and sugar to go with it, and, in case you should opt for tea, whether you would like to have lemon to go with it or cream.

The lady reporting this sentence to me also stated that she felt perplexed and out of place; in fact she was wondering if the host had something wrong with him. He later revealed that he used to be a judge and that he is a cured stutterer who compensated for his earlier speech impediment with this sort of longwinded, written style while speaking.

The 'period' answers to both its American and to its British name.

It is indeed a 'period' – an interval, if you will – during which (a) the speaker can change his mind, and (b) the hearer can get a chance to take a turn in the conversation; or rather to turn a monolog into a conversation. It also is a complete cessation of speech – a 'full STOP', since it can also be the end of an entire message followed by extended silence on the part of all participants. Sentences, beyond being grammatical constructs, are also socio-psychological events, or to use the hippie term from the 1960s, 'happenings'. Sentences hit us or caress us as we receive them, and we may return them or step aside. The game of ping-pong is not a bad analogy for human dialog. Whenever the ball comes to you at an un-expected angle, you must position yourself to be able to return it over the net so that it touches your partner's side of the table; otherwise you lose the point, and either your partner or you must serve again. Just as sentences may be short or long, 'points' in ping-pong (or in tennis, for that matter) may be longer or short-lived. If every time you serve, your opponent smashes the ball and scores a point, and gives serves that cause you to drive the ball into the net, you will lose 21–0 in 21 short exchanges. This can happen only between a cruel pro and an innocent beginner. Benevolent pros allow the novices to return the ball in order to build up their self-confidence. The same with conversation and sentences. If every time he addresses me I cruelly answer a child, 'Shut up!' I may create a clear example of how periods (exclamation marks, in this case) are arrived at, but I will also have shown that I am turning my youngster into an introverted moron who will never be able to talk freely to others.

Whereas I do not know at present how such a statistical study could be undertaken, I have a gut feeling (this expression has been rendered respectable by the writings of James D. McCawley) that there is such a thing as an 'average sentence length' in Modern American English as well as in various Commonwealth dialects. This length will probably vary with the mode (spoken or written) and the genre; but between Hemingway's short sentences and Walt Whitman's poetic mega-sentences there would be an arithmetically calculable average for written English, and presumably the same could be done for spoken varieties allowing for dialect variation both on geographical and sociological grounds. The number of verbs and nouns could be calculated per 'average sentence' (specified by mode, genre, and dialect), and the information content per 'average sentence' could be drawn in Semantic Networks. Such a study would indicate the amount and kind of information typically transmitted in one sentence where the sentences in question would always be viewed in the context of the kind of narrative in which they occur. Such a study would call for computer-parsing of sentences and the computer-parsing of various types of mechanically stored discourse.

Such a study would be an objective first step to the empirical investigation of HOW we make periods (or full stops). The WHY could be asked meaningfully only once we know the HOW.

8 Where do exclamations come from?

0. The problem: wow!

Mankind has a universal habit which is, strangely, not much discussed in the literature.[1] It starts with every human being in early infancy and accompanies us through our lives. We all EXCLAIM. The occasion may be physical pain or sudden shock, like stubbing your toe in the door, or touching a hot iron. It may be frustration or anger; you forgot your car keys and have to hike back to the office to get them. It may be the sudden realization that you have been had. But it may be the overwhelming joy of a sudden recognition; the wave of pleasure at suddenly comprehending something that used to be a mystery. It can be the pleasure of seeing an old friend or a relative. It can be the mixture of joy and embarrassment: you understand something for the first time, something that gives you great pleasure, yet at the same time you are mad at yourself because you think the recognition was long overdue. Why did I not see this four or five years ago? A friend whom we like well enough but really consider not quite our equal in many ways, gets a sudden promotion, becomes famous, or wins the Irish sweepstakes: invariably we voice our feeling and pass a judgment on the situation. The utterance produced in most of these instances is not some sort of cerebral peroration on the situation, but usually a spontaneous exclamation, phonologically well marked as such.

To put it quite simply, the number of semantically, socially, and emotionally appropriate situations for me or the readers of these lines to exclaim is so great – indeed we are in constant interaction – that it is startling how actually limited our reservoir of exclamations is. In this chapter I will try to survey the most typical English exclamations, compare them with others from languages I know, and then try to explain were these forms come from. Since the treatment attempted here will be essentially a synchronic one, the phrase 'where do they come from?' is not to be interpreted as a historical excursion which, no doubt about it, must also be undertaken but, due to the immense size of the project, must remain a future task.

1. One-word exclamations from the sublime to you know what

The exclamations *God!*, *Wow!*, *Zowie!*, *Bingo!*, *Yeah!*, *'Course!*, etc., affirmative and consentive semantically, start on the highest pitch level, say level 5, fall rapidly to a low level 2 or 1, and have a strongly felt affirmative effect. Try exclaiming them with an interrogative intonation as *God?*, *Wow?*, *Zowie?*, *Bingo?*, *Yeah?*, *'Course?*, and the effort it takes to ask these questions will clearly show that they are all telescopic declarations. The point, of course, is, that one word exclamations can also be questions, as in *Me?*, *You?*, *Him?*, *Her?*, *Us?*, *Go?*, *Stay?*, *Pay?*, *Sleep?* etc., all of which, whether personal pronouns or the overt predicates of sentences previously used in context and thus in memory between both hearer(s) and speaker(s) show surprise, indignation, unwillingness to believe what was heard and said or suggested, or a combination of them. The one word exclamation *Why?*, being an interrogative normally spoken on a falling, declarative intonation, can be exclaimed both with an interrogative and a declarative terminal contour, (*Why?* – *Why!*) with the result that they indicate different semantic antecedents. *Why???* which is angry, uptight and argumentative (especially if elongated and loud) occurs in contexts where the speaker has been making or trying to make a point but has the feeling that he is not getting through, so he says *Why???* – *I'll tell you why!* whereby he proceeds with his argument. The declarative contoured *Why!(?)* – with an orthographic question mark but a phonological falling exclamation mark – does not refer to information in memory or the subject just mentioned; qua exclamation it shows indignant curiosity or moral indignation plus disbelief. (Non-exclamatory *Why!(?)* is, primarily, a non-biased, information-seeking speech act.)

It thus seems that any personal name, lexeme for objects or actions which have been previously mentioned in context but which arouse the speaker's incredulity or indignation, can occur as a one word interrogative exclamation, e.g. *Car?*, *Gambling?*, *Arrested?*, *Drugs?*, *Escaped?*, *Psychic?*, *Already?*, *Gone?*, *Won?*, *Lost?* – the list is practically endless. Their grammatical description ('allocation' and 'provenience' in tandem) is best achieved by juxtaposition to their phonosemantically declaratively coded counterparts.

We say *God!*, *Christ!*, *Heavens!* etc., as above, which are 'positive' on the surface, but can certainly be used on a whole scale of meanings ranging from enthusiastic approval to forcefully disgusted condemnation – polar semantic opposites expressed by nothing 'grammatical' except the human voice, hence the term PHONOSEMANTIC, and its inevitable correlate to be explained below, PHONOPSYCHOSEMANTIC. Any well-trained actor or actress can perform the exclamations above so as to sound ecstatically jubilant or lugubriously downcast, bored (accompanied by yawns into a telephone receiver), resigned, pensive, or nervous and hurried. Next to these, however, we also use 'four letter words' in our exclaimings which, although all 'dirty' on the surface, can – depending on the phonopsychosemantic interaction of the speaker and the hearer – be interpreted as highly positive. Thus *Shit!*, *Fuck!*, *Damn!*, *Hell!* – the four national favorites of post-World War II America – while all almost certainly impossible as questions (*Shit?, *Fuck?, *Damn?, *Hell? – excepts as THREATS against someone who just uttered them whom we are about to scold very severely as if about 'to wash his mouth out with soap') and predominantly negative value-judgments in their semantics, can also function as exclamations of joyous surprise, the congenial envy of a gambling or a drinking buddy mixed with admiration and tacit approval, etc. As outright anger and fully negative condemnations, these exclamations tend to be realized as shorter, from highest to lowest falls on the loudest possible stress within the speaker's customary range; as admixtures of solidarity, envy, and admiration, as in the Army or around the poker table, they sound more elongated and the fall is not from highest to lowest but from mid to low. It is as if the speaker uttering these forms is about to say a MITIGATING PHRASE after them, such as *you lucky devil, you lucky dog, you lucky sonovabitch*, or *you silver-tongued devil*; perhaps, equally amiably, *you crazy nut, you disgusting genius*, etc. I personally overheard the following sentence offered as amazed and disbelieving praise from a graduate student of mathematics to a thirteen-year old: *SHIIIIIT, why of COUrse, you abso-LUTE-ly disGUSting, Miserable PROdigy!* and the youngster could not have been more pleased.

Maaaan!, the modern one word exclamation, is rarely heard with an interrogative intonation, unless it is a CONVERSATION INITIATING ADDRESS between two previously unacquainted individuals. Thus *Man?* – much shorter on the vowel than the declarative form – is heard when a stranger walks up to you at the bus stop asking for a light or a quarter; it means something like 'I want to talk to you' or 'may I engage you in conversation?'. The declarative, like most other declaratives, has the full phonopsychosemantic range of enthusiastic approval, acquiescence, admiration, disgust, or ridicule, as the case may be; the most frequently observed realization is a heavily breathed sight of relief, or the emotive interjectional use quite similar to *well . . .*, as in *Maaaan, I'm tellin' ya . . .* (cf. *all's well, I'm telling' ya . . .*) where the vowels are, of course, quite different, but the overall structure is rather similar despite the appreciable nuances in phonopsychosemantics. (It goes without saying that the phonopsychosemantic nuances of these forms positively correlate with the sociolinguistic status of these forms. Thus *Maaaan* is far more intimate than *well* or even *wehhhhl*; it is likelier to be heard from a younger Black male than from an older white male; if heard from a white female, the odds are that she is on the progressive and left-from-center side of the political spectrum, etc.)[2]

One-word imperatives, such as *Go!*, *Stay!*, *Sit!*, *Fetch!*, *Run!*, *Duck!*, *Eat!*, etc., which, of course, can only be exclaimed interrogatively AS THREATS or ACTS OF VERBAL DEFIANCE, constitute a special class of exclamations whose nature *qua* exclamation is, by virtue of our long-standing acquaintance with imperatives, the least puzzling in the whole complex family. One intuitively – and traditionally – expects a short, one-word imperative, to sound like an exclamation, though directors and actors rarely miss an opportunity to exploit these for humor by having an actor 'say them nicely', as if 'begging' a dog to stay, sit, or fetch, as the case may be. If an extremely timid, cowardly dog on a Walt Disney cartoon should be commanded by his inept master beggingly *Fehhhhhhtch* . . ., the dog could look back at him and ask back: *Fehhhhhtch????* meaning 'me, who can barely walk? You've gotta be kidding' – in which case, because of the scenario's inner structure, such an interrogatively coded one-word imperative would not be either a threat or an act of verbal defiance, but an act of BEGGING FOR SYMPATHY. (The master has issued an obviously unfulfillable command and Snoopy Sr. appeals to him via the audience for a reprieve.)

2. No kidding! *Enter* syntax

Complicated though one-word exclamations are psycho-phonosemantically, they share a certain surface-simplicity.

2.1. Approval via denial

The most frequently heard two-word exclamation starts with the negative *no* and is thus predicated to a lexeme which is supposed to be negative, e.g., *No shit!*, *No fooling!*, *No kidding!* etc., where the forms *shit*, *fooling*, and *kidding*, refer to the 'undesirables', 'nonsense', 'double-talk', generally having to do with what I propose to call DISINFORMATION. Terms of intrinsically high esteem are never heard negated; thus *No Christ!*, *No God!*, *No Heavens!* simply do not occur either in positively or negatively intended phonopsychosemantic coloring, whereas *God!*, *Christ!*, and *Heavens!* – without the *no* – all occur both as short PRAYERS ('positive coloring') or as short CURSES ('negative coloring'). This does not mean that *no* and *God*, *Christ*, and *Heavens* never co-occur in construction; but if they do, the three ecclesiastical nouns are vocatives and the succeeding *no* negates a whole previously mentioned subject of whatever length from a short sentence to an entire discourse block or even a novel. Thus we have *God, no!*, *Christ, no!* and *Heavens, no!*, but all these function as fairly specific denials of something that has been said either overtly, or suspected of the person uttering them. The likeliest situation to encounter this is listening to a person who is accused of a crime he did not commit. The likeliest statement to follow the vocative + negative structure would be something like *How could you possibly think that I could do something like that?* Less frequent, but also possible is the emotional surface denial of bad news received over the telephone, such as the sudden illness or accident of a friend or relative: *Christ, no!* . . . (*I can't believe what you're saying . . . it can't POSSIBLY be true what you are saying . . .* etc.)

Obviously then, one might think, we only deny ugly or harmful things, such as bodily refuse and the obfuscation of issues, whereas desirable entities – as the above ecclesiastical triad of nouns – is never denied. The symmetry of the situation is distorted by the fact that *no fooling!*, *no shit!*, *no kidding!*, can all function as enthusiastic exclamations of positive coloring as well; the expressions carry an admixture of surprise in such instances. The slightly incredible news that your spinster aunt Mathilda just won the Irish sweepstakes may be met with a variety of joyous and semi-incredulous exclamations such as *Wow!*, *Gosh!*, *Gee!*, *What about that!* . . . etc., all the way to *no kidding*, *no fooling*, and *no shit!* – depending, of course, on who you are, where you are, and who you are speaking to. A milder form of these is the spreading *no bull!* which, like its fellows, can be used to encode a whole range of semantic attitudes from scorn and disbelief to semi-incredulous admiration.

This can never happen to *no dice!* however, which remains hermetically sealed in its tone of complete refusal. Try to praise or semi-credulously admire someone by exclaiming *no dice!* at him! Your own eyes will throw the forbidding * to bar it from occurring.

2.2. *Some construction!*

The construction of exclamation *some* + *N* (riding the appropriate intonational contour) is, once again, a constant challenge to the grammarian, playing hide-and-seek behind the phonopsychosemantic qualities of the human voice. Take the exclamation *Some party!* – without fairly specific stage instructions of what it is supposed to sound like, and tell what it means: I will contradict whatever you say until you have actually performed it. Once I hear the exclamation on a high-fidelity tape recorder, chances are that 90 out of 100 others I should ask to listen and judge will agree with my finding. The human voice, like a most delicate musical instrument, can perform the SIMULTANEOUS CODING of such semantically contradictory attitudes as the highest degree of admiration, mild astonishment, fear ameliorated by thoughtfulness, mild scorn, sharp sarcasm, all the way to utter disdain or disgust (cf. Fónagy 1983).

The productivity of this kind of exclamation is very great and will allow, besides *Some President!*, *Some doctor!*, *Some Peace Treaty!*, *Some red herring!* etc., such forms as *Some God!*, *Some Christ!*, and *Some heavens!*, – all potentially sarcastic as well as awe-struck, contrasting sharply with the nonoccurrence of *no* in front of these very nouns.

2.3. *What a what!*

What President, *what God*, *what Peace Treaty* contrast with *what a President*, *what a God*, *what a Peace Treaty* in that the first set without the indefinite article is very hard to perform with a reverent attitude; scorn and condemnation, however, leap out vigorously in these forms. The *wh-* form carries with it a pseudo-declarative falling intonation contour, but only if *a* is absent: *What President?, What God?, What Peace Treaty?* with interrogative intonation, are not exclamations but SPECIFYING-REITERATIVE INTER-ROGATIVES: *God, President,* and *Peace Treaty* were already mentioned or are in 'memory' and the *wh-* question seeks further specification as to which one of those possible was meant. No genuine exclamation is thus possible without the indefinite article. With it, as in the second set, once again ambiguity sets in, since *What a President!* etc., can be exclaimed imparting the highest degree of praise and admiration OR the lowest degree of contempt; in between, the accomplished actor will be able to perform a whole range of psycho-phonosemantic attitudes including measured appraisal in musing reminiscence, or the bird's eye perspective of an eyewitness of long ago: *Teddy Roosevelt – what a President he was! Why, I met him in person in the African jungle . . .!*

2.4. Adjective noun!

Good Lord!, Good Heavens!, Good Grief!, are normal exclamations in American English, but the adjective *great* sounds natural only with *Heavens*; thus we have *Great Heavens!* but seldom, if ever, **Great Lord*, and certainly no **Great grief*, which is a pity, because with it we lose the alliteration of the /gr-/ cluster. Notice, incidentally, the utter unlikeliness, not to say complete impossibility of someone's coming out with an exclamation such as **good shit!, *great shit!, *good bull!, *great bull!, *good cow!, *great cow!, *good Moses!, *great Moses!, *good mackerel!, *great mackerel!,* or **good smoke!,* and **great smoke!* We are obviously facing some sort of subtle restriction on productivity here, the nature of which has escaped the attention of most investigators. If we try the adjective *holy* in front of these barred forms (or most of them), we find a whole class of ready-made and highly frequent exclamations: *holy cow!, holy Moses!, holy smoke!, holy mackerel!,* and, alas, contrapunctually desecrating the set, *holy shit!* It is strange that *holy Heavens!, holy God!* are relatively rare in English, since the holiness of both *God* and *Heavens* seems rather beyond dispute; furthermore German has *heiliger Gott!* and *heiliger Himmel!* to bear out our intuition of the collocability of these forms. The German forms cited can be used as much in the awestruck, sincerely religious mode as behind the smirk of a mundane disbeliever indulging himself in profanity: *heiliger Gott/Himmel, meine gute Frau, glauben Sie, dass ich ganz verrückt bin?* 'Holy smoke, my good woman, do you think I am completely crazy?' and not '**Good Lord/Heavens my good woman . . .*' etc. (*Heavens, my good woman . . .* sounds acceptable in a 19th-century Dickensian setting; furthermore a clever playwright can always create an acceptable context for almost anything. My observation here regarding German versus English is that English seems to take 'God' and 'Heavens' more seriously than does German; as exclamations of scolding someone, these sound archaic in 1993 especially in the USA.) The corresponding French forms *sacré Dieu!* and *sacré ciel!* are considered vulgarisms and curses despite the survival of *sacré* as 'saint, holy, consecrated' as in *sacré coeur* the 'Holy Heart (of Jesus)' and are usually rendered euphemistically as *sacré bleu*, *par bleu*, etc.

Since both French and German use their equivalent for 'holy' in exclamations, one might expect that the nouns they carry might be interchanged, but we have no such luck. The English holy class seems to be a closed set, all its own; no language I know will accept as equivalent translations (the forms Ger.) **heilige Kuh!*, **heilige Rauch!*, **heilige Makrele!*, **heiliger Moses!*, and **heilige Scheisse!*; French tolerates no literal translation into **sacrée vache!*, **sacrée fume!*, **sacrée merde!* etc. Forcing English *holy cow!* and *holy smoke!* morphologically into Russian yields the impossibilities **svjataja korova!* and **svjatoj dym!* which sound just as impossible to Russians as would the Hungarian **szent tehén!* and **szent füst!* We must, for the sake of completeness, add *holy Toledo!* to the American English set which makes no sense at all in any of the languages considered so far.

2.4.1. How about generating these? Good grief!

The reader will bear with me for a brief detour. It may seem that we are taking a walk around Robin Hood's Barn just to find that we have stood still all the while; yet as Hockett has insisted more than once (1968a, 1968b) pseudo-progress, too, is a kind of progress inasmuch as it shows with as much specificity as possible just what it is that actually makes a blind alley blind.

Let us turn the clock back mentally and imagine that we are in 1960. R.B. Lees who had recently reviewed Chomsky's *Syntactic Structures* (1957) (Lees 1957), has just finished his *Grammar of English Nominalizations* (1960). Two bold young foreigners, let us call them Günther von Nebelmacher and Gottfried von Schweinemund, respectively, bring to his attention a serious shortcoming of the book before it goes to press. Whereas Lees had discussed adjective + *N* combinations in many senses, touching even on idioms and how they defy generating (cf. Makkai (1972), 165 *et passim*), he paid no attention to exclamations: a most serious defect! Lees is tired of the project and commissions Nebelmacher and Schweinemund to write an appendix to the book so as to incorporate exclamations, as long as they do it in the spirit of generative grammar. How do our friends proceed?

Enthralled with Lees' example of *réd càp*,

'The cap is lying on its side. = = =>
WH + the cap is red. = = =>
The cap which is red is lying on its side. = = =>
The cap red is lying on its side. = = =>
The red cap is lying on its side. = = =>

[But not *the rédcàp is lying on its side, for while cap is an inanimate noun, the compound with *red* and *cap* as head (the *rédcàp*) is an animate noun' (Lees (1960), Ch. IV)], they write a series of transformational rules that generate exclamations.

A 1   The Noun WH Noun Be Adj = = ⇒
   2   The Noun is Adj = = ⇒
   3   The Noun Adj = = ⇒
   4   The Adj Noun = = ⇒
   5   Adj Noun = = ⇒
   6   *Lexicalization:*
   6a   The *cow* WH Cow Be *Holy* = = ⇒
   6b   The *cow* is *holy* = = ⇒
   6c   The *cow holy* = = ⇒
   6d   The *holy cow* = = ⇒
   6e   *Holy cow* = = ⇒
   6f   *Exclamation Transformation* (contour added):
   6g   Holy cow!
B 6   Lexicalization
   6a   *The smoke* WH smoke be *holy* = ⇒
   6b   *The smoke is* holy = ⇒
   6c   The *smoke holy* = ⇒
   6d   The *holy smoke* = ⇒
   6e   *Holy smoke* = ⇒
   6f   *Exclamation Transformation*
   6g   Holy smoke!

It takes them thirteen steps to generate *holy cow!* – where the crucial one
is, of course, 6f, the Exclamation Transformation. Controversy arises, as
some authorities near MIT do not quite see when and where the ET is to
be added, but Nebelmacher and Schweinemund insist that it is post-lexical
and comes from the phonology. The same operation is performed as in sets
A and B on a number of nouns and they thus successfully generate the
entire holy set, including *Moses, Toledo, mackerel*, and *shit*. The trouble is
that they also derive all sorts of 'exclamations' which are not commonly
recognized in the culture. They get, in fact, any adjective and any noun
after lexicalization and 6f, with the right intonation contours added,
yielding an 'exclamation', such as **yellow rose!*, **blue sweater!*, **holy table!*
*holy potato!, **holy gasoline*, **holy cat!*, **good elephant*, etc., and there is
literally nothing to block these forms from occurring.

Ten years have passed, and Nebelmacher and Schweinemund, now
disillusioned with early TG, join the ranks of the generative semanticists.
This gives them a chance to return to some earlier work and they once
again turn their attentions to the perplexing problem of English exclamations. Nebelmacher, who used to minor in comparative theology at the
University of Leipzig, comes up with a semantic restriction rule regarding
the holy set. His argument runs as follows: it is no accident that the holy
set is as restricted as it is. The reason is that the world's major religions
are represented in it. The mackerel, a fish, represents Christianity. Christ
was born in the Piscean Age, and ιχθυσ 'fish' spells Ιησουσ χριστοσ Θεου
Τιοσ Εωτηρ 'Jesus Christ, Son of God, Savior'. *Smoke*, obviously must
refer to Judaism: remember the story of Cain and Abel? But since Judaism

is ancient and strong, it has two references in case 'smoke' does not do it for you: *Holy Moses* is the obvious form. *Holy cow* takes us to India: Brahmanism and Buddhism. Toledo in medieval Spain gained its reputation via Moorish culture: Islam enters the holy set via Spain, a country also very strong in Catholicism. Most of these associations have gone unconscious in the modern age, but in our collective unconscious we are all products of one or other of these great world religions, hence the closed holy set. Everyone is impressed, and Nebelmacher is credited for inventing the 'Holiness Raising' transformation which takes its proper place next to standard 'Raising', 'Pruning', 'Sluicing', 'Feeding', and 'Bleeding'. Schweinemund, forever the devil's advocate in all matters linguistic, finds an ugly fly in the ointment: the *pièce de résistance* is the form *holy shit!* which seems to destroy the 'naturalness conditions' of the closed nature of the holy set. Excited negotiations get under way at MIT and, lo and behold, a simple solution is found: the more general rule of 'holiness raising' operates beside a minor epi-rule, known as the 'Decanonization Transformation' or 'Defrocking', for short. Defrocking applies post-cyclically after lexicalization which, in turn, can only apply after holiness raising. In other words first you raise holiness to see that the semantic naturalness condition applies; without it certain lexical items become exclamations which must be disallowed. Once the holy set is generated, the naturalness condition must be kept, and so the unwelcome occurrence of *shit* in such a noble ecumenically ecclesiastical setting must be explained. Schweinemund argues that the least holy and most reprehensible thing we know is our own human refuse which reminds us of decay and death or 'ashes to ashes, dust to dust' as it says in the Bible. It is, therefore, pseudo-holy, or quasi-holy, as it were, precisely because it is not holy at all, while appearing in its surface structure to belong to the same set. Hence the holiness raised earlier must be erased by the epi-rule of decanonization or defrocking. Prestigious journals carry the new global insight and the set is now generated as follows:

A 1   The Noun WH Noun Be Adj = ⇒
  2   The Noun is Adj = ⇒
  3   The Noun Adj = ⇒
  4   The Adj Noun = ⇒
  5   Adj Noun = ⇒
  6   *Holiness Raising*
  6a   Christianity insertion = ⇒ (Piscean Age)
  6b   Judaism₁ insertion = ⇒ (Cain and Abel)
  6c   Judaism₂ insertion = ⇒ (Ten Commandments)
  6d   Brahmanism and Buddhism insertion = ⇒ (vegetarianism, bovines)
  6e   Islam Insertion = ⇒ (The Moorish Conquest, Ibero-Arabic culture)
  7   *Lexicalization*
  7a   Christianity = ⇒ mackerel

7b   Judaism$_1$ $= \Rightarrow$ smoke
7c   Judaism$_2$ $= \Rightarrow$ Moses
7d   Brahmanism and Buddhism $= \Rightarrow$ cow
7e   Islam $= \Rightarrow$ Toledo
8   *Decanonization (defrocking)*
8a   Disgust $= \Rightarrow$ shit
9   *Exclamation Transformation*
     (contour added from phonology)
10   Output: *holy mackerel!*, *holy smoke!*, *holy Moses!*, *holy cow!*, *holy Toledo!*, *holy shit!*

In twenty steps or so, on one basic generative cycle followed by three epicycles, Nebelmacher and Schweinemund are thus able to account for the well-formed output given in step 10. (They do not mention what blocks *holy terror* from becoming an exclamation.)

The writer is anxious to emphasize that this is, of course, mere speculation, and that resemblance to any real work done by any real linguist in the USA or elsewhere is pure coincidence as no one would ever, under any circumstances, have gone to the detailed research into comparative religion and the theory of the unconscious which, I claim, alone made these derivations possible. I regret it that I was unable to offer Holiness Raising and Defrocking earlier; much futile labor could have been saved and tighter naturalness conditions would have been introduced in a controversial and emotionally loaded compartment of linguistics, the transformational study of exclamations.

2.4.2. *Oh no!* Enter *sociolinguistics and all hell breaks loose*

We are now in the sociolinguistics era. Patients in doctors' offices in poverty stricken neighborhoods are interviewed and their utterances recorded and transcribed; department store attendants are asked how they pronounce whatever they say, etc. Nebelmacher and Schweinemund are alerted to the fact that in the dialect of Robin, Batman's helper in the popular television series 'Batman and Robin', the young assistant can register his admiration and surprise at Batman's heroic exploits by naming almost any noun after *holy* – thus in the Batman and Robin dialect of North American English it is well-formed to exclaim *holy chair!*, *holy table!*, *holy window!*, *holy rope!*, and the like, especially if these objects are somehow tied to a clever escape arranged by Batman for an innocent victim. The floodgates of analogy are thus inadvertently opened and the Holiness Raising Transformation must be rewritten so as to accommodate the [+ Batman and Robin -Normal] epi-feature. Thus they create rule 7f, right after Islam Insertion, known as Batmanization. (Some disgruntled voices accusing the fearless dynamic duo that this is batty are soon silenced from headquarters near the Charles River.) The trouble lies elsewhere. Batmanization happens to be ANALOGICALLY PRODUCTIVE, and the phenomenon spreads into popular parlance when the speakers are not even Batman-wise as to what and why they are exclaiming about. *Holy kengaroo!*, *Holy Income Tax!*, *Holy Watergate!*, *Holy Pot!*, etc., appear on the scene, each living its own linguistic incarnation for as long as the population finds it useful and entertaining.

It appears that the 'holy set' is expandable in yet another interesting way. (I owe this observation to Dwight Bolinger who is, of course, not responsible for any other statement made in this chapter.) Bolinger points out (personal communication), that as long as the NP following *holy* is long, ponderous and somehow quasi-biblical, the adjective form *holy* seems all right. Thus if someone explains *holy pillars of Jerusalem!* with heavy stress on *PILars* and *jerUsalem*, saying it slowly, as if awe-struck, the phrase is quite acceptable. I have also been offered *Holy jumping jackrabbits!* by Eldon G. Lytle. I am struck by the fact that both examples have a noun that starts with /j/ (*jackrabbits, Jerusalem*) and this forces me to think that the old phrase *Holy jumping Jehosaphat*, an obvious euphemism on *Holy jumping Jesus* is at play here in the 'collective unconscious'. It is thus possible to 'create' a number of quasi-ecclesiastic exclamations of the sort:

1)   Holy walls of Jericho!
2)   Holy jingle bells!
3)   Holy Mormon Tabernacle!
4)   Holy Black Stone of Mecca!
5)   Holy Presidential jelly beans!
6)   Holy Collected Poems of Chairman Mao!
7)   Holy Watergate cover-up bullshit!
8)   Holy Bridge of Chappaquiddick!

The reader is invited to create his/her own possible expansions of the 'holy'-set. Some will sound better than others and if the reader has an interest in writing a small dialog for two interactants in a play, performing a scenario, the 'holy'-set will make more sense or less sense in direct proportion to what has preceded and what comes next. When I call the 'holy'-set essentially closed, I nevertheless state a fact about English which is well worth observing. The *adj* + *n* construction *holy terror* does not seem to yield itself to exclaiming despite the obvious presence of *holy* next to a word that describes a mental-emotional state. *Dennis the menace is a holy terror, Evil Knievel is a holy terror, John's old lady is hell on wheels on Mondays, Wednesdays and Fridays and in between she is a holy terror* all accommodate *holy terror* as an idiomatic NP with the meaning 'oppressive personal presence' or something close to it. I have been unable to get **holy terror!* as an exclamation from any native speaker, no matter what the narrative surrounding such a posited exclamation. It is simply not exclaimable; to cry *holy shit!* in a state of terror is much more likely than naming the terror itself. Maybe my imaginary character Schweinemund was onto something after all: it is certainly worth considering that the lexeme *holy*, realizing the sememe [holy, sacred] has some kind of a SEMANTIC COURT with expandable borders to accommodate new subjects who wish to immigrate into the kingdom. As all such 'immigrants', they must take certain eligibility tests ranging from phonological criteria to the lexico-semantic and the morphosyntactic.

2.5. *Famous last words!* Enter *longer Citations and* Exit *Syntax*

We bid fond farewell to Professors Nebelmacher and Schweinemund. They did their best; it was not really their fault that the paradigm they were working in burst at the seams as soon as facts were allowed to enter; in fact what happened was that it turned out it was no paradigm at all!

Having seen what difficulties even the relatively simple Adj + *N* construction can land us in, we would be well advised to give different accounts to the longer Adj + Adj + *N* construction, as encountered in the famous *famous last words!* meaning something like 'watch out, what you said may turn out the opposite' for which, of course, English has a much older and better established sememic idiom borrowed directly from Aesop, *Don't count your chickens before they're hatched!* These are, in a sense, paraphrases of one another, though of course not exact synonyms. We are confronted with the simple fact that a longer citation, learned as one unit and frequently not analyzed by speakers at all, can function as exclamations *qua* warnings, adages, proverbial summaries of folk wisdom, etc.

In a small, politically troubled country in Eastern Europe such as Hungary, where I grew up, and where Shakespearian drama translation was a vigorous force in the development of the national language in the 19th century, quotations from a given Shakespeare play are often used as exclamations.[3] One of the most frequently used ones is *Something is rotten in the State of Denmark!* meaning 'our government is up to no good again'. There is no available equivalent in American English; as a general approximation of the kind of exclamation that this is, a kind of resigned humor of the gallows, one could cite the general *O, oh! There we go again!* which can, of course, be two separate exclamations or a double one used on the same occasion. At the end of *A Midsummer Night's Dream* when the artisans hold their performance for Oberon and Titania depicting the story of Pyramus and Thisbe, a lion roars near a hedge to which Pyramus responds by saying *Well roared, lion!* In the classical translation of J. Arany, he gives Hungarian *Helyes a bőgés, oroszlán!* 'correct (is) the roaring lion!' which has become a high frequency proverbial exclamation in Hungary. Every time somebody silly says something pompous or unnecessary, the attendant grown-up or more knowledgeable person intones the Hungarian version of *Well roared, lion!* It is impossible to give the exact shade of meaning: I will call this kind of exclamation PHATIC CONDESCENSION in memory of Malinowski's term 'phatic communion'. The above quote from Hamlet *Something is rotten in the State of Denmark!*, by contrast, would be a case of PHATIC COMMISERATION.

The exclamation which heads this section, *Famous last words!* is neither phatic condescension nor commiseration; it is a different kind of phatic act. It is a friendly warning both to the interlocutor of the ego and to the ego's own self, comparable to the cultural phenomenon of 'knocking on wood' or as the British call it 'touching wood'. I will call it a PHATIC DISCLAIMER.

3. Some theoretical conclusions

I think it should be reasonably clear after reading sections 2.4.1 and 2.4.2 where our exclamations do NOT come from. They do not come from non-exclamatory noun phrases, whether the 'underlying noun phrase' (nothing, of course, lies under anything else in linguistics, nor above or beside: things co-exist) was a single word or longer construction of the types discussed above. If, in order to say *ouch!* (cf. Hockett (1958), p. 201) I need a 'performative deep structure' with a full NP and a full VP later to be deleted that says *NP: I VP: Say onto you Dependent NP: OUCH!* with everything deleted and only the *ouch!* retained, I will have spent more time on deriving the form than there was between my first shock of pain and my instantaneous exclamation of *ouch!* The performative deep structure analysis is a red herring and should be held up to public ridicule. Yet one cannot deny that *ouch!* is something the speaking ego says to others or to himself. But we know this, as it is an intrinsic part of our culture that we address each other. We are not brainless robots constantly in need of reminding ourselves of what we do: I can say *go!* to my dog without saying to myself first *'I am now saying to my dog "Go"!'* Our phatic behavior as humans (in the sense of Malinowski) renders it superfluous to 'derive' acts of a phatic nature, such as exclamations, from full sentences used elsewhere in the language. I would like to call the *ouch!* type an AUTOPHATIC EXCLAMATION. It will be uttered, instantaneously and automatically, even if no one is around to overhear it.

3.1. Exclamations as a special case of idiomaticity

I believe that exclamations, in so far as they are, to a very large extent, INSTITUTIONS IN A GIVEN CULTURE, are best viewed as a special case of idiomaticity. They qualify as such on several grounds. The meaning 'I am greatly surprised with positive and/or negative overtones' is not logically deducible either from the holiness of cows, mackerels, Moses, smoke, or the blemish in the holy set; nor is the meaning 'beware of your bragging' from *Famous last words!* This is not to deny that these meanings are partly SUGGESTED by some subset of the semantic features of the participant lexemes. More importantly, these exclamations are SET EXPRESSIONS which a person not familiar with them, even if he knows the grammar perfectly, cannot make up at will. Problems arise, as we have seen, when such semantically opaque and closed sets suddenly become productive, at least for awhile and at least in a certain section of society, as we have seen in the case of Batman and Robin's rapidly expanding *holy*-set. There is, of course, no way to predict whether this productivity will remain associated with *holy*-words thirty or forty years from now; the survival of the 'limited holy set', by contrast, seems relatively easy to foresee.

But just by saying that certain expressions are 'idiomatic' we have not really accounted for their existence, their internal structure, or their provenience. To explain the provenience of these forms could only be accomplished as a rigorous diachronic research project which would take years and is, painfully obviously, beyond the scope of this chapter. Nevertheless, certain tentative generalizations can be attempted:

1. Mankind universally exclaims as part of its PHATIC BEHAVIOR.
2. Exclamations can be divided into two types:
   a) The ego identifies with the object of his phatic act (pleasure, joy, etc.).
   b) The ego rejects the object of his phatic act (pain, anger, etc.).
3. This kind of phatic behavior antedates learned lexical and grammatical speech and starts in all human groups in the earliest infancy; it is co-ordinated with facial and bodily gestures (grimace and frown, clenched fist for rejection, smile, cooing, etc., for joy and pleasure).
4. The sensation of surprise, encountering the unexpected, factors out into the a) and the b) types (under 2) allowing a wide range of gradience between the two extremes.
5. The socially controlled logical lexico-grammatical speech which replaces the infant's arche-speech during and in the wake of primary socialization (roughly age 6), assigns certain previously used portions of the lexicon for the traditional encoding of both the identifying and the rejecting types of phatic acts. (The expression *holy Mary, mother of God* has the same lexeme *holy* in it as does the exclamation *holy cow!* which has the same lexeme *cow* in it as the sentence *the farmer bought a new cow.*) The selection of already existing lexical items for the tagging of positively or negatively colored exclamations most probably proceeds along the lines of metaphorical extension (cf. Makkai 1975), but the 'rhyme or reason' of a particular choice seems arbitrary under synchronic investigation.
6. Thus the available lexico-grammatical apparatus is much too inadequate for the expressing of the flow of human emotions. This has a dual result:
   a) People create new exclamations by analogy.
   b) People mean more than one thing by the 'same' exclamation.
7. 6b is regulated PHONOPSYCHOSEMANTICS.

4. Psychophonosemantics and multiple coding in live speech

As the pioneering research of Iván Fónagy has convincingly shown
(Fónagy (1976), (1983), and in press), the live human voice resists the
tyranny of lexico-grammatical categorizations and claims continual access
to the symbolization process, as if every individual user of a language were
engaged in an ongoing battle to expand and modify the socially agreed
upon meanings of the common lexeme stock. This tendency, of course, is
more noticeable in the area of PSYCHOSEMEMES than in the areas of the
COGNOSEMEMES and TECHNOSEMEMES (see Chapter 9). Generally,
psychosememes are the meanings of those lexemes which a child acquires
during primary socialization, up to leaving the home for kindergarten
and/or the first grade. Definitions of the lexeme stock are never verbal but
ostensive, as no one ever needs a definition for *daddy* or *mommy* as 'male
parent' and 'female parent'. They are hugged and they feed us, if things
are normal; if not they shout and hit us, etc. Thus the child acquires the
meanings of these words unconsciously; hence the term psychosememes.
Cognosememes are acquired in the grades through exposure to reading
materials. Definition are given verbally or by pictorial illustration. The
names of animals, ranging from *ostrich* to *duck-billed platypus* are such
cognosememes, so are the terms *anticipation*, *pledge*, *allegiance*, etc., which
must all be learned consciously. *Doggy* and *kitty cat* in most homes are
acquired psychosememically: the creatures are simply members of the
family. Technosememes are acquired as one acquires tools and their use;
as terms in the upper grades of high school, college and graduate school.
The terms *phoneme*, *morphophoneme*, *syntax*, and *idiom* are all technosememes.

Psychophonosemantic multiple-coding primarily affects, then, psychosememes, and the more emotionally colored lower ranges of our
cognosememes, but does not seem to have much effect on medical
discourse, the language of a well argued legal writ, a deed, or a technical
treatise on formal linguistics. I have devoted a long essay (Makkai 1975b)
to documenting how a theory of human language that fails to take multiple
coding into account is bound to be a failure. In terms of the written
language idioms, jokes, allusions, and translation, 'literature', for short,
cannot be accomplished if simultaneous multiple coding is not allowed. No
known brand of Transformational Generative Grammar is capable of
handling simulcoding to date, hence its characterization as a failure.

The human voice, in particular, Fónagy argues, is as individual as our
finger prints or our signature. Logical lexico-grammatical discourse about
business, education, and politics, in short, civilization, has become possible
because *Homo sapiens* accepted the necessity of an arbitrary code which is
traditionally learned. The ADULT and the PARENTAL ego state
(comparable to the Freudian EGO and SUPEREGO, cf. Makkai (1978)) are
particularly well suited to function via socially regulated lexicogrammatical
norms. But the individual's most creative, inner self, his CHILD
(comparable to the Freudian ID) rebels against the lexicogrammatical
norms and tries to transcend them in every possible way. The socially most

adjustable, even commercially successful, version of such rebellions may be termed POETRY. The poets e.e. cummings and Edgar Guest may have used a large number of identical lexemes and grammar, yet Edgar Guest remains a not very highly regarded poet and e.e. cummings remains the century's linguistically most rebellious genius in modern American English. Their individual styles are unmistakable. T.S. Eliot and Ogden Nash may have used words and constructions that were common to both of them as speakers of English; yet Nash's charm and verbal playfulness is all his own and Eliot's greatness in the *Four Quartets* remains unparalleled and outdone perhaps only by Ezra Pound in the *Cantos*. In each case mentioned here an artist has used his CHILD, took his rebellious attitudes, his playful inventiveness, and mapped that into novel arrangements of the available lexicogrammatical patterns for consumption by other adults in the written medium.

But not every one succeeds in translating his inner speech into socially valued art, whereas every human being appears to have this tripartition of the personality. The commonest manifestation of the inner child, then, is through our voice and the meanings it adds to or subtracts from the socially accepted, standard average dictionary meanings of our lexicons. The human voice does not lie; just like preverbal children, it does not know how to tell a lie. Thus when the lexicogrammar forces it to say something it does not quite mean, the voice compensates for it by grafting a private meaning onto the lexicogrammatically extant one at hand.

Let us revisit, with this in mind, some of our examples discussed earlier in this chapter. Let us take the example *Good grief!*, a popular exclamation in American English. Lexicogrammatically and logically, it is somewhat of a contradiction; *grief* has, usually, negative connotations such as 'sadness', 'sorrow', 'pain', 'loss', and 'mourning'; the lexeme *good*, on the other hand means 'not bad', 'joyous', 'favorable', 'advantageous for me', etc. Thus a grief that is good is hard to imagine and calls for some moral parable such as 'too much fun is bad for you because you will become irresponsible; an occasional grief, on the other hand, is good for you, because it will sober you and make you mature'. Obviously people when they exclaim *Good grief!* do not think about these matters and just use the ready-made phrase on tap, since it is a convenient pre-fab, to use Bolinger's most fitting term (1976). But this involves the ego in an emotional contradiction: should he/she emphasize the 'good' part or the 'grief' part of the exclamation? And so it happens that exclaiming *Good grief!* can be done both belly-achingly, self-pityingly, lugubriously, mournfully, pessimistically, defiantly, and delightedly, happily, light-headedly, and optimistically. (Due to Charlie Brown, whose favorite phrase it is, it is most often heard in a mood of crestfallenness and lack of self-confidence.) However it can be chuckled sarcastically and unbelievingly, as if separating the syllables into GOO-OOD GRIE-IEF; or in mock-surprise upon seeing the very largest pumpkin on Halloween Day *good GRIEF!!!* (eyes rolling in mock fear). The point of these quasi-descriptions and quasi-classifications here is that private though the inner speech is, it, too, comes

in observable patterns and these can be correlated with physically observable and recordable phonological contours. This is the essence of Iván
Fónagy's research into the functions of the live human voice. A highly
trained instrumental phonetician equally at home in Edinburgh, Ann
Arbor, Stockholm, Vienna, Paris, and Budapest – currently residing in
Paris – Fónagy, in his several studies of 1976, 1976a and 1983, has
succeeded in giving objectively quantified evaluations, 'emicizations of
allos', in a way, of what major types of multiple coding there are in human
languages. Most of his examples come from his native Hungarian but there
are also many French, German, English and other examples as well.

The child, who thrives to retain the arche-language of itself developed
prior to the acquisition of the lexicogrammatical norm of its family,
survives under the diplomas of the grown up and in constant dialectical
tension against the norm, creates new meanings by the thousands every
day. We cannot dismiss this as the 'idiolect' of the individual since the
idiolect itself is largely lexicogrammatical speech imbued and interwoven
with the inflections of the inner voice. Thus the voice, a phonologically
observable event, carries meanings into grammar and lexis, signalling
directly unobservable but in effect clearly manifest psychological states. In
other words the carrier is phonology, the content is semantics, and the
source is the individual's emotional states. There is nothing mystical or
'mentalistic' about this; the average well trained family physician knew it
a hundred years ago and said to bewildered parents 'your son talks nicely
but sounds and looks mean; have a word with him to see what's bothering
him, and his headaches will go away'.

Hence the term PSYCHOPHONOSEMANTICS. Currently still unrecognized
in America, the phenomena it promises to be able to treat will encompass
what is currently relegated to the ill defined area of 'speech acts'. There
is something Jakobsonian about it (amounting to his notion of *Gesamt-
bedeutungen*); the questions raised range from Saussure through Wells (1958)
to Halliday. American structuralists, by and large, tended to stay away
from discussing inobservables and concentrated their energy on the careful
display of overt data. This was correct scientific behavior couched in
modesty and integrity, but it also landed the profession in the turmoil of
the Transformationalist-Generativist movement which started in 1957.
Transformationalists tend to call themselves 'mentalists', but have created
some of the largest and most awkward taxonomies in the field –
taxonomies of rules instead of taxonomies of facts. Section 2.4.1 of this
chapter offers a parody of their approach to the treatment of data. As the
century progresses and previously incredible achievements of mankind,
such as the manned lunar landing in July of 1969, become household
conversation topics, we can entertain the vision of an objective cataloguing
of those facets of language which are not directly observable without falling
prey to pseudo-mentalism which is, to use Talmy Givón's adroit phrase,
'structuralism with a vengeance'. This chapter is a modest attempt at
answering Wells' question in 1958: is a Structural Description of Semantics
Possible? We have seen the pseudo results of the twenty-five years. Formal

explicitness, although a virtue, cannot account for natural language use without a theory of context, tenor, and register, as in Halliday (1978). The desired synthesis will be ecological linguistics, or ECOLINGUISTICS, for short. To understand and to practice ECOLINGUISTICS, one must approach the field with the peripathetic openmindedness and tolerance I have experienced for the first time in my life at Yale University, when I first came into contact with Rulon S. Wells. Peripatetic open-mindedness is an attitude that approaches all movements within linguistics with creative curiosity. As the first major American exponent of syntax through Immediate Constituents (Wells 1947), Wells has shown that a Harris-type structuralist approach to syntax is certainly possible; furthermore, it is reasonably clear that the study of surface structure will gain new recognition in all modes of theoretical linguistics. (Chomsky, for example, no longer seeks meaning entirely in 'Deep Structure', much of meaning is now found in surface structure as well.)

Since exclamations are, as we have seen, to a large extent idiomatic, we must recognize that live language is stored in chunks and units in memory beyond the size of the single word. Sometimes the meaning is transparent, sometimes it is opaque; in all cases there is something unpredictable either about the semantics or about the construction. We have learned from stratificational grammar (Makkai 1972a) that idioms are hard to generate and that LEXEMIC and SEMEMIC STRATA of a natural language offer convenient places for the storage and retrieval of idioms. Yet it is clear that idioms have both internal and external syntax; not to study that in detail would be to ignore overt data. Exclamation idioms in particular, however, ride on PHONOLOGICAL INTONATIONS, which, invariably, CARRY MEANING. To understand exclamations, then, we need all of the following:

a)   Knowledge of the syntax of the utterance, both internal and external.
b)   Knowledge of the morphologies involved.
c)   Knowledge of the appropriateness conditions for the exclamation; this involves:
    (i)   thorough familiarity with a theory of 'speech acts' or
    (ii)   a knowledge of the register and tenor of the explanation, and a
    (iii)   theory of context, which must be sociolinguistically and semiotically based.
d)   The meaning of the exclamation is of central importance, of course, both as a matter of lexicography (static view), and syntactic operability (dynamic view), but it rests on
e)   the phonological realization of the utterance – see the role of intonation discussed above.
f)   Meaning through phonology is in its infancy in the United States, despite major advances made by scholars such as Dwight Bolinger; furthermore, it involves the researcher in
g)   psycho-linguistics of the psychiatric-transactional type.

ECOLINGUISTICS rests on these seven foundations. Fact, overt observation; introspection, study of context, syntax, semantics, morphology, and phonology are inextricably interwoven in the study of exclamations. Would Bloomfield have shied away from studying exclamations? It is unfair to guess. He would have argued that we needed much faster and better access to much more and much better classified information. But that was in 1933, and this is sixty years later in 1993. Even the large capacity IBM computers of the 1960s are outmoded; this is the age of the microchip computer with the video-screen, easily available to all who need one. It is perhaps no accident that cognitive stratificational linguistics should be so closely tied with computer research through the work of Sydney M. Lamb: both Lamb and Halliday view human language as a large semiotic system in the last analysis. Wells' question of nearly thirty years ago, 'Is a Structural Treatment of Semantics Possible?' can now be answered with a more than tentative, cautious 'yes'. Oddly enough no single theoretical model can do the job; we need the synthesis of Tagmemics (with its -emes- and -allos, field, particle and wave modalities); Systemic-Functional Grammar (Halliday's concept of Language as Social Semiotic), Lamb's cognitive-stratificational theory via computer, and the classical theories of analogy, formation of neologisms, etc. Set theory and logic and transformational sentence derivation can also be shown to play a part, although a minor one, and often one that yields negative results. The systemization of all of these currents into a truly viable ECOLINGUISTICS calls for rigor and logic but also presupposes more than just cold-headed, detached scholarship. Could one call it a love of language?

Notes

1. For some historical insights see McDavid and Mencken (1963, pp. 395, 629, 677), etc. The form *holy jumping Jesus!* is cited as having vanished toward 1890. Bolinger (1975, p. 308), one of the best recent textbooks on general linguistics, discusses exclamations in a chapter dealing with the origin of language in connection with holophrasis. This is in essential agreement with Hockett's interesting but short treatment of exclamations in (1958, p. 201) where exclamations are treated as 'minor types' of sentences, or 'fragments'. Hockett writes: 'Strong emotion, or its simulation, may produce *exclamatory* fragments: *Ouch! Goodness gracious! The devil you say!*' Standard discussions are available in various older traditionalist treatments of English grammar. See also Wentworth and Flexner (1960, p. 264) under *holy cow!*, Boatner, Gates and Makkai (1975–1977, p. 162) under the same entry.

    Several sources, especially McDavid and Mencken, and Wentworth and Flexner treat the *holy* set as euphemisms for *Holy Jesus!*. This might have interesting consequences for section 2.4.1.

    Other, now extinct exclamations, perhaps still remembered by the older generation such as *jumpin' jimminie cricket!* and *jumpin' (holy) Jehosaphat!* were left unmentioned in this essentially synchronic treatment.

2. This situation may be changing as sentences such as *Man, I'm telling you, I'm*

beat are more frequently heard even among middle class white women in intellectual professions, such as teachers among themselves during coffee break, etc.

3. Hungary is by no means unique in having adopted Shakespeare as a national saint through literature. Shakespearian proverbs have, of course, originated in British culture and were exported with the dramatic output itself; many translators knew what lines had become proverbial in the original English which alerted them to outdo themselves in translating those particular lines. The same lines are, for those who read Shakespeare anyway, among the better known and more easily recognized ones. Generally speaking, however, in modern American English, unless one is in the company of literature majors or professors, one does not hear a great deal of Shakespearian quotation in commenting on instances of everyday life; 'to be or not to be,' and 'he shuffled off this mortal coil' have almost become forbidden as trite. I have not once in twenty-seven years in the USA encountered a spontaneous comment from any native American speaker about politics using 'something is rotten in the State of Denmark' (not even during Watergate), and I have never been able to observe 'well roared, lion' from an adult to an excessively vocal youngster. Accordingly, I try to use them myself in an attempt to find out if they are at least recognized, which they frequently are, though sometimes not. It is my understanding that even in Britain 'to exclaim in Shakespeare' is a generational phenomenon found more typical of older people and regarded as snobbery by most.

9 How does a *SEMEME* mean?

0. In customary stratificationalist parlance (Lamb 1964, 1965, 1966, Lockwood 1972, Makkai 1972, 1973, 1974, 1975; Makkai and Lockwood [Eds.] 1973) one refers to the SEMEME as the REALIZATE OF A LEXEME, or that piece of fragment of a network of man's cognitive knowledge that the given lexeme happens to realize. For technical and working purposes such a definition of the sememe is quite satisfactory and one need take no further issue with it. The evolution of the concept is fairly straight as well: in Bloomfield's *Language* (1933) the term SEMEME refers to the meaning of a morpheme. Bloomfield offered no clear distinction between morpheme and lexeme, however, and this lack of clarification, which fifty years later looks like a most useful distinction (cf. V.B. Makkai 1973, A. Makkai 1972), meant foregoing the benefit of a powerful generalization. The morpheme–lexeme problem shows up powerfully in Hockett's *Course in Modern Linguistics* (1958) especially in Chapters 36 and 37, clearly implying although not specifically mentioning sememes. In anthropological literature (Conklin 1962) the lexeme-concept is used for polymorphemic constructs whose meaning remains unpredictable from the sum of the components, thus also implying sememes as the realizates of lexemes. A great deal of unnecessary labor involving 'syntactic constraints' on certain sentences could have been avoided in transformational-generative work had the sememe–lexeme–morpheme trichotomy been understood and practiced by MIT-oriented linguists.

The reason for this neglect of a most useful principle in linguistics arises partly from the fact that it is difficult to explain to linguistics of other persuasions, to students, etc., just what it is that the stratificationalist means by the term SEMEME. One of the most frequent reactions one receives is skepticism regarding the realism of the sememe–lexeme–morpheme trichotomy, as people tend to see one-to-one isomorphism in instances such as [S]/sun/, 'the star around which Earth revolves' realized as the [L]/sun/, a noun, further realized as the basic morpheme [M]/sun/. Why not just have the morpheme /sun/ whose meaning is thus-and-such and leave it at that? It seems like wasteful and unnecessary duplication to reintroduce the element /sun/ on these various levels. Stratificationalists, of

course, simply use the labels S, L, and M as convenient shorthand notation to differentiate between the meaning, the dictionary entry, and its
basic form; but the situation, both for the skeptic and the novice, is
aggravated by the fact that the common English word *s*, *u*, *n* is somehow
present on all three of these levels. Could it be that words exist
simultaneously on three strata? Which words? Only monosyllabic and
simple ones, some, or perhaps all?

In this chapter, then, I will try to suggest some ways of looking at the
sememe–lexeme–morpheme trichotomy from the point of view of a modified
brand of stratificationalism to be called SOCIAL INTERACTION PSYCHOLOGY
(henceforth SIP) – something I consider to be a fundamental factor in the
ecology of human communication, and therefore, perhaps, a more convincing explanation of the earlier, more mechanical stratification model (cf.
Makkai 1976). Insofar as this chapter is more concerned with a detailed
description of meaning as it changes and expands than with a presentation
of structural mechanisms (which does not imply that these two are mutually
exclusive, contradictory, or irrelevant), I will use practically no relational
network diagramming such as is customary in stratificationalism. The
diagrams, in any event, do not make the theory, even if some colleagues will
disagree about this. Hockett's review (1968) of Lamb's *Outline* (1966) made
the same point. I disagreed with Hockett for roughly a decade, but have
come gradually closer to his position. Whereas relational networks do, in
certain instances, capture generalizations in a visual fashion based on the
logical operators AND, OR, ORDERED, UNORDERED, UPWARD (towards
meaning) and DOWNWARD (toward expression), if the underlying thinking
cannot be stated in commonly accessible expository prose, the diagram itself
fails to communicate. The observations offered here, then, could be regarded
as a new thrust within the family of stratificational grammars and could be
called PRAGMO-ECOLOGICAL GRAMMAR, or, following Einar Haugen's
excellent suggestion, ECOLINGUISTICS for short.

1. A very young child, still under one year of age, when asked 'where is
the sun?' can point towards the sky and say nothing. Would it be fair to
assume that such a quasi-communicator has no idea whatever about what
the sun really is? I think it would be a gross underestimation of the child's
intelligence to do so. Yet, obviously, such a child cannot DEFINE what the
sun is, somewhat as a junior in high school could. Growing older, the child
will have more and more experience of the sun. Some of these will be
enjoyable experiences, such as getting tanned on a beach, and some will
be painful, such as getting burned if over-exposed. Some people, in later
adulthood, might develop economical considerations relating to the sun, as
solar energy might be thought of as a cheap and steady replacement for
other sources of energy. Farmers and gardeners will have yet other occasions when thinking about the sun, as sunlight affects the growing season
in different parts of North America depending on the latitude. Even blind
people have certain notions about the sun; after all it can be FELT, turned
toward and followed, not just seen.

Under bilingual conditions a person of average intelligence has little difficulty translating *sun* into French *soleil*, Hungarian *nap*, German *Sonne*, Italian *sole*, Russian солнце , or whatever. On the other hand, relatively few adults, no matter how well educated, seem to feel comfortable and ready to provide a formal dictionary definition of the English lexeme *sun*, such as is found, for instance, in *Webster's New Collegiate Dictionary* (1974, p. 1167):

> The luminous celestial body around which the Earth and other planets revolve, from which they receive heat and light, and which has a mean distance from the Earth of 93,000,000 miles, a linear diameter of 864,000 miles, a mass 332,000 times greater than Earth, and a mean density about one fourth that of Earth.

(Additional cross-references are offered about the planets, the history of the knowledge developed concerning the sun, etc.) It is an interesting experiment asking fluent and well-educated native speakers to come up with definitions of common terms such as *sun*, *moon*, *mother*, *father*, *brother*, *sister*, *hand*, *arm*, *foot*, etc. Most people tend to hesitate; some feel either irritated or amused, but certainly all feel surprised and quite often remark: 'Why define these words? Any fool knows what they are.' And this is, of course, from their point of view, a completely sensible objection. Yet there is no dictionary on the market today that would omit the definitions of terms such as these. Reading these definitions one has the feeling that more information is given that necessary; that the definitions are somehow pedantic. Did you, on reading these lines, know the mean distance of the sun from Earth? How much greater its mass is, with its mean density only a quarter of Earth's? How about the sun's linear diameter? How relevant is this information to your knowledge of when to plant corn, cabbages and tomatoes? To your decision whether to go for a swim or not? I, who am engaged in the writing of this chapter, recall having had some vague familiarity with these details but certainly could not have quoted them accurately and doubt if I will, unless I purposely memorize such 'facts and figures'; I would have to look them up in a reliable reference book or dictionary. Does this mean that my sememe of the lexeme *sun* VACILLATES IN ITS FOCUS AND ITS PRECISION depending on whether I am talking in general terms about the sun or I am consulting an encyclopaedia? I am a linguist, not an astronomer, but I can use a library and get hold of a tome on the sun and read it. Does my sememic realizate of the English word *sun* change in any way during and after my reading of a special book on the sun? My two-year-old daughter, who is well on her way to speaking in full sentences but who still produces fewer words than she understands, seems to recognize the word *sun* when we walk to the window together and I ask her about it. My eleven-year-old, who just finished the 6th grade, strongly feels that 'the definition is unnecessary'; when I point out that it belongs to science education, she accepts it. The idea of ninety-three million miles – astronomically certainly no great distance – remains, however, quite ungraspable to me; I derive no appreciable difference in sensation upon hearing ninety-three million miles versus, say, one hundred ninety-six million or seventy-five million miles. It is intriguing but existentially superfluous information when I compare it to 'I live 33 miles from work', something I can feel in my tired muscles. Who, then, REALLY KNOWS what the sememe ^{S}/sun/ is? Does my two-year-old have that sememe? My eleven-year-old? I, their father, who am not an astronomer but a person who can use a dictionary? Do I have it temporarily while I read the definition, only to lose it a few seconds later? Do some astronomers specializing in our sun? Or lexicographers of various languages and nationalities congregating at some conference and comparing their definitions of their native word for English *sun*? And how can a multilingual individual, even a child, so readily translate the English word into its equivalent terms when it is not at all certain that such speakers possess an adequate definition of the lexeme at all?

I will, in this chapter, then NOT try to explain what a sememe is because, although interesting, that way of putting the question can lead to formulations that will, on the one hand, seem unmanageably profound (e.g. a Ph.D. thesis in celestial mechanics with primary emphasis on solar evolution or on solar eclipses) and, on the other, overly simplistic. Frustrated though we may feel at times with the customary statement that a sememe is the realizate of a lexeme, this definition is really not as bad as it seems, because it leaves it open to further, and not necessarily linguistic, investigation of just what the nature of the realizate in question actually is. The question to be raised is rather this: HOW does a sememe mean? Or rather, how is meaning evoked from a complex bundle of realizates by the triggering mechanism of the lexeme?

In approaching this question I would like to say that all of us, my two-year-old, my eleven-year-old, I, my colleague the astronomer, and Johann Wolfgang von Goethe, who in the opening lines of *Faust* declares that the sun is music ('die Sonne tönt, nach alter Weise, in Brudersphären, Wettgesang') k, n, o, w – each in our own way – what the sun is, but our k, n, o, w, l, e, d, g, e differs in scope, intensity, detail, style, and sophistication. It is my thesis that sememes come in a hierarchy of SOCIO-PSYCHOLOGICAL STRATIFICATION within the cognitive system of any given hearer-speaker, and that this socio-psychological stratification is not quite the same sort of stratification we are accustomed to talk about in cognitive linguistics, but one that correlates with the age at which it was acquired, with the relative frequency with which it is used in the spoken nontechnical daily language of normal human interaction, and with the SOCIO-PSYCHOLOGICAL OBVIOUSNESS (SPO) of the referent(s) in question. (Cf. Ogden and Richards 1923–1953.)

I will posit, as an initial working hypothesis, a threefold structure in the cognitive system, as follows:

I   Psychosememes
II Cognosememes
III Technosememes.

I will try to explain, expand and justify this threefold hierarchy within the cognitive system, giving due credit for the numerous exceptions that can be found in various societies around the world as well as in English-speaking North America, Britain, and other Commonwealth countries.

2. From the point of view of what follows, the question raised in section 0, i.e. whether sememe, lexeme, and morpheme 'are the same or not', seems actually irrelevant; still it would be negligent not to discuss the issue, however briefly. The case of the item *sun* is 'special' in the sense that it belongs to a class of nouns which, by virtue of being monomorphemic, do not require analysis on the morphological level. In the sense of Hockett (1958, pp. 172–3) *s*, *u*, *n* would be an idiom since *s* + *u* + *n* do not add up to 'luminous heavenly body'; but as I have argued (1972) in detail, the use of the term IDIOM here is off by one stratum; the term LEXEME accomplishes exactly what Hockett was after when making room for further analysis of complex lexemes such as *sunflower*, *sunstroke*, *sun-bath*, etc. My own analysis of idioms, it turns out, was deficient not in the sense that it separated lexemic from sememic idioms with a possibility of recognizing hypersememic idioms as well, but rather in the sense that it failed to call proper attention to MORPHEMIC IDIOMS, a feature particularly important for English. Thus it has been pointed out by Sullivan (1980) that lexemes such as *preoccupied*, *conductor*, and *conducive* are 'idiomatic' in the morphological sense: their particular combination both in terms of what occurs and what does not, has something arbitrary about it, as do the meanings. We do not have **co(n)occupied* or **preductor*, or **preducive*; the meanings that are manifest in a sentence such as *a preoccupied conductor is not conducive to a good performance* are arrived at by a tacit 'social contract' among users of these forms. *Preoccupied* COULD actually mean 'occupied in advance'; *conductor*, beside meaning 'music director', 'streetcar or subway official' and 'element that transmits electricity' COULD also mean 'tourist guide book' or 'tourist guide'; it could also be used for a compass. The restriction of *conducive* to describing certain desirable psychological states is quite arbitrary; roads could, without any violation of logic, be called conducive if it is easy to drive on them, etc. The three lexemes mentioned, then, are morphologically idiomatic, whereas *s*, *u*, *n* is not. We do have to ascertain, however, whether we are dealing with the noun *sun* or with the verb *sun*. The morphological class – verb or noun – is easy to identify: it applies to a large number of monosyllabic English nouns of AS provenience, e.g. *hand*, *man*, *wash*, etc. (*John is sunning himself by the pool*; *he has sunned himself*; *Sue can man the post better than her husband Max*; *hand me the sugar!*) In contrast, *preoccupied*, *conductor*, and *conducive*, are single lexemes of bimorphemic composition, hence MORPHEMIC IDIOMS. Longer, multiword entries such as *Human Relations Area Files*, *University of Illinois at Chicago Circle*, *dogwood*, *blackbird*, *hot dog*, *The White House*, *understand*, *go in for*, *withstand*, etc., are LEXEMIC IDIOMS as analyzed and described by Makkai (1972a). Complex lexemes of this sort frequently retain the irregular morphological behavior of a main constituent: *undergo*, *go in for* do not have

the pasts *undergoed, *goed in for, but the expected (although irregular) *under-went, went in for*; *understand, withstand*, form their respective past tenses as *understood* and *withstood*, and not as *understanded, *withstanded*. Not accounting for these facts on the morphological level amounts to missing an important generalization no school of thought in linguistics, past or present, or any other science for that matter, could possibly consider elegant. We say, then, that *undergo* 'suffer, sustain, endure' INFLECTS IDENTICALLY with the simpler root verb *go*, although synchronically there is no relationship between the sememe 'propel oneself on foot' and 'endure, suffer, sustain'. In stratificational terms we have been accounting for this by saying that the morpheme ^{M}/go/ is present in the lexeme *undergo*, whereas the lexeme ^{L}/go/ is not.

The situation is roughly comparable to a tall building that has several sets of elevator banks in it with some elevators stopping only at the 15th floor and up, and with others stopping at every floor below the 15th as well. It would depend on the needs of the person entering the building whether he took the express elevator or the local one. The lexeme *sun*, in this context, is comparable to the express elevator that does not have to stop at intermediate floors, whereas *undergo*, in order to explain how its past tense is formed, is comparable to the local elevator. Now elevator engineers face a dilemma: should they actually construct different elevator shafts for the local and the express passengers, or should they perhaps allow THE SAME ELEVATOR SOMETIMES TO GO LOCAL, AND SOMETIMES TO GO EXPRESS? Using different sets of push-buttons, the same elevator could be 'reprogrammed' to function either as local or as express, as the need arose. Natural languages such as English seem to have evolved like the sophisticated elevator that can either stop at various floors below the 15th, or go straight through. This would depend on the 'passengers', i.e. the lexemes (and their sponsors, the realizates). The lexeme *sun* (n) is an express passenger who has no need to stop at any intermediate floor, whereas *undergo*, etc. are local passengers who must stop at the intermediate floor in order to reveal how their past tenses are formed.

When a lexeme is morphologically simple, like *sun*, the sememe and the morpheme can be collapsed; or, to put it another way, the lexeme *sun (n)* functions simultaneously as its own morphological container. Morphologically complex lexemes, on the other hand, and especially in the case of inflecting languages, relate to their realizates, the sememes in a more complex fashion, especially if their constituent morphemes happen to overlap with lexemes elsewhere that have their own semantic realizates. Correct and incorrect guessing is invited in the decoding of such lexemes. The lexeme *hót dòg*, despite the special idiom-indicating stress pattern, may suggest a 'canis familiaris domesticus' whose temperature happens to be 'calidus' rather than a 'grilled or boiled frankfurter in a bun'. This happens primarily to foreigners and children; furthermore, cultural borrowing via calquing reinforces one's suspicions that the term IS misunderstandable. In countries that share a common border with the USA, the term *hot dog* tends to be calqued: in Mexico and Puerto Rico one orders a *perro caliente* (or, with the diminutive, *perrito caliente*); in Canada one hears *chien chaud* for the same. In Spain and France, on the other hand, the English term is borrowed in its original form though pronounced, of course, according to French and Spanish articulatory habits. Similarly *The White House* has been loan-translated into every language; we have *la maison blanche*, *la casa bianca*, Белый дом, to mention just a few. If these items were 'express elevator passengers' these literal calques would not exist.

Quite clearly, the number and kind of associations linked with complex nouns must be of a different kind than those linked with simple nouns. This does not contradict the additional observation that a morphologically simple noun may refer to extremely complex objects such as the sun, or to a concept that has been the subject of millennia of debate, such as God, whereas a morphologically complex noun such as *hot dog* refers to a relatively trivial cultural item. (It would be idle here to speculate that atomically and subatomically a hot dog could be as complicated as the sun, especially if we compare every atom to a miniature solar system. If one took this view, everything would become so complex as to defy description. This would violate the ecology of the human mind: basically all humans think in Gestalten, not in atomic particles, hence the fundamental error of reductionistic approaches to the study of language.)

Most of these issues are discussed, although in slightly different terms, in Makkai (1972a), hence the relative brevity of the discussion here which was meant essentially as an attempt at correcting the two idiomaticity areas of my 1973 view by adding a lower one, the morphemic idiomaticity area. It was also desirable to summarize our current thinking regarding lexemes, morphemes, sememes, and idioms, before going on to the actual topic at hand: the sociopsychological stratification of sememe types.

1. Psychosememes

The typical age for the acquisition of psychosememes appears to be from six or seven months of age to about six years of age, or the beginning of literacy, i.e., roughly post-kindergarten and first grade. The mode of the acquisition of psycho-sememes is, therefore, almost exclusively oral and coincides in terms of personality development with the process of primary socialization. Sememes are not defined during this period of development; they are felt, smelled, touched, tasted, chewed, swallowed, hugged, seen, heard, kicked – consequently also loved, feared, wanted, unwanted, etc. If we can speak of definitions during this age in any sense at all, they are invariably ostensive definitions via physical contact, resulting in a high degree of PSYCHO-PHYSICAL OBVIOUSNESS (PPO). Personal names and generic terms are routinely fused; *Kelly* means 'cat' because that is its name, and *Pogi* means 'that other creature' (the dog), because that is its name. *Daddy*, *Mommy*, *Sylvia*, the immediate members of the family, by virtue of being always around, have such a high degree of PPO that no need ever arises at tagging them via other vocal utterances.

The physical environment, however, offers constant challenges in terms of just being there; and the child already at ten to eleven months of age knows that things have names and it wants to know what those names are. It is as if an instinctual drive for cataloguing the environment, an urge to 'take inventory' around oneself, were at work: Halliday calls this the MATHETIC function (1974). Rebecca Rose is twenty-six months old at the time of this writing, her older sister Sylvia is eleven and has just graduated from the 6th grade in the Lake Bluff Central Elementary School. Both of the parents are linguists and have a special interest in children's language acquisition. Thus the observations offered here are as realistic as any one could hope for; nothing is invented *ex nihilo*. RRM's most predominant syllables at eleven months were an interrogative *dae – dae – dae?* (we interpreted it as 'what's the name of that? what is that?' since it was accompanied by a curious look and deliberate pointing, repeatedly) and a declarative *ta-ta-ta-ta* meaning something like 'that's a familiar object, I have seen that before'. She had a 'passive vocabulary' of roughly one hundred words. When asked 'where are your eyes?', 'where are your fingers?', 'where is Mommy's hand', 'where is Daddy's hand?' she would point at the appropriate objects with 95 per cent accuracy. (Every now and then she would confuse her hair with her ears.) The words *milk, bottle, bread, no-no!, tickle, hug* and *kiss* (followed by a smacking of the lips in the air, not yet on the cheeks of others) were all recognized and organically tied to some actual and sufficiently significant event – bodily motion, eating, getting picked up, being moved away from the flower pots, etc. – replete with high degrees of PPO. While RRM eats her lunch in her highchair, SM, home from school for lunch, gives me her 'vocabulary words' and asks me to drill her on them, as they will have a test of the past three week's material in the afternoon. I look at the words and notice that all of them REQUIRE VERBAL DEFINITIONS in plain, monosyllabic Anglo-Saxon; words that she learned when she was two, three and four years old. The words are not entirely randomly chosen by Mr Wiles, her teacher; some of them materialize from the readings Sylvia and her classmates do from day to day. What surprises me in these 'vocabulary words' is that I do not recall ever having done anything similar in Hungarian, the language I grew up with and spoke constantly until I was twenty-one. Whereas we did have composition and speaking exercises, somehow the 'abstract vocabulary' of Hungarian builds itself up unnoticed by the native speakers; terms are created by the compounding of many small, short, familiar Hungarian words of Finno-Ugric or thoroughly familiarized Slavic stock. Sylvia and her classmates, by contrast, almost seem to be learning a second, foreign language through their 'vocabulary words'. In what follows, I will present a limited set of last year's 5th grade 'vocabulary words' in an attempt at illustrating the next layer of sememes and lexemes, the cognosememes.

2. Cognosememes

The items listed below appear in no particular order, alphabetical or otherwise, but they do constitute the material absorbed at Lake Bluff Central Elementary School in a typical homework dosage.

Entry	Definition
amphibian	An animal or plant that can live in the water or on land.
ecstatic	Overwhelmed with joy.
distillation	The process of making liquids pure.
ferocity	Fierceness.
scavenge	To collect or eat garbage or waste matter.
carrion	Dead or decaying flesh.
regiment	A group of batallions in the Army.
Tory	In American history, a person or people who were on the British side during the Revolution.
muster	To assemble for roll call.
implement	To carry out a plan.

This was the homework for a week. Unit #17. The homework for the previous week, Unit #16, was:

calico	A kind of material.
carcass	A dead animal.
chasm	A deep or sharp-edged depression in the ground; a huge ditch or ravine.
cower	To be scared.
grouse	A kind of bird.
irreplaceable	You can't get another one.
loftily	Bravely, elegantly; with authority.
knight	A young gentleman or a nobleman who stays with or goes with a king till he himself is made a more advanced nobleman, known as a 'knight'.

An earlier set (Unit #14) included the following items:

anticipation	Can't wait.
browse	Look casually before buying (or without buying) as in book stores.
emblem	A symbol.
leech	A blood sucking worm.
livid	So angry that the face turns pale.
ordeal	Very hard time; troubles.
reckoning	Figuring out: counting.
sextant	An instrument used by navigators to figure out where they are.
solar	Having to do with the sun.

wreckage   The broken particles of something that got smashed.

Other 'vocabulary words' included *abyss, duff, dulcet, eerie, endear, lair, lupine, pungent, quicksilver, rapier, curvet, zenith, sally, sortie, heath, kelp, consternation, orb, saga, mormot, ancestor, descendent, antagonism, competent, dictation, lichen, perilous, pinion, plait, remnant, surety, desolation, esteem, flounder, mementoes, onslaught, prism, reconnoiter, re-enact, rendez-vouz,* and many more.

I asked Sylvia how she would define *father, mother,* and *milk* – 'let's pretend that they are "vocabulary words" that I don't know and you are teaching them to me – what would you say they meant?' 'No need', she said 'it's just you guys and the stuff we drink for lunch'. I asked her if she knew the *Pledge of Allegiance.* 'Of course', she said. 'It's what we say in school all the time.' 'What is *allegiance*?' I asked, and got a blank stare. So we defined it as 'you don't want to quit, you want to stay faithful' and that made sense. It was now treatable as a 'vocabulary word', that is, it revealed itself to be a COGNOSEMEME whose meaning must be elucidated by CIRCUMLEXICALIZATION. Children show embarrassment and reluctance when asked to circumlexicalize a psychosememe; when faced with unfamiliar cognosememes, they actually ask for a verbal definition. 'Daddy, what is *mentality*?' Sylvia asked one day, when we were speaking about a neighbor; one of us said 'no wonder that he does such things with that kind of mentality'. So it had to be explained as 'attitude', 'philosophy of life' which, then, led to further notions (and words) to be explained. The meaning finally sank in when we illustrated the meaning of *mentality* by placing two characters in a story, one of whom is honest and the other willing to steal.

Whereas many of the circumlexicalizations of cogno-sememes lead to items that also require further elucidation, quite a few offer old and thoroughly familiar words. Witness the 5th grade definition of *anticipate* above as 'can't wait', every element of which was acquired unconsciously before SM marched off to kindergarten. They are stored in that deepest, inner layer of her memory where RRM is now beginning to build up her basic psycho-sememes of the kind that *Mommy, Daddy, Grandma, Grandpa, Kelly, Pogi, Sister, Sylvia, yes, no-no!,* seem to be.

2.1. It is reasonably clear, I think, that the difference in sophistication and the difference in communicative competence between a two-year-old and a kindergarten graduate proudly marching off to the 1st grade is quite immense. The kindergarten graduate will have been through the basic phases of holophrastic speech, the joining stage and the recursive stage (cf. Bolinger 1975), and this effortless process of acquiring the phonology, morphology, and syntax of the mother tongue is a feat which is simply never paralleled in significance in later life. Small wonder, therefore, that exponents of the transformational-generative view of language should have made efforts at explaining language acquisition as a rule-governed type of behavior which may ultimately rest on innate genetic traits unique to the human species. The reason why transformationalist treaties on children's

language acquisition sound mostly unconvincing, however, is that no attention is paid to the fact that the child does not merely 'acquire language',
as if learning how to play chess or program a toy computer. The child
learns how to become a member of a small social circle (the family) whose
members the child tries to influence in a variety of ways. After primary
socialization the larger though not essentially dissimilar process of becoming a member of a peer-group (kindergarten and the grades) is repeated;
here again, the child is as busy establishing his or her authority and leader-
ship role, as he or she is in furthering the language acquisition process.
From a realistic anthropological and sociological point of view (Halliday
1973, 1975a) language can be seen as a tool designed to achieve certain
goals in the process of primary and later secondary socialization. Quite in
accordance with the very title of Halliday's remarkably lucid and convincing book on the topic, a child LEARNS HOW TO MEAN in order to develop
his position *vis-à-vis* his parents, siblings, and peers. Linguists have grossly
underestimated the capacity of children for memorization and repeating in
recent years. Entire pieces of text (like the Pledge of Allegiance), bed-time
prayers, songs, nursery rhymes, are memorized playfully and without any
effort. How much more likely, then, that typical syntactic patterns replete
with the typical vocabulary items riding on such syntax, should also be
unconsciously recorded, overlearned, and displayed at irregular intervals,
thus giving the impression that 'each sentence is a novel creation' based
on a 'rule' which is the output of the 'language-acquisition device'? Let us
arbitrarily imagine that home-spun Anglo-Saxon English around the family
involves being exposed to one thousand basic syntactic patterns ranging
from three-word sentences such as *Pogi is hungry* to longer sentences (in the
context of a pretending, hide-and-seek game) such as *No, I am not Rebecca
Rose, I am Rachel and I am hiding, Daddy you find me!* The unconscious
leisurely recording time at the youngster's disposal is nothing less than 6 ×
365 (day) × 16 (hours a day) = 33,040 hours = 2,102,400 minutes of
playful memorization! We must also not forget that literature in such
relatively recent times as Homer's Iliad and Odyssey was exclusively a
matter of oral tradition with the written versions having been produced
centuries later. The very idea of a 'rewrite rule' seems preposterous for
people living preliterate lives – this of course includes all of us as children
and all of our ancestors in such rather recent times as 5,000 B.C., while
mankind's age on the planet must be measured in millions of years. The
purpose of this chapter is not to offer spurious polemic against Chomsky and
his followers; nevertheless, the logic of my narrative forces me to make a
remark about transformationalist-generative theory and the practice in the
light of what has been said here about psychosememes and cognosememes
based on careful records and personal observation over many years.

Let us take the simple exclamation *ouch!* as heard from youngsters of one
year of age and up. It also occurs as a noun as in *Daddy, I've got an ouch
on my finger*. (I am not concerned with *ouch* as a neat direct object here.)
Ouch!!! the psycho-sememe, and where it comes from, is what we are after.
If we always spoke symmetrical sentences obeying the S → NP + VP

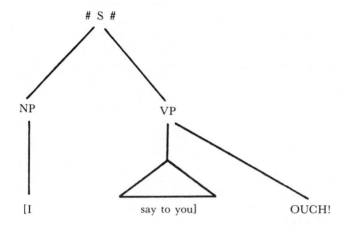

Figure 1

pattern, the explanation of this simple exclamation becomes a major problem. It is presumably a sentence which has a laboriously retrievable deep structure with *ouch!!!* (appropriate exclamatory intonation added) being the end result of a 'derivational history'. Thus the MIT-oriented linguist sets up a deep structure replete with a 'real' NP and a 'real' VP such that the utterance *ouch!!!* is a quasi-object under the VP node (see Figure 1).

(The portion in square brackets is that part of the sentence which will later be deleted by a deletion transformation leaving the quasi-object *ouch* there which, however, still does not sound like an exclamation because it has not yet been interpreted phonetically. There could be rather quiet, non-exclamatory sentences of this type as well, such as *I say to you don't, I say to you bunk, I say to you poppycock, I say to you bullshit, I say to you forget it.* Invariably the effect of actually saying *I say to you . . .* is quite noticeable; any sensible stage director who knows his business can attest to this observation.) But the child screams *ouch!!!* so spontaneously and so fast, that simply no cognitive time could have elapsed for the processing of an underlying sentence whose major portion is then to be 'deleted' in order to wind up with the utterance *ouch!!!* itself. This can only work WITH PENCIL AND PAPER IN HAND, as a kind of logical exercise but preschool children do not, and mankind in general, a few millennia ago, DID NOT WRITE; PEOPLE ONLY SPOKE. The notion of the transformationalist's 'rewrite rule', then, must be rewritten as a RESPEAK RULE. It is now likelier that children and Homeric humanity can make sentences. But this is absurd; no child or Homeric hero HAS THE COGNITIVE PROCESSING TIME to build a derivation, delete it, and THEN, finally, exclaim.

Deletions, however, do occur in written compositions. Any writer knows that the first draft is usually imperfect; a second rewriting usually helps. If there is any real sense to 'deletions' and 'rewritings', they should belong to sememic and sememic language modes of human communication which necessarily involve the written medium and hence one's ability to change what has been committed to paper.

I have discussed elsewhere in detail (cf. Chapter 1) that transformationalist's answering such observations usually claim that the critic is talking about 'performance' whereas the 'true goal of a linguistic theory is to describe competence', and it is by now common knowledge that such excuses would not do.

Transformational-Generative Grammar will simply remain doomed to irrelevance and failure when discussing children's language acquisition unless and until the basic difference between psychosememic language and cognosememic language has been properly understood. If such an understanding were to be shown by transformationalists, however, they would cease to be transformationalists. It remains to be seen whether facts or party loyalty will win in the long run, and what the social anthropology of those linguists is and will be who will go after the facts abandoning the ideology, versus those who will deny the facts in order to worship the ideology.

What matters from our point of view here is that, no matter how grammatically complex, *can't wait*, and *you can't get another one* are all built of psycho-sememic meanings whose PPO is immeasurably greater than that of *anticipation* and *irreplaceable*. In fact, the allegedly 'complicated syntax' of these two psychosememic definitions is really only two familiar constructions whose chance of occurrence during 2,102,400 minutes of the first six years of a child's life must be very high indeed.

2.2. Cognosememes, then, are seen to be acquired between the ages of six and eighteen years, during the typical time of secondary socialization. This view is, of course, based on North American culture and would vary considerably with continents and customs. The locus of secondary socialization being the elementary, the junior high, and the high school (with or without college or at least the beginnings of it), the mode of acquisition is primarily written, although spoken reinforcements follow at regular intervals in the classroom situation. 'Vocabulary Words' are looked up and deliberately memorized and drilled both in handwritten notebooks and in printed 'scholastic dictionaries' each child is required to own and learn how to use. The manner of acquisition is textual contact through reading assignments followed by possible field trips to museums, factories, farms, and the like. The result is a fair amount of need for verbal definitions, use of synonyms, and the inevitable encounter with DIGLOSSIA (i.e. the home-spun Anglo-Saxon for the explanation and Franco–Greco–Latin for the explicanda). The PPO of the explicanda is greatly decreased but is, of course, relative to the learner's situation as an urban or as a rural youth, just to mention one obvious point of difference. A city child may

have to acquire certain terms as cognosememes through reading and definition which are entirely obvious psychosememes to the child who grew up
on a farm, and vice versa. *Pheasant, bushel, trough, manure,* etc. are somehow
unreal to a child such as Sylvia, who spent the first four years of her life
on the 30th floor of a Chicago highrise building, whereas *elevator button,
coinomatic laundry, receiving room,* which were psycho-sememically obvious to
her, would belong almost in science fiction for a farmer's child from
Bushnell, Illinois.

3. Technosememes

In the book *A Dictionary of Space English* (Makkai 1972d) there are approximately 3,000 definitions and over seventy illustrations. The material was
collected two years before and two years after the first American lunar
landing in June of 1969; it involved more than two dozen people; fellow-
editors, graduate students, etc. who were in constant touch with the
engineers at the Kennedy Space Center in Florida, the Johnson Space
Center in Houston, the Pasadena jet propulsion laboratory, the Goddard
Space Flight Center, NASA; several of the astronauts; also various
embassies, including those of China and the Soviet Union. Some entries,
in encyclopeadic fashion, simply give the name of a country, followed by
the particular achievements of that country, mostly in chronological order.
Some entries throughout the dictionary are simple verbs, nouns, or adjectives; some are complex noun phrases; many of these are telescoped into
letter-spelling acronyms such as GET for 'ground-elapsed time'; syllable
acronyms such as SAM for 'surface to air missile' or SINS 'ship's internal
navigational system'; or acronyms punning on some appropriately
mnemonic or accidentally like-sounding word, e.g., STAR for 'self test
and repair', TOPS for 'thermoelectric Outer Planets Spacecraft', or
EGADS for 'Electronic ground automatic destruct sequencer', where
STAR and TOPS are mostly accidental mnemonic tags, but EGADS
echoes an actual exclamation of fright or panic. Many of the definitions are
so complex, by reason of the object or activity described, that some of the
defining words within them had to be set in boldface in order to direct the
user to the definitions of these defining words. Below there appear a few
characteristic entries from *Space English*. What they have in common is that
they are all technosememes, a fact which follows rather automatically from
the nature of this dictionary. It is interesting to note that many of these
terms have filtered down into normal American English and are now
somewhere on the borderline between cognosememic and psychosememic
lexemes for youngsters. To *pull the chicken switch*, for instance, means now
'to avail oneself to an emergency exit from any unpleasant situation'; the
original Space English term means specifically 'to activate the control lever
situated beside an astronaut's knee in an emergency in order to separate
the CAPSULE from the LAUNCH VEHICLE'. (The items in capital
letters are cross-referenced boldface entries.) Some of the original

technosememes have, additionally, become psychosememic slang for fellow astronauts who by overuse and glib self-indulgence in mock-officialese create, via these forms, a linguistic aura around themselves as elevated members of a highly selective professional fraternity.

3.1. Some typical technosememes from Space English

FITH /fiθ/	(acronym, noun compound, Apollo) 'Fire in the Hole', LM maneuver during lunar-surface liftoff, descent, or inflight abort in which the ascent engine (AE) fires while the ascent and descent stages are mated but not bound together. Lunar orbit rendezvous (LOR) follows.
AE (ac.) n.c.,	'Ascent Engine,' 3,500 lb. thrust engine of the ascent or upper stage of the LM which is used for liftoff from the lunar surface or in case of prelanding abort.
LM /lem/ (ac.) n.c.,	Apollo. 'Lunar module', one of the three main sections of the basic APOLLO spacecraft. It was originally designated the 'lunar excursion vehicle' (LEV) and later the 'lunar excursion module' (LEM). The LM, an ungainly 18-ton, two-stage vehicle, is designed to carry two astronauts from a lunar orbiting CSM to the surface of the moon and back. The lower half of the LM, the unmanned, unpressurized DESCENT STAGE, contains a descent engine (DE), used to deorbit the craft and soft-land it on the moon; propellant and supply tanks; a landing gear assembly; scientific equipment housing; and the 'lunar roving vehicle' (LRV). After lunar exploration, the descent stage serves as a launch pad for the ascent stage.

(The definition continues for fourteen more lines and is accompanied by two rather complex drawings with twenty-one explanations attached to Figure 1, and twenty-three attached to Figure 2; the two drawings together make up entire p. 35 of the Dictionary. In the fourteen lines omitted there are six more boldfaced cross references.)

I think that these few examples suffice to indicate the complexity involved in technosememic vocabulary. The case of Space English is not a special one; medicine, law, technology, to name but a few, all have their heavily technosememic vocabularies familiar enough to the practitioner of the profession involved and quite esoteric for the man in the street.

4. Sememe mobility

Metaphorical extensions of the various types known from classical rhetoric, such as PARS PRO TOTO, SYNECDOCHE, PERSONIFICATION, etc., may all play roles in the process of leading a simple Anglo-Saxon monosyllabic psychosememe into school, from school to college, and from college into one of the highly specialized professional schools, such as medicine. Take the word *foot* that every two-year-old knows with a fair amount of consistency as that lower limb on which we humans walk. (Walking may not be the first use of our feet, especially when we are still autopodophagous – a term I have coined to refer to the tendency of infants to chew on their own feet, a preoccupation that evidently brings them joy and costs no effort at all.) Later in school or perhaps still at home the child may come across the expression *the foot of the mountain* and wonder why the foot, something that he walks on, is now said to belong to the mountain. The teacher or the attending parent explains by pointing out that the mountain does not really have a foot; but if you compare the mountain to a person standing, then the bottom where you start to climb is like your foot insofar as it, too, is downward, i.e., toward the ground. Children ponder a while, may shake their heads, giggle, then give in and say 'Aha, I see'. If the same child later, in a course dealing with poetry, comes across the terms IAMB, TROCHEE, DACTYL, SPONDEE, and CHORIAMB, commonly known as metric FEET, a new setting for the lexeme *foot–feet* will have been established. The same individual may, after graduation from college, become an M.D. specializing in podiatry whose task is to diagnose diseased bone structures and tissue and prescribe corrective footwear for his patients. The lexeme *foot* will have undergone for such a person a cognitive stratification of a lifetime's learning and experience.

4.1. A Sunday on the mountain

Let us imagine the following imaginary excursion: A podiatrist, having climbed a mountain, rests on a portable three-foot stool composing light verse for entertaining purposes in iambic tetrameter under the glaring summer sun; his undergraduate major was physics and astronomy, so he knows a fair amount of solar physics. Beside him sits his younger brother, a Catholic priest. Their father, a well-known modern painter, sits further up on a ledge and is engaged in doing a pastel painting entitled 'The Eclipsing Foot'. He is doing a large psychedelic foot whose center looks like the sun and whose toes are abstract bundles of rays; the moon, resembling a human face, covers half of the sun-foot. Since I saw such a painting once among a large number of graffiti painted on the shore of Lake Michigan – in fact there was a half-mile stretch of these starting at 5701 North Sheridan Road all the way down to the Lawrence Avenue exit from Lake Shore Drive in Chicago – the example used here is much more factual than imaginary. The people on the mountain have one sensation in common: their feet ache, because the cable car they wanted to ride in had broken down, forcing them to climb. The painter father exclaims: *Boy, my dogs are barking!* Both sons answer: *Yeah, mine too.* Is this exchange totally illogical or does it have any semantic coherence with regard to the situation they are in? Since *my dogs are barking* is an idiom more frequently recognized in the Western Mountain States than in Chicago, it makes good sense to imagine that the excursion is taking place in the San Bernardino mountains of California. It means 'to have sore feet' and is, consequently, entirely *à propos* of the situation. What they refer to is the human foot in its simple-minded psychosememic, elementary meaning. This understanding of the word *foot* does not force them to use the very word *foot*, instead they choose to refer to aching feet as 'barking dogs'. At the same time they may be very well aware that the start of their climb occurred at the foot of the mountain, just as the composer of light verse remembers that his syllables come in feet and the painter knows that his psychedelic foot is not the sun and the sun has nothing foot-like about it except, of course, that in the particular, artistically idiosyncratic sense of the canvas being worked on, this very unison of sun and foot has been accomplished. The son who majored in physics when he looks at the painting knows perfectly well that equating toes with rays of sun is fanciful; yet his father's art fetches a great deal in galleries and besides he likes his father's style. Thus he feels no need to quarrel with the message of the painting. The utterance *my dogs are barking* actually reminds him of a possible rhyme in the poem he was looking for; the fact that aching feet can be referred to as dogs that bark has neither added to nor detracted from his awareness of the fact that the English word *foot* can be used for syllables, the base of mountains, and the human limb. Since they all share the sensation of fatigue and aching feet, the knowledge about the verse and the base of the mountain as well as the praeterlogical juxtaposition of the lower human limb and the star around which our planet revolves remain in the background of their internalized lexicons as if amounting to an unspoken footnote to the 'Eclipsing Foot'.

As this example is meant to illustrate, lexemes acquired in Stage I as psychosememes do frequently take on cognosememic and even technosememic status during later life, while the psychosememic sense tends to remain in the forefront of both conscious and unconscious recall – probably in that order – even if the primary psychosememic realizate 'the lower human limb' additionally manages to masquerade behind an idiomatic expression involving, in this instance, dogs that bark.

4.2. But how can this happen to terms such as Telephone *and* Computer?

One is tempted to say that *telephone* and *computer* are cognosememes acquired in Stage II through nontechnical though deliberate adult use; later perhaps they become technosememes if one becomes professionally involved with them. The American toy industry, however, achieves the effect that *telephone*, for instance, may very well crystallize in a child's consciousness as a beloved personal possession which rings if pushed, and out of which a little blond doll pops and says 'hello'. (The technical name for this toy manufactured by the Fisher-Price Toy Company is Pop-up Pal Telephone.)

It is factually observable how a child who comes from an affluent middle-class background develops the matter-of-fact but expensive habit of calling up friends long distance because the Pop-up Pal Telephone used to be a psychosememic friend before 1st grade; a child brought up on a farm with only a pay phone available half a mile down the dirt road will think of telephones as best left for emergencies.

A toy computer that rings and adds up a simple row of pears, apples, or bananas, can also become an emotionally coded psychosememe, especially if available to the child before the elementary arithmetic classes of the 1st grade. Since the toy computer is much rarer than the Pop-up Pal Phone, the likeliest time of occurrence of the lexeme and the sememe *computer* is in the psychosememic period in the later years of high school or in the first years of college.

Radio, television (TV), light, car, the *door bell,* however, can all be introduced into definitionless, but 'feelable' psychosememic memory at an early age, maybe between two and three. If the person who acquired these lexemes psychosememically chooses, in adulthood, to pursue an occupation in which these items are never consciously redefined (e.g., the ministry, or owning a chain of grocery stores) they will, for all practical purposes, remain nothing but psychosememes for that speaker throughout his adulthood. If, on the other hand, the person turns out to be a radio ham in college and later a communications engineer, the lexeme *radio,* which during his childhood may have been a bear or a doll emitting sounds, will have become a complex set of technical notions replete with advanced examinations in radio wave propagation theory.

I am afraid I am about to say a most unpopular and 'undemocratic' thing yet something which I instinctively feel is true. Despite common vocabulary items, habits of pronunciation, and grammatical conventions, people do not necessarily speak the same language. The reason is that their sememes – realized by the common lexemes – differ in scope, depth, emotional intensity, and technical sophistication. (Consider the two linguists discussing the PHONEME as a technical term – one who has just graduated from MIT where he got Halle's ideas on systematic phonology, and, say, someone of Charles F. Hockett's or Archibald A. Hill's genera-tion. Although an extreme case, there are many similar ones occurring every day.) Added to this general observation must be the fact that people are somewhat dissimilar in their needs and abilities to verbalize about certain experiences. On the one hand we have the 'idiot savant', who may be able to reproduce the structure of a large building after just one walk through it but who cannot say anything about the house. (The Nova series of Channel 11 in Chicago has just shown such a case.) We are created equal, and we are not. I know people with large vocabularies to whom talking comes easily; their style is almost facile and flippant. When pressed to explain what they mean by certain terms, they become embarrassed. I would classify them as lexeme-rich but sememe-poor; they have an unusual ability to parrot phrases, entire anecdotes and jokes. (They are usually the loudest at cocktail parties.) I also know people who are profound thinkers, scholars or poets, but are quite parsimonious with words. One of them, jokingly, describes himself as a 'dyslexic' which he of course is not.

4.3. A middle-aged immigrant's discoveries

I had already lived for twenty years in the USA, authored a major book and several articles in English along with a few poems, when I first discovered, after moving into a house in the suburbs, the following lexemes: *stud-finder, Phillips screwdriver, battery tester*. I needed stud-finders because I wanted to attach a set of book-shelves to the wall which, as I found out, was hollow. This was news to me; in the apartments where we had lived before there were no hollow walls. I now know that hollow walls are common; yet the institution of a stud-finder was like a major revelation. I now know that the little magnets on the stud-finder move only when you are over nailed wood; that is where your nails or screws will go. The Phillips screwdriver, miraculously, escaped me for twenty years in this country until I discovered, with amazement, that the storm windows in the family room can only be removed with a special screwdriver whose edge fits into a + shaped set of grooves. The need for a battery tester was more obvious; I tried to get one in fact by asking for an electrometer, an electropump, and an electric liquid gauge. After several bursts of laughter, the Arco station mechanic informed me that what I needed was a battery tester. I now know intimately what these items will do for me and have even developed a fondness for them; I especially like the stud-finder because the swiveling-pivoting action of the small magnets gives the impression of their being somehow alive and communicating with me. Insofar as I am now quite familiar with these, they have moved down from the status of technosememes to the more intimate level of cognosememes. The stud-finder, which I like, is maybe even beginning to wax psychosememic on me; I wove its name into a sonnet a few days ago *à propos* of an endowment fund raising drive that I am engaged in for the Linguistic Association of Canada and the United States; I wish the stud-finder to develop the ability to swivel when I am nearing the name of a foundation in the directory that has tappable resources. No such money-finding stud-finder exists yet, unfortunately.

5. Some experiments

Both as a matter of professional experimentation and in order to turn the tables on the Native Speaker, I decided to start asking people questions that would startle THEM for a change. I thought that in order to investigate how sememes mean, a workable idea would be to create a plausible set of circumstances described with elements of common vocabulary and then ask the informants what they think the item should be called. This is the first game. The second game is the converse: you provide an acceptable sounding term that seems phonologically and morphologically well formed, and ask the informants to guess what the thing might stand for, what it does, what its features might be, etc.

5.1. First game (circumstances given, lexeme not given)

Elicitor: Some genius in the men's shaving gear industry invented a new kind of razor blade that simply never gets dull; it is sold at very reasonable, low price. Here is how it works: Imagine an ordinary injector blade (as made by the Schick Company). The difference is that when you are through using it – after six or seven shaves – you do not dispose of it, but while ejecting it from your razor, you automatically transfer it into another injector in such a way that during the transfer the blade's molecules are rearranged and it regains its original sharpness. This can be repeated indefinitely. Give me the name of the new kind of blade. (See answers below, but do not peek before trying your own answer!)

Elicitor: The American astronauts have been given the go-ahead to explore other small bodies in our solar system, especially the moons of Jupiter and Saturn since it is easier and less costly to land on these than on the very massive planets of Saturn and Jupiter themselves where escape velocity could be technically unachievable; these moons offer excellent observation posts. They are, of course, full of craters and the astronauts cannot take Lunar Rovers ('Moon buggies') with them on such long trips. An inventor at NASA comes up with a small but powerful rocket which can be attached to an astronaut's boot and which will, when the power is turned on, catapult the astronaut across a crater of 15–25 miles in diameter, turning him into a live rocket of sorts; he can, of course, safely soft-land after decelerating his rocket's boost. What is an appropriate name for this new device? (See answers below, but do not peek just yet: try to make one up!)

5.2. Second game (lexeme given; you must guess the circumstances)

Elicitor: There is a new gadget on the market, call the *crumplink*. What do you think it does, what does it look like, and how much is it sold for? (See answers below, but do not peek just yet: develop a narrative of your own.)

Elicitor: There is a new activity people engage in all over the country; it is called *the transbibing mania*. It is 'all the thing' and it has especially affected college students from coast to coast. Can you guess what is being done? (Again, do not peek just yet and try to develop a story; see actual answer below.)

Answers to games

1. *A transjector.* (Because the blade is injected and then re-injected across a boundary separating the one container from the other.)
2. *A transjector.* (Because the rocket hurls the astronaut over or across an open space, an obstacle, or a depression (such as a crater) in space.)
3. This was made up by me; there is no such item available today. It is an Anglicized spelling of a Hungarian word *krumpli* 'potato' inflected in the possessive, i.e. *krumplim, krumplid, krumplija, KRUMPLINK, krumplitok, krumplijuk* 'my thy, his/her/its, our, your, their potato'. Because of the Angloid spelling and resultant expected phonological realization, the English words *link, crumb, cuffs*, etc., come to mind, and so people have offered such definitions as 'a new kind of cuff-link that is crush proof', or 'a new kind of unbreakable cuff-link which will fold up for easier storage', etc.
4. This is also pure fiction. Informants' answers differ according to age, sex, and major area of concentration. (The informants in these experiments are my graduate students in linguistics at the University of Illinois at Chicago Circle.) A male engineering student defined it as 'the refueling of aircraft in mid-flight such that the tanker flies in formation with but above the plane to be refueled which sucks the jet fuel via an extended pipeline "drinking it across" as it were'. A female social worker (also engaged in the writing of fiction) volunteered this: 'The sharing of a swig of alcohol via kissing by minors during the Prohibition'.

These games, incidentally, can be played in any order. Thus you can offer the test-respondents a lexeme **to transject* (v. trans. and intrans.) and make the audience guess what new invention it might refer to. Reactions will vary widely, but people who have an awareness of the Latin etymologies involved will feel somewhat constrained and hampered by their knowledge. In the case of the lexeme **transjector*, due to the two different explanations offered by my informants (I am sure, of course, that many more could be made up), we have arrived at a typical 'lexemic neutralization' of two separate sememes which, of course, are nevertheless relatable to one another hypersememically, or semantically, due to the Latin 'etymemes' present in *trans-* and *-ject*.

No one has, of course, ever seen a **transjector* either as an astronaut's rocket or as an ever-sharp razor blade; the British science fiction industry has, however, produced scenes in the 007 James Bond series where 007 jumps over a house with the help of just such a rocket. These items, therefore, have a very low chance of ever becoming psychosememes for anyone. If any such item strikes root in English, it would most likely be

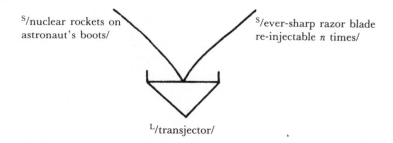

Figure 2 Neutralization of two imaginary sememes in one imaginary (though morphologically well-formed, and therefore 'possible') lexeme aided by plausible narrative and suitable Latin etymology. The node is an AND/OR since BOTH or EITHER can be realized in ANY order.

an obscure and evasive technosememe. Now, however, that the Star Wars movie series has produced offspring in The Empire Strikes Back, Heaven only knows what science fiction toys will be available for $5 on a mass production basis for pre-first-graders to wax fond of.

6. Recapitulation

Let us go back to the lexeme *sun* as discussed at the beginning of this chapter and try to show in simplified diagram format how this lexememic-sememic relationship might develop throughout the lifetime of a person who first acquires it as a child, then learns about the sun in high school science classes, later in college and graduate school eventually specializing in solar astronomy.

Since there are many Americans who, at least as a matter of curiosity and without any intent to 'predict the future', which is impossible, indulge in 'astrology', I am adding as a fourth, acquired technosememe to this imagined person's knowledge about the sun the basic information astrology has to offer about it.

7. Conclusions and future tasks

I have tried to show that sememes tend to stay mobile throughout one's cognitive development in such a way that psychosememes are acquired first, cognosememes second, and technosememes of varying kinds, last. I

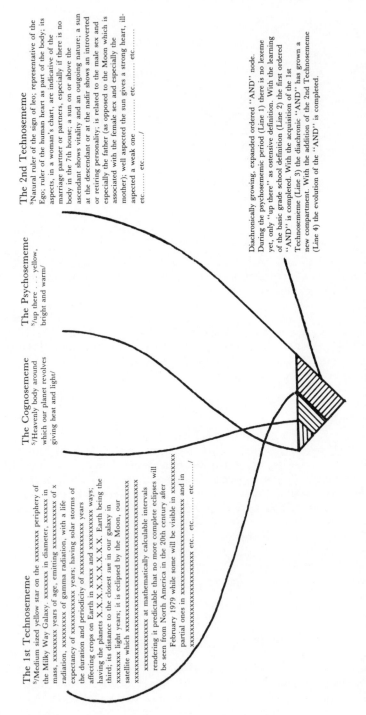

Figure 3 Abstract representation of the evolution of the sememe S/sun/ in a 'normal person' who learns Line 1 first, then in school Line 2. Later, as a physics major, he learns Line 3; and much later, after retirement, he takes up astrology as a hobby and acquires the meaning of Line 4. (1 is the psychosememe, 2 is the cognosememe, and 3 and 4 are two complimentary technosememes).

have also pointed out that what passes for a psychosememe for one person, might be only available as an obscure technosememe to another. Hence this cognitive layering of realizates is subject to sociolinguistic research.

In the section dealing with cognosememe, it may have been noticed that the explicanda are usually of non-Anglo-Saxon etymological provenience and come in multisyllables, whereas the explaining words are frequently shorter Anglo-Saxon words.

It is not far-fetched to say that learners of English really acquire more than one 'language' as they grow up. It seems as if the Anglo-Saxon base of English were acquired psychosememically, with the Latin, Greek, and other portions of English being learned cognosememically and technosememically. Reverse cases have been shown to exist for city children.

One of the most urgent tasks for Linguistics as a science for the remainder of this century and the beginning of the next will be the systematic accounting for these facts in lexicography. In order for linguists to be able to achieve these goals, however, entirely new methods of lexicography will have to be devised, justifying a respelling of lexicography with an *e* as lex*ECO*graphy (cf. Makkai 1980).

10 The passing of the syntactic age, or *take one* on *take*: lexo-ecology illustrated

> Grammar is in trouble and needs help. The problem is in the empirical foundations of grammatical theory construction. One writes a grammar on the basis of what are called grammatical judgments.
>
> *D. Terence Langendoen (1972)*

0. In a paper entitled 'The Problem of Grammaticality' (1972) D. Terence Langendoen, author of the widely used *The Study of Syntax* (1969), only three years after publishing a book aimed at textbook generality, issued an appeal to the community of the College English Association for help from the domains of logic and rhetoric. Nothing could be more telling concerning the nature of the crisis linguistics had reached by the time of the XIth International Congress of Linguists in 1972.

1. In what follows, I propose to examine some data concerning the verb *take* as presented in Langendoen (1972) based on Hankamer (1971) as well as the treatment of *take* by the generative semanticist McCawley (Quang 1971) and clarify the nature of the 'trouble' grammar is supposedly experiencing. It is my thesis that grammar is in no more nor less trouble than it has been since antiquity; that the problem with grammar does not reside in any 'empirical foundations' but that only that brand of grammar can work itself into a log-jam which has disregarded empirical facts in order to extol pseudo-mathematical abstractions in the name of a philosophically misunderstood 'mentalism'. I shall try to prove that it is Transformational-Generative Grammar alone which is in trouble, and that all the troubles it is experiencing have been created by the theory itself through its disregard of data, context, sociological stratification, and human psychology.

1.1. It would be irresponsible for people never having studied Transformational-Generative Grammar to gloat in triumph over the concern of one of the better-known practitioners of TG, for whatever went wrong with the theory during the past fifteen years, we have certainly all benefited from it. TG has made linguistics one of the most widely discussed (respected as well as scorned) disciplines in the humanities, and the number and kind of questions raised by TG grammarians needed raising, if only later to realize that they were false leads.

One should recognize in this context that Copernicus was not at fault for having erroneously posited concentric circles around the Sun in his effort to describe the planets' paths; all one can say is that it is a pity that he was unable to be a Kepler as well. But this does not subtract from the virtues of Copernicus. The nature of the present interregnum in linguistics can be made tangible for us if we state that we have come to the end of an era full of challenge and excitement, full of much progress, but also a vast number of errors and phony issues. The man whose paradoxical role it came to be to open the doors to the new era was Noam Chomsky, but we are at this point no longer in his debt, for he has turned out to be a *médecin malgré lui*, the Sorcerer's Apprentice who opened the bottle in his master's absence and now can no longer deal with the ghosts he set loose. We now know, for example, that it is impossible to posit homogeneous speech-communities describing only the ideal speaker-hearer without allowing for dialectal and socio-linguistics class variation (Labov 1966, Halliday 1973a and 1973b). That dialect geography has existed as a meaningful discipline was never questioned, but its practice was characterized by the methodology of the late 19th-century *Junggrammatiker* and was, as much, not directly relatable to a general theory of grammar and language. There is little doubt that socio-psycho-linguistics will emerge just as did the Keplerian adjustments that had to be added to early, unsophisticated heliocentrism.

But Socio-Psycho-Linguistics is only one of the positive fallouts of this War of the Wits. Perhaps the most positive fallout is the birth of two powerful movements in linguistic theory: on the one hand, that of generative semantics headed by McCawley and Lakoff and, on the other hand, a whole new way of looking at language which can nevertheless be traced back to Hjelmslev and Saussure – the birth and continual growth of Cognitive-Stratificational Grammar as practiced by Lamb, Gleason, Reich, Lockwood, and Sullivan, to mention just a few. Pike's tagmemics and Halliday's scale-and-category or systemic grammar antedate the start of TG (Chomsky 1957).

1.2. Before I proceed with an analysis of Langendoen's examples, followed by a more detailed discussion of the ecology of the verb *take*, I should like to use an analogy concerning TG and the other theories, taken from the ecology of our planet. The analogy is that of the *tsunami*, or tidal wave. Since not everyone has experienced a *tsunami*, I will quote the relevant passages about it from the *Encyclopedia Britannica* (23: 443)

> Earthquakes on the ocean bottom may produce shock waves similar to those caused by depth charges. These travel in the sea at the velocity of sound, about 5,000 ft per second. They will be felt on board ship as a shock which violently

rocks the vessel. . . . These shocks are accompanied by loud noises like thunder or cannon fire. Far more destructive are the waves caused by vertical displacements along earthquake faults on the sea bottom, by submarine land-slides and by volcanic eruptions beneath the sea. A series of so-called tidal waves (more correctly designated by their Japanese name, *tsunami*) may result. The velocity of these waves in the open sea is large and depends upon the depth of the water. . . . The *tsunami* is usually led by a small rise, followed by a distinct trough. On shore the arrival is first noticed by a fall in the sea level for a number of minutes, as if it were an abnormally low tide, followed by a rapid rise to levels far exceeding the high-tide level.

According to my personal observations in 1959–1960 on Oahu, and having spoken to survivors of the tragic 1948 Lapahoehoe (Island of Hawaii) tidal wave, the first symptom as seen from the beach is actually more dramatic than the description in the *EB* would suggest. The water actually recedes almost completely, exposing corals, shells, and suffocating fish. This happens after the leading small rise with its distinct trough. A whole school full of children, not knowing that what they saw was the first phase of a *tsunami* eagerly ran into the shallow water to pick up the fish and the exposed shells. They were all killed when the real *tsunami* struck.

The minor leading rise is comparable to the 'advent' of Trans-formational-Generative Grammar, a signal, as it were, that things are not the way they ought to be. The receding water in the wake of the leading rise is comparable to the resultant denunciation of structuralism; the emerging, previously hidden sea-goods are the data that were left untreated by the old theory that only paid attention to what was visible to the naked eye. But the work of the *tsunami* is merely begun with the leading rise and the subsequent receding of the water. This is the initial symptom of the deeper underlying unrest and the real, or 'killer wave' that is yet to come. This is the wave that will overwhelm and bury the unsuspecting who went rushing to the dry Ocean floor to pick up the free booty.

2. The second wave of the *tsunami* of modern linguistics is the COGNITIVE REVOLUTION. Transformational-Generative Grammar was merely the 'leading rise' which many people mistook for the real event that was yet to come. We can now see, in retrospect, that it was the unconscious urge to explore meaning in terms of formal structures that led to the formulation of Chomsky's *Syntactic Structures* (1957) – an avowedly nonsemantically oriented work on the surface. Specifically, the sentence *colorless green ideas sleep furiously* (whether read forwards or backwards) may have illustrated to anyone naive enough to be willing to believe it, that grammar was independent of semantics, and for a while this seemed to give enough ammunition to linguists who wished to work under such assumptions. But this claim, namely that a string may be grammatical irrespective of its also being sensical or not, must have a logical corollary: A STRING MAY BE SENSICAL IRRESPECTIVE OF ITS GRAMMATICALITY. The examples are, of course, to be found in immigrant speech and in International Broken English, dialects in which fortunes are made and the questions of war and peace are settled around us. Thus Oller (1972) and A. Makkai (1972b) have independently come to the conclusion (in English, and Hungarian, respectively) that the sentence *colorless green ideas sleep furiously* can mean a number of things depending on the richness of the reader's metaphorical system, and the context in which the sentence was uttered, if it had one at all, and was not just an INCURRENCE (i.e. an occurring non-occurrence made up by the linguist to prove a point). Oller's interpretation (1972, p. 46) reads: *insipid immature ideas lie dormant in a state of potential explosiveness*; mine (translated from the Hungarian): *unripe, unpalatable thoughts lurk in the unconscious ready to erupt and attack*. It is revealing how, entirely independently, the two interpretations, using the psychology of the unconscious, approach more or less the same content while paraphrasing Chomsky's supposedly meaningless sentence.

3. The present crisis in linguistics further implies that linguistic theorizing is far from being over. In fact the theoretical age has barely begun. Is the Space Age now over just because the USA has decided to stop its lunar exploration program by manned Apollo missions? Hardly. We now know how to land on the Moon and collect rocks; we also know that *Luna* is a desolate and inhospitable place for humans to build a permanent colony; the cost is too great in comparison to the good reaped. Thus the 'leading rise' of the *tsunami* of the Cognitive Revolution roughly coincides in time with Man's probing of outer space, and the syntactic age roughly coincides with computer-aided lunar exploration. Both have been flashy and expensive and have resulted in pollution. The quantity and kind of space garbage, abandoned motionless, or still orbiting, is only outdone by the asterisk pollution of syntactic theory (see Makkai (1971) and (1973a)).

3.1. The birth of the new theory which seems to be emerging coincides with man's increasing concern with his environment, and may thus be termed Pragmo-Ecological Grammar (PEG). The ecology of language in its exterior manifestations (termed henceforth LINGUISTIC EXO-ECOLOGY) has interested Uriel Weinreich (1953) and Einar Haugen (1972), and that pragmatics must be seriously integrated with linguistic theory is evident from the work of Oller (1969, 1971, 1972). For the ecological view of one language at a time see my 'A Pragmo-Ecological View of Linguistic Structure and Language Universals' (Chapter 2), in which the term LINGUISTIC ENDO-ECOLOGY is introduced in contrast to EXO-ECOLOGY).

4. But how does Transformational-Generative Grammar, specifically, suffer from its noncorrespondence to empirical facts? Langendoen illustrates this with sentences borrowed from Hankamer (1971). If we use the Conjunction Reduction Transformation as in (1) and (2):

(1)   The investigator examined the evidence and she found it to be inconclusive.

(2)   The investigator examined the evidence and found it to be inconclusive.

and the Gapping Transformation as in (3) and (4):

(3)   Sam got a raise and Ralph got a vacation.
(4)   Sam got a raise and Ralph a vacation.

where Conjunction Reduction 'deletes material from the beginning or the end of the second conjunct, whereas Gapping deletes material from the middle', it is possible that we may come upon a sentence whose origin (so traced) is unclear: it could have been derived either via Gapping or Conjunction Reduction, and we are faced with an unresolveable ambiguity. Langendoen cites (5) and (6) as evidence:

(5)   Mary takes Nancy seriously, but Mary takes Ollie lightly.
(6)   Mary takes Nancy seriously, but Ollie lightly.

Then it is suggested that we consider the derivation of (8) from (7) via Gapping:

(7)   Mary takes Nancy seriously, but Ollie takes Nancy lightly.
(8)   Mary takes Nancy seriously, but Ollie lightly.

The trouble is that (6) is the same as (8) and so you do not know what was meant. That is to say, is *Ollie* subject or object, 'nominative' or 'accusative', agent or goal? What further complicates matters for the TG-grammarian is that people, when asked, interpret (8) as related in meaning to (5) and that alone; 'few give their assent', Langendoen complains, 'when it is pointed out to them that it could also be related to (7)'. This, of course, seems to be entirely correct. People seem to prefer not to shift agents (subjects) from antecedent clause to the conjoined one; an enumeration of the direct objects depending on the transitive verb in the first clause with the subject left unrepeated is the preferred interpretation.

4.1. To remedy this situation, Langendoen turns to the examples where the PHRASEOLOGICALLY IDIOMATIC EXPRESSION *take life seriously* is involved.

Few transformationalists (or, for that matter, linguists of other persuasions trained in the American tradition) realize that there are, in fact, two kinds of idiomaticity. One has to recognize the difference between SEMANTIC IDIOMS and PHRASEOLOGICAL IDIOMS (see Makkai (1972), Part I, and the recent Soviet scholarship on English phraseology such as the two volumes by Kunin (1970) and (1972)). The two categories may, of course, overlap, insofar as most phraseological idioms are semantically aberrant as well. A semantic idiom is one whose meaning remains obscure despite the hearer's familiarity with its components; a phraseological idiom is one which a learner or a foreigner cannot correctly produce despite his familiarity with the basic syntax and the basic vocabulary. The entire family of the COMPULSORY ATTRACTIONS of the verb *take* are characterizable as phraseologically idiomatic. This is the key error in McCawley's work on idioms (Quang 1971) discussed in detail in Makkai (1972a, pp. 54–8). Langendoen (see below) manages to reverse the native speaker responses precisely because he unwittingly involves a phraseological idiom *to take life seriously*, where the phrase behaves differently if instead of *life* we have a personal name in the frame *take X seriously* such as Mary or Ollie. This formula, then, really breaks down into two phraseological expressions: *take* $X_{(human)}$ *seriously* and *take* $X_{(abstract\ noun)}$ *seriously*. The two phraseological formulae share the exterior phrase *take – seriously* which contrasts with *take – lightly, take – superficially*, etc. *Take* in these instances really means 'relate to', 'behave toward', and any number of languages is ready to provide further evidence that despite the great frequency of the equivalents of *take* in such constructions (cf. German *ernst nehmen*, Hungarian *komolyan venni*, etc.) the same notions can also be expressed without any verb 'take' in other instances.

The behavior of the variable X in the phrase *take X seriously* as belongs to the semantic subset 'human' or 'abstract notion' makes the expression *take life seriously* one degree more idiomatic than the expression *take Mary seriously*. If this analysis is correct, it is not surprising that the greater phraseological cohesion of *take life seriously* (which could be paraphrased in a single imaginary English verb such as **to vitasevere, *vitasevered, *vitasevering; *Mary vitaseveres but Ollie doesn't; *Mary is a vitasevering person*, etc.) does allow Gapping, whereas the weaker phrase-idiomatic cohesion of *take Mary seriously* allows only a putative Conjunction Reduction. If we have the single-verb paraphrase (as above), only the Gapping interpretation is replaceable with that single verb. Consider again:

(9)   Mary *vitaseveres,
            but Ollie doesn't.
            but not Ollie.

This can potentially mean:

(10)   Mary takes life seriously, but Ollie (takes life) lightly.

Now it must be clear to anyone that no such single verb (made up or real) seems to fit for *take Mary seriously* or *take Ollie seriously*, because here the two direct objects Mary and Ollie, must be kept separate semantically in order to get across the distinction between the persons involved; otherwise a separate verb would have to be invented for taking Nancy seriously, one again for taking Ollie seriously, such as **Nancysevere, *Olliesevere*, etc., provided that the morphology of the language permitted such compounding.

4.1.1. A great deal has been made in transformational literature of the so-called 'constraints' on syntax and the 'notion of possible lexical entry'. J.R. Ross's runaway bestseller MIT dissertation (1968) *Constraints on Variables in Syntax* introduced examples such as *blimp* being 'impossible' in the sense 'kiss a girl who is allergic to' as in the sentence *I* *blimped coconuts* where the sentence is supposed to read 'I kissed a girl who is allergic to coconuts'. The well-known argument maintains that *blimp* is not a possible lexical item in English, since English syntax does not permit a verb whose meaning includes a transitive verb, a direct object, and a relative clause with a further sentence and a dependent prepositional phrase. If the observation were to mean that 'such verbs with such meanings do not occur in English' nobody could object to the statement except for saying that it is a trivial observation. There are thousands of imaginary features that do not occur in English. Are they, too, all impossible? Yes, and no. In Hungarian I can ask: *Ki az?* 'Who's that?' and the answer: '*ő*', meaning 'he', 'she', or 'it'. No normal Hungarian ever mistakes a male for a female and vice versa. English appears to be 'constrained' to be wordy and over-exact as to sex-identification, and the word *hitch* (conflation of *he + she + it*) would be 'impossible' in a sentence such as *Who's there? – Why, *hitch*.

Yes, of course, it is immediately obvious that the very fact that Ross was at all able to think of *blimp* and that one can make up *hitch* (the all-sex pronoun) makes them EPISTEMOLOGICAL POSSIBILITIES. An epistemological possibility need not, of course, correspond to a descriptive fact.

I have introduced these observations in order to explain Langendoen's examples in terms of 'possible lexical entry' and 'syntactical constraints'.

English syntax is quite capable of admitting verbs whose semantics implies V_t + O; e.g., we have *drink* 'ingest liquid', *eat* 'ingest food', and so on. My proposed incurrences *vitasevere*, *Nancysevere*, and *Olliesevere*, must all be logically permissible forms hence admissible evidence as to the derivation of the discussed sentences either by Gapping or by Conjunction Reduction, or neither.

Let us consider the following possibilities:

(a)   Mary takes Nancy seriously, and Mary takes Ollie seriously.

This is obviously too long and awkward, though unambiguous. If we subject it to various types of Conjunction Reduction we get:

(b)   Mary takes Nancy and Ollie seriously. Or,
(c)   Mary takes both Nancy and Ollie seriously. Or,
(d)   Mary takes seriously both Nancy and Ollie. (Less preferred.)

If English had the verb-compounding feature N + *severe* yielding *Nancysevere*, *Olliesevere*, etc., we might have:

(e)   *Mary Nancyseveres and Ollieseveres.

If English were like German, however, and the compound could be split, we might get:

(f)   *Mary Nancy- and Ollieseveres.

Let us now turn to Gapping. In (15), see below, Langendoen gives *Mary takes life seriously, but Ollie lightly* as the possible result of either:

(g)   Mary takes life seriously, but Mary takes Ollie lightly.

where the direct objects differ, or:

(h)   Mary takes life seriously, but Ollie takes life lightly.

where *life*, the direct object, is the same, but one takes it seriously, and the other takes it lightly.

Let us see if, translated into logical Martian, with the N + *severe* compound, we can make this fact emerge. The neutralization would be impossible, because another noun would have to be prefixed to the stem *-severe*. Thus (15) would read:

(i)   *Mary vitaseveres but Ollie doesn't (vitasevere). Or,
(j)   *Mary vitaseveres, but Olliescorns.

(Here we have invented the verb *Olliescorn* 'to scorn Ollie', or 'not to take Ollie seriously'.) It will be argued below that *to take something + adv.* is a PHRASEOLOGICAL IDIOM in English and that the logico-epistemological 'facts of the matter', concerning who does what to whom, are on a different level from the syntax which either expresses the facts clearly or produces occasional neutralizations.

An alternate solution would be to collapse the phrase *take seriously* (with any and all intervening direct objects omitted) to a single imaginary transitive verb, say, *prosevere*. We then might have

(11)   *Mary proseveres Ollie, but not Nancy.

where both personal nouns would be interpretable only as direct objects. This, then, will have but one possible interpretation, namely Conjunction Reduction, and never Gapping. If it helps those trained in Transformational-Generative Grammar to understand what a phraseological idiom is, one may view the expression *take life seriously* as a single intransitive (hence replaceable) verb, whereas *take Nancy, Mary, Ollie, etc., seriously* is reducible to a single transitive verb which, however, must be followed by the specific direct object personal noun.

4.1.1.1. It is no wonder, then, that Langendoen is able to generate (12), (13), (14) and (15) below and find that now the trend in informant responses has been reversed: not only do people give their assent to the neutralization being derivable from Gapping (previously they allowed only the plausibility of Conjunction Reduction), but now they actually prefer Gapping:

(12)   Mary takes life seriously, but Mary takes Ollie lightly.
(13)   Mary takes life seriously, but Ollie lightly.
(14)   Mary takes life seriously, but Ollie takes life lightly.
(15)   Mary takes life seriously, but Ollie lightly.

(15), of course is the crucial neutralization. We seem to have encountered a genuine example where the native speaker respondents were willing to concede that they did break the previously preferred pattern of carrying over the subject-agent only while allowing a new direct object; the preferred analysis of (15) is that Ollie is now a new subject-agent who takes life lightly, whereas Mary takes it seriously, with the identical object, *life*, being deleted.

The answer, Langendoen suggests, lies in the question of parallelism: *taking Ollie* versus *taking life*. He writes:

> Thus, if parallel structures are more salient than nonparallel ones (as well as being more pleasing aesthetically – in fact one may be justified in saying that one's pleasure in grammatical parallelism is a consequence of its relative ease of perceptibility), then it would follow that (15) is more salient than (12) as a source of the ambiguous example (13) = (15). If some such explanation can ultimately be shown to be correct, *then we have freed the theory of grammar from the unwanted task of having to check alternative derivations.* Grammar and rhetoric, as separate components of linguistic competence, each frees the other from unnecessary theoretical burdens. (1972, p. 23) (My emphasis, A.M.)

It really matters little whether one calls it rhetoric, logic, or aesthetics, for it all boils down to the same thing: speakers in reality do not produce sentences and do not understand their meanings by analyzing the bulldozer-syntax that merely moves dirt horizontally until one heap of it becomes exactly like the other by dint of sheer force and without semantic-pragmatic hookups with the REAL COMMUNICATION SITUATION. On the contrary, what happens is that people occasionally, largely by accident, will work themselves into a syntactic log-jam of ambiguity (such as the 'ambiguous', i.e. *neutralized*, sentences above) from which then they have to burst their way out by appropriately placed semantic-contextual charges. The most frequently used stick of dynamite, of course, is the stock question, 'What do you mean?'. Upon hearing it, the speaker-encoder reformulates his message for the hearer-decoder's benefit. That in reality such is the case, has been known for ages. There is really nothing new to observe here. Whence the 'trouble' then, that grammar is in? Who put it there? Why the sudden emergency and the pushing of the panic button by a leading transformationalist in front of college English composition teachers?

If we really wish to arrive at a satisfactory answer, we must treat the actual causes of the disease, and not just its symptoms. Langendoen makes a hesitant first step in the right direction. He, too, acts under the influence of the cognitive impulse when pointing the way to 'rhetoric' and 'logic'. The trouble is that too much prestige, time, and energy have been invested in transformational-generative theory during the past fifteen years; so much in fact, that what was once a small group of idealistic and dedicated scholars fighting a formidable establishment have, perversely, transformed themselves into a worse establishment guarding its own vested interests. Thus, whatever is wrong with Transformational-Generative Grammar is supposed to be curable by inventing yet another transformation or yet another derivation in order to make it acceptable to those in power. If someone were to say 'it is TG as such that does not do justice to human language', the statement would be scornfully brushed aside and said to amount to 'not arguing one's case' but making merely an 'ad hoc' political assertion.

5. Since we seem to be touching upon the highly explosive issue of *Wissenschaftspolitik* ('the politics of science'), a fact of life Europeans are traditionally more familiar with than Americans who, at least until recently, were protected by the Anglo-Saxon institution of academic freedom, the reader will, I hope, bear with me through the brief diversion that follows.

Let us, for the sake of argument, imagine that a significant cross-section of the American public accepts, buys, extols, and eagerly consumes as good poetry the following type of linguistic noise:

(A)   Pssssssssssssssst. . . . . . .
       Hmmmmmmmm. . . . . . .
       Grrrrrrr. . . . . . .!!!!!!!
       Wow!

       Shhhhhhhhhhhhhhhhhhhhh. . . . . . .

       Wow!
       Grrrrrrr. . . . . . .!!!!!!!
       Hmmmmmmmm. . . . . . .
       Pssssssssssssssst. . . . . . .

The critics in charge of dispensing the Pulitzer, perhaps even the Nobel Prize, would have the rules of the new aesthetics all worked out: (1) the poem must consist of two parts, a beginning and an end; (2) the end must be an inverse recapitulation of Part I (the beginning); (3) and the two parts must be separated by a neutral axis which does not use the sound elements of either Part I or Part II. (4) Additionally, the poem may not use any commonly recognizable lexical entries, since the habit of writing poetry is considered to belong to the old age and is practiced by untalented reactionaries who are not deserving of the rank of poet. (5) The noises spelled out in the poem must come in multiples of 7 in the first three lines of Part I and in the corresponding inverse recapitulation of Part II; thus, we have in line 1, 2 x 7 s's. seven .'s, and seven !'s, and so on. The proposal (I hope!) sounds absurd to anyone reading these lines; yet it is not, at least theoretically, inconceivable that such a power elite might seize control of all or most presses and publishing houses concerned with the publishing of poetry. Further, imagine, for the sake of argument, that these new aesthetic rules are not actually forced on the freedom-loving American public (as certain types of 'Socialist-realist' aesthetics were, in fact, rigidly enforced on writers, poets, painters, and musicians in the USSR and controlled territories under Stalin and Zhdanov), but that it is a genuine religious fad, a free wish of the majority of poetry consumers that deems (A) a very fine poem. We would have to lay our present convictions aside and formulate a pragmatic definition of 'poetry' somewhat along the following lines: *Poetry is the kind of written or recited language material that a given society of consumers, at a given historical period, accepts as such.*[1]

Let us imagine, again for the sake of argument, that the majority of linguists decides on an international basis that the only kind of linguistics which is deserving of the name is the kind which deals with nothing but exotic languages in detailed phonetic transcription. Or, in another age-view of linguistics, it might be held that only historical studies done on a comparative basis are of any value.

The cognitive revolution's 'leading rise', that is, the fifteen years of transformational syntacticism, created an age-view according to which the only brand of linguistics deserving of the name is that which operates as a process on synchronic material in terms of partially ordered rewrite rules, or derivations. This view is called Grammar (with a capital 'G') and nothing else is interesting, insightful, relevant, or serious. (I am deliberately stating here the extreme view, while I am aware that there are many transformationalists who were and are less dogmatic about their Credo.)

The truth of the matter is that most of human science is unscientific, and the 'softer' the science, the more it is subject to quasi-religious fads that sweep the land. (See Garvin (1970) which argues essentially the same point. Further cf. Lukacs (1968), the chapter 'Heisenberg's Recognitions', discussed in Makkai (1972a), Part I, under 'Why Language is Stratified', and in detail in Makkai (1973).) What separates the 'soft sciences' from the 'hard sciences' is, of course, the ability of the latter to be lethal. Thus physics, mathematics, chemistry, and biophysics, should they malfunction in practice, can become killers on the moon, in a space capsule, or in the laboratory. I am not suggesting, incidentally, that anthropology and linguistics cannot be lethal, too; but the chances for this to happen are less. Imagine that the wrong message involving the execution of 100 men, women and children, is delivered to the wrong person in an African village: this would be anthropology and linguistics joining hands in lethal malfunctioning. But one could also argue, of course, that it was only the actual 'performance' of the messenger involved that caused the deaths and not the 'sciences' of anthropology and linguistics.

6. In actual reality, in the ecological setting of human communication via language, it does not make the least bit of difference whether the sentence *Mary takes life seriously, but Ollie lightly* 'derives' from Gapping or Conjunction Reduction or from no 'underlying sentence' at all. If the person so spoken to does not understand, he will say, 'come again', or 'what do you mean'; and the 'ambiguity' will work itself out in the socio-ecological interaction of the speaker and the hearer.

What, then, we may wonder, is the true scientific description and analysis of *Mary takes life seriously, but Ollie lightly*? Several possible answers suggest themselves:

(a) There is no true scientific answer available to this, or in the coming century; semantics cannot be handled structurally 'until human knowledge advances very far beyond its present state' (cf. Bloomfield (1993, p. 140), quoted by Hall (1972, p. 4)).

(b) It derives from the Gapping Transformation.

(c) It derives from the Conjunction Reduction Transformation.

(d) It does not derive either from Gapping or Conjunction Reduction, but from whatever the statistically significant majority of a randomly selected native speaker test-population interprets as the actual meaning of the sentence, first out of context, and then in an appropriately chosen piece of plausible narrative.

(e) The true derivation of the sentence is that in which the majority of linguists in power at the time of the analysis happen to believe whether because of (i) genuine conviction, (ii) lack of a better explanation, (iii) the inertia of conformism, (iv) fear of losing their jobs, (v) unprincipled bandwagon-jumping.

(f) The only possible scientific analysis of this sentence is the one which deals with nothing but the overt data in narrow phonetic transcription or tape recording, having elicited the sentence from a native speaker informant under natural circumstances.

(g) The true scientific explanation of the sentence is the one which shows that neutralization can also occur on the lexemic stratum between two different sememic traces thus indicating which one of the sememic traces was to have been realized by the present inadvertent or deliberate lexotactic neutralization.

(h) The true scientific analysis of the sentence is the one that seeks to explain, based on the responses as under (d), who uttered it to whom, under what circumstances, for what purpose; what the answer was, if any, to the statement; whether the statement was made *ex abrupto* and without any previous discussion of the personalities of 'Mary' and 'Ollie' and how they relate to each other in life; or was this a concluding remark after a thorough (preferably psychiatric) evaluation on the part of both discussants of all factors involved, including Mary's and Ollie's emotional maturity, educational background, possible family relationship engagement, extra-marital affairs, etc.

I believe we can all agree that (e) is a moral disaster if it is motivated by (iii), (iv), or (v); barely tolerable if motivated by (ii); and coldly cynical, as is the above pseudo-definition of the sequence (A) being poetry, if motivated by (i). Yet, of course, this latter motivation always wins as the definition of 'scientific explanation', for such are the rules of democracy and academic freedom.

The open-minded investigator who looks at language from the pragmo-ecological point of view, would prefer a combination of positions (a), (d), (g), and (h), where (h) is clearly the most context-oriented and, hence, the most difficult and most time consuming to accomplish. Under the assumptions (h), a sentence such as *Mary takes life seriously, but Ollie lightly* could be the summary (abbreviated television guide style, as in *Hamlet*: jealous royal step-son seeks revenge against step-father for his father's death) of the plot of a novel longer and deeper than Tolstoy's *War and Peace*. In this case, Mary, the tragic heroine, commits suicide (she took life too seriously), because of the incurable gambler, Ollie, who is, on top of that, an alcoholic. Conversely, the novel could be telling the story of how Ollie committed suicide (he took life so lightly that it did not matter to him whether he lived or died) leaving behind a grieving Mary (unwed mother), who ends up paying Ollie's unpaid bills.

Granting that these imaginary plots are all very arbitrary and far too easy to contrive, it must be pointed out in the name of sanity that they have more to do with potential communication in real life than any of the hair-splitting academic questions concerning the syntactic derivation of the sentence via Gapping or Conjunction Reduction. I would argue that the transformational dilemma is alien to life, irrelevant to society, deaf to human communication, ignorant of encoding and decoding, hostile to story telling and plot, and deeply afraid of psychology. Or else, it is simply callously unconcerned with all of these matters, which would be even worse.

Langendoen is correct. Transformational Grammar is in deep trouble and it needs help. But whether it deserves rescuing by literary men or linguists of other persuasions is another matter which I must leave to the reader to decide. I, for one, would like to enter a motion of no confidence. The real trouble with TG is that it has become an obscure and irrelevant predator, much like the notorious medieval theological debate centering around the question of how many Angels can turn around effortlessly on the tip of a pin.

7. The mechanism that brought TG into its present log-jam is the process view, inappropriately applied to synchronic description. What characterizes the current era is that this log-jam is now about to burst. Remove the central fixation that a 'theory of grammar has to check alternative derivations' as Langendoen himself suggests, and start with the communication situation between hearer and speaker in the appropriately described social setting, and then observe and analyze the utterance. Most 'ambiguities' will disappear through re-encoding, and whatever ambiguities remain will be the flotsam and jetsam of minor syntactic accidents rather than two consciously constructed alternative derivations.

Sociolinguistics is well on its way in the study of the communication situation. Generative semantics has taken the right first steps in its attempt at generating sentences: according to its practitioners the sememic input comes first, the sentences later. The most convincing study in this regard is that by Chafe (1970). Stratificational-cognitive theory, from its very inception, has seen a two-way bridge in communication that leads the message through phonology, morphology, sentences, and meaning, with the two human interlocutors really reaching understanding (if they do at all) through cognition.

But so far all of the criticism leveled against TG, justified as it may have been, went unheeded, because it came from outsiders, and 'scientific status' is measured, alas, not by merit, but by power, as under assumption (e). What marks this as an era of transition, then, is the fact that it is now revisionist transformationalists who are beginning to undermine the Chomskyan paradigm and move, even if ever so timidly, toward a more realistic cognitive-social view of language. (Earlier warnings came from Chafe (1968), and Hockett (1968) but apparently the influences determining the intellectual climate were less favorable then than they are now.)

Particularly noteworthy are the following transformationalists writings aimed at reforming TG:

In her article 'Language in Context' (1972) R. Lakoff begins to pay serious attention to context. In her article 'Passive Resistance' (1971), just one year earlier, she raised significant questions about *be*-passives and *get*-passives the essence of which is that it is far more realistic to view the resultant passives as situationally–semantically conditioned acts of speech-style, than 'transformations' from some kind of underlying active-type 'deep structure'.

In his paper read at the XIth International Congress of Linguists in Bologna, Italy, Morris Halle, after fourteen years of silence on the subject, introduces morphology in a generative grammar. The result is a more realistic view of the generative mechanism, since it realizes the necessity of SIMULTANEOUS COMPONENTS in the morphological sector and disallows phonological features to generate the morphemes directly. It is worthwhile to quote Halle's concluding remarks:

It seems to me significant that I have yet to come across any clear instances where word formation rules have to be ordered in that tightly constrained fashion that is constantly encountered in true phonological rules. I should like to propose therefore that the word formation component differs from the phonology by having completely different principles of interaction among rules. Whereas in the phonology this interaction is captured by means of the convention of linear order of rule application, THE INTERACTION AMONG WORD FORMATION CONSTRAINTS MAY REQUIRE A DIFFERENT PRINCIPLE ALTOGETHER; E.G. SIMULTANEOUS APPLICATION. (My emphasis, A.M.)

The objective reader will conclude that the improvement in TG via the organic inclusion of morphology in a compartment whose 'rules' basically differ from phonological rules and are, hence, self-contained, amounts to an inexplicit admission of the stratification of language in the sense of Lamb (1966), Lockwood (1972), and A. Makkai (1972a). Stratificational theory has always recognized the independence of the morphemic stratum, its semi-independent tactics, units, etc.

Andreas Koutsoudas has been engaged for some time in demonstrating that strict order is a fallacy. The result is a recognition of the fact that alternative operations, simultaneity components, and a certain residual necessity for ordering are not mutually exclusive notions in a sound description of natural languages, but that all of these possibilities must be dealt with as the data demand it. This insight has been available also since 1966, the appearance of Lamb's *Outline of Stratificational Grammar*, in which the conjunction ('AND') and the disjunction node ('OR') have both ordered and unordered versions going both from meaning to sound, and from sound to meaning. I quote the concluding remarks from Koutsoudas' paper 'Can Ordering Statements Be Eliminated from Grammars?':

Four types of arguments given in support of the assumption that rules must be extrinsically ordered have been examined and shown to be invalid. It has been shown that, without changing the proposed rules in any way, the facts in question can be accounted for, with equal or greater generality, without extrinsic ordering, given only the language-independent principles of the cycle and the notions of 'obligatory rule' and 'optional rule'. . . . This supports the proposal that although there are restrictions to be observed regarding the order of application of rules, these restrictions are predictable from language-independent principles, and extrinsic ordering therefore is not necessary for the explanation of any facts about natural languages.

7.1. I have tried to point out succinctly what the nature of the present passing of the syntactic age is. The arguments, the counterarguments, many of the examples in short, the lion's share of the action, comes from the transformationalists themselves, an altogether highly spirited and talented group of linguists who take little for granted and probe everything hitherto unprobed. This being the case, it can be predicted that some of the best students of Chomsky himself will become champions of the new paradigm for our science: Pragmo-Ecological Grammar.

8. In the remaining sections of this chapter I should like to illustrate the principle of LEXO-ECOLOGY with the verb *take* and the various tactic positions it can occupy in natural spoken American English.

8.1. A natural language is a self-contained ecological system consisting of the following sub-ecologies:

Table 1

	Estimated Population
Cognition and Semo-Ecology	millions (concepts in consciousness)
Lexo-Ecology	tens of thousands (dictionary)
Morpho-Ecology	thousands (word formatives)
Phono-Ecology	dozens (syllable formatives)

The structure of a language is its ENDO-ECOLOGY. The relationship of the language to other languages with which it is in contact, from which it borrows or to which it lends lexemes, the number of its speakers, its age, its relationship to its dialects, etc., is its EXO-ECOLOGY. The social stratification of a given language into distinct class dialects is an exo-ecological matter; the relationship of the Semo-, Lexo-, Morpho-, and Phono-Ecologies within one socially definable dialect is an endo-ecological matter.

The purpose and function of language ecology is to provide a tool for human communication. Human communication occurs in specific SOCIO-ECOLOGICAL SETTINGS which are analyzable by means of SOCIAL INTERACTION PSYCHOLOGY (SIP). An individual unit of exchange (i.e., a minimal conversation) is a TRANSACTION. Transactions come in a hierarchy of SIP which may be tabulated as follows (cf. Eric Berne, MD., *What Do you Say After You Say Hello?*):

(A) Monologs
(B) Dialogs: Strokes, Rituals, Pastimes, Games, and Informative Exchanges;
     Games subdivide into (a) Creative Games, and (b) Destructive Games.

8.2. The present study cannot address itself to Monologs, Strokes, Rituals, Pastimes, and Games of either type, for its immediate task is to illustrate primarily INFORMATIVE EXCHANGES. Informative Exchanges are transmitted from speaker to hearer (and vice versa) by lexemes which are the depositories of cognitive material nested in specific LEXO-ECOLOGICAL NESTS. Since much of the transformationalist discussion concerning Gapping and Conjunction Reduction (Langendoen 1972) has to do with the verb *take* and since McCawley in his attempt to deal with idiomaticity (Quang 1971) has also chosen to select examples that contain *take*, it seems appropriate to introduce a notion of lexo-ecological nests by example of the verb *take*.

8.3. Let us imagine an immigrant to the United States who in his place of work hears the following expressions: *take a break; take a bus; take a cab; take it to heart, take it easy; take it seriously; take it lightly; she takes to me; he takes after his father; this takes forever; the guy was on the take; how much was today's take; take one; take the case of abortion; don't take offense so easily; I dictate – you take it down; how much is your take-home pay?; are you going to just sit there and take it?; I took a swim; she took a shower; we took a nap; they took a stroll together; he took the Oath of Allegiance; did the inoculation take?; taking it one step further . . .; do you take cream and sugar?; do you take The New York Times?; Max is sluggish on the uptake; Ali took a punch at Fraser; what's the intake of that tank?; do you have any take-out sandwiches?; there are two kinds of people: givers and takers; please don't take advantage of me; what do you take me for?; I took you for granted; he took it for granted that I told the truth; is Algernon really an undertaker?; Nebelmacher undertook arguing against Schweinemund; the cops overtook the robbers; take me into your confidence!; I'll take your case under advisement; take this chair back where it belongs; let's take your argument back to the beginning, shall we?; now, let's take this step by step; you moved your head, we'll have to retake the picture; what on earth betook you?; I'll take that back; Max took a leak; Max took a shit; Max took a piss; Max took a look at Hjelmslev; Hjelmslev took pity upon Max; Spiro took on a lot of weight; Ali took on six boxers at once; Mr Murgatroyd took on twenty new employees; Aunt Mathilda is taking on too much these days; Algernon took up astrology in earnest; Algernon took Archibald down a notch or two during their telecast debate; you're taking up too much room; you'll have to take the matter up with Mrs Murgatroyd herself; I can't take any more of take.*

8.3.1. The fact that I have not subcategorized and numbered this incomplete sampling of the family of *take* was deliberate. For this is the way it comes to the unsuspecting foreigner, in a massive onslaught of actual occurrences. But this is also why the immigrant survives. The contexts help him to sort out the various meanings of *take* in their various environments. Nor is the youngster growing up with English-speaking parents entirely different from the immigrant, though he will acquire the uses of *take* and all the *take*-attractions more gradually and unconsciously, hence with greater ease.

8.4. I will not reproduce here what most dictionaries have to offer on *take*. In what follows I should like to make some concrete proposals, however, concerning LEXO-ECOLOGY and its description, LEXO-ECOGRAHY.[2]

The lexo-ecography (or lex-ecography) of the English language can be characterized by three mnemonic acronyms. The first of these is *HABIT*: the dictionaries of the present. *HABIT* stands for 'Heterogeneous Alphabetical Inventory Taxa'. The Oxford English Dictionary, The Random House Dictionary of the English Language, the various editions of Webster's are all cast in *HABIT*. In a *HABIT* dictionary *take* will be found under the letter *t* and a number of pronunciations, principal parts, parts of speech, etc., will be followed by a sampling of some of its main senses. Better *HABIT* dictionaries will give some of the most important phrasal verb idioms involving *take*, such as *take up*, *take in*, *take out*, *take back*, etc., and a few of the phraseological idioms, such as *take it to heart*, *take it seriously*, *take something lightly*, and so on. No uniformity can, of course, be found in *HABIT* dictionaries. *HABIT* gives no indication as to the frequency of the form cited, its sociological spread, its dialectal provenience, or its average spread in the various English-speaking countries.

In some European countries where there is a tradition for computational linguistics, lexicographers have started to write dictionaries in the reverse, i.e., *a tergo* volumes, which can be ear-marked by the mnemonic acronym *HARD*. *HARD* stands for 'Heterogeneous Alphabetical Retro-Depository' (see Papp 1969). The value of a *HARD* dictionary is that it provides one of the most reliable bodies of suffixes and rhymes. *HARD* is difficult to put to concrete use, hence its name. *HABIT*, on the other hand, is as old as Dr Johnson, that is, habitual, yet though of more immediate use to the public, it does not give a true picture of what goes on in the lexical jungle.

The lexo-ecography of the future will, I hope, produce *TRUE* dictionaries. *TRUE* stands for 'Thesaurus Rendered Updated Ecologically'.

8.5. Briefly, the organization of *TRUE* is as follows. In *TRUE* the elements of both *HABIT* and *HARD* are put to their best use. Entries do not come alphabetized, but according to their order of frequency in (a) the spoken standard dialect, (b) the language of public broadcasting, (c) the language of the press, (d) popular literature, and (e) the various nonstandard dialects. These frequency counts will put items starting with *a* such as *abacinate*, *ablate*, *abduct*, and *acrobatize* in the proper frequency slot in *TRUE*. Next to *TRUE* entries, however, there is a number corresponding to the *HABIT* listing, and at the back a full *HABIT* printout is provided (with no definitions or examples, however) bearing the same cross-reference number. Each *TRUE* entry also has its *HARD* number, and the appendicized *HARD* printout has the corresponding cross-reference number attached to it.

8.6. A *TRUE* sample concerning *take* follows.

8.6.1. *Take* in phrasal verbs.

Take occurs 'literally' with the following adverbial-prepositional formants: *take again*, *take alone*, *take along*, *take away*, *take back*, *take by*, (*take sg. by sy.'s place*), *take down*, 'carry downstairs', *take in* 'inside some place', *take off* 'lift off', *take out*, *take through*, and *take up* 'carry upstairs'.

Take occurs idiomatically with (at least)[3] the following prepositional-adverbial formants:

be taken aback (restricted to the passive voice) 'to be startled and/or unpleasantly surprised'; *take after sy.* 'resemble a person, by genetic inheritance'; *take back* 'rescind previous statement' as in *on second thought,*

I'll take that back; *take down* 'commit to writing, as in dictation'; *take sy. for sg.* 'consider as'; *take in₁* 'deceive, fool' as in *I really got taken in by those hoodlums*; *take in₂* 'employ or join as partner' as in *Harcourt and Brace took in Mr Jovanovich*; *take on₁* 'engage in combat' as in *Ali took on Fraser yesterday*; *take on₂* 'assume responsibilities' as in *Aunt Leona is taking on too much for her age*; *take on₃* 'add employees' as in *General Motors isn't taking on any new workers these days*; *take over* 'assume control'; *take up* 'start as a hobby or undertaking' as in *Clementine took up the harpsichord*; *take sy. up on sg.* 'make previous promise or offer come true' as in *I am sorry to have to take you up on your promise, but I really need the money now*; *take sg. up with sy.* 'discuss'; and *take to* 'feel kindly toward or attracted to'.

Nominalizations of the above phrasal verbs include:

Literal: *intake* 'capacity' (also used attributively); *take-out* (primarily used as an attributive) as in *take-out order, take-out sandwich*, but nominal occurrences also exist, as in *this is a take-out, that one isn't*.

Idiomatically we have: *take-off₁* 'parody' as in *Vaughn Meader did the best take-off on Kennedy's speech*; *take-off₂* 'state of becoming airborne'. Both of these occur as attributes: we may talk of *take-off artists* and *take-off preparations* at the airport. *Take-over* 'change in power' does not correspond to *overtake* 'pass on the highway', *uptake* 'mental alertness' fails to correspond to *take up* 'undertake a hobby', and *intake* 'capacity' has no semantic connection with *take in* 'engage as a partner'.

I know of no dictionary that makes all of these observations systematically. *TRUE*, by virtue of its multiply flexible cross-referencing system, would also send the user to the appropriate places in the dictionary where the formants *up, down, in, out, over*, etc., are discussed, somewhat as in Part II of Makkai (1972a, pp. 192–248). It is also noteworthy that some of the nominal-attributive forms of the phrasal verb begin with the formant, and others with the verb. By way of diversion, consider the lexoecology of *hold*, a verb which would be much closer to *take* in *TRUE* than it is in *HABIT*, because of their similar frequency ratings (see Makkai (1972a), Part II, Introductory Remarks). *Thus* the formant *up* can go after *hold* and we get a literal sense *hold úp* (with the stress on *up*) as in *Jack was holding the shelf up while I drilled the hole in the wall* (also possible: *Jack was holding up the shelf*, etc.).[4]

Now notice that many times when you have a V followed by a literal formant, e.g. *mock úp* as in *they mocked úp a model for visitors at the Cape*, the corresponding nominalization, *móckup* (with initial stress now) carries the same sense. This fails to happen with *hold*. Thus, if you *hold up* an item (such as a pencil) it does not become a **hóldup*. The form *hóldup* exists, of course, but it means 'robbery' and has nothing to do with an item being held in the air.[5] Yet the verb *hold* and the formant *up* have further symbioses. Whereas it is ungrammatical to say **the judge held up the Constitution* (in the sense of 'maintain, enforce' unless as a joke meant as a take-off on *uphóld*), what one says is *the judge uphéld the Constitution*. But again, notice the strange, one-way idiomatic restriction of *uphóld*. We cannot say **Jack uphéld the shelf while I drilled the hole in the wall*, though again, of course, it could be said as a joke of some sort.

Similarly, notice *fall + down*. We say *the tree fell dówn* normally, but we do not talk about the *dównfall of the tree*. *The dównfall of the Roman Empire* is, of course, normal. (*The dównfall of the tree* would imply its moral decay rather than its behavior in the Earth's gravitational field. Again, given the appropriate literary witticism, the sentence might be acceptable.)

But back to *take*. *Take + in*, yielding both a literal construct, as in *I take the milk in every morning*, and an idiom, as in *Harcourt and Brace took in Mr Jovanovich*, if reversed, yielding *intake* has no semantic connection either with 'partnership', or with the act of moving an object inside from the outside. Otherwise we ought to have **the intake of the milk occurs every morning after the milkman leaves it*, and **the intake of Mr Jovanovich by Harcourt and Brace*.

But again we have barely begun to scratch the surface of *take*. Where in a dictionary should we put an expression such as *take it out on*, meaning 'use someone as a scapegoat'? What is the role of *it* in such an expression? That of *on*?

In *TRUE* we not only describe the item itself, but also the *ecological links* that the entry has with other related entries. Thus the form *take it out on* relates *take* ecologically with several other matters at once; it relates *take* (a) to the prepositional-adverbial formants *out* and *on*, and (b) to larger size phrasal verbs and phrasal verb idioms which are characterized by two prepositional-adverbial formants instead of one, and (c) to the occurrence of the OBLIGATORY IT. Thus the entry for *take it out on*, besides giving the meaning of this phase, would send the user of *TRUE* to expressions such as *cop out on*, *drop out on*, *run out on*, and *walk out on*; but also to expressions such as *drop in on*, *listen in on*, *be in on*, *sit in on*, and so forth; furthermore, to such expressions as *step on IT*, *take IT to heart*, *have IT out with*, and so on. The various parts of the expression *take it out on* will be sub-labelled with labels such as *V*, *comp. IT*, *P/A$_1$*, and *P/A$_2$* where *V* stands for *take*, *comp IT* for 'compulsory *IT* ', and *P/A* for prepositional-adverbial formant. By virtue of having these sub-markings, *TRUE* not only exemplifies and defines as does *HABIT*, but it also gives a practical guide to the function of the elements under investigation as regards their MULTIPLE REINVESTABILITY.[6]

8.6.2. *Take* in TOURNURE IDIOMS. TOURNURE IDIOMS are larger size lexo-ecological units which are the multi-word encodings of cognitive material which, in most cases, corresponds to a single verb. Thus *to kick the bucket* 'die' is a tournure; *fly off the handle* 'lose one's temper', *seize the bull by the horns* 'come to grips with a problem, face a problem' represents another type, and so on. (For a detailed discussion of the various tournure types see Makkai (1972a).) A typical example involving *take* is *take a raincheck on sg.* 'to postpone privilege or use of invitation'. An incomplete sampling of *take* tournures appears below:

take five 'to take a five-minute break or a short rest period from whatever
   one is doing, especially a theatrical rehearsal'
take ten 'to reconsider one's point in a vociferous quarrel, as if by counting
   until ten'
take it on the chin 'to withstand punishment or abuse; to bear up under
   attack, strain or hard work'
take it in 'to see or do everything a specific locale or job has to offer'
take someone to the cleaners 'to cheat someone out of all his money'
take a bath (on something) 'to come to financial ruin'; etc.

8.6.3. The last example, *take a bath* 'to come to financial ruin' deserves
special discussion. It is the example that leads the compiler of *TRUE* from
tournure idioms into the PHRASEOLOGICAL IDIOMS involving *take*. It is
important to point out that the expression *take a bath* has a more 'predictable' meaning as well, which can be paraphrased as 'indulge oneself in a
bodily self-cleansing act by immersion in water'. This idiom, however, is
essentially different from the ones so far discussed. What is idiomatic about
take a bath in the bathing sense is not so much its semantic unpredictability,
but rather the obligatory use of the verb *take* in front of *bath* rather than
some such other possible verb as *have a bath*, *get a bath*, *do a bath*, etc.,
Baths, in addition to being had, gotten, and done, can also be bought, as
in certain Eastern European countries where bathrooms are scarce and
country folk walk up to a ticket window and literally purchase a tub bath
in a public bath house; baths can be given (as to a baby, a sick patient,
or an elderly person), and quite a few more possibilities. Why then, the
question arises, do we correct the foreigner when he laboriously says *I just
did a bath* or *I just got a bath*? Probably because the *take a bath* formula, due
to its statistically much higher frequency, is beginning to sound to us like
some kind of unit that we do not like to hear broken up. But what kind
of unit can it be? *Take* surely has one of its most frequent subsenses in the
expression – German *nehmen*, French *prendre*, Hungarian *venni*, Russian
принимать, Italian *prendere*, etc., all correspond to it.

Once again the problem seems extremely difficult to solve unless we
resort to ecological subnesting in the *TRUE* spirit. Let us, then, take a
look at the various kinds of direct objects one traditionally *takes* in English
and see if they exhibit any kind of systematic recurrence of meaning.

(1) PUBLIC CONVEYANCE FOR HIRE BY SINGLE INDIVIDUAL OR GROUP:

   *take a cab, take a/the bus, take the subway, take the Elevated, take a/the train,
   take a/the plane, take a rickshaw, take a rent-a-car.* (A subclass of this
   includes the structure *take an X ride* where X can be any of the
   conveyances listed above, as in *take a taxi ride, take a bus ride, take a
   boat ride.* The *take an X ride* structure is possible in a number of cases
   where the X (without the ride) seems not to occur; e.g. we do not say
   I took a roller coaster, but we do say *I took a roller coaster ride*; similarly
   one may speak of *taking a ferris wheel ride*, but not of *taking a/the ferris*

wheel. This becomes clear when we contrast *boat* with *pleasure boat*: we say *I took a pleasure boat ride*, but not *I took a pleasure boat*. (Of course, all the nonoccurrences CAN be justified given the right context.) The principle that emerges is this: when the conveyance is for ordinary business (exclusive of pleasure) one simply *takes* it; *ride* implies lack of business and greater likelihood of idle pleasure seeking.)

(2) IMMERSION IN A LIQUID:

take a dip, take a dive.

(3) IMMERSION IN A LIQUID WITH THE PURPOSE OF SELF-CLEANSING:

take a bath, take a shower, take a soak.

(4) DIPILLATORY ACT (used by the minority, others use *get* or *have*):

take a shave, take a hair cut.

(5) SUPPRESSED UNPLEASANTNESS EUPHEMICIZED BY IT:

take it to heart, take sg. out on sy., take it to court, take it up with sy.

(6) SELF-PROPELLING MOTION ON DRY LAND OR WATER:

take a walk, take a stroll, take a swim.

(7) SELF-INDULGENCE:

take a nap, take a break, take a rest, take a snooze.

(8) OBLIGE ANOTHER BY ACCEPTING:

take a hint, take a suggestion, take some friendly advice, take note of sg.

(9) CAUTION:

take care, take care of, take good care of.

(10) BODILY EXCRETION (all vulgarisms):

take a shit, take a piss, take a leak, take a crap.

(11) RELATE TO (inanimate or animate):

take sg. easy(ly), take sg. lightly, take sy. lightly, take sg. seriously, take sy. seriously, take sg. optimistically, take sg. pessimistically, take sg. philosophically, take sg. with equanimity. (This class seems to favor the

-ly type adverb as the obligatory attraction of take. It can be compared with *take it* + *adv.*, as in *he took it philosophically, he took it badly, he took it like a soldier*, etc., where *take it* [with compulsory *IT*] means 'accept'.)

As we can see, then, there are at least eleven reasonable subsenses that one can associate with the verb *take* depending on the nature of the direct object involved. The point that has to be make at this juncture with regard to Langendoen's use of *take*-based phraseological idiom, is that he fails to see that *take . . . seriously* and *take . . . lightly* belong in this ecological nest of *take*-attractions, where the semantics of the intervening object (person or abstract notion) forces the exterior phrase to behave differently with regard to the monoverbal paraphrasability.

9. The foregoing sketch of *take* is incomplete. As the title of the chapter suggests, it is merely a first look at the ecology of *take*, which must be followed by detailed studies. Specifically, I have omitted from the discussion the standard *HABIT* definitions of *take*, whether verb or noun, and a very large number of both semantic and phraseological idioms have been left untreated. But completeness was not my purpose. I have tried to show that by looking at language as an ecology, certain pseudo-problems forced onto language analysis by Transformational-Generative Grammar resolve themselves and yield their long unsurped place to data-oriented common sense.

Notes

1. There is reason to believe that the state of current rock music, physically harmful to the listener's ears, has almost totally eradicated the notion of 'music' in the sense of Bach, Mozart, and Beethoven from the consciousness of a vary large number of young people these days. Perhaps the analogy of (A) being poetry is not as far-fetched as all that.
2. Lest I be accused of introducing an abnormal amount of new and impenetrable terminology, I should like to point out that not one new word had been coined in this entire chapter, except for **vitasevere* and **Olliescorn* and their derivatives, when discussing Langendoen's examples above. The word *ecology* has been added to the well known terms SEMOLOGY, LEXOLOGY, MORPHOLOGY, and PHONOLOGY and the suffix *-graphy* was added to *ecology* after removing *-logy*. I have tried using LEX-ECOGRAPHY and if it pleases the reader, it is certainly available to replace LEXO-ECOGRAPHY. The meaning of this neologism is clear: it suggests an ecologically oriented overhauling of traditional lexicography thus rendering it lex-ecography.
3. No intention of completeness is intended here. The statements are minimal. The purpose of the present chapter is not to exhaust the ecology of *take* but rather to show how it would be treated in *TRUE*.
4. No satisfactory answer exists to the intriguing question of when and how a phrasal verb can be interrupted by an intervening direct object (cf. Bolinger (1971), Fraser 1970). Only trivialities are certain, such as the observation

that if the intervening object is a personal pronoun we always have the *hold him up* pattern and not the **hold up him* pattern. One would instinctively guess that idiomatic status is a force working against the interruptability of such sequences, but this seems to be the case only sporadically and without any predictability. It is certainly not systematic.

5. This is not to deny that historically there may be a connection, such as the robbers having traditionally shouted 'hold up your hands!' or some such thing, or the robbers holding their guns up, or holding up (in the sense of 'delaying') the wagon on its way in frontier days. Synchronically *hold úp* 'keep elevated by hand' and *hóldup* 'robbery' are semantically only very vaguely connected. It follows, therefore, that the nominal *hóldup* cannot possibly be a transformation of the phrasal verb *to hold úp*, even in the sense 'to delay'; if it were, the nominalization *hóldup* would have to mean 'a loss of time, a delay' and have nothing to do with a robbery.

6. See Chapter 2.

Part III. Facing the arts

11 Systems of simultaneous awareness: toward a 'musical linguistics'

'Linguistic science needs a general theory of associative sets, comparable in boldness and imaginative power to the theory of paradigms developed by Roman Jakobson.'

Rulon S. Wells (1956, p. 667)

0. Introduction

Here I am raising a question of potentially great interest not only in linguistics but in psychology, literature and music as well: how do we humans do so many things SIMULTANEOUSLY? Some of the numerous complex thing we do are carried out by the HUMAN voice; others by our HANDS and FEET, others yet by our eyes, EARS, HANDS and feet in an astonishingly rich display of what I propose to call SATCOG, the acronym for 'simultaneous awareness of transmodal cognition'.

Obviously not all human events that somehow involve simultaneity and some greater or lesser degree of AWARENESS of such simultaneity are of equal linguistic interest; yet Linguistics as a science, can only gain in realism by coming to grips with multiple awareness and multiple coding.

In order to introduce the subject from the more familiar sides of everyday life, I would like to present some well-known non-linguistic examples.

0.1. Some non-linguistic examples

A person is driving a car. He has a passenger beside him. He must watch the road, the lights, and the oncoming traffic as well as cars that pass him, pedestrian crossings, motorcycles, trucks and cyclists. The driver may be smoking and conducting an important business discussion with the passenger. The car in question, if it is a standard gear-shift car, is equipped with a clutch beside the breaks and the accelerator pedal, forcing the driver to use the clutch whenever shifting gears.

A radio or a tape player may also be on in the car; the radio may give an exact time-signal prompting the driver to look at his watch while paying various degrees of attention to all the other things he must do in this particular situation. Probably his main attention will be on the business transaction which the two happen to be discussing in the car; most of the driving will be done semi-automatically.

While talking to the passenger in the side-seat about the business at hand, the driver may also slip in an occasional word about the weather, the passenger's comfort, or the road conditions.

A typist, who is skilled in touch-typing, is listening to the evening news on television or radio while finishing a piece of work at home. Her son walks in the door and is asking for his dinner. Without stopping, she tells him where in the refrigerator he can find it and carries right on with the sentence she is typing. She is interrupted by a phone call. She answers the call, picks up the receiver and puts it on her right ear with a shoulder-rest, and then continues her work by allowing the typewriter to run out a paragraph which was previously corrected in the memory. She silently reads along the printed-out text as she talks into the receiver of the telephone.

A pianist in a night club plays the piano and sings the lyrics; alternating between French and English; the night club is in Montréal and the code-switching in mid-song is meant to emphasize the bilingual cosmopolitan nature of the establishment. He also has a drink on top of his piano-bar and takes an occasional sip of it. Beside the piano there is a set of jazz drums which he operates with his feet when he decides not to use them to manipulate the soft and 'hold' pedals of the piano itself. While engaged in all these activities he also manages to shift the quality of his voice from ordinary singing voice to the typical bar-singer's half-spoken half-sung *parlando* mode. A waiter comes up to him and asks a question: without stopping the music he listens to the waiter's question, understands it and gives a reply to it.

A mother, while cooking dinner in the kitchen and watching the evening news on a small TV set on the kitchen counter, answers a phone call while helping her daughter solve an 8th grade math problem.

All of these examples come from my personal observations of real individuals.

0.1.1. Some everyday household items that feature 'SIMUL-AWARENESS'

The most obvious example known by most people is the common telephone dial, whether touch-tone or old-fashioned, whose numbers are simul-coded with triads of the letters of the alphabet. Modern touch-tone dials also have extra button marked by 0 for 'Operator', * and # for certain types of banking and international dialling purposes.

Multi-purpose buttons abound on most modern typewriters and are also found on microwave ovens, washing and drying machines, kitchen appliances of various sorts, etc. On the average modern typewriter upper

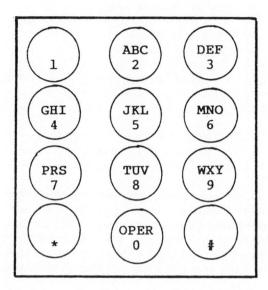

Figure 1 A typical touch-tone telephone dialing system. Notice the absence of the letters Q and Z. The arrangement may be circular, oval, or square. The actual telephone in question does not have to be a touch-tone system phone in order to have the double-coding of letters and numbers. Old-fashioned circular dialing phones in North America had double coding; telephone numbers used to begin with a word such as UN(iversity)6-4343, and the like. In many parts of the world 7-digit dialing is just now being gradually introduced.

and lower key function sit on the same button and are distinguished by the use of the SHIFT-key; numbers and other symbols usually sit together on the keys of the top row; word-processor typewriters of various vintages and models all have multi-function keys, some for bold face printing, some for underlining, and so forth.

Some people have been known deliberately to ask for telephone numbers which, due to the double-coding of numbers and letters, create English words that help people to remember the given number more readily. Such MNEMONIC TELEPHONE NUMBERS cost a little more in some states, and are free in others; from a sociological point of view they resemble 'vanity licence plates' on cars. Some are used by businesses, as the examples below from Chicago indicate:

$$
\begin{array}{lcl}
\text{C A R P E T S} & = & \text{227-7387} \\
\text{W H I S K E Y} & = & \text{944-7539} \\
\text{T I C K E T S} & = & \text{842-5387}
\end{array}
$$

Public information may use such as these:

$$\begin{aligned}
\text{W E A T H E R} &= 932\text{-}8437 \\
\text{H I G H W A Y} &= 444\text{-}4929
\end{aligned}$$

Playful individuals (some of them linguists) may use the mnemonic telephone number for their home, summer cottage or University office, as did J.R. 'Haj' Ross in Massachussetts, in the Area Code 617:

$$\begin{aligned}
\text{D U M B H U T} &= 386\text{-}3488 \\
\text{T R U E A L P} &= 878\text{-}3257 \\
\text{A L E F A C T} &= 253\text{-}3228
\end{aligned}$$

The first one was the home, the second his summer cottage, and the third his office at MIT. I have no way of knowing if our brilliant colleague wanted to indicate that there was something 'dumb' about his primary abode; that the summer cottage may have reminded him of 'true Alps' may be understandable, and as to whether or not his office at MIT was as intoxicating to him as massive consumption of 'ale' can in 'fact' do, is anybody's guess.

Notice, by the way, that these numbers have a rather simple 'syntax' with only a couple of 'constraints on variables': only 7-letter words can be used and the letters Q and Z are not in the 'lexicon'. The 'grammar' is provided by the buttons 2 through 9; but 1 is not simul-codable with any letter and the non-digital buttons marked *, # and 0 for 'Operator' are not available as alphabet-unit carriers.

The international electronics industry has created a number of different types of musical key-boards and music synthesizers whose most striking common feature is the multiplicity of available instrument voices upon the touch of a button. I will return to the various SIMULTANEITY FUNCTIONS of the typical musical keyboard in the main section on music.

Whatever the nature and use of similar household items, it is obvious that modern industry has recognized the need and appeal of such products. It may be argued, of course, that it is modern industry that creates the need for these items. One can only guess what kind of plays Shakespeare would have written on a word-processor and what kind of music Mozart would have composed on the YAMAHA SY-77 music synthesizer. Basically, however, industry imitates, albeit in a redundantly amplified way, the nature-given, basic human habit of SIMULTANEOUS AWARENESS AND MULTIPLE CODING.

0.1.1.1. In this section we will take a closer look at the letter-dialling capability of the now fairly common touch-tone dial phone. Figure 1 presents this in simple tabular form. In Figure 2, this visual reproduction of the dialling system is expanded into a relational network sign pattern and a greatly oversimplified tactics. The relational network diagrams that follow throughout the rest of this chapter are based on Lamb (1966),

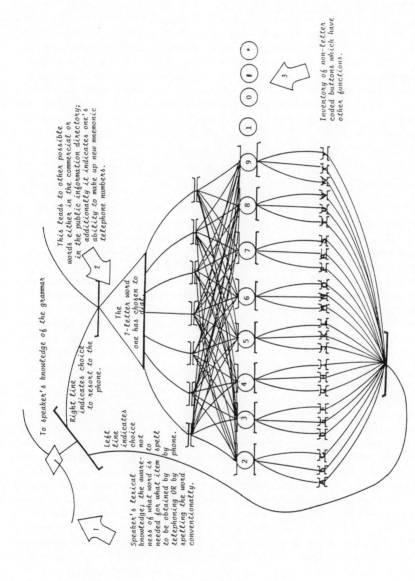

Figure 2 Simplified logical structure of the letter-coded telephone dialing system

Lockwood (1972) and Makkai and Lockwood (1972) plus the cumulative stratificational literature that can be found in the *LACUS FORUM Series* starting with 1974 and continuing.

The arrow labelled 1 in Figure 2 indicates that the user of the mnemonic telephone number has a choice of lexemes (commonly thought of as 'words') in his memory; these will include the names of many items one may go shopping for to a supermarket. The tactic diamond which, on its other side, ties his inventory of words to their behavior in grammar (the second line to the upper right) leads to an 'unordered OR node' whose left line takes precedence over the right one. In this instance the left line leads the user to 8 triads of English alphabet letters, in fact the entire English alphabet with the exclusion of the letters *Q* and *Z*. The user knows, in other words, that s(he) can spell any word in English as long as it contains no *Q* or *Z*. The MANNER OF SPELLING is up to the user: a pencil may be used, a blackboard, a set of alphabet blocks, a typewriter – literally anything. If this choice is not taken, the right-hand line prevails: The user has chosen to 'spell by phoning' as it were. This line leads to the large triangle marked arrow No. 2. This is an 'ordered AND node' with seven lines leading to eight approximately wired telephone buttons numbered 2 through 9, since 1 is left unused for multiple coding with letters and 0, left for 'Operator', is also left unused for double-coding with letters. Arrow No. 3, lower in the lower right-hand corner of the diagram shows these extra non-letter-coded buttons.

Arrow No. 2 pointing at the large triangle indicates that the user may have many such 7-digit, letter-coded words/numbers in his directory; our examples above show several of these. As J.R. 'Haj' Ross' self-made mnemonic numbers show, these 'triangles' may be increased at will by designing one's own 7-digit number and then requesting it as one's actual phone number from the phone company for a surcharge. Once the letters have 'left the triangle', so to speak, their future place in the 7-digit line-up is no longer subject to the 'rules' (i.e. the 'orderedness') of the sponsoring triangle. A telephone number may theoretically begin with any digit and may end with any digit. In other words, every telephone number that is seven digits long does, in effect, spell a 7-letter word whether that word is a recognizable English word or not. My present home phone number is 769-2207, and with the letter triads MNO, GHI, WXY, N/A, DEF, MNP, DEF one cannot quite make a decent 7-letter word because 1 is involved, which is not applicable. Word-fragments are, of course, always possible but according to our present 7-digit rule my present telephone number does not lend itself to being a mnemonic one.

If Figure 2 and the actually oversimplified relational network diagramming that accompanies it looks complicated, just think of the computational complexity of the telephone exchange of a medium-sized modern city of a million inhabitants, where there are, say, 500,000 telephones in use. With the extra features of long distance dialling, memory phones that retain up to 100 telephone numbers, the extra buttons # and * for banking and other special purposes, such computer-terminal hook-ups, you will agree that Figure 2 is a very humble exercise in industrial drawing.

1. A first linguistic approximation: the simplified structure of a tongue-twister

Let us focus our attention for a moment on a familiar English tongue-twister, the famous *Peter Piper picked a peck of pickled peppers*. Linguists seldom bother analyzing this as a sentence and understandably so, since it really does not say very much at all. Lexico-semantically it informs us that the individual called Peter Piper harvested a half-bushel of peppers. An ordinary, simple declarative sentence in the past tense, the tongue-twister offers nothing remarkable for grammatical analysis. For obvious reasons, it is remembered and fondly repeated by countless multitudes due to the difficult repetition of /p/ phonemes which, in word-initial position in English are heavily aspirated. *Peter Piper* thus makes excellent pronunciation drill material for foreigners who speak languages with unaspirated /p/ sounds. At the same time it is quite impossible to deny that the sentence does have a meaning of its own, a meaning which is easily arrived at by the compositional function of ordinary English syntax and the lexical semantics of the words in it. The question, really, is this: what part of *Peter Piper* do we pay more attention to? To the 'meaning' of this sentence, or to the machine-gun like repetition, and thus the difficulty, of the voiceless aspirated /p/-sounds? To answer the question favoring only the one side, say the lexico-grammar, against the other, is obviously just as arbitrary as denying that this tongue-twister also has a 'legal' meaning. We are thus faced with the necessity of DOING BOTH THINGS AT ONCE: we may remind ourselves of the sentence's meaning AND we may concentrate on the difficulty of the /p/-sounds. The question arises: is our attention-span likely to extend to the lexico-grammar and the phonology evenly? Here, I think, we must admit that it is the nature of tongue-twisters that they call attention to themselves more by their phonologies than by what they say. As observed above, however, this does not in any way make it impossible for us to analyze tongue-twisters syntactically. Hence, in the upper right-hand corner of Figure 3, an unordered AND-OR node reminds us that we can turn our attention evenly, on a 50–50 basis to the meaning and the syntax and to the phonology, or that, alternatively, we can turn off the one line or the other entirely or to a considerable extent. ATTENTION in this sense, is comparable to a pocket flash-light: the larger the area it illuminates, the less sharp the illumination. We can turn our attention quite like a flash-light either toward the phonology or toward the lexico-grammar.

Our ability to do this is ultimately bound to the structure of the human brain. Figure 4 shows in greatly simplified form the relationship of the human neo-cortex to that of mammalians, amphibians, etc. The feature that sets the human neo-cortex aside from the rest of the animal kingdom is the large neo-cortex that balloons out to the left. This relatively young

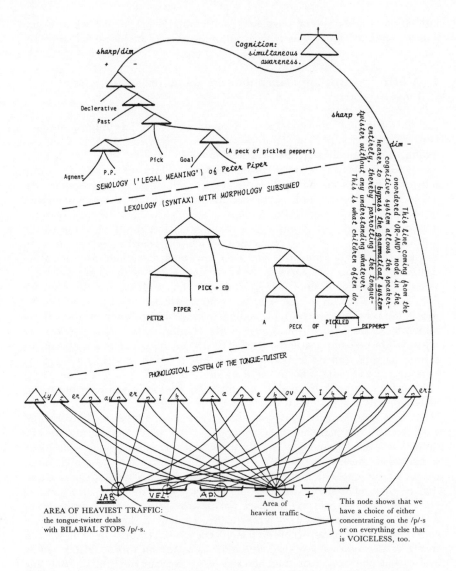

Figure 3 The relational network description of a familiar tongue-twister

and extremely large neo-cortex is, furthermore, subject to HEMISPHERIC LATERALIZATION, a feature which has received much attention in the recent literature (Koestler 1967, Janes 1976).

To paraphrase the latter, we have a situation roughly as follows. In right-handed individuals the LEFT HEMISPHERE is dominant, in left-handed individuals, the right. The dominant hemisphere is like a

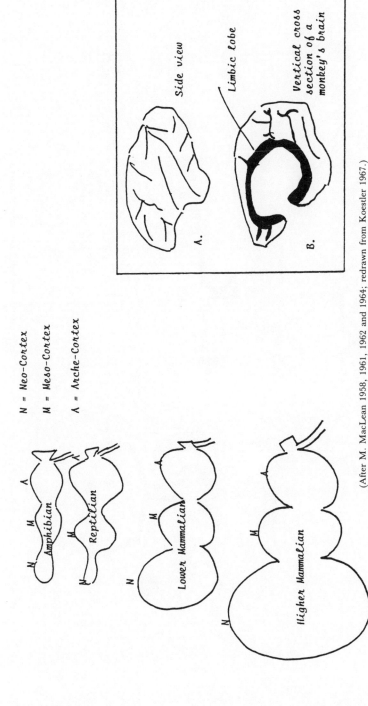

N = Neo-Cortex

M = Meso-Cortex

A = Arche-Cortex

Side view

Limbic lobe

Vertical cross section of a monkey's brain

A.

B.

Amphibian

Reptilian

Lower Mammalian

Higher Mammalian

(After M. MacLean 1958, 1961, 1962 and 1964; redrawn from Koestler 1967.)

Figure 4   Stages in the evolution of brain structures from amphibian to human

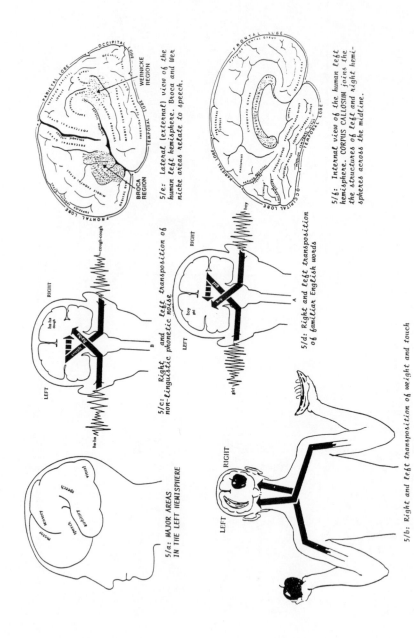

5/a: MAJOR AREAS IN THE LEFT HEMISPHERE

5/b: Right and left transposition of weight and touch

5/c: Right and left transposition of non-linguistic phonetic noise

5/d: Right and left transposition of familiar English words

5/e: Lateral (external) view of the human left hemisphere. Broca and Wernicke areas relate to speech.

5/f: Internal view of the human left hemisphere. CORPUS CALLOSUM joins the structures of left and right hemispheres across the midline.

Figure 5 Major human brain structures and hemispheric lateralization and transfer

'computer' that calculates and plots the conscious activities we engage in such as counting, solving math problems, and a great deal of speech production and reception (i.e. ENCODING and DECODING) (see Figure 5). Psychologists are fond of comparing the dominant 'left hemisphere' to the more aggressive male temperament and to equate it with day-time consciousness. The more 'submissive' right hemisphere is said to be more 'feminine', given to dreaming. It is receptive to rhythm and tunes, degrees of loudness and non-rational free association. During sleep, it is believed, the 'right hemisphere' produces images and sensations such as floating in air without falling down which the rational left hemisphere's day-time consciousness would rule out as impossible.

It cannot be the task of the present study to evaluate on biological and physiological grounds the relative merits of the debate that rages around hemispheric lateralization. It may indeed turn out as many believe that what is currently attributed to hemispheric lateralization is, to a large extent, the result of social conventions. However this may be, the evidence I am trying to present here speaks for itself: people either pay attention to the way a TONGUE-TWISTER SOUNDS, or they pay attention to its SYNTAX AND LEXICAL MEANING. Invariably, the 'meanings' and grammatical structures of tongue-twisters are somehow trivial, at best not very important, and the goal of the tongue-twister is to create difficulty in pronunciation. Some readers may object to my statement that tongue-twisters have a 'goal'. This is not meant as a teleological statement but is a factual social observation: a good deal of human language, especially what we consider children's language, is not the main vehicle for the exchange of GOODS AND SERVICES, but functions as a toy, a way to create SOCIAL AMUSEMENT. Whether social amusement is 'useful' or not is a secondary debate; my personal conviction is that everything nature endowed us with is 'useful' in a profound sense, whether we can today convince ourselves of such usefulness or not. Sleep and dreams are also 'useful', since they bring about rest and recuperation. Surely, then, the daydream and phenomena related to it are also 'useful' inasmuch as daydreams create periodic instances of rest.

The phenomenon of tongue-twisters – along with the related phenomenon of the 'nonsensical' nursery-rhyme – calls attention to an important aspect of second language learning. Adults over 21 years of age are known to have more difficulty 'mastering a native-like accent' than children under seven or fourteen. If it is true that hemispheric lateralization completes itself in stages roughly according to the metabolic cycle of seven years, it makes sense to suppose that children under seven 'will learn with BOTH HEMISPHERES' unconsciously, as if 'taking language in by its sound' – like imitating dance steps or humming a tune. That fourteen-year olds can easier imitate seven-year olds than can twenty-one-year olds is easy to observe. If your job is to teach English to a forty-five-year old Chinese engineer, you will have maximum difficulty, since such individuals are unlikely to revert to childhood behavior willingly. Successful foreign language teachers testify unanimously that SONGS, NURSERY RHYMES, etc., have a major facilitating effect on the overcoming of 'foreign accented speech'.

2. On the sound and sense of acronyms

The purpose of the present section is not to classify acronyms in English, but rather to explicate on a cognitive basis how native speakers form them. Acronym formation is essentially an innovating, creative process. It merits investigation by a formal theory of language versus 'performance', where by 'performance' we mean, of course, 'ideal performance'. Thus no outline of major or minor types of acronyms is offered here, since I assume that all possible categories are automatically implied in the treatment that follows. Such categories based on the intersection of phonological and orthographic criteria, such as the relationship that exists between speech sounds resulting from saying out loud the names of 'letters', the formation of pronouncing-syllables from a sequence of the initial letters of a complex noun phrase, or the mixing of the syllable type with pure alphabetic type, pronounced or read as a spell-out. Such a classification is urgently needed.

2.1. In this section special attention will be paid to that type of acronym in which the resultant word is an allusion by phonologic coincidence to an existing English word such that there is a logical or quasi-logical connection between the new acronym-word's old, familiar meaning and the concept or institution that it stands for. My reason for concentrating on these PUNNING ACRONYMS is that it is in this type that the deliberate act of coining with a specific purpose in mind is the most obvious. Punning acronyms can be viewed as containing all of the features of the other types, hence their analysis automatically subsume the analysis of other acronym types. The validity of this observation will be demonstrated below. Viewable as the summit-achievement of acronymy, punning acronyms include the now famous types *NOW* /náw/ 'National Organization for Women', an impatient, progressive political organization whose slogan *NOW* could not be more appropriately chosen; *ASH* /æš/ 'Action for Smoking and Health', a group devoted to the struggle against lung cancer by persuading people to stop smoking, with the word *ash* strongly associated with fire and smoke in general; *GOES* /gówz/ 'Geostationary Operational Environmental Satellite', a gadget which obviously goes, and many more. Before I attempt a stratificational formalization of acronymy, I should like to point out that the first sound, and economical treatment, one which was, in fact, a step in the direction of separating lexemic from morphemic phenomena, was laid down by Wells' now classic article 'Acronymy' (1956). In the concluding section of the paper Wells wrote (p. 667):

Saussure (1922, Part II, chs. 5–7) contrasted two 'axes' of synchronic relations, the syntagmatic and the associative. In effect (174–5) he classified associative sets into two kinds, according as the number of terms in a given set that stand in associative relation to one another is definite or indefinite. The definite ones are what we ordinarily called paradigms. Thus Saussure made a contribution toward defining paradigms, by providing a genus, of which paradigms are a species. The present paper has attempted to explore Saussure's second class, the associative sets that are NOT paradigmatic, in the belief that although Saussure's ground of distinguishing the two classes is unsatisfactory, the distinction itself into paradigmatic sets and the remainder is of value. The remainder class poses interesting problems. What other sorts of sets besides the ones that have been mentioned in this paper should be placed in this class? Since similarity (whether in sound or in meaning) is a matter of degree, shouldn't we switch to a many-valued framework? And if we did so, wouldn't this lead us into a closer alliance of linguistics with psychology than has been customary in recent years? And on the other hand, what kind of structural treatment would it permit? . . . Linguistic science needs a general theory of associative sets, comparable in boldness and imaginative power to the theory of paradigms developed by Roman Jakobson.

2.1.1. It is my contention that such a structural treatment of associative sets is now available; that such an alliance of linguistics and psychology has indeed come about; and that such a theory of associative sets considerably more general in scope than anything ever proposed by Jakobson is getting well established in linguistics: it is COGNITIVE-STRATIFICATIONAL GRAMMAR in the sense of Lamb (1964a, 1965a, 1966a); Gleason (1964, 1969); Lockwood (1972); Makkai (1972a); and Makkai and Lockwood (1973); also Reich (1970) and other publications by Reich listed therein.

2.1.1.1. Before I can proceed in proving that Wells' prophetic prestratificational insights have all come true and born fruit, I should like to reiterate a point made by Lamb (1969) concerning the theoretical ancestry of stratificational linguistics: On the one hand, we have the Boas–Sapir–Bloomfield–Harris–Chomsky tradition in linguistics. These are the linguists who have paid overwhelming attention to the *signifiants*, i.e., the 'acoustic-articulatory' side of language, at the expense of properly exploring the semantic or 'content-side', the side of the *signifié*. (This point is echoed, incidentally, in such publications as Chafe (1968b) and (1970) as well). Stratificational grammar, on the other hand, derives its intellectual ancestry from the De Saussure–Noreen–Troubetzkoy–Hjelmslev–Firth–Halliday–Lamb line. While the former tradition is characterizable as a paradigm-yielding line of thought, this latter tradition is equally capable of yielding paradigms as well as associative sets. The reason for this ability of stratificational theory to deal with both of Saussure's 'axes' is that according to the stratificational view, a language is a system of systems that mediates between cognition and the phonologic code for encoding purposes; between the phonological code and cognition for decoding purposes; and that any person within a given speech community can be speaker and/or hearer. From this it follows that stratificational theory is neither speaker-oriented as transformational-generative grammar is in its syntax; nor hearer-oriented as transformationalists are in their phonology and semantics. Rather, SG is completely neutral with regard to hearer and speaker since both are accommodated in its scheme equally. The same goes for paradigmatic sets (the formal connections in a relational network system and their relevant tactics) and for associative sets (sememes versus lexemes, lexemes versus morphemes, sememic traces versus lexotactic realizations; agnate structures on the sememic level, etc.). (See Lockwood 1972.)

2.2. Yet a claim is no better than the evidence available to back it up. Let us, then, examine the evidence.

2.2.1. In his 'Acronymy' article Wells asks the question:
. . . What process leads from *veteran* to *vet*? First suggestion: *Vet* is the same morpheme as *veteran*.

This, however, must be rejected, argues Wells, since there is no complementation in distribution between these putative allomorphs.

Second suggestion: *Veteran* is a morpheme sequence that contains the morpheme *vet* . . . and *-eran* is also a morpheme . . . we would also analyze *logarithm* into *log* and *-arithm*, *professor* into *prof* and *-essor* . . .

This alternative, too, is rejected, because of its inability to account for the remainder forms *-essor*, *-eran*, *-arithm* either as allomorphs of the same morpheme, or as individual morphemes.

Third suggestion: Take *veteran* as one morpheme and *vet* as two morphemes: *veteran* plus *minus feature*.

Here Wells points out that Bloomfield's idea of the minus feature comes, in fact, from Passy (Wells 1956, p. 664 fn. 9). There being no gain in calling features morphemes, Wells argues, 'there is no advantageous use of the morpheme concept in taking *vet* as a sequence or complex of two morphemes'.

At this point, under section 2 (p. 663) Wells reaches a conclusion truly revolutionary for 1956: He suggests that both *vet* and *veteran* be regarded as single morphemes, 'but morphemes somehow related in a grammatical way to each other'. He then suggests that the semantic relation of 'near-synonymy' which holds between *vet* and *veteran* can be called STRICT ASSOCIATION. It is pointed out that the logical denotation of an ORIGINAL and its acronym is 'identical', with connotations of familiarity, colloquiality, etc., somehow also being present in these acronym forms, as when we say *vet* and *veteran*, *Chevy* for *Chevrolet*, *Commie* for *Communist*, and so on. Unfortunately in 1956 there was no formal theory of grammar that could have shown just on what level and how forms such as *vet* and *veteran* are related, if both are independent morphemes that somehow mean the same thing, with *vet* additionally meaning 'colloquial' and 'familiar'.

3. In stratificational theory we have an elaborate formal system which can elegantly analyze such cases. The basic insight is the well-known separation

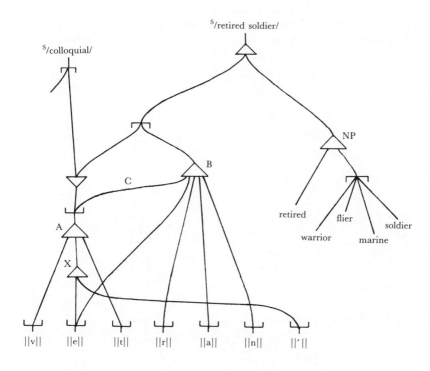

NP = retired warrior, retired marine, retired soldier, etc.
A = the acronoym *vet*
B = the full form *veteran*
C = the syllable *vet* which is shared by the acronym and the full form
X = morphemic stress / ´ / on the *é* of both *vét* and *véteran* but not on the second
     e of *veteran*

Figure 6 Relational network description of *vet* and *veteran*

of lexemic and morphemic phenomena (Lamb 1966, Becker Makkai 1969, Makkai 1972a, Lockwood 1972) which allows us to posit two or more separate morphemic realizations of the 'same' lexeme.

As Figure 6 shows, the English language allows a speaker to encode the notion 'retired soldier' in a number of ways, depending essentially on the person's vocabulary, and on the style he wishes to use. The speaker, thus, may use the compound expression *retired soldier* itself, or alternatively, *retired warrior*; or he may use the form *veteran*, or the acronym *vet*. When choosing *vet* over *veteran*, however, two things happen: The speaker has also selected the form that is a realization of the ^{S}/colloquial/, and, an observation regretfully missed by Wells, an expression which can SIMULTANEOUSLY realize yet another lexeme, namely *veterinarian*, 'animal doctor'. Figure 7 shows that portion of the relational network diagram which highlights the neutralization of *vet* 'retired soldier' and *vet* as 'animal doctor':

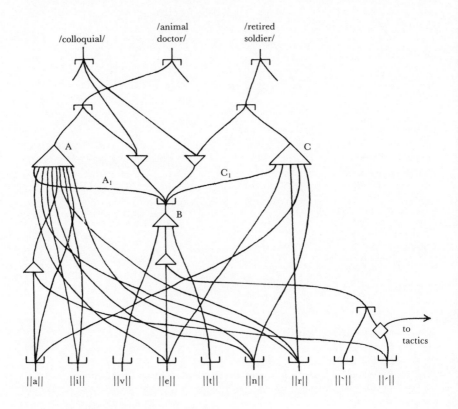

A = the lexeme *veterinarian*
A_1 = the syllable *vet* of A shared with C
B = the acronym *vet*; a neutralization of A and C
C = the lexeme *veteran*
C_1 = the syllable *vet* of C shared with A

Figure 7 Relational network description of *veteran*, *veterinarian*, and *vet* as usable for both

Figure 7 shows that the forms *veterinarian* and *veteran* have in common the syllable //v//, //e//, //t//, indicated by the lines labelled A_1 and C_1 leading from the ordered ANDs labelled A and C respectively. The diagram specifically shows that the lexemes *veteran* and *veterinarian* have morpheme composition such that they are analyzable into a sequence *vet* plus *-eran* or

-*erinarian* and that the sequence *vet*, the morphemic sign ^{MS}{//v//, //e//, //t//} labelled B on Figure 7 is both a separate morpheme having a double connection to *veteran* and *veterinarian* (unordered upward OR) and a meaningless syllable. It is the 'meaningless syllable' if we look at it as that which precedes -*eran* and -*erinarian*; but it is a 'meaningful morpheme' when we look at it alone, i.e. without paying attention to -*eran* or -*erinarian* but seeing it in actual sentence context. Thus it turns out that all of Wells' suggestions regarding the structural treatment of *vet* versus *veteran* have truth in them, but each proposal, taken by itself, covers only a part of the truth. The relational network diagram describes all of the possibilities while also showing why it was Wells' last proposal which makes the most economical sense (i.e. *vet* and *veteran* are 'separate morphemes' somehow connected to each other grammatically).

What conclusions can we draw concerning the status of *vet* if we separate, as we must, form from content? It is clear that *vet* is a separate morpheme, or more precisely a separate morphemic sign, and that this morphemic sign is the syllable *vet* whose morphons, //v//, //e//, and //t//, are identical with the first syllables of BOTH *veteran* and *veterinarian*. Since, however, this separate morphemic sign *vet* can realize both the ^{S}/Animal doctor/ as in *I took my cat to the vet* and the ^{S}/Retired soldier/ as in *Uncle Ferdinand gets a government pension as a vet of World War II* the sequence *vet* is also two separate lexemes. As such, vet_1 and vet_2 are no longer 'neutralized' (compare the two sentences above) – better said their similarity at this point is purely incidental. In fact, vet_1 could just as well be **voot* or some other form. It is primarily *qua* morphemic signs that they are in neutralization with each other since their morphonic composition realizes itself by coalescing into the same syllable *vet*. That vet_1 and vet_2 realize separate sememes should need no further elaboration.

As we can see from the contrasting senses of *vet* in a sentence such as *Uncle Algernon studied to be a vet on a scholarship he got as a vet of World War II*, the status of vet_1 and vet_2 as different lexemes is quite important, and precisely because of the neutralization on the morphemic level of 'Animal doctor' and 'Retired soldier' in the same morphemic sign. Otherwise one could argue that the morpheme–lexeme distinction is not a necessary one, since the morpheme can carry the contrasting sense.

3.1. By way of illustrating some of the knottier problems the analysis of acronyms presents, let us consider for a moment the acronyms *AAA* 'American Automobile Association', pronounced not always /êy + ey + éy/ but sometimes /trîpl + éy/; and *NAACP* 'National Association for the Advancement of Colored People' which is not often pronounced /ên + ey + ey + siy + píy/ but rather /ên + dəbl + èy + siy + píy/. What is the morphemic status of forms such as these? The spelling names of the letters of the English alphabet are separate syllables in each instance. The letter *w* is called /də́blyuw/, amounting to three syllables and it has a clearly separate morpheme *double* in it. We see this principle recurring in *AAA* and *NAACP*, with the two *A*'s of the latter called *double* and the three *A*'s of the former *triple A*. Morphologically *NAACP* seems to break down at least into five morphemes: *ên, dəbl, êy, siy*, and *píy*; *AAA*, in contrast, contains three morphemes, *trîpl* and *éy*, with two bound morphemes in *trîpl* and another in *éy*. Yet both the *AAA* and the *NAACP*, are unitary sememes and single lexemes of multilexonic realization; in the lexotactics (i.e. the sentence-syntax) one can equally use the acronym or the full name of either organization, as in: *Roy Wilkins, the President of the NAACP is also a member of the AAA*; or, *Roy Wilkins, the President of the National Association for the Advancement of Colored People is also a member of the American Automobile Association*. It is clear from examples such as this that the concepts which are INSTITUTIONS in American civilization are unitary on the pre-syntactic and syntactic levels (though quite complex, or polysemantic, of course, on the even higher cognitive level), and complex only on the expression level of the lexo-morphemic realization. It is the lengthy complexity of these expressions, incidentally, that makes people prone to want to abbreviate such forms. *NAACP* then, (though cognitively very complex) is a unitary sememe in the culture and its meaning can be rendered by defining what the *NAACP* does and what it stands for. The lexeme that realizes it is multi-lexonic, where the constituent lexons are: *nation, -al, a(d) / soci-, -ate, -ion, for, the, advance, -ment, of, color, ppl., person, pl.*, altogether fifteen lexons realizing separate morphemes in the expression system. Notice, however, that in the acronym form, *NAACP*, several of the lexons are not represented. Not participating in the abbreviation are the lexons *for, the*, and *of*, which we may define as the SUPPRESSED LEXONS OF THE ACRONYM. On the other hand, no direct higher sponsorship exists for the word *double* which arises solely by virtue of the fact that two *A*'s are describable as *double A*; something speakers of English instinctively know by virtue of the fact that they can count, so if they see two of something they can call it *double X*, just as when they see three of the same, they can call it *triple X*. (There seems to be a practical limitation on how high one can go; *quadruple A* or *quintuple A* sounds impossible in an acronym.) Hence the name *triple A* for *AAA* 'American Automobile Association'.

As Figure 8 indicates there is a complex system in the consciousness of literate native speakers of English which allows them to think of a letter (henceforth called a GRAPHO-MORPHON) as a symbol that (a) has a name, and (b) makes a certain set of noises in certain environments. This is essentially the principle that is used inexplicitly by teachers and educational television programs such as *Sesame Street* in order to teach youngsters how to read and write. It is also true, however, that the 'noises letters make' (phonemes in our sense) can also be used to spell their 'names', or conversely, the names of the letters are expressible by a recombination of SOME of the noises SOME of the letters make. Thus the grapho-morphon ||a|| makes, among other noises, the sounds /e/, /æ/, and /a/, but in 'long syllables', one version of which is describable as ||a + C + e|| with a 'mute *e*' as in *fame, same*, and *tame*, the 'noise of the letter' coincides with its name, i.e. /ey/. Similarly, the grapho-morphon ||c|| can make the noises /s/ and /k/, respectively, but in conjunction with the grapho-morphon ||h||,

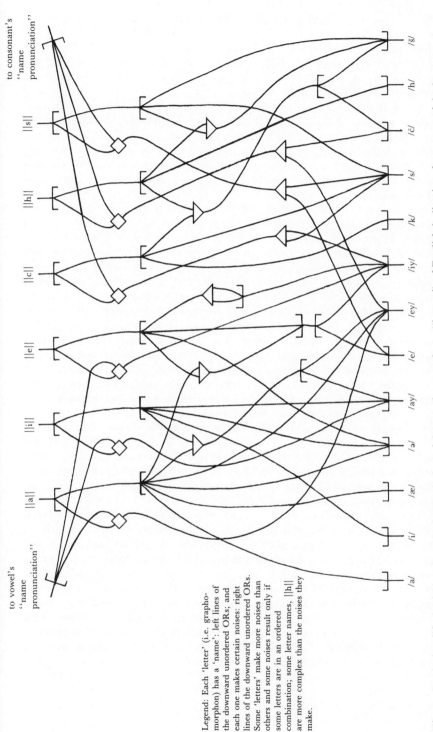

to consonant's "name pronunciation"

to vowel's "name pronunciation"

Legend: Each 'letter' (i.e. grapho-morphon) has a 'name'. left lines of the downward unordered ORs; and each one makes certain noises: right lines of the downward unordered ORs. Some 'letters' make more noises than others and some noises result only if some letters are in an ordered combination; some letter names, ||h||, are more complex than the noises they make.

Figure 8 A simplified relational network description of the grapho-morphons ('letters') of English indicating the names of the letters and the 'sounds they make'

which makes it own noise /h/ elsewhere, they make the noise /č/. The noises /ey/, the name of ||a||, and /č/, the noise of ||c|| and ||h|| in combination, however, if combined into the noise /eyč/, are the name of the grapho-morphon ||h||.

Notice that all of these grapho-morphons start in unordered downward ORs at the top of Figure 8, indicating that the speaker has a choice: he can either 'pronounce the letter' in one of the conventional ways, or he can utter the letter's 'spelling name'. It is no random coincidence, by the way, that both the names of the letters and the noises they make are realized by the same phonemic system. Figure 8 is, of course, only a crude first approximation.

We must now consider briefly the reasons why a speaker will choose the 'pronouncing name' of a letter acronym over its 'spelling name'. It was already observed by Wells that every acronym, or for that matter, every word in English, has a possible letter 'spelling name' realization, but not necessarily a word-pronunciation acronym. By this reasoning every word that begins with the grapho-morphon ||a|| could have the acronym A pronounceable as /ey/, and so on, through the twenty-six letters of the English alphabet. If an organization or institution has a multiword designation, one would use the first letter of each word. Thus if we want to acronymize *Human Relations Area Files*, we can say *HRAF*, that is /êyč/ + ar + ey + éf/ but not very likely something like */hræf/. Now whether, in case of easy pronounceability, it is the word-pronunciation or the letter-by-letter pronunciation that becomes institutionalized in the culture, is something that we may guess partially at from the syllable structure the acronym makes, but even so there are constant surprises all along the way. For *NASA* to be pronounced /nǽsə/ is more 'natural' than */ên + ey + es + éy/ though this spelling out is always possible. Consider, however, *PCCLLU* which stands for 'Pacific Conference on Contrastive Linguistics and Language Universals' with the suppressed lexons *on* and *and*. Everybody at the conference in Honolulu, Hawaii (January, 1971) assumed that the acronym was to be spelled out /pîy + siy + siy + el + el + yúw/ until we were notified by the organizing chairman that it was, in fact, pronounced /píkə luw/. This pronunciation was made possible by what I will refer to henceforth as AVI, 'ACRONYM VOWEL INSERTION'. *NASA*, in coining new space vocabulary, has been using AVI to a great extent. Notice such expressions as *PLSS* pronounced /plís/ for 'Portable Life Support System' with /i/ the inserted vowel. It seems that AVI uses ordinary English phonemes to render an unpronounceable consonant sequence pronounceable; it favors /i/ heavily. In the tactic portion of a diagram dealing with AVI it would be indicated that certain consonant sequences are interrupted by /i/ in order to form a phonologically well-formed word. To illustrate the arbitrariness with which acronyms crystallize in public consciousness as spell-outs or as pronounced words, consider *GET*, a *NASA* term for 'Ground Elapsed Time', measured during manned Apollo Moon missions. Clearly, it is a pronounceable word /get/, which also has a familiar meaning. Yet the space industry calls it /jîy + iy + tíy/.

One of the most interesting and also best known cases of a letter spell-out fully coinciding with the phonological realization of not only a word but a full phrase is the acronym *I.O.U.*

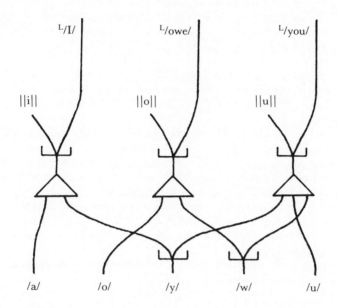

Figure 9 The structure of I.O.U., simplified

In the case of *I.O.U.* /ây + ow + yúw/ 'I owe you' the letter names fully coincide with the phonemic realizations of the 1st person sing. nom. personal pron., the verb *to owe*, and the syntactic objective of the 2nd person sing. personal pron., the whole phrase being paraphraseable as 'I am in your debt'.

Figure 9 does not go into the details of how *I owe you* works as a sentence, but merely shows that the lexical entries, *I, owe, you* coincide in their phonological realizations with the grapho-morphons ||i||, ||o||, and ||u||; the very reason they have been chosen as the popular three-letter abbreviation of the kind of note we slip to a friend for something borrowed in his absence, such as coins to make a telephone call, or something similar.

From this point on we may consider the problem of alphabetic (pronounced or spelled) acronyms essentially solved, though a detailed description and classification still needs to be carried out. Subvarieties with some first syllables spoken such as *NABISCO* 'National Biscuit Company', *CAPCOM* 'Capsule Communicator', and *NORADCOM* 'North American Defense Command' could be integrated into the description depending on how much of the pronounced form follows from the names or sounds of the participating letters and how much is a 'syllable pronunciation'; also how the placement of stress alters the pronunciation, etc.

4. There is one type of acronym which has not received attention in the past. This is the type which – for reasons of syllable structure or deliberate choice – have been institutionalized as fully pronounceable NEW WORDS. They subdivide into three clearly distinguishable subtypes:

(a) The resultant form is a word which, however, carries no mental association with any other existing word. Examples are *NASA*, *UNESCO*, *PLSS* /plís/, and *SNCC* /sník/ for 'Student Nonviolent Coordinating Committee'.

(b) The resultant new word coincides in its phonological realization with an existing word in English, but without any logical connection between the meaning of the acronym itself and the meaning of the already existing word, e.g., *SINS* /sínz/ 'Ships's Internal Navigation System', *SAM* /sæm/ 'surface-to-air missile', and so forth.

(c) The third type is certainly the most interesting and currently the most popular (at least in the United States), so it will be discussed here in somewhat more detail. It is like the second type (b) except for the fact that the resultant new word is a PUN, deliberately coined, such that the name of the group or institution that it acronymizes shares features with the original word's own independent meaning.

4.1. Consider the acronym *PUSH* 'People United to Save Humanity' in relation to the word *push*. *PUSH* could, of course, acronymize as /pîy + yuw + es + éyč/ but it is, in fact, never so pronounced. It is my intention to show that the suppression of the letter spell-out is no accident, but as a result of the organization's having been given a deliberately coined word-association acronym.

This organization, founded by the Rev. Jesse Jackson, the leader of several militant black groups, has as its purpose to exert great effort, and to make others be aware of the need of doing the same, in order to achieve social justice and equality for Blacks. The exertion of great effort has the synonymous expressions *strive*, *work*, and, of course, *push*, as in the expression *he is pushing for equal housing*, etc. Strive, work, and push, in other words, form one ASSOCIATIVE SET, whose distinguishing features point toward the common element *exert great effort*. Now it is commonly agreed that it is easier to remember a smoothly pronounceable one syllable verb which is, incidentally, quite *à propos* of what it abbreviates, than just a letter spell-out; hence when the Rev. Jackson named his organization, he, in all likelihood, considered two things at once:

(i) What words begin with the letters *p*, *u*, *s*, and *h*, to make sense as the title of this group? Notice that this method holds particularly for coiners of acronyms who have a pet word first, and then build the

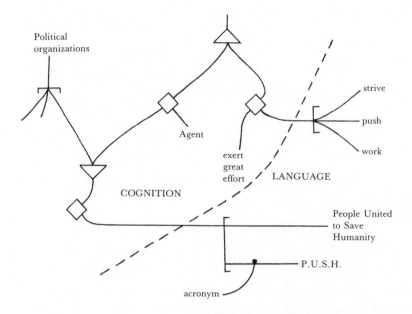

Legend: The staggered line marks the boundary between language (beginning on the right) and the cognitive system (on the left). This organization has as one of its purposes & properties that it recognizes and wants others to recognize the need for exerting great effort for which *push* is a simple, albeit polysemantic, morpheme whose grapho-morphonic composition *p, u, s, h*, (see Figure 6 and 8) if pronounced as a word, happens to coincide with that morpheme. To pronounce the name of the group as /pîy + yuw + es + éyč/ would defeat the purpose of the founder, Black militant Rev. Jesse Jackson.

Figure 10   Diagram for PUSH 'People United to Save Humanity' – cognitive portion

name of the organization around that favorite word. This is, in a way, like finding a pretty button and then having a coat tailored to match its color; BUT PEOPLE DO ACT LIKE THAT.

(ii)   What semantically *à propos* words are there, brief and easy to pronounce, that would encapsulate via acronymy the notion(s) that a progressive and active group stands for whose interest lies in exerting great effort? This, though procedurally more 'natural', is, in a way, the more difficult attack. While it resembles the more relaxed way of first having a coat made and then searching for the right color of button, it poses the problems of greater limitation.

From this bifocal orientation, then, the search in the coiner's memory

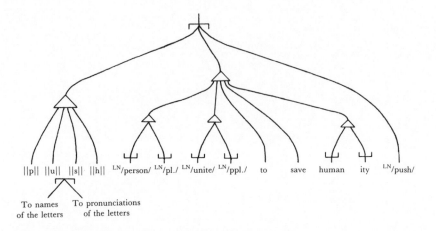

To names   To pronunciations
of the letters   of the letters

Legend: This is the linguistic portion of 'People United to Save Humanity' outlined on Figure 10. On Figure 10 we have seen ^{L}/push/ that an ordered OR from the cognition determined whether the speaker will use the full name of the group or the acronym. If he chooses the acronym, he starts with the lexon ^{L}/push/ which takes him to the grapho-morphons p, u, s, h, on the one hand, and to the lexon ^{L}/push/ on the other. The pun works automatically from here on down, but it was deliberately selected in the cognition. The grapho-morphons can, of course, be spelled out /pî + yuw + es + éyč/ as well, hence the OR node (as on Figure 8).

Figure 11 Diagram for PUSH 'People United to Save Humanity' morphemic and phonemic position

begins. Maybe it is the word *work* (under assumption ((i))) that occurs to one first, and so one tries the grapho-morphons ||w||, ||o||, ||r||, and ||k||, and takes them through one's internalized morpheme-dictionary look-up, matching each 'letter' rapidly, and perhaps with great intuitive jumps, quite UNLIKE a computer which must, of course, yield first all the possible morpheme/word combinations that have w, o, r, and k as the first letter, until one comes up with a tentative solution, say, *Warriors Organized to Rebuke the Ku-Kux-Clan*, which, at the customary cost of repressing *to* and *the* does acronymize into *work*. But it is unsatisfactory for several reasons: *Work* is a pale and unglamorous everyday term disliked by many, and the purpose of the organization would be, if so described, far too specific. Then, the coiner may try to *strive*, and through an essentially similar process of intuitive jumps by trial-and-error, intermixed with minor stretches of systematic memory search, come up with say, *Students Trying Really to Initiate Veritable Equality*. This is passable, but the organization must also have non-student members, and *strive* is a much rarer word than *push* while also lacking the currently high frequency (we live in an 'uptight' society)

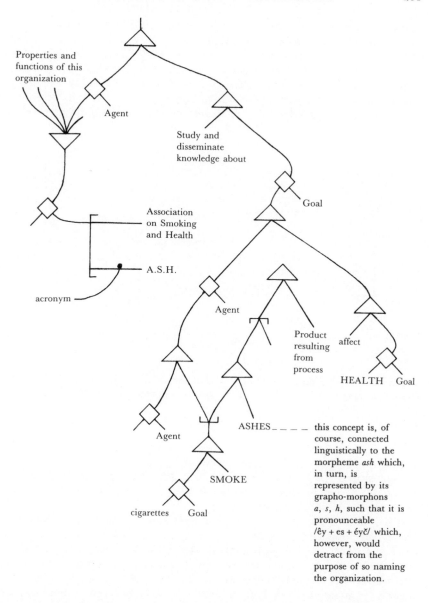

Properties and functions of this organization

Agent

Study and disseminate knowledge about

Goal

Association on Smoking and Health

A.S.H.

acronym

Agent

Product resulting from process

affect

HEALTH   Goal

Agent

ASHES _ _ _ _ this concept is, of course, connected linguistically to the morpheme *ash* which, in turn, is represented by its grapho-morphons *a*, *s*, *h*, such that it is pronounceable /êy + es + éyč/ which, however, would detract from the purpose of so naming the organization.

SMOKE

cigarettes   Goal

Legend: This association ASH studies and disseminates information about the (mostly harmful) effects of smoking (cigarettes, cigars, etc.) on health. Smoking cigarettes, cigers, etc., results in, among other things, *ashes*. Additionally, *ash(es)* and *smoke* both are further associated with *fire*, hence also with each other. What is not shown by this diagram is that *ashes* are associated with negative values, such as being burned out, used up, etc. The organization ASH deliberately exploits this association as it actually discourages rather than encourages smoking.

Figure 12   Relational network diagram for ASH 'Association on Smoking and Health'

and popular colloquial usage of the verb *push*, and the desirability of acting pushy. So one tries *push* itself. As a first, purely random and, in fact, facetious guess, one may come up with *Poor Underdogs Seeking Help*, which does yield *p, u, s, h*. After several more aborted tries, the coiner finally settles on *People United to Save Humanity* which rings of nobility of purpose and yields a powerful acronym of great currency and monosyllabic ease of pronounceability added to a high degree of semantic appropriateness.

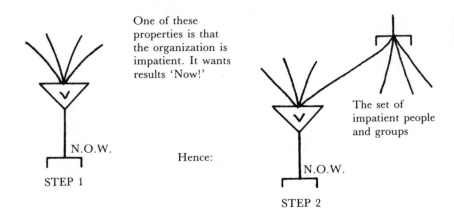

One of these properties is that the organization is impatient. It wants results 'Now!'

N.O.W.

STEP 1

Hence:

The set of impatient people and groups

N.O.W.

STEP 2

Legend: v: variable threshold indicating that the set of distinguishing features of a concept is not fixed. It amounts to a variable subset of the total features.

Figure 13

4.2. The acronym *ASH* 'Action on Smoking and Health' uses a different type of SEMANTIC APPROPRIATENESS. For *PUSH* it was a kind of DOING, for *NOW*, as we shall see presently, it is an ADVERBIAL; for *ASH* it is a by-product of the action of smoking.

Ashes are in the memory of most speakers associated with refuse, a 'dead end', the condition of being used up, burned out, etc. Thus the coiner of *ASH*, by a complicated but by no means irretrievable leap of association hits upon a word whose grapho-morphonic composition on the one hand, and semantic description on the other, offer a clever and suggestive mnemonic tag both for the name of the organization and its implied purpose, actually almost a warning, if you will.

4.3. Let us take a look at the organization *NOW* 'National Organization for Women' which, again is never pronounced */ên + ow + dʒblyuw/*, though, clearly, it could be so pronounced.

Members of this organization, the well known women's liberation movement, feel that their time has come to act; that they have been prevailed

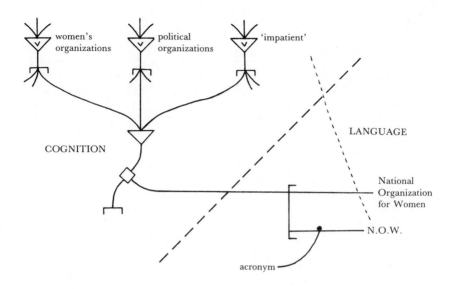

Legend: What the diagram does not show is knowledge that the concepts *now* and *impatient* are closely related. The dotted line suggests that such a connection between the concepts *now* and *impatient* exists.
As before, the two lexemes L/now/ and L/National Organization etc./ alternate at will.

Figure 14 Relational network diagram for NOW, 'National Organization for Women'

upon and exploited in the past; that their demands are so overdue that they must have results – *right now!* Thus the coiner of NOW selects this powerful adverb in order to encode the group's general IMPATIENCE with the present state of affairs and starts to scan eligible NP members with initial grapho-morphons ||n||, ||o||, and ||w||, respectively. Again as a random guess, they might have first thought of a phrase such as *Nobody Owns Watermelons*, immediately changing *Watermelons* to *Women* to make better sense, getting *Nobody Owns Women*. This is certainly closer to their aim, but sounds far too emotional and undignified for an intended national organization. This very thought, however, yields *National Organization for Women* with only one suppressed lexon, *for*, a standard minor cost in all name and title coinages. (These suppressed lexons, as is commonly know, are the definite article *the*, the indefinite article *a*, the prepositions *to*, *for*, *with*, etc.)

5. Some theoretical conclusions

The most remarkable feature of acronyms of the *PUSH, ASH,* and *NOW*-types is that both their functions as appropriately chosen mnemonic tags with an implicit allusion, and the way they were coined by means of the name versus sound dichotomy present in all English grapho-morphons ('letters') CANNOT BE EXPLAINED BY ANY THEORY OF LANGUAGE THAT POSTULATES PROCESS AND ORDERED RULES AS THE SOLE MECHANISM OF EITHER LINGUISTIC COMPETENCE OR PERFORMANCE. This simple, if to some of our colleges disagreeable, fact cannot be over-emphasized.

A structuralist treatment of these acronyms would, of course, be judged as to its success or failure by how detailed an analysis it could present of the commonly understood facts of the various relationships involved, and – in the end – one would be forced to exclaim: 'What remarkable forms they are!' – SINCE THEY SEEM TO MEAN MORE THAN ONE THING AT THE SAME TIME. But the structuralist would be forced to stop here and allow this surprise to generate its own satisfaction.

And this is precisely the point of the present chapter. *NOW, ASH, PUSH,* and the hundreds of current punning-acronyms that follow the same principle of the joint availability of a certain type of semantic appropriateness AND a grapho-morphonic abbreviatability of an organization's or a concept's name into a common word, literally depend both for understanding and for their formation on the SIMULTANEOUS AWARENESS OF TRANSMODAL COGNITION. Other commonly known human activities whose understanding and scientific description per force necessitates *SATCOG* /sǽtkàg/ – if I may be permitted to coin a mixed alphabetic-syllabic acronym of my own – are touch-typing, piano playing, singing, to say nothing of simultaneous translation as carried out by experts at the United Nations, and other types of translation as well. (For a detailed treatment of the translation process in this regard, see Makkai (1971a) reprinted in revised and expanded format in Makkai and Lockwood (1973).)

One such underexplored area is the simultaneous availability of competing etymological derivations for America's best known contribution to international acronym, our old friend *OK.*

Among current linguistic theories cognitive-stratificational grammar is the only one equipped with an adequate formalism (unfortunately still misunderstood by many) to deal with such facts of culture-based language use.

The concept of *SATCOG* is a deceivingly simple one. Yet it is immensely powerful. *SATCOG* may be described as the mode of cognition whose symbol – most likely encapsulating a REAL NEUROLOGICAL FUNCTION of the appropriate convolution of the brain – is a COINCIDENCE CONCATENATION, also known as a downward underordered AND.

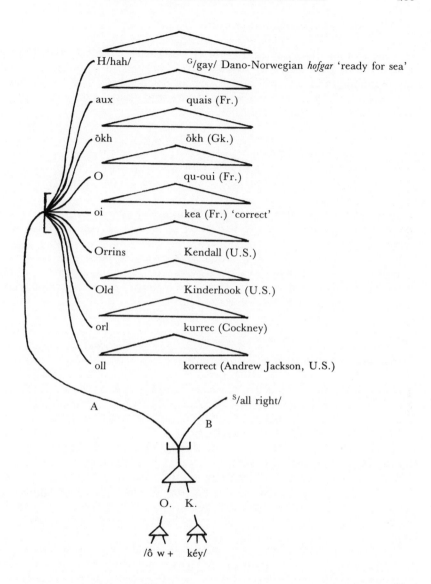

A = ordinary interpretation 'all right' without fictitious inventions or historical research
B = simultaneous availability of 'all right' and fictitious senses

Figure 15 Cognitive structure for interpreting O.K.

6. Deliberate and accidental punning

Just as acronym is an integral part of 'multiple awareness' and 'double coding', so is punning in all of its forms. The topic is by no means new or unfamiliar, and so I will not devote an extended discussion to it here. Suffice it to say that punning is not always intentional. Formulaically, we have at least the following possibilities:

PUN INTENDED : PUN RECEIVED
PUN INTENDED : PUN NOT RECEIVED
PUN NOT INTENDED : PUN NOT RECEIVED
PUN NOT INTENDED : YET PUN IS RECEIVED

Given these four alternatives the 'punster' must choose his audience carefully and be aware of the likelihood of success; indeed he must also know when to avoid puns altogether.

No matter how tempting a further exploration of puns and acronyms, I must not dwell on them here as they are by nature much more in the cognitive domain than in the auditive. In a future, more expanded treatment of the topic they will, of course, have to be included in full length and with many examples.

7. Summary of bio-theoretical preliminary observations

The human brain is organized in a most complex way, as shown in Figures 4 and 5. Figure 4 shows the evolutionary history of the human brain in comparison to the AMPHIBIAN, REPTILIAN, LOWER MAMMALIAN and HIGHER MAMMALIAN brain structures.

The human NEO-CORTEX alone shows the extremely large ballooning effect that sets us humans aside from our fellow creatures.

This typically *human neo-cortex* is organized in two major hemispheres, the left and the right hemisphere. Objects held in our right hand register in the left hemisphere, and vice versa; nonlingual noise or recognizable words picked up by the right ear are registered in the left hemisphere, and vice versa.

It follows, therefore, that if a pianist is playing with both hands, the TUNE, played by the right hand, is 'driven' by the left, more dominant and more logical hemisphere, while the ACCOMPANIMENT, played with the left hand, is driven by the more rhythm and melody-oriented, more submissively 'feminine' right hemisphere.

No claim is made in this chapter as to the ultimate validity or fallacy of the theory of hemispheric lateralization: It is merely used as one possible and altogether not implausible attempt at explaining what, on the other hand, is OBSERVATIONALLY TRUE and CORRECT: that human beings engage in activities that scatter their attentions in many directions. Scattered attention means that we have the ability deliberately to ignore SOME of what we are doing and/or to EMPHASIZE some other areas of our activities. I call this SATCOG: or the 'Simultaneous Awareness of Transmodal Cognition'.

In the rest of this chapter I will try to show that METRIC VERSIFICA-TION and the ability to CARRY A TUNE both depend on SATCOG. It will be further suggested that multi-voice instrumental music, choral singing, the sonata and the symphony would be impossible without SATCOG, our ability to do several things at once with DIRECTABLE and DIVIDED ATTEN-TION.

MULTIPLE CODING is, I suggest, an intrinsic and inescapable part of all natural languages on Earth. The phenomenon is scandalously ill-explored and callously relegated to 'incidentals' whether in 'Pragmatics' or some other convenient garbage disposal system. As a result, traditional gram-matical theory has been unable to deal with the semantics of STRESS, with INTONATION CURVES that go against the expected standard, and many other basic features of English and other languages.

Studies of POETIC LANGUAGE are altogether woefully inadequate as there is to this day no convincing study on why English metric versification has never really taken off as have its German and Hungarian counterparts. I will suggest below that this has to do with the fact that anglophones pay primary attention to STRESS ALONE while ignoring SYLLABLE LENGTH the feature of OPEN versus CLOSED syllabicity.

It will be further suggested that *musicology*, in turn, also stands to benefit from an understanding of SATCOG.

8. The case of metric versification: 'musical linguistics' in a classical setting with English imitations and approximations of various success

In the East-Central European High School (Gimnázium) tradition MEMORIZATION used to be a mandatory feature. The debate still rages in Europe itself whether this was pedagogically sound or necessary: tempers flare on each side of the argument. I, for one, never resented memorization and even eagerly participated in contests that were held at the Gimnázium of the Hungarian Reformed Church in Budapest where I was in the Latin ('Humanities') division from age eleven to sixteen.

We memorized proverbs both in prose and in hexameter form: some proverbs were famous lines form Horace's *Ars Poetica* such as the two-line distych extolling the virtues of hard work in one's youth:

> *Qi cupit optatam cursu contingere metam*
> *Multa tulit fecitque puer: sudavit et alsit.*

('He who wishes to reach the desired goal by running, carried and did much as a boy – sweated and froze.')

Latin grammar was taught to us in terms of rhyming rules: to this day I cannot forget the Latin nouns ending in *-us* that are of the feminine gender: idus, tribus, porticus, acus, manus et domus. I admit in retrospect that this was not 'useful' in a direct sense; certainly less useful for Latin itself than knowing all the prepositions that took the accusative case: *ante, apud, ad, adversus, circum, circa, cis, extra, intra, iuxta, ob, post, praeter, supra, versus, ultra* and *trans* . . . I am sure I missed some of them: I learned this forty-four years ago along with a number of Aesop's Fables, and numerous lines of Ovid, Horace and others.

The famous SAPPHIC meter, named after its inventor, the Greek poetess Sappho, registered in my memory at age thirteen by this stanza by Horace:

Integer vitae scelerisque purus
Non eget mauris iaculis neque arcu
Nec venenatis gravida sagittis
Phusce, pharetra.

('One pure of sins and with a life of integrity does not need Moorish javelins, a bow, nor a quiver heavy with poisonous arrows, Oh Phuscus!')

The ALCAEIC meter, named after the Greek Alkaios, still rings in my mind with these four lines, also by Horace:

Eheu, fugaces Postume, Postume,
Labuntur anni; nec pietas moram
Rugis et instanti senectae
Adferet indomitaeque morti.

('Alas, Oh Postumus, Oh Postumus, the fast running years (show that) piety won't bring a halt to wrinkles, instant old age, nor to untamable death' or: 'The years are running fast, and neither will piety bring a pause to wrinkles, instant old age, nor indomitable death.')

The Sapphic stanza in prose Latin would read:
Phusce! (Homo) sceleris purus et integer vitae non eget mauris iaculis neque arcu, nec gravida pharetra venenatis sagittis.

The Alcaeic stanza in prose Latin would read:
Eheu, Postume, Postume, anni fugaces labuntur; nec adferet pietas moram rugis, senectae instanti, et morti indomitae.
The relevant metric systems are:

i) *Sapphic stanza*

two trochees, dactyl, trochee,
spondee: this is repeated over 3
lines

CLOSING LINE:
dactyl, spondee.

ii) *Alcaeic stanza*

iamb, choriamb, dactyl, dactyl
(Repeated over two lines)

4 iambs and a half spondee, or 2
iambs, choriamb, full spondee

2 dactyls, trochee, spondee.

This traditional way of representing meter is very much like writing music in the traditional way on the five familiar bars; the comparison is, of course, an imperfect one since tunes can be recognized even without words whereas metric skeletons without words are meaningless. I will have to return to this major difference between music writing and other notational modes in the section on music.

One way to test the usefulness and flexibility of a given mode of description is to see if it can give a reasonable representation of diverse cognitive phenomena. Lamb's RELATIONAL NETWORK METHOD has come in for much criticism for its complexity. Admittedly, it is difficult and demanding; logical clarity needs to be coupled with a certain amount of manual dexterity and visual aesthetics. Figure 16 gives such a relational network description of the six classical metric feet, the anapaest, the iamb, the choriamb, the trochee, the dactyl, and the spondee.

The description is based on the notion of the mora or basic unit of duration, as was originally done in Greek and Latin rhetoric. A 'half' mora, represented by the 'U' equals one mora by another count, and two such morae amount to a full mora, represented by ———.

Figures 16, 17, 18, 19, 20, and 21 show in relational network format the metric structure of some of the best known stanza-types from classical Greek and Latin poetry. Figure 16 shows the basic feet of metric versification that build these stanzas by using the above-mentioned 'half' and 'full' mora as the basic building block of these metric feet. Figure 17 shows the structure of the familiar iambic pentameter: on the a side

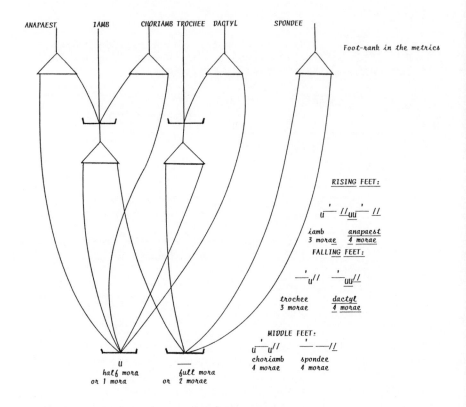

Figure 16   A relational network description of the basic feet of classical metrics. The description is based on time units or 'morae', where the 'short' is considered 'half' of the 'long'.

'masculine' and the 'feminine' lines are treated as separate types, on side b they are integrated. Figure 18, based on trochees, iambs, dactyls, anapaests and the spondee shows the structure of the Sapphic stanza, while Figure 19, similarly organized, shows the Alcaeic stanza. Figures 20 and 21 show the structures of two types of sonnet, the Italian or 'Petrarcan', and the 'Shakespearian'.

If Figures 16–21 look somewhat forbidding, the reader should feel free to skip them altogether and concentrate on what they are intended to convey: the immense difficulty in wording one's message so that it makes sense, conveys a 'poetic atmosphere', and yet fully conforms to the rigid constraints of Greek and Latin metric versification. The German Hölderlin and the Hungarian Berzsenyi have produced a large number of excellent poems in these meters. English metric versification, on the other hand, is imperfect at best.

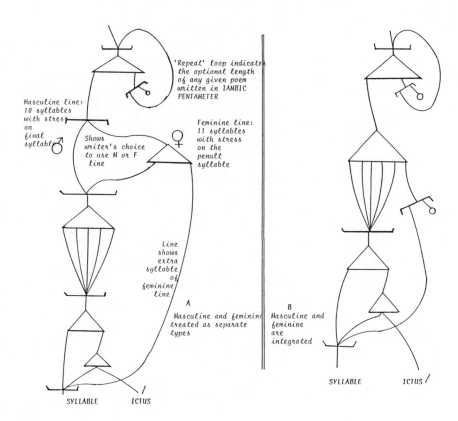

Figure 17 A relational network description of the traditional iambic pentameter M & F.

English has a HAMMER-BLOW ACCENT that tends to obscure in native ears the difference between OPEN and CLOSED SYLLABLES. A syllable in Greek and Latin meter is considered open if it does not contain a consonant cluster and starts and ends with a vowel. A syllable may be long, of course, by virtue of containing a long vowel, such as -ae- in Latin. In the line by Horace:

IN-te GER-vi-TAE scele-RIS-que PU-rus

the syllables typed in capital letters are considered both stressed and long. The stress is obvious, the length – to English ears – is not.

In the first word cluster of /n/ + /t/ creates the length; /ger/, although not long in itself becomes long next to /v/, /ae/ is naturally long; /ris/ becomes long next to the /kw- of *que*, and the /pu-/ or 'purus' is naturally long. Can

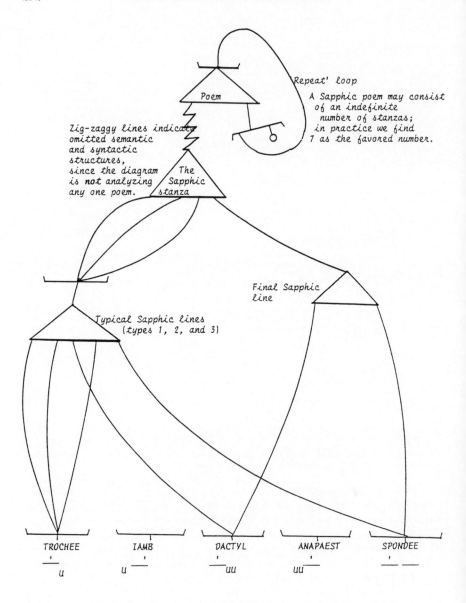

Figure 18 A relational network description of the Sapphic stanza

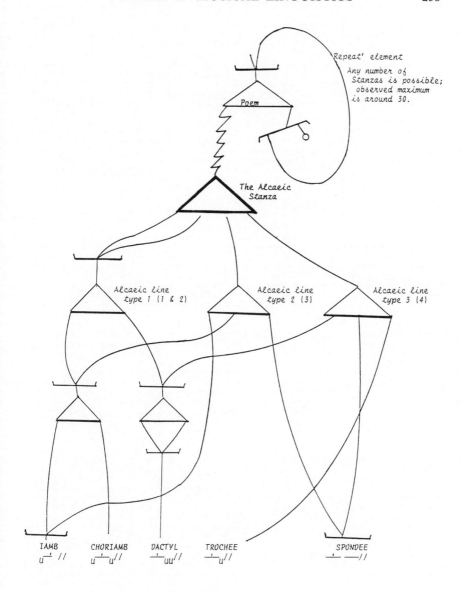

Figure 19   A relational network description of the Alcaeic stanza

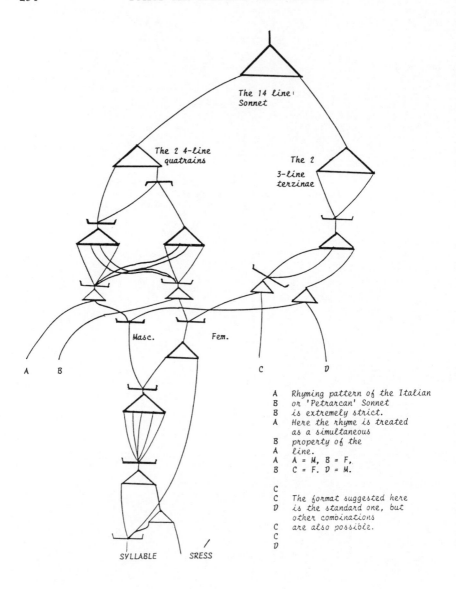

Figure 20   A relational network description of the Italian or 'Petrarcan' sonnet

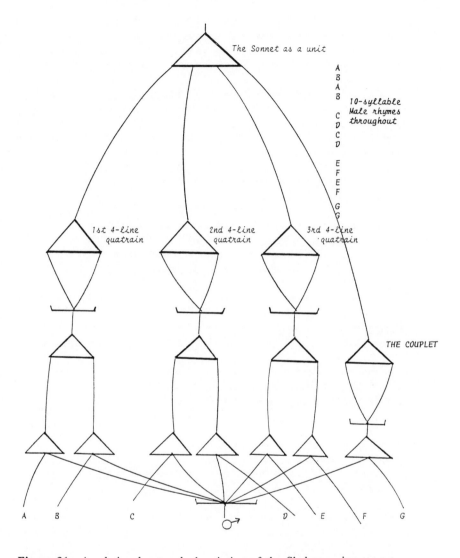

Figure 21   A relational network description of the Shakespearian sonnet

this be faithfully imitated in English? Endless generations of poets have tried in various ways and with various degrees of success. John F. Nims, the noted poet, former editor of *Poetry* and excellent translator of Horace, allows himself a Sapphic 4th line that says *figure the hell with*; it is one of Horace's bawdy odes on commercial love (Nims 1980). What is wrong with this line? It is five syllables long as it should be, and the stress is certainly in the right place. The problem is that he does not hear the lack of length in the word *figure*. Finger would be a lot better; why, we would have an /ng-g/ cluster; if this still sounds unconvincing try the 'blind words' *let* ——— *me be wholesome*, or some such phrase. The lining of /t/ + /m/ between 'let' and 'me' creates the needed length; 'wholesome' has a naturally long /o/.

Being a non-native speaker of English, the temptation to write a 'perfect' Sapphic poem was dwarfed by my diffidence: how could I possibly succeed? After many years of hesitation, I finally tried.

The general technique I can suggest to anyone interested in doing the same is to start saying meaningless words in a more or less random order paying minute attention, however, to whether they sound right or not. Certainly English stress placement must not be violated, but you must train your ears to length. I wrote:

Metri(c)ks: a Sapphic Meditation on the Openness or Closedness of Certain Syllables and the Mouths and Minds of Those who Uttered Them
For M.A.K. Halliday

Why should metric verse be a major problem
in such lovely speech as a 'Standard English',
    English clearly pronounced, perceived and spelled, that
       nobody loses

slumber over? Why should a major master
– John F. Nims, Ralph Mills, Teddy Hughes, Paul Carroll
    Roethke, Lowell, Plath – what a list! It's endless!
       limp to the rescue

minding only STRESS, never once perceiving
what there lurks inside in a Grecian stanza
    I mean LENGTH, where vowels hug a consonne cluster
       multisyllabic?

English ears don't hear for a rhyme (nor reason!)
blind Love's labor lost on a line Alcaeic;
    English lips won't say for a Pound (nor Dollar!)
       SAPPHIC IS ALWAYS –

ancient Lesbos waits with a ruseful vengeance,
right inside your home, whether it's Manhattan,
    rain-soaked London Town, chilly Leeds, Lancaster,
       or sunny Sydney.

Upwards! Forwards! Run, run an Anglo gauntlet –
all our stress must roost in a cloak of timing –
*   no more pounds, no miles, not an ounce; no gallons:*
*   life is a METRIC*

SLAUGHTER-HOUSE OF SCALES: whether always open,
half-way closed, shut tight – not an UNDERSTATEMENT
*   must escape untossed with a ten-foot pole of*
*   high on a Sapphic!*

The poem was never intended as some kind of reprimand to American and British poets who mind only stress and ignore the length: what happened, in all probability, was what happens invariably when the mind grows half-way unconscious under the influence of a rhythm or a rhyme pattern and the 'meaning' of what is said gets adjusted to the dictates of the form.

That this particular Sapphic exercise should have turned into a minor lament against 'English ears and mouths' is a natural consequence of the topic; the long-awaited conversion of American miles, ounces and gallons to the metric system still years in the future seemed, in retrospect, as an appropriate coda to the foregoing remarks. I eventually dedicated the poem to M.A.K. Halliday who, as inventor/leader of the Systemic-Functional Grammar is also known to be fond of the Classics and is a matchless phonologian.

But my task was not over: I needed to produce credible Alcaeic verse as well. I wrote:

The Kremlagon: an Alcaeic Mediation on 'Brains' versus 'Hearts'

We've lost the wager – nobody, nobody
can turn the clock back; crossing the 'Rubicon'
*   the die'd been cast and every player*
*   is but a dot to emerge at random*

whether 't 's a SIX, a FIVE, or a lonely ONE,
a DEUCE, a THREE; Ah! FOUR is a terrible
*   result: uncompromising anger*
*   nobody knows were it incubated*

before impacting here on an innocent
and softish ball with many a cavity
*   which hides inside the skull's enclosure*
*   known as a BRAIN that is ours to garden . . .*

Beware the brain! It's glued to a booby-trap!
Castrate the rogue! Get COMMISSURRECTOMY!
    Go, scale the lobes from where the lowland
        seems as a maze that, in awe, meanders

from LEFT to RIGHT and back: An ACCORDION,
whose sounds are muted, stuck in a medium,
    whose only way of sound-emission
        is the parade of a blind machine-gun.

For KILL we must; yes, nobody, nobody
can turn the years back; dropping the Atom Bomb
    we 'cast the die' and every victim
        was but a dot's billiard-statistics.

Beware the BRASS who sit in the KREMLAGON:
Arrest the chiefs who lavishly defecate
    on every dream our softer hearts are
        set to behold as a gift from Mozart.

I was not trying to write a peace-poem that was even-handedly critical of the Americans and the Russians: the word *Kremlagon* just arose from the metric, quite unconsciously. It was already there as a metric unit when I realized that I had concocted a blend of the *Pentagon* and the *Kremlin*.

I distinctly remember that it was Horace's repetition of the vocative *Postume, Postume* that rhythmically suggested *nobody, nobody* to me; this repetition of a dactyl, on the other hand, aided by the word's lexical semantics, brought in a mood of doom and resignation. *Crossing the Rubicon* came to mind as yet another dactylic ending – since line 2 has to be identical with L/1 and 'Rubicon' as one is likely to remember from Caesar's life, means 'war'. The rest followed almost automatically. I was still under the influence of writing the Sapphic poem, whose major thrust is about stress, length and reason, so the 'heart–brain' dichotomy was not at all an illogical or an unexpected one. *Mozart*, as the closing word of the poem was very well in keeping with my intentions of saying something about both music and language and, having somewhere in the back of my mind what I had said earlier about the brain, it made sense to accuse the 'brain' of aggressiveness ('war') and the 'heart' of being in tune with music, a gift from Mozart. The word *commissurrectomy* perhaps deserves brief comment: when a brain-damaged patient needs an operation to save his life, or an epileptic can no longer tolerate his *grands maux* seizures, a separation of the brain's two hemispheres is performed by means of a 'commissurrectomy' or excision of the commissures (which link the hemispheres). The word, with its two stresses, is a fortuitous instance of two dactyls and, as such, was not be missed.

Interested readers who may wish to experiment with this mode of versification will also find that once they get into the mood of the rhythm, all sorts of associations become possible that would not surface to consciousness under other circumstances. I know of no better or more modern statement about poetic language than the one made back in 1929 by László Németh, a Hungarian physician who, like Chekhov, gave up his medical practice and became a major writer. Németh is, alas, not translated into English although several of his novels have enjoyed great success in German translation. About the nature of poetic language he wrote (I am translating from Hungarian) in 1929:

> Anyone who has ever seriously wondered why it is so difficult to become aware of the many facets of our own mental life will sooner or later come to realize that the reason is this: *language falsifies our thinking.*
> The very moment I say 'thinking' I have falsified, because I have separated the content of the mental process from its emotional coefficients. Such a separation, however, never really takes place in the Life of the Mind, since the two, 'content' and 'emotional coefficients' are but the two qualities of the same process.
> Even the expression 'the two qualities' partitions and severs in the same way as my referring to 'thinking' on the one hand and to 'feeling' on the other. Language is like a butcher's knife: it is used to cut up things into chunks. We get so used to our own words that we re-project them onto the mental processes themselves and so we wind up by seeing 'concepts' in the place of nouns, the joining of concepts in the place of verbs, and we look for 'souvenirs' and 'memories' in the place of ordinary past tense.
> We believe that we think according to the grammar – and grammar is indeed a visualization of mental processes. Language itself, however, does *not illustrate but merely alludes at* thinking. The same situation exists with logic: it never shows how a truth was discovered, only how it is to be communicated according to the prevailing conventions. *Nobody finds truths by pursuing logic and no one weaves his associations according to sentence patterns.* Language is a sign system standing in for thinking and it has no more to do with the processes of the human mind and soul than does any writing system with the live word. The word, formerly the slave of the mind, now captures and imprisons it just as certain lower animals incarcerate themselves in their own discarded and calcified secretions. The mind, however, is less satisfied with its jail than those lower life-forms with their calcium prisons, and so it starts to protest time and again against the falsifications endured, and tries to reveal itself more deeply and with greater plasticity. *The name of this tragic and, in the final analysis, hopeless experiment, is:* POETIC LANGUAGE. The poet wishes to project his thought in all its shades, in its more profound essence; this is why he uses cunning and all sorts of tricks; this is why he twists and molds language, the lazy servant, so that it will proclaim the right of its master all the louder. *Paradoxically, poetic language is the more touching, the more it does away with conventional language, the more it sends to the reader the thought itself – or let us bravely call it the mental state of the author.* Poetic style is a mental state rendered palpable despite the language being used. (Emphases mine (A.M.).)

Later in the same essay Németh goes into detailed analysis of the effects of metric constraints on the unconscious of the poet. Although writing metric verse is like dancing in a straitjacket, at the same time the rhythm puts the semantics and the lexico-grammar 'to sleep', and as a result all sorts of associations start to surface that would otherwise, without the constraining of the meter, have remained underneath the surface.

I was most anxious to see if this is also true in the case of a sonnet. The Petrarcan, with which I have had some experience in Hungarian, seemed much too difficult for a beginner, so I opted to try my hand at a (formally) Shakespearean Sonnet. I wrote:

Profane Prayer for Health

'Heavenly Father, who graciously assignest
our souls to one container lasting but one lifetime,
kindly permit me to state: mine ain't the finest,
in fact, sometimes I wonder if it's worth a bright dime.

I suffer insomnia, the runs, gout, constipation;
worry-transformations stomachic and spinal:
many a straightforward bathroom-visitation
threatens to tear me up; in fact, to be the final . . .

That this here hull o' dust hath zero trade-in value
I most humbly accept . . . Forgive my words informal . . .
What I must needs protest: Why can't it function normal?!'
And then He Spake: 'Thou pleadest tough, I tell ya!

If Thou wilt jog a mile a day and practice meditation,
to wholesome turds will I restore thy foul liquifecation!'

I make no apology for the bawdy overtones of this sonnet; after all, it was only a metric experiment and as far as the content was concerned, I felt rather sure that with the sonnet being a somewhat tired and over-worked form of lyric poetry in English, a different mode of playfulness, mixing the modern colloquial with certain King Jamesian forms would be a relief to some readers. (See Chapter 15 for a fuller account.)

None of these three pieces of verse presented here amount to good poetry. Poetry, meter and rhyme schemes may or may not find one another in a given piece: neither metrics nor rhyming is any guarantee of success in poetry. Most modern poets, in fact, try to steer clear of ancient metrics and elaborate rhyming schemes such as the sonnet altogether.

My purpose in showing a Sapphic and an Alcaeic poem followed by a 4-quatrain sonnet with a couplet ('Shakespearian') was to illustrate the relational network diagrams describing these metric and rhyming structures.

In texts whose primary function is not logical communication, but 'musical language' that allows through the daydream-materials of the 'right hemisphere' which the left hemisphere would have filtered out and rejected, a subordination of content to form opens up unusual lines of association which, in turn, color the content of the resultant piece in question.

9. Trying to get close to music: pitch patterns and rhythm patterns

One way to illustrate the complex and multiply stratified nature of music is to take a familiar tune and play it to an audience ignoring all the customary rhythm patterns associated with the piece. Evening out everything into full notes and half notes and further ignoring all places where the usual melody gets faster, then slower again, louder and softer, has the desired effect of shocking everyone present. The player must do violence to him/herself as well: this takes practice and is not a pleasurable activity.

The reverse can also be done: take the familiar tune you will play with one finger at the piano, and give all the needed rhythm patterns; speed up where needed and slow down where necessary, but never change the pitch! Keep one finger firmly attached to one single note and play the whole song on that single note. Some of the most knowledgeable listeners who can be credited with knowing the piece you are trying to play will become nervous and resentful after a few seconds of this acoustic attack. It reminds most people of a novice trying to practice the Morse Code.

I have chosen to do the famous *Ode to Joy* from Beethoven's 9th Symphony, because it is universally well known; it is short; it can be played with one finger in D Major starting on F sharp (or any other signature for that matter). The pitch sequences are: mi, mi, fa, sol, sol, fa, mi, re, do, do, re, mi, mi, re, re; mi, mi, fa, sol, sol, fa, mi, re, do, do, re, mi, re, do, do. Re, re, mi, do, re, mi, fa, mi, do, re, mi, fa, mi, re, do, re, *sol*; mi, mi, fa, sol, sol, fa, mi, re, do, do, re, mi, re, do, do.

If you are not familiar with 'solfeggio', you will have difficulty following this notation; taking the C Major scale as an example, the correspondences are:

C	D	E	F	G	A	H	C
Do	Re	Mi	Fa	Sol	La	Ti	Do

The *Ode to Joy* can, therefore, be also presented as E,E, F, G, G, F,E, D etc.

The audience reactions as well as the player's own violated intuition cries out for a rectification, a putting back together of what belongs together and what has been artificially picked apart during this brief experiment. By the time you play *Freude, schöner Götterfunken* in normal tempo and with the normal rhythm patterns, a sigh of relief will be heard from the audience. At the same time you will become aware of the fact that just in order to CARRY A SIMPLE TUNE, you had to do SEVERAL THINGS AT ONCE. You had to pay attention to the pitch alternations – the raw material for the 'melody' – but this, you now realize, comes inextricably interwoven with a rhythm and stress ('musical ictus') pattern which is intrinsic to the melody. In a sense, it is harder to pick the 'melody' and the 'rhythm' apart for artificial demonstration purposes than it is to remember them as a unit and so to perform them, the value of the picking apart is precisely the fact that after having done so you will come to realize that when you play, hum or sing a simple unaccompanied tune, you really are doing several things at once. I am not suggesting at all that we learn songs (a) by their pitch alternations first and then (b) proceed to add the rhythm to them or vice versa; on the contrary; such a learning and listening procedure would be most counter-intuitive. Yet the nature of music-writing itself is such that (c) the location of the notes on the bars, together with the signature, gives the 'melody', the length-value of the note, full, half, quarter, eighth, sixteenth, etc., plus whatever dots are added for syncopation, indicate the rhythm. Sheet music, in fact, gives these things to us as *Gestalten*, units which we recognize and play. But just as it is possible to remove the rhythm notations from notes on the bars and leave just the bare outline of the melody, so can you at the keyboard play only the pitch-variations and equalize the rhythm to everyone's pain and discomfort.

In what follows, I will try to give a quasi-linguistic description of the events that lead from one's recognition that it was the *Ode to Joy* from Beethoven's 9th that has been played to one's ability to account in detail of WHAT IT IS WE DO when we produce/perform the melody ourselves either by humming it, singing it, or playing it on a piano with one finger, two hands, or full accompaniment.

Figure 22 is a general chart of a music performance in general: The top triangle indicates the basic piece, in this case the *Ode to Joy*. It is an 'unordered AND' indicating that singing voice and instrumentation coincide in time as the performance progresses. The instrumentation (left hand 'unordered AND') shows that the instrumentation itself is complex: the right hand may play the main tune alone; on the present diagram it is implied that it is accompanied by a chord-playing left hand. The singer may be a coloratura soprano or a meso soprano; an alto, a tenor, countertenor, etc., down to a deep bass; beside solo singing the 'Ode' may be sung by a traditional mixed choir for four voices, or an all-male choir, an all-female choir, etc. This general scheme is valid for any other piece of music as well, e.g. the *Star-spangled Banner* or *I've Been Working on the Railroad*, the piece in question does not have to be a revered classic.

Figure 23 shows the nature of the *Ode to Joy* in more detail: the left branch of the top 'unordered AND' node leads to the possible languages in which the Ode can be sung. (In Figure 24, where the piece is given in regular sheet music, the text is written out in English, German and Hungarian.) The 'unordered OR' node shows the choice of language; it also allows for simultaneous singing in more than one language. It happens rather frequently in opera houses all over the world that an invited star would sing in Italian while the rest of the cast sing in the local language. I have personally observed this happening at the Budapest opera house on

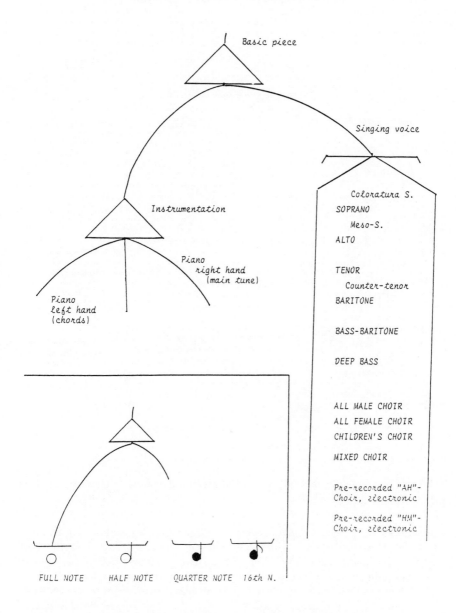

Figure 22   Simplified logical structure of musical performances in general

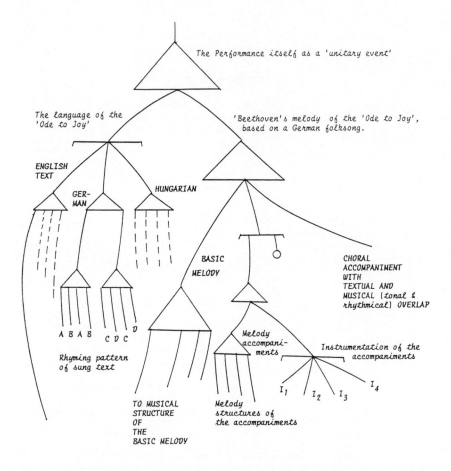

Figure 23   Simplified logical structure of a performance of the *Ode to Joy* from the last movement of Beethoven's IXth (Choral) Symphony in D-Minor

a number of occasions when a visiting Yugoslav tenor would sing the lead role of *Aida* in Italian while the rest of the cast sang everything in Hungarian translation. The phenomenon is an extreme case of *qui pro quo*, the operatic situation where two, three, maybe up to six characters all say their own words relating to the plot at hand in diverse ways while all harmonizing in the given musical setting; duos, trios, quartets, quintets, sextets, even octets are known in classical opera.

The text has a rhyming scheme, as indicated by the ABAB CDCD lettering under the second 'unordered AND' triangle suspended under the 'unordered OR'. The singing of the text coincides with the BASIC MELODY which, in turn, coincides with the INSTRUMENTAL and the CHORAL ACCOMPANIMENTS as indicated by Beethoven's score.

Figure 24 *Ode to Joy* from Beethoven's IXth Symphony in traditional sheet-music notation, in E-flat Major

In Figure 24 the tune of the *Ode to Joy* is written out in traditional sheet music. I have chosen to write it out in E-Flat Major for two reasons: first, I wanted to indicate that, given the assumptions of 'solfeggio', DO is relative and, second, it simplified the music writing as G, the second line from the bottom, makes a convenient MI, the start of the song. The texts appear underneath the bars in English, German and in Hungarian. Whereas the Hungarian text is a rather faithful translation of Schiller's original poem, the English text, which has become a religious hymn in its own right, is not a translation of Schiller's *An die Freude* in any sense, it is more a pastiche-like adaptation or a re-composition.

Figure 25 shows the logical structure of note-length in music in relational network format from the Full Note to the Half, Syncopated Half, Quarter, Eighth, Sixteenth and Sixty-fourth with a possible inclusion of the 1/128 note available on faster metronomes even if not too often used in reality. The reader is asked to turn the pages back to Figure 16, where the basic feet of classical metrics were shown based on the notion of the Mora; here in music we have the same logical structure with the 1/64 note being

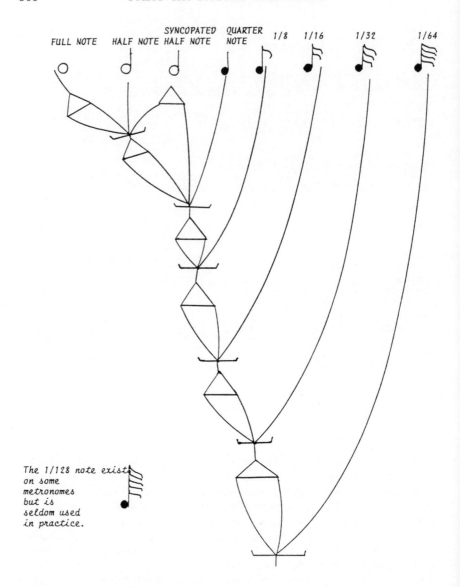

Figure 25   Simplified logical structure of 'musical length' from the full note to the 128th note in a relational network description

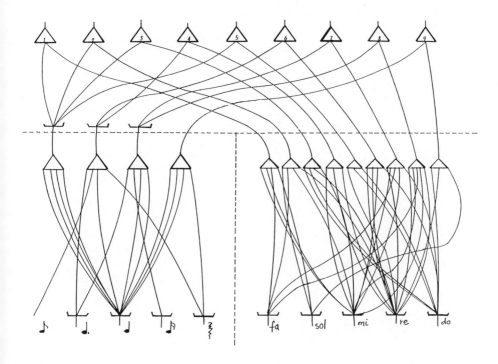

Figure 26   Relational network of the 'lower-quasi-trace' of the *Ode to Joy*: Measure types leading to pitch-patterns and rhythms patterns

viewable as the basic musical mora, multiples of which 'generate' (or describe) the familiar notes of sheet-music.

Let us return now to the torture-session I described above in which a skilled player subjects an audience to the playing of the pitch-patterns of the *Ode to Joy* on even half notes or full notes omitting all rhythm and 'stress' indications. What would such a pitch-pattern look like in a relational network diagram? Could it be drawn? We can indeed play the *Ode to Joy* in such a rhythmless way and, therefore, this way of playing it can also be logically represented. Figure 26 gives the alternations of the pitches (ranging from lower Sol to Do, Re, Mi, Fa and Sol). The upper 'unordered AND' node shows the four lines of the 'Ode'; the 'OR' nodes and Repeat elements added also appropriately indicate that in memory no new trace has to be engraved in order to reiterate the vocal chords and/or the hand to carry out the characteristic repetitions. This is a truly cumbersome way of reading music and no suggestion is made that we should abandon traditional sheet-music writing for relational network diagrams. By the same token it must also be said that a melody is not registered in human memory in sheet-music notation form! Cumbersome, even

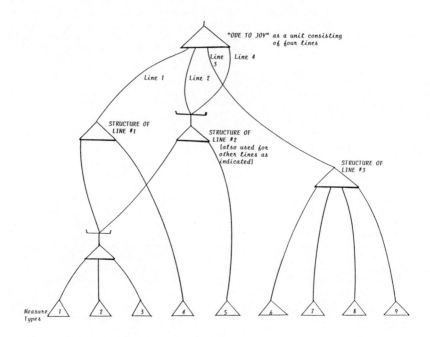

Figure 27 Simplified logical structure of the 'upper quasi-trace' of the *Ode to Joy* leading to the measure types

awkward though the relational network diagram is, it does better justice to what is likely to be stored in human memory than any other notational system devised so far. Where an element is repeated, RN diagramming omits the repeated element and indicates where the new material starts.

As stated above, however, this description does not represent the true song, only its pitch-alternations. What we need is a more sophisticated diagram that is able to account for both the rhythm patterns and the pitch alternations. Hence Figures 27 and 28 which are designed to accomplish that goal.

Figure 27 shows the 'Upper Quasi-Trace' of the *Ode to Joy*: the four line-poem set to four musical lines is describable in terms of nine measurable types (numbered 1–9 in the bottom triangles) which on Figure 18 are shown to be 'unordered AND' nodes, that lead to pitch-patterns (right-hand side) and rhythm patterns (left-hand side) simultaneously. Clearly Figures 27 and 28 are equivalent to the traditional sheet-music notation (Figure 24), and the reader is invited to take a little time out and compare the two. The obvious advantage of the traditional sheet-music notation is that pitch and rhythm together with musical stress are all given together, in a *Gestalt*, and we are used to reading music in this familiar form. The

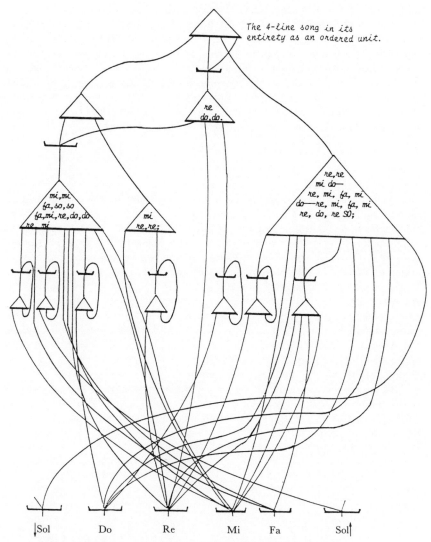

The 4-line song in its entirety as an ordered unit.

re do, do.

re, re mi do— re, mi, fa, mi do—re, mi, fa, mi re, do, re SO;

mi, mi fa, so, so fa, mi, re, do, do re mi

mi re, re;

Sol   Do   Re   Mi   Fa   Sol

Readers are invited to compare this rendition of the pitch alternations to the traditional sheet-music in Figure 24. Whereas the sheet-music is easier to follow, it is full of redundancies handled here by the 'repeat loops'.

Figure 28   The pitch-patterns of the *Ode to Joy* without rhythm and 'ictus'

advantage of the RN diagrams, if any, is that like computer flow-charts, they take nothing for granted and therefore explain as separate systems that which we usually swallow as a ready-made entity. This has no aesthetic appeal for music publishers or for composers; my reason for converting traditional musical notation into RN is that the basic cognitive similarity of music and language could best be shown by a notational system that can handle both. This notation system is the Relational Network method now in common use by cognitive linguists who have learned it from its inventor, Professor Sydney M. Lamb.

Conclusions

If a conceptual system, representable in a consistent notation form is sufficiently flexible to be able economically and logically to describe a telephone dialling system, a tongue-twister, acronyms of various types ranging from letter-spelling to word-acronyms and deliberately coined punning-acronyms, English metric versification with the relevant feet; can give a coherent picture of the Sapphic and Alcaeic meter, iambic pentameter, two kinds of sonnet ('Petrarcan' and 'Shakespearian'); if, furthermore, the same system based on logic can describe the structure of a musical performance, the structure of a song by factoring out pitch-patterns and rhythm-patterns, while also being able to show that certain portions of rhymed language coincide in time with solo or accompanied music, we must conclude that the system of description is adequate to the cognitive organization of both language and music.

This being the case, we can be reasonably optimistic of our chances of developing a cognitively adequate musical linguistics, a field of inquiry that can apply musical insights to language and linguistic insights to the description of music.

12 The transformation of a *Turkish pasha* into a big, fat dummy

This chapter[1] deals with the process of creating a verse translation of a didactic-performative nursery rhyme from Hungarian to English, and evaluates the adequacy of contemporary linguistic theories in coping with translation problems in general.

I intend to show, with a simple concrete example involving two unrelated languages, that, among familiar theories, transformational-generative grammar is hard put, if at all able, to handle translation, and that the most reliable scientific hypothesis of the nature of translation will in all likelihood be a stratificational model if that theory manages to incorporate in its hypersememic system the cultural taxonomy of Pike's behavioremes.

By way of illustration I shall present a brief text in a foreign language:

Pont, pont, vesszőcske,
Készen van a fejecske.
Kurta nyaka, nagy a hasa,
Készen van a Török Pasa.

The text is Hungarian, and consists of two sentence: (1) *Pont, pont, vesszőcske, készen van a fejecske*, and (2) *Kurta nyaka, nagy a hasa, készen van a Török Pasa*. A raw, undoctored morpheme-for-morpheme translation yields the following in English:

period, period, comma, diminutive, suffix,
ready, adverbial suffix, is, the, head, diminutive suffix.
short, neck, possessive suffix, large, the belly, possessive suffix,
ready, adverbial suffix, is, the Turkish, pasha.

Rearranging the content units of the text in accordance with their usual appearance in English, we get the following literal translation:

Period, period, little comma,
The little head is ready.
His neck is short, his belly is big,
The Turkish pasha is ready.

This is a completely accurate literal translation of the original yet it somehow fails to communicate.

If I tell you that I last heard it uttered by my twenty-seven month old daughter Sylvia, otherwise a developing native speaker of English, you will have little difficulty in guessing that it must be some kind of nursery rhyme. Now nursery rhymes are known to be flimsy in the well-formedness of their semological progressions, which they usually counterbalance with catchy imagery and sound patterns. What is significant about THIS piece is that it is not a simple nursery rhyme, but what we may call a didactic-performative one. Sylvia was last heard saying it while attempting to draw a human figure with a crayon on a sheet of paper. It is important to observe here that the saying of the various portions of the nursery rhyme is designed to coincide in time with the various drawing motions. Thus during the uttering of *Pont, pont, vesszőcske* (i.e., 'period, period, little comma'), the child draws two eyes and a nose, and perhaps also a mouth, depending on her degree of skill and coordination of verbal rhythm with manual rhythm:

Figure 1

During the pronunciation of the seven syllables *Készen van a fejecske* ('the little head is ready'), the child draws a circle around the eyes and nose, and we have the abstract representation of a human head:

Figure 2

During the next four syllables, *kurta nyaka*, meaning 'his neck is short', the child draws two vertical strokes stemming downward from the circle:

Figure 3

while *nagy a hasa* ('his belly his big') coincides with the drawing of a large circle below, representing the belly:

Figure 4

The next eight syllables, *készen van a Török Pasa*, 'the Turkish pasha is ready' with their rhythmical breaks into four pairs of two syllables each, provide the child with the exterior stimulus to draw two stick arms and two stick legs:

Figure 5

We now know a fair amount about the nursery rhyme, what it is used for and what it means literally, but we have not really TRANSLATED it. The problem became a very real one when Sylvia approached me and requested, 'Daddy, I want to draw the Török Pasa in mommy language' (that is English).

The task is really more complicated than it appears, because a great deal of cultural substitution must take place. Turkish pashas are meaningless for American children. This aspect of the translation problem may seem linguistically irrelevant, but it cannot be ignored if one is interested in obtaining the best possible translation.

At this point we must, by necessity, enter the suspicious world of poetic license. We must make value judgments. What is more important? The rhyming and the number of syllables, or the exact cultural connotations a Hungarian child would have when drawing his Turkish pasha in Hungarian? Having discovered that we are concerned with the rendition in English of a Hungarian nursery rhyme of the didactic-performance type, the translator must decide in favor of the rhymes, the rhythm, and the completion of the human figure, over the preservation of the exact, if at all available, cultural connotations of the lexemes involved.

Briefly, and to start with the second line first, the translation *ready is the little head* covers *Készen van a fejecske* rather well; as a matter of fact even the word order corresponds. The translator is now committed, however, to the word *head* being at the end of the line; thus whatever the translation of the line above, it must end with a word that rhymes with *head*. The word *thread* appears to fill the bill, and thus we get:

Dot, dot, tiny thread,
Ready is the tiny head.

Through essentially similar calculations, resulting in the omission of *Turkish pasha*, and aided by the discovery that *tummy*, a fair synonym for *belly*, rhymes reassuringly with *dummy*, we come up with the following English version:

Dot, dot, tiny thread,
Ready is the tiny head.
Short his neck, and huge his tummy,
Ready is the big fat dummy.

It may not be great poetry, but then neither was the original. Once in pronounceable and meaningful shape, Sylvia was confronted with the English version. Delighted, she went through the same drawing motions as with the Hungarian, and completed the drawing, on schedule, on the twenty-eighth syllable.

It is my contention that Transformational-Generative Grammar, in its present shape, is unable to account, not only for how the present translation was accomplished, but for translation in general. If we believe, as Chomsky asserts, that the syntactic component is creative, and the semantic and phonological components interpret what the syntax generates, translation could only be accomplished under one of the following procedures:

(1) The phonological output of Hungarian is algorithmically mapped onto an English phonological output. But this is absurd. Phonologies, being interpretive of the syntaxes that generate them, cannot be mapped onto one another without control from the syntactic components.

(2) The second possibility is that the surface structure of the Hungarian is mapped onto the surface structure of the English, after the appropriate dictionary look-ups have been made. But that is exactly what we got when we substituted literally morpheme for morpheme. We must abandon this approach also, since it does not yield comprehensible English.

(3) Thirdly, if we try to map deep structure onto deep structure we might come up with the adjusted literal translation:[1]

Period, period, little comma,
The little head is ready.
His neck is short, his belly is big,
The Turkish pasha is ready.

The problem is that the rhymes are lost, as is also the knowledge of the fact that the nursery rhyme is a didactic-performance game in the source language. These are the most obvious objections to the Transformational-

Generative approach. But there are more basic ones as well. If the syntax generates and the semantic component interprets, what exactly happens in translating into the target language? The translator does not interpret anything. He in fact takes the semantic interpretation of the source language and re-encodes it in the target language. Furthermore, he must re-encode it with discretion, as the case of our omission of *Turkish pasha* shows. One might argue that what happens in the target language is not the same as what happens in the source language; that in the source language one starts with syntax and then interprets it, whereas in the target language the semantic interpretation comes over ready-made from the source language, and the syntax must follow it. The problem with such a view is that it supposes a double standard: we describe a person's COMPETENCE in the source language, whereas the only way his ability to translate into the target language can be handled is by ascribing it to PERFORMANCE. The transformationalist would, in fact, have to say that translation belongs to performance, not to competence. But is it not a logical contradiction to suppose that a person can outperform his own competence? (See Chapter 3.) And yet the mappings attempted above, of phonology onto phonology, etc., do not produce an adequate result.

If one cannot go directly from the phonology of language A to the phonology of language B, or from the surface structure of A to the surface structure of B, or from the deep structure of A to the deep structure of B, the only recourse is to go from the phonology of A to the surface structure of A, then to the deep structure of A, and then to the semantic component of A; and ONLY THEN can one transfer to B. This obviously must be on the semantic or cognitive level. Thus from the semantic component of A we go the semantic component of B, then to its deep structure, its surface structure, and down to its phonological component. But at this point we have really abandoned Transformational-Generative Grammar.

In fact, this amounts to a recognition of the stratification of language. The translator actually proceeds as is illustrated in the following diagram:

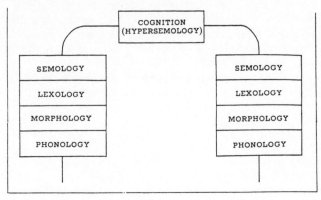

Figure 6   A stratificational interpretation of the directionality of the translation process

The knowledge that the source text is a traditional nursery rhyme is stored in the hypersemology, as is the awareness that it is a didactic-performative rhyme, and that Turkish pashas are not meaningful for English speaking children. This knowledge causes the translator to adjust, correspondingly, the semology and the lexology of the test in the target language. In terms of Tagmemics, such a nursery rhyme would be a Behavioreme in the source culture, with its feature and manifestation modes.

Rhyming is essentially a phonological matter. In most instances of verse translation it so happens that the translator, upon some concentration and effort, finds a pair of words in the target language that makes sense in the context set up by the source language and which ACCIDENTALLY HAPPEN TO RHYME. In our case this was the discovery that *tummy* and *dummy* were such words in English, suitable both phonologically and semantically. But as most verse translators will testify, such discoveries usually occur BEFORE one commits the discovered, semantically available target-language rhymes to perform any task in the emerging target-language sentence-syntax at all. Far from being INTERPRETIVE, then, it is precisely the phonology of the target language that will 'co-generate', by the power of suggestion as it were, the sentence that will result. Or alternatively, the finding of the acceptable target-language rhyme pair may occur just about the same time one is building the sentence structure that must carry the rhymes. This allows us to choose between two alternatives only: (1) Either the rhyme (a phonological matter of the target language) can have a delimiting and determining effect on the outcome of the sentence, or (2) the finding of the appropriate rhyme is co-synchronous with the building of the sentence. What in fact NEVER HAPPENS is the third alternative, namely (3) whereby the sentence structure *qua* syntax, would determine the outcome of the rhyme. THAT IS, HOWEVER, PRECISELY WHAT TRANSFOR-MATIONAL THEORY CLAIMS! Thus we see transformational theory claim-ing the absurd while not being able to account for the obvious, i.e., the commonly observed fact that rhymes can 'dominate' sentence production or be co-synchronous with it. The reason why transformational theory cannot account for cosynchronicity and/or the possible occasional supremacy of phonological criteria over syntactical ones is the central fixation of rule ordering. What happens in verse translation is that the independent features of various levels (rhyme : phonology; number of syllables : phonotactics; available words per meaning form classes : morph-ology; available lexemes per context-defined sense and their tactics : syn-tax; availability of cross-cultural context-defined sememes : semology AND cognition) are amalgamated by the translator into ONE COHERENT TEXT. Hence the only theory that can account for verse translation is one that can account for SYSTEMS OF SIMULTANEOUS AWARENESS. Pending further details of elaboration, this problem has been solved, at least in PRINCIPLE, by stratificational theory in which we have both ordered and unordered nodes. In the translator's cognitive system there is an 'unordered AND' node which allows him to explore the rhyming possibilities and the sentence building in any order, or simultaneously, as many times as necessary. This is also the only sensible way to explain how a child actually sees such a rhyming didactism: In the child's consciousness there is, again, an unordered AND node one line from which activates the speech mechanism (i.e., the child says the verse out loud), while the other activates the muscular co-ordination center of the central nervous system resulting in the drawing motions. The pedagogical value of such didactisms rests precisely in the fact that they reinforce drawing ability by the mnemonic aid of the verse, and verbal memorization by the aid of the drawing. Note, however, that this varies with age. For Sylvia at 27–28 months it was far easier to say the words in two languages than to draw a half-way decent Pasha, whereas at the age of three and a half the drawing skill got much better co-ordinated. This difference in verbal versus manual skill in the very young, however, does not invalidate my suggestion that at the actual time of performing a drawing-rhyming didactism the person so doing must, by necessity, use a mental ability whose abstract representation is, as far as analogies go, adequately captured by the notion of the UNORDERED AND node.

Note also that this process of translation, as illustrated above, does not apply only to poetry. Consider English *How do you do?*, whose French equivalent *enchanté* (literally 'enchanted'), while in Indonesian it is *apa kabar* 'What is the news?'. In the case of greetings we lexicalize the entire form and simply utter the corresponding form in the target language, since the cognitive adjustments have been made for us by the social situation in which the greeting occurs. In the translation of new texts however, we must determine by cognitive means what the situation is, and then recreate its proper expression in the target language.

A stratificational grammar, in fact, handles all types of translation: literal prose, slightly idiomatic texts, traditional sayings, and poetry, with the same directionality illustrated on the diagram. If the text is straightforward, as in *dogs bark*, the cognitive system does not signal to the speaker that additional cultural material needs to be added or suppressed. The cognitive system functions as a flexible monitoring device: without it we can translate only as if we were incompletely programmed computers; with it we are able to translate straightforward prose, if that is our task, but also complicated texts which would not otherwise reach the target language in a contextually adequate format.

POSTWORD: Mr Igor Miletić of the University of Illinois at Chicago Circle brought to my attention the fact that in Serbo-Croatian there exists a similar didactic-performative nursery rhyme. The text is as follows:

Točka, točka, točkica,
Gotova je glavica.
Male uši, dugi vrat,
Trbuh mu ko crkven sat.
Male noge ko u miša
Gotovi je čika Gliša.

Literally it means:

Period, period, little period,
Ready is the little head,
Little ears, long neck,
His belly is like the church clock.
Small legs like a mouse,
Ready is Uncle Glisha.

The reader is invited to create his own verse translation. The author would sincerely appreciate word of similar nursery rhymes in other languages.[2]

Notes

1. The 'deep structure' of both the Hungarian original and the 'adjusted English prose translation' can be worked out in several ways by lexicalist-interpretivist, and generativist transformational readers depending on their vintage of graduation and personal preferences. Labelled trees, bracketed strings, Katzian semi-sentences, deep word order mapped onto surface word order by transformations can all be used as well as pre-lexical predicate raising and semantic feature syntax. Whatever the outcome, you will find that given the ideally 'best' deep structure for the Hungarian version and the 'best' version for the English, the translator has still not fulfilled his goal of translating the given didactism AS VERSE.

2. In addition to Hungarian, Serbo-Croatian and English (translated) versions, I now have a Danish, two Austrian German, and one Bavarian German version in addition to Cantonese, Mandarin and Burmese rhyme-drawings, and a native Midwestern American rhyming-drawing didactism involving a fish (April, 1993).

13 On the meaning of Noel Coward's '*Venice*'

1. The text:

Last Wednesday on the *Piazza*
Near San Marco's rococo *duomo*,
I observed *una grassa ragazza*
With a thin, Middle Western *uomo*.

He was swatting a *piccola mosca*
She was eating a chocolate *gelato*,
While the orchestra played (from *La Tosca*)
A flat violin *obbligato*.

They stared at a dusty *piccione* –
They spoke not a single *parola*;
She ordered some *tè con limone*,
He ordered an iced Coca-Cola.

And while the *tramonto del sole*
Set fire to the *Grande Canale*,
She scribbled haphazard *parole*
On a glazed *cartolina postale*.

2. The problem:

a) What linguistic explanation are we able to provide about a writer's ability to generate essentially English sentences, capped with Italian rhymes?

b) Are there two 'deep structures' involved? If the answer to (b) is 'yes', where and how does the proposed DS signal to the surface structure to 'interpret' the line-final word(s) not according to English, but according to Italian phonology?

c) Is there only one deep structure involved? If the answer is 'yes' to (c), where does the single underlying deep structure provide the signal to the surface structure and the phonology to switch the code?

d) Is the 'English' part of the poem the author's 'competence' and the

Italian rhymes his 'performance', or the other way round?

e) Is the poem *in toto* a matter of unusual performance, cleverly super-imposed on an essentially identical deep structure?

f) Could it be that the deep structure–surface structure dichotomy is simply irrelevant to this poem, and so we must seek an alternative explanation?

g) Could the stratificational model account for this poem by suggesting that the poem is a code-switched realization of the same set of sememic reticula? Is such an explanation not basically similar to (c) outlined above, with only a minor difference in terminology?

h) Even if one should choose to take the stratificational explanation over the transformational one, JUST WHERE EXACTLY DOES CODE-SWITCHING OCCUR and HOW IS IT CARRIED OUT?

2.1. There is no easy answer to these eight questions which, if gone into in detail, could amount to a vast study on code-switching from a variety of points of view, including neurology and socio-psycholinguistics.

Whether the poem is BASICALLY in English or in Italian can, I believe, be relatively easily decided by rewriting it once in English, and once in Italian. The rhymes – i.e. the fact that this text is a poem – could only be kept if the English material before the rhyming words would allow themselves to be put in Italian which will not work because possessives, such as *San Marco*'s and Adj + N combinations such as *rococo duomo* would have to be turned around to yield *il duomo rococo di San Marco* thereby changing the final word and thus upsetting the rhyming scheme. Let us, then, suppose that the poem is basically in English with the rhymes merely added in Italian for some sort of special effect. If this hypothesis is correct, we should have no difficulty rewriting the poem all in English:

Last Wednesday on the market place
Near San Marco's rococo house (church),
I observed a fat girl
With a thin Middle Western man.

He was swatting a small fly
She was eating a chocolate ice cream,
While the orchestra played (from *La Tosca*)
A flat violin counterpart. (Or 'obbligato').

They stared at a dusty pigeon
They spoke not a single word –
She ordered some tea with lemon
He ordered an iced Coca-Cola.

And while the setting of the sun
Set fire to the Grand Canal,
She scribbled haphazard words
On a glazed post card.

The rhymes are, of course, lost, and with them the author's purpose of writing the poem bilingually in the first place. The poem COULD, of course, be rewritten in Italian as well; minor syntactic adjustments would have to be made to accommodate the word order conventions of Italian.

2.2. Let us approach now the poem from the 'literary' point of view, exploring, as it were, the 'stylistics' and the 'message' of it to see if these might shed some light on the universe of discourse this piece belongs to allowing us to penetrate the grammar of the poem from 'above', as it were.

I think we can easily agree that we are not dealing with a profound or a great poem in any sense of the word, but rather with a spoof, a kind of fun-poking at human foibles that Coward, both as a movie director and as a writer, was well known for. The poem gives us certain clues as to the author's point of view and his intentions: the man is not a Japanese or a German tourist, nor is he British. He is a Middle Western *uomo*, that is, an American on a Venetian holiday with his fat – i.e., not irresistably attractive – girl friend. Coward, the British humorist, observes the couple and comments on their comically common-place and rather dull behavior in the over-publicized and over-romanticized setting of the famous square in front of Saint Mark's, a scene frequently seen on travel agents' posters. One wonders actually why Coward did not add a couple of additional stanzas drawing a caricature of the famous Venetian gondola and its ruseful skipper, the tip-hungry gondolier: he could have got the couple wet falling into the canal as the thin Middle Westerner ushers his obese bride out of the gondola, etc. Apparently four stanzas were all he wanted to make his sketch, and perhaps adding other stanzas would have been too much. It is fairly clear, however, that he is MAKING FUN OF THE AMERICANS while at the same time giving the connoisseur's cunning smirk about Venice itself; here the sophisticated European is WARNING THE AMERICANS that the place is over-rated and not really so glamorous, after all. His attitude is not one of criticism or of reproach, he is more the passive observer (stanza 1, line 3); and by the time the *dramatis personae* are introduced (stanza 1, lines 3 and 4) he, the observer, has already put HIMSELF into the same ridiculous situation as those he observes: he was on the *piazza*, not the market place, near San Marco's *rococo duomo*, not his church, or house. The observer is an integral part of the act of observation, overtly and admittedly, and hence the mild ridicule and the warning to the Americans is, at the same time, self-irony and self-warning as well. ('What on Earth am I doing here if this is the kind of dull scene I am going to be witnessing . . .'.) The Englishman, the 'Joker', is just as 'estranged' from the over-publicized romantic scenery as are the American tourists, who are the 'straight-men' in this little scenario, primarily because they do not seem to realize how utterly out-of-place they are in Venice with Venice, of course, being the 'culprit' for offering such dull amusement as a dusty pigeon, and the American invention, iced tea. Coke, which has become so universal, can be pronounced in flawless Italian as *una Coca-Cola*, rhyming perfectly with *parola*. (The underlined words in the original text, *San Marco's*, *rococo*, and *La Tosca* are Italian words that the English and the Americans have adopted and which can be pronounced both according to English or Italian phonology; *Coca-Cola* is an English-based internationalism receiving as many foreign phonological realizations as it has commercial adoptions the world over, with such internationalisms usually being 'bent' towards whatever the host-speakers interpret as 'cool', i.e., Latinoid.)

The sequence of 'events' shows the Middle Western Man and the fat girl as a couple who are either bored with one another, or who do not really belong to each other, having perhaps only met recently with not much chance of a great romantic love. The description moves from 'he' to 'she' (stanza 2); then twice 'they' (stanza 3); then the order is reversed: 'she' and 'he'. An act by 'she' closes the poem. Whether the 'camera' focuses on him or her, it also gives us a 'cut' to the side: first the orchestra, then the dusty pigeon, and finally the setting of the sun over the Grand Canal. The last stanza is a coda in a sense: the setting sun, while suggestive of the end of the day, also suggests the falling of the curtain on the little scenario, and the post card she is scribbling haphazard words on tie her (perhaps also him) in with whoever was left behind, probably in the Midwest of the USA.

We learn in stanza 2 that he is active (he swatted a tiny fly) while she eats – this duality of behavior is underscored by the 'flat violin obbligato' from one of the world's more sentimental (and somewhat overrated) operas, La Tosca. When they are together (stanza 3) the COUPLE DOES EXACTLY NOTHING, i.e., they are actively engaged in doing nothing ('they stared at a dusty pigeon, they spoke not a single word'). Then they both fill their stomachs again; she with more refinement, orders tea with lemon, he orders an iced coke. The 4th stanza, as mentioned above, lets the curtain fall with the setting of the sun and the post card acts as the *envoi* calling back home, and therefore to us, the readers, the end of the scenario. (The poem was originally published in 1969 in the *New Yorker*.)

2.2.1. The Italian rhymes (replete with *La Tosca* and *Coca-Cola*, the first already international and the second an English-based internationalism) can now be seen as fulfilling a BASIC FUNCTION in the entire poem: without them we would not get the sensation of being POTENTIAL SUBJECTS TO RIDICULE when we are out of our own NATURAL LINGUISTIC MILIEU. These people are not at home on Saint Mark's Square in Venice, and the local culture (*'flat* violin obbligato') does not embrace them with the best it can offer. 'They spoke not a single parola' either means that they do not speak Italian, or that the trip has got them sufficiently down so that they no longer care to converse even in English with each other. What they do instead is rather atypical of the ideal Venice one thinks of: staring at a dusty pigeon and swatting a fly, eating ice-cream and drinking a coke can be done anywhere in the world including any MacDonald's stand anywhere in the USA. Whatever 'haphazard parole' she may be writing on her local post cards probably exaggerate the trip: they are 'glazed', a word that alliterates and readily associates with *glitter* and, as we know, not all that glitters is gold. (Read: not every trip to Europe is as glamorous as the travel agent's ad might have you believe.)

The role of the rhymes is, then, strategic-functional: they are the constant reminders at the end of each line of the CULTURAL DISPLACEMENT of the participants in this four-act mini-drama.

2.2.1.1. The author could have written a brief prose paragraph about 'cultural displacement' of Midwestern Americans in Europe, and the 'intellectual message' of such a paragraph would be easily understood by any reader. The present poem, however, while informing us implicitly about 'cultural displacement' explicitly PERFORMS for the reader the very fact of cultural displacement: as each sentence and each line, begun in English, carries us toward an expected English noun, NP, or N compliment (out of the sixteen Italian rhymes six are complex NPs, *una grassa ragazza*, *piccola mosca*, *La Tosca*, *tè con limone*, *Grande Canale*, and *cartolina postale*, one is an adjective, *gelato*, and counting English-based Coca-Cola a simple N, the rest are simple nouns) we are sixteen times subjected to the 'culture shock' the fictionalized foreign traveler feels. This observation is, of course, a direct consequence of the very nature of poetry, whether of an elevated, serious nature, or of the light *vers de société* type, of which *Venice* undoubtedly belongs, since a poem, from Greek ποεϊν 'do', 'make', is always more than its meaning given in prose paraphrase: it is as much of a HAPPENING for the reader who lives through it while reading it as it was for the poet who wrote it. In poetry, typically, the language-user reverts to that archaic state of language use which Fónagy (1974a,b) calls the primitive arche-language, a cognitive state in mankind's intellectual development in which language was much less abstract than today and much more of an iconic recapitulation of events in the real world. (The reader is invited to compare this observation with Chapter 10, 'The Origin of Language' of Bolinger (1975b) and Chapter 2 of Halliday (1975a).)

From a literary point of view, a significant part of the meaning of this poem is what it DOES to the reader; and what it does to the reader is EXPOSE HIM SIXTEEN TIMES to the actual crossing of a cultural and linguistic barrier moving us back and forth, as it were, between the English-speaking world and Italy. Coward may have realized that one could easily tire of this which may partly explain why he did not enhance the ridicule with a possible gondola scene, or something similar.

2.3. But from a linguistic point of view, if an integral part of the meaning of the poem is what it DOES to the reader – i.e., move him back and forth between English and Italian – then a major part of the poem's meaning must be its SPECIAL PERFORMANCE QUA POEM. Yet this special performance *qua* poem co-exists simultaneously with the recoverability of the basic syntax and semantics of the poem which can be expressed either in homogeneous English (as given above) or in Italian. In a strange sense, then, this poem is actually impossible and should not exist at all. On the one hand, its 'meaning' is derivable from its syntax and the dictionary definition of each lexeme in the text, whether English or Italian; on the other hand this legal 'meaning' misses the point of the poem entirely which is, as we have seen, that the reader must be shifted back and forth between *Italica* and *Anglica* and be made fun of (while making fun of) the protagonists in the tiny play. We are additionally puzzled by the fact that here apparently ONE SINGLE UNDERLYING SYNTAX is capable of carrying English material on the one hand, and Italian on the other. Strictly speaking the two languages are not entirely equivalent here. The English, which determines the shape of the sentences, and of which there is quite simply more per stanza, definitely dominates the text; secondly, the rhymed words, by virtue of being in the sensitive position of being rhymes, all seem to fall into the same syntactic category of noun or nominal group. A noun, or nominal group, is always more reified, more 'tangible', than a verb or a verbal group; it is more 'concrete'. It can be compared to a point of arrival at the end of a journey: the English-speaking travellers arrive in Venice, they are in Italy, where the objects they touch, consume, or are surrounded by, either visually or aurally, are (in) Italian. In other words the TRIP is in English, but the TRAIN STATIONS are in Italian sixteen times throughout the four stanzas. Could it be that the syntax itself, which prepares these Italian endpoints of arrival, was so conceived by Coward in its very Englishness, as to reach culturally and semantically pregnant nouns and nominal groups which can only deliver their intended effect if they are code-switched? Quite possibly. But if this is the case, we must be ready to face the consequence that some of the English syntax of the poem was occasioned by the anticipated Italian rhyme. It is well known poetic practice on both sides of the Atlantic to be 'pregnant with a promising rhyme' and then to construct a poem around that rhyme.

2.3.1. In order for a transformationalist deep structure derivation to be able to account for just monolingual poetry alone, where by poetry I mean rhyming and meter in dominant position over the ordinary sentence syntax, the deep structure would have to be so adjusted and re-explained theoretically, as to be able to take directions from the phonological component of the grammar. It is, strictly speaking, not a responsible statement to make that this is intrinsically impossible. The way deep structure has been conceived of up till recently, however, it is difficult to see how such a partial subordination of the DS to the phonology would be accomplished. Part of the difficulty is the unidirectional nature of DS derivations which map onto surface structures from left to right which, then, are interpreted phonologically, again from left to right. What would be needed would be a set of RETRO-REWRITE RULES, or some such device, that would allow the phonological component to map backwards onto the surface structure which, in turn, would map backwards onto the deep structure. I can think of no inherent logical reason why such a model would be impossible though I am not aware of such rules ever having been proposed in writing.

(Barbara Hall Partee (personal communication) apparently gave an oral paper on 'reverse rewrite rules' but has not published the paper.) Additional problems would arise since the TG theorist would have to account for the author's having chosen a rhyme before having chosen a sentence structure that would accommodate that rhyme in whatever syntactic position was appropriate for it. It seems that whatever solution one might come up with would be highly suspect of being arbitrary and *ad hoc* in the extreme.

Given the fact that Italian and English are both Indo-European languages with considerable genetic and typological affinity, the same-deep-structure-hypothesis could perhaps be maintained and justified up to a certain point. Given the appropriate *IE reconstructions, the poem could actually be rewritten in Proto-Indo-European and both the English and the Italian version could be 'derived' from this (historically) underlying *PIE poem by a long and complicated set of 'derivational rules', in the spirit of Lightner (1975). (For a reply to Lightner's suggestions, see Lockwood 1975, 1976.) Only an extremely erudite Indo-Europeanist could equate the notion of 'same underlying deep structure' with a reconstructed *PIE version of the text, and Noel Coward is not a historical linguist.

2.3.2. Useful models of the stratificationalist account of poetry and bilingualism are available in Makkai (1973) and Paradis (1976). The bilingual individual has in his memory parallel sets of phonological, morphological, lexical, and sememic material, which he can switch and correlate by virtue of certain extralinguistic considerations housed in that part of his cognitive system which has been called 'gnostemics'. 'hypersememic', or the 'pragmo-sememic interface'. The stratificational model would allow one to speculate about how *Venice* was conceived in some such manner as follows:

(1) Coward knew the basic plot of his poem before he began writing it. The idea was not yet entirely clear in his mind, and the sentences as they now actually appear in print were not ready yet as he began writing. He probably decided, however, that the main sentence structure would be English and that the rhymes would be in Italian. This must have been in direct response to the CONTEXT OF SITUATION which occasioned the poem.

(2) Being probably stronger in English than in Italian, he picked nouns and nominal groups to be the Italian rhymes.

(3) Being nevertheless knowledgeable in Italian, he knew that the words *piazza–ragazza*, *duomo–uomo*, *mosca–Tosca*, *gelato–obbligato*, *piccione–limone*, *parola–Coca-Cola*, *sole–parole*, and *canale–postale*, were good, if trite, rhymes. It is not possible at this stage to reconstruct just in what order these occurred to him, but by rereading the English with the Italian rhymes left off we get: Last Wednesday on the _____ near San Marco's rococo _____, I observed _____ _____ _____ with a thin Middle Western _____. He was swatting a _____ _____,

she was eating a chocolate _____, while the orchestra played (from La Tosca) a flat violin _____. They stared at a dusty _____, they spoke not a single _____; she ordered some _____ _____ _____, he ordered an iced Coca-Cola. And while the _____ _____ _____ set fire to the _____ _____, she scribbled haphazard _____ on a glazed _____ _____.

(4)   What we now have are two matrices, the English sentences with the gaps to be filled in, and the Italian rhymes asking for sentences to be carried by, to be housed in.

(5)   As a 'bilingual' in this situation, Coward knew, of course, the 'meanings' of the Italian words as well as the meanings of the English words which, as we saw above, are easily translatable into one another. The translation of the words of L_1 into the words of L_2 seems to occur by taking the corresponding sememe of L_1 and comparing it to the sememe of L_2 to see if they fit. In the case of *tè con limone* = 'tea with lemon' and *Grande Canale* = 'Grand Canal' the translation process is facilitated by the fact that the words involved are close cognates, but no great difficulty is encountered by such non-cognate material as *una grassa ragazza* = 'a fat girl' and *une piccola mosca* = 'a small fly' either, as the lexemes (and the corresponding sememes) involved are common in both cultures and exist essentially within the same scope of boundary. Serious problems of translation always occur when the item to be translated is unique to one or other of the cultures, i.e., imagine Coward's having had to deal with *hominy grits*, *bubble and squeak*, *pecan pie*, and/or *prosciutto*, *frutti di mare* or some such quasi-proverbial institutionalized Italian attitude as *dolce far niente*. We can hypothesize, then, that Coward's task was a relatively easy one, insofar as he dealt with CULTURALLY RELATED SEMEMES whose respective Italian and English lexemic realization could be accomplished rather rapidly, by using the sememe more or less as an unconscious token merely rather than a laborious technical definition. Common lexemes such as *sun, moon, mother*, and *father* are immediately and unconsciously translatable into whatever language one is dealing with, because the sememes of which they are the lexemic realizations came into our consciousness not by technical definitions but by primary bio-physical contact during early childhood. The reader should try to translate the English terms *filibuster, gerrymander, lame duck President*, and *wild cat strike* into the foreign language of his choice, right after translating *sun, moon, mother* and *father* to appreciate the difference between what I propose to call a BIO-PSYCHO-SEMEME and a SOCIO-TECHNO-SEMEME. The only socio-techno-sememe in *Venice* is the word *obbligato*, a technical term pertaining to counterpoint in music. (See Chapter 9 in this volume.)

(6)   Coward, then, wrote the poem in two languages at once, displaying a double competence and double performance, localizing the point of the code-switch always in rhymed, line-final position, with these positions always coinciding with a noun or a nominal group.

(7)   Coward must have been counting on a bilingual audience when he wrote the poem. (Bilingual in the sense that the reader, basically an Anglo-American, would be able to understand the Italian words in the rhymed positions.) The poem falls rather flat for a reader who has to look up every word in an Italian–English dictionary and who does not know how to pronounce them. This is essentially an upper-middle class elitist attitude; this is not working class humor, but bourgeois humor.

3. The meaning of this poem can only be approached if we take all of these considerations into account simultaneously. As it is by now plainly evident, the author's cognitive system, his 'gnostemics' or his 'hypersemology' is the crucial area where everything else must be co-ordinated. These elements, roughly, are:

(a)   The plot,
(b)   The syntax,
(c)   The knowledge of the setting,
(d)   Familiarity with the sociology of the participants,
(e)   Knowledge of the syllabic pattern of English,
(f)   Knowledge of the Italian lexemes, their meanings, and the fact that they are eligible rhymes, although somewhat trite,
(g)   Anticipation of the derived effect on Anglo-American readers.

There could be many more; these few points are the inevitable necessities. The dynamics of shifting the reader between English and Italian has been discussed before and falls into the areas of a-b-c above.

3.1. Creative language use is extremely complex and does not readily yield itself to routine grammatical analysis of no matter what vintage and no matter what theoretical bent. Linguists have been reluctant to look at creative language use precisely because it poses so many problems and difficulties. Far from being fanciful and idle, however, the study of poetic language and imaginative language use is perhaps the most important aspect of linguistic research, because people do indulge in creative language use all the time, whether wittingly or unwittingly. It is also to be expected that once linguistics faces up to the task of dealing with the unusual, it will have a much better chance of dealing with the ordinary, than the other way round.

14 'Lexical insertion' as a socio-psychological event: evidence from poetic behavior

The thesis of this chapter is that we human beings are all poets, whether or not we actually practice poetry in a professional sense or not. Whether one is engaged in a matter-of-fact prosaic transaction with a sales clerk, a waiter, or during a university lecture on linguistics, one is constantly confronted with the necessity of CHOOSING THE RIGHT WORD for what one has to say. The choosing of the right word, however, is a mysterious process shrouded in theoretical obfuscation and controversy. I have no intention of arbitrating in this chapter on whether the transformational-generativists are right or wrong in their various notions of 'lexical insertion', and I will not take sides in the glamorous debate between the Chomsky–Katz-type 'lexicalist-interpretivists' and the McCawley–Lakoff-type 'generative semanticists'. (If I had to choose between these two versions of TG, I would probably choose generative semantics, however, because even though its practitioners disavow such intentions, it seems to imply a greater likelihood for psychological realism by 'starting' the sentence-generating process in the semantics and not in the deep structure. If 'creativity' and generation start in the deep structure, lexical insertion becomes, I think, an appendage of the syntactic string whereby the sentence structure chosen would seem to dictate the choice of words to be used, a possible consequence of TG which seems to me to be entirely counter-intuitive.)

Nor will this chapter be any attempt at redeeming stratificationalism, a movement with which I have been associated in a major way for some time (Makkai 1972, 1973). Stratificationalism, I believe, suffers from the same deficiency as the various versions of TG do: there is no believable model offered regarding the mysterious relationship between SENTENCE STRUCTURE and VOCABULARY.

Thus, when a generative grammarian comes up with a pre-lexical terminal string of the type (this being a rough oversimplification for the sole purpose of illustration; see Figure 1), there is never any convincing reason offered in the literature to indicate whether this derivation is there

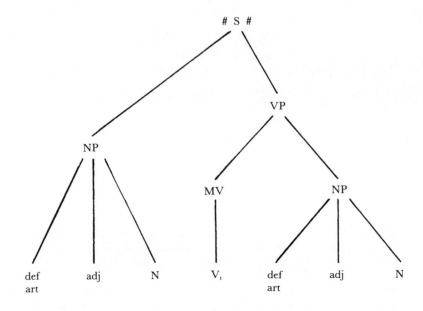

Figure 1

because one of the possible sentences it describes was virtually present in the consciousness of the person (i.e., the linguist) who constructed it (e.g., *The naughty boy swallowed the ecstatic goldfish*) or whether it is this kind of structure which somehow elicits vocabulary from the conscious and the subconscious mind of the speaker. I am reasonably sure, of course, that the 'man-in-the-street' would never find himself in the situation of having to find suitable words for skeletal sentence structures, unless hired for the explicit purpose by an experimenter. From an intuitive psychological point of view, it seems to me that sentence structures materialize quasi-automatically partially after, and partially simultaneously with, our having selected the wording of what we are about to say.

Similarly, stratificationalism gives us no indication regarding the precise nature, the timing, or the choices to be made when a SEMEMIC RETICULUM is about to be realized as a lexemic network. (It does not matter, for the purposes of this discussion, whether we draw relational networks or directed graphs. For simplicity's sake I will adopt here the latter.) Any sememic reticulum, that does not somehow exhibit actual WORDS in it, remains undecodable, or multiguous. Consider the example in Figure 2.

The only thing this network will tell the decoder is that the agent is an ancient male human being (who can be further identified if you look up

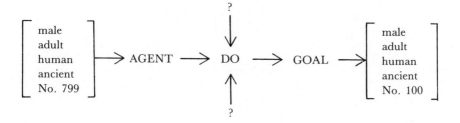

Figure 2

his identification number) engaged in some doing the goal of which is another ancient male human being. We have no idea what the doing entails; we do not know whether the doing takes place in the past, the present, or the future (unless the word 'ancient' suggests the past, but we could be dealing with a contemporary play which has not yet been performed); furthermore, not even this much would be known, if we had not used the 'words' *male, adult, human,* and *ancient.* One possible realization of this sentence is *Brutus killed Caesar,* or, without any passive transformation, *Caesar was killed by Brutus,* if we adjust the sememic focus (cf. Lockwood 1972).

In another mode of stratificational representation, one does not draw 'directed graphs' but 'relational networks' for 'sememic trace'. Such traces, in simple cases, may consist of 'unordered AND' nodes (also known as coincidence concatenations or conjunctions). Figure 3 shows such a 'sememic trace' but does not give any lexical hints whatever what it is we may be talking about. All the network says is that there is an agent whose identification number is X, engaged in doing something with regard to a goal. We do not know what the goal is, we do not know whether the agent is animate, like a person or an animal, or inanimate (as in *the wind shut the door* which, of course, is also analyzable as containing an instrument rather than an agent); we are not told whether the doing is in the present, the past, or the future.[2]

This kind of lexically uninformative structure can be contrasted with syntactically unstructured lists of words, such as *quick–police–dead–man; man, dead, police, quick; dead, police, man, quick; man, quick, dead, police,* or any combination of these four words. Whereas, clearly, some ordering of these words will sound more like what we expect for *quick, the police! The man's dead!* it is disproportionately easier to make sense of these four words than it is to find out what the network of Figure 3 is trying to tell us. Single words, without any syntax whatever, may carry much richer communicative function than pages worth of syntactically well-formed sentences. Compare the one word items *go!, Fire!, Now!, Stop!* with some such elegant but semantically empty sentence as *previous information to the contrary notwithstanding, the*

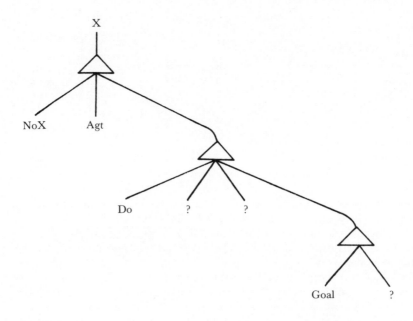

Figure 3

statements made in the case at hand will remain mere allegations unless additional
evidence can be adduced to support dissident views on the matter.

The trouble is that, exactly as in the case of TG, the network makes
sense after we know the sentence in question, but the sentence, as given,
is only one possible outcome of the network. I am forced to conclude that
all theoreticians have been either deliberately joking or that they simply
have not faced the simple fact that the communicative intent of normal
people rests with loosely structured words and not with lexical strings or
sememic reticula. (If I must choose between any brand of lexical string as
a lexeme eliciting matrix and sememic reticular, I will choose the sememic
reticula, because they offer a greater freedom of choice and seem to do the
'lexeme eliciting' from the unconscious more in accordance with some
plausible measure of psychological realism.) I must now explain a few
unfamiliar notions, such as 'lexeme elicitation'.

This is an experiment anyone can perform either on oneself or on
subjects willing to try. The experimenter is free to choose between TG-ish
eliciting matrices or stratificationally styled ones; the results will be surprisingly similar. Since surface structure oriented terminal strings are very

specific, there is less freedom to insert words (and make sense); with the sememic reticula one's freedom of choice depends on the specifications given in the reticulum. If the reticulum is reasonably vague, the inserter's freedom remains proportionately larger; the more specifications appear in the reticulum, the more compliance in choice will be required on the part of the inserter. Both the elicitor and the inserter have to be willing to play this game, of course, but the benefits are considerable and the game is entirely harmless.

Let us try two different eliciting matrices, one in the transformationalist style, and one in the stratificationalist mode. An eliciting matrix is a set of instructions given by the analyst (the elicitor) to his patient, the inserter, somewhat as if the former were a psychiatrist, and the latter his patient, lying on the office couch. I am reasonably certain that the eventual use of such techniques by real psychiatrists on real patients would yield valuable insight into personality structures, types of mental disorder, etc.

FIRST GAME, TRANSFORMATIONAL STYLE

Analyst: How many sentences can you make out of the simple the N v-ed the N pattern?

Patient: Oh, that's easy! Here we go: *the boy threw the ball, the man saw the girl, the girl saw the man, the elephant trampled the grass, the tiger chased the tourist* . . .

Analyst: You're slowing down . . . Anything the matter? . . . What were you going to say?.

Patient: (Blushing): I was going to say *the boy hates his father*.

Analyst: That's all right. You can say anything you want.

SECOND GAME, TRANSFORMATIONAL STYLE

Analyst: How many sentences can you make of the simple passive pattern the N was v-ed by the N?

Patient: Oh, that's easy, too! OK: *the boy was whipped by the father, the rock was thrown by the boy, the dirt was smeared by the boy, the tire was punctured by the boy, the father was feared by the boy* . . . Why do I keep coming back to that boy?

Analyst: That's what we're trying to find out. How many sentences can you make of the somewhat more complicated pattern, without thinking, the adj N which v-ed the adj N, v-ed the Ns.

Patient: Can you give me an example?

Analyst: Sure, take for instance, *the shaggy dog that stole the old bone, frightened the chickens.*

Patient: Ah, I get it . . . Let' see . . . *the angry father who whipped the boy, shut the windows* . . . *the crying mother who washed the dishes, broke the jar* . . . *the tired father who fixed the garage door, moved the benches* . . . *the angry teacher who* . . .

Analyst: You're omitting the adjectives before your second noun. Try again.

Patient: OK, let's see: *the angry father who whipped the crying baby, shut the windows . . . the crying mother who washed the dirty dishes moved the benches . . .*

This can go on for an hour twice or three times a week, and by the end of a month or two, the analyst would have a fairly good insight into a variety of traumas the patient is carrying around in his unconscious. The skeletal sentence structures, dubbed 'transformational style' here (although there is nothing truly transformational about them, as they also seem perfectly straightforward as traditional grammatical categories) can start out as very simple and gradually become more and more complex. Just how many instructions an actual patient on an actual couch can absorb will, of course, differ from person to person, but for the purposes of our experiment(s) these can be two linguists who are not in an analyst–patient relationship in real life, but colleagues on the same campus. The faster the 'patient' has to reply, the better the chances that some real, hard 'sense' will emerge from the eliciting matrix and not some fanciful contrivance such as *the supermarket aardvark, which denigrated the Chairman, circumambulated the edifice*. Note that this highly unlikely sentence is just as grammatical as is the much simpler *the crying mother, who washed the dirty dishes, broke the jar*, furthermore, that they are exactly structurally identical, or to use Gleason's term ENATE. The difference between the aardvark-sentence and the mother-sentence is that the former lacks any real socio-psychological reality and is a mere mental exercise; the latter can be a real sentence reporting a real event from one's suppressed or forgotten past, despite the present tense, as if viewing one's life on a movie screen, here and now.

I will now try to show similar games in the 'stratificational' style.

THIRD GAME, STRATIFICATIONAL STYLE

Analyst: Close your eyes. There is a doer, and a done-to; technically an agent and a patient, and the doer does something to the done-to. What do you see?

Patient: *A boy throws a rock, the father spanks the boy, the mother is breaking the jar . . .*

Analyst: Excellent, you've got it. Now try this: there is a doer, an agent, who has certain qualities, technically known as attributes. The done-to also has some qualities or attributes. Bear in mind that these qualities or attributes can be a single item like kind, noisy, honest, or naughty, or longer statements about something they did in the past, for instance, who loves ginger ale or who can't stand Coca Cola, because both the short items and these longer statements describe, and characterize that person. Got it?

Patient: How about *the angry father spanked the frightened boy, the father who drank too much spanked the boy who was screaming for help, the mother who broke the jar scolded the boy who was crying?*

Analyst: You've got it. Now let's try this: there is a doer, you know, the agent, and the done-to, or the patient, but we are more interested in the done-to than in the doer, so we want to give him the courtesy, so to speak, to appear first on the stage; think of the father spanking the boy, but favor the boy in your statement. Can you do that?

Patient: Let's see . . . *the boy* . . . *the boy* . . . we want him first, don't we?

Analyst: That's right.

Patient: *The boy was spanked by the father, the rock got thrown by the boy, the jars were broken by the mother* . . .

Analyst: You've got it.

FOURTH GAME, STRATIFICATIONAL STYLE

Analyst: Imagine the following situation. There is a doer and a done-to, as before, and a doing which affects the done-to. They both have qualities, as before, and they can be short item qualities or longer statement qualities. The difference is this: You don't want to tell me what happens, but you're asking questions about it, trying to find out if it really happened, then next, you're denying that it happened, and lastly, you're trying to question about denying that it happened. Can you do this?

Patient: (After several trials) *did the father spank the boy? Did the father who drank too much spank the screaming boy? Didn't the father spank the screaming boy? Didn't the screaming father who drank too much spank the miserable boy who ran away? Did the sad mother break the jars? Didn't the sad, crying mother, who broke the jars, scold the miserable boy who ran away? The father didn't spank the boy . . . The sad mother didn't break the jars . . . The sad boy, who was spanked by his father who drank too much, didn't run away* . . .

Analyst: You mixed up the order a bit there – notice that all your denials were clustered at the end. Does that mean something?

Patient: Maybe. I made it, didn't I? I didn't run away, in the long run, if you know what I mean . . .

And this is probably how it would go between our imaginary 'analyst' and 'patient'. Notice that the 'analyst' here always provides the 'primary input'; once in the 'transformationalist' or rather 'syntacticist' style, and once in the 'stratificationalist', or more accurately 'semanticist' style. The 'patient' by verbalizing about his experiences takes the individual words, as they come to his mind, and 'inserts' them into the eliciting framework provided by the analyst.

But this is an artificial situation, one might object; a situation which is restricted to the practice (or a semblance thereof) of psychotherapy. My reply to such an objection would be that the situation is only apparently artificial insofar as we actually put two people on the stage, dubbed here the 'analyst' and the 'patient'. I would also contend that ordinary people engaging in dialog, or in monolog, are in fact each other's (linguistic) 'analysts' and 'patients' when they converse with one another, and the analysts and patients themselves, when they soliloquize. The basic difference between our imaginary conversations above and what happens in real life is that people do not give each other grammatical hints when they talk and a person thinking out loud or writing is essentially unaware of grammatical constructions. The analogy of the conversations between the 'analyst' and the 'patient' will become useful later: we shall see that in the process of encoding (verbalization) people unwittingly force themselves into grammatical structures which, then, exert a fair amount of tyranny on what is, or what CAN be, said later.

The best known kind of association game is the single word elicitation method where grammatical structures and sentences are quite irrelevant. An example follows below:

Analyst: Tell me what you think of when I give you the words I will
            pronounce, one by one. Don't speculate. Just try to see and feel
            what wants to come out and just enumerate these things. I'll
            give you an example: I say lemon, and you say sour and yellow,
            get it?

Patient: Let's try it.

Analyst: Father.

Patient: *Angry, screams, booze, . . . scarred . . . bangs . . . money . . . money
            . . . money . . . screams . . . not enough . . .* Is that what you want?

Analyst: You're doing OK. Just see, and enumerate, all right?

Patient: All right.

Analyst: School.

Patient: *Kids . . . boys . . . snow-balls . . . chalk . . . math . . . scared . . .
            hungry . . . lunchbag . . . empty . . . hungry . . . teasing . . . kids
            . . . teasing . . . hungry . . . math . . . scared . . . pushing . . . teas-
            ing . . . mud . . . snow . . . falling . . . hurts . . . bell . . . ringing
            . . . hungry*

Analyst: That was during the War in Europe, wasn't it?

Patient: You know it.

(Cf. Eric Berne (1969).)

It is becoming more and more widely known and generally appreciated that hemispheric lateralization may have a good deal to do with the conscious and the unconscious.[3] During sleep, when we dream, associations flow freely and without logical control. We can be in more than one place simultaneously, step out the window and not fall down, but just float away, etc. These are generally believed to be 'right hemispheric functions' (with the right hemisphere dominating the left hand, the left eye, and being, generally, the 'weaker', or 'sinister', artistic-feminine part of the person's mind).[4] Passing a course in computer programming, driving a car and stopping at the red light, ordering supplies over the telephone, etc., are said to be 'left hemispheric functions' (Bolinger 1975, Jaynes 1976). It makes sense to compare, by analogy, grammatically correct sentence construction and poetic free-association of single words to the left (strong) and right (weak) hemispheres, respectively, and further to imagine that, somewhat as Julian Jaynes suggests, a modern poet, when he turns his imagination loose and writes a poem in the modern mode of stream-of-consciousness, is relying more on right-hemispheric functions than on left-hemispheric ones, and that, conversely, when next day he rewrites his poem 'with a cold head', he is more under the influence of the left (sober, quasi-mathematical) hemisphere. But it does not really matter if it does not quite work this way technically as far as the biology of the brain is concerned; what matters from our point of view here is that people do exhibit poetic behavior, something which is, strictly speaking, 'superfluous' – or seems to be superfluous from the point of view of material survival. (I firmly believe that we would actually die if we were always and only logical and never allowed our brains to 'rest', by wandering off in the direction of 'sleep', even when we are technically awake.)

Thus we find ourselves giving one another (as well as ourselves) eliciting matrices which we then proceed to fill with words (= lexemes) which are arranged in certain traditional ways. These eliciting matrices range from the very exactly prosaic (*How much for that pair of shoes? – Thirty nine dollars, Sir*) to the surrealistic and the esoteric (*who can see love in a rancid prune in February? – Anyone who has a wrinkled face*). Abstract structures, such as The Adj. Ns. that/who V-ed the Adj. Ns. 'elicit' variously eligible lexemes, while concrete lexemes, such as lemon, father, school, war, love, and jail, tend to 'elicit' word association sets, and/or grammatical patterns, insofar as they materialize wearing these grammatical patterns. It is as if grammar and lexis co-selected one another both consciously and unconsciously at a very rapid rate.

In the opening sentence of this chapter I stated that we humans are all poets, whether we professionally engage in poetry or not. I hope that this statement is a little more meaningful now after what has been said, but I know that further elucidation is in order. I do not know of any better way to show what I mean than by retracting my own steps in what I did when I wrote what eventually turned out to be a sonnet. It appears *in toto* towards the end of the chapter written out in the traditional fourteen lines, three quatrains and a couplet with an ABBA, BAAB, CCDD, AA rhyme pattern consisting of iambic pentameters (A = 10 syllables; B = 11 syllables; C = 11 syllables; D = 10 syllables).

The various 'matrices' that 'elicited' these 114 words (a word is defined as one graphic unit between spaces, i.e., eight-foot, ain't, and I'd are single words) were some physical events that took place; some things I saw; certain tasks I had to perform, and certain monologs that started here and there during the performance of those tasks. I had absolutely no idea that I was about to write a sonnet, and once I got into it, I had no idea how it would start and how it would end, or how the lines and rhymes would exactly be organized. Nor was I conscious of writing well-formed clauses and sentences in the declarative, the negative, or the conditional – I actually became aware of these structures as the sonnet unfolded itself first in my head, later on paper. Here is what happened: I had to shovel an enormous amount of snow on my drive-way in order to be able to open the garage door and get the car out. I have a dog who has been cooped up inside the house for a long time; it is impossible to walk him over the 4–5 foot drifts. We take him out for a few minutes, put him in a hole in the snow, and then put him back in. The poor animal relieves himself where and how he can; the visible traces are greenish-yellow discolorations in the snow. I was thinking of Professor Ornstein's beautiful house in El Paso, Texas, where I spent a wonderfully active and happy week in August of 1976 during the Third LACUS Forum (cf. Di Pietro and Blansitt (eds) 1976) and remembered what a precious commodity water was in the arid Southwestern desert climate and how beautifully green the vegetation was around the Ornstein home. The only green I could see now was the yellowish discoloration left by my miserable dog. The temperature was – 20 F and I was in considerable physical discomfort. The two words devoid of any syntactic role, that kept coming back to me were *snow* and *green*, *green* and *snow*; *green*, *green*, *snow*, *snow*, *snow*, in alarming simultaneity and without any apparent logic. During a moment's pause my logical self rebelled against this colonization of my attention and I actually loudly spoke out the words *there is no such thing as green snow*. Then I shovelled some more, and the words *green* and *snow* kept coming back. Then I asked myself the question: *Could there be such a thing as green snow?* The answer – after three shovels full of the white stuff – *If snow were green it wouldn't be snow.* But then what would it be? *This is nonsense, let's get back to work. I'll fix a cup of constant comment tea when I get inside. If snow were green . . . Wait! That's iambic! if SNOW were GREEN . . . if SNOW were GREEN . . . I* stopped and bent over the shovel. I felt hot. What else could snow be that it is not? Why, hot, of course. It is terribly cold, yet I am hot, because I have to bend over shovelling the stuff. *If Snow were GREEN and HOT . . . that's iambic, too! Three feet, in fact.* But snow is neither, it isn't, it isn't. *It ain't.* That's inelegant: I teach how to avoid <u>ain't</u> to my foreign students. Of course the dean said it in a meeting a couple of weeks back; being the dean who was signalling, in a way, that he can afford to say <u>ain't</u> and that he was 'cool' by using this form . . . *If SNOW were GREEN and HOT which is SURE AIN'T . . . not perfectly iambic, you can't say which IT sure AIn't, the natural way to say it is which it SURE AIN'T . . .* How about *which sure it ain't?* That sounds better, now I have a good iambic line, *which SURE it AIN'T.* I was dizzy, my pulse was racing. I am not going to pass out, not out here. *Faint, faint, faint!* somebody shouted inside my head, and I heard a full line answered by a ghostline that ended in <u>faint</u>:

> *If snow were green and hot which sure it ain't,*
> ta TUM ta TUM ta TUM ta TUM ta faint.

I did not know what this was shaping up to be. I was glad that <u>ain't</u> and <u>faint</u> had announced their desire to be united as a rhyming couple but, not being at all sure what form this whole message was going to take, I felt resentment against the words. They're not going to tell <u>me</u> what to do![5]

Just like the snow which I am forced to move against my wishes. This heap is really tall. I am angry, and the heap is very tall. Very tall heap. I am mad.

As it happens, I watch a fair amount of television, especially on Thursday nights, when *Hawaii Five-0* and *Barnaby Jones* are aired. This was Friday, and the night before during the breaks some vegetable company ran their Jolly Green Giant ad, *à propos* of some green peas. So I suppose the JGG must have been on my mind subliminally, because without further ado I momentarily imagined that I became the JGG who blew all the snow away in one fell swoop. I suppose this further increased my resentment at the inexorable reality of the nearly eight-foot drift at the end of the drive-way, as I overheard myself saying to the snow drift: *I feel mad and defiant, because I am not a giant.* It was time to go in. I took a piece of paper and jotted down in pencil:

> *If snow were green and hot (which sure it ain't)*
> *ta TUM ta TUM ta TUM ta TUM ta TUM defiant*
> *ta TUM ta TUM ta TUM ta TUM ta TUM ta giant*
> *ta TUM ta TUM ta TUM ta I will faint.*

But this is like the first quatrain of a sonnet – I realized; all right then, I might as well accept that challenge and actually make this into one. But sonnets have a structure and, therefore, a will of their own; anyone wishing to write one, must obey the dictates of the iambic pentameter, the rhyming scheme, etc.

At this point, I made a deliberate decision: the second quatrain will use the same 'rhymes', except in the reverse order, instead of ABBA, I would use BAAB. While I was out in the snow, I almost swore out loud a couple of times, but decided not to when I saw one of my neighbors go by. This reminded me of the word silent which, I found, would do for an assonance with giant and defiant, but I needed one more to fill the pattern. Why is it, I wondered, that native speakers get away with using four-letter words in mixed company, even evoking laughter, and immigrants usually don't? Is it the accent? Or could it be that it is just not expected of a 'foreigner' to indulge himself in some of the luxuries of the native? I know that when I hear a non-native speaker of Hungarian proudly perform one of our obscenities for my benefit, I feel embarrassed. It strikes me the wrong way; it sounds too 'loud', somehow, no matter how 'softly' spoken otherwise . . . I've got it! My next word will be strident. A colleague once observed that part of my foreign accent is that my rate of speech is considerably faster than that of native Americans. This would seem more natural if I were French or Italian, not all Hungarians speak as fast as I do. I now had silent and strident as two elicitors placed in line-final strategic positions; and they were conveniently polarized in meaning, somewhat like soft is to hard or harsh. The A-rhymes quaint and restraint almost leapt out of the unconscious automatically and simultaneously; I actually have no recollection which came first. All I knew was that I had moved out of the snow and into the area of language; I was no longer concerned with snow at all, but rather with my possible verbalizations on the subject of snow and how they might affect my English-speaking listeners. I put down the assonance end-words in the format:

$$
I \left\{
\begin{array}{l}
\text{ain't} \\
\text{defiant} \\
\text{giant} \\
\text{faint}
\end{array}
\right.
\qquad
II \left\{
\begin{array}{l}
\text{silent} \\
\text{restraint} \\
\text{quaint} \\
\text{strident}
\end{array}
\right.
$$

I had, at this point, probably made two subconscious decisions regarding syntax: the words faint and strident should be spoken on a falling (period) intonation, indicating the end of a sentence each. I was not sure at all, though, whether there might be just two full sentences in the first two quatrains, or more than two. At this point I went back to the beginning, and for the first time consciously realized that I had worked myself into an if-clause of the past subjunctive, unreal type. If I were king of France, I would eat roast partridge for breakfast every morning – the old school pattern rang all too forcefully to ignore. What, really, would I do, if snow were green, which it sure ain't? I'd be glad, I guess. That is all right, but I must end the line in defiant which is an adjective. Maybe be defiant? Act defiant? No, be less defiant, or act less defiant. But I needed a conditional to answer to present condition contrary to fact and it must all be in good iambic scansion. The words I'd leap for joy and would be/feel less defiant seemed to fill the bill, so I wrote down the first two lines:

If snow were green and hot (which sure it ain't)
I'd leap for joy, and would feel less defiant . . .

but less defiant about what? Well, the snow, obviously; but I had used the word snow already and repeating it is dull; there must be other words to refer to it. What did I do out there? I attacked two snow mountains. One of them was well over my head, at least eight feet. I wrote: when tackling eight-foot drifts. This made sense with the would feel less defiant of the previous line, but made me make a period, and I was not having a full line ending in the target word, *giant*. So I had to start a new sentence in mid-line. Some sonnet writers regard this as bad form, some actually praise the practice and call the device enjambment, the art of the grammatically run-on line whose syntactic boundary does not coincide with the metric line. So be it; I've worked myself into an enjambment; let's see how do I get out of it? Giant must be the subject of the new sentence, but it must be introduced by three syllables, otherwise I am falling out of the iambic pentameter, one of whose tolerated poetic licences is that choriambic, anapaestic, dactylic, and trochaic feet may occasionally be interspersed with pure iambs. One does not do iambic scansion saying onLY a GIant, the natural rhythm is ONly a GIant. What about Only a giant grammatically, as a subject? Well, that's what I wanted to be, to move the snow. The giant can move it. Only he can move it. I had it: *Only a giant . . . can move this. Not me. Faint.* That's it; I will faint. *Only a giant can move it, I will faint.* The words can move this, I will faint seemed to fill in the last portion of the fourth line, but I needed four syllables at the beginning of the fourth line. Maybe describe the giant, I thought, and the words jolly and green went down on the paper almost automatically. They are actually 'wrong', they should go in scansion as jolLY and GREEN, while in fact they go JOlly and GREEN $\perp \cup \cup \perp$; a dactyl and a half spondee. With can move this: I will faint, however, the iambs are restored. Moreover, uninterrupted, pure iambs tend to get monotonous, so I felt thrilled with my new 'mixed' quatrain:

If snow were green and hot (which sure it ain't)
I'd leap for joy, and feel much less defiant
when tackling eight-foot drifts. Only a giant
jolly, and green, can move this: I will faint.

I now had the four-word rhyming outline (silent–restraint–quaint–strident) of the second quatrain. Have I said enough about what I might do if snow were green and hot? What other magic might one use to make the snow go away? When I was a nine-year-old boy, I was stricken by polio. It was the summer of 1945, and we were in a village in the county of Somogy near Lake Balaton, where my mother had a modest summer house that survived the end of the war. All the local boys were climbing trees, going swimming, or playing soccer, the Hungarian national sport; I was sitting in a wheelchair and was reading books. Whatever I could get my hands on. My mother gave me the *Kalevala* in Hungarian translation. Its principal hero, Väjnemöjnen, is a magician who can make things happen by verbal incantations. When faced by people physically much stronger than he, he sings an incantation at them, and they are drilled into the ground up to their necks and cannot get out for several days. 'What a neat trick' – I used to think – what he cannot do with his body, he does through the power of words. I became a precocious, somewhat smart-allecky and overly verbal youngster who would flail his tongue at older men, stronger boys, anybody who was foolish enough to listen, and when they wanted to slap me for my arrogance, I accused them of cruelty and base ignobility for maligning a poor polio victim. In short, I was blackmailing and punishing the world for the great wrong that had befallen me and considered verbal prowess to be the best means to get even. Going into linguistics instead of comparative literature after graduation from Harvard (where I first met Dr Ornstein, who was the first American to speak to me in fluent Hungarian, out of his wheelchair, he being a less fortunate victim of polio than I was) may have had to do with an unconscious desire to master the language better before I tried my hand at writing literary prose or poetry in it; I do not know for sure. But this was all subliminally in the background for the next line, *If singing melted snow, I'd sing.* I am not a good singer; I have a hoarse tenor voice mixed with infelicitous falsettos.

Aha! I had just worked myself into yet another enjambment. Not too bad; this gives me the chance to start a new sentence with silent, all I need is a syllable – OK, it's a, the indefinite article. I now had *If singing melted snow, I'd sing. A silent* – a silent what? Whatever it will be, it must lead to restraint, because I put that word down there as a mile stone which I must reach. What should restraint be? The end of a sentence? The direct object of a sentence? Maybe a new subject? I had no idea. A silent what?, I continued. I thought of various deletable expletives including 'hell' and other, less printable ones; I visualized these as appearing between quotes in order to indicate that these are the silent exclamations I am making inwardly so that only I can hear them. Then it occurred to me that perhaps I do not have to cite an exclamation: unspoken swear-word materialized rather soon and without much conscious speculation. I now had a sentence start which read a silent, unspoken swear-word – what am I to do with this so that I can let the line end in restraint? Predicate them to one another? As I said the word restraint out loud a few times, I realized that it sounded best when I imagined that it was an order, sort of an exhortation said to me encouragingly and warningly, by someone else. I wrote: – – – – – – – – – – 'Restraint / my boy!' I now saw that restraint was both the beginning of a new sentence and quoted rather than direct speech; this must be my social super-ego talking to me through another persona. That is fine; but I still have not finished the sentence with a silent, unspoken swear-word. What can a silent unspoken swear-word do or be? What should it do or be? Must it do or be anything? I am trying to disallow myself to shout out loud, therefore the silent swear-word must be enough; it must do. I tried: a silent swear-word must be enough . . . I didn't like the sequence must be enough; it was too choppy and dactyilic. What other way is there to say 'be enough' in English? The adjective sufficient came to mind; a moment later the verb suffice. I now wrote:

> *If singing melted snow, I'd sing. A silent*
> *unspoken swear-word must suffice: 'Restraint*
> *my boy!'*

and looked at what I had so far. I was now into the third line of the second quatrain, and my goal was to reach the word quaint to close the second stanza. Someone here, perhaps my super-ego, my parental ego-state, is warning me not to swear out loud, but to swallow my anger. It is a privilege of native speakers to use four-letter words; I have to be on my best behavior. What is going to be quaint? The foreigner's use of 'hell' or some of its fellow four-letter words? A fellow graduate student once, back in 1962, after a two-hour car ride from Boston to New Haven, told Professor Isidore Dyen, who sat in the back seat: 'Adam speaks a quaint brand of English'. Mr Dyen was laughing. The student, Al Stevens, explained: 'He compared the Indonesian lady, Mrs Dardjowidjodjo, to an "apparition" . . . he meant that she was very pretty'. I was laughing, too, and asked my riders: 'Would you please tell me what <u>quaint</u> means? I never heard the word'. This was true. 'Does it mean funny?' More laughter. 'Keep guessing' – they said. 'Awkward', I volunteered. 'No, not really'. 'Antiquated?' – more laughter. 'Well,' I asked, 'tell me Mr Dyen, is Al praising me, or is he criticising me?' They were roaring with laughter. Mr Dyen said: 'it is mildly offensive, Adam. Look it up in a good dictionary when you get home.' We were driving back to Yale from the Ninth International Congress of Linguists which was held at MIT, and people generally did not make allowances for me in their speech. 'I take you as a straight American, Adam' Mr Dyen said, 'that's why it jars us when you don't know a common word'. I doubt that I was consciously aware of all of this, but I caught myself writing: *'Your friends may find your English quaint – your accent jars, your speech is fast and strident.'* But this is two full quatrains already! Let's see what I've got here:

If snow were green and hot (which sure it ain't)
I'd leap for joy, and feel much less defiant
when tackling eight-foot drifts. Only a giant
jolly and green, can move this: I may faint.

If singing melted snow, I'd sing. A silent
unspoken swear-word must suffice: 'Restraint
my boy! Your friends may find your English quaint . . .
your accent jars, your speech is fast and strident'.

I was getting quite annoyed at myself. What is this poem about, anyway? Who am I kidding? I start out with snow; my desire to get rid of it; I think of the Jolly Green Giant, and then, suddenly, find myself feeling sorry for myself because I cannot swear gracefully in English. What is this? Who is writing this stupid sonnet, anyway? Adam Makkai, the professor of linguistics, or the little boy who had polio and is feeling sorry for himself, whenever the occasion arises? I had no intention of talking about my accent and what it means to me; I was going to talk about snow, how I hate it, and how nice it would be to be communing with a yucca plant near Jack Ornstein's house in El Paso. I've got to get back to that snow somehow. This is imperative if there is to be any cohesion in the inane text. SOMEHOW I MUST GET BACK INTO THAT SNOW SHOVELLING SITUATION. But I am enjoying my second cup of instant comment tea and I've really had it for today. No more shovelling – outside that is. Oh, wait a minute. Could I bring some snow in? No, nonsense; 'don't track in', we say to the ten-year-old. (She used to bring in snow balls and put them into the refrigerator to see how long they would keep. I had difficulty robbing her of her little frozen toys, but eventually managed to explain that there will be other winters and real, new snow outside.) Snow, snow, snow – but I am talking about language, aren't I? My own language, my accent, and my feelings about it.

'What's wrong with this term paper, Mr Dyen?', I once asked my respected teacher, and he answered: 'It's a snow job.' 'I am sorry,' I said, 'I don't understand'. He explained. I acquired the expressions to snow someone under, to do a snow job; later I also learned that snow can refer to illegitimate cocaine.

I suddenly saw the light. It is no accident that I have drifted into a discussion of language from the snow shovelling; it had to happen this way. Talking about actual snow was a 'snow-job'; I was just warming up to the occasion to express my feeling of estrangement in Midwestern suburbia where I live. I belong, and I do not. I get invited to my neighbours' cocktail parties, and I manage to entertain them; but I never really feel truly relaxed with them; I do not know what they think of me. One of the most difficult things here in Lake Bluff is to explain to the orthodontist, the real estate broker, the lawyer, the physical therapist, the medical supplies wholesale dealer and importer, the commodities trader, and the retired Navy Captain what my wife and I do for a living: we are linguists. 'What is that?' they invariably ask us, and since theory would instantly put them to sleep and a flat assertion such as 'we teach English to foreigners' would really be underselling ourselves, we sometimes indulge in stories about the Summer Institute of Linguistics and how the missionary tagmemicists create alphabets for unwritten languages; translate the Bible and bring penicillin to pre-literate peoples in strange corners of the world. This gets some attention and exclamations of the sort 'Oh, how interesting! You must like to travel a lot? Have you been to Africa? My husband and I went to Kenya's Serengeti for a safari last year . . .'.

I usually feel quite phony in these situations. If I wax too technical, I bore them; if I tell light stories, I feel cheap myself: it is a no-win situation. I must make the most of it, and making the most of it means choosing the benefit of the audience over my own satisfaction; so I entertain them.

I was penning out the four corner-stones of the third quatrain, reasonably sure that my neighbors must be mentioned. I wrote: neighbors – arbitrators – hot, and Hottentot. But how shall I start the third quatrain? This is an important point in the unfolding of a sonnet's internal plot; something new must come in. But the something 'new' cannot be disconnected from what I started with; I must get back to that snow out there. No. Not out there. The line jumped at me like a tiger from behind a bush. The snow's inside. Maybe I AM a snow-artist, as Mr Dyen suggested in one of his intimidating moods. If I was, I probably would not be able to admit it. If I admit that I must act that way sometimes, maybe I'll get free of it eventually. At any rate, I must change the focus of the scenery. I'll make this the semantic axis of my story: here is where I'll really shift pace. All right then. What do I do with the 'snow' (my loose talk about my profession) that affects my neighbors? I throw it at them, not with the shovel, of course, but at the 4th of July parties with a drink in my hand. I wrote:

The snow's inside. I throw it at my neighbors,
these gentle and bewildered arbitrators – – – – –

arbitrators of what? I looked at the line-final call-word, and saw that it was
hot. This reminded me that I had used hot earlier, in line 1, in its primary
sense 'high in temperature'. Next to it, in line 1, is the word green also
in its primary physical color sense. Can it mean anything else? I thought
of Chomsky's colorless green ideas sleep furiously and all the fun we have
had with it during the past twenty years. Dell Hymes had rhymed it
forwards and backwards in a variety of sonnets; John Oller interpreted it
psychiatrically as meaning 'bleak immature ideas lurk in the unconscious
ready to break out and attack'; and I interpreted it once similarly for a
Hungarian audience in Szeged in 1972. 'Immature', 'juvenile' (as in
greenhorn) is a good sense of green, and so is boasting of foreign travel
and the excessive seeking of adventures abroad. Cool in its socio-
psychological sense of 'detached, elegant, unhurried, relaxed, clever' etc.,
announced its availability by juxtaposition to hot, and so before I knew it
I wrote:

of why it's 'cool' and yet so 'green' and 'hot'
selling linguistics to the Hottentot – –

except I did not know whether to make a period or to go on. What makes
people decide to make a period or to go on? Does anyone know? Does
Chomsky know? Do Pike and Lamb know? Hockett? Halliday? My
dilemma was solved by my great desire to bring the sonnet to a close with
a couplet. I am a frustrated musician; I play rather mediocre piano, and
when no one is around, I indulge in composing songs. I like recapitula-
tions. So I wrote down faint and ain't, which made me ask the question
who is fainting? I already said that I would; maybe the Hottentot should
faint. But if he faints, Hottentot cannot end the sentence and I am going
to be stuck with a who-clause. So be it: selling linguistics to the Hottentot
/ who ta TUM ta TUM ta TUM ta TUM would faint. All right, let's see
what this adds up to: who TUM ta TUM ta TUM would surely faint.
What would make a Hottentot faint that is connected with snow (or
'snow', as the case may be) and that is somehow connected to linguistics?
Chances are that Hottentots never see real snow; if they saw it, without
previous explanation, they would not know what it was. It would literally
– as well as figuratively – snow them under. Could this be happening to
them with 'snow', i.e. idle Western chatter about progress, technology,
mass distribution of goods, and the like? Quite likely. We Westerners
really think we are rather mature; even though we eagerly disavow
colonialism and disown the 'white man's burden' we colonize the peoples
of Africa in other ways. And we use a lot of propaganda in doing this.
Certainly the Soviets do, and so do the Americans, in other, perhaps less
immediately harmful ways. Propaganda is seldom 'cool'; the propagator
has an axe to grind, while much of what he says is nonsense, 'hot air', as

another saying goes. Then I looked at the words in the first line and saw
snow, green, and hot, in that order. 'Maybe I could just reverse them and
see what I get,' I thought, and wrote:

> *who, – – – – – – – – – would surely faint,*
> *hot words are snow that's green (which sure it ain't).*

This, however, did not make sense. The trouble was that it was unclear
who thinks or says the last line. If I say it, it does not make any sense
at all; but the Hottentot cannot say it either. So maybe a third person
must enter and talk to the Hottentot, whereby the last line can become
quoted speech. I put quotation marks around the last line, changed it to
they, and now had:

> *who – – – – – – would surely faint:*
> *'hot words are snow that's green' (which sure they ain't).*

But what am I to do with – – – – – ? Everything depends on it. I tried
various things, such as if some one told him, if he found out, and many
more. What I need is five syllables that introduce what I have got between
quotation marks as quoted speech: what about if he heard the truth? I
penned out the whole sequence from I throw it at my neighbors reinserting
it again for they:

> *I throw it at my neighbors,*
> *these gentle and bewildered arbitrators*
> *of why it's 'cool' and yet so 'green' and 'hot'*
> *selling linguistics to the Hottentot*
> *who, if he heard the truth, would surely faint:*
> *'hot words are snow that's green' (which sure it ain't).*

I had to see it in a variety of formats. One went like this:

> *If snow were green and hot (which sure it ain't)*
> *I'd leap for joy, and feel much less defiant*
> *When tackling eight-foot drifts. Only a giant*
> *Jolly, and green, could move this: I would faint.*

> *If singing melted snow, I'd sing. A silent*
> *Unspoken swear-word must suffice: 'RESTRAINT*
> *MY BOY!' YOUR FRIENDS MAY FIND YOUR ENGLISH QUAINT –*
> *YOUR ACCENT JARS, YOUR SPEECH IS FAST AND STRIDENT.'*

> *The snow's inside. I throw it at my neighbors.*
> *These gentle and bewildered arbitrators*
> *of why it's 'cool' and yet so 'green' and 'hot'*
> *selling linguistics to the Hottentot*

Who, if he heard the truth, would surely faint:
'Hot words are snow that's green' ((which sure it ain't)).

Later I changed the format to a solid, indented block of fourteen lines, could to can and would to will in the first quatrain. I threw out it for they for the last time, and added a title:

The Mad Foreign Linguist Speaks to His
Straight American Neighbors During Chicago's
Great Blizzard of '79 in Commemoration of
Jack Ornstein's 65th Birthday

If snow were green and hot (which sure it ain't)
I'd leap for joy, and feel much less defiant
when tackling eight-foot drifts. Only a giant
jolly, and green, can move this: I will faint.
    If swearing melted snow, I'd swear. A silent
    regurgitation must suffice: 'Restraint
    my boy!' Your friends may find your English quaint – – –
your accent jars, your speech is fast and strident.'
The snow's inside. I throw it at my neighbors,
these gentle and bewildered arbitrators
of why it's 'cool' and yet so 'green' and 'hot'
selling The Grammar to the Hottentot
    who, if he heard the Truth, would surely faint:
    'hot words are snow that's green' (which sure they ain't).

I have no illusions about the intrinsic literary merit of this text and I certainly do not expect a great emotional reaction from the reader as one might in the case of less structured heart-poetry. I have edited out the line if singing melted snow, I'd sing. A silent / unspoken swear-word and substituted If swearing melted snow, I'd swear. A Silent / regurgitation must suffice. Transincantation (not to be found in any dictionary) for regurgitation may say more for 'verbal magic'; regurgitation, however, better explains what immigrants do to vocabulary primarily used by natives. It is like forced feeding that has difficulty settling in the stomach. My goal was to illustrate, by writing, explaining and editing this sonnet, what the phenomenon of 'lexical insertion' might look like in a performance model that seeks to attain maximum psychological realism. None of the attendant circumstances were invented; 'ALL IS TRUE', as they used to say on the front page of certain historical novels.

Situations correlate with certain institutionalized bundles of meaning (sememes), which have a variety of ways of being expressed in the vocabulary (as lexemes). One, two, or more lexemes, idiosyncratically or logically relevant to a given situation, tend to line up both in the conscious and the unconscious, thereby forming two kinds of 'elicitors' at once: a word-association elicitor (unconscious), and a more deliberate phrase,

clause, and eventually sentence elicitor (see the various possible games
described earlier in this chapter). A person indulging in poetic behavior is
simultaneously his own analyst and his own patient and the game is played
in terms of soliloquy or internal monolog eventually reinforced by paper
or pencil and typewriter. Once a combination of words is put down on
paper, they assume a force of their own, bringing to mind suggestions and
possibilities of which the 'poet' was not at all, or only most vaguely,
conscious at the beginning. Most poetry is like finding a shiny button on
the street, falling in love with it, and then having a coat tailored to suit
the button. This being the case, the notion of 'lexical insertion' evaporates
in thin air, if viewed as a part of poetic behavior – if by lexical insertion
we mean a reasonably specific deep structure and/or surface structure
derivation replete with categorical markers which then somehow conjure up
real lexemes in order to become real sentences. Note that there is
something of this sort going on, insofar as the text, as it evolves, creates
certain patterns which then need to be filled. The search for the right word
becomes quite deliberate in these cases as I have tried to show above, but
this is actually incidental to the poetic process. Lexical insertion, however,
can be interpreted entirely differently. Let us imagine a high school
chemistry laboratory: there is a thin, tall jar, filled with water that has a
high concentration of salt in it. The teacher INSERTS A THREAD from the
top and tells the students that a few days later, when they remove the
string, small salt crystals will be visible along the string. The string is
usually called a catalyst during such simple demonstrations. The body of
the lexical knowledge a fluent speaker has of his/her language may be
compared to the solution containing the high concentration of NACl
(kitchen salt), and the inserted string to a number of actual situations;
conversely, the physical chemistry of the kind of salt in use may be
compared to the speaker's unconscious knowledge of his grammar, and the
inserted string may be compared to association-set call-words. Both
analogies leak, and both contain a fair amount of truth. Looked at with
tolerance and dialectical stereo-vision, they reveal something about
language that we, as speakers all know intuitively, but as linguists have a
hard time facing and explaining. The truth is that a single word can be
a syntactic event, and the entire grammar can be viewed as a collection
of words. At the same time, of course, a single word can, and frequently
must, be seen as an isolated item in an inventory, and the grammar can
be seen as a highly complex network of relations (if one is stratificationally
oriented) or as a large body of rewrite rules (if one is transformationally
oriented). Words tend to create their own syntax, and syntactic patterns
cause words to crystallize in the right places. Words secrete tactic patterns
and tactic patterns cause words to crystallize at crucial junctures. Lexical
insertion, I suggest, ought to be renamed LEXEMIC CRYSTALLIZATION
and syntax ought to be renamed LEXEMIC SECRETION.

The 'chemistry' of it all is enormously complex. Involved in it are the
speaker's self-image as a member of society; his self-image as a complex
bundle of emotions; his ability or inability to avail himself of certain

lexemes, all of which are social products and bear distinguishing marks of prestigious, stigmatized, colloquial, technical, common, or rare status (Ornstein, 1975). The grammar, of course, has its own tremendous complexities, but it must be seen as strictly secondary in importance during the communication process. This is not to downgrade grammar. Without it lexis can only limp along, as if on crutches. Frequently of course, two steps will do the job – will you drive a Cadillac to your neighbor's house twenty yards away to borrow two eggs? The single utterance /mmmmmmmmmmm!/ as produced by my ten-month old daughter achieves most things she cares to achieve; by pointing at the milk bottle, the bread, she orders us to give them to her; it can also mean 'get me out of the high chair', 'change me', 'I am sleepy', and a variety of other manipulatory functions (cf. Halliday 1975a).

To call /mmmmmmmmmm!/ a lexeme, a morpheme, a word, a sentence, or a proposition would be just as absurd as denying that it contains germinally all of these and, given her social situation in the family, it delivers her all the goods and services she wants.

But ARE we all poets, in fact, as I suggested? I think we are. Certainly my ten-month old is. Beside her command word /mmmmmmmmmm!/ and a more recent /dae-dae-dae/ (on a rising intonation) meaning something like 'what is the name of that?', she plays a number of vocal games with us at the breakfast table. She looks at me and says /ghaaaaaaa/. I look back at her and /ghaaaaaaa/. She smiles, happily, and now says /ghaaaaa/, /ghaaaaaa/. I repeat after her /ghaaaaaa/, /ghaaaaaaa/. We go up to three or four /ghaaaaaa/s, make them at lower and higher pitches, of shorter or longer duration. It is an intense and lively exchange, everyone gets involved, and it makes us feel good. Sometimes we call it the 'Let's be Lions' game, or just /ghaaaaaaa/. There are no words, no lexemes, and no grammatical patterns to act as 'elicitors' or as 'insertions'; /ghaaaaaa/ just HAPPENS, it just IS. She can get carried away with /ghaaaaaaa/; when I am receiving a long distance phone call and she won't stop, it is downright irritating. /ghaaaaaa/ can be felicitous, and it can be *mal à propos*.

Maybe it is a poem.

Notes

1. This chapter owes a good deal to Charles F. Hockett, William M. Christie, Jr., and Michael Eric Bennett who have given me valuable suggestions on how to improve the original version. They are not to be blamed for any errors, oversimplifications, and the like, which remain in here solely as my own fault; nor do they necessarily agree with my presentation and my conclusions.

2. My criticism of stratificationalism here pertains primarily to the older standard model represented in Lamb (1966a) and Lockwood (1972); SG was up to the mid-1970s essentially a static COMPETENCE MODEL. There is some rather promising recent work, however, which seems to indicate that actual PERFORMANCE, how the networks actually work, can be successfully modelled and diagrammed. Thus Dell and Reich (1977) suggest a SPREADING ACTIVATION

MODEL and Christie (1977) proposes a MEMORY CELL MODEL replete with synapses, excitatory terminals and inhibitory terminals. Here is a simplified summary of these latest developments: Dell and Reich envisage a model where activation flows through the relational network to decode/encode utterances. In addition, the flow is TWO-WAY, not just one-way. The result is that activation 'spreads' from activated nodes to neighboring activated nodes. Thus are substitutions accounted for in slips of the tongue, as in, say, 'Second Hungarian Restaurant' for 'Second Hungarian Rhapsody'. In the following simplified network, then, let us assume that the darkened diamond is activated, either through encoding or decoding:

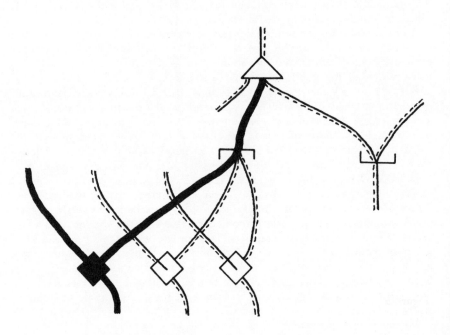

Figure 4

Assuming that the dominant flow of activation is shown by the thick black lines, according to Dell and Reich (1976) activation may spread here as shown by the dotted lines. Thus other members of the class represented by the downward OR are 'semi-activated' as are the other parts of the construction represented by the AND. In relation to what goes on in word association sets (whether conditioned by the semantics or the phonology, as is the case in poetry and in composition in general), the 'spread' of activation represents the unconscious 'suggestion' of related words, clauses, etc. It seems sensible to believe that the activation can spread at all levels of the grammar. Thus if the word one is encoding or decoding is *glow*, the activations spread at the phonotactic level (because of the /gl/ cluster) will also suggest such words as *gleam*, *glitter*, *glower*, *glimmer*, etc. On the other hand, at the semotactic level it might result in activation of related concepts such as 'light', 'fire', 'sun', and so on. The theory of spreading activation may also be able to account for associated sentence structures, not just word association sets. Let us consider the following piece of simplified network:

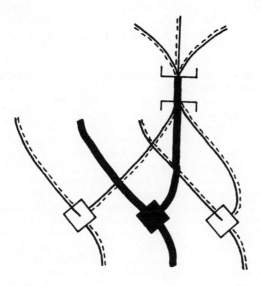

Figure 5

The lines leading up from the upward OR, let us say, lead to different tactic configurations at a certain level of the grammar. Activation, once more, is shown by the thick lines, and spreading activation by the dotted thinner lines. Notice that there may arise an instance where one member of a class is activated, but the rest of the construction is not. In this case, let us say that the activated diamond represents the word *cat*. You may have just seen a cat, or for some reason thought of one, so this concept is salient in your mind and is, consequently, receiving activation. You can now begin to 'fill in' the rest of the sentence structure, but as the diagram indicates you can 'plug in' the word *cat* in more than one place; you have a choice. (We have known this to be intuitively correct all the time.) You can say *cats annoy me, I am allergic to cats, uncle Algernon keeps two smelly cats in his basement, where's that miserable cat?* or even *there's that elusive siamese that the mailman so cruelly kicked yesterday*. The point is that the spread of activation from the diamond places these (and other) tactic constructions on 'stand-by', as it were, ready to accept what other things you might have to say. Of course, the word exercises some control over the possibilities. For instance, it is likely that the connections all lead to various nominal constructions thus eliminating *cat* as a verb **I am going to cat all day*, or as an adverb **this sonnet is likely to be rather catly done*. Of course, given the proper stimulus, be it 'poetic licence' or simple intoxication, the network can be modified to produce these as well as many other unlikely utterances (cf. Makkai (1971b)). I am heavily indebted to Michael Eric Bennett for this explanation (personal communication). Christie's view on the subject (personal communication) is as follows: We have in SG two competing models of the connection between the tactics and the realization portion. The standard model (as in Lockwood (1972)), has each lexical item connect with all necessary diamonds at each stratum. The alternative (sketched in Christie (1977)), is to have a SEPARATE LEXICON, with only categories determined in the main section, and then at the bottom of the morphotactics a signal goes up that such-and-such a type of lexical item is wanted. In the standard version the item and its role were selected at the top, then the item waited while the role got moved around into its surface place, and then the item was called up in the proper surface sequence. For reasons too complicated to enter here, if we assume 5,000 nouns and 3,000 adjectives (a conservative estimate), we would need 15 million AND nodes to handle every combination of this sort alone. As Christie points out, this problem has not been noticed before because networks were looked at as tactic arrangements (i.e., as competence) without giving detailed consideration of how they might actually work. The point is that the association of a noun and a role (e.g., agent or goal) or of an adjective and a noun is not something that can be built into a network: it has to be a REAL TIME ACTIVITY OF THE NETWORK RATHER THAN A PART OF ITS STRUCTURE. What this means is that the grammar has to set out the surface roles in order and THEN it has to associate with each one an item that was being selected simultaneously. Thus the combination occurs at the bottom, not at the top. Important conclusions are to be drawn if this is the case: first, the stratal bypass has to be chosen. It is compatible with combination at top or bottom, whereas the standard theory requires combination at the top only. Second, it explains the relative independence of grammar and lexicon that this chapter is essentially about, a fact that all writers and poets have known intuitively for ages. Third, and most important, it explains a very general and troubling phenomenon of linguistic analysis in all models to date. Of all the levels of language, phonology is the most tractable, with morphology, syntax, and semology basically sloppy and intractable. There seems to be a quantal leap from phonology to morphology, a fact noticed by traditional grammarians who excluded 'Lautlehre' from 'Grammatik' as a separate matter. The recent stratificational model as Christie perceives of it explains this problem and offers a solution. Whereas in the phonology the areas of grammar and the lexicon can be integrated with a single structure taking care of matters, it seems that from the morphology upward the grammar operates independently from the lexicon. Each does its separate work and only at the bottom do they converge. Analysts have viewed the totality of language and have thus had difficulty separating the two parts. Part of the problem is characterized by Halliday's statement:

'The grammarian's dream is (and must be, such is the nature of grammar) of constant territorial expansion. He would like to turn the whole of linguistic form into grammar, hoping to show that lexis can be defined as "most delicate grammar".'

Thus more and more material that belongs in the lexicon has been shifted over to the grammar which should be kept separate. The generative semantics movement, in particular, could be characterized as a desperate effort to inject grammar into lexis, hence the pre-lexical 'trees' or 'senteceoids', such as CAUSE, BECOME, NOT, and ALIVE for *kill*. In English in particular, the grammar is rather simple and the lexicon is overwhelmingly complex. Thus many constraints and restrictions that have been put forward as grammatical are not 'grammatical' at all but rather restrictions on the co-occurrence of words, i.e., lexis.

On the same point British anthropologist I. Bronowksi writes (quote courtesy of Prof. C.F. Hockett): 'The relation (. . . of words and sentences) has the formal duality of an abstract plane geometry: the words are joined in sentences and the sentences intersect in words, in mutual definition like that between points and lines. And this mutual dependence cannot be gotten rid of; the words are not defined except by the sentences into which they fit, and fitting into a sentence means obeying a grammatical scheme which formalizes in a syntax the laws of behavior which the object obeys in our experiences. Thus vocabulary and grammar are not separable.'

3. I may be technically wrong about this, though it is one logical inference to be drawn from Jaynes (1976). Insofar as dreams are 'unconscious' rather than 'conscious' (which sounds intuitively sensible to me) and insofar as dreams are typical 'right hemisphere activity' the correlation seems to exist. This is not to deny that certain 'right hemisphere activities' such as car driving or typing cannot become 'unconscious' due to routine activities, overrepetition, and the like. I have come across people who add up long columns of numbers while talking on the phone quasi-unconsciously. Future research not available to me at the present will have to settle the physiological loci of the conscious and the unconscious and the above statement should be taken metaphorically.

4. 'Mind' is used here in its general or sloppy sense since I cannot use 'brain'; *mentality, outlook, personality,* and *consciousness* all say too much and too little; thus the sloppy sense of 'mind' offers the least offensive intersection of the senses I need.

5. Professor Hockett points out (personal communication) that in the literature of aesthetics there are several important statements regarding how poets feel about the interaction between the piece they write and their own intentions. To Robert Frost, for instance, the making of a genuine poem was that it had to be a discovery in the poet's experience with the language, as surprising to the poet as to his audience. It is rather rare in world literature to find a major master who actually wrote a doctoral dissertation on how he composes, but this is the case with Hungary's undisputed leading poet laureate Sándor Weöres (1913–1991) who translated most of Western lyrics into Hungarian. In his doctoral dissertation *The Birth of the Poem* (*A vers születése*, Pécs 1933, published as Weöres 1970) under the chapter 'The Development', W. contrasts Coleridge's *Kubla Khan* and Poe's *The Raven* as two types of poems that had attendant circumstances well documented in the literature. Coleridge wrote in a trance, almost unconsciously, while Poe himself describes *The Raven* as a precalculated and almost mathematical progression. Weöres points these out as two extremes and suggests that most poets use both intuition and premeditation. An English

translation of W.'s dissertation is in progress by myself and will reach print within a year. The phenomenon also exists in musical composition and the visual arts; both compositions and paintings as well as sculptures have a way of unfolding themselves to the utter surprise of the artist at work.

15 How to put the pieces of a formal poem, e.g. a 'sonnet', together

The thesis of this chapter is that 'half-writtenness' functions as a semantic and stylistic midway station of action and reaction between the author and the text '*in statu nascendi*' – as the Romans would have put it. I wish to show that the half-written text plays a meaningful role during its own production by influencing many of the author's subsequent choices. This is perhaps most strikingly true in the case of the writing of formal poetry (e.g. the sonnet); but it also occurs in 'free verse', iambic pentameter; furthermore, the half-writtenness effect also occurs in prose, both technical, scientific and research-oriented, and in belletristic prose.

The composition process is one in which the linguistic terms DELETION, METATHESIS and TRANSFORMATION would make, or would have made, the most sense; yet linguists have neglected the many opportunities to make these terms usably meaningful in composition and text-production theory. Linguistics applied these notions to one-sentence-long utterances, that is to say, to text-fragments in isolation. It was thus meaningless to ask 'who is saying this?', 'In what context do you wish to determine if the given sentence is grammatical or not?', because linguists, especially in the United States where the influence of MIT was felt the strongest, did not concern themselves with COHESION, PLOT-STRUCTURE the tracing of NARRATIVE THREADS, etc. Consequently, the well-known terms of MODE, LEXIS, PERSONAL TENOR, or REGISTER, FIELD OF DISCOURSE and FUNCTIONAL TENOR have been totally ignored by Chomsky and his followers as if these extremely important pillars of information on which an entire composition must rest were somehow intrinsically alien to the tasks of linguistics. Luckily for the discipline as a global undertaking, the influence of the tagmemicists in the United States, and that of the Systemic-Functionalists throughout the Commonwealth and select, if somewhat isolated, spots in America, did not ignore plot-structure and the 'Context of Situation'. In other parts of Europe as well, especially the Scandinavian countries and West Germany, TEXT LINGUISTICS reached sophisticated techniques both as traditional scholarship aided by modern linguistics and as the brand new field of computational linguistics (e.g. the work of J. Petöfi and Sture Allén).

I am deeply convinced that Language can interact with the writer as much, if not more, as a slab of marble or a large oak trunk reacts to the sculptor's chisel and hammer, whether the sculptor is a Michelangelo or a Hawaiian Kahuna carving the statue of a ghostly ancestor, known as a 'tiki'. In Michelangelo's world-famous statue of David, the sculptor did, in a literal sense, add nothing to David himself. Rather, Michelangelo took away all of the unnecessary pieces and fragments of marble that 'contained David' in a concrete, physical sense. The artist's vision 'liberated' the shape of David from its marble prison. At the risk of running an over-worked analogy more into the ground, I would like seriously to insist that all artistic creation actually consists in the REMOVAL OF UNWANTED MATERIAL from around the 'object' which, then, can be seen as arising from two directions simultaneously: the direct action and vision of the artist and, second, the quasi-autonomous collaboration or resistance of the material of the piece of art work at hand.

The objection could be raised that this is acceptable perhaps in sculpture and, *mutatis mutandis*, in painting, but how do we explain music and writing in this sense? I believe that the PHONEMIC PRINCIPLE can provide a meaningful answer. What is a phoneme, really? To a certain extent it is an approximation of a set of related speech sounds. The English phoneme /t/, as commonly understood, is a kind of 'apico-alveolar voiceless stop'. It has, of course, a large number of allophones, such as the well known [tº], the [t⁼], and the [t ˀ], each one predictable by its environment in the word. A 'real /t/', then, is a fiction; there is no such 'actual sound'. What is, nevertheless, POSITIVELY FUNCTIONAL about this fictitious entity called /t/ is that it is not the fictitious entity /k/ or /p/, or any other conceivable sound. A phoneme, in this view, is the EXCLUSION OF ALL OTHER MEANING-DISTINGUISHING SOUNDS from a given morpheme and allomorph set. In other words, what is SEMIOTICALLY RELEVANT about /t/ is more what it is NOT, than what it IS; /t/ can be coded as the number '20' (which it happens to correspond to in the Latin alphabet); or I can arbitrarily designate its code number in the reverse as '02'. An entire text can be written all with numbers; each number corresponds to a given phoneme; if one has to work with people not trained in linguistics, one can designate a number for any key of an English typewriter and send a message coded in that particular way. Speech, then, if seen as an actual realization in space-time of a string of meaning distinguishing phonemes who owe their SEMIOTIC SIGNIFICANCE more to what they are NOT than what they ARE, can also be seen as EMERGING FROM THE PRISON OF ITS OWN MEDIUM, WHICH IS AN ALLOY OF SILENCE AND ALL CONCEIVABLE NOISES. This analogy is made in order to liken Language to sculpture. The medium of sculpture is so much more obvious that the validity of the analogy may seem to be wanting; I really think, however, that it is a valid analogy. Speech, as it emerges from silence, comes about because my interlocutor is NOT SAYING WHAT HE IS

NOT SAYING. He can only say what he DOES say, because he does not say something else. I beg the reader's kind indulgence for seemingly stretching my point. As I type this text, visible and legible English words and sentences appear in black on a white surface. But what is the REALITY of this text? The words are certainly not new that I am using. The letters of this typewriter have been typing many different texts; letters, notes, parts of essays. The letters are also not new. Some of my sentences, in all likelihood, will resemble some other sentences that I have written in other texts on other occasions for, after all, a person has a 'style' (*le style c'est l'homme* – as the French put it). I cannot become someone else or write in someone else's style. There is, fortunately or unfortunately, such a thing as 'Makkai's essays on language', just as there are identifiable passages written by other linguists. We all tend at least partially to repeat ourselves or to vary themes mentioned elsewhere. This particular text is, nevertheless, this particular text, solely and precisely BECAUSE IT IS NOT ONE OF MY OTHER ESSAYS OR ARTICLES; this is what distinguishes it from any other possible text that I am capable of producing. In the writing of this essay on half-writtenness I am 'removing' from my 'mind' all other possible arguments that I could make in a variety of styles. This is plain dry prose, as far as I can tell; I am certainly unaware of any feet in iambic tetrameter, pentameter or trimeter that might have sneaked in without my knowledge.

When I was presented with the challenge to write an essay on written language, many ideas crossed my mind that were later rejected. First, I was considering the effect of funny spellings on readers' aesthetic judgements. Another idea, a much more challenging one, was to investigate James Joyce's use of made-up 'nonsense words' in *Finnegan's Wake*. This plan is simmering on one of my back-burners; co-operation with a skilled computational linguist seems necessary to succeed with it. Another idea I rejected was whether a G.B. Shaw-like 'simplification' of English spelling might lead to greater literary creativity among minority dialect users whether in the United States or in the Commonwealth.

I am one of the few non-native speakers of English who have succeeded in producing a certain type of publishable poetry in English. I certainly lay no claim to any greatness or excellence in these writings; one reason for opting to analyse my own progress is that the linguist in me has never been blinded by the Hungarian poet and the English would-be poet. I think I can render account rationally of how a sonnet is formed by me as its medium whether in my native Hungarian or in my acquired English. What follows in this chapter, then, is a kind of linguistic introspection and exegesis. The poem first appeared in *The Earthquake on Ada Street* (Carroll (ed.) 1979) and was later reprinted in an anthology of poetry written by linguists (Napoli and Rando (eds) 1981).

The noted major American poet, Paul Carroll, my colleague in the English Department of the University of Illinois at Chicago, was kind enough to hold a series of workshop sessions in his home on Ada Street, where Mrs Carroll, a noted sculptress, had been creating large statues from metal pieces welded together. The Carroll home on Ada Street is, in fact, on top of an abandoned factory which Mrs Carroll transformed into her studio which, due to the unusual dimensions of her original and striking statues, had to be an unusually large one. When Paul Carroll gave his blessing to our cumulative efforts to bring out an anthology of our poetry, he suggested that we read out loud every piece he selected as if we had seen it then and there for the first time. His arrangement of the poets and their material is in itself quite remarkable; material we all felt we knew intimately suddenly appeared in another light. It turned out that the poems, in accumulated manuscript form, created a context of continuity from one poet to the next throughout the anthology. We were also consulted about possible titles. Some liked the idea of *Poetry from the Sculpture Factory*; someone else suggested *The Massacre on Ada Street*. Another suggestion I remember was *Oncoming Traffic has Longer Green*, and yet another member suggested *We Knew You – When*. Since the preparing of the camera-ready manuscript was left to me (I owned and operated an IBM Electronic Selectric Composer under our aegis of Jupiter Press), I was allowed to suggest the compromise title: *The Earthquake on Ada Street*. Ada Street had become a second home to us; leaving that out was out of the question. 'Massacre', avidly pursued by its proponent, sounded too harsh and unrealistic; as a joking reminder of the Al Capone days of Chicago it was a bit too overworked and we, after all, did not 'knock anyone dead' with the quality of our lyrics. 'The mouse that roared' somehow seemed more appropriate, and so the title 'The Earthquake on . . .' suggested itself. The designer of our book cover, James Axeman, a wonderful artist, who worked in the Publications Department of our university, immediately understood the goal of the title, that is self-irony. He drew the perfect cover for the book: You see a spreading crack in the pavement of a city street gradually widening out. It has the characteristic zigzag structure of lightning from above, yet it spreads on the ground. 'You want something stark and funky,' Jim Axeman said, and out of a few sheets of paper, wax and an assortment of crayons there emerged one of the finest book covers I ever saw. The cover itself now corresponded in a visual context to what the poetry was trying to say through the individual pieces and the particular way Paul Carroll had arranged them. In order to understand this macro-context of the entire anthology, one has to know that Paul Carroll asked everyone for about thirty poems. The restriction was that everything submitted has to have been written in the workshop; he would choose the best pieces of each contributor, and no one would be represented by more than ten poems. In other words, he WAS REMOVING UNWANTED PIECES from our various contributions, somewhat as Michelangelo was removing unwanted pieces of marble from the slab containing the germinal and yet undeveloped David.

At this point I am tempted by my own argument to take off in another direction, namely to strike out and explain how an anthology is edited. I must resist this for now. Well, maybe just for the moment I could allow myself an interjection. All I want to do is show how the text affects the writer. When you have an anthology to edit, you are dealing with a whole collection of texts, texts that were written by others. Some anthologies contain scholarly articles; some contain short stories; and then there are the poetry anthologies. The editor of a journal, for that matter, creates each issue by rejecting a certain number of submissions. I hope my point is clear: Once again, in order to create the 'positive end result', the shaper of an anthology proceeds by excluding a certain amount of material. I believe that Paul Carroll saw several poems in a new light as he looked at our submissions in context. My sonnet, *Prayer for Health*, did not earn me great praise a year earlier during the actual workshop sessions; in fact he seemed somewhat irritated by it. After a number of minor changes (which I will explain later), I decided, nevertheless, to submit it in my particular batch. To my great surprise, Paul Carroll, as he handed me the manuscript for typesetting, said: 'By the way, your *Prayer for Health* is really funny, I decided to include it.' I was puzzled. I reminded him that he had not liked it. 'True', he said, 'it sounded a bit morbid and gross in your oral presentation and right after a nice, serious religious poem by X' – he was referring to one of the other participants in the workshops. 'But now, you see', he said, 'it picks up a different flavor in the context of what comes before it and after it in the book. I didn't see what you were trying to do that evening, but it is rather clear now. You are getting away with a mixture of profanity and Elizabethan expressions and this is a novum of sorts. That's why I chose the poem.'

It was in 1980, a year after the appearance of the anthology, that a noted Illinois reviewer pointed out the same mixing of profanity and Biblical language as 'refreshingly new'. Abashed and grateful, I filed the article away with the rest of the paper that had anything to do with the anthology, and paid little attention to it. Now, however, as it has become my task to show how the poem, in a sense, 'wrote itself despite my interference', I am forced to rethink the steps I took during its composition. I will be trying to explain in the rest of this chapter how the text interacted with me, and thereby 'wrote itself' into a finished product from a state of half-writtenness. But I must backtrack and start with our family physician, Dr Barton K. Adams, who abandoned his general practice in Lake Forest, Illinois, and retrained himself, partly in Switzerland's Jung Institute and partly at Loyola Medical School in Chicago, to become a full-time psychiatrist.

I am basically in reasonably good health. I do, however, sit too much and do not exercise much. This is worse in my case than ordinarily, because as a former polio victim, I should have been paying much more attention to my physical fitness. Some of my symptoms have been rapid heartbeats (technically known as tachycardia) and allergic reactions to certain food items, resulting in headaches and an upset stomach. Dr Adams, a regular jogging fan, did not mince his words: 'A man in his forties, like you, ought to jog regularly. Why, you're a regular garbage dump of tablets. So you have headaches . . . Jog it out of your system, or do some meditating. In fact, why don't you do both?' As you can begin to guess, the voice of the 'Heavenly Father' in the sonnet was the elevation of our doctor to the status of divinity. But why did I do that? Well, that, too, is interesting in its own way. I admired Dr Adams for his physical fitness and his good, down-to-earth common sense. Here was a man, five years my senior, in far better shape than I ever would be. I admired his erudition and his strength. Patients have a tendency to turn their favorite family physician into some kind of father figure. All the greater was our disappointment when Dr Adams declared that he was closing down his family general practice in order to become a Jungian psychoanalyst. We missed him sorely. I, too, was having second thoughts about my regular profession, linguistics, and secretly wished that I could somehow get out of it. Linguistic argumentation was much too polemical and much too logic-oriented; our campus was not developing new, interesting courses; the Head of the Department and I disagreed on questions of personnel, theory, even politics. What was I really doing in this strange field? My own family physician is leaving his clientele, his security and his high income . . . He is pursuing a dream . . . The dream of reaching the patient's emotional problems and his unconscious . . . What a brave man!

Thus began Dr Adams's apotheosis and emulation in my mind.

With my favorite physician gone, my headaches continuing, and poetry my only solace, one day, as I prepared for Paul Carroll's poetry workshop, I heard an inner voice say: 'mine ain't the finest . . .' I was not sure WHAT of mine was not the finest; but soon I realized that I was complaining about my body. *Ain't* is such a stigmatized expression that well-educated people do not use it, unless, of course, they are in actually very highly intelligent company, where it no longer matters whether they use 'correct grammar' or not; everyone knows that they are merely playing. I heard the Dean once say: 'We ain't got no money and nobody can do nuttin' about it.' The Dean was no Appalachian; he was merely tired and disgusted. Any other way of registering his frustrations would have seemed labored and unfriendly. After all, he was talking to his colleagues, all holders of the Ph.D. Why shouldn't he say *ain't* if he so pleases? This led to the thought of 'elegant company'. Surely the CREATOR must be on the top of ANY hierarchical listing of educators, private or public. Doesn't the Bible say that he created Man in his own image? I have a special handicap here, since my name is Adam. Would the original Adam have dared speak to HIM UP THERE and point out that not all was well? Who could say? All I can remember is that the word *assignest* announced its availability to rhyme with *the finest*. I now had two potential lines bound by a rhyme, *ain't the finest* and *who assignest*. The ending in *-est* bothered me a bit. This sounds too much like some Shakespearean lines I knew from the famous dramas; also it rang like verses from the Bible read from the pulpit. 'So why not?' I thought, 'God talks in Shakespearean English, so we, too, must address him in 16th-century English.' The trouble spot was the *ain't*. How can I reconcile the informality of *ain't* with the solemnity of the King James version of Scriptures?

'God may have a strong sense of humor,' a voice now said in my head.

'What? God . . . having a sense . . . of . . . humor?' Who said that? I was
frantically trying to remember. Then in a sudden flash: 'But of course,
that's Doc Adams trying to persuade me not to hate my own body so
much.' I used to complain to him during various physical examinations,
such as a long and painful rectal internal examination with various tiny
lights and lenses hooked up to a television screen whose task it was to
determine if I had malignant tumours or benign polyps or just plain old
haemorrhoids. 'Why did we get so goddam screwed up', I asked, 'that our
digestive system has to be so closely linked with the organs of reproduction? Wouldn't it be neater if holding hands could deliver more pleasure
than sex and conceiving or not conceiving would be a voluntary act?' –
'A philosophical patient, eh?' the nurse interjected. 'Dr Makkai is a
Professor of Linguistics', Doc Adams came to the rescue. 'Sorry, I didn't
know', the nurse hastened to soothe me. 'Well', Doc Adams added, 'I
guess you could make a reasonable argument that the Old Man Upstairs
did a bit of sloppy engineering here and there . . . I guess that's what you
mean, right?' I do not remember how the rest of the conversation went
because I had to concentrate very hard in order not to faint. I was bent
over in a 90-degree angle over an examining table, a five-foot-long chord
inserted into my intestines; my head was awhirl with dizziness and a good
deal of discomfort, if not unbearable pain. On another occasion I
mentioned to Doc Adams that it is not fair that we live such short lives.
'An average of two hundred years would seem much more realistic than
seventy-five to eighty-five', I said while he was sticking a nasty, thick
needle into my vein in the left arm to draw ten cubic centimetres of blood.
'What about reincarnation?' Doc Adams asked, and that genuinely
surprised me. I have found that nine out of ten physicians are materialists
and do not even believe in the immortal soul, let alone trump the wise-
guy-patient by referring to reincarnation. 'Well', I said, 'if there is reincarnation, that gives us a chance to finish in another lifetime what we missed
earlier . . . I am not really able to believe in it, though . . . I think that
one body per one life is all we get.' 'But of course', Doc Adams mused,
'you wouldn't want the same old lousy body back the second time round
now, would you?' That was the end of that argument. The entire conversation was forgotten and pushed down into my subconscious, but now, stir-
red up by the desire to write a sonnet and the rhymes *ain't the finest* and
thou assignest, I was now able to take a pencil and actually write down the
first line:

Heavenly Father, who graciously assignest . . .

'*Assignest*', all right, but what doest Thou assign and to what? Well,
maybe certain souls deserve better bodies than others. Maybe I had been
a sinner in an earlier life and my not-too-perfect body was the 'punishment' or the 'corrective challenge' that 'God', whoever or whatever, 'He'
is, gave me. This word *lifetime* now surfaced. Yes, it probably works like
this; one gets one body per lifetime. The body 'contains' the soul, like

wrapping paper. I came from war-torn Eastern Europe, Budapest, Hungary. Nothing was ever properly wrapped. Going shopping in Budapest without a basket or a nylon bag was asking for trouble; only twenty years after the war did the nationalized food stores start to sell paper and plastic bags for shoppers. A good container was a real necessity. The analogy was obvious: The soul gets the kind of container it deserves; luckily (or unluckily) for us, it has to dwell in its container only one lifetime. I sat down and wrote:

> Heavenly Father, who graciously assignest
> our souls to one container lasting only one lifetime . . .
> > [hmm, hmmm, hmmm]
> > a bright dime.

I do not quite know where *the bright dime* came from, but I suspect that the expressions *not worth a dime, not worth the paper it is written on* and *not worth a damn* were at least partially responsible for what I now heard as the needed rhyme to close off the first quatrain. 'Quatrain', I say, with a certain degree of embarrassment. I had never managed to write a sonnet in English before this, whereas in my native language, Hungarian, I have been credited not only with handling the sonnet rather well, but I am also credited with having invented a new type of sonnet, in which all the vowels of all the fourteen lines rhyme with one another in an ABAB relationship scheme. Surely a fairly traditional rhyming scheme in English has to be easier than that . . . Some members of the workshop had expressed a certain dislike for fixed forms – 'the sonnet is such a bore and such a nuisance', Y once remarked. 'Have you ever written one?' I had the unwise idea to ask. Y and I have been correct and polite acquaintances ever since, but I cannot boast of a very close and warm friendship between the two of us. Proving that I can do a sonnet and that it is worth doing, because it can deliver an unusual punch, was now a categorical imperative for me. I thus sat down and penned out the first quatrain:

> Heavenly Father, who graciously assignest
> our souls to one container lasting but one lifetime,
> permit me to complain 'mine ain't the finest'
> I actually wonder if it's worth a bright dime.

I was not really satisfied with this stanza, but thought – as we probably all do – that I can always change some words later. The 'first draft' is really one of the most important steps in the creating of any text, prose or poetry. 'Well now, let's see', I thought, 'what can I tell the "Old Man Upstairs" in more or less concrete terms that was bothering me?' I made a short check-list: (1) headaches, (2) frequent diarrhoea alternating with days of constipation, (3) when I get nervous about something my heart-beats per minute can double up; for this Doc Adams gave me the wonder-ful drug valium, (4) I have a hard time falling asleep as well as waking up. Now came the problem of how to make these miseries rhyme and fit into the second stanza. In a really tightly woven classical sonnet form, known as the 'Petrarchan Sonnet', one must continue the rhyme scheme established by the first stanza. Thus I would have needed words rhyming with *assignest*, *lifetime*, *finest*, and *bright dime*; but in the reverse order of the first stanza, e.g. *my lime*, *Thou mightest*, *the brightest*, and maybe *light mime*. But I was not ready for this much punishment in English; after all, this was my first English sonnet and no lesser bard than Shakespeare himself did not conform to the rigid rules of the Petrarchan sonnet. In fact there is a 'Shakespearean sonnet' whose characteristics include three four-line stanzas with ABAB CDCD EFEF and a GG couplet at the end. (For a formal description of the Shakespearian and the Petrarchan Sonnet see Chapter 11.) This I did not want to do – partly because of respect for The Bard, and because I wanted to see two quatrains and two terzinae. But how then should I proceed? The name of my first complaint came to mind rather quickly; it was the word *constipation*. Rhymes with *-ation* can be dull and trivial; if I was to use it, I needed another *-ation* to rhyme with it, but not necessarily a customary one. *Visitation* – I heard from the inside Reverse Morphicon. (The 'morphicon' is the dictionary of the morphemes in English, just as the lexicon is the depository of its lexemes; the semicon would be the Thesaurus of English that contains semantically nested meanings.) What *visitation*, though? – I wondered. The idea of the *bathroom* came a few minutes later; after all that is where *constipation* is noticed in its acute form. But I also have the opposite problem aggravated by sleeplessness and aches and pains. I penned out the line:

I suffer from sleeplessness, the runs, gout, constipation
[NEW RHYME NEEDED]
bathroom visitation
[NEW RHYME NEEDED]

Where do all my troubles really come from? Doc Adams more than implied that they are probably of a psychosomatic nature. 'You worry too much', he said. 'This can affect both the stomach and the vegetative nervous system attached to the spine. How many sit-ups are you doing every morning?' 'Just a few', I lied sheepishly. The truth was that I was doing no sit-ups at all. But where then DID all my troubles come from? From worry. 'I transform my worries into medical symptoms.' The word *transformation* sounded particularly promising; with it I can make an allusion to Transformational-Generative Grammar, my least favored mode of speculating about language, and I do not even have to mention Chomsky or MIT. The pen started to write almost automatically and despite my presence:

I suffer insomnia, the runs, gout, constipation,
worry-transformations Ta Tum Ta TUM and spinal . . .

or did not Doc Adams say that even the spinally linked vegetative nervous system gets involved? I was three syllables short of a usable second line. Not too long ago I saw a label on dried camomile tea in the Lake Bluff pharmacy. It said 'camomile is the ideal stomachic'. I never heard or read the word *stomachic* before, but it sounded heavy, medical and somewhat obscure. Why not try it out? I wrote:

> worry-transformations, stomachic and spinal

'If the natives don't like it, they will tell me', I thought; 'after all, that's what the workshop is all about'. But what should rhyme with *spinal*? A number of /aynəl/ syllables ran through my head, but the word *final* seemed to make the most sense. It had to appear as a predicate adjective, however, to fit syntactically at the end of the sentence which was also a quatrain-ending word. *Was the final* [*one*], *to be the final* [*act of something*] were some of my available choices. Maybe if bathroom visitations could be the subject of a sentence, I could get enough clause-structure in the last line so that I could end the stanza with *final* in the predicate adjective position. (Needless to say that this kind of reasoning is much easier in retrospect than during the actual act of writing itself. A good deal of this speculation goes on quasi-unconsciously and at great speed.) I sat down and wrote out the whole quatrain:

> I suffer insomnia, the runs, gout, constipation . . .
> worry-transformations, stomachic and spinal;
> many a straightforward bathroom visitation
> looks as if it will kill me, in fact to be the final.

I was not happy with this, but I now had two first-draft stanzas, both quatrains, and this point during the writing of a sonnet usually brings the writer to the SEMANTIC FULCRUM of this rather tight form of verse. One presents the 'topic' or the 'problem', as it were, in the two quatrains, and then two following six lines; the two terzinae offer a solution to these problems. Another way of putting it would be to say that the first quatrain specifies the TOPIC; the second is an amplification of the topic, or COMMENT on the topic; the two terzinae offer their lexical and phonological space to 'solve the problem' proposed in the quatrains or to pour a bucket full of ice-water on them, depending on how one's day predisposes one to any possible 'solution'. The patient has not said everything yet that he had to say; the first terzina must somehow act as the 'mailman' who takes my letter to the Old Man Upstairs. 'You can't trade it in for a new one', I knew it only too well. The expression *trade-in value* came to mind, as during the quarter century I have lived in America I had numerous occasions to bargain with used car dealers. The pencil started to move once more:

> That this exhausted body has zero trade-in value
> I had better accept. I know I am being informal.

The word *normal* rang a fairly obvious bell somewhere in Wernicke's or Broca's area; the sentence it forced itself into as its last word went as:

What I must ask you now's why can't it function normal?

This, then, would be the end of the speech to the Old Man Upstairs, and if this sonnet had any chance of amusing any reader with a punchline, the last terzina ought to be used for giving the Old Man Upstairs a chance to respond. I have become aware over the years that the word *you* sometimes sounds like [ya] in colloquial English. *I tell you* comes out as *I tell ya*. The *tell* was a useful syllable: if God answers and says *I tell ya*, he is performing a well-known speech-act, known as a direct address, an illocutionary act, as in *I hereby declare that* . . . The pencil started to run:

And he replied: 'Your words are sharp, I tell ya.

With this I will have established that God (*mutatis mutandis*, Doc Adams) has heard me and is willing to reply; He reprimands me mildly for my boldness in addressing HIM as a plaintiff sues someone in court. The last two lines of the second terzina must, therefore, be the real punch-line of this conversation with God Almighty (disguised as Doc Adams) who gives this lazy patient a piece of his mind for living such a sedentary and lazy life. *Jogging* and *meditation* were the two key words. If I could only bring myself to do some regular jogging and some meditating, maybe the headaches would pass, I could lose some weight, the hypertension would go away, and I would gradually start to feel better. *Meditation* sounded like an excellent line-final, but the trouble was that, as yet another *-ation* word, it called for an *-ation* rhyme, and I have already used that option in *constipation – visitation* in the second quatrain. What I needed was a new *-ation* word; something that would be a novelty in an English sonnet. Here I was helped by a paper by James D. McCawley who, in a mimeographed paper once discussed the difference between *shit* as a genetic term and *turd* as an 'individuation' of generic *shit*. Going to the bathroom can be called *defecation* in English and that would be a great *-ation* word, except that it is too common. What if I invented a new word for *diarrhoea*? *Liquid* plus *-ation* . . . I've got it! I will try the non-existent yet understandable word *Liquifecation*. The Old Man Upstairs was now ready to respond, and my pencil registered it as:

If you will jog a mile a day and practice meditation,
to normal turds will I restore your sad liquifecation.

This was all right as a working version, as in-between text, as it were. I had it now on four different sheets of paper and I had never yet seen it in one piece. This is the stage in a composition when a unified draft may be presented. One should pretend that the piece may be 'finished', knowing perfectly well, of course, that it is not. The tentative quasi-final version, however, must not be skipped. It shows all the previous elements in a NEW CONTEXT; the writer can now imagine what the final version would look like in typescript or in printed form. Words that do not seem right can be altered at this point; the scaffolding can be removed from the building. There is no paint on the walls and the doors and windows are not yet in place, making the 'building' uninhabitable. Yet the working crew can take a break; they can climb up to the roof and celebrate the fact that the basic structure is there. So I wrote down the following imperfect version:

PRAYER FOR HEALTH

Heavenly Father, who merrily assignest
our souls to one container, lasting but one lifetime,
please look and realize that mine ain't the finest,
I actually wonder if it's worth a bright dime.

I suffer insomnia, the runs, gout, constipation . . .
worry-transformations stomachic and spinal;
many a straightforward bathroom visitation
feels as if it will kill me, in fact, to be the final.

That this too tired body has zero trade-in value
I had better accept. So sorry I'm being informal.
What I must ask you now's, why can't it function normal?

And He replied: 'Your tongue is sharp, I tell ya.
If you will jog a mile a day and practice meditation,
to normal turds will I remake your pained liquifecation.

It looked barely passable. I was deeply disappointed and wanted to tear it up and throw it away. It was tiring work to put this all together and still it lacked a certain tone, a voice, the *je ne sais quoi* that make a poem hang together.

A couple of weeks later I took it out from the drawer and looked at it as if it had been written by someone else. 'But of course!' I thought, 'this is wrong because I have an old, 16th-century verb form in stanza 1 in 'assignest' but don't carry through with that in the rest of the conversation'. The *you* of the second terzina became *thou*, the *will* turned into *willst*; the word *your* automatically coming as *thy*. *Please look and realize* was much too prosaic; I crossed it out. The words *That this too tired body* was also wrong; I remembered the *this here* . . . construction. *Ashes to Ashes, dust to dust*, remembered from the burial ceremony and the Bible, suggested *That this here hull of dust*. *Has* became *hath*. *What I must ask you now* also had to go; it was too prosaic and did not live up to the expectations of a serious protest directed at the Almighty.

These and similar considerations in editing the poem have produced a version that I was at last able to read to the members of the workshop and get some feedback from them. It now read as follows:

PRAYER FOR HEALTH

Heavenly Father, who graciously assignest
our souls to one container lasting but one lifetime,
kindly permit me to state mine ain't the finest,
in fact, sometimes I wonder, if it's worth a bright dime.

I suffer insomnia, the runs, gout, constipation,
worry-transformations stomachic and spinal;
many a straightforward bathroom visitation
threatens to tear me up; in fact, to be the final.

That this here hull o' dust hath zero trade-in value
I most humbly accept. Forgive my words informal.
What I must needs protest: Why can't it function normal?

And then He spake: 'Thou pleadest tough, I tell ya.
If Thou willst jog a mile a day and practice meditation,
to wholesome turds will I restore thy foul liquifecation.

The changes in word order, such as *forgive my words informal* for normal
forgive my informal words seemed to have added a bit of antiquity to the style,
as did *spake* for the earlier *replied*.

Some theoretical conclusions

Every text exists in simultaneously minimally two contexts: (1) the INTER-
NAL CONTEXT of the text itself, and (2) the EXTERNAL CONTEXT, that is
the context of the situation that the text appears in. I say 'minimally two'
because there are numerous other contexts, e.g. temporal and social
dialect, that enter into the *Gesamtbedeutung* of any text, if I can borrow
Roman Jakobson's term. This sonnet, as I have tried to show, went
through a number of stages of 'half-writtenness' until it reached its pre-
final first draft form which, then, was edited further. The Internal Context
in this case can be identified as QUATRAIN 1, QUATRAIN 2, 1st TERZINA
and the 2nd TERZINA, from a formal point of view. In terms of dialog
(another aspect of the text's Internal Context), the two quatrains constitute
the 'Plaintiff's Plea'. The first two lines of the first terzina is the 'Confession of the Plaintiff', in which he concedes that the item (his body) that
he is complaining about is not really worth the trouble. The line *What I
must needs protest: Why can't it function normal?* is the 'Sub-Plea', the plaintiff's 'Fall-back Position'. (If he cannot get a 'new body', could the one
he has function normally, at least?)

The first four words of the second terzina *And then He spake* is the structural bridge introducing the role of the 'antagonist–interlocutor', the 'Old
Man Upstairs'. His first utterance is not the verdict itself, but a comment
on the plaintiff's behavior; *Thou pleadest tough, I tell ya* is an admission on
the part of the God–Physician–Super-ego that the plaintiff has made a

strong and convincing argument for his case. He then closes his side of this mini-trial in the rhyming couplet of the second terzina by issuing the verdict; a 'condition for the cure' as it were. If plaintiff will do so and so, He then, will reciprocate and do so-and-so. This would be, sketching it out roughly, the 'rhetorical thread' or the 'inner context' of these fourteen lines.

This 'Inner Context', however, is merely the Progression of the Plot. It coincides in time and space with the fact that this sonnet is in the WRIT-TEN MODE, although in a written mode that imitates speaking out loud. It is thus in a mixed Written–Spoken mode. The DEIXIS of the piece shows a funny mixture of extremely formal and extremely informal; this duality co-exists, furthermore, with the 'Modern Colloquial/Slang' and the 'Archaic-Elizabethan', especially in the words *assignest*, *spake*, *Thou*, *willst*, and *thy*. These archaic *thou*-forms tend to pile up towards the end, when God answers the plaintiff. In terms of archaisms the plaintiff uses only a few; besides the already mentioned *assignest* he uses the form *this here hull o' dust* (harking back to *this here my son was dead and is now alive* from the story of the Prodigal Son), the form *hath* for *has*, and the quaint locution *must needs* which originated in all likelihood from the fuller and longer *must [by] needs*; where *needs* is a pluralized noun and not the familiar verb. The plaintiff's use of *ain't* is jarring in a speech to God as is *trade-in value*, but he then catches himself just in time to apologize and says *Forgive my words informal* in an antiquated, inverted word order for *forgive my informal words*.

Why do I say these things under the heading of 'Theoretical Conclu-sions'? Doesn't this belong in the previous section explicating the sonnet's plot progression? The answer to that question must be a cautious 'yes/no' answer wired around with numerous caveats and semi-stylistic hook-up links. The simple fact of this rather complex matter is that the temporal–social dialect mixture, riding the lexis, CO-EXISTS IN SPACE/TIME THROUGHOUT THE ENTIRE TEXT. In other words, besides the Internal Context we also have the External or 'Diatypical' Context of FORMAL versus INFORMAL, *thou* versus *you*, 'folksy' versus 'academic', and 'made-up' versus 'real'. This last remark concerns the ending word *liquifecation*, a blend of *liquid* and *defecation*. This newly coined nonsense word would be quite meaningless in isolation, but as a summation of the plaintiff's miseries, it makes sense.

Deletions, transformations and rewritings

These three terms used to be the Pillars of Hercules on which Chomsky's Transformational-Generative Grammar rested for two and a half decades. Invariably, these potentially useful words – useful, that is, in RHETORIC and COMPOSITION THEORY – were callously ignored in the very place where they could have done the most good. None of these three plays any really significant role in the human act of generating speech from memory traces and yet unspoken intentions. I respectfully invite all scholars of different persuasions to tell me what exactly 'Prayer' should be called in Linguistics. Is it 'speech'? Why, yes and no, of course. Is it 'interaction with another member of one's speech community'? Yes and no again, depending on what status we assign to the Old Man Upstairs in our particular speech community. A destructive fellow He was, wasn't he? After all, he confused all the human tongues because of the naughty Tower of Babel. Nevertheless, one prefers to think that He can understand ANY language – 5,103 of them. The pseudo-theological question concerning whether God understands loudly spoken prayer better than silently meditated prayer has to remain a moot one; we just do not know the answer, as linguists. As a private citizen, I believe, of course, that written prayers, especially in sonnet form, are the best way to get the Old Man's attention.

There is so much wrong with the TGG mutation view of language that it would take several volumes to make just the most necessary corrections. It is, furthermore, considered bad manners to flog a dead horse. I beg to differ. TGG may be a 'dead horse', but it is one with a very vicious kick. More flogging is in order; indeed we perhaps need to drive a wooden stake through its vampire heart.

At the same time, the theory and practice of teaching English as a Foreign Language and the theory and practice of Composition were disenfranchized by the 'theoreticians'. Chomsky's numerous disclaimers about any pedagogical applicability of his theories are only too well known. It is indeed in the area of 'social accountability' (to quote Halliday) that TGG has been the guiltiest. Chomsky's clever manoeuvring of all pedagogical and related issues to the convenience excess of 'special performance' is but an all too obvious escape-hatch built into TGG rhetoric in order not to have to account of HOW people use Language WHEN, in WHAT MODE, and for WHAT PURPOSE.

I have deliberately chosen one of my own sonnets, written in a mixed oral-printed mode, and with mixed personal tenors, and mixed temporal and social dialects to show that if such texts are analysed carefully, the inevitable need for SIMULTANEOUS AWARENESS and THE CONTEXTUAL ADJUSTABILITY PRINCIPLE arises.

Whereas poetry used to be recited aloud accompanied by musical instruments (from Homeric days to the present, e.g. in Yugoslavia), most modern poetry exists primarily in the WRITTEN MODE. Poetry reading by the author (frequently followed by the autographing of books sold under the impact of the poet's live voice) cannot make up for the amount of what one has to read. Poems, furthermore, are hardly ever 'ready' when one writes them down for the first time. There is thus every reason why modern theoretical linguistics should start to pay more attention to poetry than has been the case hitherto. The self-analyses of practising poets should be eagerly sought and invited, as they will undoubtedly reveal much about the composition process in a rich variety of various forms.

16 The '*illumination*' of Giuseppe Ungaretti: a linguistic meditation on phonetics, semantics and the explication of text

0. Preliminary Remarks

The object of the present analysis – if you can justifiably call what follows here 'analysis' in the usual linguistic sense – is a two-line poem by one of Italy's 20th-century masters of modern poetry, Giuseppe Ungaretti. The poem has been characterized by many researchers[1] as memorable, untranslatable; a unique specimen of the hermetic tradition,[2] a literary style in modern Italian *belles lettres* which was born in the wake of the famous 'poets of the twilight', *i crepuscolari*,[3] who, in turn, can be seen as followers of the symbolist tradition *à la* Rimbaud, Mallarmé, and others.[4]

It would not be necessary to protect this first paragraph with the artillery of four heavy notes under normal circumstances; but as the meditation on Ungaretti's two-word poem gets under way, it will become evident that no amount of literary and historical circumnavigation can even begin to do justice to the intricacies involved. But before I attempt to scale the walls of the fortress of *explication de texte*, let us stare the poem squarely in the face as an ordinary text, and ask some sensible, if all too trivial questions about its morphological structure and its syntax. The phonology of the poem must be left to a section all by itself because, as I shall presently try to show, a large portion of the 'meaning' of this poem is directly realized by its unique phonological structure.

The text itself is deceptively simple and short, and reads as follows:

1. The text and its grammar

MATTINA
M'illumino
d'immenso

No exclamation mark, dashes, or period suggest that a sentence final intonation is to be spoken or heard; neither is there a question mark following the two words making it seem to be a question. The date of the composition is given as 26 January, 1917; the place was Santa Maria La Langa. The place and the time, as I intend to show later, are also relevant to the total meaning of this poem.

On the surface, the grammar of this two-line, two-word poem is rather simple. We are dealing with a declarative sentence of which the unexpressed grammatical subject is *Io* 'I'; unexpressed in the sense that expressing it is 'superfluous' due to the unmistakable grammatical ending on the verb *illumino*. The direct object of the sentence is *mi* 'myself'; that is, we are dealing with the familiar reflexive construction well-described and understood in the Romance languages. The morpheme *di* – with the *i* elided – marks the *agent* of the illumination. One can, thus, easily 'translate' the legal sense of Ungaretti's poem as 'I illuminate myself through the immense' or 'I become illuminated by immensity'; in the active voice in English one can certainly say 'immensity illuminates me' and not be guilty of having drastically altered Ungaretti's legal and grammatical meaning.

If one regards the reflexive morpheme *me-m'* as a 'word' and the genitive *di-d'* as another, the text may be said to contain four words, but the elision of the vowels forces Italians to pronounce the poem as two phonological words. The legal–grammatical translatability of the poem into English is, of course, further facilitated by the fact that both *illumino, illuminare*, and *immenso* have well known and frequent cognates in the words *illuminate–illumination* and *immense–immensity–immensely*. There is no need to go into historical explanation of how these words came to be cognates; the heavily Romance upper layer of English texts has created multifarious examples of this sort over the centuries and presents no mysteries for linguistic scholarship.[5] Since English has no enclitic reflexives, *m'illumino* can, nevertheless, only be rendered awkwardly as 'I illuminate myself' or 'I become illuminated'; rendering the Italian *di* as *by*, marking the agent in English, is entirely matter of course. The legal prose translation thus obtained says, nevertheless, very little about Ungaretti's poem *qua* poem; and offers no insight whatever into the deeper meanings that can be found in this often quoted two-liner. The active rendering of the original in English, would seem to suggest an active construction in the Italian itself since there are many other ways 'I become illuminated by the immense' can be said in grammatical Italian as long as all one wants to do is speak grammatical prose. The *immense illuminates me*, then, can easily be imagined as stemming from an Italian *L'immenso m'illumina*, but reciting this prose sentence aloud in juxtaposition to Ungaretti's original, one can immediately sense the enormous difference that exists between the two versions.

At this point I must make a few remarks about what the original poem sounds like in Italian.

In the standard literary language, most likely Ungaretti's native dialect[6], it sounds as follows:

/m i l: ú m i n o + d i m: é n s o/

The main stress is on the /u/ of *m'illúmino*; and the /-ns-/ cluster is spoken as indicated with a voiceless /s/ following the voiced nasal apical continuant /n/. However, other pronunciations of the poem are also possible. In certain areas of Italy the stress in the first word is found on the /i/ (*m'illumíno*); and the /-ns-/ cluster produces different realizations depending on the region of Italy one considers. In Rome, one can hear /-*nts*-/; farther south, especially around Naples, /imme*ndzo*/ may be heard, and south of Naples even /imme*nzo*/.[7]

Whatever the case may be in dialects other than the standard one, I will look in this chapter primarily at the standard (Tuscan) rendering of the two words, since Ungaretti was born in Alexandria, Egypt, and would not have been exposed to nonstandard Italian speech.[8] We will treat the /s/ as the only voiceless consonant in this poem with the possibility of occasional lenis pronunciations via -*dz*- leading to an occasional /z/ pronunciation. At one time I considered the possibility that part of the complex evocative meanings of the poem may reside precisely in the fact that it contains not a single voiceless consonant, but on further thought I concluded that if the /s/ was in fact voiceless in Ungaretti's speech, this does not destroy the 'phonosemantic argument' I am about to develop in this chapter; it rather adds emphasis to it by virtue of the place of the /s/ phoneme in the poem as a whole. I shall return to the phonosemantic role of /s/ in the 'illumination' further below and will devote a few words here to the rhythmic pattern of the poem.

If one takes the main stress to reside on the /u/ of *m'illúmino* as expected from speakers of literary Tuscan, the rhythmic pattern of the poem shapes up as follows: v ´ vv v ´ v. This pattern is quite obviously neither purely 'rising' nor 'falling'; the main stress is always in the middle surrounded by unstressed vowels. As a result, the lines are simultaneously quasi-iambic and quasi-trochaeic. The two v-s followed by the stressed syllable give a 'rising' iambic effect; the accented syllable followed by two rapid unaccented ones in the first word is dactylic and the second word is literally both iambic and trochaeic, depending on how you look at it. Intercepted stresses of this sort are usually referred to as CHORIAMBIC STRESS PATTERNS,[9] so if we follow the north-Italian habit of stressing the /u/ here, we can speak of two choriambic lines.

Another native rendering of the poem, however, shows the main accent of the first word on the /i/ phoneme; the reading now is v v ´ vv ´ -, or v v ´ v v ´ v. Reading the poem in this fashion, one sees clearly rising or anapaestic structure, expressionistically renderable as *ta-ta-TUM ta-ta-TUM-ta*.

Let us consider some of the possible Italian sentences that the original could be related to syntactically. I deliberately make no claim that any of the following sentences are 'transformations' of any other sentence listed here.

1. M'illumino d'immenso – the original.
2. L'immenso m'illumina – 'the immense illuminates me'.
3. Sono illuminato dall'immenso 'I am illuminated by the immense/immensity'.
4. Sono illuminato immensamente 'I am immensely illuminated'.
5. Sono illuminato dall'immensità 'I am illuminated by the immensity'.
6. È dall'immensità che sono illuminato 'It's by the immensity that I am illuminated'.
7. È l'immensità che m'illumina. } 'It's the immense/immensity
8. È l'immenso che m'illumina. } that illuminates me'.
9. Sono stato illuminato dall'immenso/immensità/immensamente 'I have been illuminated by the immense/immensity/immensely'.
10. ?È stata l'immensità ad illuminarmi? 'It has been the immensity that illuminates me'.
11. ?È stata l'immensità che mi a illuminato? 'It has been the immensity that has illuminated me'.
12. (Io) sono quello che e stato illuminato dall'immensità 'I am the one who has been illuminated by the immensity'.
13. Io sono l'illuminato dall'immenso/immensità 'I am immensity's illuminated one'.

As these thirteen examples show, there is no dearth of syntactic devices in modern Italian to foreground *immensity*, the doer; *mi*, as the goal/recipient/ undergoer; the being of an illuminated state (*sono*), and *is* (È) in the various compound tenses. Everyone would agree, we think, that none of these sentences offer any improvement over Ungaretti's original; all of them show some straining and forcing of the language. All of them, with the possible exception of (10) and (11), are 'grammatical', and I think everyone would agree that the 'legal meaning' of the statement remains discernable from these various lexotactic re-encodings of the main message.

According to literary legend,[10] Ungaretti, when a soldier in World War I, was in a fox-hole for several days and nights and woke up one morning to the sight of the rising sun over a radiant Adriatic. It was then, the legend goes, that this poem was first conceived in his mind. Reportedly he carried it along inside him for several years before he finally wrote it down in its published version in his collection entitled *L'Allegria*. The sentence *M'illumino d'immenso*, then, can be seen as a SPONTANEOUS EXCLAMA-TION, that is, as a specific (though descriptively not too well understood) grammatical phenomenon which must, despite the theoretical obscurity that surrounds it, be regarded as somehow PRIMARY rather than DERIVATIVE. Whether exclamations, as spontaneous speech acts, have grammatical derivations of their own is a topic better left for another occa-sion.[11]. Generally, it seems unrealistic to posit a 'deep structure' for an exclamation such as English *ouch!* or *Gosh!* Positing a 'well-formed gram-matical deep structure' that somehow 'underlies' such exclamations results in a striking loss of psychological realism. If the exclamation *ouch!*, for example, is left dangling as the dependent object noun phrase of a deep structure sentence such as the following where one must delete everything in a series of steps to be left with the object of the analysis *ouch!*, one has the sensation that too much time has elapsed since a swift stab of pain would be reacted to. Counter-arguments suggesting that the performance of *ouch!* realized in REAL TIME has nothing to do with its logical and grammatical derivation are like saying that expressing the simple arithmetic function $1 + 1 = 2$ is inelegant. Sophisticated people ought to express it as a long and complicated equation which is mathematically and logically correct, but somehow psychologically vacuous.[12]

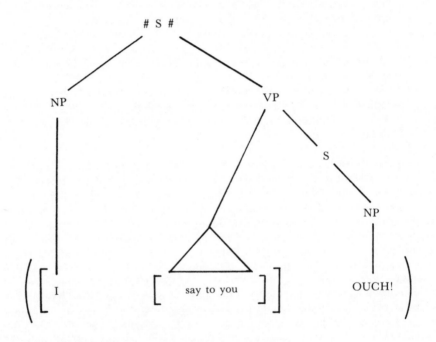

Figure 1

I therefore, believe that Ungaretti had no grammatical processes running through his head (even though anyone can easily 'rewrite' his poem in any of the 'transformations' offered above in sentences (1) through (13)) and that he made a spontaneous exclamation in the simplest possible form available to his consciousness at the time of the birth of the poem. Nor was this any kind of formal greeting of the sun as in some imaginary though possible society of Sun worshippers because he would have said, had he wanted to, something like:

14.   Caro sole, buona mattina!, or

15.   Buona mattina, (caro) sole!, or
16.   Sono (molto) lieto di vederti, (caro) sole!

I suggest that none of these possibilities of 'addressing the Sun' amounts to poetry, let alone good poetry. Ungaretti's original is not only good poetry, but uniquely captivating and frequently quoted poetry, poetry that has given critics and students of poetry much food for thought.

The question must, nevertheless, be answered: Why and how is anyone able to 'transform' Ungaretti's poem, or to translate it into a related Romance language, such as French, in which

17.   Je m'illumine de l'immense

is about as good a translation as one can get of this sentence *qua* sentence.

The question of why two autoglottic statements are acceptable paraphrases of one another and why two xenoglottic ones are acceptable translations is, of course, a tumultuously ancient one, and I cannot attempt to answer it here *à propos* of Ungaretti's poem. Suffice it to say, therefore, that sentences, whether in order to be autoglottically paraphrased or xenoglottically to be translated, 'carry linguistic meaning' and that this 'linguistic meaning' – a composite result of lexical meanings and grammatical meanings residing in the morphology and the syntax of the text in question – is a semantic construct. This would be the 'legally translatable' semantics of the words and their syntax with regard to one another. It is of secondary importance whether one represents this 'meaning of a sentence' according to the tree-like structures of the transformationalists, the 'sememic traces' of the stratificationalists, or the 'directed graphs' of various European functionalist schools of thought, such as the dependency-syntactitians who follow LeCerf and Tesnière. In order to be as objective about this as possible, I will give three versions of the 'legal semantics' of *M'illumino d'immenso* according to the three modes mentioned: The first will be a transformationalist-style deep-structure tree; the second a Lambian-Lockwoodian 'sememic trace', and the third a 'directed graph'. I do not claim that these are the only possible or 'the correct' versions of the representation of the meanings of these sentences; I am only trying to show alternative possibilities.

In Figure 2 the agent Np is *Io*, the transitive verb is *illuminare* (later to be inflectionally adjusted to *illumino*) and the direct object is also logically *Io* (the same *Io* as was the doer) which will be expressed by a morphological reflexivization rule in Italian orthography as *mi/m'* + *v*; in this case *m'illumino*. The last node to the right of the tree bears the label Agt./instr, which must be expressed in surface structure as *di* + *N* in Italian, and as *by* + *N* in English. Several awkward features emerge: such trees do not seem to handle elegantly the recursive nature of agents acting on themselves. Logically, *Io* is both subject (nominative) and object, rendered in the accusative as *me/m'*, but in this tradition several intermediate steps are needed in the course of the actual derivation before

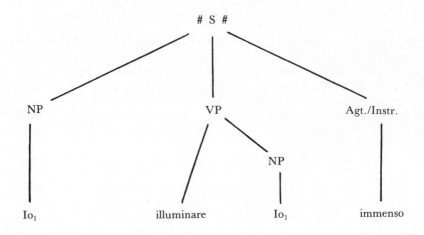

Figure 2

one reaches the sentence itself; the sentence, I might add, which was there in the first place offering the analyst the various insights he has.

The 'sememic trace' in Figure 3 indicates that the Speaker, who is the Ego, is the same Ego as the object/goal of the action; the agency of the speaker is marked for declarative in the present tense. The trace is 'neutral' in the sense that it does not favor the Ego thematically over the goal or the action. This trace, then, is best seen as the state of affairs stored in memory prior to the speaker's committing himself to any particular way of saying what is on his mind. If the sentence desired were (18) *C'est bien moi-même qui est illuminé de l'immense*, the trace would have to indicate that the identity of the Ego has been questioned by an interlocutor and that for this reason the speaker insists on (or reiterates with whatever French syntax allows) underscoring his identity as 'new information'. (For simplicity's sake, I assume that in the memory of a multilingual, the 'sememic trace' shows the same logical relationships insofar as the typologies involved permit it; heteroglottic relexicalization might already start at the sememic level.)

Directed graphs, unlike 'sememic traces' and tree-like 'deep structures' can visually represent the identity of subject and object by virtue of the closed loop visible on Figure 4, where the line starting out of *Io* goes through *fare*, and after reaching *Object* loops right back to the start, *Io*. They can be found, nevertheless, in preliminary work by Hockett[13] and in Makkai (1972a).

Both autoglottic paraphrasing and xenoglottic re-encoding (i.e., translation) proceed in an analogous manner (a fact writers and translators have

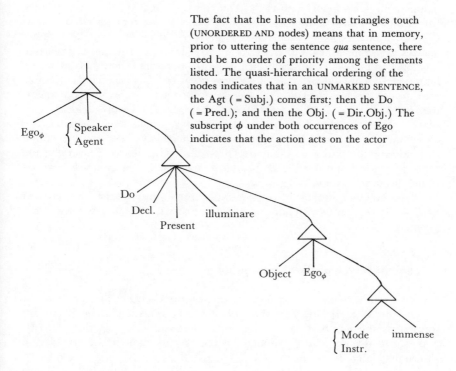

The fact that the lines under the triangles touch (UNORDERED AND nodes) means that in memory, prior to uttering the sentence *qua* sentence, there need be no order of priority among the elements listed. The quasi-hierarchical ordering of the nodes indicates that in an UNMARKED SENTENCE, the Agt (= Subj.) comes first; then the Do (= Pred.); and then the Obj. (= Dir.Obj.) The subscript φ under both occurrences of Ego indicates that the action acts on the actor

Figure 3   Quasi-stratificational 'sememic trace'

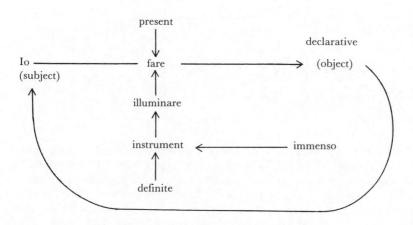

Figure 4   The sentence in 'directed graph' format

instinctively known for centuries). The semantic structure of the sentence (in whatever form, though mostly in an unconscious manner) is somehow decoded and kept in memory by the speaker-translator who, then, relexicalizes the same 'trace' either by the nearest available lexemes in the same language or by the semantically nearest corresponding lexemes of the target language. To say, then, that *M'illumino d'immenso* is properly translatable into French as *Je m'illumine de l'immense* is not an act of legally consequential prevarication. If this sentence had, for some obscure reason, ever played a part in a trial such that the sentence would have been the key to solving a mystery, a French interpreter would have been quite accurate in rendering the phrase in his native French as given above. Naturally, the same goes for English *I am illuminated by the immense*. What these translations, accurate though they may be, fail to accomplish is the poetry inherent in Ungaretti original. We must, then, turn to the original text itself and examine as carefully as possible just what holds it together as a poem.

2. The phonology of the 'Illumination'

First, let us examine the consonantal orchestration of the 'illumination'. It stands out as a striking fact that all of the consonants in the poem are formed by the lips or the alveolar ridge. /m/, /l/, /m/, /n/, /d/, /m/, /n/, and /s/, in this sequence, employ the places and manners of articulation shown in Table 1.

Table 1

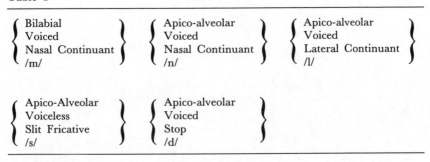

Bilabial	Apico-alveolar	Apico-alveolar
Voiced	Voiced	Voiced
Nasal Continuant	Nasal Continuant	Lateral Continuant
/m/	/n/	/l/

Apico-Alveolar	Apico-alveolar
Voiceless	Voiced
Slit Fricative	Stop
/s/	/d/

The phoneme /m/ occurs twice in *M'illumino* as a single sound, and as a geminate in *d'immenso*. One can say, then, that the 'illumination' contains four /m/-sounds. The nasal /n/ occurs once in each phonological word, as the next-to-last sound in the first line followed by the vowel /o/, and in the second word and line right after /s/, the only voiceless sound in the poem, followed by the /o/. (I will return to the significance of both lines ending in the /o/ sound when discussing the vowels.) This gives us two /n/-s which, added to the four /m/-s, gives us six instances of nasal resonance in the 'illumination'. The apical lateral continuant /l/, geminated into /ll/, occurs in the first word and is immediately followed by the stressed /u/, which also functions as the syllabic peak of the first line's 'choriambic' structure. The related voiced /d/ (the only stop in the poem), formed by the tip of the tongue at the alveolar ridge, introduces the second word-line of the poem *d'immenso*. The consonantal structure of the 'illumination', then, rests on the features Cl(osed), Lab(ial), Alv(eolar), Na(sal), Lat(eral), Fric(ative), and Unv(oiced).

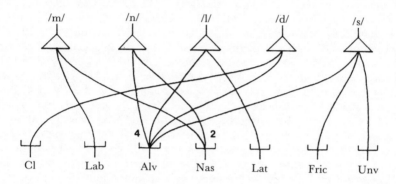

Figure 5

Viewing the phonemes /m/, /n/, /l/, /d/, and /s/ as complexes of these features, we can draw a simplified relational network diagram that shows which of the features are the most frequently employed in the formation of these sounds. Alveolarity leads with four lines; Nasality follows by two; the others (each) occur once. A frequency hierarchy of the consonantal features of the poem, then, might look as follows:

Alv 4	Cl 1	Lat 1	Unv 1
Nas 2	Lab 1	Fric 1	

This exercise in simplified statistics bears out one's intuitive feelings about the 'illumination' as being a heavily front-consonantal poem. There are no /k/, /g/, or other back sounds of any sort. There is also quite a dearth of stops in the entire poem, /d/ a voiced apical, being the only one. The entire consonantal sequence /m ll m n d mm ns/ gives the definite impression of effortlessness and an easy, airy floating. As far as this sequence's location in the human mouth, it is concentrated in the front region.

It has been argued successfully by many phonosymbolists, but perhaps most convincingly by Wescott (1980) and Iván Fónagy ((1976) and 1983),[14] that the human mouth can be viewed as a micro-universe in which sounds iconically represent events taking place in the outside world. I do not imply a teleological *Weltanschauung* by this and do not wish to take sides in the essentially mechanism–mentalism controversy.[15] What I state here is objectively demonstratable: there are no stops and no back consonants in the 'illumination'. The feature of 'back-ness', as we shall see presently, is, however, realized by the vocalism of the poem.

Anthropological linguists (e.g. Wescott (1980)) have proven with great success, that iconicity and sound-symbolism are objectively existing phenomenon, indeed on a universal scale. Wescott's investigations show striking similarities between Bini, a west African language, and English, a Germanic language with a large Romance lexical layer on top of it.

Before we integrate the picture presented by the consonantal orchestration of the poem with its vocalic orchestration, it is necessary to take a separate look at the vowels. We are dealing with the 'classical vowel triangle' minus its least marked low central member, the /a/ phoneme, which is strikingly absent from the 'illumination'. By observing the absence of /a/ in the poem, we have, therefore, also said that 'low-centrality' in vocalic terms is absent from the poem. It is as if the consonants, all of which are front ones, were entering a cave without falling down in the middle of the pit inside. The vowels represented, then, are /i/, /e/, /o/, and /u/, in order of frontness to backness and openness and closedness. The features H(igh), F(ront), B(ack), M(id), L(ow) and R(ounded) may be observed here and represented in a relational network diagram (Figure 6).

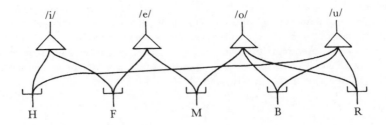

Figure 6

The spoken sequence is /i/, /u/, /i/, /o/ ——— /i/, /e/, /o/. /i/ is used three times, /o/ twice, creating a quasi-rhyme.

The feature-diagram (Figure 6) of the participant phonemes /i/, /e/, /o/, and /u/ shows that the formants High, Front, Mid, Back, and Rounded occur in equal distribution (all five of them are used twice to make connections to the phonemes). The phonemes themselves are realized, in turn, by

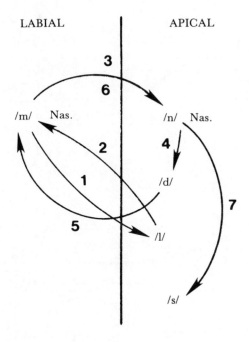

1 = *m* to *l* *M'il* = reciprocal of 2
2 = *l* to *m* *lu(+m)* = reciprocal of 1
3 = *m* to *n* *mi(+n)* = anticipation of 6
4 = *n* to *d* *no(+d)* = nasal to only STOP
5 = *d* to *m* *dim* = ONLY STOP to nasal
6 = *m* to *n* *men* = repetition of 3
7 = *n* to *s* *(+n)so* = nasal to ONLY UNVOICED

Figure 7 Consonantal movement in the 'illumination' between 4 instances of bilabial nasal /m/ and the apical phonemes of the poem

the two features /i/, and /e/, and the three /o/, and /u/, these last two being also Rounded while /i/ and /e/ are not.

What we now need to do is visualize both the consonants and the vowels of the poem in MOTION, that is, the way they make the articulatory organs move back and forth inside the human mouth.

The most obvious consonantal movement occurs between Labiality and Apicality (Figure 7).

If we envisage the geminate /ll/ of the 'illumination' as occupying a

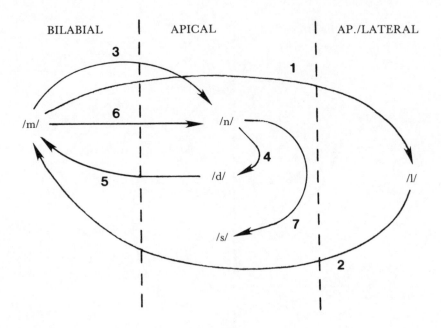

Figure 8

position farther back in the mouth due to the anticipation of the high back vowel /u/, we can place LATERAL into a third column beside Bilabial and Apical as in Figure 8.

In terms of visual progression following the orthography, this looks as in Figure 9.

There are exactly seven CONSONANTAL PASSES performed by the articulators during the speaking out loud of the poem; they are numbered 1 through 7 on Figure 9 and repeated in the sequential spell-out below. The first pass goes from /m/ to /ll/ in the syllable *M'il*; the second pass takes us back from /ll/ to /m/ in the syllable *lum-*; the third one is between the two nasals /m/ and /n/ in *-min-*; the fourth pass is between the related alveolars /n/ and /d/ in *-no d'*. In the fifth pass we move back to the frontal bilabial /m/ in *no d'im*; the sixth pass leads from the nasal /m/ to /n/ again in *men*, and the last movement, the seventh, lands us on the only voiceless phoneme of the entire poem, the final voiceless alveolar slit fricative /s/, which is followed by the second and closing /o/ of the poem.

It would be worthwhile to line up the syllables in terms of frontness and backness in order to see if there is perhaps a symmetry at work here. It turns out that out of the poem's seven syllables, three *mil-*, *mi-*, and *dim-*, are indeed riding the front high vowel /i/; whereas *lu-*, *no-*, and *so-* are back vowel-dominated syllables creating an even 50–50 per cent distribution

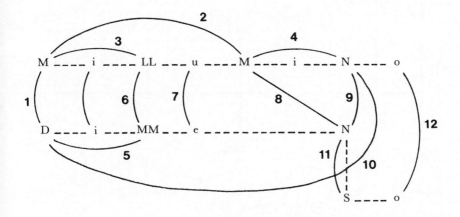

1 = *m* to *d*, voiced frontal C̲ onsets
2 = *m* to *m*, *bridge of labiality/nasality*
3 = *m* to *ll*, *voiced C onset to geminate ll̲*
4 = *m* to *n*, *bridge of nasality*
5 = *d* to *mm*, *voiced C onset to geminate m̲m̲*
6 = *ll* to *mm*, *3rd place bridge between geminate pairs ll̲ and m̲m̲*
7 = *u* to *e*, *front to back contrast before onset of coda cluster*
8 = *m* to *n*, *bridge of nasality*
9 = *n* to *n*, *bridge of nasality/alveolarity*
10 = *n* to *d*, *bridge of alveolarity*
11 = *n* to *s*, *alveolarity (−Voice)*
12 = *o* to *o*, *final coda and quasi-rhyme*

Figure 9

between front and back vowels. Even more striking is the fact that only
the vowel /e/, which is formed in the general frontal region but lower down
and also a bit farther back, can be seen as the mid-point here. The result
of this line-up produces a seven-pronged structure that looks very much
like the Menorah of Judaism, an ancient symbol for 'equilibrium' or
'equality'.

It could be objected, however, that this quasi-Menorah is not a true
sequential representation of Ungaretti's vowels but merely shows the
numerical distribution of frontness and backness in the poem. Furthermore, the status of /e/ could be questioned as an honorary Central vowel
by virtue of its mid-height position. As we have observed earlier, however,
the vowel /a/, the least marked in classical vowel triangles, is strikingly
absent from the poem. This exaggeration is, therefore, excusable since the

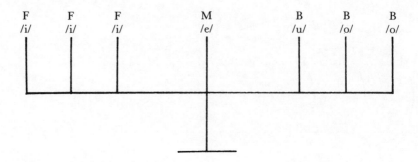

Figure 10

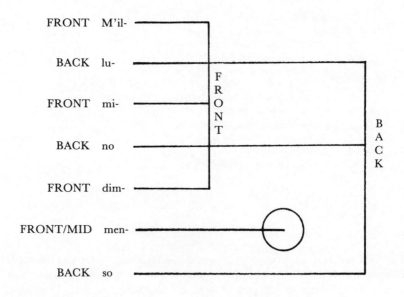

Figure 11

seven syllables do, in fact, naturally divide into three front vowels and three back vowels with the /e/, both by articulatory position and by frequency in the poem, occupying a quasi-neutral position. Another way to represent the syllables is shown in Figure 12.

The temporal sequencing of the motions is Front to Back; Front to Back;

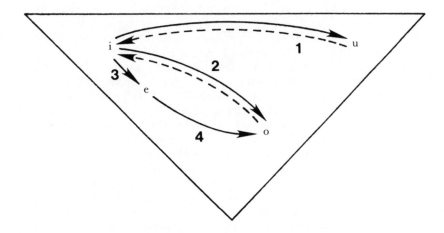

1 = *M'illu*
2 = *mino*
3 = *d'im*
4 = *menso*

Notice that there is no repositioning required between 3 and 4 as the tongue can go on directly from *e* to *o*, coming down to *e* from *i*.

Figure 12   'Vocalic passes' in the 'illumination'. The solid lines indicate actual articulation, the dashed lines indicate the respositioning of the tongue for the next pass.

Front to Front/Mid, and to the final resting point, Back. Let us imagine a person exploring a cave from the entrance to the darkest place in the back. The exploration is conducted in seven steps, sweeping the area of the cave in seven motions, FRONT, BACK, FRONT, BACK, FRONT, FRONT/MID, BACK. If we visualize FRONT as 'light' or as 'beginning' and BACK as 'darkness' or the 'end' (and these are not very far-fetched); we begin to witness a ceremonial dance taking place inside the human orifice. The dance is iconically performed by virtue of its unique choreography, the very act of illumination itself, insofar as true 'illumination' can only occur by having lived through both periods of darkness and light such that periodic movements between the two extremes come to a resting point in an ENLIGHTENED DARKNESS, that is, a voluntarily accepted and unfeared death of the ego.

It is noteworthy here that the only consonant cluster of the 'illumination' occurs just before the second, and final, /o/; this is the cluster /ns/, the *pièce de résistance*.

As I have remarked before, /ns/ in standard literary Italian based on Tuscan, is a genuine voiced apical nasal followed by an unvoiced alveolar slit fricative. I have also mentioned that in the dialect of Rome this may

become /-nts-/ and that in Naples and farther south it may show up as
/-ndz-/ or even, though rarely, as /-nz-/. There is reason to believe that
Ungaretti did not speak with a southern accent. He was already in his
early twenties when he first set foot in Europe on his way to France from
Alexandria. His French was native-like; he wrote a great deal of poetry in
French as well. The French word *l'immense* has a voiceless /s/ in it, and
so there is reason to believe that Ungaretti's own dialect also contained a
voiceless /s/. The phonemes /n/ and /s/, however, despite their difference
in voicing, are at least partially homorganic as the apex of the tongue and
the alveolar ridge are involved in the production of both. The transition
from the voice /n/ to the voiceless /s/, therefore, does not involve a great
deal of distance to be travelled by the tongue; rather it is the onset of the
fricativity of the /s/ and the simultaneous turning off of the voice that
characterizes this cluster. The cluster, as was pointed out before, leads us
into the final quasi-rhyme, /o/, and functions, in this light, as a coda
before it. Voicelessness and fricativity are, furthermore, familiar sounds in
the human death-rattle and thus /-ns-/, not only due to the fact that it is
the only cluster in the poem and the only voiceless phoneme, but also
because of the strategic position it occupies, can be seen as the 'last breath
of life'.

The first syllable, *M'il-* is, by contrast, the positive, upbeat, optimistic
thesis; the first burst of air in the human lung. Perhaps it symbolizes birth
itself. It is immediately followed by its antithesis, the syllable *lu-* which
takes us back into the farthest recesses of the oral cavity. This motion itself
is like breathing in and breathing out – despite the fact, of course, that
during normal speech one talks on expelled air in terms of physiology. The
third syllable *mi-* takes us back to 'being born' and breathing in; its
antithesis, *no-* takes us back again in the oral cavity but at a lower height
of elevation than the /u/ of the second syllable. It is as if climbing a mountain for the second time were more tiring than doing it for the first time.
Similarly, if you are born twice, the second birth may be followed by some
fatigue and lethargia. When we go back to /i/ for the third time in *d'im-*,
we have reached middle age and passed adulthood. Our vital energy is
less; the running in and out of the cave is more tiresome. Nor does the
next syllable take us right back into the dark side of the cave, we drop
from /i/ to /e/ in the syllable *men-* which sets the stage for old age and
death, through the cluster -ns- and alighting on the second and final /o/.

Let us now take a look at the combined vocalic and consonantal
orchestration of the 'illumination' (Figure 13).

The syllables also form an unusual ARTICULATORY PROGRESSION
seldom, if ever, encountered in other types of poetry. It merits special
attention. It may be represented as in Figure 14.

This striking feature-perpetuation from syllable to syllable gives the
'illumination' yet another unique textual homogeneity which is neither
grammatical (i.e. morphological or syntactic) nor stylistic-semantic, but
exclusively phonological. The phenomenon deserves to be given its own
name. I suggest PHONOTEXTUALITY or PHONOTEXTUAL COHESION.

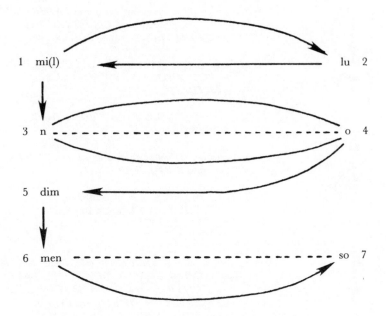

The numbers indicate the syllable in question (there being 7 in the entire poem) and the arrows indicate the front-back-front-back-front-front/mid-back progressions. Regarding the significance of the number 7, see the last section of this paper dealing with hermeticism in general.

Figure 13

Laterality, nasality, and alveolarity stand out as the most frequently used bridges from one syllable to the next; while the front–back and back–front contrast is constantly present in the vocalic orchestration, with the sole exception of syllables 5 to 6 where we have the lowering of /i/ to /e/ instead.

It is no exaggeration to state, I believe, that the more one looks at Figure 14 the more evident it becomes that not one iota of Ungaretti's poem could be changed; nor could this unique line-up of phonological events be due to accident. Poets are, of course, seldom, if ever, aware of what they actually do when composing in an inspired state of consciousness. The question, therefore, of whether Ungaretti knew what he was doing or not, is both irrelevant and unanswerable. The FACTS ARE that these progressions are OBJECTIVELY PRESENT in the poem.

Segmental phonemes, representable by actual elements of the Roman alphabet and certain modifications thereof, never occur without stress and pitch in live speech. We must, therefore, lay Figure 14 on its side and add

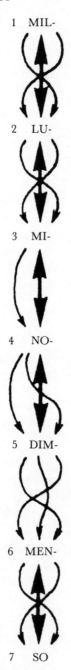

1   MIL-

2   LU-

3   MI-

4   NO-

5   DIM-

6   MEN-

7   SO

1–2: *l* to *l*: preservation of geminate *LATERALITY*;
m to *u*: preservation of *LABIALITY*; *i* to *u*: first
instance of *FRONT-BACK CONTRAST*;

2–3: *u* to *m*: LABIALITY; *l* to *i*: *APICO-LATERALITY*
to *FRONTNESS*; *u–i*: *BACK-FRONT
CONTRAST*;

3–4: *m* to *n*: *NASALITY*; *i–o*: *FRONT-BACK
CONTRAST*;

4–5: *n* to *m*: *NASALITY*; *n* to *d*: *ALVEOLARITY*;
o–i: *BACK-FRONT CONTRAST*;

5–6: *m* to *m*: preservation of geminate
LABIALITY/NASALITY; *d* to *n*:
ALVEOLARITY; *i–e*: *HIGH-to-MID
LOWERING*;

6–7: *n* to *s*: *FINAL INSTANCE OF PRESERVATION
OF ALVEOLARITY + DEVOICING; NASAL* to
FRICATIVE; m to *o*: *FINAL INSTANCE OF
PRESERVATION OF LABIALITY*; *e* to *o*:
*FINAL INSTANCE OF FRONT-BACK
CONTRAST*. /*s*/ is the only voiceless phoneme
in the poem; the last /*o*/ functions as quasi-
rhyme and coda.

Figure 14 A visual representation of the articulatory progressions, or PHONO-
TEXTUALITY of the '*Illumination*'

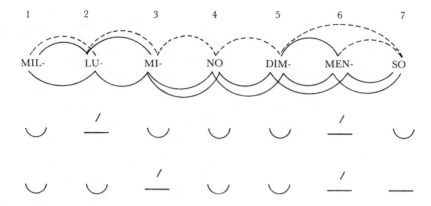

Figure 15 Combined representation of the PHONOTEXTUAL COHESION of Ungaretti's '*Illumination*' with two possible stress patterns, the standard (stress on the /u/), and the non-standard, (stress on the /i/). The solid lines correspond to the arrow-bearing lines of Fig. 14 (feature perpetuation). The dashed lines show the vocalic contrasts.

the metrics to it underneath. The emerging picture is seen in Figure 15.

3. Towards an integrated description of the 'Illumination'

In the foregoing sections of this chapter I have attempted to outline relevant portions of the poem's deep syntax, its surface syntax, its syllable structure, and its phonology at some length, since I believe that the meaning of the poem is intrinsically tied to its phonology.

The question arises as to whether some kind of an integrated description might be possible via the relational network model of the description of language and texts. Figure 16 attempts to provide such a simplified description. The slanted double line separating the 'semantics and semology' from the 'lexology and morphology', i.e. the grammar, may be seen as the demarcation line between the content and the form of this two-word poem. The upper portion of the diagram is, essentially, a repetition of Figure 3 which characterized as 'quasi-stratificational' and regarded as functionally equivalent to the directed graph and, *mutatis mutandis*, the 'deep structure tree' of transformational grammar. The basic difference between Figure 3 and the upper portion of Figure 16 is that the sememes ILLUMINATE, EGO, and IMMENSE are encircled. Inside each circle there is a 'relay switch', drawn as a diamond, that leads you to the various

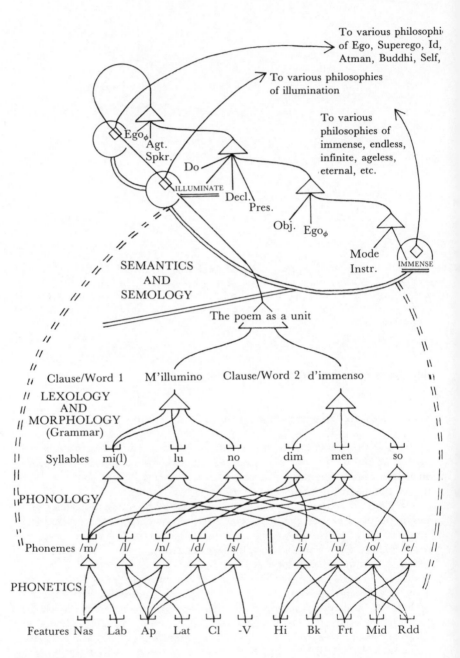

Figure 16

philosophies involved. Thus, the arrowed line leading up and away from EGO leads one to the various philosophies of the Ego: the Super-ego, the Id, the Atman, the Buddha, the Self, and other notions connected with the 'Ego'. The sememe /illuminate/ is surrounded by a power-box with a diamond-relay in it that leads the reader to the various philosophies one can associate with 'illumination'. Enlightenment, renaissance, scientific advancement, spiritual enlightenment, mystical experiences (such as seeing of an Angel of God) may be involved. For others, enlightenment may simply mean an increase in materialistic knowledge and a loss of fearful superstitions. The arrow leading out of the sememe IMMENSE leads the materialistic non-believer to ideas of mathematical infinity, astronomy, and the like. The religiously or mystically inclined may easily move to concepts such as God, creation, endlessness (in a spiritual sense), the eternal, etc. As we shall see presently, it is these various possibilities (some of them contradictory), that make the job of the analyst of hermetic poetry so uncommonly difficult.

Underneath the double slanted line there is a large ordered AND-triangle, the poem as a whole, consisting of two clauses expressed as two words in Italian. (This is an over-simplification, to be sure. On an intermediate level *Mi illumino di immenso* could be shown as four words which then coalesce into two phonological words.) Treating the two constituents as clause-words enables one to move to the syllabic level, the last units in the morphology, since syllables coincide with morphemic signs (cf. Lamb 1966, Lockwood 1972). The syllables are realized by the phonemes /m/, /l/, /n/, /d/, /s/, /i/, /u/, /o/, and /e/ which, in turn, are realized by the features on the bottom of Figure 16, which leads us into the area of phonetics.

The heavy double curved lines uniting the circles of EGO, ILLUMINATE, and IMMENSE leading down on the sides in similar double curved lines to the phonology indicate that the notions of EGO (*Mi-* in the accusative form of Italian *Io*), 'illuminare' and 'immenso' are also connected to the sound system. This PHONAESTHEMIC LINK is a feature of SIMULTANEITY that runs through the poem. This diagram cannot show the consonantal and the vocalic motions or the phonotextual cohesion as discussed in section 2 of this chapter; it merely serves as a reminder that the meanings of these philosophically far-ranging concepts are also somehow realized by the phonology of the expressive medium of the Italian language.

Having attempted such an 'integrated description' of the poem, I still have said nothing about what 'illumination' and 'immensity' mean; even less of how a person may illuminate himself through the immensity, or by means of it. In order to arrive at some kind of an understanding of what the 'Illumination' is really all about, we must take leave of semology, lexology, syntax, morphology, syllables, phonemes, and phonetic features and literally transcend the poem in its tangible manifestations. Description and analysis may come close to one another, yet neither analysis nor description can even approximate *explication de texte*. Paradoxically, the best *explication de texte* is nevertheless the kind that does take description and accurately detailed analysis into consideration.

The attempted 'integrated description', then, must be understood in this light. It is merely an integrated description FROM THE LINGUISTIC POINT OF VIEW which must now yield its place to other concerns.

4. What was Ungaretti trying to say?

The question may be raised why and how seven syllables amount to 'poetry'. In North American culture, in particular, one expects a longer piece of writing with recurrent syllabification, say, iambic pentameter, and a certain rhyming scheme; if one builds a mental bridge from Edgar Allan Poe through Walt Whitman to Ezra Pound and Robert Lowell, it is easy to see why a short sequence of seven syllables would strike one as an odd candidate for a real poem.

Not so in the Far East. The Japanese *haiku*, a well-established and much appreciated form of poetry consisting of three lines of five, seven and again five syllables, uses devices similar to what we find in Ungaretti's 'Illumination'. A short poem, such as the one under discussion here, achieves the status of poetry not because of a recurrent stanza-structure, the orchestration of rhymes, and the plot of a story told (compare Kipling's popular *Gunga Din* as a poem that has those features), but by virtue of a strikingly original image, or an unusually highly condensed metaphor that challenges the imagination of the reader and the would-be critic. Bearing this in mind, it stands to reason to suspect that Ungaretti was, first and foremost, trying to verbalize an inner experience that happened to him one early morning in 1916. His lexico-grammar, his semantics, and his phonology, preserved as printed text, tell us that the 'immense', whatever it may be, 'illuminated' him, whatever illumination means to people who experience it. The use of the present tense suggests that this may have been a habitual experience.

There is little question about deliberate plotting on Ungaretti's part: it is hard, indeed impossible, to imagine the author sitting down with a handbook on articulatory phonetics trying cleverly to plot the phonotextual progressions in the poem as outlined in Figures 14 and 15. This is an important observation, since part of the meaning of the poem – perhaps the major part if it – is directly expressed by the unique phonological pattern. An inspired state of consciousness which can be visual or auditory and is, therefore, most likely a 'right hemispheric phenomenon' in the sense of Julian Jaynes (1976), is not simultaneously a logically premeditated scheming and planning state of consciousness. Whether the poem was written by Verlaine and has words such as *les sanglots longs des violons de l'automne blessent mon coeur d'une longeur monotone*, or by Goethe who, according to generations of studious admirers, depicted in sound the very act of returning to nature and the primordial restfulness in the words of the Wanderer's Night Song . . . *kaum einen Hauch, warte nur, balde ruhest du auch*, the poem, if genuinely successful, surprises the author as much as his audience. When Robert Frost wrote his famous *Stopping by Woods on a*

Snowy Evening, he had no idea that in the fourth stanza he would break the pattern established in the first three and repeat the last line giving the words *but I have promises to keep / And miles to go before I sleep, / And miles to go, before I sleep* that strange quality that makes this poem so memorable. The repetition of 'And miles to go before I sleep' causes a subtle shift in meaning: whereas the first time around, it literally means 'a distance to be covered before turning in for the night', in the second instance the miles become metaphoric expressions of tasks unfinished in life and 'before I sleep' alludes to personal death. It makes sense that such *trouvailles* are not attainable through premeditation. It makes the poet a more understandable and therefore more likeable individual. We see him as an experimenter, someone quite like ourselves. Once the words that carry the unusual effect are somehow written down, the analyst's conscious and educated mind (with its analytical tendencies well anchored in the computer-like left hemisphere) can take over and the analyst is free to find any and all correspondences – as long as they are objectively there. The phonotextual progressions (as well as the other phonological effects) described in Figures 14 and 15 are not our fabrication: these facts yield themselves freely and without coercion out of the text as found by the reader who approaches the material without any preconceived notions. Ungaretti, then, was both 'conscious' of what he was doing and 'unconscious'; conscious in the inspired but not very self-analytical sense and probably rather unconscious in the philological, feature-counting sense that I have tried to reproduce (especially in Figures 14 and 15).

Ungaretti's larger meaning relating to the concepts of 'illumination', 'ego' (the self), and 'immense' can perhaps best be approached by comparing this poem to another famous four-word mind-bender of his, the oft-quoted:

Cerco un paese
innocente

written roughly at the same time and also originally published in *Allegria*. Whatever the translation, *Je cherche un pays innocent, ich suche ein unschuldiges Land*, or *I am seeking an innocent country*, the mind's eye cannot help but see a Diogenes-like character who, with a torch lit in broad daylight, has set out 'in search of reason' in the streets of Athens both as a shocker to his fellow citizens and as a powerful means of passing judgment on contemporary affairs. Was Ungaretti trying consciously to imitate Diogenes in *Cerco on paese innocente*? It hardly matters. It is altogether likely, of course, that the brilliant young man, born and raised in Alexandria, should have known of the founder of 'cynicism'; the one who lived like a dog. If one says *I am looking for an innocent country* one, wittingly or unwittingly, says simultaneously several things, added to which must be the fact that some of the things said are said by unsaying certain other things. This is, in a sense, similar to the double-bind revealed in trick questions of the sort *When did you stop beating your wife?*. The fact that I am (note the present tense) looking for an innocent country implies that the search continues; that is, I have not found the object of my search; there may very well never be an end to it. If I imply this, I also imply that there is no such thing as an innocent country, ergo all countries are guilty of something or other. What they are guilty of, imperialism, racism, Marxism, Fascism (the list is endless), hardly matters; what matters is that the reader-hearer is left to guess if Ungaretti actually meant that there can be no such thing as an innocent country, and what the possible crimes that the countries are guilty of may be. The poet says overtly only a very few things which, by logical implication, bring attention to the lack of something which the poet suggests ought to exist, but does not. A huge and potentially endless chain-reaction of thought is thus provoked by minimal means bordering on being taciturn. It is interesting to note here that some of Ungaretti's critics consider *M'illumino d'immenso* and *Cerco on paese innocente* to be his flashy material from the days of his youth (Francesco Flora (1936), pp. 104–5 *et passim*).

But in order to get beyond this point, we must say a word about the hermetic tradition and how some understanding of it might help the explication of texts as we *qua* linguists-philologists conceive of this art.

5. The Hermetic Tradition

According to William Rose Benét's *The Reader's Encyclopedia* (Vol. I:461):

> Hermeticism is a name applied to a 20th-century school of Italian poets. It was first used by the noted Italian critic Francesco Flora to characterize the difficult, 'occult-meaning' verse of a group of Italian poets headed by Salvatore Quasimodo, Giuseppe Ungaretti, and Eugenio Montale. The verse of these poets originated in the French symbolist school of 'pure poetry' as practiced by Mallarmé and Valéry. Decadent poetry entered Italy through the CREPUSCOLARI poets (q.v.), and it is from them that 'the hermetics' have evolved.
>
> Typical of hermetic poetry is a deliberate rarefaction of poetic language; this is the result of the poet's attempt to verbalize a personal impression that seems to transcend common experience in a language that conveys it with the maximum fidelity and immediacy. The hermetics reject rhetoric and the stylistic mechanics of formal traditional poetry. They adopt instead a vocabulary that is extremely personal, idiosyncratic, and, to the uninitiated, abstruse and often meaningless.

As the linguist-philologist draws back one curtain, he finds three new ones to draw back if some of the newly found terms used in the definition are to make any sense. Let us suppose, for the sake of argument, that we have entered this investigation as 'truly modern linguists', that is, people who are basically naive about literature and literary movements. Hermetic writings, it turns out, go back to the Egyptian god Thoth, whose name in Greek was Hermes Trismegistos, i.e., the thrice-great Hermes, as used by

Neo-Platonians. This gives us pause, of course. Does a modern linguist need to know who the Neo-Platonians were? The original Plato, for that matter? Did not all philosophy, that is all philosophy worth knowing about, start with Descartes? I can easily identify a few dozen dashing matadors of the US linguistics scene who would, and indeed have, as has Newmayer (1980), claim that '. . . Linguistics learned more during the past 25 years than during the past 2,500.'

But let us assume that the researcher whose steps I am reconstructing here is genuinely curious and has an open mind. He goes on reading:

> The name was also applied, from about the third century, to the supposed author of a body of alchemic, occult, and mystical writings. Until the 17th century he was thought to have been a contemporary of Moses, and his writings were considered Christian and almost as sacred as the Bible. Actually the Hermetic books were composed by a group of teachers who lived in Alexandria in the first two centuries B.C. or A.D.; they were a composite of Egyptian magical writings, Jewish mysticism, and Platonism. The 20th century is seeing a revival of interest in the Hermetic writings, notably in the work of the French symbolists and the occult system of William Butler Yeats.

At this, the open mind of our imaginary young researcher rebounds and boggles. Has not he just learned that Ungaretti was born in Alexandria of Italian expatriate parents? Is he not one of the standard-bearers of hermeticism according to Francesco Flora? Was it an accident that the original Hermes Trismegistos cult started from the very same city? Is it an accident that the 20th century produced Yeats in Ireland and the French symbolists in France, the same symbolists who inspired the Italian Crepuscolari, who, in turn, were the intellectual ancestors of the hermeticists? How is the grammarian going to handle all of this information in his scheme of 'underlying beliefs' and 'logical presuppositions'? Should one write symbols of logic, upside down capital E-s, 'implies' and 'entails' signs borrowed from set-theory? Is there somewhere in the world out there an ill-defined notion belonging to Lakoff's 'fuzzy grammar' that has a nebulous entity in it identifiable as the ongoing transformation that takes Plato as the deep structure, the Neo-Platonists as the infra-structure, the Hermes Trismegistos cult as the shallow deep structure, French symbolism as the surface structure, and Italian hermeticism as the morphology at hand? What prevents one from weaving a quixotic yarn positing such steps in cognitive development, well intended, of course, to explicate Ungaretti's seven syllables? Or should one write up a barn-door's worth of stratificationalist relational networks building this information into the hyper-semology? (I believe that if it belongs anywhere at all, it perhaps belongs there, but for practical reasons linguists need not go further than is hinted at by the arrows at the top of Figure 16.) Just how much of an Alexandrian-based, conscious 'hermeticist' was Ungaretti? Is it an accident that the *Illumination* has exactly seven syllables, like the Jewish *Menorah* (Figure 10)? Is it an accident that the words, save this excursus into intellectual history, say less about the poem than its phonology? But let us follow the 'research steps' of our *Fachbarbar* colleague who has been rendered sufficiently aware of Hermes Trismegistos and why Francesco Flora chose him to designate Ungaretti's group by. He now turns to the entry *I Crepuscolari* (Benét, Vol. I:235) and reads:

> *Ital.*, 'the twilight poets,' a name coined by the critic G.A. Borgese. A group of Italian poets of the early 20th century whose work is notable for its use of musical and mood-conveying language and its general tone of despondency. Their attitude represents a reaction to the content-poetry and rhetorical style of Carducci and D'Annunzio, favoring instead the unadorned language and homely themes of Pascoli. An affinity existed with the French symbolists, Valéry, Rimbaud, and Mallarmé. Guido Gozzano was the most competent exponent of the movement.

Our young but diligent researcher is really in trouble now. He is beginning to wonder if he should perhaps have gone into comparative literature instead of linguistics. How much should he know about Carducci and D'Annunzio? Gozzano? Pascoli? Should he also have taken French Literature of the *fin de siècle* and the second half of the 19th century? Should he wonder why, for instance, Benét omitted Baudelaire from his list of relevant French poets? Is hermeticism a conscious, deliberate adherence to the philosophy and poetic practice of a group which consciously identifies with all of the French and Italian poets mentioned starting the intellectual lineage with the God Hermes of actual Greek mythology, shifting the emphasis to Thoth in Alexandria, and then to the Neo-Platonists? Or is it perhaps enough to observe the fact that some poets prefer to give their audience pretty riddles rather than elaborate harangues with political overtones?

While some of these observations are obviously rhetorical questions used here in an attempt to bring home the fact that modern linguists will, for better or for worse, be forced to re-embrace classical philology in the best sense of the term, they are also real and tantalizing questions since literary scholarship, as far as one can tell, has not attempted the kind of detailed linguistic analysis of poetry as given in the earlier parts of this chapter concerning Ungaretti's seven famous syllables. One could, perhaps, then settle for a compromise solution such as the following: just as we do not search in vain for insight into what was actually present in Ungaretti's consciousness when he produced the *Illumination*'s phonocontextual sequences, neither will we here seek an answer to the question of whether he could have passed an examination on Plato and Neo-Platonic philosophy or not, no matter how likely it may have been that he was knowledgeable in these areas. We shall satisfy ourselves with the observation that IN TERMS OF POETIC PERSONALITY TYPES, Ungaretti was a hermeticist. The ability to identify an author as a 'hermeticist' can, in fact, be on synchronic evidence alone, even if this evidence must, of necessity, be more negative than positive. Seen in this light, a 'hermeticist' is the poet who BEGS SEVERAL QUESTIONS IN ONE BRIEF STATEMENT thereby unleashing an avalanche of possible free-associations as well as associations depending on the reader–hearer's specific education relevant to the topic at hand. This begging of questions is brought about by making statements that are, taken by themselves, vacuous or somehow intangible. *Cerco on paese innocente* begs the question of why he cannot find one; it also begs the question of what all the countries he has found are guilty of. In terms of specific education, it begs the question of whether Ungaretti knew of Diogenes or whether the allusion to the ancient Greek was deliberate or not. By virtue of being anchored in historical time around World War I, *Cerco on paese innocente* begs the question of whether this was a disguised pacifist statement, or whether Ungaretti's search for innocence would also have continued had there been no war, thus referring to a quest for a transcendental innocence of a pre-Adamic, paradisiacal state? In *M'illumino d'immenso* Ungaretti leads his audience down the primrose path again showing vistas by hinting at them rather by telling us what we have just been shown. On the lowest possible level of interpretations, remaining entirely on the mundane–physical level of sensory perception, we could believe that he is describing the sunrise as perceived from a fox-hole during World War I after a sleepless night full of anguish. Self-illumination could simply equal inundation by sunlight and thus the immense could be the sun itself around which we revolve, as the physical source and sustenance of our material existence. But having said this, one becomes aware of the lack of interest of such an obvious interpretation. The sunrise does not go away thereby, rather it becomes the hole in the wall through which we may peek at the broader vistas beyond. A flight in space, more easily imagined in the wake of television pictures reaching us in July of 1969 on the Moon, and the resultant expansion of human consciousness may come to mind as experiences standing behind 'illumination' and the 'immense'. The modern television industry has achieved some remarkable effects in this regard: we have been shown as one of many planets in one of many possible solar systems, and this insight leads to modesty and a desire for peace. We are but one possible, not too large 'flying saucer'; spoiling or exploding our one vehicle would be the ultimate Tragedy of Man. Was Ungaretti even remotely aware that there is a famous play, cast in a series of visions entitled *The Tragedy of Man*, written by Imre Madách in the 1880s? Could he have heard of Madách, referred to by his countrymen as the 'Hungarian Goethe', was the first writer in Europe to describe a flight in space? Or, to go one step further, was Ungaretti joking when he told Hungarian poet Gyula Illyés that his name meant 'from the place of those little Hungarians'? (Illyés told an interviewer in the Fall of 1971 that he teased Ungaretti about his name. *Ungharese*, *Ungheria*, etc., do refer to Hungary, and so, according to Paul Tabori (to whom Illyés gave the interview), Ungaretti admitted that a small Hungarian colony existed near Venice going back to the Tartar invasion of 1242, as a result of which a small colony of settlers from Hungary remained in the northern outskirts of Venice. They forgot the Hungarian language but did not mind bearing the name that meant 'those little Hungarians' i.e. *i ungaretti*. I was present in Ireland, Dun Loaghaire in September of 1971, when Illyés recounted the story to Paul Tabori who later wrote it up in connection with the International P.E.N. Club meeting held there that year.) Note that there is nothing 'pessimistic' about *M'illumino d'immenso*. It is, in fact, an optimistic and outgoing poem, comparable in emotional overtones to nomadic hunters chasing elk into the sunset. The Hungarian 'national temperament' is said to be 'Sagittarian' in nature, while oriental, or at least Near-Eastern in its inspiration. Could there be such a thing as an EXTROVERTED HERMETICISM as opposed to an anguished, introverted kind? Even in *Cerco on paese innocente* we feel a touch of tenaciousness, the presence of a will that has not yet given up that search. How wrong would one be if one attempted to formulate a hypothesis of the joint Hungarian–Egyptian underpinnings of a special brand of hermeticism that could only be found in the poetry of Ungaretti, descendant of 'those little Hungarians', who, by the vicissitudes of immigration, was born in Alexandria, Egypt of Italian parents?

One of the most important elements of *M'illumino d'immenso* is the declarative mode of the verb *illuminare* with *mi* as both its subject and its object. In philosophical terms, the human self, the higher Ego, is at work in order to bring about the act of illumination. A pidgin-English morphological rendering would bring this out as *myself-illuminate-I of the immense*, an unattractive but faithful funny-mirror rendition of the original that I deliberately omitted from the possible English translations at the beginning. The Italian *m-illumin-o* uses *m* for the accusative morpheme of *io* and the *o* at the end of the verb signalling the first person singular. Symbolically, then, EGO-ILLUMINATE-EGO is what we have here, or in a pidgin Latin closer to what we recognize as correct, *Ego illuminate me*. (The classical Latin would probably say *Ego me illumino*, though other rethematicizations would also be possible.) What interests us now, from the philosophical perspective is, that the Ego that does the illuminating, and the Ego that receives it, cannot be the same, even if existentially they are, paradoxically, both the source and the target. An Ego that is a shedder of light, and Ego that is the recipient of such illumination may be existentially the same, but they must surely represent TWO DIFFERENT STATES of that Ego's inner evolution. The first Ego takes the step into the sunlight, the second Ego arrives in the desired state of illumination. The first, in other words, is the active, mundane, personal Ego, and the second is the contemplative, higher, spiritual Ego, or the Sacred Self, the Atman of the Vedic tradition. The Ego undergoes an upgrading, an *éducation sentimentale*, as it were, and the scale by which it grows, or the terrain on which it runs out this course of self-growth, is the 'immense'. We are now ready to translate *M'illumino d'immenso* from Tellurian into Interstellar: 'My personal self becomes a second, divine, sacred Self, as it unfolds itself on the scale of the "immense"'. What is needed is a better understanding of what the 'immense' stands for. Immense is that which cannot be endured or born by the micro-individual, only the macro-individual. The personal self, or the starter-Ego is the micro-individual, and the second, the Sacred Divine Self is the macro-individual, or supra-individual. This is, of course, also implied in Christ's ministry on Earth: '*Be ye therefore perfect as your Heavenly Father is perfect*' is either an impossible task, or a task only to be accomplished if one accepts the possibility that one's *person* is no more than that word's proper etymology entails, *a container through which something sounds or re-sounds*. Just as sound can be amplified, our persona, catcher of the 'vibrations' from the other world, can develop lower and higher octaves in its capacity as a resonator, depending on how closed or how open it presents itself to those impulses reaching it from below and from above. One need not be a schizophrenic to have a mundane Ego and a spiritual Ego; we have only one Ego existentially, but this Ego is like a musical instrument with unexplored possibilities in its range both in the lower and the higher frequencies. The physical-personal Ego 'becoming' the higher, spiritual Self, therefore, is no contradiction at all, nor is it an impossible task. It is, however, difficult to understand what it is exactly because it can only be achieved by doing it, as the French proverb reminds us, *c'est en forgeant qu'on devient forgeron*, or the Latin proverb: *dicendo doscimus*.

If, however, there are states in our consciousness that can only be attained by aspiring to them, rational explanation becomes its own worst enemy, and the language that describes such an event must be an iconic language that does not just arbitrarily 'mean' what it means, but 'does it for you' in front of your ears and eyes. Hence hermetic language is not an arbitrary choice, a cool or decadent option that the poet has at his disposal, it is, in fact, inevitable, it is pre-ordained and inescapable. The poet, then, has no choice of how he will say what he is about to say; he either has it, or he has not. Whether he had it or not is there for those to see 'who have eyes to see and ears to hear'.

This is where the phonology of the *Illumination* becomes both vehicle and content for what it says, justifying the unusual length and detail devoted to it in section 2 of this chapter.

Let us go back to our interstellar translation as we had it above: 'My personal self becomes a second, divine, sacred Self, as it unfolds itself on the scale of the IMMENSE'. Let us try to tiptoe around the word IMMENSE and then add our pitifully inadequate definition of this term into the sentence above. The IMMENSE, as may be guessed by the foregoing observations, is the experience of becoming, or of *rebecoming (i.e. becoming again) in the continuum of space-time, where the act of becoming and *rebecoming separate and reunite the individual with the cosmic world substance of which we are all variously cognizant parts. Adding the definition, we obtain:

MY PERSONAL SELF BECOMES A SECOND, DIVINE, SACRED SELF, AS IT UNFOLDS ITSELF ON THE SCALE OF THE EXPERIENCE OF BECOMING AND *REBECOMING IN THE CONTINUUM OF SPACE-TIME, WHERE BECOMING AND *REBECOMING SEPARATE AND REUNITE THE INDIVIDUAL WITH THE COSMIC WORLD – SUBSTANCE OF WHICH WE ARE ALL VARIOUSLY COGNIZANT PARTS.

What can I say in closing? That I have produced material proof of the hidden meaning of a hermetic poem, opened up to the public through the marvellous tools of modern linguistics? Certainly not. The poem need not mean this at all. Or it could mean even more, elaborated even more taxingly along the lines of alien philosophies we have not yet even heard of. This enlarged 'interstellar' paraphrase of the tellurian original is by no means shockingly new; it reminds one rather easily of the mature work of Carl Gustav Jung who, especially towards the last two decades of his life, paid increasingly serious attention to Sanskrit mandalas, and a spiritual reinterpretation of the notion of the 'collective unconscious'. In simpler, more familiar terms, let us simply say that the beauty of the poem lies inexorably in the eyes of the beholder. It means whatever you see in it. And what you see is codetermined by the way you look. This is another way of saying that the meaning of the *Illumination* is its own language-specific performance *viva voce*, while walking in the morning (or in the evening). *M'illumino d'immenso*, you see, is really a modern mantra. It will work for those who are willing to accept it as such, and it will, in all likelihood, remain a silent mystery for those who shy away from saying mantras and other outlandish modes of behavior.

Mantras are to be SAID ALOUD. *M'illumino d'immenso* has had real therapeutic effect on me: it has cured me of headaches, depressions, and has changed my outlook from negative to positive in many difficult situations. It works at midnight under the starry sky when I walk my dog; it works in the morning, and it works extremely well as I look into the setting sun.

But do not believe me. All I ask is that you try it – at least once.

Notes

1. See Creagh (1971, p. 9), Flora (1936, pp. 106–14), De Robertis in Patronio (1971, pp. 532–43) and many others.
2. Flora (1936 *in toto*, but particularly Chapter III 'L'Analogista ermetico' (pp. 102–72)); also Benét (1965 I:461 *et passim*).
3. Benét (1965 I:235).
4. Benét (1965 II:980).
5. For a standard reference work on the subject see Pyles (1971) and subsequent updated editions, but particularly Chapter XII 'Foreign Elements in the English Word Stock'.
6. Ungaretti was born in Alexandria, Egypt, on 8 February, 1888. His parents, Antonio Ungaretti and Maria Lunardini came from Lucca, Italy, just south of Firenze in the vicinity of Siena, Cortona, and Arezzo – that is in plain Tuscany, the cradle of the 'literary language' of Italy. Dialectal versions of Umbria and Latium are not likely to have been present in the senior Ungaretti's speech. Giuseppe attended the École Suisse Jacot where he was instructed in standard literary Italian and Parisian French. His readings of Leopardi, Baudelaire, Mallarmé, Nietzsche, and the avant-garde poets of France and Italy were all imparted to him according to the standard Tuscany and Paris speech patterns of this élite school. An excellent and detailed chronology of Ungaretti's career is available in Mandelbaum (1975, p. xviixx).
7. I have this on the authority of several native speakers, e.g. Robert Di Pietro,

who, although American-born, commands native Italian and has observed such pronunciations around Rome and Naples. Standard Italian (communication of R.A. Hall, Jr.) does not generally have an /nz/ cluster.

8. It is a generally observable phenomenon that expatriate private schools tend to teach 'Bühnensprache' literary standards and not regional varieties. On the continent of Europe mostly British English is taught – it is the exceptional department of English that has special courses in American English phonology. German schools abroad do not reach *Schwitzerdütsch* or Viennese slang but the Bavarian Radio Broadcaster's dialect. Italian schools abroad, similarly, do not teach Neapolitan or Sicilian speech forms but the standard Tuscany literary dialect.

9. Technically, a choriamb is a Choree followed by an Iamb (- vv -). This does not strictly fit the *Illumination* except in parts, as in LU-mi-no, but *no*, a weak syllable, is not followed by a stressed one. The 'choriambicity' of the *Illumination*, is not a pure one, and is suggested there merely due to the intercepted stress pattern of the poem which does not allow one to classify it either as 'rising' or as 'falling'. In other words, you can find Iambs, Dactyls, Trochees and Anapaests in the seven syllables as well, but the start is never a clean, absolute one. I have, then, deliberately stretched the sense of 'choriambic' to describe rhythmic interception.

10. The poem was written in Santa Maria La Lunga, 26 January, 1917 in 'zona di guerra' cf. Piccioni (1970, p. 68).

11. See my 'Where Do Exclamations Come From?' (See Chapter 8 in this volume.)

12. The mathematical equation (see Chapter 4, p. 135) describing $1 + 1 = 2$ in 'more elegant form' appeared in *Forum Linguisticum* I:2 (173), December, 1976. Several mathematicians attested to its accuracy and agreed that it was an appropriate example of the futility of excessive formalism.

13. Particularly Hockett (1967, the chapter on 'Conversion Grammars'). Makkai (1972a) emphasizes that 'directed graphs' are rather useful and should be re-introduced into stratificationally oriented relational grammars.

14. These are articulatory features as developed by structuralists and put to further use in stratificational theory as can be found in Lamb (1966), Lockwood (1972), Makkai (1972a), and Makkai and Lockwood (eds) (1973). The fact that the lines touch at the same point under the triangles indicated LACK OF ORDERING, i.e. the 'features' below are present in the 'AND' nodes above SIMULTANEOUSLY.

15. About the futility of the 'mentalism–mechanism controversy' and its solution according to the principles of Pragmo-Ecological Grammar see Chapter 2 in this volume.

It is no exaggeration to state that in not a single paper written by Chomsky, for instance, or any of his disciples, do literary considerations play any part worth mentioning. They are, of course, not alone in such provincial isolationism from the world of *belles lettres*: the oft-criticized 'Neo-Bloomfieldians', who are far easier to draw premanufactured caricatures of than to find in real life and who, perhaps, may be identified with Prof. Zelig Harris in the mid-1950s (perhaps not entirely accidentally Chomsky's teacher at the University of Pennsylvania), were also unconcerned with literary styles and poetic language. Small wonder, then, if transformationalists, who are in truth the real Neo-Bloomfieldians, that is, *die Fachbarbaren der Philologie*, have no need to explicate hermetic texts. But a younger linguist could, and often is, innocently ignorant of terms such as 'hermeticism'. So what can he do? Look up more terms in Benét.

List of abbreviations

AA	AMERICAN ANTHROPOLOGIST, Journal of the American Anthropological Association
ACLS	AMERICAN COUNCIL OF LEARNED SOCIETIES, New York City
ALH	ACTA LINGUISTICA HUNGARICA, Journal of the Hungarian Academy of Sciences
ASTHLS	Amsterdam Studies in the Theory and History of Linguistic Science
CAL	CENTER FOR APPLIED LINGUISTICS, Washington, D.C.
CEA	COLLEGE ENGLISH ASSOCIATION, Baton Rouge, Louisiana
CILT	Current Issues in Linguistic Theory
CLS	CHICAGO LINGUISTIC SOCIETY, Department of Linguistics, University of Chicago
ESMSLCC	EDWARD SAPIR MONOGRAPH SERIES IN LANGUAGE CULTURE AND COGNITION, Supplement to ForLing (q.v.)
EUQ	EMORY UNIVERSITY QUARTERLY, Atlanta, Georgia
FndtnsLg	FOUNDATIONS OF LANGUAGE, Dordrecht, The Netherlands (now defunct)
ForLing	FORUM LINGUISTICUM, Triquarterly Journal, Jupiter Press, Lake Bluff, IL.
IJAL	INTERNATIONAL JOURNAL OF AMERICAN LINGUISTICS, University Chicago Press
ILD	INSTITUTO LINGUISTICO DE VERANO, Spanish name of the Summer Institute of Linguistics (SIL)
IURCAFL	INDIANA UNIVERSITY RESEARCH CENTER IN ANTHROPOLOGY FOLKLORE AND LINGUISTICS
JL	JOURNAL OF LINGUISTICS, Journal of the Linguistic Society of Great Britain
JVLVB	JOURNAL OF VERBAL LEARNING AND VERBAL BEHAVIOR

Lg	LANGUAGE, Journal of the Linguistic Society of America (LSA)
LgSci	LANGUAGE SCIENCES, originally Indiana University, Bloomington, IN., subsequently International Christian University, Tokyo, Japan, & Pergamon Press, UK.
LP	LANGUAGES FOR PEACE, Jupiter Press, Lake Bluff, IL.
Lua	LINGUA, Leyden, The Netherlands
LSA	LINGUISTIC SOCIETY OF AMERICA and its annual conventions, the papers read at these
Lx	LINGUISTICS, Journal of Mouton & Co.
MSLL	MONOGRAPH SERIES ON LANGUAGES AND LINGUISTICS, Georgetown University, Washington, D.C.
PCCLLU	PACIFIC CONFERENCE ON CONTRASTIVE LINGUISTICS AND LANGUAGE UNIVERSALS, University of Hawaii (January 1971)
PPhilSoc	PUBLICATIONS OF THE PHILOLOGICAL SOCIETY, London, UK.
PICL	PROCEEDINGS OF THE Nth INTERNATIONAL CONGRESS OF LINGUISTS
PUF	PRESSES UNIVERSITAIRES DE FRANCE, Paris
RomPhil	ROMANCE PHILOLOGY, Department of Linguistics, University of California, Berkeley, CAL.
Sem	SEMIOTICA, Mouton & Co.
SILTA	STUDI ITALIANI DI LINGUISTICA TEORICA ED APPLICATA, Liviana Editrice, Padova, Italy
Wd	WORD, Journal of the International Linguistic Association (ILA) formerly the Linguistic Circle of New York

Bibliography

Aarsleff, H. (1970) 'The History of Linguistics and Professor Chomsky', *Lg* 46: 570–85.
——— (1971) 'Cartesian Linguistics: History or Phantasy?', *LgSci* 17: 1–12.
Abercrombie, D. (1980) 'Fifty Years in Phonetics', *ForLing* 5/2: 169–78.
Algeo, J. (1970a) *English: An Introduction to Language*, New York, Harcourt Brace & World.
——— (1970b) 'On Defining a Stratum', *EUQ* 23: 263–96.
——— (1972) 'Stratificational Grammar' in Makkai and Lockwood (eds), 1973: 9–14.
Anttila, R. (1974) 'Revelation as Linguistic Revolution' in *The First LACUS FORUM*: 171–6.
——— (1977) Preface to Maher 1977: ix–xx.
Bach, E. (1971) 'Syntax Since *Aspects*', *MSLL* 24: 1–17, Washington, D.C., Georgetown University Press.
Beekman, J., and Callow, J. (1974) *Translating the Word of God*, Grand Rapids, MI, Zonderman.
Benét, W.R. (1965) *The Reader's Encyclopedia* (2nd edn), New York, Thomas Y. Crowell.
Bennett, D.C. (1968) 'English Prepositions', *JL* 4: 153–73. (Reprinted in Makkai and Lockwood (eds) 1973: 267–96.)
——— (1973) 'A Stratificational View of Polysemy', in Makkai and Lockwood (eds) 1973: 297–306.
Benson, J.D., and Greaves, W.S. (1973) *The Language People Really Use*, Agincourt, Ont., The Book Society of Canada, Ltd.
Berger, P.L., and Luckmann, T. (1967) *The Social Construction of Reality: A Treatise in the Sociology of Knowledge*, London, Allen Lane (The Penguin Press).
Berne, E.M.D. (1966) *Games People Play*, New York, Grove Press.
——— (1972) *What Do You Say After You Say Hello?*, New York, Grove Press.
Binnick, R.I. (1974) Review of Makkai 1972a, *IJAL* 40:2: 155–7.
Birnbaum, H. (1977) 'Toward a Stratificational View of Deep Structure' in Makkai, A., Makkai, V.B., and Heilmann, L. (eds) 1977: 104–19.
Bloch, B. (1948) 'A Set of Postulates for Phonemic Analysis', *Lg* 24: 3–46.
Bloch, B., and Trager, G.L. (1942) *Outline of Linguistic Analysis*, Baltimore, Waverley Press.
Bloomfield, L. (1933) *Language*, New York, Henry Holt and Co.
Boatner, M.T., Gates, E.J., and Makkai, A. (eds) (1975) *A Dictionary of American*

Idioms, Woodbury, N.Y., Barron's Educational Series.

—————— (1987) *A Dictionary of American Idioms* (2nd Revised and updated edition by A. Makkai), Hauppaug, N.Y., Barron's Educational Series.

Bolinger, D.L. (1975a) 'On the Passive in English', *The First LACUS FORUM*: 57–80.

—————— (1975b) *Aspects of Language*. (2nd edn), New York, Harcourt Brace Jovanovich.

—————— (1976a) 'Meaning and Memory', *ForLing* 1/1: 1–14.

—————— (1976b) 'Truth is a Linguistic Question' *LSA* Presidential Address, *Lg* 49/3: 539–50.

—————— (1977a) 'Idioms Have Relations', *ForLing* 2/2: 157–69.

—————— (1977b) *Meaning and Form*, New York and London, Longman.

Cambon, G. (1967) *Giuseppe Ungaretti*, New York and London, Columbia University Press.

Capra, F. (1980) *The Tao of Physics*, New York, Bantam Books.

Carnap, R. (1960) *Introduction to Symbolic Logic*, New York, Philosophical Library.

Carroll, J.B. (ed.) (1956) *Language, Thought, and Reality: Selected Writings of Benjamin Lee Whorf*, Cambridge, Mass., MIT Press and New York, John Wiley.

Carroll, P. (ed.) (1979) *The Earthquake on Ada Street. An Anthology of Poetry from the 'Sculpture Factory'*, Lake Bluff, IL., Jupiter Press.

Cassierer, E. (1938) *Einführung in die Logik der Symbolischen Formen*, Wien, Doblehoff.

Castaneda, C. (1975) *The Teachings of Don Juan; A Separate Reality; Journey to Ixtlan; Tales of Power* (A tetralogy), New York, Braziller.

Chafe, W.L. (1967) 'Language as Symbolization', *Lg* 43: 57–91.

—————— (1968a) Review of Lamb 1966a, *Lg* 44: 593–603.

—————— (1968b) 'Idiomaticity as an Anomaly in the Chomskian Paradigm', *FndtnsLg* 4: 109–27.

—————— (1970) *Meaning and the Structure of Language*, Chicago, University of Chicago Press.

Chomsky, N. (1957) *Syntactic Structures*, The Hague, Mouton.

—————— (1964a) *Current Issues in Linguistic Theory*, The Hague, Mouton.

—————— (1964b) 'Degrees of Grammaticalness' in *Structure of Language*, Fodor, J.A., and Katz, J.J. (eds): 384–9.

—————— (1965) *Aspects of the Theory of Syntax*, Cambridge, Mass., MIT Press.

—————— (1966) *Cartesian Linguistics: A Chapter in the History of Rationalist Thought*, New York, Harper & Row.

—————— (1968) *Language and Mind*, New York, Harcourt Brace & World.

—————— (1980) *Rules and Representations*, New York, Columbia University Press.

Chomsky, N., and Halle, M. (1968) *The Sound Pattern of English*, New York, Harper & Row.

Christie, W.M. Jr. (1977) 'A Stratificational View of Linguistic Change', *ESMSLCC* 4, Lake Bluff, IL., Jupiter Press.

—————— (1980) Preface to a Neo-Frithian Linguistics, *ESMSLCC* 7, Lake Bluff, IL., Jupiter Press.

Conklin, H.C. (1962) 'Lexicographical Treatment of Folk Taxonomies' in *Problems in Lexicography*, Householder, F.W., and Saporta, S. (eds) Bloomington, IURCAFL, 21: 119–41.

Creagh, P. (ed. and trans.) (1971) *Selected Poems of Giuseppe Ungaretti*, Harmondsworth, Penguin Books.

Dell, G.S., and Reich, P.A. (1976) 'A Model of Slips of the Tongue', *The Third LACUS FORUM*: 448–55.

De Robertis, G. (1971) 'Sulla formazione della poesia di Ungaretti', *Antologia della critica letteraria* (Giuseppe Petroni (ed.)) Bari, Editoria Laterza: 532–43.

Dinneen, F.P. (S.J.) (1967) *An Introduction to General Linguistics*, New York, Holt Rinehart & Winston.

Di Pietro, R.J. (1971) *Language Structures in Contrast*, Rowley, Mass., Newbury House.

–––––– (1972) 'The Need to be Practical' in Makkai A., Makkai, V.B., and Heilmann, L. (eds) 1976: Reprinted in *LP* 6–8.

Eckhardt, S. (1953) *Francia-magyar szótár*. (French-Hungarian Dictionary.) Budapest, Akadémiai Kiadó.

Firth, J.R. (1957a) *Papers in Linguistics* (1934–1951). London, Oxford University Press.

–––––– (1957b) 'A Synopsis of Linguistic Theory' in *Studies in Linguistic Analysis*, Oxford, Blackwell.

Flora, F. (1936) *La poesia ermetica*, Bari, Giuseppe Laterza & Figli.

Fónagy, I. (1971) 'Double Coding in Speech', *Sem* 3: 189–222.

–––––– (1976a) *Öregség – Dallamfejtés*. (*Old Age – Melody Semantics.*) Budapest, Akadémiai Kiadó.

–––––– (1976b) 'The Voice of the Poet' in Makkai, A. (ed. and trans.) 1976: 81–143.

–––––– (1983) *La vive voix*, Paris, PUF.

Fraser, B. (1970) 'Idioms Within a Transformational Grammar', *FndtnsLg* 6: 22–42.

Fulton, R. (ed. and trans.) (1966) *An Italian Quarter (Un quartetto italiano: Saba, Ungaretti, Montale, Quasimodo)*, London, Alan Ross' London Magazines Editions 6(6).

Garneau, J.-L. (1972) 'A Study of Two Aspects of Semantic Divergence in Anglo-French Cognates', *Equivalences*, Bruxelles, Institut Supérieur des traducteurs et interprêts.

–––––– (1975/76) 'Anglo-French Misleading Transfer Items: A Semantic Analysis', *The Second LACUS FORUM*: 567–83.

–––––– (1985(1973)) *Semantic Divergence in Anglo-French Cognates. A Synchronic Study in Contrastive Lexicography*, ESMSLCC 14, Lake Bluff, IL., Jupiter Press.

Garvin, P.L. (ed.) (1970a) *Cognition: A Multiple View*, New York, Spartan Books.

–––––– (1970b) 'Moderation in Linguistic Theory', *LgSci* 9: 1–4.

Gleason, H.A. Jr. (1964) 'The Organization of Language: A Stratificational View', *MSLL* 17: 75–95.

–––––– (1965) *Linguistics and English Grammar*, New York, Holt Rinehart & Winston.

–––––– (1969) 'Contrastive Analysis in Discourse Structure', *MSLL* 21: 39–63. Reprinted in Makkai, A., and Lockwood, D.G. (eds) 1973: 258–76.

Greenberg, J.H. (1957) 'The Nature and Use of Linguistic Typologies', *IJAL* 23: 68–77.

–––––– (1963) *Universals of Language*, Cambridge, Mass., MIT Press.

–––––– (1966) *Language Universals*, The Hague, Mouton.

Hall, R.A. Jr. (1944) *Hungarian Grammar* (Language Monograph 21, LSA.), Baltimore, Md., Waverley Press.

–––––– (1977) 'Italian *pregno*, English *preggy* and Derivational Morphology', *LgSci* 46: 24–6.

–––––– (1981) Review of Newmeyer 1980, *ForLing* 6: 177–88.

Halle, M. (1972) 'Morphology Within a Generative Grammar', *PICL* XI: Reprinted in Makkai, A., Makkai, V.B., and Heilmann, L. (eds) 1976.

Halliday, M.A.K. (1959) 'The Language of the Chinese "Secret History of the Mongols"', *PPhilSoc* 17, Oxford, Basil Blackwell.

——— (1961) 'Categories of the Theory of Grammar', *Wd* 17: 241–92.

——— (1966) 'Lexis as a Linguistic Level' *In Memory of J.R. Frith*, Bazell, C., Catford, I., Halliday, M.A.K., and Robbins, H. (eds), London, Longman: 148–62.

——— (1967) *Intonation and Grammar in British English* (Series practica 48.), The Hague, Mouton.

——— (1972) 'Towards a Sociological Semantics', *Working Papers and Prepublications* C-14, Urbino, Centro Internazionale di Semiotica e Linguistica, Università di Urbino.

——— (1973) *Explorations in the Functions of Language*, London, Edward Arnold.

——— (1975a) *Learning How to Mean*, London, Edward Arnold.

——— (1975b) 'Language as Social Semiotic: Towards A General Socio-linguistic Theory', *The First LACUS FORUM*: 17–46.

——— (1976) 'Anti-languages', *AA* 78(3): 570–84.

——— (1978) *Language as Social Semiotic*, London, Edward Arnold.

——— (1985) *Introduction to Functional Grammar*, London, Edward Arnold.

Halliday, M.A.K., and Hasan, R. (1976) *Cohesion in English*, London, Longman.

Hankamer, J. (1971) 'Unacceptable Ambiguity', *LSA*, Saint Louis.

Harris, R. (1973) *Synonymy and Linguistic Analysis*, Oxford, Blackwell.

——— (1989) 'The Semiotic Basis of Applicative Grammar', *Semiotica* 74 1/2: 121–32.

Harris, T.A. (1967) *I'm OK, You're OK*, New York, Harper & Row.

Harris, Z. (1951) *Methods in Structural Linguistics*, Chicago, University of Chicago Press.

Haugen, E. (1972) *The Ecology of Language*, Stanford, Stanford University Press.

Herrick, E.M. (1984) *Sociolinguistic Variation: A Formal Approach*, University, Ala., University of Alabama Press.

Hjelmslev, Louis (1943–1961) *Omkring sprogteoriens grundlaeggelse*, Copenhagen, Einar Munksgaard. Translated in 1953 as *Prolegomena to a Theory of Language* by Francis J. Whitfield (Indiana University Publications in Anthropology, Folklore and Linguistics, Memoire 7 of *IJAL*), Revised English edn 1961, Madison, University of Wisconsin Press.

Hockett, C.F. (1955) *Manual of Phonology*. (Indiana University Publications in Anthropology, Folklore and Linguistics, Memoire 11 of *IJAL*; Vol. 21/4, Pt. 1.) Baltimore, Waverley Press.

——— (1958) *A Course in Modern Linguistics*, New York, Macmillan.

——— (1961) 'Linguistic Units and their Relations', *Lg* 27: 29–53.

——— (1967) *Language, Mathematics, and Linguistics*, The Hague, Mouton.

——— (1968a) Review of Lamb 1966a, *IJAL* 34: 145–53.

——— (1968b) *The State of the Art*, The Hague, Mouton.

——— (1969) 'The Problem of Universals in Language' in Greenberg 1966: 1–30.

Howard, I. (1971) 'On Several Conceptions of Universals', *PCCLLU, Working Papers* 3/4: 243–8, Honolulu, Hawaii.

Humboldt, W. von (1836) *Über die Verschiedenheit des menschlichen Sprachbaues und ihren Einfluß auf die geistige Entwicklung des Menschengeschlechtes*, Berlin, Druckerei der königlichen Akademie der Wissenschaften.

James, W. (1907–1965) *Pragmatism: Collected Harvard Lectures*, New York, World Publishing. (Originally published in 1909.)

Jaynes, J. (1976) *The Origin of Consciousness in the Breakdown of the Bicameral Mind*, Boston, Houghton Mifflin.

Joyce, J. (1976 (1920–1939)) *Finnegan's Wake*, New York and London, Faber & Faber.

Karácsony, S. (1938) *Magyar nyelvtan társaslélektani alapon* (*Hungarian Grammar Based on Social Interaction Psychology*), Budapest, Exodus.

Katz, J., and Fodor, J.A. (1963) 'The Structure of Semantic Theory', *Lg* 39: 170–210.

Katz, J., and Postal, P.M. (1963) 'Semantic Interpretation of Idioms and Sentences Containing Them', *MIT Research Laboratory in Electronics, Quarterly Progress Report* 70: 275–82.

Koestler, A. (1967) *The Ghost in the Machine: The Urge to Self-destruction: A Psychological and Evolutionary Study of Modern Man's Predicament*, New York, Macmillan.

Kuhn, T. (1962) *The Structure of Scientific Revolutions*, Chicago, University of Chicago Press.

Kunin, I.V. (1970) *Anglijskaya frazeologiya (teoretičeskij kurs)*, Moscow, Izdatel'stvo 'Vysšaya Škola'.

———— (1972) *Frazeologiya sovremennogo anglijskogo jazyka*, Moscow, Isdatel'stvo 'Meždunarodnye otnošeniya'.

———— (1984) *Frazeologičeskij Slovar' sovremennogo anglijskogo jazyka*. Moscow, Izdatel'stvo Nauka.

Labov, W. (1966) *The Social Stratification of English in New York City*, Washington, D.C., CAL.

———— (1976) 'On the Use of the Present to Explain the Past' in Makkai, A., Makkai, V.B., and Heilmann, L. (eds) 1976.

LACUS FORUM SERIES

———— (1974) *The First LACUS FORUM*, Makkai, A., and Makkai, V.B. (eds) Columbia, S.C., Hornbeam Press.

———— (1975) *The Second LACUS FORUM*, Reich, P.A. (ed.) Columbia, S.C., Hornbeam Press.

———— (1976) *The Third LACUS FORUM*, Blansitt, E.L., and Di Pietro, R.J. (eds) Columbia, S.C., Hornbeam Press.

———— (1977) *The Fourth LACUS FORUM*, Paradis, M. (ed.) Columbia, S.C., Hornbeam Press.

———— (1978) *The Fifth LACUS FORUM*, Wölck, W., and Garvin, P.L. (eds) Columbia, S.C., Hornbeam Press.

———— (1979) *The Sixth LACUS FORUM*, McCormack, W., and Izzo, H.J. (eds) Columbia, S.C., Hornbeam Press.

———— (1980) *The Seventh LACUS FORUM*, Copeland, J.E., and Davis, P.W. (eds) Columbia, S.C., Hornbeam Press.

———— (1981) *The Eighth LACUS FORUM*, Gutwinski, W., and Jolly, G. (eds) Columbia, S.C., Hornbeam Press.

———— (1982) *The Ninth LACUS FORUM*, Morreal, J. (ed.) Columbia, S.C., Hornbeam Press.

———— (1983) *The Tenth LACUS FORUM*, Manning, A., Martin, P., and McCalle, K. (eds) Columbia, S.C., Hornbeam Press.

———— (1984) *The Eleventh LACUS FORUM*, Hall, R.A. Jr. (ed.) Columbia, S.C., Hornbeam Press.

———— (1985) *The Twelfth LACUS FORUM*, Marino, M.C., and Pérez, L.A. (eds) Lake Bluff, IL., LACUS, Inc.

———— (1986) *The Thirteenth LACUS FORUM*, Fleming, I. (ed.) Lake Bluff, IL., LACUS, Inc.

———— (1987) *The Fourteenth LACUS FORUM*, Embleton, S. (ed.) Lake Bluff, IL., LACUS, Inc.

—— (1988) *The Fifteenth LACUS FORUM*, Brend, R.M., and Lockwood, D.G. (eds) Lake Bluff, IL., LACUS, Inc.

—— (1989) *The Sixteenth LACUS FORUM*, Jordan, M. (ed.) Lake Bluff, IL., LACUS, Inc.

—— (1990) *The Seventeenth LACUS FORUM*, Della Volpe, A. (ed.) Lake Bluff, IL., LACUS, Inc.

Lakoff, G. (1965) *The Nature of Syntactic Irregularity*, Harvard University Computation Laboratory, Report #NSF-16.

—— (1968) 'Counterparts on the Problem of Reference in Transformational Grammar', *LSA*, Urbana, Summer. (Mimeographed, Indiana University Linguistics Club.)

Lakoff, R. (1971) 'Passive Resistance', *CLS* 7: 149–61.

—— (1972) 'Language in Context', *Lg* 48: 907–27.

Lamb, S.M. (1961) 'Machine Translation Research at the University of California, Berkeley', *Proceedings of the National Symposium on Machine Translation*, Edmundson, H.P. (ed.): 150–64. Englewood Cliffs, N.J., Prentice-Hall.

—— (1964a) 'Stratificational Linguistics as a Basis for Machine Translation' in Makkai, A., and Lockwood, D.G. (eds) 1973: 34–59.

—— (1964b) 'The Sememic Approach to Structural Semantics', *AA* (66:3, Pt. 2): 57–78. Reprinted in Makkai and Lockwood (eds): 207–28.

—— (1965a) 'Kinship Terminology and Linguistic Structure', *AA* (67:5, Pt. 2): 37–64. Reprinted in Makkai and Lockwood (eds): 229–57.

—— (1965b) 'The Nature of the Machine Translation Problem', *JLVLB* 4: 196–210.

—— (1966a) *Outline of Stratificational Grammar*. (Revised edn) Washington, D.C., Georgetown University Press.

—— (1966b) 'Epilegomena to a Theory of Language', *RomPhil* 19: 531–73.

—— (1967) Review of Chomsky 1964 and 1965, *AA* (69): 411–15.

—— (1969) 'Linguistic and Cognitive Networks' in Garvin 1970: 195–222. Reprinted in Makkai and Lockwood (eds): 60–83.

—— (1975a) 'Mutations and Relations', *The First LACUS FORUM*: 540–57.

—— (1975b) 'Semiotics of Language and Culture: A Relational Approach', *Wenner-Gren Symposium* #66, Burg Wartenstein, Austria. Revised version in Fawcett, Halliday, Lamb and Makkai (eds).

—— (1990) 'Linguistic Model and Linguistic Thought: The Case of Either-or Thinking', *The Seventeenth LACUS FORUM*: 250–62.

—— (1991) *Language and Illusion*, Department of Linguistics, Rice University, Houston, Texas (prepublication copy of work in progress).

Langendoen, D.T. (1972) 'The Problem of Grammaticality', *CEA Chap Book: Selected Papers from the 33rd Annual Meeting of the CEA*: 20–3.

Larson, M.L. (1984) *Meaning-based Translation: A Guide to Cross-language Equivalences*, Lanham, MD., University Press of America.

Leech, G.N. (1974) *Semantics*, Harmondsworth, Penguin Books.

Lees, R.B. (1957) Review of Chomsky 1957, *Lg* 33: 375–408.

—— (1960) *The Grammar of English Nominalizations*, IURCAFL, 12 (*IJAL* XXVI, No. 2 II).

Lightner, T. (1975) 'Morphology Within a Generative Grammar', *Lg* 51: 617–38.

Lockwood, D.G. (1969) 'Markedness in Stratificational Phonology', *Lg* 45: 300–8.

—— (1972) *Introduction to Stratificational Linguistics*, New York, Harcourt Brace & World.

—— (1973) '"Replacives" Without Process' in Makkai and Lockwood (eds): 166–80.

—— (1975) 'Quasi-Etymological and "Natural Phonology" as Two Varieties of the Same Mistake', *The First LACUS FORUM*: 446–57.

—— (1976) 'A Stratificational Interpretation of Phonological Change' in Makkai, A., Makkai, V.B., and Heilmann, L. (eds).

Longacre, R.E. (1964) 'Prolegomena to Lexical Structure', *Lx* 5: 4–24.

Lounsbury, F.G. (1956) 'A Semantic Analysis of the Pawnee Kinship Usage', *Lg* 32: 158–94.

—— (1964a) 'A Formal Account of the Crow and Omaha-type Kinship Terminologies' in *Explorations in Cultural Anthropology: Essays in Honor of George Peter Murdock*, Ward H. Goodenough (ed.), New York, pp. 351–93.

—— (1964b) 'The Structural Analysis of Kinship Semantics' *Proceedings of the IXth International Congress of Linguists*, Horace G. Lunt (ed.), The Hague, Mouton, pp. 1073–93.

—— (1965) 'Another Look at the Trobriand Kinship Categories', *AA*, 67/5, Pt. 2, 142–85.

Lukacs, J. (1968) *Historical Consciousness*, New York, Harper & Row.

—— (1972) *The Passing of the Modern Age*, New York, Harper & Row.

Lytle, E.G. (1977) 'An Overview of the Junction Grammar Model of Language', *Junction Theory and Application* 1/1: 3–24, Provo, Translation Sciences Institute, Brigham Young University.

Maher, J.P. (1969) 'The Paradox of Creation and Tradition in Grammar: Sound Pattern of a Palimpsest', *LgSci* 7: 15–24.

—— (1977) *Papers on Language Theory and History: Creation and Tradition in Language*, *ASTHLS* IV, *CILT*, Vol. III, Amsterdam, John Benjamins.

—— (1985) 'The Transformational Paradigm: A Silver Anniversary Polemic', *ForLing* 5/1: 1–35.

Makkai, A. (1965) *Idiom Structure in English*, Unpublished Yale University Doctoral Dissertation.

—— (1971a) 'The Transformation of a "Turkish Pasha" Into a Big, Fat Dummy', *PCCLLU* Papers: 267–73, Honolulu, Hawaii. Reprinted in Makkai and Lockwood (eds): 307–15.

—— (1971b) 'Degrees of Nonsense, or Transformation, Stratification, and Contextual Adjustability Principle', *CLS* 7: 479–91.

—— (1972a) *Idiom Structure in English*, The Hague, Mouton.

—— (1972b) Review of Wallace L. Chafe 1970, *AA* 74: 91–4.

—— (1972c) Review of Geoffrey N. Leach, 'Toward a Semantic Description of English', *AA* 74(1/2): 92–4.

—— (1972d) *A Dictionary of Space English*, Chicago, English Language Institute of America (Consolidated Book Publishers).

—— (1973) 'A Pragmo-Ecological View of Linguistic Structure and Language Universals', *LgSci* 27: 9–22.

—— (1974a) 'Take One on *TAKE*: Lexo-Ecology Illustrated', *LgSci* 31: 1–6.

—— (1974b) 'A Stratificational Re-Examination of Acronymy in English', XIth *PICL*: 345–63.

—— (1974c) 'Madison Avenue Advertising: A Scenario', *The First LACUS FORUM*: 197–208.

—— (1974d) 'Grammatica Pragmo-Ecologica (PEG): Per una nuova sintesi della linguistica e dell' antropologia', *SILTA* 3(1/2): 7–55.

—— (1975a) 'Stratificational Solutions to Unbridgeable Gaps in the TGG

Paradigm: Translation, Idiomaticity and Multiple Coding', *ASTHLS* IV, *CILT*, Vol. I: 27–85, Amsterdam, John Benjamins.

———— (1975b) (ed. and trans.) *Toward a Theory of Context in Linguistics and Literature*, Proceedings of the Kelemen Mikes Hungarian Cultural Soc. Maastricht (Sept. 21–25, 1971), De Proprietatibus Litterarum, Series Minor 18, The Hague, Mouton.

———— (1975c) 'The Cognitive Organization of Idiomaticity: "Rhyme" or "Reason"?', *Georgetown University Working Papers in Language and Linguistics* 11, Robert J. Di Pietro (ed.) 10–29.

———— (1975d) *A Dictionary of American Idioms*, Woodbury, New York, Barron's Educational Series.

———— (1976a) 'Idioms, Psychology, and the Lexemic Principle', *The Third LACUS FORUM*: 467–78.

———— (1976b) 'Towards an Ecological Dictionary of English', *The Second LACUS FORUM*: 52–9.

———— (1976c) *A Dictionary of American Idioms*, Taiwanese edition (pirated), printed in Taipei by Ch'eng Wen Publishers.

———— (1976) (with V.B. Makkai) 'The Nature of Linguistic Change and Modern Linguistic Theories', *Proceedings of the 2nd International Congress of Historical Linguistics*, William M. Christie Jr. (ed.), Amsterdam, North Holland Publishing Co.: 235–65.

———— (1977) Review of L. Zgusta 1971, *Kratylos* XX: 13–19.

———— (1978a) 'Pragmo-Ecological Grammar (PEG): Towards a New Synthesis of Linguistics and Anthropology' in *Approaches to Language, Anthropological Issues*, William C. McCormack and Stephen A. Wurm (eds), The Hague, Mouton: 327–62.

———— (1978b) 'Idiomaticity as a Language universal' in *Universals of Human Language*, Joseph H. Greenberg, Charles A. Ferguson and Edith A. Moravcsik (eds) Vol. III, *Word Structure*: 401–48. Stanford, Stanford University Press.

———— (1978c) *A Dictionary of American Idioms*, First Chinese edition with definitions translated, Beijing (pirated).

———— (1979) 'Lexical Insertion as Socio-Psychological Activity: Evidence from Poetic Behavior' in *Festschrift for Jacob Ornstein*, A.L. Blansitt, Jr., and V.R. Teschner (eds), Rowley, Mass., Newbury House: 189–210.

———— (1980) 'Theoretical and Practical Aspects of an Associative Lexicon for Twentieth Century English' in *Theory and Method in Lexicography: Western and Non-Western Perspectives*, Ladislav Zgusta (ed.), Columbia, S.C., Hornbeam Press: 125–46.

———— (1981) 'What does a Native Speaker Know About the Verb KILL?' in *Festschrift for 'Native Speaker'*, Florian Coulmas (ed.), The Hague, Mouton: 237–44.

———— (1982) *A Dictionary of American Idioms*, Japanese edition, Tokyo, Shubun International.

———— (1983a) Second revised edition of Makkai 1975.

———— (1983b) *Languages for Peace. To Honor Kenneth L. Pike, Candidate for Nobel Peace Prize*, Lake Bluff, IL., Jupiter Press.

———— (1984) *Handbook of Commonly Used American Idioms*, Woodbury, New York, Barron's Educational Series.

———— (1985a) *Amerikai angol idiomatikus szólások és kifejezések tára* (Dictionary of American English Idioms), Budapest, International House.

———— (1985b) 'Where do Exclamations Come From?' in *Essays in Honor of Rulon S. Wells*, Makkai, A., and Melby, Alan K. (eds), Amsterdam, John Benjamins.

———— (1986) 'The Lexo-centric Approach to Descriptive Linguistics' in *Language in Global Perspective, Papers in Honor of the 50th Anniversary of the Summer Institute of Linguistics*, 1935–1985, B.F. Elson (ed.), Dallas, SIL, pp. 47–61.

———— (1988a) *A Dictionary of American Idioms* (2nd Revised Edition) Hauppaug, N.Y., Barron's Educational Series.

———— (1988b) Review of William Frawley (ed.), 1984 *Lg* 64/1: 180–7.

———— (1991a) Second revised edition of Makkai 1984. Hauppaug, N.Y., Barron's Educational Series.

———— (1991b) 'Systems of Simultaneous Awareness: Towards a "Musical Linguistics"', *The Sixteenth LACUS FORUM*: 40–82.

Makkai, A., and Lockwood, D.G. (eds) (1973) *Readings in Stratificational Linguistics*, University, Ala., University of Alabama Press.

Makkai, A., Makkai, V.B., and Heilmann, L. (eds) (1977) *Linguistics at the Crossroads*, Padova, Liviana Editrice, and Lake Bluff, IL., Jupiter Press.

Makkai, V.B. (1969) 'On the Correlation of Morphemes and Lexemes', *CLS* 5: 159–66.

———— (1972) (ed.) *Phonological Theory, Evolution and Current Practice*, New York, Holt Rinehart & Winston.

———— (1975) 'Are Autonomous and Systematic Phonemics Really Contradictory? The Outline of a New Synthesis' XIth *PICL* II: 783–8.

Malinowski, B. (1923) 'The Problem of Meaning in Primitive Languages' Supplement No. #1 to *The Meaning of Meaning* by C.K. Ogden and I.A. Richards, London, Routledge and Kegan Paul.

———— (1934) *Coral Gardens and their Magic* Vol. II, London, Allen and Unwin.

Malkiel, Y. (1975) 'Etymology and Modern Linguistics' *Lua* 36: 101–20.

Mandelbaum, A. (ed. and trans.) (1975) *Selected Poems of Giuseppe Ungaretti*, Ithaca and London, Cornell University Press.

McCawley, J.D. (1967a) 'The Respective Downfall of Deep Structure and Autonomous Syntax', *LSA* 1967 (December, Chicago).

———— (1967b) Review of Owen Thomas: *Transformational Grammar and the Teacher of English*, New York, 1965, Holt Rinehart & Winston. Mimeographed, Department of Linguistics, University of Chicago.

———— (1968a) 'The Role of Semantics in a Grammar' in *Universals of Linguistic Theory*, Bach, Emmon and Harms, Robert (eds), New York, Holt Rinehart & Winston: 124–69.

———— (1968b) *The Annotated 'Respective'*. Mimeographed, Department of Linguistics, University of Chicago.

McCormack, W., and Wurm, S.A. (eds) (1978) *Approaches to Language: Anthropological Issues*, The Hague, Mouton.

McDavid, R.I. (ed.) (1963) *The American Language*. (Abridged edn) Original by H.L. Mencken. New York, Knopf.

Napoli, D.J., and Rando, E.N. (eds) (1981) *The Linguistic Muse* (An Anthology of Poetry by Linguists) Edmonton, ALB., Canada, Linguistic Research, Inc.

———— (1983) *Meliglossa* (The 2nd Anthology of Poetry Written by Linguists) Edmonton, ALB., Canada, Linguistic Research, Inc.

———— (1989) *Linguafranca* (The 3rd Anthology of Poetry by Linguists) Lake Bluff, IL., Jupiter Press.

Neilson, W.A. (ed.) (1942) *The Complete Plays and Poems of William Shakespeare*. Cambridge, Mass., Houghton Mifflin at Riverside Press.

Newmeyer F.J. (1972) 'The Insertion of Idioms', *CLS* 8: 294–302.

——— (1980) *Linguistic Theory in America: The First Quarter Century of Transformational-Generative Grammar*, New York, Academic Press.

Nida, E.A. (1974) *Towards a Science of Translating with Special Reference to Principles and Procedures Involved in Bible Translation*. Leyden, Brill.

Noss, R.B. (1972) 'The Ungrounded Transformer', *LgSci* 23: 8–14.

Ogden, C.K., and Richards, I.A. (1953) *The Meaning of Meaning*, New York, Harcourt Brace & World. (Paperback edn based on original edition of 1923, Cambridge University Press.)

Oller, J.W. Jr. (1971) *Coding Information in Natural Languages*, The Hague, Mouton.

Oller, J.W. Jr., Sales, B.D., and Harrington, R.V. (1969) 'A Basic Circularity in Current and Traditional Linguistic Theory', *Lua* 22: 317–28.

Ornstein-Galicia, J. (1975) 'The Need for a Sociolinguistic Marking System and a Proposal', *The Third LACUS FORUM*: 514–28.

Országh, L. (1969–70) *Hungarian-English and English-Hungarian Dictionary* (II Vols), Budapest, Akadémiai Kiadó.

Palmer, F.R. (1968) Review of Lamb 1966a, *JL* 4: 287–95.

Papini, G. (1944) *Ritratti italiani* (1904–1931), Firenze, Vallecchi Editore.

Papp, F. (1969) *A magyar nyelv szóvégmutató szótára* (The A Tergo Dictionary of the Hungarian Language), Budapest, Akadémiai Kiadó.

Paradis, M. (1976) 'The Stratification of Bilingualism', *The Third LACUS FORUM*: 237–47.

Piccioni, L. (1970) *Vita di una poeta: Giuseppe Ungaretti*, Milano, Rizzoli Editore.

Pike, K.L. (1967) *Language in Relation to a Unified Theory of the Structure of Human Behavior* (2nd edn), The Hague, Mouton.

——— (1979) 'Pike on Language: Into the Unknown'. One of four 45-minute television tapes made by the television studios of the University of Michigan at Ann Arbor.

Pyles, T. (1971) *The Origins and Development of the English Language* (2nd edn), New York, Harcourt Brace Jovanovich.

Reich, P.A. (1970) *A Relational Network Model of Language Behavior*, Unpublished Ph.D. Thesis, Ann Arbor, University of Michigan.

——— (1978) 'The House that Noam Built', *ForLing* 2/1: 63–4.

Ross, J.R. (1967) *Constraints on Variables in Syntax*, MIT Doctoral Dissertation, Mimeographed. Indiana University Linguistics Club.

Sapir, E. (1921) *Language: An Introduction to the Study of Speech*, New York, Harcourt Brace.

Shaumyan, S.K. (1976) 'Linguistics as a Part of Semiotics', *ForLing* 1: 60–5.

——— (1983) 'Inaugural Thought on the Philosophy of Linguistics, Semiotics, and Communication as it Relates to a New Philosophy of Physics', *LP* 1: 28–31.

——— (1987) *A Semiotic Theory of Language*, Bloomington, Indiana University Press.

Steiner, R. (1861–1925)

——— *Outline of Occult Science* (1920, 1925, 1960, 1972);

——— *The Philosophy of Freedom* (1899, 1917, 1979);

——— *The Puzzles of Philosophy* (1923, 1945, 1968, 1979);

——— *The Gospel of St. John* (1920, 1969, 1984).

(All books by Steiner were written originally in German and are being systematically published in English in the USA, available from the Anthroposophic Press, Bell's Pond, Hudson, N.Y. 12534.)

Sullivan, W.J. (1975) 'Alternation, Transformation, Realization, and Stratification Revisited', *The First LACUS FORUM*: 472–522.

—— (1977) 'A Stratificational View of the Lexicon', *LgSci* 46: 11–22.

—— (1980) 'Some Logical Consequences of Makkai's "Idiomaticity as a Language Universal"', *Papers in Cognitive Stratificational Linguistics*, Rice University Studies 66/2: 143–54.

Thomas, O. (1966) *Transformational Grammar and the Teacher of English*, New York, Holt Rinehart & Winston.

Thorndike, E.L. (1920) *The Teacher's Manual of the 20,000 Most Frequent Words in English*, New York. (Revised in 1952 with the co-authorship of P. Lorge.)

Troubetzkoy, N.S. (1939) *Grundzüge der Phonologie*. Prague, TCLP 7. (Reprinted in 1958 by Vandenboeck and Ruprecht, Göttingen. French translation *Principes de phonologie* (J. Cantinean, trans.), Paris, 1949, Libraire Klincksieck.)

Ungaretti, G. (1975)

—— *Vita d'un uomo: 106 poesie* (1914–1960)

—— Mondadori.

—— *L'allegria* (1914–1919), *Sentimento del tempo* (1919–1935),

—— *Il dolore* (1937–1947), *Le terra promessa* (1935–1950),

—— *Un grido e paesaggi* (1939–1951), *Il tacuino del vecchio* (1952–1960).

Verhaar, J.W.M. (1971) 'Philosophy and Linguistic Theory', *LgSci* 14: 1–11.

Vico. G. (1770–1961) *The New Science (La szienza nuova)*. (Translated from the Italian by Max Fisch and Eugen Bär, Ithaca, N.Y., Cornell University Press.)

Weinreich, R. (1953) *Languages in Contact*, New York, Columbia University Press.

Wells, R.S. (1947) 'Immediate Constituents', *Lg* 23: 81–117.

—— (1956) 'Acronymy', in *For Roman Jakobson*: 662–7, The Hague, Mouton.

Wentworth, H., and Flexner, S.B. (1960) *Dictionary of American Slang*, New York, Thomas Y. Crowell.

Weöres, S. (1970) *A vers születése (The Birth of the Poem)*. Összegyűjtött írások (Collected Writings) Budapest, Magvető Kiadó.

Wescott, R.W. (1962) *Linguistics as a Tool in African Studies*, Annals of the New York Academy of Sciences, New York.

—— (1969) *The Divine Animal*, New York, Funk & Wagnalls.

—— (1980) *Sound and Sense: Essays on Phonosemic Subjects*. ESMSLCC 8, Lake Bluff, IL., Jupiter Press.

Whitney, W.D. (1889) *Sanskrit Grammar*, Leipzig, Breitkopf und Härtel. (Reprinted by Harvard University Press in 1947, 1957, 1960.)

Winter, W. (1965) 'Transforms Without Kernels?', *Lg* 41: 484–9.

Yngve, V.H. (1969) 'On Achieving Agreement in Linguistics', *CLS* 5: 455–62.

—— (1975a) 'The Dilemma of Contemporary Linguistics', *The First LACUS FORUM*: 1–16.

—— (1975b) *Introduction to Human Linguistics*. Unpublished to date, circulated in mimeographed format, Department of Linguistics, University of Chicago.

—— (1986) 'To Be a Scientist', *The Thirteenth LACUS FORUM*: 5–25.

Index of names

Index of subjects